该专著为"教育部人文社科研究项目，一般项目（规划基金项目）"成果，项目号：15YJA740034

多学科专业英语论文体裁对比分析

实验方法写作

钱杨 著

中国社会科学出版社

图书在版编目（CIP）数据

多学科专业英语论文体裁对比分析：实验方法写作 /
钱杨著. -- 北京：中国社会科学出版社，2024. 10.
ISBN 978-7-5227-3931-1

Ⅰ. H315

中国国家版本馆 CIP 数据核字第 2024PB5867 号

出 版 人	赵剑英
责任编辑	张冰洁
责任校对	王佳玉
责任印制	李寡寡

出　　版	中国社会科学出版社
社　　址	北京鼓楼西大街甲 158 号
邮　　编	100720
网　　址	http://www.csspw.cn
发 行 部	010-84083685
门 市 部	010-84029450
经　　销	新华书店及其他书店

印　　刷	北京明恒达印务有限公司
装　　订	廊坊市广阳区广增装订厂
版　　次	2024 年 10 月第 1 版
印　　次	2024 年 10 月第 1 次印刷

开　　本	710×1000　1/16
印　　张	45.5
插　　页	2
字　　数	680 千字
定　　价	198.00 元

前　　言

　　"实验方法"是实证性学术论文的重要组成部分。该部分的主要作用是为读者提供验证和再现研究的手段，同时也是确立研究信度与效度的重要途径。

　　现有对于学术论文写作的研究主要集中在对论文摘要和引言部分的宏观结构分析，对于实验方法部分的研究不足。已有研究主要存在以下几点问题：

　　一、类型单一：已有研究只将传统实验类论文作为研究对象；

　　二、学科单一：已有研究主要针对单一学科论文，缺少对多个学科的对比研究；

　　三、内容单一：已有研究多为宏观的结构分析或微观的词汇特征分析，未能将两者结合起来。

　　随着科学的不断发展，人们收集数据的方法也不再局限于实验室研究法，而是变得多样化，以满足不同学科、不同性质研究问题的需要。不同研究方法的写作在篇章结构或语步的构成、词汇的使用等方面必然存在一定的差异。本研究将论文分为问卷调查、传统实验和建模实验三种类型分别研究。

　　同一学科不同类型研究方法在收集数据的方法上会存在一定的差异，不同学科同一种类型研究方法的写作也会存在一定的差异。语步研究者当初的出发点是学术论文的语步模式具有跨学科的普遍性，但是很多学者后来发现，不少学科的学术语篇往往会表现出对常见语步模式的偏离。Swales 发现学科间学术论文最大的差异并不存在于人们以为的引言和讨论部分，而是方法和结果部分。本研究将不同学科同一种类型论文进行对比研究，研究的论文涉及 13 个一级学科。

不同语步有着不同的语篇功能，而语言是为交际服务的，离开语步的语言研究没有意义。本研究主要从宏观语步特征方面和微观语言特征方面分析三类实验方法写作的体裁特征。宏观语步特征主要包括语步种类、各语步包含的步骤种类、各步骤在各个语步及所有语步中占比、不同语步占比及分布轨迹。微观语言特征主要包括句子结构、不同类型句子长度分布、句子类型与语步相关性、时态种类及组合、时态组合与语步相关性、语态种类及组合，以及语态与语步相关性。

本书共有五个章节。第一章为总论，主要概述目前国内外学术语篇研究现状，特别是有关实验方法写作的研究，并在此基础上提出了本研究的研究目的、具体研究问题和研究的必要性。第二章主要阐述本研究使用的方法，其中包括语料库建设、语步框架制定、语料标注及数据统计及作图软件。第三章主要分析管理科学与工程和外国语言学及应用语言学两个领域学术英语论文中问卷调查方法的写作特征。本章由三个小节构成，其中第一小节和第二小节分别为两个学科中问卷调查法写作的体裁特征分析，第三小节对比分析两个学科在体裁特征方面的异同。第四章主要涉及生物学、临床医学、基础医学、海洋地球物理科学、环境科学与工程、化学学科、材料工程与科学、土木工程与科学和外国语言学及应用语言学多个领域传统实验方法写作的体裁特征分析。本章由十个小节构成，前九个小节是针对各学科的研究，最后一个小节是针对各学科的对比分析。第五章主要涉及管理科学与工程、电子信息工程、交通运输工程、车辆运输工程及软件工程与科学这五个领域建模实验方法写作的体裁特征分析。本章由六个小节构成，前五个小节是针对各学科的研究，最后一个小节是针对各学科的对比分析。

本书不仅能为各专业研究人员撰写专业学术英语论文提供指导，同时还能为语言文学领域从事学术语篇分析的学者提供一定的帮助。

本研究主要依托教育部人文社科项目（一般），自立项到专著完成共经历了六个年头，研究过程中得到了相关专业大批博士生、英语

专业研究生及同行的鼎力帮助。同时感谢中国社会科学出版社的大力
支持，也感谢同济大学外国语学院在出版费用及其他条件方面的支
持。由于作者水平有限，书中疏漏之处在所难免，恳请广大读者批评
指正。

语言标注符号

使用时态符号：

T1 = do/does/is/are

T2 = have/has done

T3 = did/was/were

T4 = will /shall do

T5 = had done

T6 = would/should/could/might have done

T7 = is/are doing

T8 = was/were doing

T9 = has/have been doing

T10 = would/should/could/might do

T11 = would/should/could/might be doing

T12 = had been doing

T13 = will be doing

T14 = may may/can have done

使用语态符号：

V1：主动语态

V2：被动语态

使用句类符号

S 简单句

P 复杂句

C 复合句

Eq. 省略的公式

CP 复合复杂句

F 片段

R 有语法错误

BCP	复杂句＋括号内复杂句
BCPF	复合复杂句＋括号内片段
BCPP	复合复杂句＋括号内内复杂句
BCPS	复合复杂句＋括号内简单句
BCS	外复合句＋括号内简单句
BPC	复杂句＋括号内复合句
BPF	复杂句＋括号内片段
BPFS	复杂句＋括号内片段/简单句
BPFW	复杂句＋括号内片段及词组
BPP	复杂句＋括号内复杂句
BPS	复杂句＋括号内简单句
BSF	简单句＋括号内片段
BSISW	简单句＋括号内［简单句＋i. e.＋词组］
BSP	简单句＋括号内复杂句
BSS	简单句＋括号内简单句
BWAS	简单句/内简单句＋从句
BWF	词组＋括号内片段
BWHC	复合句＋括号内公式或从句
IBSWS	简单句＋i. e.＋词组＋括号内简单句
ICPS	复合复杂句＋i. e.＋简单句
ICPWA	复合复杂句＋i. e.＋词组及从句
ICS	复合句＋i. e.＋简单句
INPC	复杂句＋冒号＋i. e.＋复合句
IPC	复杂句＋i. e.＋复合句
IPF	复杂句＋i. e.＋片段
IPP	复杂句＋i. e.＋复杂句

IPS	复杂句 + i. e. + 简单句
IPWA	复杂句 + i. e. + 词组 + 从句
IPWH	复杂句 + i. e. + 公式 + 从句 where 引导的从句
ISBFF	简单句 + i. e. + 片段 + 括号内片段
ISC	简单句 + i. e. + 复合句
ISCP	简单句 + i. e. + 复合复杂句
ISF	简单句 + i. e. + 片段
ISNWHS	简单句 + i. e. + 简单句 + 冒号 + 公式 + 从句 where 引导的从句
ISP	简单句 + i. e. + 复杂句
ISS	简单句 + i. e. + 简单句
ISWH	简单句 + i. e. + 公式 + 从句
NBWPP/S	复杂句 + 冒号 + 词组 + 括号内复杂句或简单句
NCC	复合句 + 冒号 + 复合句
NCPF	复合复杂句 + 冒号 + 片段
NCPP	复合复杂句 + 冒号 + 复杂句
NCPS	复合复杂句 + 冒号 + 简单句
NCS	复合句 + 冒号 + 简单句
NPC	复杂句 + 冒号 + 复合句
NPCBP	复杂句 + 冒号 + 复合句 + 括号内复杂句
NPCP	复杂句 + 冒号 + 复合复杂句
NPF	复杂句 + 冒号 + 片段
NPP	复杂句 + 冒号 + 复杂句
NPS	复杂句 + 冒号 + 简单句
NPW	词组 + 冒号复杂句
NSC	简单句 + 冒号 + 复合句
NSCIW	简单句 + 冒号 + 复合句 + i. e. + 词组
NSCP	简单句 + 冒号 + 复合复杂句
NSF	简单句 + 冒号 + 片段
NSIWS	简单句 + 冒号 + 词组 + i. e. + 简单句

NSP	简单句 + 冒号 + 复杂句
NSS	简单句 + 冒号 + 简单句
NSW	词组 + 冒号 + 简单句
NSWHIWH	简单句 + 冒号 + 公式 + where 引导的从句 + i. e. + 公式 + where 引导的从句
NWABPF	复杂句 + 括号内片段 + 冒号 + 词组 + 片段
NWAP	复杂句 + 冒号 + 词组 + 从句
NWAS	简单句 + 冒号 + 词组 + 从句
NWBSF	简单句 + 冒号 + 词组 + 括号内片段
NWBSS	简单句 + 括号内简单句 + 冒号 + 词组或公式
NWC	复合句 + 冒号 + 词组
NWCP	复合复杂句 + 冒号 + 词组
NWHC	复合句 + 冒号 + 公式 + where 引导的从句
NWHP	复杂句 + 冒号 + 公式 + where 引导的从句
NWHS	简单句 + 冒号 + 公式 + where 引导的从句
NWHW	词组 + where 引导的从句
NWHWW	词组 + 冒号 + 公式 + where 引导的从句 + 词组
NWISF	简单句 + i. e. + 片段 + 冒号 + 词组
NWP	复杂句 + 冒号 + 词组
NWS	简单句 + 冒号 + 词组
PCS	复合句 + 破折号 + 简单句
PPC	复杂句 + 破折号 + 复合句
PPP	复杂句 + 破折号 + 复杂句
PSC	简单句 + 破折号 + 复合句
PSS	简单句 + 破折号 + 简单句
PSW	简单句 + 破折号 + 词组
SP	特殊句类无法归类

目　　录

第一章 总论

随着国际学术交流变得日益广泛，撰写学术论文成为"科研学术交流的主要渠道"（Holmes，1997）。发表文章的数量和质量已经成为衡量一个国家、一个机构乃至一个科学工作者学术水平和地位的重要标志之一。然而，随着稿件数量与日俱增，期刊的拒稿率已高达95％以上（Soyer Patlas & Bluemke，2022）。英语作为一门国际性语言也已成为发表国际期刊论文最常用的语言（Swales，1990）。而在全球化时代，用英语以外的任何语言发表文章都是"一方面把自己隔离于国际社会之外，另一方面不利于自己的职业发展"（Flowerdew，1999：125）。

撰写好专业学术英语论文变得至关重要。怎样有效地、有针对性地提高我国学者学术英语论文质量，无疑是一个既紧迫又现实的问题。学术论文作为特殊语篇也得到了广泛研究，特别是自 Swales（1990）提出体裁分析理论以来。

"体裁"（genre）这一术语最早来自法语，是指任何一种形式和方式的交流。随着时间的推移，它的意思也发生了变化。这一术语在古希腊时期开始用于对古希腊文学分类。逐渐地，随着读者和创作者人群的变化，体裁的含义不断发展，它成了一种动态工具，帮助公众理解不可预测的艺术，现在已经发展成为现代语言学中语篇分析与教学的研究框架——体裁理论。

体裁是语篇的重要特征，它的研究可追溯到 20 世纪 60 年代，并在 90 年代初得到了迅速发展。对于什么是体裁许多学者都给出了各自定义。Swales（1990：45—58）认为体裁是交际事件的一种分类，体裁理论对语篇的内容和形式起着制约的作用，同一领域的人都承认并力图遵守这种制约。所谓交际事件就是按照特定的目的和特定程式运用语言在社会生活中办事的示例（秦秀白，1997：8）。Bhatia（1993：13—16）认为体裁是一种有着鲜明特征的内部结构，高度约定俗成的交际事件，体裁对于语篇的构成具有制约的作用。在构建语篇时必须遵循某种特定体裁所要求的惯例，体裁分析的目的是通过分析语篇的内部结构，弄清语轮是如何被组织起来并实现交际目的。Ventola（1995）认为体裁是生成特定语篇结构的符号系统，使用语言进行交际的过程可以分成若干具有规律的"步骤"。

不同学者对于体裁的界定虽然存在一定的差异，但可以归结为：体裁由一系列交际事件构成，它与交际目的密切相关，是一种可辨认的、具有鲜明内部结构特征及高度约定俗成的交际事件；同一种体裁具有相同的结构，有着相同交际目的或同一领域的人都遵循某种特定的要求。

体裁分析的根本宗旨是研究语篇的交际目的和语言使用策略（秦秀白，2000：43）。不同体裁的文章因其交际目的不同，文章实现的形式也各不相同，各种体裁的文章在结构、语言和修辞等方面都有着各自的特点。体裁分析能帮助读者解析语篇的组织模式，从而挖掘特定语篇所具有的特定的宏观认知结构。

近三十年来，该理论引起多学科、多领域的共同关注，形成了众多的研究学派。到20世纪80年代体裁理论主要有三个流派（梁文花、康淑敏，2012）：1. 以 Miller（1984）、Freedman & Medway（1994）以及 Bazerman（2009）为代表的北美新修辞学派（North American New Rhetoric Studies）；2. 以 Swales（1990）和 Bhatia（1993）为代表的专门用途英语（English for Specific Purposes）或学术用途英语学派（English for Academic Purposes），即斯威尔斯学派（Swalesian School）；3. 以 Martin（1993）为代表的澳大利亚学派（Australian School），即系统功能语言学学派（Systemic Functional Linguistics）。

北美新修辞学派反对以劝说为中心的修辞观以及其他两个学派的

体裁观。认为不能把体裁仅仅理解为大同小异的语篇组合，而应把它看作社会交际过程中编码与解码的事件（温植胜，2005）。北美新修辞学派围绕体裁所能完成的社会行为来界定体裁，试图在修辞情景和修辞体裁之间做出区分（梁文花、康淑敏，2012）。澳大利亚学派最早研究体裁的是 Halliday & Hasan（1989），他们认为"体裁"是语篇的类型，是由结构的必要成分来定义的，其中体裁结构是语篇的意义结构，而不是形式结构。Martin（1993）认为体裁是一种有步骤的交际过程。澳大利亚学派重点分析交际事件的图式结构。

国内外现有对于学术语篇体裁的研究主要可以分为对论文各部分宏观语步特征的分析和微观词汇特征的分析。其中对于宏观语步特征的分析主要集中在对引言和摘要部分的研究，对于论文其他部分的研究较少。

第一节　学术语篇体裁特征研究

一　语步特征研究

（一）引言和摘要研究

专门用途英语的语言研究可以追溯到 20 世纪 60 年代。1964 年 Halliday 就提出了进行特殊用途英语教学的必要性，但是体裁这一概念是 80 年代由 Taron et al.（1981）和 Swales（1981）首次引入专门用途英语领域的。斯威尔斯学派在分析语篇时通常以语步（move）和步骤（step）作为语篇分析的出发点，每一个语步都有着明确的目的和为实现总体交际目的的各自功能，主要研究对象为学术语篇和职业语篇。

王丽萍、吴红云、张军（2017）运用 CiteSpace 对 Web of Science-SSCI 核心合集中 2176 篇有关学术英语写作文献进行深度分析，发现在国际学术英语写作研究中影响力最大的前三项文献是 Swales（1990），Biber et al.（1999）和 Hyland（2000）。

Swales 被称为"体裁分析之父"（Pèrez-Llantada，2004：140）。Swales（1981）首次对学术语篇引言的宏观结构进行了研究，提出语步和步骤概念。指出学术论文引言包括四个语步的模式，即界定研究领域—总结前人研究成果—介绍本课题研究的准备情况—介绍本课题的研究。1990 年他对该模式进行了修订，提出学术英语论文引言包括三个不同的语步，即确定研究范围—提出研究空白—填补研究空白。同时，每个语步又包括不同的步骤。这就是人们通常说的 CARS Model。

2014 年 Swales 又出版了另一部有关学术研究性论文体裁分析的著作，成为体裁研究的另一个里程碑（Séror & Zappa-Hollman，2005：351）。该著作对作者以往关于体裁的认识，探索体裁生产者、消费者以及体裁所出现的语境等多个方面问题进行了重新评估。

早期对学术论文宏观结构研究的主要还有 Stanley、Hutchins、Bruce 等。Stanley（1984）把论文的宏观结构归纳为"问题—解决"模式。Hutchins（1977）给出了 dogma（信条）—dissonance（不一致）—crisis（危机）—search（探讨）—new model（新模式）的模式。Bruce（1983）认为 IMRD 格式体现了学术论文归纳研究的逻辑顺序，即 Introduction（引言）—Methods（方法）—Results（结果）—Discussion（讨论）。

近期对于引言宏观结构的研究主要是对于不同学科的对比研究，如 Samraj（2002）运用了 Swales（1990）的 CARS model 对比了 Wildlife Behavior 和 Conservation Biology 两个相关领域引言的特征。在此基础上对 Swales 的 CARS Model 中的步骤进行了修改，认为语步一主要包括：Step 1：Claiming centrality（in research/in the real world）；Step 2：Presenting background information。语步二主要包括：Step 1A：Counter-claiming or Step 1B：Indicating a gap（in research/in the real world）；Step 1C：Question-raising or Step 1D：Continuing a tradition；Step 2：Presenting positive justification。语步三主要包括：Step 1：Presenting goals of present research—giving background information on species or site；Step 2A：Announcing principal findings or Step 2B：predicting results；Step 3：indicating RA structure。

Kanoksilapatham（2012）基于 Swales（2004）的语步模式研究了

工程领域三个分支的学术论文引言部分语步的异同，研究发现这三个分支有着共同的大框架，但是同时也存在学科差异。Lin（2014）对30 篇土木工程类文章的引言进行分析，根据论文主要的交际目的、结构流程及研究的性质将论文分类，对其中两种类型论文的引言进行了系统的对比，即"Two-move Orientation"类型和"Research-oriented Traditional Creating a Research Space"类型，发现这两种类型的引言在长度、功能和结构上有着较大的差异。当引言后出现文献回顾时，引言写作较为灵活，同时结构也较为简单，包含的步骤种类较少。有些学者针对不同引言语步模式在具体学科中的使用进行了深入研究，如Bahadoran et. al.（2018）分析了生物医学领域论文引言写作模式，发现该学科中通常使用到的典型写作模式为从宽泛到具体的漏斗式结构。

国内学者对于引言的研究主要是不同语言论文之间的对比，如Loi（2010）从英语学术期刊 *Journal of Educational Psychology* 和中文学术期刊《心理发展与教育》中分别选取了二十篇英语国家作者和中国作者撰写的论文，根据 Swales（1990，2004）语步框架进行对比，发现这两类论文中均包括了三个语步，但是 Swales 的 CARS 模型不能涵盖英语国家和中国学者使用到的所有步骤。此外，中国学者撰写的论文引言中涉及的步骤类型少于英语国家学者。Hirano（2009）同样也借助 Swales（1990）的语步模型对比分析了葡萄牙语应用语言学论文的引言与英语应用语言学论文引言的结构。研究发现葡萄牙语论文的引言在结构上没有使用到 Swales 的语步模型，而英语论文与该模型结合密切。

除了学术语篇引言外，同样受到关注的还有学术语篇摘要的写作。摘要普遍被认为是独立的语篇，Swales（1990：179）、Salager-Mayer（1990：367）和 Kaplan et al.（1994：405）分别使用"distillation，crystallization，summary"来表述摘要的功能。Hyland（2000：67）采用语料库和访谈等手段，对八个学科国际期刊中 800 篇学术论文摘要进行了语步特征分析，总结得出了一个包含"Introduction（I）—Purpose（P）—Method（M）—Product（Pr）—Conclusion

（C）"的模式。从这一模式的名称可以看出，Hyland 把摘要看成了论文的缩影，从结构上来说它是一个微型篇章。此外，Hyland 还发现不同论文摘要常出现的语步组合有：I-P-M-Pr［C］；P-M-Pr［C］；I-P-Pr［C］；P-Pr［C］；I-Pr 及其他。可以发现，虽然不同学科在摘要的语步特征上有着一定的相同之处，但同时也存在一定的差异。物理学科和工程类摘要多采用 P-M-Pr 语步模式（60%），人文和社会学科多采用 I-P-Pr 语步模式（75%）。Saeeaw & Tangkiengsirisin（2014）利用 Hyland（2000）的摘要模板对比分析了环境和应用语言学两个学科论文摘要特征，发现这两个学科摘要中主要差异是环境学科中通常包含五个语步，而应用语言学中较少包含"Introduction"。

国内学者对于摘要的分析主要是对比分析中国学者和以英语为母语的外国学者英语论文摘要写作的语步特征及时态特征，目的是为国内学者撰写高质量学术英语论文提供指导。刘永厚、张颖（2016）从五种国际期刊上分别选取了 50 篇中国大陆学者撰写的学术英语论文摘要，从摘要的宏观和微观两个方面对比分析，发现以英语为母语的作者撰写的摘要中包含的语步类型较多，但是两类摘要在时态和语态的使用上较为一致，一般现在时和主动语态均较高，不同语步中时态的使用有所差异。

（二）结果、讨论和结尾研究

对于论文结果、讨论和结尾部分的体裁研究相对较少，尤其是论文结尾部分。论文结果部分的研究主要有 Brett（1994）和 Williams（1999）就单一学科论文结果部分的研究及 Bruce（2009）和 Lim（2010）对两个学科论文结果部分的对比分析。Brett（1994）从功能、语法形式和词汇方面分析了社会学科 20 篇研究性论文的结果部分，总结出了该部分写作的典型的范畴（即语步）模式及循环模式，发现常用到的模式为：Pointer—Statement of Finding—Substantiation of Finding，同时还发现该部分的写作模式与硬科学研究论文讨论部分有着相似之处。Williams（1999）对 Brett（1994）的范畴模式进行了修改，并用于分析八篇医学论文，发现有 77% 的句子属于 Statement of Finding 范畴，该范畴同时出现在循环的和线性的范畴模式中。文章的种类和研究内容与语篇结构及呈现的模式有关。Yang & Edwards（1995）对结果部分分析得出的结论与 Brett 一致，同时指出结果部分的语步经常会重复出现。

Dubois（1997）和 Lewin, Fine & Young（2001）分别研究了生物医学、化学工程和社会科学领域论文的讨论部分，发现虽然不同学科之间讨论部分包含的语步种类和数量存在差异，但是这些差异有可能不是学科间的差异，而是研究者使用的研究手段和定义不同造成的。研究还发现讨论部分有一个有别于其他部分的特点，即该部分会包含多个从研究发现到研究问题的语步循环（Hopkins & Dudley-Evans, 1988；Swales, 1990；Holmes, 1997；Dubois, 1997；Peacock, 2002；Yang & Allison, 2003；Kanoksilapatham, 2003；Basturkmen, 2009）。Holmes（1997）对比分析社会科学中历史、政治和社会学三个学科论文讨论部分，发现虽然它们与自然科学有着共性，但是社会科学有着独特的特点，其中历史学科论文与自然学科差异最大。此外，Basturkmen（2012）分析牙科专业论文讨论部分发现，该部分很大程度上可以用语步和步骤框架来解释。

论文结尾部分在有些文章中不作为单独的部分，而是包含在讨论部分。Weissberg and Buker（1990：161）认为论文的最后部分通常以"Discussion"作为标题，有时候也会使用"Conclusions"作为标题。Yang & Allison（2003）对于文章结尾部分语步特征做了开创性研究，归类总结出三个语步框架。Bunton（2005）对多个学科博士学位论文结尾部分语步分析，总结出自己结尾部分的语步模板，但是发现自然科学和工程领域存在一定的差异。Aslam & Mehmood（2014）在 Yang & Allison（2003）和 Bunton（2005）语步模板基础上对比分析了巴基斯坦学者撰写的自然和社会两个学科中论文结尾部分的语步特征，分析发现这两个学科之间既存在共性，也存在差异。

二 学术语篇语言特征研究

学术词汇在书面学术体裁的意义构建中起着重要作用（Omidian

& Siyanova-Chanturia，2021）。学术词汇主要由专业词汇和非专业通用学术词汇构成。非专业通用学术英语词汇对于英语作为母语和外语的学生均会造成困难（Spencer, et al.，2017；Evans & Green，2007）。非专业通用学术词汇广泛使用在不同学科论文中（Coxhead，2000）。对于非专业通用学术英语词汇的研究主要有以下几个方面：1. 针对不同学科的对比研究（如管李鑫、胡志清，2019；王华、胡志清，2020；Durrant，2016；Hyland & Tse，2007；Martínez，Beck & Panza，2009）；2. 针对特定学科的研究（如 Gardner & Davies，2014）；3. 针对词汇研究方法及研究对象的研究（如 Baker & Egbert，2016）；4. 针对某一类学术论文的研究（如 Omidian & Siyanova-Chanturia，2021）；5. 针对某一类词汇的研究（如 Parkinson & Musgrave，2014；刘国兵、张孝莲，2021；姜峰，2019）；6. 针对文章不同部分词汇特征的研究（如 Wright，2019）；7. 针对词汇与语步关联性的研究（如 Omidian，Shahriari & Siyanova-Chanturia，2018；Cortes，2013；Kanoksilapatham，2003；Yang & Allison，2003；Brett，1994；Swales，1981；Williams，1999）；8. 针对中外学者论文中语步词块使用特征的对比研究（如李梦骁、刘永兵，2017）；9. 针对英语学习者学术词块使用及发展的研究（如徐昉，2012）。近年来，学术英语词汇教学得到了更多的关注，越来越多学者开始研究学术词汇教学材料的选取及方法（如陈浩、文秋芳，2020；Skoufaki & Petrić，2021；Otto，2021）。此外，还有针对英语为外语的作者学术论文中句子特征的研究。Wu，Mauranen & Lei（2020）对比研究英语为母语和非英语国家的作者在学术文章中的语言特征，发现后者多使用长句、并列连词及复杂的名词性从句。在词组使用方面，后者多使用名词性词组。

三 方法部分体裁特征研究

目前，国内外学者对于学术语篇，特别是学术论文语篇的研究主要集中在引言和摘要方面，而对方法部分的研究较少。Bazerman（1988）发现论文中方法部分的演变是一个由简入繁的过程。最初方法描述的作用仅是告知读者实验中采取何种方法，但是随着实验的深入和复杂程度的增加，该部分已经成为论文结论部分的重要支撑，同时也是作者引导和"控制"读者以及对潜在的反对观点进行防范的重要手段。

一般来说，科学研究主要包括三个步骤，即提出问题、收集与问题相关的数据及回答问题。科学研究必须有着系统的数据收集方法。因此，研究方法作为学术论文的重要组成部分对研究的信度与效度有着较大的影响。研究的设计是否恰当与研究方法密切相关。作者可以使用方法部分来证明其研究结果的可信度，避免同行对其研究设计、研究结果及相关的结论提出批评或产生怀疑。Lim（2006：283）认为如果方法部分写不好就不能说服读者获得研究结果所使用的手段的有效性。方法部分的写作显得极其重要，作者在该部分必须清晰、恰当地描述实验步骤及理据，并提供足够的信息确保同行可以重复该实验来验证是否可以得到同样的实验结果，同时确保读者可以评判结果和结论是否有效（Azevedo et al.，2011）。

在学术语篇体裁分析方面，Bloor（1998）、Brett（1994）、Nwogu（1997）、Posteguilo（1999）、Yang & Edwards（1995）及 Swales（1990）对于学术论文方法部分体裁研究都进行过描述。以上学者都是将方法部分与文章其他部分一起分析。Nwogu（1997）和 Yang & Edwards（1995）给出的方法部分的主要语步基本相同（见表 1.1.1），但是后者指出有可能会出现另外一个语步，即 Describing instruments。Posteguilo（1999）分析计算机科学论文发现，该学科论文在引言和结果之间不使用"Method"这一词汇作为标题，这一点与医学和应用语言学明显不同。Berkenkotter & Huckin（1995）对 1944—1989 年发表的论文进行了历时研究，发现在生物和物理学科方法部分有弱化的趋势，通常将方法部分以比文章其他部分小一号的字体呈现，或者将其放在论文的最后。此外，Bruce（2008）对研究性论文的方法部分进行了认知体裁分析。

表 1.1.1 　　医学论文方法部分语步框架（Nwogu, 1997：135）

	Move	Step
1	Describing Data-Collection Procedure	1. Indicating source of data
		2. Indicating data size
		3. Indicating criteria for data collection
2	Describing Experimental Procedure	1. Identification of main research apparatus
		2. Recounting experimental process
		3. Indicating criteria for success
3	Describing Data-Analysis Procedure	1. Defining terminologies
		2. Indicating process of data classification
		3. Indentify anlytical instrument/procedure
		4. Indicating modification to instrument/procedure

　　Lim（2006）第一个将方法部分单独进行具体的语步分析，他从两个国际知名的管理学科期刊上选取了 20 篇论文，发现大部分论文的方法部分均包含以下三大语步（见表 1.1.2）。Kanoksilapatham（2015）对比分析了工程领域中土木、软件和生物医学三个学科中 180 篇论文各部分语步特征，给出了这三个学科方法部分语步模板（见表 1.1.3）。

表 1.1.2 　管理学科论文方法部分语步框架（Lim, 2006：287）

Rhetorical Move	Constituent Step
Move 1 Describing Data Collection Procedure/s	Step 1：Describing the sample
	a. Describing the location of the sample
	b. Describing the size of the sample/population
	c. Describing the characteristics of the sample
	d. Describing the sampling technique or criterion
	Step 2：Recounting steps in data collection
	Step 3：Justifying the data collection procedure/s
	a. Highlighting advantages of using the sample
	b. Showing representativity of the sample

续表

Rhetorical Move	Constituent Step
Move 2 Delineating Procedure/s for Measuring Variables	Step 1: Presenting an overview of the design
	Step 2: Explaining method/s of measuring variables
	a. Specifying items in questionnaires/databases
	b. Defining variables
	c. Describing methods of measuring variables
	Step 3: Justifying the method/s of measuring variables
	a. Citing previous research method/s
	b. Highlighting acceptability of the method/s
Move 3 Elucidating Data Analysis Procedure/s	Step 1: Relating (or 'recounting') data analysis procedure/s
	Step 2: Justifying the data analysis procedure/s
	Step 3: Previewing results

表 1.1.3　　　　工程领域三个学科论文方法部分语步框架
（Kanoksilapatham，2015：81）

Move	Step
Describing Procedures	Step 1: Announcing objectives
	Step 2: Specifying protocolized procedures
	Step 3: Detailing procedures
	Step 4: Providing procedural background
	Step 5: Justifying procedures
	Step 6: Describing research sites
	Step 7: Declaring ethical statements
Featuring Other Methodological Issues	Step 1: Describing materials and participants
	Step 2: Setting apparatus
	Step 3: Identifying data sources
Reporting and Consolidating Findings	Step 1: Stating findings
	Step 2: Interpreting findings
	Step 3: Comparing findings
	Step 4: Explaining findings

　　Cotos，Huffman & Link（2017）结合前人研究成果，分别对艺术、人文和社会科学领域八个学科共 240 篇论文及自然和应用科学中 22 个学科中 660 篇论文方法部分进行语步特征分析，给出了以下语步模板（见表 1.1.4）。

表 1.1.4　　　　　　多学科论文方法部分语步框架
（Cotos，Huffman & Link，2017：97—98）

Move	Step
Contextualizing Study Methods	Step 1：Referencing previous works
	Step 2：Providing general information
	Step 3：Identifying the methodological approach
	Step 4：Describing the setting
	Step 5：Introducing the subjects/participants
	Step 6：Rationalizing pre-experiment decisions
Describing the Study	Step 1：Acquiring the data
	Step 2：Describing the data
	Step 3：Describing experimental/study procedures
	Step 4：Describing tools
	Step 5：Identifying variables
	Step 6：Rationalizing experiment decisions
	Step 7：Reporting incrementals
Establishing Credibility	Step 1：Preparing the data
	Step 2：Describing the dataanaysis
	Step 3：Rationalizing data processing/analysis

　　国内学者对于论文方法部分的研究较少，杨瑞英（2014）分析了 20 篇应用语言学论文，总结得出以下语步和步骤（见表 1.1.5），发现该部分语步和步骤对于收集数据的方法很敏感。此外，她还发现对于实验性论文，表中的 5 个语步均有可能出现，同时有的语步和步骤也会重复出现。

表 1.1.5 应用语言学论文方法语步框架（杨瑞英，2014：151—152）

Move	Step
（M）Move 1 – Preliminary information	Presenting overview
	Reviewing relevant literature
	Providing justification
	Describing research setting
（M）Move 2 – Describing data	Indicating type and/or size of data
	Introducing criteria of data collection
	Introducing instrument of data collection
	Introducing background of interviewers
	Introducing procedure of data collection
（M）Move 3 – Describing subjects	Introducing background of subjects
	Introducing the criteria of subject selection
	Introducing the criteria of subject classification
（M）Move 4 – Describing experiment	Describing the timing and location of experiment
	Introducing experimental techniques
	Defining experimental variables
	Interpreting experimental variables
	Introducing apparatus
	Introducing tasks
	Describing the procedure of experiment
（M）Move 5 – Introducing the method of analysis	Defining concept/terminology
	Introducing the criteria of analysis
	Introducing procedure of analysis
	Indicating preliminary results
	Setting up the framework of analysis

综上所述，现有对于学术论文方法部分写作的研究不仅不足，同时还存在以下几个问题。

1. 现有研究主要是针对传统实验方法写作的研究。然而，随着科学的不断发展，人们收集数据的方法也不再局限于传统实验室方法，而是变得多样化以满足不同学科、不同性质的话题及研究问题的需要。除了传统实验方法，在研究中还会用到问卷调查法和数学建模。不同研究方法的写作在篇章结构或语步的构成、词汇的使用等方面必然存在一定的差异，如果不将它们区分开来研究就不可能真正看清该部分的写作特征。

2. 以往传统实验方法的写作类似菜谱，需要详细精确地描写实验步骤。现有的针对传统实验研究方法部分写作的研究主要集中在这种类型的写作。但就针对传统实验方法的写作目前已不再局限于菜谱式一种，根据研究的重点、实验方法的创新程度及学科的特点，实验部分的写作可分为详细阐述型（expounded）、标签型（labeled）及标题型（captions to figures or charts）；方法部分的呈现方式也不仅仅局限于在引言之后，而是也可以出现在论文的结尾后，作为论文的补充材料，以比论文其他部分小一号字体的形式呈现。

3. 现有研究主要是对单一学科或几个学科传统实验方法写作的研究，缺乏对多个学科同一种实验方法写作的对比研究及同一学科不同实验方法写作的研究。不同类型研究方法收集数据的方法存在差异；但是，不同学科同一种类型研究方法的写作也会有所区别。语步研究者当初的出发点是：学术论文的语步模式具有跨学科的普遍性。但不少学者后来发现，不少学科的学术语篇往往会表现出对常见语步模式的偏离（姜亚军、赵刚，2006）。Swales（1990：168）发现学科间学术论文最大的差异并不存在于人们以为的引言与讨论部分，而是方法与结果部分。他在回顾社会语言学家 Gilbert & Mulkay（1984）、Myers（1985）及语言学家 Bruce（1983）和 Weissberg（1984）研究结果的基础上指出，物理学与社会科学或诸如应用语言学这类交叉学科在方法部分的写作存在学科间的差异。在物理学科，方法部分比较粗略，语篇的连贯性主要依靠读者与作者共有的对于步骤和可能的顺序知识，即连贯是通过认知而不是通过最初的名词短语的语篇发展来实现的。相反，社会科学领域论文的方法部分通常是对步骤的详细描述，同时通过前指照应及词汇重复实现语篇的连贯。

4. 现有对于学术论文语言的研究很少涉及句子结构、时态和语态，特别是较少将语言特征与语步结合起来。不同语步有着不同的语篇功能，而语言是为交际服务的，离开语步的语言研究没有意义。论文写作中必须确保英语语义使用正确（Soyer，2017）。本研究将语言的研究建立在语步研究的结果上，可以为人们在撰写学术英语论文方法部分提供较大的帮助。

5. Berkenotter & Huckin（1995）通过对物理学和生物学的学术语篇研究得出了方法部分的历时发展变化等。姜峰（2020）考察了学术语篇语体特征的历时变化，发现学术语篇语体特征会随着社会情境演变而变化。而对于近十年来学术语篇体裁研究，特别是论文方法部分的研究严重缺乏。

第二节　本研究目的和研究问题

本研究主要分析近十年不同学科研究性论文中主要用到的几种实验方法的写作特征，即问卷调查法、传统实验（实验室/现场）和数学建模，旨在分析不同学科同一种实验方法写作的异同。特定的语言体裁具有其特定的语篇结构模式，社会文化差异制约了我们对英语语篇体裁的识别。通过对英语学术语篇方法部分进行体裁分析可以为中国学生撰写英语科研论文提供指导。

本研究主要从宏观语步特征方面和微观语言特征方面对比分析三类实验方法写作的体裁特征和不同学科同一种实验方法体裁特征的异同。宏观语步特征主要包括语步种类、各语步包含的步骤种类、各步骤在各个语步及所有语步中占比、不同语步占比及分布轨迹。微观语言特征主要包括句子结构、不同类型句子长度分布、句子类型与语步相关性、时态种类及组合、时态与语步相关性、语态种类及组合以及语态与语步相关性。

第二章　研究方法

　　本章主要从语料库建设、语步框架制定、语料标注、数据统计及作图软件四个方面介绍本研究方法。语料库建设主要涉及用于分析文章的来源、数量、学科、发表时间及作者相关信息。语步框架制定主要涉及三种类型实验方法，即传统实验、问卷调查和数学建模。这三种类型语步框架制定的方法略有不同，但是主要都是借助现有文献，选取不同学科一定数量论文进行分析，在此基础上对现有语步框架进行修改和完善，最终得出本研究的语步框架。语料标注分为两个部分。第一部分为语步标注，其中涉及语步标注模板、标注人及标注方法；第二部分为语言标注，涉及句类、时态和语态标注方法及标注人。数据统计及作图软件主要介绍数据统计内容、工具及作图软件。

第一节　语料库建设

　　本研究根据研究内容分别自建了三个小型语料库，即问卷调查语料库、传统实验语料库和数学建模语料库。问卷调查语料库包含管理科学与工程和英语语言文学两个一级学科共四十篇论文，用于研究的句子共计 1605 句，单词数约为 40599 个。传统实验语料库包含生物、临床医学、基础医学、海洋、市政、化学、材料、土木和语言学八个学科多个专业共 186 篇论文，用于研究的句子共计 7498 句，单词数约为 170929 个。数学建模语料库包含经管、电信、交通、车辆和软件五个学科共 116 篇文章，用于分析的句子共计 10822 句，约 251069

个单词。

语料库建设历经两年半时间，论文均由以上提到的各学科正在修读本论著作者所教授的学术英语论文写作课程的在读博士研究生收集，语言学论文由作者指导的 2 名在读英语专业硕士研究生完成，该 2 名硕士研究生也跟读了该门课程。

论文均选自各学科国际核心期刊。此外，论文的选取还必须符合以下几点要求。

1. 论文必须为实证性或应用型论文，同时各篇文章中方法部分必须有明显的标题，与论文的其他部分是分开的；

2. 论文必须从高因子国际期刊中选取，因为这样才能最大程度地保证论文质量，研究结果才有价值；

3. 选取的论文中必须有80%以上的文章为2010年后发表的，但是对于一些学科经典的论文发表时间不限；

4. 选取的论文中第一作者通信地址必须为英语国家或以英语为官方语言的国家。目的是保证语言使用的地道性，从而可以将语言方面的研究结果用于学术英语写作的教学中。

在选取以上提及的三种不同类型实验方法的论文前，首先要求各学科学生翻阅所在学科学术期刊，总结各学科不同类型实验方法论文情况，在此基础上布置学生论文选取任务。

第二节　语步框架制定

借助现有文献语步模板，从传统实验语料库不同学科论文中各选取五篇进行分析，在此基础上对现有语步进行增减和修改形成最终传统实验语步模板（详见第四章）。

问卷调查作为一种研究手段在写作上与传统实验性论文具有一定的差异，但是通过对比发现它们在写作中使用的语步存在诸多相似之处，因此我们在传统实验语步框架的基础上，结合对问卷调查写作部分的分析总结得出了本研究的语步框架（详见第三章）。

随着计算机技术的发展，建模实验目前已经成为很多学科的一种主要研究手段，但是目前还没有研究该类实验写作特征的文献。本研究在现有语步理论的指导下，在分析多个学科一定数量论文的基础上最终得出了本研究的语步模板（详见第五章）。

第三节　语料标注

语料标注人均为负责选取论文的学生本人。对于语料的标注主要分三个阶段，即准备阶段、语步标注和语言标注。

准备阶段：在课程开始2周的时间内学生按照要求完成文章的选取，本研究负责人从论文的选题，到总体结构，再到各部分结构逐一讲解，但把重点放在实验方法部分语步的分析上，特别是本研究涉及的问卷调查、传统实验和数学建模三种类型语步讨论上。此外，句子类型的讲解和讨论也是课堂教学的重点，在各部分讲解的过程中带领学生分析各自所选文章。

语步标注：根据语步模板，逐句标注步骤代码，如遇模板中不包含的内容，则修改模板添加步骤。

语言标注：主要标注出句子类型、时态和语态。句子类型根据结构划分为简单句、复杂句、复合句和复合复杂句。如果句子中出现冒号，"i. e."后或括号内或破折号后出现非词组的句子或从句则归为特殊句类，使用特殊代码标注（详见符号说明）。需要特别说明的是，如果括号中句子为"See Figure…"则忽略不计，如果括号中有i. e.则归为i. e类句子。

第四节　数据统计及作图软件

本研究对论文实验方法写作在正文中的占比进行了统计。正文是指从引言到结尾部分，即不包括摘要、参考文献和附录。此外，由于考虑到文章中图表的因素，对于占比的计算不是按照字数而是按照版面来计算。

研究中使用到的作图软件主要涉及用于绘制语步轨迹的 Windows

2018 AntConc 3.5.7，用于绘制词汇云图的 WordArt（https：//wor-
dart. com/），以及用于绘制步骤与句类、时态和语态可视化网络关系
图的 Gephi 绘图软件。

第三章　问卷调查方法写作特征

　　问卷调查是调查法中最常用的一种研究手段，它是由伦敦统计学会（Statistical Society of London）于 1838 年发明的。与其他调查法相比，问卷调查的优点在于它可以从大量的人中获得信息，成本低、速度快，易于分析、允许人们花时间慢慢思考。问卷多以无记名方式进行，因此参与者可以陈述自己的真实观点或感受，而不必顾忌别人的反应。但是使用问卷收集数据的缺点在于回收率通常比较低，不能确保人们是否正确理解问题。此外，有些问题的答案选项有限，答题者的答案未必包括在内。

　　问卷主要分为结构型和非结构型两种。非结构型问卷（Unstructured questionnaire）用于收集定性数据，即可以观察和记录的信息，但不是数字性质的。它用于获取近似值及特征描述。结构型问卷（Structured questionnaire）用于收集定量数据，即以计数或数值形式记录的信息。

　　问卷是由一系列问题构成的，问题主要有以下几种类型：开放式问题（Open ended questions）；多项选择题（Multiple choice questions）；二分法问题（Dichotomous questions）；尺度问题（Scaled questions）；图像问题（Pictorial questions）。

　　开放式问题让受访者可以更自由地回答，想写多少就写多少，主要用于收集定性数据的非结构型问卷。多项选择题为受访者提供了一系列的答案选项，他们可以选择一个或多个，这种类型潜在的问题在于提供答案选项可能不全面，为了弥补这一缺陷，选项中会加入"其他"这一答案。二分法问题只包括两种可能的答案，比如"是/否"，"同意/不同意"或"真/假"。当研究需要的只是基本的验证而不需要太深入的动机时，可以使用这种问题。尺度问题通常用来判断一种感觉的程度，在问卷中很常见，在两种类型的问卷中均可以使用。尺度问题还可以细分为诸如评分表（Rating scale）、量表（Likert scale）、语义差分表（Semantic differential scale）等不同的类型。图像问题主要是向受访者展示图片而不是文字供其选择回答问题，它通常比其他类型问题的回答率高。

　　问卷作为一种收集数据的手段，使用的学科有管理科学与工程、电信、交通、机械与能源、汽车、外国语言学及应用语言学等。其中使用的最多的学科是管理科学与工程，其次是外国语言学及应用语言学中的语言教学。本章节选取管理科学与工程和外国语言学及应用语言学在外语教学中以问卷作为研究手段的英语学术论文，对文章中问卷调查写作进行体裁分析。

　　本研究共从两个一级学科中的 23 种国际期刊中选取了 40 篇论文，通过对论文语步分析，发现这两个学科在问卷调查方法的写作基本上包括以下三大语步，即问卷调查对象及相关情况、问卷设计及变量测量、数据分析相关内容。但是不同学科各个语步中所包含的步骤在种类方面存在一定的差异。此外，某些步骤在方法部分出现的语境也存在一定的差异。具体语步和步骤如下。

语步一　问卷调查对象及相关情况：

　　使用该研究方法的意义；被调查对象数量及来源；被调查对象招募知情权；前人调查对象选取方法；被调查对象选取方法；被调查对象分组及预处理；被调查对象选取的科学性；被调查对象选取的局限性；被调查对象相关信息；问卷填写要求及说明。

语步二　问卷设计及变量测量：

　　问卷设计概述；调查目的；问题涉及维度/题项；问卷类型；定义变量；使用某种类型问卷的理由；测量变量的方法；前人测量变量方法；预调查；预调查后的修改；问卷设计潜在问题；问卷设计过程；确定相关控制因素；问卷分发时间段；问卷分发/回收途径；细节参见图表/期刊/网站；问卷回收率；回收率分析；问卷设计/数据

测量的科学性；填写问卷的时长。

语步三　数据分析相关内容：

分析软件/工具；数据分析方法；前人数据分析方法；数据信度与效度；预览主要结果。

第一节　管理科学与工程

管理科学与工程（以下简称管理学）主要包括管理与工程、工商管理学、农林经济管理学、公共管理学四个一级学科，涉及多个研究方向。本研究从 13 种 SCI 国际期刊上选取了 20 篇论文，这些文章主要涉及管理科学与工程、企业管理、教育经济与管理三大方向。第一作者单位主要为美国、澳大利亚及加拿大，除 1 篇论文外，其他论文发表时间均为 2000 年以后，其中 60% 为 2015 年以后发表的文章。本研究只分析各篇文章中有关问卷调查部分的写作特征，所选论文中绝大部分论文只使用了问卷调查一种方法，极少数论文同时使用了访谈。用于研究的句子共计 1014 个，约合 26868 个单词。方法部分在正文中占比最大值为 39%，最小值为 8%，平均值为 20%，标准差为 0.087。同一种期刊不同文章中该部分占比存在一定的差异，占比情况与期刊及论文发表时间没有显著关联性。

一　标题特征分析

图 3.1.1 为本学科二十篇论文方法部分一级大标题中词汇使用情况。如图所示，绝大部分文章使用了 method，共出现过 10 次；其次是 methods 和 methodology，分别出现过 5 次和 3 次。有两篇文章中标题分别为 data source 和 research design and procedure。所选的文章中有 80% 的文章方法部分使用了二级小标题，最多的有 5 个，最少的有 2 个。图 3.1.2 是二级小标题词汇分布，使用频率最高的是 measure，一共有 13 篇文章中使用了该词汇，其次为 sample（10 次）、data（7 次）和 procedure（7 次）。有 35% 的文章会将二级小标题 measure 进一步细化，

使用三级标题。从图 3.1.3 中可以发现，出现最多的是 job（8 次），其次是 variables（6 次）、work（5 次）和 control（5 次）。有一篇文章中使用了四级小标题，主要涉及变量测量细节。

图 3.1.1　一级大标题词汇云图

图 3.1.2　二级小标题词汇云图

图 3.1.3　三级小标题词汇云图

综上所述，管理学领域论文方法部分均包含一级大标题。大部分文章中包含二级小标题，较少的文章使用三级小标题，极少部分文章使用四级小标题。第一、二级标题与文章研究主题均没有显著的相关性，但是小标题中词汇与使用的研究方法关系更密切。第三、四级小标题与研究内容之间呈现一定的相关性。此外，不同文章中包含的小标题数量存在一定的差异。

二　语步特征分析

本节主要分析所研究论文问卷调查方法部分的语步特征。分析发现该学科论文该部分写作的总体语步框架与语言学基本一致，即该部分写作均可分成三个大的语步；但是两个学科各语步中包含的步骤种类存在一定的差异。本节各语步列表中只列出该学科论文中出现的步骤。

（一）语步一特征

表3.1.1是本学科语步一中所包含的步骤。如表所示，语步一中共包括了十个步骤。表3.1.2是各篇文章语步一中各步骤在该语步中的占比情况。如表所示，除一篇文章外，其他各篇文章中均包含了语步一。主要原因是该篇文章中研究方法同时包括了访谈和问卷两个部分，访谈的描述在问卷前，访谈中涉及访谈对象的来源、特点及招募办法等数据收集相关情况。问卷部分涉及的被调查对象等信息与访谈一致，所以作者在问卷部分的写作省略了调查对象相关信息。在包含该步骤的文章中，该语步中各步骤在各篇文章中占比情况不一。此外，同一个步骤在不同文章中的占比情况也有所差异。以下是针对每个步骤占比情况的具体分析及提供的实例。各章节例句后括号中为该例句所在语篇代码。

表3.1.1　　　　　　　　　　**语步一各步骤列表**

M	语步一、问卷调查对象及相关情况		
1.1	被调查对象数量及来源	1.3a	被调查对象分组及预处理
1.1A	使用该研究方法的意义	1.4	被调查对象选取的科学性

续表

M	语步一、问卷调查对象及相关情况			
1.2	被调查对象招募知情权		1.5	被调查对象选取的局限性
1.2a	前人调查对象选取方法		1.6	被调查对象相关信息
1.3	被调查对象选取方法		1.7	问卷填写要求及说明

表 3.1.2　　　　　　　　　语步一各步骤占比

M	1.1	1.1A	1.2	1.2a	1.3	1.3a	1.4	1.5	1.6	1.7
GW-01	25%	—	—	—	13%	—	38%	13%	13%	—
GW-02	50%	—	—	—	38%	—	—	—	13%	—
GW-03	18%	—	9%	1%	10%	15%	32%	9%	3%	3%
GW-04	20%	—	27%	3%	10%	—	27%	13%	—	—
GW-05	20%	—	14%	4%	4%	—	45%	—	14%	—
GW-06	20%	—	25%	3%	5%	—	28%	—	20%	—
GW-07	14%	—	—	—	—	—	—	—	86%	—
GW-08	18%	—	27%	—	—	—	9%	—	45%	—
GW-09	12%	—	—	6%	3%	6%	33%	—	39%	—
GW-10	10%	—	6%	—	3%	—	—	—	77%	3%
GW-11	10%	—	13%	3%	31%	3%	8%	—	33%	—
GW-12	41%	—	15%	—	—	—	7%	—	7%	30%
GW-13	14%	—	7%	—	7%	7%	14%	—	52%	—
GW-14	80%	—	20%	—	—	—	—	—	—	—
GW-15	56%	—	—	—	—	—	—	25%	19%	—
GW-16	7%	16%	—	—	—	—	—	—	67%	10%
GW-17	6%	28%	—	—	8%	—	58%	—	—	—
GW-18	13%	—	—	—	27%	—	40%	—	20%	—
GW-19	21%	21%	—	—	11%	—	11%	—	37%	—
GW-20	—	—	—	—	—	—	—	—	—	—

M 1.1 被调查对象数量及来源：所选文章中有 95% 的文章包含该步骤。在包含该步骤的文章中，该步骤在语步一中的占比最大值为 80%，最小值为 6%，平均值为 24%，标准差为 0.19。实例如下：

A total of 150 respondents were identified (75 contractor representatives and 75 owner representatives), of whom 92 returned completed surveys for a 61% response rate. (GW – 02)

The preliminary data was collected from a total of 15 medium to large construction firms in Australia. (GW – 18)

M 1.1A 使用该研究方法的意义：所选文章中有三篇文章包含该步骤。在这三篇文章中，该步骤在语步一中的占比分别为 28% 、16% 和 21% 。实例如下：

This method was chosen because it can efficiently reach a large sample, and allowed ease of response. (GW – 16)

Mixed methods from multiple sources provide research rigidity (Sekaran, 2003) which allows researchers to overcome the inherent weaknesses associated with each method (Dawson, 2009). Therefore, mixed methods were adopted in this research by combining qualitative and quantitative research approaches to identify ways of improving WM practices in non-residential building projects as shown in Fig. 1. (GW – 19)

M 1.2 被调查对象招募知情权：所选文章中有一半的文章包含该步骤。在包含该步骤的文章中，该步骤在语步一中的占比最大值为 27% ，最小值为 6% ，平均值为 16% ，标准差为 0.08 。实例如下：

All participants received a hard copy of the survey pack which described the aim of the study and stated that participation was both voluntary and anonymous. (GW – 08)

One week prior to the beginning of the data collection, the director of the division sent an e-mail to all division employees (n = 312), which included an invitation to participate in the survey and a brief message that his intentions were to enact positive changes suggested by the results of the study. (GW – 12)

M 1.2a 前人调查对象选取方法：所选文章中有 30% 的文章包含该步骤。在包含该步骤的文章中，该步骤在语步一中的占比最大值为 6% ，最小值为 1% ，平均值为 3% ，标准差为 0.01 。实例如下：

Following previous researchers, we assessed the key informant quality in our survey to make sure that respondents to our survey were indeed CEOs and/or senior executives of SBUs (Heide & Weiss, 1995, Phillips, 1981). (GW – 09)

This procedure for data collection has been used in several studies (e. g. Grant & Mayer, 2009) and allows for testing of the model from individuals in an assortment of organizations and industries to enhance generalizability. (GW – 11)

M 1.3 被调查对象选取方法：所选文章中有 65% 的文章包含该步骤。在包含该步骤的文章中，该步骤在语步一中的占比最大值为 38% ，最小值为 3% ，平均值为 13% ，标准差为 0.11 。实例如下：

After contacting and conducting detailed interviews with 20 of these purchasing managers to gain a better understanding of the specific research context, we identified 1, 050 NAPM members who were eligible to participate in our study. (GW - 04)

If a participant indicated he or she worked more hours per week at the second job, the participant was omitted from analysis as we could not be certain which job was actually the primary job and which job was actually the second job. (GW - 11)

M 1.3a 被调查对象分组及预处理：所选文章中有 20% 的文章包含该步骤。在包含该步骤的文章中，该步骤在语步一中的占比最大值为 15%，最小值为 3%，平均值为 8%，标准差为 0.04。实例如下：

For comparison purposes, the total sample was split into two groups; those received before the second wave of mailing and those received after the second wave. (GW - 09)

We classified universities on the basis of the Chinese national projects of the "211 university" and "the 985 university". (GW - 13)

M 1.4 被调查对象选取的科学性：所选文章中有 65% 的文章包含该步骤。在包含该步骤的文章中，该步骤在语步一中的占比最大值为 58%，最小值为 7%，平均值为 27%，标准差为 0.16。实例如下：

All participants voluntarily completed the surveys. (GW - 06)

A comparison between the responding and nonresponding firms using multivariate analysis of variance indicated no significant differences in terms of key firm characteristics (i. e. , industry type, firm ownership, number of employees, and annual sales revenues) (Wilks's $\Lambda = 0.83$; $F = 1.26$; $p = 0.49$), which suggested that nonresponse bias was not a concern. (GW - 05)

M 1.5 被调查对象选取的局限性：所选文章中有 20% 的文章包含该步骤。在包含该步骤的文章中，该步骤在语步一中的占比最大值为 25%，最小值为 9%，平均值为 15%，标准差为 0.06。实例如下：

Although we received an equal number of responses from buyer and supplier organizations, not all of the questionnaires were matched within a given dyad because some of the buyer responses were for dyads for which we did not receive supplier responses (and vice versa). (GW - 04)

The sample was comprised of 6, 828 (83.2%) females and 1,300 (15.8%) males while 83 (1%) failed to provide their gender. (GW - 15)

M 1.6 被调查对象相关信息：所选文章中有 80% 的文章包含该步骤。在包含该步骤的文章中，该步骤在语步一中的占比最大值为 86%，最小值为 3%，平均值为 34%，标准差为 0.25。实例如下：

Members of each team were geographically dispersed. Many members worked from offices in their homes. All of the day-to-day work carried out by teams was virtual in nature. (GW - 10)

The respondents' firms engaged between 10 and 6000 employees, with an average of 975 employees. Results showed that more than 50% of the respondents' firms had 500 or fewer employees. Annual revenue averaged $70M. (GW – 16)

M 1.7 问卷填写要求及说明：所选文章中有 20% 的文章包含该步骤。在包含该步骤的文章中，该步骤在语步一中的占比最大值为 30%，最小值为 3%，平均值为 11%，标准差为 0.11。实例如下：

We asked respondents to navigate to and complete the survey within 30 days of the date that the e-mail was sent. To further encourage participation, during the 30 days that the survey was a-vailable for completion, the director sent a follow-up e-mail encouraging participation, and we sent two reminder e-mails that included a link to the survey. (GW – 12)

Respondents were requested to base their responses on one particular China-based project of their choice. However, projects must be recently (after 2000) completed AEC projects so that the data is not outdated. (GW – 16)

综上所述，在所分析的文章中除一篇文章外，其他文章中均包含了该语步。在该语步中，涉及文章数最高的步骤是 M1.1，最低的是 M1.1A，分别占所有文章的 95% 和 15%。除一篇不包含语步一的文章外，其他各篇文章中语步一各步骤涉及篇章数平均值为 9.2 篇，占所有文章的 48%，标准差为 5.79。在这些文章中涉及步骤种类最多的有 9 种，最低的只有 2 种，分别占语步一中所有步骤的 90% 和 20%。各篇文章中语步一中各步骤种类的平均值为 4.6 种，占所有步骤的 46%，标准差为 2.01 种。不同文章中包含的步骤种类存在一定的差异，同一个步骤在不同文章中的占比也存在一定的差异。在包含该步骤的文章中，步骤占比平均值最高的是 M1.6，为 34%，最低的是 M1.2a，仅有 3%。各步骤在不同文章中占比平均值之间的标准差为 9.41。

（二）语步二特征

表 3.1.3 是该学科所分析文章中语步二中包含的步骤种类。该语步共包括 16 种步骤。表 3.1.4 是各篇文章语步二中各步骤在该语步中的占比情况。如表所示，所有文章均包括了该语步，但是该语步中各步骤占比情况不一。此外，同一个步骤在不同文章中使用的情况也存在差异。以下是每个步骤占比的具体分析及实例。

表 3.1.3　　　　　　　　　　语步二各步骤列表

M	语步二、问卷设计及变量测量		
2.1A	问卷设计概述	2.1g	问卷设计潜在问题
2.1B	调查目的	2.2	确定相关控制因素
2.1a	问题涉及维度/题项	2.3	问卷分发时间段
2.1b	问卷类型	2.4	问卷分发/回收途径
2.1c	定义变量	2.5	细节参见图表/期刊/网站
2.1d	测量变量的方法	2.6a	问卷回收率
2.1e	前人测量变量方法	2.6b	回收率分析
2.1f	预调查	2.7	问卷设计/数据测量的科学性

表 3.1.4　　　　　　　　　　语步二各步骤占比

M	2.1A	2.1B	2.1a	2.1b	2.1c	2.1d	2.1e	2.1f	2.1g	2.2	2.3	2.4	2.5	2.6a	2.6b	2.7
GW-01	14%	—	18%	—	9%	4%	23%	4%	11%	—	—	—	2%	4%	2%	11%
GW-02	—	—	43%	—	—	20%	13%	—	10%	—	—	13%	—	—	—	—
GW-03	—	—	33%	—	4%	14%	—	—	26%	—	—	4%	—	—	—	20%
GW-04	2%	1%	1%	—	2%	23%	10%	—	33%	—	4%	1%	2%	—	—	20%
GW-05	—	—	19%	—	3%	10%	29%	—	25%	—	—	—	10%	—	—	3%
GW-06	—	—	41%	—	6%	41%	—	—	—	—	—	—	—	12%	—	—
GW-07	—	7%	30%	—	11%	—	37%	—	—	—	—	—	7%	7%	—	—
GW-08	—	—	16%	—	16%	21%	—	—	—	4%	—	—	4%	9%	—	30%
GW-09	—	—	8%	—	—	37%	19%	9%	9%	—	8%	3%	3%	—	—	3%
GW-10	—	2%	13%	—	—	42%	9%	—	—	1%	—	—	3%	1%	—	29%
GW-11	10%	—	13%	—	—	32%	12%	—	13%	—	2%	—	—	—	—	19%
GW-12	—	—	31%	4%	—	29%	8%	—	16%	—	12%	—	—	—	—	—
GW-13	—	—	19%	—	2%	31%	13%	—	—	—	4%	4%	4%	—	—	23%
GW-14	—	—	22%	—	—	7%	—	7%	11%	—	—	—	7%	—	—	44%
GW-15	—	—	35%	—	3%	33%	3%	—	8%	3%	—	—	7%	—	—	8%
GW-16	20%	4%	8%	—	18%	6%	—	—	—	12%	2%	—	4%	2%	—	22%
GW-17	29%	—	—	—	—	29%	13%	—	—	—	8%	4%	—	8%	—	8%

M	2.1A	2.1B	2.1a	2.1b	2.1c	2.1d	2.1e	2.1f	2.1g	2.2	2.3	2.4	2.5	2.6a	2.6b	2.7
GW－18	—	22%	19%	—	—	—	15%	—	—	—	—	4%	15%	19%	7%	—
GW－19	11%	22%	—	—	—	22%	—	—	—	—	—	22%	22%	—	—	—
GW－20	14%	—	—	—	—	29%	—	14%	—	—	—	14%	—	4%	4%	6%

M 2.1A 问卷设计概述：所选文章中有 35% 的文章包含该步骤。在包含该步骤的文章中，该步骤在语步二中的占比最大值为 29%，最小值为 2%，平均值为 14%，标准差为 0.08。实例如下：

In the first stage, theoretical constructs were based on a thorough review of the literature and are well grounded in existing theory. Acknowledging the inherit complexities of the constructs considered in this study, all of them constituted latent variables, thus requiring indirect measurement from multi-item reflective scales. (GW－01)

We tested both theoretical models in two samples: Sample A and Sample B. Sample A is a cross-sectional model in which all measures were self-reported and collected at the same time. To mitigate concerns of common method variance and to conduct a replication of Sample A, we collected a Time 1 and Time 2 survey, spaced one week apart, for Sample B. In the Measures section, we note at which time each scale was administered to the participant in Sample B (i. e., Time 1 or Time 2). (GW－11)

M 2.1B 调查目的：所选文章中有 30% 的文章包含该步骤。在包含该步骤的文章中，该步骤在语步二中的占比最大值为 22%，最小值为 1%，平均值为 10%，标准差为 0.09。实例如下：

It is worth noting that the intent of the questionnaire was clearly communicated with the respondents in a plain language statement (PLS), which requested them to provide specific and objective responses to the relevant variables or indicators aimed to measure only the performance of the WBPM systems but isolating any other associated issues affecting the performance of projects. (GW－18)

We conducted a field study to test the (1) direct effects of team empowerment on virtual team process improvement and customer satisfaction and (2) moderating effects of face-to-face interaction on the relationships between team empowerment and both process improvement and customer satisfaction. (GW－10)

M 2.1a 问题涉及维度/题项：所选文章中有 85% 的文章包含该步骤。在包含该步骤的文章中，该步骤在语步二中的占比最大值为 43%，最小值为 1%，平均值为 22%，标准差为 0.12。实例如下：

A sample item includes "I have left work early without permission". (GW – 12)

Organizational Commitment: Six items developed by Meyer and Allen (1991) were used to capture organizational commitment. A sample item is "I do not feel a strong sense of belonging to my organization". (GW – 06)

M 2.1b 问卷类型：所选文章中只有一篇包含该步骤。在该篇文章中，该步骤在语步二中的占比为4%。实例如下：

The supervisor surveys were personalized and displayed in matrix format. (GW – 12)

M 2.1c 定义变量：所选文章中有30%的文章包含该步骤。在包含该步骤的文章中，该步骤在语步二中的占比最大值为18%，最小值为2%，平均值为6%，标准差为0.06。实例如下：

To ensure the robustness of results, this study also included several control variables to limit extraneous effects that might offer alternative explanations of BPE and SCI. These include firm size (number of employees), industry type and revenue (annual sales) (Liu et al., 2016). (GW – 01)

Section A of the questionnaire requested information of the project in China and its level of success in six areas (Y1 – Y6 in Table 1). The level of performance was assigned based on an anchored seven-point Likert scale (Table 1). (GW – 16)

M 2.1d 测量变量的方法：所选文章中有95%的文章包含该步骤。在包含该步骤的文章中，该步骤在语步二中的占比最大值为42%，最小值为4%，平均值为21%，标准差为0.12。实例如下：

All but one measure employed a 7 – point scale ranging from (1) strongly disagree to (7) strongly agree. (GW – 07)

A five-point Likert-scale was used to elicit the level of agreement where (1 = strongly disagree, 2 = disagree, 3 = neutral, 4 = agree, and 5 = strongly agree). (GW – 17)

M 2.1e 前人测量变量方法：所选文章中有75%的文章包含该步骤。在包含该步骤的文章中，该步骤在语步二中的占比最大值为41%，最小值为3%，平均值为18%，标准差为0.11。实例如下：

Prior studies have used a similar approach to capture SCI (Terjesen et al., 2012; Danese and Bortolotti, 2014). (GW – 01)

Available options for collecting data from respondents are qualitative, quantitative or a combination of both using mixed-methods (Creswell et al., 2003). (GW – 17)

M 2.1f 预调查：所选文章中有20%的文章包含该步骤。在包含该步骤的文章中，该步骤在语步二中的占比最大值为15%，最小值为4%，平均值为10%，标准差为0.05。实例如下：

To conduct a pretest, a random selection of 15 CEOs or senior executives was contacted by one of the authors. After obtaining their consent to participate, the 15 CEOs or senior executives were asked to evaluate the draft questionnaire. (GW – 09)

The quantitative data collection was conducted in two phases: the first phase was a pilot survey with 35 respondents to ensure functionality, reliability, and response rate of the research instrument. (GW – 20)

M 2.1g 问卷设计潜在问题：所选文章中只有三篇文章包含该步骤。在这三篇文章中，该步骤在语步二中的占比分别为 11%、7% 和 8%。实例如下：

Although we hypothesize that both TPT and TPP are antecedents of SCI, it can be argued that SCI may be affected by other factors beyond the ones considered in this study. (GW – 01)

Scholars have argued that it is difficult to separate the effects of age and generation (Macky et al., 2008; Twenge & Campbell, 2008), and this is a challenge for all generational research (Parry & Urwin, 2011). (GW – 15)

M 2.2 确定相关控制因素：所选文章中有 45% 的文章包含该步骤。在包含该步骤的文章中，该步骤在语步二中的占比最大值为 33%，最小值为 3%，平均值为 16%，标准差为 0.09。实例如下：

A number of control variables were expected to influence the work engagement exhibited at the primary job. (GW – 11)

Previous research has also shown that tenure in the organization is related to trust (Perrone et al. 2003). (GW – 04)

M 2.3 问卷分发时间段：所选文章中只有一篇文章包含该步骤。在该篇文章中，该步骤在语步二中的占比为 4%。实例如下：

To minimise potential common method bias, data were collected at two points in time separated by a four-week interval (cf. Podsakoff, MacKenzie, & Podsakoff, 2012). (GW – 08)

M 2.4 问卷分发/回收途径：所选文章中有 55% 的文章包含该步骤。在包含该步骤的文章中，该步骤在语步二中的占比最大值为 22%，最小值为 1%，平均值为 8%，标准差为 0.06。实例如下：

A follow-up letter with an additional copy of the questionnaire was sent to non-respondents four weeks after our initial mailing. (GW – 09)

Our next course of action was to send each potential respondent a personalized e-mail that reiterated the information mentioned in the initial e-mail sent from the director. Also included in this e-mail was a link to the online survey. (GW – 12)

M 2.5 细节参见图表/期刊/网站：所选文章中有 70% 的文章包含该步骤。在包含该步骤的文章中，该步骤在语步二中的占比最大值为 22%，最小值为 1%，平均值为 7%，标准差为 0.06。实例如下：

A summary of terminations by generation is given in Table 3. (GW – 15)

Appendix A lists the items for each measure. (GW – 03)

M 2.6a 问卷回收率：所选文章中有 65% 的文章包含该步骤。在包含该步骤的文章中，该步骤在语步二中的占比最大值为 19%，最小值为 2%，平均值为 7%，标准差为 0.04。实例如下：

A total of 280 out of 333 team members responded to surveys representing 35 teams, giving us a response rate of 84 percent. (GW – 10)

Follow up calls resulted in receiving 101 duly completed questionnaires (a response rate of around 24%). (GW – 17)

M 2.6b 回收率分析：所选文章中有 25% 的文章包含该步骤。在包含该步骤的文章中，该步骤在语步二中的占比最大值为 7%，最小值为 1%，平均值为 3%，标准差为 0.02。实例如下：

In addition, for all 35 teams, more than half of the team members responded, which supported the use of the data at the team level of analysis. (GW – 10)

Such a response rate was primarily due to the selection of the sample and the interaction between the researchers and the respondents in confirming willingness and participation in the study. (GW – 18)

M 2.7 问卷设计/数据测量的科学性：所选文章中有 70% 的文章包含该步骤。在包含该步骤的文章中，该步骤在语步二中的占比最大值为 44%，最小值为 3%，平均值为 18%，标准差为 0.11。实例如下：

This method for measuring work orientation was developed by Wrzesniewski et al. (1997) and has been used by other researchers (e. g., Berg et al., 2010). Although a variety of well-validated calling scales exist in the literature (for a review see Duffy, Autin, Allan, & Douglass, 2015), we chose the paragraph method for two primary reasons. (GW – 11)

Cronbach's α is 0.94 for procedural and informational justice, 0.92 for distributive justice, 0.93 for interpersonal justice and 0.95 for OJ as a whole, indicating good measurement reliability. (GW – 13)

综上所述，在所分析的文章中均包含了该语步。该语步中各步骤涉及篇章数最高的是 M2.1d，最低的是 M2.3，分别占所有文章的 95% 和 5%。各篇文章语步二中各步骤涉及篇章数平均值为 9.1 篇，占所有文章的 45%，标准差为 5.76。各篇文章中涉及步骤种类最多的有 11 种，最低的为 4 种，分别占语步二中所有步骤的 69% 和 25%。各篇文章中包含步骤种类的平均值为 7.25，占语步二中所有步骤的 45%，标准差为 1.89。不同文章中包含的步骤种类存在一定的差异，同一步骤在不同文章中的占比也存在一定的差异。除去只涉及一篇文章的步骤，其他步骤占比平均值最高的是 M2.1a，最低的是 M2.6b，分别为 22% 和 3%。各步骤在所有文章中占比平均值之间的标准差为 6.22。

（三）语步三特征

表 3.1.5 是所分析的该学科论文语步三中包含的步骤种类。如表所示，该语步中共包括了 5 个步骤。表 3.1.6 是各篇文章语步三中各步骤在该语步中的占比情况。如表所示，有一部分文章不包含该语步。在包含该步骤的文章中，该语步中各步骤占比情况不一。此外，同一个步骤在不同文章中的占比情况也有所差异。以下是针对每个步骤占比情况的具体分析及实例。

表 3.1.5 语步三各步骤列表

M	语步三、数据分析相关内容		
3.1	分析软件/工具	3.4	数据信度与效度
3.2	数据分析方法	3.5	预览主要结果
3.3	前人数据分析方法		

表 3.1.6 语步三各步骤占比

M	3.1	3.2	3.3	3.4	3.5	M	3.1	3.2	3.3	3.4	3.5
GW－01	—	—	3%	97%	—	GW－11	—	—	—	—	—
GW－02	—	9%	5%	86%	—	GW－12	17%	47%	22%	15%	—
GW－03	—	—	7%	87%	5%	GW－13	7%	22%	11%	56%	4%
GW－04	—	—	—	—	—	GW－14	—	—	—	—	—
GW－05	—	—	12%	88%	—	GW－15	—	92%	4%	4%	—
GW－06	—	—	—	—	—	GW－16	3%	97%	—	—	—
GW－07	—	—	9%	91%	—	GW－17	—	—	—	100%	—
GW－08	—	—	—	—	—	GW－18	4%	96%	—	—	—
GW－09	—	—	—	—	—	GW－19	4%	51%	29%	16%	—
GW－10	—	—	—	—	—	GW－20	—	—	—	—	—

M 3.1 分析软件/工具：所选文章中有 25% 的文章包含该步骤。在包含该步骤的文章中，该步骤在语步三中的占比最大值为 17%，最小值为 3%，平均值为 7%，标准差为 0.05。实例如下：

We used Mplus 7.3 (Muthén & Muthén, 2012) to test the relationships hypothesized in the current study. (GW – 12)

SEM was chosen as the analytical technique to examine the model fit and test hypotheses. (GW – 13)

M 3.2 数据分析方法：所选文章中有 35% 的文章包含该步骤。在包含该步骤的文章中，该步骤在语步三中的占比最大值为 97%，最小值为 9%，平均值为 59%，标准差为 0.34。实例如下：

As the sample contained a mix of facility types and different services provided by respondents, Analysis of Variance (Anova) was also conducted. (GW – 16)

Due to the different response formats associated with our items (i. e., interval, ordinal, etc.), we used a variety of analyses to test our hypotheses. (GW – 15)

M 3.3 前人数据分析方法：所选文章中有一半的文章包含该步骤。在包含该步骤的文章中，该步骤在语步三中的占比最大值为 29%，最小值为 3%，平均值为 11%，标准差为 0.08。实例如下：

A rigorous process was followed to validate the measures, modeled on previous empirical studies (Zhao et al., 2008; Shi et al., 2016). (GW – 01)

There are two broad methods of conducting SEM being covariance-based (CB-SEM) and partial least squares (PLS-SEM) (Hair et al., 2014). (GW – 17)

M 3.4：数据信度与效度：所选文章中有 50% 的文章包含该步骤。在包含该步骤的文章中，该步骤在语步三中的占比最大值为 100%，最小值为 4%，平均值为 64%，标准差为 0.36。实例如下：

Additionally, estimating the CFA model using maximum likelihood estimation (MLE) and asymptotically distribution-free (ADF) interval estimation did not reveal any significant differences, thus making it safe to assume that the model was stable even if the data violated assumptions of multivariate normality. (GW – 03)

As recommended by researchers, oblique rotation was used in this research since it allows correlation of factors (Fabrigar et al., 1999; Field, 2009; Izquierdo et al., 2014). (GW – 19)

M 3.5 预览主要结果：所选文章中只有两篇包含该步骤。在这两篇文章中，该步骤在语步三中的占比分别为 5% 和 4%。实例如下：

Table 2 displays descriptive statistics and correlations for all variables. (GW – 03)

Table III presents the results of the CFA tests. (GW – 13)

综上所述，在所分析的文章中有60%的文章包含该语步。在这些文章中，涉及文章数最高的步骤是M3.4，最低的是M3.5，分别占所有文章的50%和10%。各步骤涉及篇章数平均值为6.6，占所有文章的33%，标准差为3.21。在包含该步骤的文章中涉及的步骤种类最高的有5种，最低的只有1种，分别占所有步骤的100%和20%，各篇文章中包含的步骤种类平均值为1.65种，占语步三中所有步骤的33%，标准差为1.63。不同文章中包含的步骤种类存在一定的差异，同一步骤在不同文章中的占比也存在一定的差异。在包含该步骤的文章中，各步骤占比平均值最高的是M3.4，最低的是M3.5，占比分别为64%和5%。各步骤在不同文章中占比平均值之间的标准差为29.62。

（四）语步占比及轨迹

图3.1.4是所分析各篇文章中三个语步的总体占比。如图所示，所有文章均包含语步二，分别有95%和60%的文章包含了语步一和语步三。70%的文章语步二占比最高，分别有20%和10%的文章语步一和语步三占比最高。在语步二占比最高的文章中，有一篇只包含语步二，其他文章中有三篇语步三高于语步一，占该类文章的21%。在其他语步二占比最高的文章中语步一均高于语步三。在语步一占比最高的文章中，语步二占比均高于语步三。而在语步三占比最高的两篇文章中，其中一篇文章语步一占比高于语步二，另一篇文章则相反。

就各步骤在所有语步中占比平均值来看，占比最高的前三个步骤依次为M2.1d、M2.1a和M3.4。占比最低的是M2.1b，其次是两个占比相同的步骤，分别为M2.3和M3.5。

就各步骤涉及的篇章数而言，最高的为19篇，占所有文章的95%，分别是M1.1和M2.1d；最低的是M2.1b，仅出现在1篇文章中，占所有文章的5%。

就各篇文章中包含的步骤种类来看，最多的有19种，占所有步骤种类的61%，仅有1篇。最低的仅有8种，占所有步骤种类的

26%，有 2 篇。各篇文章中包含步骤种类的平均值为 13.55 种，占所有步骤的 44%，标准差为 3.22。

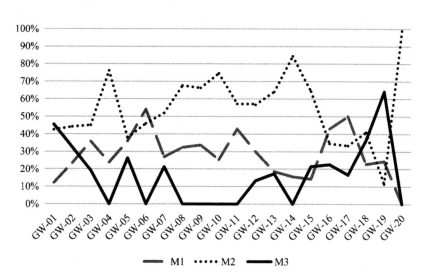

图 3.1.4 各篇文章中三个语步占比

图 3.1.5 至图 3.1.7 分别为是语步一、语步二和语步三的分布轨迹。如图所示，在所分析的二十篇文章中有一篇只包含语步二，有七篇只包含语步一和语步二两个语步，其他十二篇文章中均包含了三个语步。

在七篇只包含语步一和语步二的文章中，除一篇文章外，其他各篇文章中语步二占比均高于语步一，分布也最广，但是两个语步集中程度均存在篇章差异。除两篇文章外，其他各篇文章最前的位置均为语步一。此外，各篇文章中语步一主要分布在文章前部，有两篇文章中语步一中少部分语句分布在了文章较后的位置。语步二分布范围较广，大部分文章中语步二中少部分语句会分布在文章前部、语步一中或之前，但是主要以分布在语步一后为主。除一篇文章中语步二全部分布在语步一后，两个语步之间没有交叉，其他各篇文章中两个语步均有交叉。

在十二篇包含三个语步的文章中，除了分别有一篇文章中语步一

图 3.1.5　语步一分布轨迹

和语步三占比最高外，其他各篇文章中占比最高的均为语步二。有一半文章中语步一占比高于语步三，在另一半文章中这两个语步的占比刚好相反。总体来说，语步一主要分布在文章的前部，大部分文章最前的语句为语步一，极少数文章中语步一中部分语句会分布在文章的中间及偏后的位置。语步二分布最广，大部分文章中语步二主要分布在语步一后、语步三前，但是会有少部分语句出现在语步一和语步三中。语步三分布最集中，以文章的后部为主，但是在极少数文章中会分布在文章的中间。在绝大多数文章中语步一和语步二有交叉，但是只有一篇文章中语步一与语步三有交叉，该篇文章中三个语步均有交叉。一半的文章中语步二与语步三有交叉。

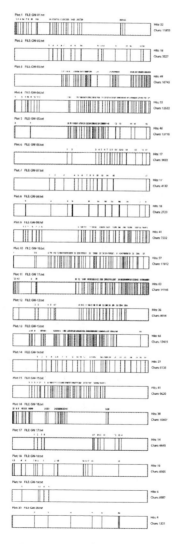

图 3.1.6　语步二分布轨迹

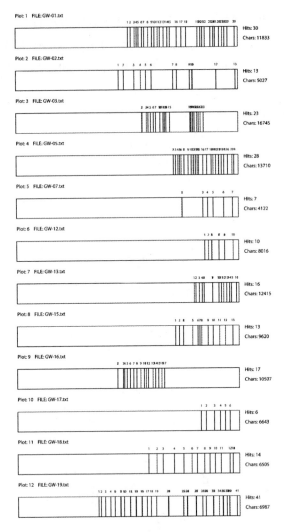

图 3.1.7　语步三分布轨迹

　　综上所述，同一学科不同文章中语步占比和分布轨迹既有相同之处，也存在一定的差异。所有文章中均出现了语步二，在绝大部分文章中该语步占比明显高于其他两个语步。语步一和语步三相比，各有一半文章中占比高于对方。就这三个语步在方法部分的分布而言，语步二分布最广，几乎覆盖了方法部分的前部、中间及偏后的位置，也就是语步一和语步三之间。语步一以文章最前和前部为主，语步三则以文章后部及最后为主。在绝大多数文章中语步二中有少量语句会与语步一有交叉，语步二与语步三交叉的情况少于语步一与语步二交叉的情况。三个语步均有交叉的情况极少发生。

三　语言特征分析

本小节主要分析该学科二十篇论文中问卷调查写作部分的语言特征。主要从句子特征、时态特征和语态特征三个大的方面进行分析。针对句子特征的分析主要包含句子类型、四类主要句子长度分布及四类句子与语步的关系。针对时态特征的分析主要包含时态种类、不同时态组合及占比最高的三种主要时态组合与语步的关系。针对语态特征的分析主要包含语态种类、不同语态组合及各语态组合与语步的关系。

（一）句子特征

A. 句子类型

表3.1.7是本学科二十篇文章中所包含的句子类型及各类句子占比。如表所示，简单句、复杂句、复合句及复合复杂句四类句子占所有句子的96.54%；有1句有语法错误，占所有句子的0.10%；其他为带有冒号及括号的各类特殊句子。四类句子中简单句占比远高于其他三类句子，其次是复杂句。其他两类句子占比均较低，其中复合句占比略高于复合复杂句。特殊类型句子形式多样，共有13种，其中NWS和NWP占比较高，其他的均较低。以下例句为特殊类型的句子。

表3.1.7　　　　　　　　　　　句类及占比

句类	句数	占比	句类	句数	占比
S	614	60.61%	NCPS	1	0.10%
P	246	24.28%	NSCP	1	0.10%
C	89	8.79%	NSS	1	0.10%
CP	29	2.86%	NWAP	1	0.10%

续表

句类	句数	占比	句类	句数	占比
BCPP	1	0.10%	NWAS	3	0.30%
BPF	1	0.10%	NWHS	2	0.20%
BPP	1	0.10%	NWP	5	0.49%
BSF	2	0.20%	NWS	14	1.38%
NPC	1	0.10%	R	1	0.10%

BCPP：One was a general recommendation item（"I would recommend the organization because I predict a good future for the organization"）; the other was a targeted, stakeholder specific recommendation item, with respondents being asked whether they would recommend to friends that they buy, invest, work for, or work with the organization.（GW – 03）

BPF：Although we cannot fully discount the possibility of response bias in such a survey（e. g., that the most and least trusting stakeholders were more likely to answer the survey）, such concerns are mitigated for two reasons.（GW – 03）

BPP：We adapted the original items（e. g., "I am aware of a time when this subordinate left work early without permission."）so that the supervisors could use the scale.（GW – 12）

BSF：All stakeholders were contacted via e-mail or through direct contact（in which case they were asked to fill out paper surveys）.（GW – 03）

NPC：Next, the participant had to indicate that his or her employment arrangement met one of two scenarios: 1）have a job as a wage or salary worker with two or more employers or 2）combine a wage or salary job with self-employment.（GW – 11）

NCPS：If the participant selected a third scenario: 3）receive a wage or salary from one employer, the participant was not classified as a dual jobholder and was removed from analysis.（GW – 11）

NSCP：This approach has four advantages:（a）it allowed supervisors to rate employees efficiently because each item had to be read only once to provide ratings for all subordinates on that item;（b）each supervisor had the ability to compare subordinates on each question asked, providing more varied and accurate ratings across the subordinates;（c）confidentiality was improved by having the pen-and-paper surveys personally distributed and collected by the researchers; and（d）it protected the employees from retaliation as supervisors were asked to rate all of their direct reports so they would not know which direct reports chose to participate.（GW – 12）

NSS：The quantitative data collection was conducted in two phases: the first phase was a pilot survey with 35 respondents to ensure functionality, reliability, and response rate of the research instrument.（GW – 20）

NWAP：Alternatively, we followed the approach suggested by Ketokivi and McIntosh (2017), where a chi-square difference statistic comparison between two nested structural equation models is conducted：an unconstrained model between the error terms of the endogenous variable (SCI) and the dependent variable (BPE) versus a second model where the error terms are correlated. (GW – 01)

NWAS：To ensure the robustness of our results, we included a number of control variables：age, gender, organization type, and whether the respondent interacted with the organization in more than one capacity. (GW – 03)

NWHS：Accordingly, we calculated the following mathematical equation for each TMT based on the information obtained from the SBUs：$H = 1 - \sum pi2$, where $i = 1$, $s = 9$, where H = functional diversity and pi = the percentage of TMT members in each functional area. (GW – 09)

NWP：Finally, for communication frequency items, respondents indicated on average how often they used a given communication media：face-to-face, telephone, email, and Sametime. (GW – 07)

NWS：Consequently, we identified nine functional backgrounds：marketing, sales/customer service, finance/accounting, general management, human resources/personnel, information technology, operations/distribution/logistics, R & D, and administrative support. (GW – 09)

B. 句类与语步

图 3.1.8 是四种句子类型与语步的关系。如图所示，复合复杂句中出现的步骤较分散，出现步骤较多的只有一种，共出现过 7 次，为 M3.4。该步骤同时也是复杂句和简单句中占比最高的前三个步骤之一，但是该步骤在这三类句子中排序不完全一致。在简单句、复合句和复杂句三类句子中占比最高的前三种步骤存在一定的差异，没有一种是三类句子中共有的，M1.6 和 M2.1A 分别为两类句子共有，但是它们在这两类句子中排序不完全一致。此外，由于这四类句子在文章中占比不同，即使相同步骤在这四类句子中排序一致，数量和占比也不相同。

这四种类型句子中包含了三个语步，就各类句子包含的三个语步中步骤种类而言，简单句中包含了三个语步中所有步骤，复杂句、复合句、复合复杂句中包含的步骤种类分别占三个语步中所有步骤种类的 91%、65% 和 52%。

总体来说，不同句子类型与步骤之间的关系存在异同，句子与步骤关系紧密度与该类句子在所有句子中的占比有关，同时也与该步骤在所有步骤中的占比有关，但是不完全成一一对应的关系，句类与步骤之间没有明显的相关性。

以下是四类句子中步骤占比最高的前三个步骤的例句。由于复杂复合句中步骤较分散，只给出占比最高的一个步骤的例句。

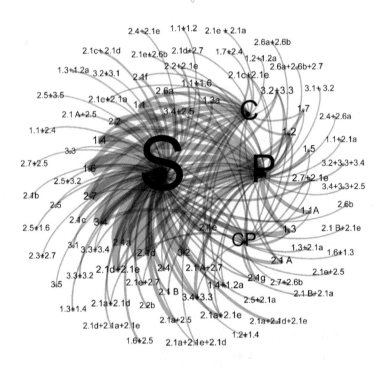

图 3.1.8　句类与步骤关系网络图

【S】

M 2.1d： Responses were marked using a five-point scale with endpoints labeled "strongly disagree" (1) and "strongly agree" (5). (GW – 03)

M 2.1a： However, as described previously, we deconstructed the Mayer et al. construct of integrity to include transparency and identification as separate constructs. (GW – 03)

M 3.4： The convergent and discriminant validity of the measures was then calculated using the full participant sample. (GW – 03)

【P】

M 3.4： First, we tested to ensure that the concept of trust was not understood differently across stakeholder groups. (GW – 03)

M 1. 6：To accomplish this, the MNC created project teams that operate 24 hours a day across multiple time zones with a primary focus on worldwide cross-culturally managed product development. (GW – 07)

M 2.7：Because the survey was conducted in German-speaking parts of Europe, we had the items translated and back-translated to ensure accuracy (Chapman and Carter 1979). (GW – 03)

【C】

M 1. 6：The average project budget was $853 million (Canadian) and average project duration was 54 months. (GW – 02)

M 3. 2：We obtained bootstrapped estimates of the indirect effect across levels of the moderator and provide confidence intervals (CIs) around the indirect effect to further test our hypotheses. (GW – 12)

M 1. 1：Organization 1 is a small to medium-sized manufacturing firm in Switzerland, Organization 2 is a large logistical company in Germany, Organization 3 is a western European branch of an international consulting firm, and Organization 4 is a public university in Switzerland. (GW – 03)

【CP】

M 3. 4：The maximum likelihood estimation technique was used in the measurement model, where each item was linked to its corresponding construct, and the covariances among the constructs were freely estimated. (GW – 01)

C. 句类与句长

表 3. 1. 8 是四种类型句子长度占比情况。如表所示，不同类型句子长度分布占比存在一定的差异。简单句中句子长度占比最高的是单词数介于 11—20 的句子，其次是介于 21—30 的句子；复杂句和复合句占比最高的均为单词数介于 21—30 的句子，但是在这两类句子中占比排在第二的有所不同，前者为介于 11—20 的句子，后者为介于 31—40 的句子。复合复杂句中占比最高的则是单词数介于 31—40 的句子，其次是介于 21—30 的句子。就各类句子覆盖范围而言，复合句最广，其次是简单句，复合复杂句跨度最小也最集中。

就句子长度最大值和最小值而言，复合句最长，与其他三类句子差异较大，其他三类句子较接近，句子长度最小值简单句最低，复合复杂句最高，其他两类句子居中，没有差异。如果不排除特殊类型的句子，将每个公式算为一个单词的话，所有句子中最长的仍然是复合句，最短的为简单句。

综上所述，四种类型句子长度分布在不同方面相似度不同。各类句子长度主要集中在 11—40 之间，但是四种类型句子长度分布存在一定的差异，简单句和复合句长度跨度均高于其他两类句子，相比而言，简单句以短句为主，复合复杂句以长句为主。句子长度最大值上，复合句与其他三类句子差异较大，其他三类句子较接近；最小值中复杂句和复合句相同，其他两类句子差异较明显。以下是四类句子中最长和最短句子的例句。

表 3.1.8　　　　　　　　　四类句子长度分布

句长范围		1—10	11—20	21—30	31—40	41—50	51—60	61—70	71—80	101—110	MAX	MIX
S	句数	96	296	158	48	13	2	1	*	*	62	4
	占比	15.64%	48.21%	25.73%	7.82%	2.12%	0.33%	0.16%	*	*		
P	句数	*	66	103	46	19	9	*	*	*	58	11
	占比	*	27.16%	42.39%	18.93%	7.82%	3.70%	*	*	*		
C	句数	*	16	40	25	4	4	*	1	1	104	11
	占比	*	17.58%	43.96%	27.47%	4.40%	4.40%	*	1.10%	1.10%		
CP	句数	*	*	10	16	4	1	*	*	*	52	24
	占比	*	*	32.26%	51.61%	12.90%	3.23%	*	*	*		

S/ [**Max：62**] Following suggestions of SEM experts (e. g. Hu and Bentler, 1999; Kline, 2005), multiple model fit indices were examined to test the level of model fit, including the traditional χ^2 statistic, the relative χ^2 *CMIN/DF* (χ^2 /df, χ^2 /degree of freedom ratio), the root mean square error of approximation (RMSEA), the standardized root mean square residual (SRMR), the Tucker Lewis coefficient (TLI) and the comparative fit index (CFI). (GW – 13)

S/ [**Min：4**] Cronbach's α is 0.81. (GW – 16)

P/ [**Max：58**] It is worth noting that the intent of the questionnaire was clearly communicated with the respondents in a plain language statement (PLS), which requested them to provide specific and objective responses to the relevant variables or indicators aimed to measure only the performance of the WBPM systems but isolating any other associated issues affecting the performance of projects. (GW – 18)

P/ [Min：11] Reliability analyses also showed that these measures possess satisfactory coefficient reliability. (GW – 05)

C/ [Max：104] Sixty-nine percent of the respondents were female; 4 percent were less than 25 years old, 17 percent were 26 – 35 years old, 45 percent were 36 – 45, 28 percent were 46 – 55, and 6 percent were over 55; 5 percent were African-American, 4 percent were Asian-American, 1 percent were Pacific Islanders, 12 percent were Hispanic-American, and 78 percent were Caucasian; 10. 5 percent of the respondents had high school degrees or less, 12 percent had associate's degrees, 3. 5 percent had technical degrees, 32 percent had some college beyond an associate's degree, 38. 5 percent had bachelor's degrees, and 3. 5 percent of the employees had graduate degrees. (GW – 10)

C/ [Min：11] Survey packages were distributed through HR managers and collected in person. (GW – 13)

CP/ [Max：52] We do not believe this adjustment influenced our results considering the model parameters in an ordinal logistic regression are invariant to collapsing adjacent categories (Greenland, 1994; Murad, Fleischman, Sadetzki, Geyer, & Freedman, 2003), and doing so when some categories are very sparse can improve the asymptotic fit of the maximum likelihood analysis. (GW – 15)

CP/ [Min：24] One irregularity was uncovered where a lone satisfaction item loaded with the three performance items, and it was included as a project performance item. (GW – 07)

（二）时态特征

A. 时态种类及组合

表3.1.9 是该学科论文中使用的时态类型及组合形式。如表所示，除去有语法错误的句子，该学科文章中共出现了11 种不同时态，其中 T4、T9 和 T12 没有单独使用，与其他时态共同出现在一个句子中。由不同时态构成的组合共有13 种，其中由两种时态构成的组合共10 种，由三种时态构成的组合共有3 种。不同时态组合中包含最多的是 T3，其次为 T1、T10 和 T2，分别占所有组合的79%、43%、29% 和21%，其他时态在组合中占比均较低。

各种时态组合中，全部由一种时态构成的句子中占比最高的是 T3，其次为 T1。由不同时态构成的句子中占比最高的是由 T1 和 T3 两种不同时态构成的句子，其他相同或不同时态组合占比均较低。

以下是按照四种类型句子给出的相同时态和不同时态组合的例句，但不是所有时态组合中都包含这四类句子。

表 3.1.9　　　　　　　　　　时态类型及组合

时态	T1	T2	T3	T5	T6	T8	T10	T13	T1T2	T1T2T3	T1T3
句数	224	10	630	3	1	2	6	1	13	1	68
占比	22.13%	0.99%	62.25%	0.30%	0.10%	0.20%	0.59%	0.10%	1.28%	0.10%	6.72%

时态	T1T3T10	T1T4	T1T10	T2T3	T3T5	T3T6	T3T8T10	T3T9	T3T10	T3T12
句数	5	2	4	7	9	1	1	1	22	1
占比	0.49%	0.20%	0.40%	0.69%	0.89%	0.10%	0.10%	0.10%	2.17%	0.10%

【T1】

S： Results indicate an adequate convergence with inter-judge raw agreement scores of 89 percent, overall placement ratios of items 90 percent, and Kappa scores of 89 percent, consistent with previous studies (Gu et al., 2017). (GW – 01)

P： Data for this study comes from an ongoing international research initiative led by the authors that include other countries (e. g. the USA, Vietnam and Singapore). (GW – 01)

C： Organization 1 is a small to medium-sized manufacturing firm in Switzerland, Organization 2 is a large logistical company in Germany, Organization 3 is a western European branch of an international consulting firm, and Organization 4 is a public university in Switzerland. (GW – 03)

CP： The seemingly low response rate is typical when the target respondents hold executive positions within a firm and is comparable to studies using a similar population frame (Gu et al., 2017). (GW – 01)

【T2】

S： The use of a composite measure of project performance has been validated in previous studies (e. g., Aga et al., 2016; Dulaimi et al., 2005). (GW – 06)

【T3】

S： The sample for this study was selected from a set of project owners and contractors for 44 large construction projects in northwest Canada. (GW – 02)

P： The final sample size was 175 after 11 responses were removed due to incomplete data. (GW – 01)

C： Overall, all factor loadings were significant at the 0.001 level, their standardized loadings were above the 0.5 cutoff value, and most above 0.7 (Hair et al., 2010). (GW – 01)

CP： The final questionnaire included general instructions about the objective of the study, and the measures were framed by statements that referenced the firm's position concerning their trading partners in the context of Web-enabled supply chains. (GW – 01)

【T5】

S: On average, respondents had worked for 11. 3 years in the industry and 6. 9 years with their company. (GW – 05)

【T6】

S: Ideally, in evaluating respondents' willingness to accept vulnerability, we would have asked them to provide their own willingness to interact with the organization. (GW – 03)

【T8】

S: The MNC, the target organization for our study, was shifting its domestic product focus to grow revenues in the United States and in the BRIC (Brazil, Russia, India and China) markets. (GW – 07)

【T10】

S: According to 2SLS, the endogenous variable (SCI) should be regressed on all exogenous variables, instrumental variables, and control variables. (GW – 01)

【T13】

S: Thus, for the balance of this paper, we will be reporting on two forms of trust: Integrity and Competence. (GW – 02)

【T1T2】

P: We also cannot exclude the possibility, albeit remote, that some respondents may have responded as a stakeholder for more than one organization (e. g., as a client for one organization and as an investor for another). (GW – 03)

C: This procedure for data collection has been used in several studies (e. g. Grant & Mayer, 2009) and allows for testing of the model from individuals in an assortment of organizations and industries to enhance generalizability. (GW – 11)

CP: Scholars have argued that it is difficult to separate the effects of age and generation (Macky et al. , 2008; Twenge & Campbell, 2008), and this is a challenge for all generational research (Parry & Urwin, 2011) . (GW – 15)

【T1T2T3】

P: Additionally, IT use (ITU), measured as a composite of IT tools needed to facilitate Web-based interactions between trading partners (see Appendix 2 for ITU items), was selected as an additional instrumental variable because it has been linked SCI but does not necessarily correlate with BPE. (GW – 01)

【T1T3】

P: In order to obtain a truly representative sample that matches the characteristics of the Chinese university population, we conducted purposive sampling based on accessibility and university types. (GW – 13)

C：In the first stage, theoretical constructs were based on a thorough review of the literature and are well grounded in existing theory. (GW – 01)

CP：We followed the latent common method factor analysis (Podsakoff et al. , 2003) by building a second measurement model that contains an unconstrained latent common method factor (CMF) and compared it against a fully constrained measurement model. (GW – 01)

【 T1 T3 T10 】

P：Archival research was not conducted because firms do not always record their PM practices in detail, while opinion research would be too subjective to fulfill the aim of identifying relationships between PM practices adopted and project performance. (GW – 16)

【 T1 T4 】

P：Second, and even more problematic, existing scales consist of items that already presume which dimensions of trustworthiness will be relevant (Dietz and Den Hartog, 2006). (GW – 3)

【 T1 T10 】

P：Second, although response bias could affect the mean level of trust in our sample relative to the overall population, our analysis does not focus on mean trust levels. (GW – 03)

CP：However, the χ statistic is extremely sensitive to sample size, and a very small difference between the observed model and the perfectly fit model could result in a statistically significant χ statistic when the sample size is 400 or more (Kline, 2005). (GW – 13)

【 T2 T3 】

P：As the implementation of web-based systems in their organizations was a prerequisite for providing responses and most firms have adopted such systems over the past 5 – 7 years, the respondents were able to provide informed judgments based on their experiences from before and after web-based systems implementation. (GW – 18)

C：The items were originally developed by McKnight et al. (2002) in the area of impersonal trust in electronic commerce and have been used in previous empirical studies (Hoffmann et al. , 2014; Ou et al. , 2014). (GW – 01)

CP：Parallel analysis (PA) was used as the factor retention criteria in this research and the "rawpar" programme, which was developed by O'Connor (2014) has been used to determine the number of factors to be retained in the factor analysis. (GW – 19)

【 T3 T5 】

P：Owner representatives were defined as senior, on-site executives for the firm that had contracted to have a large facility constructed. (GW – 02)

CP：For illicit drugs other than marijuana and nonmedical use of pills and tranquilizers, respondents were shown a card, read a list of drugs, and asked for each whether or not they had ever used it. (GW – 14)

【T3T6】

P：Although it would have been preferable to use existing scales for measuring trust among our respondents, a review of existing trust scales revealed two problems (see also Dietz and Den Hartog, 2006). (GW－03)

【T3T8T10】

P：This item asked applicants how often their most recent supervisor would say they were willing to work overtime. (GW－15)

【T3T9】

P：We operationalized Tenure as the number of years the boundary spanner has been working for their respective organization. (GW－04)

【T3T10】

P：For example, if a team had a goal of 90 percent customer satisfaction and then actually achieved a 90 percent score, that team's customer satisfaction percentage would be 100 percent (90/90, 100). (GW－10)

CP：We told team members that their responses were confidential and anonymous, assured them that the data would be collected and maintained in an off-site computer system to help guarantee confidentiality, and explained that management would receive a summary report without individual identification. (GW－10)

【T3T12】

P：In this organization, which had been collecting process improvement data for two years prior to our data collection, process improvement was viewed as an objective assessment of team learning, or a team's ability to continually refine processes and develop innovative solutions to shorten the cycle time needed to deliver and install reservation systems. (GW－10)

B. 时态与语步

图 3.1.9 是该学科文章中三种占比较高的时态组合与语步的关系，有语法错误的句子除外。如图所示，这三种组合中步骤占比最高的前三个存在较大的差异，但是 T1 中的三个步骤分别出现在了其他两个组合中，其中 M2.7 和 M3.4 出现在了 T1T3 组合中，M2.1a 出现在了 T3 组合中，但是它们在各组合中的排序不完全一致，数量和占比相差也较大。其他几个步骤均不相同。

此外，这三种时态组合中包含了三个语步，就它们包含的步骤种类而言，T3 最高，包含了三个语步中所有步骤。其次为 T1 和 T1T3，包含的步骤种类分别占所有步骤种类的77%和65%。

总体来说，不同时态组合的句子与语步的联系存在一定的差异，时态与步骤关系紧密度与该时态组合在所有句子中的占比有关，同时也与该步骤在所有步骤中的占比有关，但并不是决定性的。

以下是按照四种类型句子给出的三种时态组合中占比最高的前三个步骤的例句，但是有些步骤中不包含所有类型的句子。

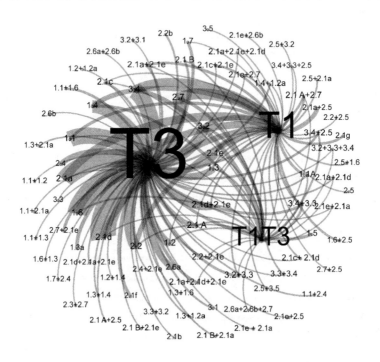

图3.1.9 时态与步骤关系网络图

【T1】

M 2.7

S: By using parallel items in the surveys, we are able to capture the distinctions in trust antecedents and exchange hazards across the dyad. (GW - 04)

P: A key methodological strength of the dyadic research design is that it limits single-source bias (Podsakoff and Organ, 1986) because our measures are drawn from different surveys. (GW - 04)

C: Using this formula, higher process improvement percentages were better, and scores in our study ranged from a low of 112 percent to a high of 200 percent. (GW - 10)

CP: Whereas exchange hazards combines asset specificity with uncertainty, power imbalance is based solely on asset specificity and, more importantly, captures the relative difference between exchange partners in relationship-specific investments. (GW – 04)

M 3.4

S： The measurement fit measures indicate a reasonable model fit (χ2 = 958.33, df = 573, CFI = 0.917, NFI = 0.817; RMSEA = 0.062; SRMR = 0.057) (Hair et al., 2010). (GW – 01)

P： Model 1 in Table V indicates that the R^2 for this regression is 0.470. (GW – 01)

M 2.1a

S： It examines supplier performance in the focal exchange relationship with respect to product quality, timeliness of delivery, after-sales support, and total value received. (GW – 05)

P： The benevolence items (six items) measure the beliefs of the firm that their trading partner is motivated to act in the best interest of their business relationship. (GW – 01)

【T1 T3】

M 3.4

P： The results of this test were non-significant (p > 0.100) suggesting that the estimates of the OLS and 2SLS models (Table V) do not differ from one another. (GW – 01)

CP： We followed the latent common method factor analysis (Podsakoff et al., 2003) by building a second measurement model that contains an unconstrained latent common method factor (CMF) and compared it against a fully constrained measurement model. (GW – 01)

M 1.4

P： Overall, the sample composition seems adequate, with approximately 65 percent of the respondents holding top/middle management positions and over 75 percent in the SCM field, which gave us confidence that the key respondents had adequate knowledge of the subject matter. (GW – 01)

M 2.7

P： This process gave us sufficient confidence that the scales used in this research possess adequate levels of face and content validity. (GW – 01)

C： With this formula, higher customer satisfaction percentages are better, and scores in our study ranged from 71 to 119 percent. (GW – 10)

【T3】

M 2.1d

S： To assess the influence of the sources of trust from each side of the dyad, we collected data using two separate questionnaires, one for the purchasing manager of the buyer firm and the other for the supplier representative of the supplier firm. (GW – 04)

P： If a function was not represented ($i = 0$), its value was assigned 0. (GW – 09)

C： We pretested a preliminary set of measures with local purchasing managers from the same industry and incorporated their feedback into a revised set of measures included in the final question-naire. (GW – 04)

CP： The final questionnaire included general instructions about the objective of the study, and the measures were framed by statements that referenced the firm's position concerning their trading partners in the context of Web-enabled supply chains. (GW – 01)

M 1.6

S： Each virtual team consisted of members with different roles, including account executives (selling the reservation systems), field service technicians (installing the systems), training representatives (training end users on the systems on-site), installation operation coordinators (setting up installation appointments), account management specialists (handling customer billing), and customer service representatives (fielding customer phone calls and questions). (GW – 10)

P： Each team reported virtually to a general manager who had overall responsibility for monitoring team performance, supporting team training, and evaluating individual contributions to the team's objectives. (GW – 10)

C： Sixty-nine percent of the respondents were female; 4 percent were less than 25 years old, 17 percent were 26 – 35 years old, 45 percent were 36 – 45, 28 percent were 46 – 55, and 6 percent were over 55; 5 percent were African-American, 4 percent were Asian-American, 1 percent were Pacific Islanders, 12 percent were Hispanic-American, and 78 percent were Caucasian; 10.5 percent of the respondents had high school degrees or less, 12 percent had associate's degrees, 3.5 percent had technical degrees, 32 percent had some college beyond an associate's degree, 38.5 percent had bachelor's degrees, and 3.5 percent of the employees had graduate degrees. (GW – 10)

M 2.1a

S： To validate and/or modify, in our empirical context, the trustworthiness dimensions suggested by the ABI framework, we interviewed 32 stakeholders with regard to their understanding of trust in the organizational context and with regard to their specific stakeholder experiences. (GW – 03)

P： We also found that stakeholders who mentioned ability or competence seemed to clearly distinguish between managerial and technical dimensions of competence. (GW – 03)

C： Some interviewees provided responses from more than one stakeholder perspective, and we therefore ended with 16 narratives regarding employee relationships, 18 narratives regarding customer relationships, and 5 narratives each for supplier and investor relationships. (GW – 03)

（三）语态特征

A. 语态种类及组合

表 3.1.10 是该学科文章中使用的不同语态组合类型，一句有语

法错误的句子没有计入其中。如表所示，该学科文章中同时包含了两种语态及这两种语态的组合形式。只包含 V1 的句子数量和占比远高于其他两种类型的句子，只包含 V2 的句子数量和占比略高于包含两种不同语态的句子。所有文章中均有这三种形式语态组合。由同一种语态构成的句子中均包含了四种类型的句子，两种不同语态组合的句子中不包含简单句。

以下是按照四种类型句子给出的三种语态组合中的例句，但是有些语态组合中不包含所有类型的句子。

表 3.1.10　　　　　　　　　语态类型及组合

语态	V1	V1V2	V2
句数	326	102	163
占比	55.16%	17.23%	27.53%

【V1】

S： Thus, for the balance of this paper, we will be reporting on two forms of trust: Integrity and Competence.

P： We also cannot exclude the possibility, albeit remote, that some respondents may have responded as a stakeholder for more than one organization (e. g. , as a client for one organization and as an investor for another). (GW – 03)

C： Organization 1 is a small to medium-sized manufacturing firm in Switzerland, Organization 2 is a large logistical company in Germany, Organization 3 is a western European branch of an international consulting firm, and Organization 4 is a public university in Switzerland. (GW – 03)

CP： Of the respondents, 51% reported that they had been in contact with the organization for more than seven years, 23.3% reported four to seven years of contact, and 18.6% reported one to three years. (GW – 03)

【V1V2】

P： It is worth noting that these performance measures were specifically reported based on perceived benefits of WBPM systems being implemented in the completed projects depicted in the first subcolumn. (GW – 18)

C： Cronbach's Alphas for all eight resulting factors were above 0.75 and are reported in Table 1. (GW – 07)

CP：We told team members that their responses were confidential and anonymous, assured them that the data would be collected and maintained in an off-site computer system to help guarantee confidentiality, and explained that management would receive a summary report without individual identification. (GW – 10)

【V2】

S：The survey was administered to 650 team members working on transport infrastructure projects. (GW – 08)

P：Secondary data sources were not used due to lack of archival data while objective measures were not used as the projects, based in China, had been completed. (GW – 16)

C：In the first stage, theoretical constructs were based on a thorough review of the literature and are well grounded in existing theory. (GW – 01)

CP：Parallel analysis (PA) was used as the factor retention criteria in this research and the "rawpar" programme, which was developed by O'Connor (2014) has been used to determine the number of factors to be retained in the factor analysis. (GW – 19)

B. 语态与语步

图 3.1.10 是该学科文章中两种语态及组合与语步的关系。如图所示，除去一句有语法错误的句子，这三种组合中步骤占比最高的前三个存在一定的差异，M1.6、M3.2 和 M3.4 分别为两种不同组合共有，其中 M1.6 和 M3.2 在两种组合中排序一致，但是数量和占比不同，M3.4 在两种组合中排序、数量和占比均不同。各组合中其他几个步骤均不相同。就这三种组合中包含的语步种类而言，它们均包含了三个语步，但是它们包含的步骤种类在所有步骤中占比不同。V2 占比最高，为 94%，其次为 V1V2，V1 最低，分别占比 77% 和 68%。总体来说，语态与步骤关系紧密度与该语态在所有句子中的占比有关，同时也与该步骤在所有步骤中的占比有一定的关系。

以下是按照四种类型句子给出的三种语态组合中占比最高的前三个步骤的例句，但是有些步骤中不包含所有类型的句子。

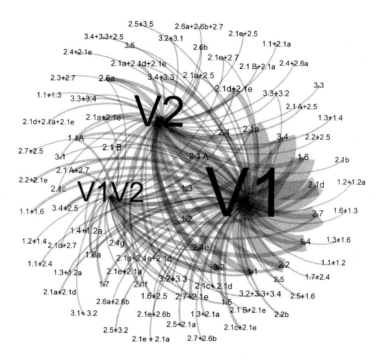

图 3.1.10　语态与步骤关系网络图

【V1】

M 1.6

S: Each virtual team consisted of members with different roles, including account executives (selling the reservation systems), field service technicians (installing the systems), training representatives (training end users on the systems on-site), installation operation coordinators (setting up installation appointments), account management specialists (handling customer billing), and customer service representatives (fielding customer phone calls and questions). (GW-10)

P: Specifically, we studied a high-technology service organization in the travel industry that had formally implemented virtual teams. (GW-10)

C: Sixty-nine percent of the respondents were female; 4 percent were less than 25 years old, 17 percent were 26-35 years old, 45 percent were 36-45, 28 percent were 46-55, and 6 percent were over 55; 5 percent were African-American, 4 percent were Asian-American, 1 percent were Pacific Islanders, 12 percent were Hispanic-American, and 78 percent were Caucasian; 10.5 percent of the respondents had high school degrees or less, 12 percent had associate's degrees, 3.5 percent had technical degrees, 32 percent had some college beyond an associate's degree, 38.5 percent had bachelor's degrees, and 3.5 percent of the employees had graduate degrees. (GW-10)

CP：The organization develops, installs, and services computer travel reservation systems for travel agencies and holds a majority ownership position in a company that offers Web-based travel services. (GW – 10)

M 3. 4

S：A seven-factor structure emerged explaining 67. 65 percent of the variance (Table II). (GW – 01)

P：Model 1 in Table V indicates that the R2 for this regression is 0. 470. (GW – 01)

C：Overall, all factor loadings were significant at the 0. 001 level, their standardized loadings were above the 0. 5 cutoff value, and most above 0. 7 (Hair et al. , 2010). (GW – 01)

CP：Third, we inspected the average variance explained (AVE) for each of the constructs and determined that their values were all above the suggested 0. 5 threshold. (GW – 01)

M 2. 1a

S：To validate and/or modify, in our empirical context, the trustworthiness dimensions suggested by the ABI framework, we interviewed 32 stakeholders with regard to their understanding of trust in the organizational context and with regard to their specific stakeholder experiences. (GW – 03)

P：We also found that stakeholders who mentioned ability or competence seemed to clearly distinguish between managerial and technical dimensions of competence. (GW – 03)

C：Some interviewees provided responses from more than one stakeholder perspective, and we therefore ended with 16 narratives regarding employee relationships, 18 narratives regarding customer relationships, and 5 narratives each for supplier and investor relationships. (GW – 03)

【V1V2】

M 1. 4

P：No significant differences between the two groups were found, leading us to conclude that non-response bias was not a likely threat. (GW – 09)

M 3. 2

P：It is worth noting that these performance measures were specifically reported based on perceived benefits of WBPM systems being implemented in the completed projects depicted in the first subcolumn. (GW – 18)

C：The remaining 29% (7% for 16 – 20 years and 22% over 20 years) respondents had experience over 15 years and were considered fairly senior among the participants. (GW – 18)

M 3. 4

P：Given that this study has more than 600 cases, it assumed the χ is inflated and cannot be used to reject CFA models. (GW – 13)

C：Two items did not load significantly on any of the three proposed dimensions of trust and so were dropped from the subsequent analysis. (GW – 02)

CP：Third, we inspected the average variance explained（AVE）for each of the constructs and determined that their values were all above the suggested 0.5 threshold.（GW－01）

【V2】

M 1.1

S：The US data were obtained from two sources：the institute for supply management and a third-party marketing company.（GW－01）

P：The sample was selected from project managers who were registered in the Australian Institute of Project Management（AIPM）, the Australian Institute of Building（AIB）and LinkedIn business networking website.（GW－19）

C：Blacks（N = 2, 172）, His-panics（N = 1, 480））and economically disadvantaged white youths（N = 1, 643）were oversampled for a supplemental sample, and 1, 280 young persons in the military（as of September 1978）were also included.（GW－14）

M 3.2

S：In order to check the influence of a PM practice on project performance, Pearson's correlation analysis was conducted.（GW－16）

P：As the sample contained a mix of facility types and different services provided by respondents, Analysis of Variance（Anova）was also conducted.（GW－16）

M 2.1d

S：In turn, functional diversity was measured using a variation of the Herfindal-Hirschman index.（GW－09）

P：If a function was not represented（i = 0）, its value was assigned 0.（GW－09）

第二节　外国语言学及应用语言学

外国语言学及应用语言学（以下简称语言学）是英语语言文学一级学科下设的一个二级学科。本学科以音系学、语音学、句法学、形式语义学和语言习得等为主要研究对象，同时从事应用语言学具体领域的教学与研究。本研究主要分析英语教学类实证性论文问卷调查方法部分写作的体裁特征，共从 11 种 SCI 国际期刊上选取了 20 篇外语教学方向英语学术论文，所选文章中有 90% 为 2015 年后发表的论文，第一作者通信地址基本上均为英语国家或以英语为官方语言的国家。

外语教学研究中一般不单独使用问卷调查法，该方法通常与访谈和课堂教学实验同时使用，本研究主要分析方法部分问卷调查法的写作特征，因此本研究不仅统计了论文研究方法部分在全文的占比，同时还统计了问卷调查法在方法部分的占比。分析发现 20 篇论文方法部分在全文中的占比最大值为 42%，最小值为 13%，平均值为 22%，标准差为 0.08。不同文章之间占比差异不大，总体占比不高。问卷调查部分在方法部分的占比平均值为 40%，最大值为 78%，最小值为 21%，标准差为 0.16；用于研究的句子共有 591 句，约 13731 个单词。同一种期刊不同文章中该部分占比存在一定的差异，占比情况与期刊及论文发表时间没有显著关联。

一　标题特征分析

图 3.2.1 为本学科论文方法部分一级大标题中词汇使用情况。如图所示，大标题中使用最多的词汇是 method，一共出现了 13 次，其次是 methods 和 methodology，均出现过 3 次，study 出现过 1 次。图 3.2.2 是该部分二级小标题词汇云图，可以发现使用频率最高的是 participants，共出现了 18 次，其次是 procedure、analyses、data 三个单词，分别出现了 12 次、12 次和 11 次。总体来说，不同文章中一级大标题中词汇差异较小，二级小标题中存在一定差异，二级小标题中的词汇与研究内容关系更密切。此外，所分析的文章中均使用了二级小标题，数量从 1 个到 6 个不等，平均值为 3.37 个，标准差为 1.26。

综上所述，该学科论文研究方法部分均包含了一级大标题和二级小标题。各篇文章中一级大标题使用的词汇相似度极高，但是二级小标题中词汇分布既有共性也有差异。不同文章中大小标题词汇的使用与文章研究主题没有直接关系，但是二级小标题中词汇与研究涉及的内容关系更密切。不同文章中包含的小标题数量存在一定的差异。

图 3.2.1　一级大标题词汇云图

图 3.2.2　二级小标题词汇云图

二　语步特征分析

本小节主要研究论文问卷调查写作部分的语步特征。分析发现，该学科论文这部分写作的总体语步框架与管理学科基本一致，即主要包括问卷调查对象及相关情况、问卷设计及变量测量和数据分析及相关内容三个语步。但是两个学科各语步中包含的步骤种类存在一定的差异，本小节各语步列表中只列出所分析的该学科论文中出现的步骤。

（一）语步一特征

表 3.2.1 是本学科语步一中所包含的步骤种类。如表所示，语步一中共包括了 8 个步骤。表 3.2.2 是各篇文章语步一中各步骤在该语

步中的占比情况。如表所示，各篇文章中均包含了语步一，但是该语步中各步骤在各篇文章中占比情况不一。此外，同一个步骤在不同文章中的占比情况也有所差异。以下是针对每个步骤使用情况的具体分析及实例。

表 3.2.1　　　　　　　　**语步一各步骤列表**

M	语步一　问卷调查对象及相关情况		
1.1	被调查对象数量及来源	1.4	被调查对象选取的科学性
1.2	被调查对象招募知情权	1.5	被调查对象选取的局限性
1.3	被调查对象选取方法	1.6	被调查对象相关信息
1.3a	被调查对象分组及预处理	1.7	问卷填写要求及说明

表 3.2.2　　　　　　　　**语步一各步骤占比**

M	1.1	1.2	1.3	1.3a	1.4	1.5	1.6	1.7
YW－01	13%	—	—	—	—	—	88%	—
YW－02	—	—	5%	—	—	—	95%	—
YW－03	8%	8%	—	—	8%	—	77%	—
YW－04	16%	2%	2%	—	—	—	79%	—
YW－05	31%	6%	—	—	—	—	63%	—
YW－06	33%	33%	—	—	—	—	33%	—
YW－07	30%	—	—	—	30%	10%	30%	—
YW－08	50%	—	—	—	—	—	50%	—
YW－09	14%	—	—	—	—	—	86%	—
YW－10	6%	—	—	—	—	—	94%	—
YW－11	6%	—	13%	—	—	—	81%	—
YW－12	13%	38%	—	—	—	—	50%	—
YW－13	7%	—	7%	41%	—	—	45%	—
YW－14	10%	—	—	20%	—	—	70%	—
YW－15	17%	—	—	—	—	—	83%	—
YW－16	27%	2%	20%	31%	—	—	20%	—
YW－17	13%	6%	—	—	—	—	56%	25%

M	1.1	1.2	1.3	1.3a	1.4	1.5	1.6	1.7
YW－18	6%	—	—	—	—	—	94%	—
YW－19	14%	—	7%	—	—	—	79%	—
YW－20	7%	—	7%	14%	—	—	72%	—

M 1.1 被调查对象数量及来源：除一篇文章外，其他文章均包含了该步骤。在包含该步骤的文章中，该步骤在语步一中的占比最大值为50%，最小值为6%，平均值为17%，标准差为0.12。实例如下：

A total of 232 upper-intermediate EFL university students participated in the present study.（YW－12）

Writing teachers and their students in levels two through five（high beginning to advanced）at the Brigham Young University（BYU）English Language Center（ELC）were invited to participate in this study.（YW－05）

M 1.2 被调查对象招募知情权：所选文章中有35%的文章包含该步骤。在包含该步骤的文章中，该步骤在语步一中的占比最大值为38%，最小值为2%，平均值为14%，标准差为0.14。实例如下：

Before participating in the study all participants provided informed consent for extra course credit. They were recruited from three universities in two major cities in the northeast of Iran.（YW－12）

Participation in the experiment was both compulsory and rewarded by a gift certificate of 10 euros.（YW－06）

M 1.3 被调查对象选取方法：所选文章中有35%的文章包含该步骤。在包含该步骤的文章中，该步骤在语步一中的占比最大值为20%，最小值为2%，平均值为9%，标准差为0.05。实例如下：

For the analyses, we excluded students who did not take part in the achievement tests at either T1 or T2. In addition, we excluded one school in Switzerland which had not reported the full scope of background information or class membership of participating students.（YW－16）

Only students who agreed to take part in the study attended the questionnaire sessions.（YW－13）

M 1.3a 被调查对象分组及预处理：所选文章中有20%的文章包含该步骤。在包含该步骤的文章中，该步骤在语步一中的占比最大值为41%，最小值为14%，平均值为26%，标准差为0.11。实例如下：

To control for the effects of task, the research took a counterbalanced approach to the distribution of the writing tests. At T1 half the students were given Task 1, and the other half were given Task 2; this was reversed at T2. (YW – 13)

On the data collection day, the participants first completed the TOEFL Junior Comprehensive test, which was 2 hours and 14 minutes long. (YW – 14)

M 1.4 被调查对象选取的科学性：所选文章中只有两篇包含该步骤。在这两篇文章中，该步骤在语步一中的占比分别为 30% 和 8%。实例如下：

Thus, all fit the "Generation 1.5" demographic profile (see Ferris, 2009; Roberge et al., 2009). (YW – 03)

Because the FL subjects completed the questionnaire in their L1 (English), they experienced no difficulty comprehending its contents. (YW – 07)

M 1.5 被调查对象选取的局限性：所选文章中只有一篇包含该步骤。在该篇文章中，该步骤在语步一中的占比为 10%。实例如下：

Because of the difficulty of accounting for primary language literacy, data related to this variable were not available. (YW – 07)

M 1.6 被调查对象相关信息：所选文章中均包含了该步骤。该步骤在语步一中的占比最大值为 95%，最小值为 20%，平均值为 67%，标准差为 0.22。实例如下：

All student participants were in the first two years of their degree, and half were in their first or second semester. (YW – 20)

The study was conducted in three large Mexican public universities, located in three distinct, geographically representative areas (north, center and south). These institutions prepare future foreign language teachers in accredited BA and MA programs, recognized for their quality by the National Council of Science and Technology (Contact, by its Spanish acronym). (YW – 08)

M 1.7 问卷填写要求及说明：所选文章中只有一篇包含该步骤。在该篇文章中，该步骤在语步一中的占比为 25%。实例如下：

Prior to administering the questionnaire, an explanation sheet describing the research was provided to students in their native language (i. e., Korean). (YW – 17)

综上所述，所分析的文章中均包含了该语步。该语步中涉及篇章数最高的是 M1.6，所有文章中均包含了该步骤，最低的是 M1.5 和 M1.7，分别只有一篇文章中包含这两个步骤。各篇文章语步一中各步骤涉及篇章数平均值为 7.6 篇，占所有文章的 38%，标准差为 7.71。就各篇文章中涉及步骤种类数量而言，最多的包含了 5 种，最低的只包含 2 种，分别占语步一中所有步骤的 63% 和 25%。

各篇文章涉及的步骤种类平均值为 3.1 种，占语步一中所有步骤的 38%，标准差为 0.94。不同文章中包含的步骤种类存在一定的差异，同一步骤在不同文章中的占比也存在一定的差异。除去只涉及一篇文章的两个步骤，其他各步骤占比平均值最高的是 M1.6，最低的是 M1.3，占比分别为 67% 和 9%。各步骤在不同文章中占比平均值之间的标准差为 18.69。

（二）语步二特征

表 3.2.3 是所分析文章语步二中包含的步骤种类。该语步共包括 19 种步骤。表 3.2.4 是各篇文章语步二中各步骤在该语步中的占比情况。如表所示，所有文章中均包括了该语步，但是该语步中各步骤占比情况不一。此外，同一个步骤在不同文章中的占比情况也存在差异。以下是针对每个步骤占比情况的具体分析及实例。

表 3.2.3　　　　　　　　　　语步二各步骤列表

M	语步二问卷设计及变量测量		
2.1A	问卷设计概述	2.1g	问卷设计潜在问题
2.1B	调查目的	2.1h	问卷设计过程
2.1C	使用某种类型问卷的理由	2.2	确定相关控制因素
2.1a	问题涉及维度/题项	2.3	问卷分发时间段
2.1b	问卷类型	2.4	问卷分发/回收途径
2.1c	定义变量	2.5	细节参见图表/期刊/网站
2.1d	测量变量的方法	2.6a	问卷回收率
2.1e	前人测量变量方法	2.7	问卷设计/数据测量的科学性
2.1f	预调查	2.8	填写问卷的时长
2.1ff	预调查后的修改		

M 2.1A 问卷设计概述：所选文章中有 25% 的文章包含该步骤。在包括该步骤的文章中，该步骤在语步二中的占比最大值为 12%，最小值为 3%，平均值为 9%，标准差为 0.03。实例如下：

Originally 16 items were entered into the survey but two were removed during factor analysis. A resulting 14-item writing strategies questionnaire was created. (YW - 17)

表3.2.4　　语步二各步骤占比

M	2.1A	2.1B	2.1C	2.1a	2.1b	2.1c	2.1d	2.1e	2.1f	2.1ff	2.1g	2.1h	2.2	2.3	2.4	2.5	2.6a	2.7	2.8
YW-01	—	7%	43%	—	—	—	7%	3%	—	—	—	—	—	2%	—	7%	—	31%	—
YW-02	8%	17%	—	50%	—	—	—	—	—	—	—	—	—	25%	—	—	—	—	—
YW-03	—	—	—	67%	—	—	—	—	—	—	—	—	—	—	—	33%	—	—	—
YW-04	—	—	—	—	—	—	—	—	—	—	—	—	—	67%	—	—	33%	—	—
YW-05	—	—	2%	31%	—	—	19%	5%	—	—	—	—	—	24%	5%	5%	—	10%	—
YW-06	—	7%	—	47%	—	—	12%	17%	—	—	—	—	—	7%	2%	—	—	9%	—
YW-07	—	30%	—	22%	17%	—	4%	4%	—	—	—	—	—	10%	—	22%	—	—	—
YW-08	10%	—	—	20%	20%	—	20%	—	—	—	—	—	—	—	—	20%	—	—	—
YW-09	—	14%	—	21%	—	—	7%	—	14%	—	—	—	7%	29%	14%	—	—	—	—
YW-10	—	11%	—	57%	7%	—	7%	11%	—	—	—	—	—	8%	—	—	—	—	—
YW-11	—	8%	—	17%	8%	—	58%	—	24%	—	—	—	—	—	21%	7%	—	14%	7%
YW-12	—	—	7%	21%	—	6%	21%	—	22%	—	—	—	3%	—	3%	6%	—	24%	3%
YW-13	3%	3%	6%	18%	—	—	4%	11%	—	9%	—	—	—	—	3%	5%	—	3%	3%
YW-14	12%	—	9%	12%	—	—	5%	6%	—	—	—	6%	—	6%	—	6%	—	13%	—
YW-15	—	19%	—	13%	13%	—	25%	—	—	—	—	—	—	8%	15%	—	—	15%	—
YW-16	—	15%	—	15%	—	—	31%	10%	—	—	5%	25%	10%	—	5%	8%	—	—	—
YW-17	10%	—	—	15%	—	—	—	—	—	—	—	—	—	—	—	—	—	10%	3%
YW-18	—	19%	—	11%	—	—	41%	7%	—	—	—	12%	—	7%	6%	15%	—	—	—
YW-19	—	6%	6%	47%	6%	—	12%	6%	—	—	—	—	—	—	—	—	—	—	—
YW-20	—	67%	—	—	11%	—	—	—	—	—	—	—	—	—	—	22%	—	—	—

The questionnaire consisted of two main sections that focused on specific task-types: one section on the Listen-Write task, and the other section on the Listen-Speak task type. (YW – 14)

M 2.1B 调查目的： 所选文章中有 65% 的文章包含该步骤。在包括该步骤的文章中，该步骤在语步二中的占比最大值为 67%，最小值为 3%，平均值为 17%，标准差为 0.16。实例如下：

As mentioned earlier, the retrospective questionnaire aimed to assess the frequency of five metacognitive processes during the planning and writing stages. (YW – 01)

To establish a profile of the test-takers participating in the study, a personal background questionnaire was designed with conventional biodata questions, including on participant's age, gender, first language, current activity (study, work) and years of learning English. (YW – 10)

M 2.1C 使用某种类型问卷的理由： 所选文章中有 30% 的文章包含该步骤。在包括该步骤的文章中，该步骤在语步二中的占比最大值为 43%，最小值为 2%，平均值为 12%，标准差为 0.14。实例如下：

This questionnaire was also selected because it incorporated the key theoretical components of test and task motivation outlined by Baumert and Demmrich (2001; see above). (YW – 14)

An open-ended questionnaire was conducted to understand the numeric figures obtained from the questionnaire. (YW – 19)

M 2.1a 问题涉及维度/题项： 所选文章中有 85% 的文章包含该步骤。在包括该步骤的文章中，该步骤在语步二中的占比最大值为 67%，最小值为 11%，平均值为 28%，标准差为 0.17。实例如下：

An example of a planning question is: "Before writing a text, I write down some notes and elaborate them later". (YW – 06)

All factors in question 5 are related to three domains of influence: personal, practice-related, and external (see Clarke & Hollingsworth, 2002). (YW – 02)

M 2.1b 问卷类型： 所选文章中有 35% 的文章包含该步骤。在包括该步骤的文章中，该步骤在语步二中的占比最大值为 20%，最小值为 6%，平均值为 12%，标准差为 0.05。实例如下：

Following that, an open-ended questionnaire which was developed by the researchers was distributed to them. (YW – 11)

Most questions in the second part of the questionnaire were open-ended and served to answer the research questions as well as identify themes for the student interviews. (YW – 20)

M 2.1c 定义变量： 所选文章中只有一篇包含该步骤。在该篇文章中，该步骤在语步二中的占比为 6%。实例如下：

Metacognitive strategies are defined as 'thinking about thinking' (Anderson, 2002) and relate to a learner's reflections and awareness of the self-regulatory strategies that they employ during a task (Anderson, 2005). (YW – 13)

M 2.1d 测量变量的方法：所选文章中有 75% 的文章包含该步骤。在包括该步骤的文章中，该步骤在语步二中的占比最大值为 58%，最小值为 4%，平均值为 18%，标准差为 0.15。实例如下：

Each of the three questions was provided with a four-point Likert scale: not at all, a little, somewhat, and a lot. (YW – 15)

The descriptions were supplemented with percentages that further clarified the categories: 0%, 30%, 50%, and 100%, respectively, of the amount of feedback the teachers thought was the total possible they could give. (YW – 05)

M 2.1e 前人测量变量方法：所选文章中有一半的文章包含该步骤。在包括该步骤的文章中，该步骤在语步二中的占比最大值为 17%，最小值为 3%，平均值为 8%，标准差为 0.04。实例如下：

The items emanated from existing questionnaires (Cassidy & Bailey, 2018; Kao & Reynolds; Maarof & Murat, 2013; Zhang & Qin, 2018) and were placed in the planning, problem-solving, and corrective feedback categories. (YW – 17)

Item writing was guided by Cross's work (2011); some of them were adapted from the questionnaire this author designed to explore the understanding of literacy of teachers of English as an L2 in Australia. (YW – 18)

M 2.1f 预调查：所选文章中有三篇文章包含该步骤。在这三篇文章中，该步骤在语步二中的占比分别为 24%、22% 和 14%。实例如下：

The questionnaire went through two rounds of piloting, with different students at each stage of piloting. (YW – 13)

For validity purposes, the questionnaire was piloted to a number of students after it was first designed and its items were later amended accordingly. (YW – 09)

M 2.1ff 预调查后的修改：所选文章中只有一篇包含该步骤。在该篇文章中，该步骤在语步二中的占比为 9%。实例如下：

However, the pilot results indicated that the learners were not able to distinguish or differentiate their answers between the Academic and Non-Academic tasks, providing the same answers for both. Thus, for the main study it was decided to collapse the task-motivation questions on the two Listen-Speak tasks and elicit young learners' views on both of these together. To compensate for this, in the main study, we added an additional open-ended question on what differences the learners perceived in the two versions (Academic/Non-Academic). (YW – 14)

M 2.1g 问卷设计潜在问题：所选文章中只有一篇包含该步骤。在该篇文章中，该步骤在语步二中的占比为 5% 。实例如下：

Due to the idiosyncratic nature of writing strategies, this is hardly an exhaustive list. (YW – 17)

M 2.1h 问卷设计过程：所选文章中有三篇包含该步骤。在这三篇文章中，该步骤在语步二中的占比分别为 25% 、12% 和 6% 。实例如下：

In the questionnaire development phase, we first wrote the questionnaire items in English, which were then translated in the participants' L1 Hungarian by the first author of the paper whose L1 is also Hungarian. (YW – 14)

The questionnaire experienced some revisions considering the characteristics of students participating in the study. (YW – 19)

M 2.2 确定相关控制因素：所选文章中有三篇包含该步骤。在这三篇文章中，该步骤在语步二中的占比分别为 10% 、7% 和 3% 。实例如下：

As an incentive to complete the tests to the best of their ability, the participants were provided with feedback and a diagnostic report on their performance (on the operational, paper-based exam format), and were provided with a retail voucher for their time and effort. (YW – 10)

Students were asked to give their gender, academic major, L2 proficiency, L2 writing skills, and years studying English. (YW – 17)

M 2.3 问卷分发时间段：所选文章中有 55% 的文章包含该步骤。在包括该步骤的文章中，该步骤在语步二中的占比最大值为 67% ，最小值为 2% ，平均值为 18% ，标准差为 0.18。实例如下：

At the end of the semester, the participants were given a postquestionnaire, and focus-group interviews with randomly chosen participants (n = 39) were implemented by two trained researchers. (YW – 11)

The teacher and student questionnaires were distributed at the end of the semester after students had completed all their compositions and had turned in their portfolios and after the teachers had finished grading the portfolios. (YW – 05)

M 2.4 问卷分发/回收途径：所选文章中有 40% 的文章包含该步骤。在包括该步骤的文章中，该步骤在语步二中的占比最大值为 21% ，最小值为 2% ，平均值为 9% ，标准差为 0.07。实例如下：

The first author was present in order to answer any questions the students may have had about any of the questions. (YW – 05)

After each writing task, students completed a retrospective questionnaire about their perceived mental effort while working on the argumentative text. (YW – 06)

M 2.5 细节参见图表/期刊/网站：所选文章中有 60% 的文章包含该步骤。在包括该步骤的文章中，该步骤在语步二中的占比最大值为 33% ，最小值为 5% ，平均值为 13% ，标准差为 0.09。实例如下：

Means and standard deviations for both the FL and ESL groups appear in Table l. (YW - 07)

Table 1 displays items for the three writing strategy scales. (YW - 17)

M 2.6a 问卷回收率：所选文章中只有一篇包含该步骤。在该篇文章中，该步骤在语步二中的占比为 33%。实例如下：

Ninety seven (56 at University A and 41 at University B) accepted the invitation, giving a response rate of 68. 3% overall (77. 8% from University A and 58. 6% from University B). (YW - 04)

M 2.7 问卷设计/数据测量的科学性：所选文章中有 45% 的文章包含该步骤。在包括该步骤的文章中，该步骤在语步二中的占比最大值为 31%，最小值为 3%，平均值为 14%，标准差为 0.08。实例如下：

Despite the methodological drawbacks of retrospective questionnaires, they were used in this present study for several reasons. First, it was the least intrusive method for examining the writers' metacognitive processes as this method minimized disruption of their cognitive processes while they composed. (YW - 01)

These categories were used instead of exact numerical counts because it is possible that if actual feedback quantities were asked, participants would have felt intimidated and unsure that they could give an accurate assessment. (YW - 05)

M 2.8 填写问卷的时长：所选文章中有 20% 的文章包含该步骤。在包括该步骤的文章中，该步骤在语步二中的占比最大值为 7%，最小值为 3%，平均值为 4%，标准差为 0.02。实例如下：

Next, the participants filled out the task-motivation questionnaire 2 and a short bio-data questionnaire which together took about 10 minutes to complete. (YW - 14)

The questionnaire sessions lasted for up to one hour and were run after the writing task sessions in a lecture theatre. (YW - 13)

综上所述，在所分析的文章中均包含了该语步。该语步中各步骤涉及篇章数最高的是 M2.1a，占所有文章的 85%，最低的只涉及一篇，有 4 个步骤，分别为 M2.1c、M2.1ff、M2.1g 和 M2.6a。各篇文章语步二中各步骤涉及篇章数平均值为 6.8 篇，占所有文章的 34%，标准差为 5.06。各篇文章中涉及步骤种类最多的有 12 种，最低的为 2 种，分别占语步二中所有步骤的 63% 和 11%。各篇文章中包含步骤种类的平均值为 6.5 种，占语步二中所有步骤的 34%，标准差为 2.65。不同文章中包含的步骤种类存在一定的差异，同一个步骤在不同文章中的占比也存在一定的差异。除去只涉及一篇文章的四个步骤，其他各步骤占比平均值最高的是 M2.1a，最低的是 M2.8，分别为 28% 和 4%。各步骤在所有文章中占比平均值之间的标准差为 6.22。

（三）语步三特征

表 3.2.5 是所分析的该学科论文语步三中包含的步骤种类。如表所示，该语步中共包括了 4 个步骤。表 3.2.6 是各篇文章语步三中各步骤在该语步中的占比情况。如表所示，有一部分文章不包含该语步。在包含该步骤的文章中，该语步中各步骤占比情况不一。此外，同一个步骤在不同文章中的占比情况也有所差异。以下是针对每个步骤占比情况的具体分析及实例。

表3.2.5　　　　　　　　语步三各步骤列表

M	语步三数据分析相关内容		
3.1	分析软件/工具	3.3	前人数据分析方法
3.2	数据分析方法	3.4	数据信度与效度

表3.2.6　　　　　　　　语步三各步骤占比

M	3.1	3.2	3.3	3.4	M	3.1	3.2	3.3	3.4
YW－01	—	—	—	—	YW－11	—	—	—	—
YW－02	—	75%	13%	13%	YW－12	100%	—	—	—
YW－03	—	—	—	—	YW－13	—	—	—	—
YW－04	—	—	—	—	YW－14	4%	96%	—	—
YW－05	—	100%	—	—	YW－15	—	—	—	—
YW－06	—	—	—	—	YW－16	—	—	—	—
YW－07	29%	57%	—	14%	YW－17	75%	—	—	25%
YW－08	—	—	—	100%	YW－18	25%	75%	—	—
YW－09	—	100%	—	—	YW－19	25%	75%	—	—
YW－10	50%	50%	—	—	YW－10	13%	88%	—	—

M 3.1 分析软件/工具：所选文章中有 40% 的文章包含该步骤。在包含该步骤的文章中，该步骤在语步三中的占比最大值为 100%，最小值为 4%，平均值为 40%，标准差为 0.31。实例如下：

Data analysis was carried out using the statistical software packages SPSS 23.0 and AMOS 24.0.（YW - 17）

In order to analyze the effect of the variables of interest in this study（i. e.，working memory capacity，writing self-efficacy，and writing anxiety）on measures of L2 writing，a particular type of structural equation modeling（SEM），path analysis，was used.（YW - 12）

M 3.2 数据分析方法：所选文章中有 45% 的文章包含该步骤。在包含该步骤的文章中，该步骤在语步三中的占比最大值为 100%，最小值为 50%，平均值为 80%，标准差为 0.17。实例如下：

An independent sample t-test was conducted to identify possible difference before and after self and peer review with respect to responsibility，motivation，ability，and learning activities.（YW - 19）

Following the principal component analysis，we examined the descriptive statistics for the task-appraisal，task-related emotion，task-related anxiety and task effort scales and of the single item that tapped into subjective competence（see Research Question 1）.（YW - 14）

M 3.3 前人数据分析方法：所选文章中只有一篇包含该步骤。在该篇文章中，该步骤在语步三中的占比为 13%。实例如下：

Second，to determine in what situations inside and outside the classroom the student teachers use the TL in junior and senior classes（Research question 1b）we used-analogous to Oosterhof et al.（2014）-Kwakernaak's（2007）so-called 'Target Language Ladder' （see Table 3）.（YW - 02）

M 3.4 数据信度与效度：所选文章中有 20% 的文章包含该步骤。在包含该步骤的文章中，该步骤在语步三中的占比最大值为 100%，最小值为 13%，平均值为 38%，标准差为 0.36。实例如下：

Reliability analysis for the planning，problem-solving，and corrective feedback strategies resulted in sufficient Cronbach alphas of 901，707，and 926 respectively.（YW - 17）

To estimate the reliability of the instrument the Cronbach's Alpha test was run，obtaining a reliability coefficient of .855.（YW - 08）

综上所述，在所分析的文章中有 60% 的文章中包含该语步。在这些文章中，涉及文章数最高的步骤是 M3.2，最低的是 M3.3，分别占所有文章的 45% 和 5%。各步骤涉及篇章数平均值为 5.5 篇，占所有文章的 28%，标准差为 4。在包含该步骤的文章中，涉及的步骤种类最高的有 3 种，最低的只有 1 种，分别占所有步骤的 75% 和 25%。各篇文章中包含步骤数量的平均值为 1.05 种，占语步三中所有步骤的 21%，标准差为 1。不同文章中包含的步骤种类存在一定的差异，同一个步骤在不同文章中的占比也存在一定的差异。在包含该步骤的文章中，除去只涉及一篇文章的步骤，其他各步骤占比平均值最高的是 M3.2，最低的是 M3.4，分别为 80% 和 38%。各步骤在所有文章中占比平均值之间的标准差为 27.71。

（四）语步占比及轨迹

图 3.2.3 是所分析各篇语步文章中三个语步总体占比。如图所示，所有文章均包含了语步一和语步二，有 60% 的文章包含语步三。就三个语步占比而言，分别有 60% 的文章语步二占比最高，35% 的文章语步一占比最高，有 5% 的文章语步一和语步二占比相同。在语步二占比最高的文章中，只有一篇文章语步三占比高于语步一，占该类文章的 8%。在语步一占比最高的文章中，有两篇文章语步三占比高于语步二，占该类文章的 29%。

就各步骤在所有语步中占比平均值来看，占比最高的三个步骤分别为 M1.6、M2.1a 和 M3.2；占比最低的是 M2.6a，其次是两个占比相同的步骤，分别为 M1.5 和 M2.1g。

就各步骤涉及的篇章数而言，最高的为 20 篇，占所有文章的 100%，为 M1.6；最低的仅涉及一篇，占所有文章的 5%，共有七个步骤，分别为 M1.5、M1.7、M2.1c、M2.1ff、M2.1g、M2.6a 和 M3.3。

就各篇文章中包含的步骤种类来看，包含步骤最多的有 17 种，占所有步骤的 55%，共有一篇文章；最少的有 6 种，占所有步骤的 19%，有两篇文章。各篇文章中包含步骤种类的平均值为 10.65 种，占所有步骤的 34%，标准差为 2.96。

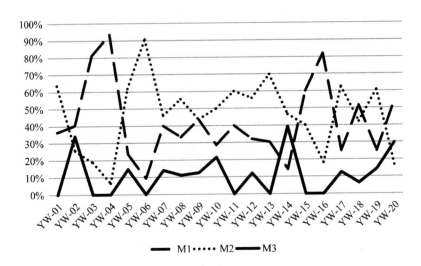

图 3.2.3　各篇文章中三个语步占比

图 3.2.4 至图 3.2.6 分别是各篇文章中三个语步的分布轨迹。如图所示，所分析的文章中均包含了语步一和语步二，但是有八篇文章不包含语步三。

在只包含语步一和语步二的文章中，有一半的文章中语步一占比高于语步二，分布也比语步二广；在另一半文章中情况则相反。这些文章中有一半的文章中语步一全部分布在语步二前，两个语步之间没有交叉；而在另一半文章中语步一分布较广，除一篇文章中语步二中有部分语句出现在语步一后，其他各篇文章中，语步二均全部分散分布在语步一中，两个语步之间有交叉。

在包含所有三个语步的十二篇文章中，有三篇文章中语步一占比最高，分布也较广，有一篇文章中语步一和语步二占比相同，均高于语步三。在其他各篇文章中语步二占比均最高，分布也最广。在语步二占比最高的文章中有一篇文章语步三占比高于语步一。其他文章中，语步三占比均最低，分布也最集中。总体来说，语步一中各步骤主要集中在方法部分的前部、语步二前，但是在少数文章中会集中分布在文章中间、语步二中，还有一部分文章中分布较广，几乎分布在文章的各处。语步二总体分布比较广，大多数文章中语步二出现的位置在语步一后、语步三前，但是在个别文章语步二中有部分语句出现在了方法的最前部；在个别文章中出现在了方法较后的位置。语步三主要集中分布在文章的最后。

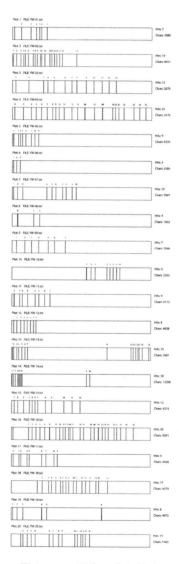

图 3.2.4　语步一分布轨迹

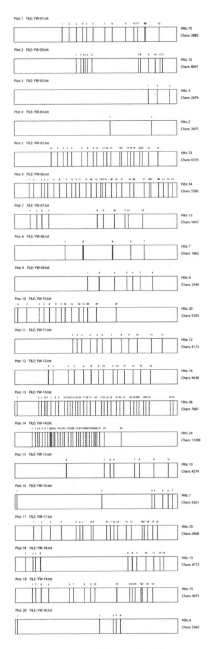

图 3.2.5　语步二分布轨迹

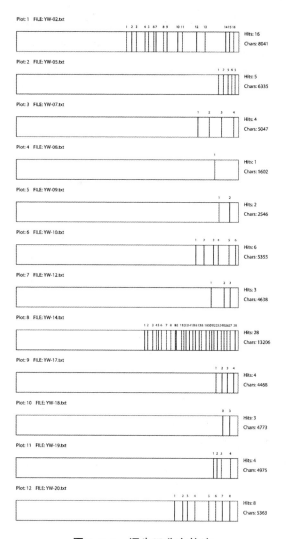

图 3.2.6　语步三分布轨迹

综上所述，同一学科不同文章中语步占比和分布轨迹既有相同之处，同时也存在一定的差异。所有文章中均出现了语步一和语步二，有一部分文章中不包含语步三。在绝大部分文章中语步二占比明显高于其他两个语步，分布也最广。三个语步中语步三占比总体最低，分布也较其他两个语步集中。语步一分布主要以文章最前和前部为主，但是有少部分文章中分布较广，也会出现在文章的中间及较后的位置。语步三以文章最后为主，语步二主要介于其他两个语步之间，但是语步二中也会有部分语句分布在文章前部及较后的位置。大部分文章中语步二与语步一有交叉，语步二与语步三交叉的情况较少，语步一和语步三之间没有交叉。

三　语言特征分析

本小节主要分析问卷调查写作部分的语言特征。主要从句子特征、时态特征和语态特征三个大的方面进行分析。针对句子结构的分析主要包含句子类型、四类主要句子长度分布及句子类型与语步之间的关系。针对时态的分析主要包含时态种类、不同时态组合及时态与语步的关系。针对语态的分析主要包含语态种类、不同语态组合及语态与语步的关系。

（一）句子特征

A. 句类及占比

表3.2.7是本学科二十篇文章中所包含的句子类型及各类句子占比。如表所示，简单句、复杂句、复合句及复合复杂句占所有句子的94.57%，其他为带有冒号及括号的各类特殊句子。四类句子中简单句占比远高于其他三类句子，其次是复杂句，其他两类句子占比均较低，其中复合句占比略高于复合复杂句。特殊类型句子形式多样，共有11种，其中NWS和BSS占比较高，其他均较低。以下例句为特殊类型的句子。

表 3.2.7　　　　　　　　　　句类及占比

句类	句数	占比	句类	句数	占比
S	334	56.51%	NWAP	2	0.34%
P	158	26.73%	NWAS	3	0.51%
C	45	7.61%	NWC	3	0.51%
CP	22	3.72%	NWP	3	0.51%
BPF	1	0.17%	NWS	11	1.86%

句类	句数	占比	句类	句数	占比
BSS	4	0.68%	NCPP	1	0.17%
NBWPP/S	1	0.17%	NPP	1	0.17%
NSC	2	0.34%			

BPF：Where possible, classes were selected which had different "special subjects" (i. e. , subjects which receive special attention in the curriculum and are given extra lessons in certain semesters such as modern languages, science, and economics) in order to maximise the representativeness of the sample. (YW – 16)

BSS：The principal components analysis revealed the presence of two components with eigenvalues exceeding 1, explaining 36.78% (task-related emotions) and 22.97% (task-related anxiety) of the variance respectively (the total variance explained was 64.72%). (YW – 14)

NBWPP/S：Developed by Bruning, Dempsey, Kauffman, McKim, and Zumbrunn (2013), the SEWS is a 16-item questionnaire with items that represent self-efficacy for performing in three writing-related dimensions：ideation ("I know exactly where to place my ideas in my writing"), conventions ("I can punctuate my sentences correctly"), and self-regulation ("I can avoid distractions while I write"). (YW – 12)

NSC：For both the student and teacher questionnaires, numerical values were assigned to the four quantity options given on each question："a lot" of feedback was coded as a 3, "some" as a 3, "a little" as a 2, and "none" as a 1. (YW – 05)

NWAP：The focus of analysis for this study is the midterm essay exam, which is a task similar to class essay assignments and the final essay exam and serves both formative and summative purposes in these classes：formative by providing feedback to the students so that they can continue to improve for the remainder of the course and summative by measuring student achievement at the midpoint of the course and contributing 20% to the students' course grade. (YW – 20)

NWAS：Section IV describes for each student teacher the following three things：1. the amount of TL use, 2. in which classroom situations he/she generally uses the TL and how much the TL is used, and 3. how their TL use develops regarding the 16 situations. (YW – 02)

NWC：These results are compared to reveal potential differences between self-report and external observations; this is done as follows：S1 – CO1, S2 – CO2, and S3 – CO3. (YW – 02)

NWP：The questionnaire consisted of two main sections that focused on specific task – types：one section on the Listen – Write task, and the other section on the Listen – Speak task type. (YW – 14)

NWS: In particular, it covered five areas: writing and language abilities; report writing abilities; situation and purpose; audiences and feedback; and planning, drafting and revising. (YW – 09)

NCPP: The format of the survey was intended to reflect a draft – revise – resubmit instructional sequence, with all questions worded so that respondents could express their agreement or disagreement with statements such as: "In a first draft, I think the instructor should always comment on my ideas and how they are developed" and "Generally, I learn the most when my instructor highlights grammatical mistakes." (YW – 07)

NPP: Additionally, an open-ended question was used to supplement the third closed-ended question to collect accounts of why and how students thought they had changed in the way they did: *"To the students who chose either a little, somewhat, or a lot in the third question, how and why do you think you have changed in the way you did?"* (YW – 15)

B. 句类与语步

图 3.2.7 是四种句子类型与语步的关系。如图所示，复合复杂句中步骤较分散，出现最多的步骤是 M1.6，共出现过 6 次。复合句中步骤分布也较分散，出现最多的也是 M1.6，共出现过 23 次，但是排在第二的 M2.1a 只出现了 5 次，其他均很低。四类句子中占比最高的步骤均为 M1.6。除复合复杂句，其他三类句子中占比最高的前三个步骤中均包含 M2.1a，但是该步骤在这三类句子中排序不完全一致，数量和占比相差也较大。简单句和复杂句中步骤占比最高的前三个步骤种类相同，但是三个步骤的排序不完全一致，同一步骤数量和占比也不相同。

这四种类型句子中均包含三个语步，就各类句子中包含的三个语步中步骤种类而言，简单句中包含了四个语步中所有步骤，复杂句、复合句、复合复杂句中包含的步骤种类分别占三个语步中所有步骤种类的 88%、47% 和 41%。

综上所述，不同句子类型与步骤之间的关系存在异同，句子与步骤关系紧密度与该类句子在所有句子中的占比有关，同时也与该步骤在所有步骤中的占比有关，但是不完全成一一对应的关系，句类与步骤之间没有明显的相关性。

以下是四类句子中步骤占比最高的前三个步骤例句，由于复合句和复杂复合句中步骤较分散，分别只给出占比较高的一到两个步骤例句。

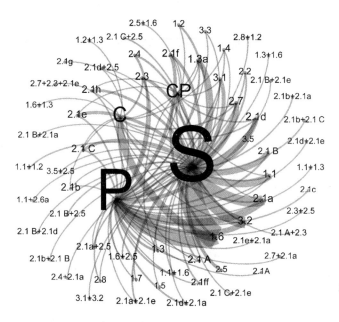

图 3.2.7 句类与步骤关系网络图

【S】

M 1. 6： The participants in this study are university students, freshmen to juniors, majoring in English language at a local university in South Korea. （YW – 19）

M 3. 2： To gain insights into test-takers' perceptions of delivery mode, descriptive and comparative statistics were run on the Likert scale and MC items of the perception questionnaire. （YW – 10）

M 2. 1a： The third set of questions asked for test-takers' views on the fairness of the test depending on the delivery mode. （YW – 10）

【P】

M 1. 6： Therefore, all of the teachers know many of the issues discussed in the field of L2 writing and what type of feedback is preferred by the ELC. （YW – 05）

M 2. 1a： How do you think the quality of self and peer review can be improved? （YW – 19）

M 3. 2： On the basis of those results, an exploratory factor analysis was performed with a view to proposing a more parsimonious three-factor model that would explain students' perceptions of, and preferences for, instructor feedback on their writing assignments. （YW – 07）

【C】

M 1. 6： To work at the ELC, the teachers must have at least a bachelor's degree and must either be working on or have completed a master's in TESOL. (YW – 05)

M 2. 1a: (1) "To what degree did you have prior experience of writing emails in English before taking this class?" (2) "Compared with the beginning of the semester, to what degree do you think that you have improved your ability to write emails in English?" and (3) "Compared with the beginning of the semester, to what degree do you think that you have changed your way of thinking about writing emails in English?" (YW – 15)

【CP】

M 1. 6: They had studied English for at least seven years, and they were placed in the lower-intermediate class based on their scores in a school-developed placement exam that focused on listening, grammar, vocabulary, and reading. (YW – 15)

C. 句类与句长

表 3. 2. 8 是四种类型句子长度占比情况。简单句中句子长度占比最高的是单词数介于 11—20 的句子，其次是介于 21—30 的句子；其他三类句子占比最高的均为介于 21—30 的句子，但是在这三类句中占比排在第二的有所不同，其中复杂句和复合句均为介于 11—20 的句子，但是复杂句中这个句长范围的句子占比与介于 31—40 的句子非常接近，而复合句中介于 11—20 的句子占比远高出介于 31—40 的句子。复合复杂句中占比排在第二的为介于 31—40 的句子，该类句子中不包含低于 21 个单词数的句子。

就各类句子覆盖长度范围而言，简单句和复杂句覆盖的长度范围相同，也最广；复合句和复合复杂句覆盖范围略低，复合句主要分布在 50 个单词内，复合复杂句则分布在 21 个单词到 80 个单词之间。

就句子长度最大值而言，最长的是复合复杂句，最短的是复合句，其他两类相近，介于其中。就最小值而言，最短的是简单句，最长的是复合复杂句，其他两类居中，没有差异。如果不排除特殊类型句子，将每个公式算为一个单词的话，所有句子中最长的句子是 NWAP，共有 76 个单词，最短的是简单句，共有 4 个单词。

综上所述，四种类型句子长度分布在不同方面相似度不同。就占比而言，简单句与其他三类句子差异较大，而在这三类句子中复杂句和复合句较相似。就覆盖范围来说，简单句和复杂句相同。就句子长度最大值而言，简单句和复杂句相近；就句长最小值而言，复杂句和复合句相同。

以下是所有句子中最长的 NWAP 例句及四类句子中最长和最短的句子。

表 3.2.8　　　　　　　　　四类句子长度分布

句长范围		1—10	11—20	21—30	31—40	41—50	51—60	61—70	71—80	MAX	MIX
S	句数	41	165	94	25	6	2	1	*	67	4
	占比	12.28%	49.40%	28.14%	7.49%	1.80%	0.60%	0.30%	*		
P	句数	1	39	73	36	6	1	1	*	69	10
	占比	0.64%	24.84%	46.50%	22.93%	3.82%	0.64%	0.64%	*		
C	句数	1	15	21	5	4	*	*	*	49	10
	占比	2.17%	32.61%	45.65%	10.87%	8.70%	*	*	*		
CP	句数	*	*	11	5	2	3	*	1	74	21
	占比	*	*	50.00%	22.73%	9.09%	13.64%	*	4.55%		

NWAP/〔**Max：76**〕The focus of analysis for this study is the midterm essay exam, which is a task similar to class essay assignments and the final essay exam and serves both formative and summative purposes in these classes: formative by providing feedback to the students so that they can continue to improve for the remainder of the course and summative by measuring student achievement at the midpoint of the course and contributing 20% to the students' course grade. (YW - 20)

S/〔**Max：67**〕They are student A, 25 year old male student in the 3rd year with a 700 TOEIC score, student B, 20 year old female student in the 2nd year with a 650 TOEIC score, student C, 19 year old female student in the 1st year with a 750 score, and student D, 23 year old male student in the 2nd year with over a 900 TOEIC score. (YW - 19)

S/〔**Min：4**〕What are the implications? (YW - 19)

P/〔**Max：69**〕In addition, given the study's focus on exploring the potential of the ISE writing test in computer-based online format, participants were also asked for how many years they had been using computers and to indicate on Likert scales (1) how often they had used computers in the last year, (2) how good they felt they were at using computers, and (3) how well they could type on a computer. (YW - 10)

P/〔**Min：10**〕It was conducted with a teacher who implemented the class. (YW - 19)

C/［**Max：49**］Additionally, some research studies (e. g, Tillema, van den Bergh, Rijlaars-dam, & Sanders, 2011; Torrance, Thomas, & Robinson, 1999) reported reasonably moderate correlations between learners' self-reported questionnaire and their actual on-line writing behavior; this raises our confidence in using the retrospective questionnaire as an instrument to elicit learners' metacognitive processes. (YW – 01)

C/［**Min：10**］Both schools are state-owned and education is free of charge. (YW – 14)

CP/［**Max：74**］Since the target students for these classes have only partially met the university's proficiency requirement and therefore need further ESL training in an academic setting, students in these classes do not learn discipline-specific EAP or genres but develop their academic writing skills more generally, focusing on the "common core" (Hyland, 2006, p11) of academic writing skills (ie, the common underlying language forms and skills) in a course with students from different faculties and programs. (YW –20)

CP/［**Min：21**］The other five were born and educated in Sacramento but raised in homes in which the primary language was not English. (YW –03)

（二）时态特征

A. 时态种类及组合

表 3.2.9 是该学科论文中使用的时态类型及组合形式。如表所示，该学科文章中共出现了 12 种不同时态，其中 T6、T7、T9、T10、T11 和 T12 这 6 种时态没有单独使用，而是与其他时态共同出现在一个句子中。由不同时态构成的组合共有 18 种，其中两种时态组合共 11 种，三种时态组合共 4 种，四种时态组合共 3 种。不同时态组合中包含 T3 的最多，T1 略低于 T3，其次依次为 T10 和 T2，分别占所有组合的 68%、63%、32% 和 21%，其他时态在组合中占比均较低。

各种时态组合中，全部由一种时态构成的句子中占比最高的是 T3，其次为 T1。由不同时态构成的句子中占比最高的是由 T1 和 T3 两种不同时态构成的句子，其他相同或不同时态组合占比均较低。以下是按照四种类型句子给出的相同时态和不同时态组合的例句，但是不是所有时态组合中均包含这四类句子。

表 3.2.9 时态类型及组合

时态	T1	T2	T3	T4	T5	T8	T1T2	T1T2T7
句数	120	2	372	1	5	1	5	1
占比	20.30%	0.34%	62.94%	0.17%	0.85%	0.17%	0.85%	0.17%
时态	T1T3	T1T3T5T10	T1T3T6T10	T1T3T9	T1T3T10	T1T4	T1T8	T1T10
句数	33	1	1	1	1	1	1	3
占比	5.58%	0.17%	0.17%	0.17%	0.17%	0.17%	0.17%	0.51%
时态	T2T3	T3T5	T3T5T8	T3T5T10T12	T3T8	T3T10	T3T11	T3T12
句数	3	15	1	1	4	16	1	1
占比	0.51%	2.54%	0.17%	0.17%	0.68%	2.71%	0.17%	0.17%

【T1】

S： The teacher education program of the University of Groningen consists of two stages. (YW – 02)

P： At bothuniversities, language work is assessed by two language papers at the end of the year, which also test essay writingskills. (YW – 04)

C： In the weekly EFL methodology course, students reflect on their questions and dilemmas related to their teaching practice and they discuss one or two general topics in FL teaching methodology, such as grammar instruction, corrective feedback, and the role of literature in FLT. (YW – 02)

CP： Furthermore, one of the sessions is dedicated entirely to TL use and the topic is discussed regularly when students raise their questions and dilemmas. (YW – 02)

【T2】

S： Reliabilities for all three factors have been found to be high (above.80) (Bruning et al., 2013). (YW – 12)

【T3】

S： Their mean age was 18 years. (YW – 01)

P： Four teachers used overt corrections (providing corrections for errors), while one teacher categorised errors with error codes. (YW – 04)

C： All students had no prior experience of contract grading and they completed the semester with passing grades. (YW – 08)

CP： For validity purposes, the questionnaire was piloted to a number of students after it was first designed and its items were later amended accordingly. (YW – 09)

【T4】

S： The higher the percentage and mean score, the closer the response to the statement will be.

（YW - 09）

【T5】

S： By that time, the participants had been employed as EFL teachers in secondary education for one year. (YW - 02)

C： None had ever been to an English-speaking country, and they had reported little opportunity to use English outside the language classroom. (YW - 01)

【T8】

S： The participants were majoring in either biotherapy or animal husbandry. (YW - 15)

【T1T2】

P： The approach to teaching writing is what has been called the post-process approach (e. g. , Ferris & Hedgcock, 2005; Polio & Williams, 2009). (YW - 20)

CP： The analysis of S1-S3 reveals developmental tendencies and distinguishes between situations that have remained stable (no change or maximum 1 point change over three measurements), situations that have developed gradually (for example: $1 - 2 - 3$ or $4 - 3 - 2$), and situations that show an irregular development (for example: $1 - 3 - 1$ or $4 - 1 - 3$). (YW - 02)

【T1T2T7】

C： To work at the ELC, the teachers must have at least a bachelor's degree and must either be working on or have completed a master's in TESOL. (YW - 05)

【T1T3】

P： Participants' task motivation towards the two integrated task types (Listen-Write and Listen-Speak) was assessed using a questionnaire adopted from Boekaerts (2002), which is one of the most widely used instruments for assessing task motivation. (YW - 14)

C： Additionally, some research studies (e. g, Tillema, van den Bergh, Rijlaarsdam, & Sanders, 2011; Torrance, Thomas, & Robinson, 1999) reported reasonably moderate correlations between learners' self-reported questionnaire and their actual on-line writing behavior; this raises our confidence in using the retrospective questionnaire as an instrument to elicit learners' metacognitive processes. (YW - 01)

CP： The scale consisted of 13 items and in our study the reliability coefficient was a $= 0.88$, which can be considered as very good (DeVellis, 1991). (YW - 06)

【T1T3T5T10】

P： Although there was no time constraint for completing the questionnaires, the directions stipulated that "when most of the participants had finished," they could suggest that all participants try to complete "in the next minute or two." (YW - 12)

【T1T3T6T10】

P： These categories were used instead of exact numerical counts because it is possible that if actual feedback quantities were asked, participants would have felt intimidated and unsure that they could give an accurate assessment. (YW – 05)

【T1T3T9】

CP: The teachers at the BYU ELC who participated in this study were all writing teachers, and many of them have been teaching L2 writing for several years, although some are new teachers recently admitted into the TESOL master's program. (YW – 05)

【T1T3T10】

P: Although the students' views and opinions in response to this type of question may be subjective, it was expected that such data would complement the analysis of the students' actual written products. (YW – 15)

【T1T4】

CP: I am anxious that I will make grammar mistakes when writing in English, I am worried that my grade will be low when writing in English, I am confused when writing in English within a time limit, and I am worried that I will make mistakes when writing in English. (YW – 17)

【T1T8】

P: The bulk of students were entering into degrees in the Management School which includes courses such as accounting and finance. (YW – 13)

【T1T10】

C: This level of reliability is considered to be the boundary for acceptability (DeVellis, 1991) and thus results should be taken with caution. (YW – 06)

【T2T3】

P: These constructs were chosen due to their prominence in both the theoretical and empirical literature on task motivation, and the positive impact that they have been shown to have on students' writing task performance (Kormos & Wilby, 2019). (YW – 13)

C: Interestingly, the students' L1 writing experience was also limited; these limitations have also been reported by Kobayashi and Rinnert's (2002) nationwide survey of Japanese students' literacy experience. (YW – 15)

【T3T5】

P: They also indicated for 12 word processor writing functions (e. g. generating a table of contents, headings, outline function) whether or not they had used it previously. (YW – 06)

C: They all had experience doing research in the field of language learning and teaching, and had published at least one of these academic products: dissertations, articles, books or chapters of books. (YW – 18)

CP: They had studied English for at least seven years, and they were placed in the lower-intermediate class based on their scores in a school-developed placement exam that focused on listening, grammar, vocabulary, and reading. (YW – 15)

【T3T5T8】

C: Some of them were members of the SNI, National Researchers System (n = 14) or had obtained the recognition of the Professional Teacher Development Program from the Ministry of Education, PRODEP (n = 53) and were working in a registered research group (CA) with different level of consolidation. (YW – 38)

【T3T5T10T12】

P: In addition, given the study's focus on exploring the potential of the ISE writing test in computer-based online format, participants were also asked for how many years they had been using computers and to indicate on Likert scales (1) how often they had used computers in the last year, (2) how good they felt they were at using computers, and (3) how well they could type on a computer. (YW – 10)

【T3T8】

P: They were professors who were working at these institutions (NU, n = 33, CU = 32, SU = 35), either as part time or full time teachers. (YW – 18)

C: They were majoring in ELT and were sampled using convenience sampling. (YW – 11)

【T3T10】

P: For each medium, students could indicate whether and how often they used it, varying from 'I never use this medium' to 'I use this medium several times a day.' (YW – 06)

C: 'Did you immediately understand how to use the outlinetool?'; 'Would you use the outline tool in subsequent writing tasks?' (YW – 06)

【T3T11】

P: After final exams, students were approached and asked if they would be willing to fill out a short survey. (YW – 05)

【T3T12】

C: The test-takers at all three test levels had been using computers for many years, and did so on a very frequent basis. (YW – 10)

B. 时态与语步

图 3.2.8 是该学科文章中三种占比较高的时态组合与语步的关系。如图所示，在这三种时态组合中，占比最高的前三个步骤种类完全一致，但是这三个步骤在这三种时态组合中排序不完全一致，数量和占比也不同。

　　此外，这三种时态组合形式中均包含了三个语步，但就它们包含的步骤种类而言，T3 最高，其次是 T1 和 T1T3，它们包含的步骤种类分别占所有步骤的 97%、59% 和 47%。

　　总体来说，不同时态形式的句子与语步的联系既存在共性，也存在一定的差异。时态与步骤关系紧密度与该时态在所有句子中的占比有关，同时也与该步骤在所有步骤中的占比有关，但并不是决定性的。

　　以下是按照四种类型句子给出的三种时态组合中占比最高的前三个步骤的例句，但是有些步骤中不包含所有类型的句子。

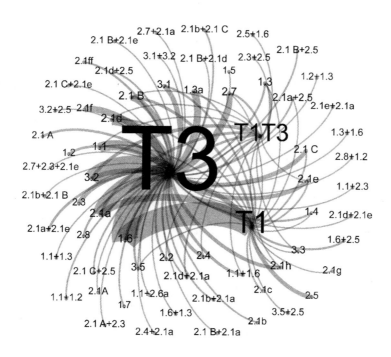

图 3.2.8　时态与步骤关系网络图

【T1】

M 1.6

S：The teacher education program of the University of Groningen consists of two stages.（YW –

02）

P：The teacher education program prepares participants to teach EFL in secondary education at all levels, that is from vocational to pre-university level. (YW – 02)

C：In the weekly EFL methodology course, students reflect on their questions and dilemmas related to their teaching practice and they discuss one or two general topics in FL teaching methodology, such as grammar instruction, corrective feedback, and the role of literature in FLT. (YW – 02)

CP：Furthermore, one of the sessions is dedicated entirely to TL use and the topic is discussed regularly when students raise their questions and dilemmas. (YW – 02)

M 2.1a

S：Regarding the context of our study, the external domain is restricted to the institutional subdomain. (YW – 02)

P：How do you think students' perceptions of self and peer review effect learners' choices in the learning process activities? (YW – 19)

C：Before writing a text, I write down some notes and elaborate them later. (YW – 06)

M 3.2

S：This is done both for the period during teacher education (S1 – S3) and the period after graduation (S3 – S4). (YW – 02)

【T1T3】

M 3.2

P：These were extended with external factors pertaining to the teacher education program, which we label 'institutional.' (YW – 02)

CP：At the same time, I used axial coding; this means that I related the emerging concepts to each other to understand the relationships among them (Corbin & Strauss, 2008). (YW – 20)

M 2.1a

P：The TL policy and practice of the secondary schools at which the student teachers served their apprenticeships, the teaching materials used, and learners' responses to TL use are included in the practice-related domain. (YW – 02)

M 1.6

P：Table 2 also indicates that, overall, the participants' self-reported computer familiarity was high. (YW – 10)

【T3】

M 1.6

S：Thus, the stakes for passing this course in a timely manner were high. (YW – 03)

P：In the English Preparatory Program from which the participants were sampled, the students received intensive English instruction adopting a skill-based approach. (YW – 11)

C：The participants were intermediate level freshmen students at the time of data collection and their ages ranged between 17 and 30 （M ＝ 18. 89）. （YW － 31）

CP：The other five were born and educated in Sacramento butraised in homes in which the primary language was not English. （YW － 03）

M 3. 2

S：The final factor solution for task-related emotion and anxiety constructs met the required statistical criteria. （YW － 14）

P：The analyses also showed that two items referring to how relieved the participants were and how satisfied they felt after they completed the tasks had to be omitted due to low commonality values. （YW － 14）

C：For the items referring to the Listen-Speak tasks, the KMO value was . 701 , and Barlett's Test of Sphericity reached statistical significance （p ＜. 001）. （YW － 14）

CP：They showed that there were outliers in all three tasks, and these outliers scored zero （n ＝ 1） and one point （n ＝ 1） in the Non-Academic Listen-Speak and one point （n ＝ 5） in the Academic Listen-Speak tasks, and zero （n ＝ 2） and one point （n ＝ 1） in the Listen-Write task. （YW － 14）

M 2. 1a

S：All students in the two classes completed questionnaires about their writing and language backgrounds during the first class meeting. （YW － 03）

P：The questions were followed by a prompt asking further explanations or clarifications for the preferences they stated. （YW － 11）

C：This was a standard questionnaire regularly used in all classes in this department; however, for these two sections, we added three extra questions at the end specifically related to WCF. （YW － 03）

（三）语态特征

A. 语态种类及组合

表 3. 2. 10 是该学科文章中使用的不同语态组合类型，其中不包含有语法错误的句子。如表所示，该学科文章中均包含了两种语态，同时还包含了这两种语态的组合形式。只包含 V1 的句子数量和占比远高于其他两种类型的句子，只包含 V2 的句子数量和占比略高于包含两种不同语态的句子。各篇文章中均包含这三种形式的语态组合。由同一种语态构成的句子中，V1 组合中包含了四种类型的句子，V2 组合中不

包含复杂复合句，V1V2 组合中不包含简单句。

以下是按照四种类型句子给出的三种语态组合中的例句，但是有些语态组合中不包含所有类型的句子。

表3.2.10 　　　　　　　　语态类型及组合

语态	V1	V1V2	V2
句数	326	102	163
占比	55.16%	17.23%	27.53%

【V1】

S：The Technical Report Writing course is the last in a series of English language courses offered in this academic program. （YW－09）

P：These were the only students who attended the course during the first semester of the academic year 2012/2013. （YW－09）

C：For the items referring to the Listen-Speak tasks, the KMO value was.701, and Barlett's Test of Sphericity reached statistical significance （p＜.001）. （YW－14）

CP：At the same time, I used axial coding; this means that I related the emerging concepts to each other to understand the relationships among them （Corbin & Strauss, 2008）. （YW－20）

【V1V2】

P：This study followed sophomore students who were enrolled in a compulsory undergraduate writing course for two credit hours in one semester. （YW－15）

C：Of the original 97, three students （all from University A） were native speakers of German and their reasons for studying German were considerably different from those of the other students; they were therefore excluded from the data set. （YW－04）

CP：If students indicated two or more home languages, they were classified as bilingual; if they only indicated one language, they were classified as monolingual. （YW－16）

【V2】

S：NU and SU are located in the border area with English speaking countries （US and Belize）. （YW－18）

P：Prior to their admission to a degree programme at the university level, they were required to attend the English Language Programme, in which they were taught how to write argumentative essays and were often instructed to plan their essays before writing. （YW－01）

C：These results are compared to reveal potential differences between self-report and external observations; this is done as follows: S1－CO1, S2－CO2, and S3－CO3. （YW－02）

B. 语态与语步

图 3.2.9 是该学科文章中两种语态及组合与语步的关系。如图所示，这三种语态组合中占比最高的前三个步骤中均包含了 M1.6 和 M3.2，但是它们在三个组合中的排序不完全一致，数量和占比也不同。此外，V1 和 V1V2 组合中均包含 M2.1d，该步骤在这两个组合中的占比均排在第三位，但是数量和占比不同。就这三种组合中包含的语步种类而言，它们均包含了三个语步，但是它们包含的步骤种类在所有步骤中占比不同。V1 包含了所有步骤，V2 和 V1V2 中分别包含了所有步骤的 81% 和 72%。总体来说，语态与步骤关系紧密度与该语态在所有句子中的占比有关，同时也与该步骤在所有步骤中的占比有一定的关系。

以下是按照四种类型句子给出的三种语态组合中占比最高的前三个步骤的例句，但是有些步骤中不包含所有类型的句子。

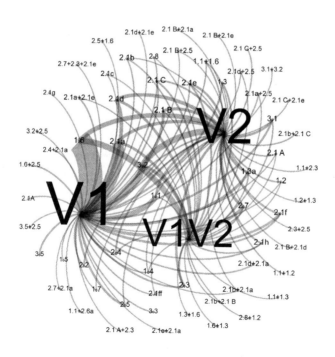

图 3.2.9　语态与步骤关系网络图

【V1】

M 1. 6

S： The sample comprised 52 males and 54 females. （YW－01）

P： Five of the ten students had immigrated to the U. S. with their families when they were young, with arrival ages ranging from 4 to 11 years old. （YW－03）

C： None had ever been to an English-speaking country, and they had reported little opportunity to use English outside the language classroom. （YW－01）

CP： Since the target students for these classes have only partially met the university's proficiency requirement and therefore need further ESL training in an academic setting, students in these classes do not learn discipline-specific EAP or genres but develop their academic writing skills more generally, focusing on the "common core" （Hyland, 2006, p11） of academic writing skills （ie, the common underlying language forms and skills） in a course with students from different faculties and programs. （YW－20）

M 2. 1a

S： The survey involved questions about TL use in junior and senior classes and intervening factors. （see Appendix 1）（YW－02）

P： Students indicated since how many years and how often they work with a computer and word processor. （YW－06）

C： Before writing a text, I write down some notes and elaborate them later. （YW－06）

CP： I am anxious that I will make grammar mistakes when writing in English, I am worried that my grade will be low when writing in English, I am confused when writing in English within a time limit, and I am worried that I will make mistakes when writing in English. （YW－17）

M 3. 2

S： We also checked the reliability of these two scales. （YW－14）

P： The analyses also showed that two items referring to how relieved the participants were and how satisfied they felt after they completed the tasks had to be omitted due to low commonality values. （YW－14）

C： For the items referring to the Listen-Speak tasks, the KMO value was $.701$, and Barlett's Test of Sphericity reached statistical significance （$p < .001$）. （YW－14）

CP： They showed that there were outliers in all three tasks, and these outliers scored zero （$n = 1$） and one point （$n = 1$） in the Non-Academic Listen-Speak and one point （$n = 5$） in the Academic Listen-Speak tasks, and zero （$n = 2$） and one point （$n = 1$） in the Listen-Write task. （YW－14）

【V1V2】

M 1. 6

P： This course is intended to qualify learners to write project reports （PRs）, which are graduation requirement projects needed in the eighth （final） semester of the computer science program.

（YW – 09）

C：The course is offered in 15 weeks, two times a week, and each class is 75 minutes. （YW –29）

CP：Under state law, all university students have one year after matriculating to successfully complete any required developmental courses in English and mathematics; if they fail to do so, they are disenrolled from the university until they can meet the requirements elsewhere. （YW – 03）

M 3. 2

P：We excluded the participants with a score of zero（n = 3）from the correlational analyses which were used to assess the link between task-motivational factors and task scores. （YW – 14）

C：Data for many of the investigated scales and items were skewed and showed a somewhat restricted range of distribution. （YW – 14）

M 2. 1d

P：Before completing the questionnaire, the participants were informed that they needed to complete the writing self-efficacy questionnaire according to their ability to write in the second language（and not their ability to write in their mother tongue）. （YW – 12）

C：For conducting pair and collaborative writing tasks in the classroom, necessary instructions regarding collaborative writing tasks were also provided by the instructor, and she answered the students' questions regarding these conditions. （YW – 11）

CP：The participants were told that they were free to express themselves in any language that they felt comfortable with, and all of them responded to the questions in Turkish. （YW – 11）

【V2】

M 3. 2

S：The teachers' responses on the questionnaire were also converted to numerical scores. （YW –05）

P：After the numerical values were assigned, the students' responses for each teacher were averaged for each response item. （YW – 05）

M 1. 6

S：The participants can be considered a fairly homogeneous group of ESL learners interms of their instructional background. （YW – 01）

P：Prior to their admission to a degree programme at the university level, they were required to attend the English Language Programme, in which they were taught how to write argumentative essays and were often instructed to plan their essays before writing. （YW – 01）

M 2. 1d

S：Prior to the study, the participants were then given an open-ended pre-questionnaire in order to explore their perceptions about writing individually, as a pair, and as a group. （WJ – 11）

P：Numerical figures were assigned so that statistical comparisons between the two questionnaires and the actual teacher feedback could be performed. （YW – 05）

第三节　学科间对比分析

本节主要对比分析管理学和语言学两个学科论文中问卷调查方法写作的体裁特征。分析主要涉及该部分在全文中的占比、标题特征、语步特征及语言特征。其中标题特征包括大小标题词汇使用情况及小标题数量。语步特征主要包括语步种类及各语步中步骤种类，同一语步中各步骤涉及篇章数及占比，各篇文章中不同语步总体占比及分布轨迹。语言特征主要包括句子、时态和语态特征。句子特征主要包括句子类型、四类主要句子长度分布及它们与语步的关系。时态特征主要包括时态种类、时态组合形式及三种占比最高的时态组合与语步之间的关系。语态特征主要包括两种语态、不同语态组合形式及它们与语步之间的关系。

一　篇幅占比

在所分析的两个学科论文中，文章的结构都遵循了 IMRD 的格式。就论文中方法部分总体篇幅占比而言，这两个学科较为接近，语言学略高。两个学科在学科内论文之间的差异也较为接近。但就论文中有关问卷调查研究方法来说，语言学中占比远低于管理学。问卷调查在管理学科中常作为主要研究方法，本研究选取的管理学科中的论文大部分只使用问卷调查一种方法，有少部分论文中会包含访谈。而在语言学中，问卷调查主要用作研究的辅助手段，写作中占据的篇幅也较少。本研究所选取的语言学论文均为外语教学研究类论文，各篇文章中涉及教学实验、访谈及问卷调查三种研究方法。

二　标题特征

这两个学科在方法部分均使用了一级大标题，使用最多的单词均是 method，其次是 methods，同时也都使用了 methodology。就二级小标题使用情况而言，管理学中有 80% 的文章使用了二级小标题，最多的有 5 个，最少的有 2 个，使用最多的词是 measure（13 次），其次是 sample（10 次）、data（7 次）和 procedure（7 次）。语言学论文全部都使用了二级小标题，最多的有 6 个，最少的有 2 个，使用最多的词汇是 participants（18 次），其次是 questionnaire（16 次）、proce-dure（9 次）、analyses（8 次）、data（7 次）。此外，管理学科中有35% 的文章使用了三级小标题，有一篇文章使用了四级小标题；而语言学文章中只包含二级小标题。

总体来看，这两个学科在大标题方面具有高度的一致性；在二级小标题使用数量方面同一学科不同文章之间存在一定的差异，学科间差异不明显。两个学科中一级大标题和二级小标题中使用的词汇与文章研究主题均没有显著的相关性，二级小标题中词汇与使用的研究方法关系均更密切。管理学科文章中三级小标题和四级小标题中的词汇与文章具体研究主题密切相关。

三 语步特征

本小节主要讨论这两个学科论文中三个语步在以下三个方面的异同：第一，不同语步中包含的步骤种类；第二，各步骤涉及的篇章数；第三，各语步中不同步骤占比及分布轨迹。步骤占比中，平均值和标准差只涉及包含该步骤的文章。分别用"＊"代表涉及篇章数在一篇的步骤，用"—"表示文章中不涉及该步骤。

A. 语步一

表 3.3.1 是两个学科语步一中各步骤涉及篇章数及在所分析的文章中占比。如表所示，管理学论文中语步一涉及的步骤种类大于语言学。有八个步骤为两个学科共有，管理学中包括了语言学中所有步骤。就各步骤涉及篇章数而言，少数步骤相同，大部分步骤中管理学均明显高于语言学。两个学科中不同步骤涉及的文章数量均存在一定的差异。两个学科中 M1.1 和 M1.6 涉及篇章数均较高，M1.3a、M1.5 和 M1.7 均较低。差异最大的是 M1.4。

表3.3.1 各学科语步一中各步骤涉及篇章数及占比

M	GW 篇数—占比	YW 篇数—占比	M	GW 篇数—占比	YW 篇数—占比
1.1	19%—95%	19%—95%	1.3a	4%—20%	4%—20%
1.1A	3%—15%	—	1.4	13%—65%	2%—10%
1.2	10%—50%	7%—35%	1.5	4%—20%	1%—5%
1.2a	6%—30%	—	1.6	16%—80%	20%—100%
1.3	13%—65%	7%—35%	1.7	4%—20%	1%—5%

表3.3.2是这两个学科不同文章中语步一各步骤在该语步中占比最大值、最小值、平均值和标准差。如表所示，就步骤占比最大值而言，两个学科共有的步骤之间均存在一定的差异，最大值均不相同，但同时也存在一定的共性。总体来说，在一个学科中占比高的步骤在另一个学科中占比也较其他步骤高，但不是完全一一对应的关系。在最小值方面，除去三个步骤外，其他各步骤中管理学总体均低于语言学。平均值和标准差与两个极值及篇章数有一定的关系，两个学科中不同步骤之间平均值和标准差关系不一。

B. 语步二

表3.3.3是两个学科中语步二中各步骤涉及篇章数及在所分析的文章中占比。如表所示，语言学论文中语步二涉及的步骤种类大于管理学。就各步骤涉及篇章数而言，两个学科中多个步骤具有较高的相似性，M2.1a、M2.1d、M2.1e和M2.5涉及篇章数均较高，但是管理学占比总体略高于语言学。有些步骤在两个学科中存在较大的差异。

表3.3.2 各学科语步一中各步骤占比四项指标

M	MAX（%）		MIN（%）		Mean（%）		SD	
	GW	YW	GW	YW	GW	YW	GW	YW
1.1	80	50	6	6	24	17	0.19	0.12
1.1A	28	—	16	—	22	—	0.05	*
1.2	27	38	6	2	16	14	0.08	0.14

续表

M	MAX（%）		MIN（%）		Mean（%）		SD	
	GW	YW	GW	YW	GW	YW	GW	YW
1.2a	6	—	1	—	3	—	0.01	*
1.3	38	20	3	2	13	9	0.11	0.05
1.3a	15	41	3	14	8	26	0.04	0.11
1.4	58	30	7	8	27	19	0.16	0.11
1.5	25	10	9	10	15	10	0.06	*
1.6	86	95	3	20	34	67	0.25	0.22
1.7	30	25	3	25	11	25	0.11	*

表3.3.3　　　　各学科语步二中各步骤涉及篇章数及占比

M	GW	YW	M	GW	YW
	篇数—占比	篇数—占比		篇数—占比	篇数—占比
2.1A	7%—35%	5%—25%	2.1g	3%—15%	1%—5%
2.1B	6%—30%	13%—65%	2.1h	—	3%—15%
2.1C	—	6%—30%	2.2	9%—45%	3%—15%
2.1a	17%—85%	17%—85%	2.3	1%—5%	11%—55%
2.1b	1%—5%	7%—35%	2.4	11%—55%	8%—40%
2.1c	6%—30%	1%—5%	2.5	14%—70%	12%—60%
2.1d	19%—95%	15%—75%	2.6a	13%—65%	1%—5%
2.1e	15%—75%	10%—50%	2.6b	5%—25%	—
2.1f	4%—20%	3%—15%	2.7	14%—70%	9%—45%
2.1ff	—	1%—5%	2.8	—	4%—20%

　　表3.3.4是这两个学科不同文章中语步二各步骤在该语步中占比最大值、最小值、平均值和标准差。如表所示，就各步骤占比最大值和最小值而言，两个学科存在较大的差异，其中语言学中最小值总体高于管理学。平均值和标准差与两个极值及篇章数有一定的关系，两个学科中相同步骤之间平均值和标准差不同。

表 3.3.4　　　　　　各学科语步二中各步骤占比四项指标

M	MAX（%）		MIN（%）		Mean（%）		SD	
	GW	YW	GW	YW	GW	YW	GW	YW
2.1A	29	12	2	3	14	9	0.08	0.03
2.1B	22	67	1	3	10	17	0.09	0.16
2.1C	—	43	—	2	—	12	—	0.14
2.1a	43	67	1	11	22	28	0.12	0.17
2.1b	4	20	4	6	4	12	*	0.05
2.1c	18	6	2	6	6	6	0.06	*
2.1d	42	58	4	4	21	18	0.12	0.15
2.1e	41	17	3	3	18	8	0.11	0.04
2.1f	15	24	4	14	10	20	0.05	0.04
2.1ff	—	9	—	9	—	9	—	*
2.1g	11	5	7	5	9	5	0.01	*
2.1h	—	25	—	6	—	14	—	0.08
2.2	33	10	3	3	16	7	0.09	0.03
2.3	4	67	4	2	4	18	*	0.18
2.4	22	21	1	2	8	9	0.06	0.07
2.5	22	33	1	5	7	13	0.06	0.09
2.6a	19	33	2	33	8	33	0.05	*
2.6b	7	—	1	—	3	—	0.02	—
2.7	44	31	3	3	18	14	0.11	0.08
2.8	—	7	—	3	—	4	—	0.02

C. 语步三

表 3.3.5 是两个学科中语步三中各步骤涉及篇章数及在所分析的文章中占比。如表所示，语言学中不包含 M3.5。就各步骤涉及篇章数而言，两个学科存在一定的差异。管理学中 M3.3 和 M3.4 较高，而语言学中则是 M3.1 和 M3.2 较高。

表3.3.5　　　　　各学科语步三中各步骤涉及篇章数及占比

M		3.1	3.2	3.3	3.4	3.5
GW	篇数—占比	5%—25%	7%—35%	10%—50%	9%—45%	2%—10%
YW	篇数—占比	8%—40%	9%—45%	1%—5%	4%—20%	—

表3.3.6 是这两个学科不同文章中语步三各步骤在该语步中占比最大值、最小值、平均值和标准差。如表所示，就步骤占比最大值和最小值而言，两个学科中 M3.2 和 M3.4 最大值较接近，最小值除 M3.1 较接近外，其他的差异均较大。平均值和标准差与两个极值及篇章数有一定的关系，相同步骤平均值 M3.4 中管理学高于语言学，但是其他几个步骤中恰好相反。M3.4 中两个学科标准差相同，其他步骤中差异均较大。

表3.3.6　　　　　各学科语步三中各步骤占比四项指标

M	MAX（%）		MIN（%）		Mean（%）		SD	
	GW	YW	GW	YW	GW	YW	GW	YW
3.1	17	100	3	4	7	40	0.05	0.31
3.2	97	100	9	50	59	80	0.34	0.17
3.3	100	13	3	13	20	13	0.28	*
3.4	97	100	4	13	60	38	0.36	0.36
3.5	5	—	4	—	5	—	0.01	—

D. 语步占比及分布轨迹

对比管理学和语言学可以发现，两个学科论文中涉及三个语步的篇章数差异不大。两个学科所有文章中均包含语步二，包含语步三的文章占比也相同，但是语言学各篇文章中同时也包含了语步一，而管理学中有一篇文章中不包含语步一。

就三个语步在各篇文章中占比而言，两个学科中绝大多数文章中语步二占比最高，其次为语步一，但是管理学中语步二占比最高的文章数量略高于语言学。就各步骤在所有语步中占比平均值来看，占比最高的前三个步骤两个学科中均包含了 M2.1a，但是其他两个步骤均不相同。此外，M2.1a 在两个学科中占比排序也不相同。占比最低的三个步骤均不同。

就各步骤涉及的篇章数而言，这两个学科中涉及文章最多的步骤不相同，篇章数也略有差异。管理学为 19 篇，语言学为 20 篇，分别占所有文章的 95% 和 100%。两个学科中涉及篇章数最少的均为一篇，但是涉及的步骤不同。此外，管理学中有一个步骤中只包含一篇文章，而在语言学中有七个步骤。就各篇文章中包含的步骤种类来看，两个学科也存在一定的差异，管理最大值、最小值、平均值和标准差均略高于语言学。

就这三个语步在方法部分的分布轨迹而言，两个学科之间的差异不大于同一学科中不同文章之间的差异。总体来说，语步一以文章最前和前部为主，语步三则以文章后部及最后为主，语步二主要介于其他两个语步之间，但是语步二中也会有部分语句分布在文章最前及较后的位置。大部分文章中语步二与语步一有交叉，语步二与语步三交叉的情况较少。在管理学文章中，极少数文章中三个语步均有交叉，但是在语言学文章中，语步一和语步三之间没有交叉。

四　语言特征

本小节主要对比分析这两个学科论文在句子结构、时态和语态三个方面的语言特征。针对句子结构的分析主要包含句子类型、四类主要句子长度分布及句子类型与语步之间的关系。针对时态的分析主要包含时态种类、三种时态组合及它们与语步的关系。语态的分析主要包含语态种类及不同语态组合与语步的关系。

（一）句子特征

A. 句类及占比

表 3.3.7 是两个学科中四类句子在所有句子中占比、特殊句子种类及占比最高的三类特殊句子。如表所示，两个学科中简单句、复杂句、复合句和复合复杂句这四种类型的句子占比均较高。四种类型句子中简单句均远高于其他三类句子，其次是复杂句，其他两类句子占

比均较低，其中复合句占比略高于复合复杂句。两个学科在这四类句子的占比上也存在细微的差别，管理学简单句和复合句占比均略高于语言学，其他两类句子则正好相反。

就特殊类型句子而言，两个学科的特殊类型句子中均包含带冒号和带括号的句子。管理学中特殊类型句子种类高于语言学。占比最高的前两个特殊句类相同，占比排在第三的句类不同。

表3.3.7 各学科句类及占比

学科	S	P	C	CP	特殊句类			
					种类	第一	第二	第三
GW	60.61%	24.28%	8.79%	2.86%	13	NWS	NWP	NWAS
YW	56.51%	26.73%	7.61%	3.72%	11	NWS	BSS	NWP/NWC/NWAS

B. 句类与语步

表3.3.8是两个学科中四种类型句子与步骤之间的关系。"种类比"一栏表示该类句子中出现的步骤种类在该学科所有步骤种类中的占比。右边三栏为各类句子中占比最高的前三个步骤。单元格中用 * 表示有多个步骤占比相同，但均较低。

如表所示，总体来说，两个学科四类句子中包含步骤种类最高的均为简单句，其次为复杂句，复合句次之，复合复杂句最低。两个学科简单句中均包含了所有步骤，但是其他三类句子中管理学包含的步骤种类均高于语言学。

就四类句子中出现的占比最高的前三个步骤而言，除复合复杂句外，其他三类句子中两个学科分别有一种步骤相同，但是在简单句和复杂句中相同步骤排序不同，数量和占比也均不相同。在复合句中相同步骤虽然排序相同，但是该步骤在两个学科中数量和占比均不相同。

表3.3.8　　　　　　　　　各学科四类句子与高占比步骤

句类	学科	种类比	第一	第二	第三
S	GW	100%	2.1d	2.1a	3.4
	YW	100%	1.6	3.2	2.1a
P	GW	91%	3.4	1.6	2.7
	YW	88%	1.6	2.1a	3.2
C	GW	65%	1.6	3.2	1.1
	YW	47%	1.6	2.1a	*
CP	GW	52%	3.4	*	*
	YW	41%	1.6	*	*

C. 句类与句长

表3.3.9是两个学科中四类句子长度分布占比及句长最大值和最小值。如表所示，总体来说，两个学科中四类句子之间的句长分布较为相似。但就同一类句子长度分布而言，这两个学科之间既有共性，也存在一定的差异。

就简单句而言，两个学科中句长占比从高到低排序具有较高的一致性，句长跨度和最小值也相同，句长最大值语言学略高。

就复杂句而言，两个学科中句长占比从高到低排序具有较高的一致性，排序也相同。该类句子在语言学中长度范围大于管理学，句长最小值相近，最大值语言学略高。

就复合句而言，两个学科中占比最高的均为介于21—30个单词的句子，其他均不同。管理学句长分布范围比语言学更广。两个学科句长最小值相似，但是管理学句长最大值远高于语言学。

就复合复杂句而言，两个学科差异较大，管理学中介于31—40的句子占比最高，而语言学中则为介于21—30的句子。此外，语言学中句长分布范围更广。两个学科句子长度最小值相似，管理学略高；但是句长最大值语言学明显高于管理学。

表3.3.9

各学科四类句子长度分布

句类	学科	句长范围									MAX	MIX
		1—10	11—20	21—30	31—40	41—50	51—60	61—70	71—80	101—110		
S	GW	15.64%	48.21%	25.73%	7.82%	2.12%	0.33%	0.16%	*	*	62	4
	YW	12.28%	49.40%	28.14%	7.49%	1.80%	0.60%	0.30%	*		67	4
P	GW	*	27.16%	42.39%	18.93%	7.82%	3.70%	*	*	*	58	11
	YW	0.64%	24.84%	46.50%	22.93%	3.82%	0.64%	0.64%	*		69	10
C	GW	*	17.58%	43.96%	27.47%	4.40%	4.40%	*	1.10%	1.10%	104	11
	YW	2.17%	32.61%	45.65%	10.87%	8.70%	*	*	*		49	10
CP	GW	*	*	32.26%	51.61%	12.90%	3.23%	*	*	*	52	24
	YW	*	*	50.00%	22.73%	9.09%	13.64%	*	4.55%		74	21

（二）时态特征

A. 时态及组合

表 3.3.10 至表 3.3.12 为两个学科中不同时态组合类型及占比。如表所示，语言学论文涉及时态种类略高于管理学。两个学科中均包含的时态有 10 种，其中有些时态在其中一个学科中只出现在不同时态组合中。就不同时态组合种类而言，由两种不同时态构成的组合种类两个学科相同，均为 11 种；由三种不同时态构成的组合语言学多于管理学，而语言学论文中还包含 3 种由四种不同时态构成的组合。就构成不同时态组合的时态类型而言，这两个学科中由 T3 构成的组合均最多，其次均为 T1、T10 和 T2，但是语言学中由 T1 构成的组合略低于由 T3 构成的组合，而在管理学中由 T3 构成的组合远高于由 T1 构成的组合。

就各时态组合占比而言，这两个学科中由相同时态构成的组合中 T3 占比均最高，其次是 T1，其他均较低。由不同时态构成的组合中，占比最高的均为 T1T3 组合，同时该组合占比也高于除 T1 和 T3 以外的其他由一种时态构成的组合。

表 3.3.10　　　　　　　　各学科相同时态组合及占比

学科	时态组合								
	T1	T2	T3	T4	T5	T6	T8	T10	T13
GW	22.13%	0.99%	62.25%	*	0.30%	0.10%	0.20%	0.59%	0.10%
YW	20.30%	0.34%	62.94%	0.17%	0.85%	*	0.17%	*	*

表 3.3.11　　　　　　　　各学科两种时态组合及占比

学科	时态组合						
	T1T2	T1T3	T1T4	T1T8	T1T10	T2T3	T3T5
GW	1.28%	6.72%	0.20%	*	0.40%	0.69%	0.89%
YW	0.85%	5.58%	0.17%	0.17%	0.51%	0.51%	2.54%

学科	T3T6	T3T8	T3T9	T3T10	T3T11	T3T12	
GW	0.10%	*	0.10%	2.17%	*	0.10%	
YW	*	0.68%	*	2.71%	0.17%	0.17%	

表3.3.12　　　　　**各学科三种及以上时态组合及占比**

时态	时态组合								
	T1T2T3	T1T2T7	T1T3T9	T1T3T10	T3T8T10	T3T5T8	T1T3T5T10	T1T3T6T10	T3T5T10T12
GW	0.10%	*	*	0.49%	0.10%	*	*	*	*
YW	*	0.17%	0.17%	0.17%	*	0.17%	0.17%	0.17%	0.17%

B.　时态与语步

表3.3.13是各学科中三种主要时态组合与步骤之间的关系，"时态"一栏表示同一个句子中出现的时态组合形式。"种类比"一栏表示该时态组合形式中出现的步骤种类在该学科所有步骤种类中的占比。右边三栏为各学科时态组合中占比最高的前三个步骤。

如表所示，两个学科中步骤占比最高的均为T3组合，其次为T1组合，最低的为T1T3组合。在这三个组合中管理学占比均高于语言学。就各学科时态组合中占比最高的前三个步骤而言，在T1组合中只有M21.a为两个学科共有，但是排序不同。在T3组合中两个学科均包了M1.6和M2.1a，但是M1.6在这两个学科中排序不同。在T1T3组合中两个学科中占比最高的前三个步骤均不相同。即使同一个步骤在两个学科中排序一致，该步骤在两个学科中数量和占比也不相同。

表3.3.13　　　　　**各学科三种类型时态组合与高占比步骤**

时态	学科	语步			
		种类比	第一	第二	第三
T1	GW	77%	2.7	3.4	2.1a
	YW	59%	1.6	2.1a	3.2
T3	GW	100%	2.1d	1.6	2.1a
	YW	97%	1.6	3.2	2.1a
T1T3	GW	65%	3.4	1.4	2.7
	YW	47%	3.2	2.1a	1.6

（三）语态特征

表 3.3.14 是两个学科中三种不同语态组合及涉及的步骤情况。"组合占比"一栏表示相对应语态组合在所有语态组合中的占比。"种类比"一栏表示该语态组合形式中出现的步骤种类在该学科所有步骤种类中的占比。最右边三栏分别是该语态组合中占比最高的前三个步骤。

如表所示，这两个学科中均包含三种类型语态组合。两个学科中全部为主动语态构成的句子占比远高于其他两类句子，由两种不同语态构成的句子占比均最低。管理学中完全由主动语态构成的句子占比高于语言学，其他两类组合则相反。

就各个语态组合中涉及步骤种类而言，两个学科存在一定的差异。在管理学科中，包含步骤种类最高的是只包含被动语态的句子，其次为两种不同语态组合的句子，最低的是只包含主动语态的句子。而在语言学中则刚好相反。就三种组合中占比最高的前三个步骤而言，两个学科每一种语态组合中均有一个相同的步骤，且排序一致，但是其他两个均不相同。

表 3.3.14　　　　　　　　**各学科语态组合与步骤**

语态	学科	组合占比	语步			
			种类比	第一	第二	第三
V1	GW	62.45%	68%	1.6	3.4	2.1a
	YW	55.24%	100%	1.6	2.1a	3.2
V2	GW	26.19%	94%	1.1	3.2	2.1d
	YW	27.53%	81%	3.2	1.6	2.1d
V1V2	GW	11.36%	77%	1.4	3.2	3.4
	YW	17.23%	72%	1.6	3.2	2.1d

第四章　传统实验方法写作体裁特征

　　传统的实验方法历史最悠久，现代意义上最早的实验方法之一可在阿拉伯数学家和学者伊本·海瑟姆（Ibnal-Haytham）的著作中见到。他是最早使用归纳实验方法取得实验结果的学者之一。他在著作 *Book of Optics* 中从实验的角度描述了全新的知识和研究方法：

　　We should, that is, recommence the inquiry into its principles and premises, beginning our investigation with an inspection of the things that exist and a survey of the conditions of visible objects. We should distinguish the properties of particulars, and gather by induction what pertains to the eye when vision takes place and what is found in the manner of sensation to be uniform, unchanging, manifest and not subject to doubt. After which we should ascend in our inquiry and reasonings, gradually and orderly, criticizing premises and exercising caution in regard to conclusions—our aim in all that we make subject to inspection and review being to employ justice, not to follow prejudice, and to take care in all that we judge and criticize that we seek the truth and not to be swayed by opinion. We may in this way eventually come to the truth that gratifies the heart and gradually and carefully reach the end at which certainty appears; while through criticism and caution we may seize the truth that dispels disagreement and resolves doubtful matters. For all that, we are not free from that human turbidity which is in the nature of man; but we must do our best with what we possess of human power. (https://en. wikipedia. org/wiki/Experiment)

传统实验方法从观察实际存在的可见事物出发，区分具体事物的属性，通过归纳法，收集所观察到的及感知到的统一、不变、明显和不容怀疑的东西。传统实验方法与其他方法相比较为成熟，同时也是运用最广的一种方法，不仅在自然科学中经常用到，也是语言学和社会科学中运用最多的研究方法。目前传统实验方法主要分为实验室实验和现场实验。传统实验研究者可以通过操纵自变量来观察因变量的变化，还可以通过设立控制组来判断操纵的强度，因此它比其他方法能更令人信服地估计因果关系。

本章主要研究理学、工学、医学和文学四大学科门类中生物、海洋、化学、医学、环境、土木、材料及英语语言文学 8 个学科论文中传统实验方法的写作特点，旨在探讨不同学科传统实验类论文研究方法部分写作方面的异同。

通过对这 8 个一级学科共 127 种国际核心学术期刊中 186 篇传统实验类论文中研究方法部分进行语步分析发现，各个学科论文方法部分基本上均不超出以下三个语步，即实验准备、变量测量及数据分析。但是，不同学科各语步中所包含的步骤在种类上存在一定的差异。具体语步和步骤如下：

语步一、实验准备：

文章概述；重述研究目的；交代实验时间/场所；被试者来源/数量/特征；被试者招募方法；样本来源/数量/特点；材料/数据/试剂来源/数量及特点；样本/材料/数据选取方法；样本/材料/数据预处理或培养方法；实验条件及注意事项；样本/材料/数据局限性；分组变量标准评价系统；前人实验准备方法；强调实验准备的合理性；符合伦理要求/注册信息；付给参与者的薪酬。

语步二、变量测量：

概述变量测量设计；交代仪器/设备/工具/理论/方程/模型；实验参数设置；定义变量；测试/获取相关变量；测量变量的原因；概

述变量；描述变量测量步骤；前人变量测量方法；强调变量测量方法的科学性；实验/治疗效果评价；介绍实验原理；说明文字符号指代内容；对比实验；试样后处理。

语步三、数据分析：

描述数据分析工具/符号；描述数据统计方法；前人数据分析方法；获取本研究数据/所研发软件途径；分析实验结果；强调数据分析方法的合理性；数据处理步骤；概述数据类型；描述实验结果；预估的实验结果；突出实验结果的有效性；对预估结果的解释；本研究不足之处；解释实验数据与模型/理论的偏差；实验前数据相关计算；描述应用；数据可靠性相关证明。

第一节　生物学

生物学（简称生物或生命科学）是探索生命现象和生命活动规律的科学，是自然科学中的一门基础学科。其研究对象是生物的结构、功能、发生和发展规律。生物学的研究手段可分为干实验和湿实验。干实验是指不进行实验室的操作，主要通过计算机模拟以及生物信息学方法来进行研究，如运用不同的软件和统计学方法对测序数据进行数据挖掘和分析。湿实验是真正在实验室进行的，即传统实验方法。通过在实验室采用分子、细胞、生理学实验方法进行研究。本研究主要分析生物学传统实验类论文方法部分的体裁特征。

本研究从生物领域 18 种国际期刊上选取了 20 篇该类型研究论文，其中 17 篇论文第一作者通信地址为英语国家，大部分文章为近十年发表的论文。实验方法部分共有 979 句，约 21169 个单词，句子数量最多的论文中有 160 句，最少的只有 10 句，各篇平均值为 49 句，标准差为 37。方法部分在正文中篇幅占比平均值为 10.79%，最小值为 2.14%，最大值为 33.3%，标准差为 0.08。分析发现，该领域实证性论文正文部分的结构主要包括引言、方法、结果、讨论和结尾五个部分，但不是所有论文均遵循 IMRD（C）的顺序。有九篇论文的方法部分在正文的最后，有两篇在全文的最后，即不在正文中，而是在附录中。

一　标题特征分析

图 4.1.1 和图 4.1.2 分别是方法部分大小标题中词汇使用情况。有两篇文章中实验方法由三个平行的部分构成，即包含三个大标题，其他各篇文章中只包含一个大标题。图 4.1.1 显示，大标题中主要使用的词汇有 methods、materials、experimental 和 details，其中 methods

图 4.1.1　一级大标题词汇云图

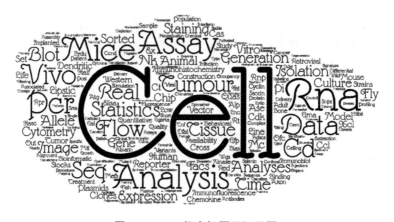

图 4.1.2　二级小标题词汇云图

使用频率最高，共出现了 16 次，其次是 materials，共出现了 8 次，experimental 和 details 分别出现了 4 次。进一步分析发现，使用最多的大标题是 Materials and Methods，共出现过 9 次，占所有标题的 38%；其次是 methods，共出现过 7 次，占所有标题的 29%。所有文章中均包含二级小标题，最多的有 22 个，最少的有 2 个。此外，有一篇文章中使用了三级小标题。图 4.1.2 显示，二级小标题中 cell 一词使用频率最高，细胞是生物领域实验中主要使用的研究对象。

综上所述，该学科论文方法部分均包含一级大标题和二级小标题，个别文章中会使用三级小标题。一级大标题与学科没有显著的相关性，但是二级小标题中词汇与研究对象和研究手段关系更密切，三级小标题与所要测量的具体变量有关。此外，不同文章中包含的小标题数量存在一定的差异。

二　语步特征分析

本节主要研究该学科论文实验方法写作的语步特征。分析发现该学科论文这部分写作的总体语步框架可以分为三个大的语步，与本研究中涉及的其他几个学科相似。但是不同学科各语步中包含的步骤种类存在一定的差异，本节各语步列表中只列出该学科论文中出现的步骤。

（一）语步一特征

表 4.1.1 是语步一中所包含的步骤种类。如表所示，语步一中共包括了 7 个步骤。表 4.1.2 是各篇文章语步一中各步骤在该语步中的占比情况。如表所示，除了一篇文章，其他各篇文章均包括该语步。但在包含该步骤的文章中，该语步中各步骤在各篇文章中占比情况不一。此外，同一个步骤在不同文章中的占比情况也有所差异。以下是针对每个步骤占比情况的具体分析及实例。

表 4.1.1   **语步一各步骤列表**

M	语步一、实验准备			
1.2a	样本来源/数量/特点		1.5	前人实验准备方法
1.2b	材料/数据/试剂来源/数量及特点		1.6	强调实验准备的合理性
1.2d	样本/材料/数据预处理或培养方法		1.7	符合伦理要求/注册信息
1.3b	样本/材料/数据局限性			

表 4.1.2   **语步一各步骤占比**

M	1.2a	1.2b	1.2d	1.3b	1.5	1.6	1.7
SW－01	17%	—	83%	—	—	—	—
SW－02	43%	—	22%	9%	—	—	26%
SW－03	87%	—	13%	—	—	—	—
SW－04	64%	—	27%	—	9%	—	—
SW－05	32%	—	68%	—	—	—	—
SW－06	76%	—	24%	—	—	—	—
SW－07	100%	—	—	—	—	—	—
SW－08	33%	—	50%	—	17%	—	—
SW－09	61%	—	33%	—	6%	—	—
SW－10	100%	—	—	—	—	—	—
SW－11	—	—	—	—	—	—	—
SW－12	64%	—	22%	6%	3%	—	6%
SW－13	71%	—	—	—	—	—	29%
SW－14	50%	—	33%	7%	2%	—	7%
SW－15	45%	25%	15%	—	8%	1%	5%
SW－16	55%	—	25%	—	20%	—	—
SW－17	—	—	100%	—	—	—	—
SW－18	48%	27%	22%	—	—	—	3%
SW－19	62%	—	29%	—	—	—	10%
SW－20	40%	—	13%	—	7%	—	40%

    M 1.2a 样本来源/数量/特点：所选的文章中有90%的文章包含该步骤。在包含该步骤的文章中，该步骤在语步一中的占比最大值为100%，最小值为17%，平均值为58%，标

准差为 0. 22。实例如下：

For measuring ASE, we used the RNA-seq data of 77 unrelated northern and western Europe-an individuals（CEU）whose phased SNP information is available through the 1000 Genomes project（phase 1）.（SW – 07）

B1-8hi（Ref. 27），JHT（Ref. 28）and OT-II TCR transgenic（Y chromosome）29 mice were originally provided by M. Nussenzweig（Rockefeller University）.（SW – 14）

M 1.2b 材料/数据/试剂来源/数量及特点：所选的文章中只有两篇包含该步骤。在这两篇文章中，该步骤在语步一中的占比分别为 25% 和 27%。实例如下：

Nocodazole（M1404）and taxol（T7402）were purchased from Sigma，thymidine（50 – 89 – 5）and cycloheximide（66 – 81 – 9）from Acros Organics，palbociclib（PD0332991，S1116）and ribociclib（LEE011，S7440）from Selleckchem and Abmole，and MG132（BML – PI102 – 0005）from Enzo Life Science. MLN4924 was a gift from W. Kaelin.（SW – 15）

All sequences of the new constructs were confirmed by DNA sequencing with the technical support from Sangon Biotech（Shanghai，China）.（SW – 18）

M 1.2d 样本/材料/数据预处理或培养方法：所选文章中有 80% 的文章包含该步骤。在包含该步骤的文章中，该步骤在语步一中的占比最大值为 100%，最小值为 13%，平均值为 36%，标准差为 0. 25。实例如下：

All constructs were cloned into the pMP71 vector19，which was modified to express a fluo-rescent reporter（eGFP or Tomato）followed by the porcine teschovirus-1 self-cleavable 2A pep-tide20 and the protein of interest.（SW – 14）

Antibodies were injected daily from P14 – P17 in 200 μl of sterile saline subcutaneously.（SW – 06）

M 1.3b 样本/材料/数据局限性：所选的文章中只有三篇包含该步骤。在这三篇文章中，该步骤在语步一中的占比分别为 9%、6% 和 7%。实例如下：

Note that the lack of sensitivity of this ELISA precluded analysis of XCL1 protein in tumor extracts.（SW – 12）

No statistical methods were used to predetermine sample size. The experiments were not ran-domized and the investigators were not blinded to allocation during experiments and outcome as-sessment.（SW – 14）

M 1.5 前人实验准备方法：所选文章中有 40% 的文章包含该步骤。在包含该步骤的文章中，该步骤在语步一中的占比最大值为 20%，最小值为 2%，平均值为 9%，标准差为 0. 06。实例如下：

A focal demyelinating spinal cord lesion was induced as previously described.（Woodruff et al. ，2004）（SW – 16）

shAR，shERG，shTrim24，shDEK and sgSPOP constructs（sgSPOP 1：CCACTCGACATTTCT-

GCCGG；sgSPOP 2：TAACTTTAGCTTTTGCCGGG；sgSPOP 3：GCTGTCCAAAGAGTGAAGTT）have been described previously[31]. (SW – 15)

M 1.6 强调实验准备的合理性：所选文章中仅有一篇包含该步骤。在该篇文章中，该步骤在语步一中的占比仅为1%。实例如下：

All cell lines were routinely tested for mycoplasma contamination and found to be negative. (SW – 15)

M 1.7 符合伦理要求/注册信息：所选文章中有40%的文章包含该步骤。在包含该步骤的文章中，该步骤在语步一中的占比最大值为40%，最小值为3%，平均值为16%，标准差为0.13。实例如下：

Animal experiments were performed under the guidance of the Principles of Laboratory Animal Care established by the National Institutes of Health and approved by the Animal Care and Use Committee at Shandong University. (SW – 18)

All animal experiments were performed in accordance with national and institutional guidelines for animal care and were approved by the Francis Crick Institute Biological Resources Facility Strategic Oversight Committee (incorporating the Animal Welfare and Ethical Review Body) and by the Home Office, UK. (SW – 12)

综上所述，在所分析的文章中除一篇文章外，其他文章中均包含了该语步。在这些文章中，涉及篇章数最高的步骤是 M1.2a，最低的是 M1.6，分别占所有文章的90%和5%。除一篇不包含语步一的文章外，其他各篇文章中语步一各步骤涉及篇章数平均值为8篇，占所有文章的42%，标准差为6.76。在这些文章中涉及步骤种类最多的有6种，最低的只有1种，分别占语步一中所有步骤的86%和14%。各篇文章中语步一各步骤种类的平均值为2.9种，占所有步骤的42%，标准差为1.43。不同文章中包含的步骤种类存在一定的差异，同一个步骤在不同文章中的占比也存在一定的差异。

（二）语步二特征

表4.1.3是所分析的该学科文章语步二中包含的步骤种类。该语步共包括6种步骤。表4.1.4是各篇文章语步二中各步骤在该语步中的占比情况。如表所示，所有文章中均包括该语步，但该语步中各步骤占比情况不一。此外，同一个步骤在不同文章中使用的情况也存在差异。以下是针对每个步骤占比情况的具体分析及实例。

表4.1.3　　　　　　　　　　**语步二各步骤列表**

M	语步二、变量测量			
2.1	概述变量测量设计	2.4	描述变量测量步骤
2.2a	交代仪器/设备/工具/理论/方程/模型	2.5	前人变量测量方法
2.3a	定义变量	2.6	强调变量测量方法的科学性

表4.1.4　　　　　　　　　　**语步二各步骤占比**

M	2.1	2.2a	2.3a	2.4	2.5	2.6
SW－01	1%	—	—	97%	2%	—
SW－02	—	3%	—	93%	—	3%
SW－03	—	10%	—	81%	10%	—
SW－04	—	—	—	93%	7%	—
SW－05	—	—	11%	89%	—	—
SW－06	—	7%	—	89%	4%	—
SW－07	—	3%	—	96%	1%	—
SW－08	—	—	—	79%	7%	14%
SW－09	—	—	—	95%	5%	—
SW－10	1%	7%	—	85%	6%	—
SW－11	—	—	—	85%	15%	—
SW－12	—	6%	3%	91%	1%	—
SW－13	3%	1%	11%	77%	6%	2%
SW－14	—	1%	—	98%	1%	—
SW－15	—	—	—	98%	2%	—
SW－16	—	—	—	95%	5%	—
SW－17	—	7%	—	93%	—	—
SW－18	2%	4%	2%	80%	5%	6%
SW－19	—	13%	6%	81%	—	—
SW－20	—	2%	—	85%	9%	4%

M 2.1 概述变量测量设计：所选文章中有 20% 的文章包含该步骤。在包含该步骤的文章中，该步骤在语步二中的占比最大值为 3%，最小值为 1%，平均值为 2%，标准差为 0.01。实例如下：

The phase 1b portion of the MASTERKEY-265 study was an open-label, multicenter, single-arm study that primarily evaluated the safety of intralesional talimogene laherparepvec in combination with intravenous pembrolizumab. (Figure S1)(SW – 13)

Eventually, we chose 3 pair NC and OV cell clones to conduct our experiments and the results were similar, so we showed only one pair in this article. (SW – 18)

M 2.2a 交代仪器/设备/工具/理论/方程/模型：所选文章中有 60% 的文章包含该步骤。在包含该步骤的文章中，该步骤在语步二中的占比最大值为 13%，最小值为 1%，平均值为 5%，标准差为 0.03。实例如下：

For temporal transgene expression we used the Gal4/Gal80TS system. (McGuire et al., 2003)(SW – 06)

To quantify ALP, Ostase® BAP Immunoenzymetric Assay (Immunodiagnostic Systems Ltd, Scottsdale, AZ, USA) was used following the manufacturer's instructions. (SW – 17)

M 2.3a 定义变量：所选文章中有 25% 的文章包含该步骤。在包含该步骤的文章中，该步骤在语步二中的占比最大值为 11%，最小值为 2%，平均值为 7%，标准差为 0.04。实例如下：

CD103 + cDC1 were identified as live CD45 + CD103 + CD11b_ CD11c + MHCII + cells. Quantification of total cell numbers by flow cytometry was done using fluorescent beads (Beckman Coulter). (SW – 12)

The combination would be declared tolerable if the incidence of DLTs was < 33% during the DLT evaluation period. (SW – 13)

M 2.4 描述变量测量步骤：所选文章均包含该步骤。该步骤在语步二中的占比最大值为 98%，最小值为 77%，平均值为 89%，标准差为。实例如下：

After removing low-quality SNPs using the filtering scheme described above, we applied a simple ASE calling for each heterozygous site. (SW – 07)

Both total luminescence and BRET signal (acceptor channel 460/60 nm, donor channel 610 nm longpass) were recorded on a GloMax Discover System using 0.5 s integration time. (SW – 01)

M 2.5 前人变量测量方法：所选文章中有 80% 的文章包含该步骤。在包含该步骤的文章中，该步骤在语步二中的占比最大值为 15%，最小值为 1%，平均值为 5%，标准差为 0.04。实例如下：

Paired-end RNA-seq. experiments were performed in biological replicate as described previously. (Trapnell et al., 2010)(SW – 9)

In vivo laser axotomy of PLM neurons was performed as described[22]. (SW – 11)

M 2.6 强调变量测量方法的科学性:所选文章中有 25% 的文章包含该步骤。在包含该步骤的文章中,该步骤在语步二中的占比最大值为 14%,最小值为 2%,平均值为 6%,标准差为 0.04。实例如下:

We could not isolate cell clones with drug selection for vector GV118 had no selection gene in mammalian cells. So we applied a mixed population to perform our experiments. The knock-down effect of lnc-U90926 was checked by qPCR. (SW – 18)

All experiments were repeated a minimum of three times. (SW – 20)

综上所述,选取的所有文章均包含语步二。在这些文章中,涉及篇章数最高的步骤是 M2.4,所有文章均包含了该步骤,最低的是 M2.1,有 20% 的文章包含该步骤。各篇文章中语步二各步骤涉及篇章数平均值为 10.3 篇,占所有文章的 52%,标准差为 6.71。各篇文章中涉及步骤种类最多的有 6 种,最低的只有 2 种,分别占语步二中所有步骤的 100% 和 33%。各篇文章语步二各步骤种类的平均值为 3.1 种,占所有步骤的 52%,标准差为 3.1。不同文章中包含的步骤种类存在一定的差异,同一个步骤在不同文章中的占比也存在一定的差异。

(三) 语步三特征

表 4.1.5 是语步三中所包含的步骤种类。如表所示,该语步共包含 4 个步骤。表 4.1.6 是各篇文章中语步三各步骤在该语步中的占比情况。如表所示,有一部分文章不包含该语步。在包含该步骤的文章中,该语步中各步骤占比情况不一。此外,同一个步骤在不同文章中的占比情况也有所差异。以下是针对每个步骤占比情况的具体分析及实例。

表 4.1.5 语步三各步骤列表

M	语步三、数据分析		
3.1	描述数据分析工具/符号	3.3	前人数据分析方法
3.2	描述数据统计方法	3.4	获取本研究数据/所研发软件途径

表 4.1.6 　　　　　　　　　　语步三各步骤占比

M	3.1	3.2	3.3	3.4
SW – 01	—	—	—	—
SW – 02	—	—	—	—
SW – 03	50%	50%	—	—
SW – 04	—	—	—	—
SW – 05	50%	50%	—	—
SW – 06	—	—	—	—
SW – 07	—	—	—	100%
SW – 08	13%	38%	25%	25%
SW – 09	—	83%	17%	—
SW – 10	18%	73%	9%	—
SW – 11	—	—	—	—
SW – 12	14%	86%	—	—
SW – 13	—	97%	3%	—
SW – 14	27%	36%	—	36%
SW – 15	22%	44%	—	33%
SW – 16	50%	50%	—	—
SW – 17	—	100%	—	—
SW – 18	30%	70%	—	—
SW – 19	—	100%	—	—
SW – 20	25%	75%	—	—

M 3.1 描述数据分析工具/符号：所选文章中有一半的文章包含该步骤，另有五篇论文将该步骤放在了论文结果部分。在包含该步骤的文章中，该步骤在语步三中的占比最大值为 50%，最小值为 13%，平均值为 30%，标准差为 0.14。实例如下：

All statistical analyses were performed using GraphPad Prism software (GraphPad). (SW – 12)

Analysis and graph generation was done using GraphPad Prism 7.03. (SW – 03)

M 3.2 描述数据统计方法：所选文章中有 70% 的文章包含该步骤。在包含该步骤的文章中，该步骤在语步三中的占比最大值为 100%，最小值为 36%，平均值为 68%，标准差为 0.22。实例如下：

Data are presented as individual responses ± SE and analyzed using One-way ANOVA. (SW – 10).

Correlation analyses were performed using Pearson correlation. The log-rank (Mantel-Cox) test was used to determine statistical significance for overall survival in cancer patient data from TCGA. (SW – 12)

M 3.3 前人数据分析方法：所选文章中有20%的文章包含该步骤。在包含该步骤的文章中，该步骤在语步三中的占比最大值为25%，最小值为3%，平均值为13%，标准差为0.08。实例如下：

For a given pathway or gene set, the distribution of distances from the TSS of each gene to the nearest binding site for a given factor was compared to the distribution of TSS to nearest binding site distances for the entire transcriptome as previously described (Savic et al. , 2016) and significance was determined using the nonparametric Kolmogorov-Smirnov test. (SW – 08)

All results were normalized to the reference gene act-1 and relative expression determined using the Livak ΔCt method [100]. (SW – 10)

M 3.4 获取本研究数据/所研发软件途径：所选文章中有20%的文章包含该步骤。在包含该步骤的文章中，该步骤在语步三中的占比最大值为100%，最小值为25%，平均值为49%，标准差为0.3。实例如下：

All other data are included within the article and the Supplementary Information or are available upon request from the corresponding author. (SW – 14)

The ASE mapping software we developed is available for download at http: // genetics. cs. ucla. edu/ase. (SW – 07)

综上所述，在所分析的文章中有25%的文章不包含语步三，在其他包含语步三的文章中，涉及篇章数最高的步骤是M3.2，占所有文章的70%。最低的有两个，分别是M3.3和M3.4，占所有文章的20%。各篇文章中语步三各步骤涉及篇章数平均值为8篇，占所有文章的40%，标准差为4.9。在包含该步骤的文章中，涉及步骤种类最多的有4种，最低的只有1种，分别占语步三中所有步骤的100%和25%。在包含语步三的文章中，各步骤种类的平均值为2.1种，占所有步骤的53%，标准差为0.83。不同文章中包含的步骤种类存在一定的差异，同一个步骤在不同文章中的占比也存在一定的差异。

（四）语步占比及轨迹

图 4.1.3 是所分析各篇文章中三个语步总体占比。如图所示，所有文章均包含语步二，分别有 95% 和 75% 的文章包含语步一和语步三。就各个语步占比而言，90% 的文章语步二占比最高，5% 的文章语步一和语步二占比相同，也最高，另外有 5% 的文章语步一占比最高。在语步二占比最高的文章中，有一篇文章只包含语步二。有 65% 的文章语步一占比高于语步三，有 20% 的文章语步三占比高于语步一。在语步一占比最高的一篇文章中，语步二占比高于语步三。

就三个语步中各步骤在所有语步中占比平均值来看，占比最高的前三个步骤依次为 M2.4、M1.2a 和 M1.2d，最低的是 M1.6。就各步骤涉及的篇章数而言，最高的为 M2.4，所有文章均包含该步骤。最低的是 M1.6，只有 5% 的文章包含了该步骤。就各篇文章中包含的步骤种类来看，最多的有 12 种，占所有步骤种类的 71%。最低的仅有 2 种，占所有步骤种类的 12%。各篇文章中包含步骤种类的平均值为 7.5 种，占所有步骤种类的 44%，标准差为 2.78。

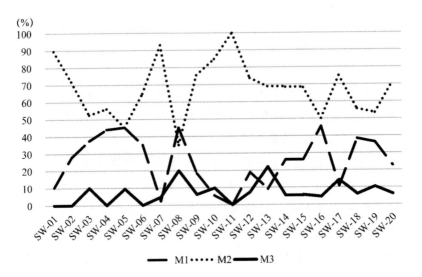

图 4.1.3　各篇文章中三个语步占比

　　图4.1.4至图4.1.6为各篇文章的三个语步分布轨迹。如图所示，所有文章均包含了语步二，有一篇文章没有语步一，五篇文章不包含语步三。不包含语步一的文章中同时也不包含语步三。

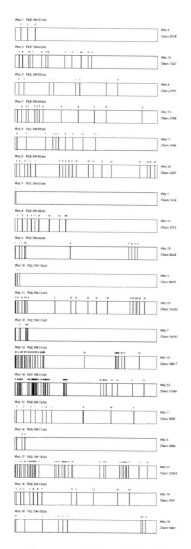

图4.1.4　语步一分布轨迹

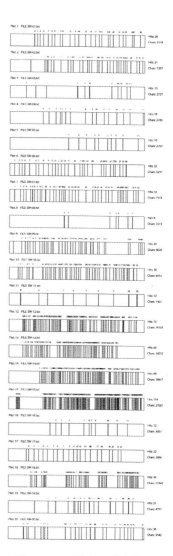

图4.1.5　语步二分布轨迹

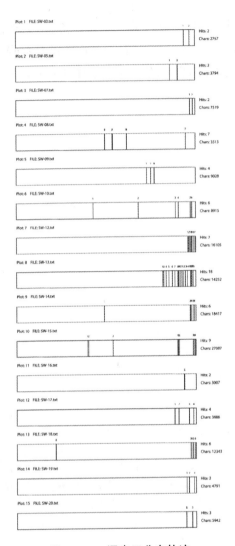

图4.1.6　语步三分布轨迹

在只包含语步一和语步二的四篇文章中，语步二占比均高于语步一，分布也均比语步一广。文章最前部全部为语步一，但是只有一篇文章中语步一全部分布在语步二前，两个语步之间没有交叉，其他三篇文章中这两个语步均有交叉，两篇文章中语步一分布也较广，同时分布在文章的前、中和后多个位置，其中有一篇文章中语步二均分布在语步一中间，两个语步有多处交叉。

在包含三个语步的 15 篇文章中，语步二占比均最高，分布也最广，其次是语步一，语步三均最低。所有文章的最前部均为语步一，其中有五篇文章中语步一全部集中分布在文章的前部、语步二前，与其他两个语步没有交叉。在其他十篇文章中语步一分布较分散，与语步二均有交叉，其中三篇文章中三个语步之间均有交叉。15 篇文章中除两篇文章外，文章的最后均为语步三，其中有八篇文章中语步三全部集中分布在文章的最后，与其他语步没有交叉。在其他文章中语步三中有部分语句分布在了文章的中部，极少数文章中出现在文章的前部，这些文章中除三篇与语步一有交叉，其他均与语步二有交叉。语步二分布最广，主要分布在语步一后、语步三前，但是在两篇文章中有部分语句出现在了文章的最后，在多数文章中语步二与其他两个语步之间有交叉。

综上所述，同一学科不同文章中语步占比和分布轨迹既有相同之处，同时也存在一定的差异。所有文章中均出现了语步二，在绝大部分文章中该语步占比明显高于其他两个语步。语步一占比高于语步三的篇章数量略高于语步三占比高于语步一的篇章数。就这三个语步在方法部分的分布而言，语步二分布最广，几乎覆盖了方法部分的前部、中间及偏后的部位，语步一和语步三之间。语步一以文章最前和前部为主，语步三则以文章后部及最后为主。在绝大多数文章中语步二中会有少量语句会与语步一有交叉，语步二与语步三交叉的情况少于语步一与语步二交叉的情况。三个语步均有交叉的情况较少。

三　语言特征分析

本小节主要分析该学科论文实验方法部分的语言特征。主要从句子、时态和语态三个大的方面进行分析。针对句子的分析主要包含句子类型、四类主要句子长度分布及四类主要句子与语步之间的关系。针对时态的分析主要包含时态种类、不同时态组合及三种占比最高的时态组合与语步的关系。针对语态的分析主要包含语态种类、各语态组合与语步的关系。

（一）句子特征

A. 句子类型

表 4.1.7 是本学科文章中包含的句子类型及各类句子占比。如表所示，简单句、复杂句、复合句及复合复杂句占所有句子的 96.83%。有语法错误的句子占所有句子的 0.72%。其他为带有冒号及 i.e. 的各类特殊句子。四类句子中简单句占比远高于其他三类句子，其次是复合句。其他两类句子占比均较低，其中复合复杂句最低。特殊类型句子共有 6 种，其中 NWS 占比较高，其他的均较低。以下例句为特殊类型的句子。

表 4.1.7 句类及占比

句类	句数	占比	句类	句数	占比
S	740	75.59%	NWC	2	0.20%
P	79	8.07%	NWHS	1	0.10%
C	123	12.56%	NWISF	1	0.10%
CP	6	0.61%	NWBSS	3	0.31%
			NWS	16	1.63%
R	7	0.72%	ICPWA	1	0.10%

NWC: The following transgenes are all inserted on chromosome 2 and were crossed into the scrib/RasV12 background for analysis: UAS-lacZ（Bloomington, BL3955）, UAS-Duox RNAi and UAS-hCatS（a kind gift of Won-Jae Lee）（Ha et al., 2005a; Ha et al., 2005b2005）, UAS-Catalase（BL24621）, UASSOD1（BL24754）, UAS-SOD2（BL24494）, UAS-p35（BL5072）, UAS-dronc RNAi and UAS-drICE RNAi（a kind gift of Pascal Meier）（Leulier et al., 2006）.（SW - 03）

NWHS: For each individual and transcribed SNP, we made ASE calls by computing the ratio between allelic counts from maternal and paternal chromosomes using the following equation: Eq. where Cm is the read count from the maternal chromosome and Cp is the read count from the paternal chromosome.（SW - 07）

NWISF: To do so, we randomly assigned disease association among the phased（i.e., where the inheritance of each allele is unambiguous）heterozygousvariants in GM12878, controlling for observation biases in GWAS studies in three ways:（i）maintaining a matched distribution of minor allele frequencies（with 5% absolute value difference），（ii）maintaining a matched distance to the TSS of the nearest RefSEq gene（with 1 kb），and（iii）maintaining both similar minorallele frequency（within 10% absolute value difference）and similar distance to the nearest RefSEq TSSs（within 2 kb）.（SW－09）

NWBSS：The sequence of the dsDNA template for chimeric Cd40lgSrtA sgRNA transcription was as follows（protospacer sequence is underlined）：CGCTGTTAA TACGACTCACTATAGGAGAGTTG-GCTTCTCATCTTTGTTTTAGAGCTAGAAATAGCAAGTTAAAATAAGGCTAGTCCGTTATCAACTT GAAAAAGTGG CACCGAGTCGGTGCTTTT.（SW－14）

NWS：The following antibodies were used：cleaved caspase-3（CC3；Cell Signaling Technology）；NimC（kind gift of I. Ando'）（Kurucz et al. ，2007）；MMP1（Developmental Studies Hybridoma Bank（DSHB））and pJNK（Promega）.（SW－03）

ICPWA：We then aligned all such reads to the maternal and paternal genomes，and noted every genomic position that did not have a unique 36-bp alignment for either the maternal or paternal version（i. e. ，reads for which the maternal or paternal variant could also align elsewhere in the genome，or could originate from elsewhere in the genome）.（SW－09）

B. 句类与语步

图 4.1.7 是四种类型句子与语步的关系。如图所示，各类句子中步骤占比最高的均为 M2.4。除复合复杂句外，其他三类句子中占比最高的前三个步骤中均包含了 M1.2a，但是该步骤在这三类句子中排序不完全一致。复杂句中除两个步骤外，其他各步骤占比均较低。复合复杂句中只有一个步骤占比较高，其他均较低。简单句和复合句中占比最高的前三个中有两个相同，但是排序不完全一致。此外，由于四类句子在文章中占比不同，即使相同步骤在这四类句子中排序一致，数量和占比也不相同。

这四类句子中除复合复杂句外均包含了三个语步。就这三类句子中包含的三个语步中步骤种类而言，复合句中包含了三个语步中所有步骤，简单句和复杂句中包含的步骤种类分别占三个语步中所有步骤种类的94%和71%。复合复杂句只有一句，该句涉及的是 M2.4 一种步骤，占所有步骤的6%。

总体来说，不同句子类型与步骤之间的关系存在异同，句类与步骤关系紧密度与该类句子在所有句子中的占比有关，同时也与该步骤在所有步骤中的占比有关，但是不完全成一一对应的关系，句类与步骤之间没有明显的相关性。

以下是四类句子中步骤占比最高的前三个步骤的例句。由于复杂句和复合复杂句中步骤较分散，分别只给出占比较高的一到两个步骤例句。

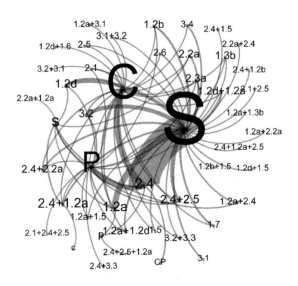

图 4.1.7　句类与步骤关系网络图

【S】

M 2.4： SVMs were trained on replicate-concordant narrow peak sites from the adult liver using a method previously established (Ghandi et al. , 2014; Lee 2016). (SW – 08)

M 1.2a： Antibodies used for ChIP-sEq. assays are listed in Supplemental Table S16. (SW – 08)

M 3.2： Statistical analysis was based on individual responses to treatment with n values given where appropriate. (SW – 10)

【P】

M 2.4： The recording electrode, which had a tip diameter of 10 – 20 mm, was connected to a 200B Ax-opatch Amplifier (Molecular Devices) and a DP-301 differential amplifier (Warner Instruments). (SW – 05)

M 1.2a： Other stocks that were used include UAS-TNTin and UAS-TNT (Sweeney et al. , 1995), UAS-Kir2. 1 (Baines et al. , 2001), UAS-mCD8-GFP (Bloomington stock number 5137),

UAS-mCD8-tomato（F. Schnorrer and B. J. D. , unpublished data），lexAop-myrGFP（Pfeiffer et al. , 2010），UAS > stop > mCD8-GFP；fruFLP（Yu et al. , 2010），UAS-NaChBac（Wang and Anderson, 2010），UAS > stop > trpA1；fruFLP（von Philipsborn et al. , 2011），and ppk23e03639, ppk23f02390, and ppk23D（Chen et al. , 2010）.（SW－05）

【C】

M 2. 4：We aligned reads to the GM12878-specific reference genome using Bowtie（Langmead et al. , 2009）with options "-n 2 -l 36 -k 1-best", and removed alignments mismatching at any heterozygous SNP.（SW－09）

M 1. 2d：Then, C57BL/6 mice were divided into 3 groups randomly, the mice in one group were fed with a basal diet and the other 2 groups were fed with a high-fat diet（HFD）.（SW－18）

M 1. 2a：Lnc-U90926 overexpression lentivirus was constructed and produced by Shanghai GenePharma（Shanghai, China）and lnc-U90926 knockdown lentivirus was constructed and produced by Shanghai Genechem（Shanghai, China）.（SW－18）

【CP】

M 2. 4：Flies were raised at 18℃, where the driver Gal4 is inhibited by the tub-Gal80, and the larvae were shifted at 29℃ at different time points to initiate Gal4 activity.（SW－06）

C. 句类与句长

表4. 1. 8是四类句子长度占比情况。如表所示，各类句子之间在长度分布方面相似度不同。在长度分布占比方面，简单句与其他三类句子差异较大。简单句中句子长度占比最高的是单词数介于11—20的句子，其次是介于21—30的句子。其他三类句子占比最高的均为单词数介于21—30的句子。但是，复杂句和复合句中占比第二的均为介于11—20的句子，复合复杂句中介于11—20和介于41—50的均只有1句，占比相等。就各类句子长度覆盖范围而言，复合句长度跨度最广，其次依次为简单句、复杂句和复合复杂句。

就句子长度最大值而言，从高到低依次为复合句、复杂句、简单句和复合复杂句，各类句子之间差异较明显。句子长度最小值简单句最低，其他依次为复合句、复杂句和复合复杂句。总体来说，简单句和复合句差异不大，复杂句和复合复杂句较接近。如果不排除特殊类型的句子，将每个公式算为一个单词的话，所有句子中最长的句子为NWS，最短的为简单句。

以下是 NWS 例句和四类句子中最长和最短句子的例句。

表 4.1.8　　　　　　　　　　四类句子长度分布

句长范围		1—10	11—20	21—30	31—40	41—50	51—60	61—70	71—80	81—90	MAX	MIX
S	句数	128	333	184	67	23	4	1	*	*	62	5
	占比	17.30%	45.00%	24.86%	9.05%	3.11%	0.54%	0.14%	*	*		
P	句数	*	22	26	19	6	2	3	*	*	70	11
	占比	*	28.57%	33.77%	24.36%	7.79%	2.60%	3.90%	*	*		
C	句数	3	33	56	21	6	3	*	1	1	88	7
	占比	2.40%	26.40%	44.80%	16.94%	4.80%	2.40%	*	0.80%	0.80%		
CP	句数	*	1	4	*	1	*	*	*	*	48	14
	占比	*	16.67%	66.67%	*	16.67%	*	*	*	*		

NWS/〔**Max：92**〕Dose-limiting toxicities were defined as any of the following treatment-related toxicities occurring during the 6-week period from the beginning of pembrolizumab treatment：grade 4 nonhematologic toxicity；grade 3/4 pneumonitis；grade 3 nonhematologic toxicity lasting > 3 days despite optimal supportive care（except grade 3 fatigue）；grade 3/4 nonhematologic laboratory value requiring medical intervention/hospitalization or persisting >1 week；grade 3/4 febrile neutropenia；thrombocytopenia < 25 109/L if associated with a life-threatening bleeding event or bleeding event requiring platelet infusion；any grade 5 toxicity；or any toxicity requiring permanent discontinuation of talimogene laherparepvec or pembrolizumab.（SW – 13）

S/〔**Max：62**〕pcDNA3-PD-L1，pCMV-GST-PD-L1-tail（cytoplasmic amino acids），HA-PD-L1-ΔC-tail，HA-PD-L1-Δ283-290，HA-PD-L1-S283A，HA-PD-L1-S285A，HA-PD-L1- T290M，wild-type pLenti-PD-L1，pLenti-PD-L1-Δ283-290，pLenti-PD-L1 T290M，pET-28a-His-SPOP（wild-type，S6A，S222A and S6A/S222A mutants），Flag-SPOP with ΔD-box（ΔRXXL），pLenti-HA-Myc（wild-type and T58A/S62A mutant），pLenti-HA-cyclin D1，pLenti-HA-cyclin D2，pLenti-HA-cyclin D3，Flag-SPOP S6A，HA-tagged CDK2，CDK4 and CDK6 were generated in this study.（SW – 15）

S/〔**Min：5**〕Nuclei were counterstained with DAPI.（SW – 16）

C/〔**Max：88**〕The gpa-4∷nlp-14〔leader sequence〕∷nlp-9∷gfp included the 2.6 kb gpa-4 promoter, nlp-14 leader sequence（the first 66 bp），full-length nlp-9 cDNA（minus the first 69 bp）and gfp∷unc-54 3' UTR；the gpa-4∷nlp-9〔leader sequence〕∷nlp-14∷gfp included the 2.6 kb gpa-4 promoter, nlp-9 leader sequence（the first 69 bp），full-length nlp-14 cDNA（minus the first 66 bp) and gfp∷unc-54 3' UTR; the truncated gpa-4∷nlp-14 (1-95)∷gfp included the 2. 6 kb gpa-4 promoter, the first 285bp nlp-14 cDNA and gfp∷unc-54 3' UTR and the transcriptional Pgpa-4∷gfp included 2. 6 kb gpa-4 promoter and gfp∷unc-54 3' UTR. (SW – 10)

C/〔Min:7〕 Clones were outlined and signal intensity determined. (SW – 03)

P/〔Min:11〕 We removed all SNPs for each individual whose coverage was < 10. (SW – 07)

P/〔Max:70〕 If the SNP of an individual from the 1000 Genomes Project data was heterozygous, we filtered out the SNP when (1) the frequency of the alternative allele was higher than two alleles recorded in the 1000 Genome Project data or (2) the total frequency of the third and fourth alleles combined was greater than 5%, where the third and fourth alleles are not recorded in the 1000 Genomes Project data. (SW – 07)

CP/〔Min:14〕 Controls were all time-matched and consisted of mice that received normal drinking water only. (SW – 02)

CP/〔Max:48〕 B cells and CD4$^+$ T cells were isolated from mouse spleens as described above; B cells were activated with 25 μg ml^{-1} LPS and 10 ng ml^{-1} IL-4, whereas CD4$^+$ T cells were activated with CD3/CD28 dynabeads and rat T-STIM conditioned medium (both from Thermo Fisher Scientific). (SW – 14)

（二）时态特征

A. 时态种类及组合

表 4. 1. 9 是该学科论文中使用的时态类型及组合形式。如表所示，除去有语法错误的句子，该学科文章中共出现了 7 种不同时态，其中 T4、T5 和 T6 没有单独使用，而是与其他时态共同出现在一个句子中。由不同时态构成的组合共有 5 种，其中两种时态组合的共 4 种，三种时态组合的共 1 种。不同时态组合中均包含 T3，占所有组合的 80%，其他时态在组合中占比均较低。

各种时态组合中，全部由一种时态构成的句子中占比最高的也是 T3，其次为 T1。由不同时态构成的句子中占比最高的是由 T1 和 T3 两种不同时态构成的句子，其他相同或不同时态组合占比均较低。

以下是按照四种类型句子给出的相同时态和不同时态组合的例句，但不是所有时态组合中均包含这四类句子。

表4.1.9 时态类型及组合

时态	T1	T2	T3	T10	T1T3	T1T3T6	T3T4	T3T5	T3T10
句数	49	2	887	4	21	1	1	1	6
占比	5.04%	0.21%	91.26%	0.41%	2.16%	0.10%	0.10%	0.10%	0.62%

【T1】

S: Antibodies used are listed in Supplemental Table 1. (SW – 09)

P: If the ratio is greater than 0.65, then the paternal chromosomeis more expressed. (SW – 07)

C: All other data are included within the article and the Supplementary Information are available upon request from the corresponding author. (SW – 14)

CP: We then count the number of unique variants that overlap TF binding from ourstudy, and describe the resulting distribution in Supplemental Table 9. (SW – 09)

【T2】

S: MYC-tagged cullin 1, cullin 2, cullin 3, cullin 4A, cullin 4B and cullin 5; Flag-tagged wild-type SPOP and mutants (Y87C, F102C and W131G); delta MATH; delta BTB; HA-tagged wild-type SPOP (pLenti-HA-SPOP) and mutants (Y87C, F102C and W131G); pGEX-4T-1-SPOP; Flag-Keap1; Flag-Cop1; shScramble; shCullin 3; shSPOP; and His-ubiquitin constructs have been described previously[31]. (SW – 15)

【T3】

S: Discs were then mounted in Vectashield (Vector Laboratories, Burlingame, CA). (SW – 06)

P: All flies were raised in standard fliy food at 25℃ unless indicated otherwise. (SW – 06)

C: Cryostat sections (10 μm) were placed on Superfrost Plus Stain slides, and samples were then permeabilized in 0.1% Triton X-100/PBS for 10 min. (SW – 15)

CP: Percentage tumor area was first assessed and either all tissue was scraped for isolation or if < 50% tumor area was present, tumor tissue was macrodissected for isolation. (SW – 13)

【T10】

S: Pembrolizumab could be withheld or discontinued per protocol-specified rules consistent with the US prescribing information. (SW – 13)

【T1T3】

P: We created a simulated dataset consisting of all possible 75-bp reads (369 million reads in total) that overlap the 1000 Genomes Project exonic SNPs. (SW – 07)

C: prosβ2DTS7 encodes a DTS allele of prosβ2; however, in this work, we used it in genetic mosaics using FRT80B DTS7, not applying a temperature-shift. (SW – 04)

CP：Flies were raised at 18℃, where the driver Gal4 is inhibited by the tub-Gal80, and the larvae were shifted at 29℃ at different time points to initiate Gal4 activity. (SW – 06)

【T1T3T6】

P：Next, we filtered reads that aligned to positions in the genome for which either the maternal or paternal sequence were not unique and could have therefore arisen from a different location, as sequences aligning to such positions are inherently biased to a single allele (Degner et al. , 2009). (SW – 09)

【T3T4】

P：We then combined overlapping sequences such that any read aligning to a parental sequence will overlap a heterozygous SNP and vice versa. (SW – 09)

【T3T5】

P：Eligible patients (R18 years) had histologically confirmed, surgically unresectable, stage IIIB to IV cutaneous melanoma; measurable disease (R1 melanoma lesion with longest diameter R10 mm); and R1 injectable cutaneous, subcutaneous, or nodal melanoma lesion (s) R10mmin longest diameter, either alone or in aggregate, for which surgery was not recommended. (SW – 13)

【T3T10】

P：To do so, we simulated every possible 36-bp read that would overlap a heterozygous variant. (SW – 09)

C：Up to 4 mL (total volume) of talimogene laherparepvec could be administered by intralesional injection at each treatment visit; the volume delivered to each injected lesion was contingent on the diameter of the lesion (Hoffner et al. , 2016). (SW – 13)

CP：If toxicity occurred, talimogene laherparepvec doses could be delayed for up to 4 weeks; delays > 4 weeks resulted in permanent discontinuation. (SW – 13)

B. 时态与语步

图 4.1.8 是该学科文章中三种占比较高的时态组合与语步的关系，不包含有语法错误的句子。如图所示，T1 和 T3 中步骤占比最高的前两个步骤一致，但是排在第三的不同。T1T3 组合中步骤分布较分散，占比最高的是 M2.4，与其他两个时态组合一致，其他步骤占比均较低。虽然 T1 和 T3 中前两个步骤排序一致，但是这两个步骤在这两种时态组合中的数量和占比相差较大。

此外，这三种时态组合形式中均包含了三个语步。就它们包含的步骤种类而言，T3 最高，包含了三个语步中所有步骤，T1 和 T1T3

中包含的步骤种类均分别占所有步骤种类的41%。

总体来说，不同时态形式的句子与语步的关系存在一定的差异，时态与步骤关系紧密度与该时态在所有句子中的占比有关，同时也与该步骤在所有步骤中的占比有关，但并不是决定性的。

以下是按照四种类型句子给出的三种时态组合中占比最高的前三个步骤的例句，但是有些步骤中不包含所有类型的句子。此外，由于T1T3中步骤较分散，因此只列举了占比最高的一种步骤。

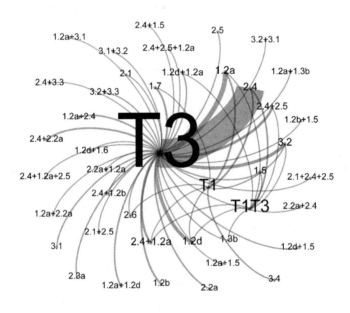

图4.1.8 时态与步骤关系网络图

【T1】

M 2.4

S：Lesion volume measurements are described in the Supplemental Experimental Procedures. (SW – 16)

P：If the ratio is greater than 0.65, then the paternal chromosome is more expressed. (SW – 07)

CP：We then count the number of unique variants that overlap TF binding from ourstudy, and describe the resulting distribution in Supplemental Table 9. (SW – 09)

M1.2a

S：A list of the antibodies used is provided in the Supplemental Experimental Procedures.

（SW – 16）

M 3. 4

S： RNA-sequencing data are deposited in GEO under accession number GSE107643. （SW – 14）

C： All other data are included within the article and the Supplementary Information are available upon request from the corresponding author. （SW – 14）

【T1T3】

M 2. 4

P： We created a simulated dataset consisting of all possible 75-bp reads （369 million reads in total） that overlap the 1000 Genomes Project exonic SNPs. （SW – 07）

CP： Flies were raised at 18℃, where the driver Gal4 is inhibited by the tub-Gal80, and the larvae were shifted at 29℃ at different time points to initiate Gal4 activity. （SW – 06）

【T3】

M 2. 4

S： Discs were then mounted in Vectashield （Vector Laboratories, Burlingame, CA）. （SW – 06）

P： If the SNP of the individual from the 1000 Genomes Project data was homozygous, we filtered-out the SNP when （1） the frequency of the alternative allele was higher than an allele recorded in the 1000 Genomes Projectdata, （2） the total frequency of the combined third and fourth alleles was. 5%, or （3） the total frequency of the combined second, third, and fourth alleles was. 5%. （SW – 07）

C： Cryostat sections （10 μm） were placed on Superfrost Plus Stain slides, and samples were then permeabilized in 0. 1% Triton X-100/PBS for 10 min. （SW – 15）

CP： B cells and $CD4^+$ T cells were isolated from mouse spleens as described above; B cells were activated with 25 μg ml^{-1} LPS and 10 ng ml^{-1} IL-4, whereas $CD4^+$ T cells were activated with CD3/CD28 dynabeads and rat T-STIM conditioned medium （both from Thermo Fisher Scientific）. （SW – 14）

M 1. 2a

S： Blood samples were collected from each partner of the parabiotic pair directly before sacrifice. （SW – 16）

P： Patients were excluded if they had uveal/mucosal melanoma; had previously received talimogene laherparepvec or any prior systemic anticancer treatment （i. e., chemotherapy, immunotherapy, targeted therapy） given in a nonadjuvant setting for unresectable, stage IIIB to IV melanoma; Eastern Cooperative Oncology Group performance status R 2; active brain metastases; active herpetic skin lesions; prior complications from herpetic infection; or required systemic antiherpetic treatment other than intermittent topical use. （SW – 13）

C: Of the 21 patients included in this study, 13（62%）were female and 8（38%）were male.（SW – 13）

M 1. 2d

S: Reacted peptides were purified by HPLC.（SW – 14）

P: Finally, we identified all suchvariants that also had significant differential allelic occupancy by one or more TFs at the same SNP.（SW – 09）

C: SVF was incubated overnight, and non-ad- herent cells were removed.（SW – 17）

（三）语态特征

A. 语态种类及组合

表4.1.10是该学科文章中使用的不同语态组合类型，不包含有语法错误的句子。如表所示，该学科文章中均包含了这两种语态，同时还包含了这两种语态的组合形式。只包含 V2 的句子数量和占比最高，同时包含 V1 和 V2 的句子数量和占比最低。有两篇文章中不包含 V1 及七篇文章中不包含 V1V2 组合，分别占所有文章的10% 和35%。但是所有文章中均包含了 V2。同一种语态构成的句子中均包括了简单句、复杂句、复合句和复合复杂句这四种类型的句子。两种不同语态构成的句子中包括了除简单句以外的三种类型的句子。

以下是按照四种类型句子给出的三种语态组合中的例句，但是有些语态组合中不包含所有类型的句子。

表 4.1.10 语态类型及组合

语态	V1	V1V2	V2
句数	170	37	765
占比	17. 49%	3. 81%	78. 70%

【V1】

S: To ensure stringency, we only considered genes with reads aligning to at least three heterozygous SNPs.（SW – 09）

P: We then removed any alignments that resulted in mismatches atheterozygous SNPs.（SW –09）

C: Of the 21 patients included in this study, 13（62%）were female and 8（38%）were male.

（SW - 13）

CP：We then count the number of unique variants that overlap TF binding from our study, and describe the resulting distribution in Supplemental Table 9. （SW - 09）

【V1 V2】

P：An IFN-g gene signature score was obtained using a calculation that compared a calculated normalized value to a predefined weighted score for each gene within the signature. （SW - 13）

C：Up to 4 mL（total volume）of talimogene laherparepvec could be administered by intralesional injection at each treatment visit；the volume delivered to each injected lesion was contingent on the diameter of the lesion（Hoffner et al. , 2016）. （SW - 13）

CP：Percentage tumor area was first assessed and either all tissue was scraped for isolation or if < 50% tumor area was present, tumor tissue was macrodissected for isolation. （SW - 13）

【V2】

S：Mice skin harvested at P16 and P17 was embedded in OCT. （SW - 06）

P：Late third instar larvae were dissected after different periods of time at 29℃, as mentioned in the text. （SW - 06）

C：The following day secondary antibodies were used and sections were mounted with Vectashield（Vector Laboratories）. （SW - 06）

CP：Flies were raised at 18℃, where the driver Gal4 is inhibited by the tub-Gal80, and the larvae were shifted at 29℃ at different time points to initiate Gal4 activity. （SW - 06）

B. 语态与语步

图 4.1.9 是该学科文章中两个语态及组合与语步的关系。如图所示，V1 和 V2 中步骤占比最高的前两个步骤一致，但是排在第三的不同。V1V2 组合中语步分布较分散，占比最高的是 M2.4，与其他两个语态组合一致，其他均较低。虽然 V1 和 V2 中前两个步骤排序一致，但是这两个步骤在这两种语态组合中的数量和占比相差较大。

就这三种组合中包含的语步种类而言，它们均包含了三个语步，但是它们包含的步骤种类在所有步骤中占比不同。V2 最高，包含了所有步骤；其次是 V1，最低的是 V1V2，分别为 88% 和 53%。

总体来说，语态与步骤关系紧密度与该语态在所有句子中的占比有关，同时也与该步骤在所有步骤中的占比有一定的关系，但是不存在一一对应的关系。

以下是按照四种类型句子给出的三种语态组合中占比最高的前三个步骤的例句，但是有些步骤中不包含所有类型的句子。此外，由于V1V2中步骤较分散，因此只列举了最高的一种步骤。

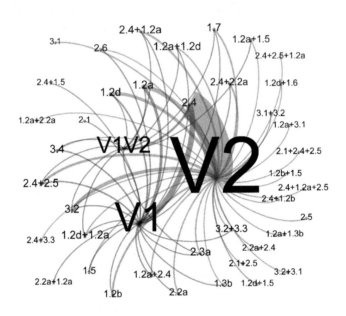

图 4.1.9　语态与步骤关系网络图

【V1】

M 2.4

S：To ensure stringency, we only considered genes with reads aligning to at least three heterozygous SNPs. (SW – 09)

P：We then removed any alignments that resulted in mismatches atheterozygous SNPs. (SW – 09)

C：We aligned reads to the GM12878-specific reference genome using Bowtie (Langmead et al., 2009) with options "-n 2 -l 36 -k 1-best", and removed alignments mismatching at any heterozygous SNP. (SW – 09)

CP：We then count the number of unique variants that overlap TF binding from ourstudy, and describe the resulting distribution in Supplemental Table 9. (SW – 09)

M 1.2a

S：We selected factors to include both ubiquitous TFs and cofactors (e. g., SP1 and EP300), and factors specific to the development of B-cells (e. g. , POU2F2, SPI1, PBX3, BCL3, and EBF1). (SW – 09)

P：For measuring ASE, we used the RNA-sEq. data of 77 unrelated northern and western European individuals (CEU) whose phased SNP information is available through the 1000 Genomes project (phase 1). (SW – 07)

C：Of the 21 patients included in this study, 13 (62%) were female and 8 (38%) were male. (SW – 13)

M 1. 2d

S：UAS-Atg7RNAi targets Atg7 by RNAi. (SW – 04)

P：Comparing the list with resequencing of the GM12878 genome, we identified all disease-associated variants that are heterozygous in GM12878. (SW – 09)

【V1V2】

M 2. 4

P：An IFN-g gene signature score was obtained using a calculation that compared a calculated normalized value to a predefined weighted score for each gene within the signature. (SW – 13)

C：Insl5-deficient mice (29) were housed under normal conditions at an ambient temperature in a 312-h light/12-h dark cycle, and mice had free access to standard mouse chow and tap water. (SW – 02)

CP：Percentage tumor area was first assessed and either all tissue was scraped for isolation or if < 50% tumor area was present, tumor tissue was macrodissected for isolation. (SW – 13)

【V2】

M 2. 4

S：The reaper and p35 inserts were PCR amplifed from genomic DNA from flies containing the UAS-p35 and UAS-rpr transgenes using the primers ATAGAGGCGCTTCGTCTACGG and CCCAT-TCATCA GTTCCATAGGTTG. (SW – 06)

P：Late third instar larvae were dissected after different periods of time at 29℃, as mentioned in the text. (SW – 06)

C：The following day secondary antibodies were used and sections were mounted with Vectashield (Vector Laboratories). (SW – 06)

CP：Flies were raised at 18℃, where the driver Gal4 is inhibited by the tub-Gal80, and the larvae were shifted at 29℃ at different time points to initiate Gal4 activity. (SW – 06)

M 1. 2a

S：All tissues were collected at the Department of Surgery, University of Halle, Germany, by surgical resection for clinical indications. (SW – 02)

P：All strains were obtained from the Caenorhabditis Genetics Center (University of Minnesota, Minneapolis, MN) except nlp-9 (tm3572) and nlp-14 (tm1880) which was received from the National Bio-Resources Project（Tokyo Women's Medical University, Tokyo, Japan）. (SW – 10)

C: Nocodazole（M1404）and taxol（T7402）were purchased from Sigma, thymidine（50-89-5）and cycloheximide（66-81-9）from Acros Organics, palbociclib（PD0332991, S1116）and ribociclib（LEE011, S7440）from Selleckchem and Abmole, and MG132（BML-PI102-0005）from Enzo Life Science. (SW – 15)

M 3.2

S: All data values were shown as mean ± standard deviation（SD）. (SW – 17)

C: Comparison of all other results was performed by one-way analysis of variance（ANOVA）with Tukey's comparison analysis and the statistical significance was analyzed using Student T test and analysis of variance. (SW – 17)

第二节　临床医学

医学类学术文章中实验类型可分为以下两大类：一类是临床试验类研究，即 Clinical Research；另一类是基础医学类实验研究，即 Basic Research。临床试验通常是以患者或受试人群为主要对象，围绕用药、疾病的诊断、治疗、预后、病因和预防等问题进行。该类型实验比较广泛，因临床医生有大量机会接触病患，有大量的临床材料可以搜集，但考虑到安全性，临床试验类研究主要应用于已经较为成熟的手术或药物，其他具有风险的研究多使用动物为研究对象。本研究主要分析该领域论文实验方法部分的体裁特征。

本研究共从 15 种医学领域国际期刊选取了 20 篇临床医学论文，用于分析的句子共有 896 句，单词数约 20628 个。包含句子最多的论文有 75 句，最少的有 23 句，平均值为 44.8 句，标准差为 14.06。在所选的文章中有 75% 的文章为 2015 年后发表的论文，第一作者通信地址主要为英语国家或以英语为官方语言的国家。论文的结构主要遵循了 IMRD（C）的模式，实验方法部分在正文中的平均占比近 70%，最低值为 54%，最高值为 79%，各篇文章在占比上差异不大，标准差为 0.067。

一　标题特征分析

图 4.2.1 和图 4.2.2 分别是本学科二十篇文章实验方法部分的大

小标题词汇云图。如图所示，大标题中出现的词汇一共有 5 种，其中 methods 占比最高，共出现过 19 次，其次是 materials，共出现过 14 次，experimental、section、patients 各出现过 1 次。有十篇文章大标题使用了 materials and methods，有四篇使用了 methods，使用 experimental section 和 patients and methods 的分别为一篇。除一篇文章外，其他各篇中均包含二级小标题，最多的文章中共有 14 个，最少的为 2 个。小标题中使用最多的词是 analysis，其次是 statistics。analysis 共出现过 18 次，statistics 出现过 16 次。此外，小标题中出现频率较高的还有 study、clinical、measures 和 assay，各出现过 6 次。

图 4.2.1　一级大标题词汇云图

图 4.2.2　二级小标题词汇云图

综上所述，各篇文章中均包含一级大标题。大部分文章中包含二级小标题。一级大标题与文章研究主题没有显著的相关性，但是二级小标题中词汇与研究所涉及的内容关系更密切。此外，不同文章中包含的小标题数量存在一定的差异。

二 语步特征分析

本节研究对象为该领域论文实验方法写作的语步特征。分析发现，该学科论文这部分写作的总体框架可以分为三个大的语步，与本研究中涉及的其他几个学科相似，但是不同学科中各语步中包含的步骤种类存在一定的差异。本节各语步列表中只列出该学科论文中出现的步骤。

（一）语步一特征

表4.2.1是语步一中所包含的步骤种类。如表所示，语步一中共包含10个步骤。表4.2.2是各篇文章中各步骤在语步一中的占比情况。如表所示，所有文章中均包含语步一，但该语步中各步骤占比情况不一。此外，同一个步骤在不同文章中使用的情况也存在差异。以下是针对每个步骤占比情况的具体分析及实例。

表4.2.1　　　　　　　　　　语步一各步骤列表

M	语步一、实验准备		
1.1B	重述研究目的	1.2d	样本/材料/数据预处理或培养方法
1.1C	交代实验时间/场所	1.3a	实验条件及注意事项
1.2a	样本来源/数量/特点	1.4	分组变量标准评价系统
1.2b	材料/数据/试剂来源/数量及特点	1.5	前人实验准备方法
1.2c	样本/材料/数据选取方法	1.7	符合伦理要求/注册信息

表4.2.2　　　　　　　　　　语步一各步骤占比

M	1.1B	1.1C	1.2a	1.2b	1.2c	1.2d	1.3a	1.4	1.5	1.7
LC－01	—	—	18%	—	64%	—	—	—	—	18%
LC－02	10%	—	20%	—	30%	—	—	20%	10%	10%
LC－03	—	—	—	—	36%	—	—	—	—	64%

续表

M	1.1B	1.1C	1.2a	1.2b	1.2c	1.2d	1.3a	1.4	1.5	1.7
LC－04	—	8%	—	—	46%	—	—	31%	—	15%
LC－05	—	10%	—	—	37%	—	—	40%	—	13%
LC－06	—	—	—	—	38%	—	—	48%	—	14%
LC－07	—	4%	4%	—	—	—	8%	65%	4%	15%
LC－08	—	—	15%	—	50%	—	—	—	15%	20%
LC－09	—	—	3%	—	81%	5%	—	3%	4%	5%
LC－10	—	—	11%	39%	22%	6%	—	—	—	22%
LC－11	—	11%	—	21%	—	56%	—	—	—	11%
LC－12	—	—	11%	25%	50%	—	—	—	—	14%
LC－13	—	—	54%	22%	12%	8%	—	—	4%	—
LC－14	—	—	22%	—	43%	—	13%	—	13%	9%
LC－15	—	—	63%	—	25%	—	—	13%	—	—
LC－16	—	—	38%	19%	25%	—	6%	—	13%	—
LC－17	—	—	7%	54%	21%	—	11%	—	—	7%
LC－18	—	—	22%	11%	28%	—	—	—	17%	22%
LC－19	—	—	18%	82%	—	—	—	—	—	—
LC－20	—	—	6%	—	81%	—	—	—	—	13%

M 1.1B 重述研究目的：所选文章中只有一篇包含该步骤。在该篇文章中，该步骤在语步一中的占比为10%。实例如下：

The protocol was designed to measure changes in the lung volume at resting functional residual capacity（relaxation volume）caused by a change in posture by measuring the expiratory reserve volume in both positions, the position-dependent difference in expiratory reserve volume indicating the change in relaxation volume.（LC－02）

M 1.1C 交代实验时间/场所：所选文章中有20%的文章包含该步骤。在包含该步骤的文章中，该步骤在语步一中的占比最大值为11%，最小值为4%，平均值为8%，标准差为0.03。实例如下：

It was approved by the Regional Ethics Committee in Uppsala（Dnr 2015/338）and was registered with ClinicalTrials. govon September 1, 2015（NCT02548416, principal investigator Erland Östberg）.（LC－04）

The study was performed at an orthopedic teaching hospital.（LC－05）

M 1.2a 样本来源/数量/特点：所选文章中有75%的文章包含该步骤。在包含该步骤的文章中，该步骤在语步一中的占比最大值为63%，最小值为3%，平均值为21%，标准差为0.17。实例如下：

The study population were children aged 2 to 3 y who were registered with 22 National Health Service (NHS) general dental practices in Northern Ireland. (LC - 08)

Forty subjects were recruited from 2 centers, the Universities of Bern (20 patients) and Geneva (20 patients), Switzerland. (LC - 09)

M 1.2b 材料/数据/试剂来源/数量及特点：所选文章中有40%的文章包含该步骤。在包含该步骤的文章中，该步骤在语步一中的占比最大值为82%，最小值为11%，平均值为34%，标准差为0.22。实例如下：

Ziv-aflibercept 100mg/4ml was purchased as the commercial solution Zaltrap® from Regeneron, Tarrytown, New-York, USA. (LC - 10)

Monoclonal antibodies (mAb) were purchased from Serotec (Oxford, UK) except CD4 and fibrinogen mAbs were from Becton Dickinson (Franklin Lakes, NJ, USA). (LC - 11)

M 1.2c 样本/材料/数据选取方法：所选文章中有85%的文章包含该步骤。在包含该步骤的文章中，该步骤在语步一中的占比最大值为81%，最小值为12%，平均值为41%，标准差为0.19。实例如下：

Bone marrow-derived MSC were isolated from 6 to 8 weeks old female C57BL/6 mice. (LC - 13)

All animals were allowed at least five-to-seven days of acclimatization after shipment to the animal stable before the actual experiments. (LC - 17)

M 1.2d 样本/材料/数据预处理或培养方法：所选文章中有20%的文章包含该步骤。在包含该步骤的文章中，该步骤在语步一中的占比最大值为56%，最小值为5%，平均值为19%，标准差为0.22。实例如下：

After the provisional phase and final impression, 1-piece screw-retained single crowns were fabricated using 2 different zirconium dioxide abutments and 2 different veneering ceramic techniques. (LC - 09)

The thickness of the RHCIII-MPC hydrogels was 100-150 mm and prior to grafting, they were sterilized in penicillin/streptomycin solution overnight at 4℃. (LC - 13)

M 1.3a 实验条件及注意事项：所选文章中有20%的文章包含该步骤。在包含该步骤的文章中，该步骤在语步一中的占比最大值为13%，最小值为6%，平均值为9%，标准差为0.03。实例如下：

Patients were instructed to refrain from mechanical cleaning at the surgical site. (LC - 07)

The cycling conditions were as follows: 10 min at 95℃ and 45 cycles of 10 s at 95℃, 20 s at 65℃ (single acquisition of fluorescence signals) and 20 s at 72℃. (LC - 14)

M 1.4 分组变量标准评价系统：所选文章中有 35% 的文章包含该步骤。在包含该步骤的文章中，该步骤在语步一中的占比最大值为 65%，最小值为 3%，平均值为 31%，标准差为 0.2。实例如下：

Patients eligible for implant therapy had to be >18 y of age and able to comply with study procedures. (LC – 07)

The patients were randomly assigned to either group A or B by the use of a sealed envelope, which had been prepared by an independent person. (LC – 09)

M 1.5 前人实验准备方法：所选文章中有 40% 的文章包含该步骤。在包含该步骤的文章中，该步骤在语步一中的占比最大值为 17%，最小值为 4%，平均值为 10%，标准差为 0.05。实例如下：

An additional nine isolates of six clinical strains that had been described in a previous study[21] were subjected to re-evaluation. (LC – 16)

The sputa were digested, decontaminated, and concentrated as recommended by the WHO [24]. (LC – 14)

M 1.7 符合伦理要求/注册信息：所选文章中有 80% 的文章包含该步骤。在包含该步骤的文章中，该步骤在语步一中的占比最大值为 64%，最小值为 5%，平均值为 17%，标准差为 0.13。实例如下：

Ethical approval was provided by the Ethics Committee of the State of Bern (approval no. 061/10). The informed consent document was written in accordance with the "Declaration of Helsinki". (LC – 09)

The experiments were approved by the Norwegian Animal Health Authority and were performed under the principles of laboratory animal care (Guide for the Care and Use of Laboratory Animals published by the United States National Institute of Health, NIH Publication no. 85 – 23, revised 1996). (LC – 17)

综上所述，所分析的文章中均包含语步一。该语步中涉及篇章数最高的步骤是 M1.2c，最低的是 M1.1B，分别占所有文章的 85% 和 5%。语步一各步骤涉及篇章数平均值为 8.4 篇，占所有文章的 42%，标准差为 5.68。这些文章中涉及步骤种类最多的有 6 种，最低的只有 2 种，分别占语步一中所有步骤的 60% 和 20%。各篇文章中语步一包含的步骤种类的平均值为 4.2 种，占所有步骤的 42%，标准差为 1.24。不同文章中包含的步骤种类存在一定的差异，同一个步骤在不同文章中的占比也存在一定的差异。

（二）语步二特征

表4.2.3是语步二中所包含的步骤种类。该语步共包括8种步骤。表4.2.4是各篇文章语步二中各步骤在该语步中的占比情况。如表所示，所有文章中均包括了该语步，但该语步中各步骤占比情况不一。此外，同一个步骤在不同文章中使用的情况也存在差异。以下是针对每个步骤占比情况的具体分析及实例。

表4.2.3　　　　　　　　　　语步二各步骤列表

M	语步二、变量测量		
2.1	概述变量测量设计	2.4	描述变量测量步骤
2.2a	交代仪器/设备/工具/理论/方程/模型	2.5	前人变量测量方法
2.3a	定义变量	2.6	强调变量测量方法的科学性
2.3b	测试/获取相关变量	2.6a	实验/治疗效果评价

表4.2.4　　　　　　　　　　语步二各步骤占比

M	2.1	2.2a	2.3a	2.3b	2.4	2.5	2.6	2.6a
LC-01	—	14%	23%	45%	18%	—	—	—
LC-02	5%	5%	—	20%	70%	—	—	—
LC-03	8%	—	—	50%	42%	—	—	—
LC-04	—	8%	—	—	90%	—	3%	—
LC-05	—	6%	—	9%	54%	—	—	31%
LC-06	10%	16%	—	—	59%	2%	—	12%
LC-07	2%	14%	2%	5%	66%	2%	10%	—
LC-08	6%	—	12%	52%	26%	5%	—	—
LC-09	—	—	8%	2%	71%	7%	12%	—
LC-10	—	6%	—	—	91%	3%	—	—
LC-11	—	—	—	—	93%	5%	1%	—
LC-12	—	17%	—	—	75%	8%	—	—
LC-13	—	9%	—	3%	76%	11%	—	—
LC-14	—	32%	—	—	59%	8%	—	—

M	2.1	2.2a	2.3a	2.3b	2.4	2.5	2.6	2.6a
LC－15	2%	17%	—	—	65%	15%	—	—
LC－16	—	3%	—	—	73%	23%	—	—
LC－17	—	5%	—	—	94%	2%	—	—
LC－18	—	6%	10%	—	78%	6%	—	—
LC－19	1%	6%	—	1%	89%	3%	—	—
LC－20	—	—	70%	10%	20%	—	—	—

M 2.1 概述变量测量设计：所选文章中有 35% 的文章包含该步骤。在包含该步骤的文章中，该步骤在语步二中的占比最大值为 10%，最小值为 1%，平均值为 5%，标准差为 0.03。实例如下：

This single-blind, 2-arm, parallel-group RCT, approved by the London-South East research ethics committee and registered with the National Health Service (NHS) England Research Authority (14/LO/0880, Integrated Research Application System [IRAS] project ID 156456; ClinicalTrials. gov NCT03071588), was designed to have 80% power and a type I error probability α = 0.05 to detect a difference between the 2 arms. (LC－06)

This study was designed as a 2-center RCT following the CONSORT guidelines regarding the design and conduct of an RCT, and it encompassed 94 patients. (LC－07)

M 2.2a 交代仪器/设备/工具/理论/方程/模型：所选文章中有 75% 的文章包含该步骤。在包含该步骤的文章中，该步骤在语步二中的占比最大值为 32%，最小值为 3%，平均值为 11%，标准差为 0.07。实例如下：

A LightCycler (version 96; Roche Life Science, Mannheim, Germany) system was used for the real-time PCR, and three channels were used for the experiment. (LC－14)

A cDNA library of M, abscessus subsp, massiliense JCM 15300T, containing fragments of approximately 500 bp in length, was prepared using a genomic DNA Sample Prep kit (Illumina, San Diego, CA). (LC－15)

M 2.3a 定义变量：所选文章中有 30% 的文章包含该步骤。在包含该步骤的文章中，该步骤在语步二中的占比最大值为 70%，最小值为 2%，平均值为 21%，标准差为 0.23。实例如下：

Various definitions of t aPL status were also defined: (a) any positive single antibody test, (b) two positive tests in any combination, (c) aCL IgG positive (d) aCL IgM positive, (e) ab2-GP1-IgG positive or (f) ab2-GP1-IgM positive. (LC－01)

A DT was defined as a tumor that was substantially larger than other ground glass nodules and contained radiographic features. (LC－20)

M 2.3b 测试/获取相关变量：所选文章中有50%的文章包含该步骤。在包含该步骤的文章中，该步骤在语步二中的占比最大值为52%，最小值为1%，平均值为20%，标准差为0.2。实例如下：

Sensory and motor tests were administered to test normal peripheral nerve function. (LC－05)

NHS costs were subdivided into those related to the intervention, those associated with other oral health care (checkups, pulpectomies, etc.), and those associated with care provided by other health service professionals. (LC－08)

M 2.4 描述变量测量步骤：所选文章中均包含该步骤。该步骤在语步二中的占比最大值为94%，最小值为18%，平均值为66%，标准差为0.23。实例如下：

Ziv-aflibercept (25 mg/ml) treatment was administered by a singlesub-conjunctival injection of 0.08 ml (2 mg), at 4 weeks following SM exposure in eyes displaying corneal NV. (LC－10)

After excision and rinsing in cold cardioplegic solution, the aorta was cannulated and a PE-50 catheter was pushed across the mitral valve into the left ventricle, and secured in place. (LC－18)

M 2.5 前人变量测量方法：所选文章中有70%的文章包含该步骤。在包含该步骤的文章中，该步骤在语步二中的占比最大值为23%，最小值为2%，平均值为7%，标准差为0.06。实例如下：

The clinical observations were scored, documented by digital photography (using a video camera connected to the slit-lamp microscope) and analyzed semi-quantitatively using our clinical scoring scale (evaluating corneal transparency, conjunctival hyperemia and eyelidedema), as described previously(Kadar et al., 2001). (LC－10)

For induction of myocardial infarction, in vivo permanent occlusion of the left anterior descending coronary artery was performed after a left-sided thoracotomy, as previously described in detail [28]. (LC－17)

M 2.6 强调变量测量方法的科学性：所选文章中有20%的文章包含该步骤。在包含该步骤的文章中，该步骤在语步二中的占比最大值为12%，最小值为1%，平均值为6%，标准差为0.05。实例如下：

After the first coronal bone-to-implant contacts were marked on the radiographs, 2 authors (N. N. and P. S.) had to reach a consensus in terms of the marks. These were cross-checked with the aforementioned examiner and only thereafter the measurements were performed. (LC－07)

This cast analysis technique has been previously used in clinical studies (Buser et al., 2009; Buser, Chappuis, Bornstein, et al., 2013). (LC－09)

M 2.6a 实验/治疗效果评价：所选文章中只有两篇包含该步骤。在这两篇文章中，该步骤在语步二中的占比分别为31%和12%。实例如下：

The PADS is designed to determine home readiness and was assessed every 15 minutes by trained research assistants in conjunction with the PACU nurses. (LC – 05)

For each tooth, a periapical radiograph/CBCT scan that best confirmed the presence/absence of PA radiolucency was selected and assessed by a consensus panel comprising 2 experienced endodontists who were unaware of the objectives of the trial. (LC – 06)

　　综上所述，所分析的文章中均包含语步二。在该语步中，涉及篇章数最高的步骤是 M2.4，最低的是 M2.6a，分别占所有文章的100%和10%。各篇文章中语步二各步骤涉及篇章数平均值为9.75篇，占所有文章的49%，标准差为6.16。各篇文章中涉及步骤种类最多的有7种，最低的只有3种，分别占语步二中所有步骤的88%和38%。各篇文章语步二中包含步骤种类的平均值为3.9种，占所有步骤的49%，标准差为1.07。不同文章中包含的步骤种类存在一定的差异，同一个步骤在不同文章中的占比也存在一定的差异。

　　（三）语步三特征

　　表4.2.5是语步三中所包含的步骤种类。该语步共包括7种步骤。表4.2.6是各篇文章语步三中各步骤在该语步中的占比情况。如表所示，有极少数文章中不包含该语步。在包含该步骤的文章中，该语步中各步骤占比情况不一。此外，同一个步骤在不同文章中的占比情况也有所差异。以下是针对每个步骤占比情况的具体分析及实例。

表4.2.5　　　　　　　　　　**语步三各步骤列表**

M	语步三、数据分析		
3.1	描述数据分析工具/符号	3.7a	描述实验结果
3.2	描述数据统计方法	3.9b	实验前数据相关计算
3.4	获取本研究数据/所研发软件途径	3.9d	数据可靠性相关证明
3.5	分析实验结果		

表 4.2.6　　　　　　　　　　语步三各步骤占比

M	3.1	3.2	3.4	3.5	3.7a	3.9b	3.9d
LC – 01	7%	53%	—	7%	33%	—	—
LC – 02	13%	88%	—	—	—	—	—
LC – 03	5%	53%	—	—	—	21%	21%
LC – 04	10%	70%	—	10%	—	10%	—
LC – 05	4%	96%	—	—	—	—	—
LC – 06	—	100%	—	—	—	—	—
LC – 07	7%	93%	—	—	—	—	—
LC – 08	—	—	—	—	—	67%	33%
LC – 09	14%	86%	—	—	—	—	—
LC – 10	—	100%	—	—	—	—	—
LC – 11	—	100%	—	—	—	—	—
LC – 12	—	100%	—	—	—	—	—
LC – 13	25%	75%	—	—	—	—	—
LC – 14	—	—	—	—	—	—	—
LC – 15	—	—	100%	—	—	—	—
LC – 16	—	—	—	—	—	—	—
LC – 17	—	100%	—	—	—	—	—
LC – 18	—	100%	—	—	—	—	—
LC – 19	—	100%	—	—	—	—	—
LC – 20	10%	90%	—	—	—	—	—

M 3.1 描述数据分析工具/符号：所选文章中有 45% 的文章包含该步骤。在包含该步骤的文章中，该步骤在语步三中的占比最大值为 25%，最小值为 4%，平均值为 11%，标准差为 0.06。实例如下：

The significance level was set to α = 0.05, and the entire statistical analyses were performed with R (R Core Team, 2015), including the survival package (Therneau, 2015). (LC –07)

All calculations were done with R, version 3.3.1 (The R Project for Statistical Computing;

www. r-project. org）. （LC－09）

M 3.2 描述数据统计方法：所选文章中有 80% 的文章包含该步骤。在包含该步骤的文章中，该步骤在语步三中的占比最大值为 100%，最小值为 53%，平均值为 88%，标准差为 0.16。实例如下：

Mortality was analyzed by χ2/Fisher exact test；biomarkers were evaluated by delta values, relative values, and absolute differences at 24 and 48 hours（Mann-WhitneyU test）. （LC－03）

A t-test was used when data were evenly distributed, while a Mann-Whitney test was used for data with a non-gaussian distribution. $p < 0.05$ was considered significant. （LC－17）

M 3.4 获取本研究数据/所研发软件途径：所选文章中只有一篇包含该步骤。在该篇文章中，该步骤在语步三中的占比为 100%。实例如下：

The DNA sequences of the 16S rRNA（1, 468-bp）, hsp65（401-bp）, rpoB（409-bp）, and ITS（298-bp）fragments from the reference strains ⋯ were deposited into the International Nucleotide Sequence Databases（INSD）through the DNA Databank of Japan（DDBJ）under accession numbers AB548592 to AB548611（see Table 2）. （LC－15）

M 3.5 分析实验结果：所选文章中只有两篇包含该步骤。在这两篇文章中，该步骤在语步三中的占比分别为 10% 和 7%。实例如下：

We acknowledge that these categories overlap, but because they have different diagnostic strategies, we found it useful to analyze all of them. （LC－01）

Areas of different aeration were erroneously preregistered as additional primary outcomes, but were considered secondary outcomes throughout the study. （LC－04）

M 3.7a 描述实验结果：所选文章中只有一篇包含该步骤。在该篇文章中，该步骤在语步三中的占比为 33%。实例如下：

Preclinical loss was loss prior to clinically confirmed pregnancy via ultrasound visualization of an embryo. （LC－01）

M 3.9b 实验前数据相关计算：所选文章中有三篇文章包含该步骤。在这三篇文章中，该步骤在语步三中的占比分别为 67%、21% 和 10%。实例如下：

The sample size calculation was based in part by data collected in a quality control investigation with the use of the endothelial marker sTM in OctaplasLG-treated TADpatients. （LC－03）

A series of sensitivity analyses were undertaken. These included reestimations of cost-effectiveness when：Parental costs were included；Measured delivery time ⋯ as opposed to that reported by dentists；Fluoride was assumed to have been applied by a dental nurse or a hygienist rather than a dentist⋯ （LC－08）

M 3.9d 数据可靠性相关证明：所选文章中只有两篇文章包含该步骤。在这两篇文章中，该步骤在语步三中的占比分别为 33% 和 21%。实例如下：

Baseline balance was assessed in baseline parameters by Mann-Whitney Utest or χ2/Fisher exact test as appropriate. (LC - 03)

　　Cost effectiveness acceptability curves were generated with respect to each outcome to examine uncertainty around the threshold. (LC - 08)

　　综上所述，在所分析的文章中除两篇文章外，其他均包含语步三。在这些文章中，涉及篇章数最高的步骤是 M3.2，占所有文章的80%，最低的是 M3.4 和 M3.7a，占所有文章的5%。在包含该语步的各篇文章中，各步骤涉及篇章数平均值为 4.86 篇，占所有文章的24%，标准差为 5.64。在包含该步骤的文章中，涉及步骤种类最多的有 4 种，最低的只有 1 种，分别占语步三中所有步骤的 57% 和14%，平均值为 1.9 种，占所有步骤的 27%，标准差为 1.08。不同文章中包含的步骤种类存在一定的差异，同一个步骤在不同文章中的占比也存在一定的差异。

（四）语步占比及轨迹

　　图4.2.3 是所分析各篇文章中三个语步总体占比。如图所示，所有文章均包含语步一和语步二，有两篇文章不包含语步三。就各个语步占比而言，有80%的文章语步二占比最高，分别有5%和10%的文章语步一和语步三占比最高。此外，有一篇文章语步二和语步三占比相同，均高于语步一。在语步二占比最高的文章中，除一篇文章语步三占比高于语步一外，其他各篇文章语步一占比均高于语步三。在一篇语步一占比最高的文章中，语步二占比高于语步三。在语步三占比最高的两篇文章中，一篇语步一和语步二占比相同，另一篇语步一占比高于语步二。

　　就各步骤在所有语步中占比平均值来看，占比最高的前三个步骤依次为 M2.4、M3.2 和 M1.2c。就各个步骤涉及的篇章数而言，涉及的篇章数最高的三个步骤与占比最高的步骤基本一致。所有文章中均包含了 M2.4。此外，M1.2c、M3.2 和 M1.7 占比也较高，分别占所有文章的 85%、80% 和 80%。涉及的篇章数最少的步骤为 M1.1B、M3.4 和 M3.7a，它们均只出现在一篇文章中，占所有文章的 5%。就各篇文章中包含的步骤种类来看，最多的包括 15 种，占所有步骤

种类的 60%，最少的包括 8 种，占所有步骤种类的 32%，平均值为
9.8 种，占所有步骤的 40%，标准差为 1.96。

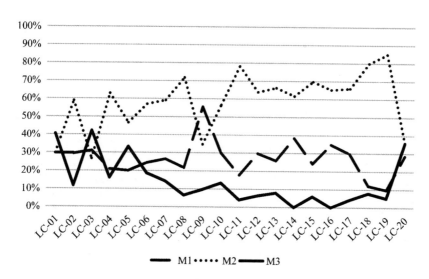

图 4.2.3　各篇文章中三个语步占比

　　图 4.2.4 至图 4.2.6 是各篇文章中三个语步的分布轨迹。如图所
示，有两篇文章不包含语步三。

　　在不包含语步三的两篇文章中，语步二占比均高于语步一，分布
也最广。语步一主要集中分布在文章的最前、语步二前，但是有少量
语句分布在了文章的中间及后部、语步二中间。两个语步均有交叉。

　　在其他 18 篇包含三个语步的文章中，语步二总体占比较高、分
布也较广，其他两个语步较相似，低于语步二。语步一主要集中在文
章的前部，语步三主要集中分布在文章的最后，语步二主要分布在语
步一和语步三之间，但是有少部分文章语步一中有少量语句分布在了
文章其他位置、语步二中。各篇文章中语步三均集中分布在文章的最
后，与其他语步没有交叉。在七篇文章中语步二与语步一之间没有交
叉，其他 11 篇文章中语步二与语步一均有交叉。

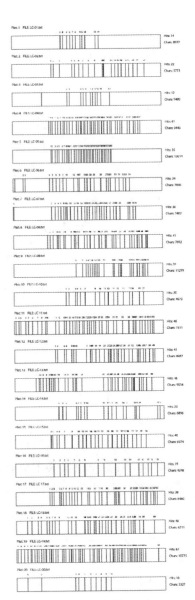

图 4.2.4　语步一分布轨迹　　　　图 4.2.5　语步二分布轨迹

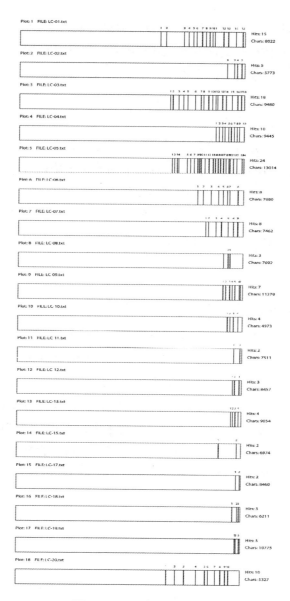

图 4.2.6　语步三分布轨迹

综上所述，同一学科不同文章中语步占比和分布轨迹既有相同之处，同时也存在一定的差异。所有文章中均出现了语步一和语步二。绝大部分文章中语步二占比明显高于其他两个语步。三个语步中分布最广的是语步二，语步三分布最集中。总体来看，三个语步依次从前往后分布，但是有些文章中语步一和语步二之间会出现不同程度的交叉。语步三与其他两个语步均没有交叉。

三 语言特征分析

本小节主要分析实验方法部分的语言特征。主要从句子、时态和语态三个大的方面进行分析。针对句子的分析主要包含句子类型、四类主要句子长度分布及四类主要句子与语步之间的关系。针对时态的分析主要包含时态种类、不同时态组合及三种占比最高的时态组合与语步的关系。针对语态的分析主要包含语态种类、各语态组合与语步的关系。

（一）句子特征

A. 句子类型

表4.2.7是本学科二十篇文章中所包含的句子类型及占比。如表所示，简单句、复杂句、复合句及复合复杂句占所有句子的93.75%。片段和有语法错误的句子占所有句子的3.46%。其他为带有冒号及i.e.的各类特殊句子。四类句子中简单句占比远高于其他三类句子，其次是复合句。其他两类句子占比均较低，其中复合复杂句最低。特殊类型句子形式共有4种，其中NWS占比较高，其他的均较低。以下例句为特殊类型的句子。

表4.2.7 句类及占比

句类	句数	占比	句类	句数	占比
S	617	68.86%	NSC	1	0.11%
P	74	8.26%	NWC	5	0.56%
C	136	15.18%	NWS	18	2.01%
CP	13	1.45%	F	27	3.01%
ISC	1	0.11%	R	4	0.45%

ISC：Identification of mycobacterial infections in all sputum samples（30 samples were culture positive for M. abscessus complex strains and 30 samples were culture positive for other mycobacteria）was previously determined by rpoB PRA analysis of the same cultures.（LC – 14）

NSC：Flow cytometry and immunofluorescent staining were performed using the following antibodies：hamster anti – mouse CD11c – FITC（HL3），rat anti – mouse CD11b – PerCPCy5. 5（M1/70），rat anti – mouse CD45 – APC（30 – F11），rat anti – mouse Gr – 1 – APCCy7（RB6 – 8C5），purified rat anti – mouse fibrinogen and purified rat anti – mouse CD45（30 – F11）were purchased from BD Pharmingen，UK；purified rabbit anti – mouse alpha – smooth muscle actin from Novus Biologicals，USA.（LC – 13）

NWC：The mice had conventional microbial status and were kept under regulated temperature 22 – 23℃ and relative humidity 55% ±5%，with an alternating light：dark cycle（12：12）.（LC – 17）

NWS：Various definitions of t aPL status were also defined：（a）any positive single antibody test，（b）two positive tests in any combination，（c）aCL IgG positive（d）aCL IgM positive，（e）a – b2 – GP1 – IgG positive or（f）ab2 – GP1 – IgM positive.（LC – 01）

B. 句类与语步

图 4. 2. 7 是四种类型句子与语步的关系。如图所示，各类句子中语步占比最高的均为 M2.4。除复合复杂句外，其他三类句子中占比最高的前三个步骤中均包含了 M1. 2c，但是该步骤在复合句中占比排序和其他两类句子不同。此外，简单句和复杂句中还包含 M3. 2，这两类句子中占比最高的前三个步骤排序完全一致。复合句中不包含 M3. 2。由于四类句子在文章中占比不同，即使相同步骤在这四类句子中排序一致，数量和占比也不相同。

四类句子中均包含了三个语步。就各类句子包含的三个语步中步骤种类而言，简单句中包含了三个语步中所有步骤，复杂句、复合句、复合复杂句中包含的步骤种类分别占三个语步中所有步骤种类的 64%、68% 和 36%。

总体来说，不同句子类型与步骤之间的关系存在异同。句子与步骤关系紧密度与该类句子在所有句子中的占比有关，同时也与该步骤在所有步骤中的占比有关，但是不完全成一一对应的关系，句类与步骤之间没有明显的相关性。

以下是四类句子中步骤占比最高的前三个步骤例句。由于复合复杂句中步骤较分散，只给出了占比较高的一个步骤例句。

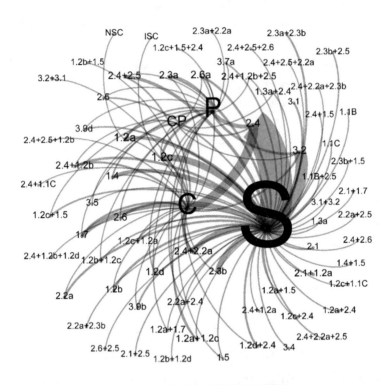

图 4.2.7　句类与步骤关系网络图

【S】

M 2.4： Free beta hCG was measured in these urine samples to enable more sensitive detection of very early pregnancy than possible with conventional urine pregnancy testing. (LC – 01)

M 3.2： Outcomes were compared using the varying definitions for taPL status. (LC – 01)

M 1.2c： Furthermore, we excluded patients with known hypersensitivity to OctaplasLG, known severe deficiencies of protein S and with confirmed pregnancy on arrival. (LC – 03)

【P】

M 2.4： Then, the temperature was increased from 37℃ to 80℃ at a temperature transition rate of 0.07℃/s during which time the fluorescence signal was continuously acquired. (LC – 14)

M 3.2： Women who withdrew prior to pregnancy outcome ascertainment were not included in this analysis. (LC – 01)

M 1. 2c：Patients were excluded if they had a history of chronic obstructive pulmonary disease, ischemic heart disease, or were smokers or previous smokers with a history of more than six pack years. (LC – 04)

【C】

M 2. 4：Tracheal intubation was performed 6 min after the start of preoxygenation, and was facilitated by rocuronium, 0. 5 mg/kg of ideal body weight. (LC – 04)

M 1. 2c：Animals were housed one animal per cage, in a temperaturecontrolled environment and a 12 h light/dark cycle (lights on at 6 a. m.) was maintained. (LC – 10)

M 1. 7：All participating centers obtained Institutional Board approval for the primary study and informed consent was obtained from all participants. (LC – 01)

【CP】

M 2. 4：The inspired oxygen fraction was set to 1. 0, and preoxygenation lasted for at least 3 min or until the end-tidal oxygen concentration was greater than or equal to 90%. (LC – 04)

C. 句类与句长

表 4. 2. 8 是四类句子长度占比情况。如表所示，各类句子之间在长度分布方面相似情况不同。在长度分布占比方面，简单句中长度占比最高的是单词数介于 11—20 的句子，其次是介于 21—30 的句子。其他三类句子占比最高的均为介于 21—30 的句子，但是复杂句和复合句中占比排在第二的均为介于 11—20 的句子，复合复杂句则为介于 41—50 的句子。就各类句子覆盖范围而言，简单句长度跨度最广，其次是复杂句，复合复杂句跨度最小，也最集中。

就句子长度最大值而言，从高到低依次为简单句、复杂句、复合句和复合复杂句，其中复合句和复合复杂句较接近，简单句和复杂句之间及与另两类句子差异均较大。句子长度最小值简单句最低，复杂句和复合句较接近，复合复杂句最长。如果不排除特殊类型句子，将每个公式算为一个单词的话，所有句子中最长的和最短的均为简单句。

以下是四类句子中最长和最短的句子的例句。

表 4.2.8

四类句子长度分布

句长范围		1—10	11—20	21—30	31—40	41—50	51—60	61—70	71—80	81—90	91—100	111—120	MAX	MIN
S	句数	86	282	161	51	20	8	4	2	*	3	1	111	4
	占比	13.92%	45.63%	26.05%	8.25%	3.24%	1.29%	0.65%	0.32%	*	0.49%	0.16%		
P	句数	*	18	27	16	7	3	*	*	2	*	*	82	11
	占比	*	24.66%	36.99%	21.92%	9.59%	4.11%	*	*	2.74%	*	*		
C	句数	2	35	58	24	14	3	*	*	*	*	*	58	9
	占比	1.47%	25.74%	42.65%	17.65%	10.29%	2.21%	*	*	*	*	*		
CP	句数	*	1	5	3	4	*	*	*	*	*	*	49	17
	占比	*	7.69%	38.46%	23.08%	30.77%	*	*	*	*	*	*		

S/〔Max：111〕 The mRNA expression level of the chemokines monocyte chemoattractant protein（MCP）-1, macrophage inflammatory protein（MIP）-1, MIP-1, MIP-2, and interferon-γinducible protein（IP）-10, the IP-10 receptor, CXCR3, the cytokines tumor necrosis factor（TNF）-α, interleukin（IL）-1β, IL-6, leukemia inhibitory factor（LIF）and IL-10, the growth factors transforming growth factor（TGF）-β1, 2, and 3, stem cell factor（SCF）, granulocyte macrophage-colony stimulating factor（GM-CSF）and macrophage-colony stimulating factor（M-CSF）, the adhesion molecules intercellular adhesion molecule（ICAM）-1, CD31/platelet endothelial cell adhesion molecule（PECAM）-1 and E-selectin, the matricellular protein osteopontin（OPN）-1, and the cytokine receptors IL-10 receptor（IL-10R）, and GM-CSF receptor was determined using a ribonuclease protection assay（RiboQuant；PharMingen）according to the manufacturer's protocol.（LC – 19）

S/〔Min：4〕 No premedication was used.（LC – 04）

P/〔Max：82〕 Pregnancies were identified using spot urine pregnancy tests at the clinical sites〔Quidel Quickvue, Quidel Corporation, sensitive to 25 mIU/mL human chorionic gonadotropin（hCG）〕, as well as urine hCG testing that was performed later in the laboratory on the last 10 days of each woman's first and second cycle of study participation（using daily first-morning urine collected at home）, and on spot urine samples collected at all visits scheduled to occur at a woman's next expected menses（day 2 – 4 of cycle）.（LC – 01）

P/〔Min：11〕 No changes were made in the protocol after the trial started.（LC – 05）

C/〔Max：58〕 Rabbits were provided with food and tap water ad libitum during the study and were maintained in accordance with the principles enunciated in the Guide for the Care and Use of Laboratory Animals, Eighth Edition, National Academy Press, Washington DC, 2010 and in accordance with the ARVO statement for the Use of Animals in Ophthalmic and Vision Research.（LC – 10）

C/〔Min：9〕 Eyes were then embedded in OCT medium and frozen.（LC – 13）

CP/〔Max：49〕 As spleen cells contained the receptor for IL-17, but not IL-22, spleen cells were isolated and incubated with recombinant murine 250 ng/mL IL-17A（PeproTech EC Ltd., England）over night, compared with unstimulated cells, and sorted by FACS to evaluate the expression of CCR2, CCR4, CCR5, CCR6, CCR7, CXCR3 and CXCR4.（LC – 17）

CP/〔Min：17〕 Then, the supernatant was removed and the cells were cultured for 12 – 14 days until they were confluent.（LC – 12）

（二）时态特征

A. 时态种类与组合

表4.2.9是该学科论文中使用的时态种类及组合形式。如表所

示，除去片段和有语法错误的句子，该学科文章中共出现了 6 种不同时态，其中 T8 没有单独使用，与其他时态共同出现在一个句子中。由不同时态构成的组合共有 6 种，其中两种时态组合的共 4 种，三种时态组合的共 2 种。不同时态组合中包含 T3 的最多，占所有组合的83%，其他时态在组合中占比均较低。

各种时态组合中，全部由一种时态构成的句子中占比最高的是 T3，其次为 T1。由不同时态构成的句子中占比最高的是由 T1 和 T3 两种不同时态构成的句子，其他相同或不同时态组合占比均较低。

以下是按照四种类型句子给出的相同时态和不同时态组合的例句，但不是所有时态组合中均包含这四类句子。

表 4.2.9 时态类型及组合

时态	T1	T2	T3	T5	T10	T1T2
句数	23	5	801	5	1	2
占比	2.66%	0.58%	92.60%	0.58%	0.12%	0.23%
时态	T1T2T3	T1T3	T3T5	T3T5T8	T3T10	
句数	1	15	7	1	4	
占比	0.12%	1.73%	0.81%	0.12%	0.46%	

【T1】

S: This secondary analysis is a prospective cohort study from the Effects of Aspirin in Gestation and Reproduction (EAGeR) randomized-controlled trial of preconception low-dose aspirin. (LC-01)

P: The substantially negative transpulmonary pressure causes exhalation to the minimum air volume of the lung, at which time all the airways are collapsed and the alveoli are isolated from the pressure in the endotracheal tube. (LC-02)

C: Details of the radiographic assessment are described in Appendix Section 2, and an example of images is given in Appendix Figure 1. (LC-06)

【T10】

S: Exhalation to expiratory reserve volume would normally be achieved by active exhalation, raising the pleural pressure to a highly positive value. (LC-02)

【T1T2】

P: We have therefore used a grading system, which is similar to that for allograft. (LC-11)

【T1T2T3】

P: To identify macrophages, we used immunohistochemical staining with the mouse anti-human macrophage antibody PM-2K (Biogenesis, Kingston, NH), which crossreacts with canine species[21] and detects infarct macrophages as we have previously demonstrated[22]. (LC – 19)

【T1T3】

P: We included preeclampsia, SGA and preterm birth as outcomes because preterm birth due to preeclampsia or placental insufficiency is also part of APS. (LC – 01)

C: The PADS is designed to determine home readiness and was assessed every 15 minutes by trained research assistants in conjunction with the PACU nurses. (LC – 05)

CP: We acknowledge that these categories overlap, but because they have different diagnostic strategies, we found it useful to analyze all of them. (LC – 01)

【T2】

S: This cast analysis technique has been previously used in clinical studies (Buser et al. , 2009 ; Buser, Chappuis, Bornstein, et al. , 2013). (LC – 09)

【T3】

S: University of Utah Institutional Review Board application "Effects of Aspirin in Gestation and Reproduction (EAGeR)" (#00021732) was approved on 7 February 2008. (LC – 01)

P: Women were randomized to receive 81 mg aspirin (LDA) daily or placebo, starting after bio-specimen collection at the enrollment visit, through up to six menstrual cycles of attempting pregnancy and until 36 weeks of pregnancy if pregnancy was achieved within six menstrual cycles. (LC – 01)

C: Finally, the patient was turned prone, and all measurements at both PEEP concentrations were repeated. (LC – 02)

CP: Patients were only enrolled after informed consent, but because the enrolled patients were temporarily incapacitated, they were all included after proxy consent by 2 independent physicians (a legal surrogate) according to Danish legislation. (LC – 03)

【T3T10】

P: With an alpha error of 0. 05 and a power of 80% , we calculated that a sample size of 24 subjects would be sufficient. (LC – 04)

C: Internal sinus floor augmentation (Summers technique) could be performed if needed, but no lateral bone augmentation was allowed. (LC – 07)

CP: Odds ratios were calculated in some cases when the number of cases was too small; in some scenarios, no models could be estimated due to insufficient cases. (LC – 01)

【T3T5】

P: Participants were recruited from the same patient population that had previously received dental implant treatment and a screw-retained implant-supported provisional restoration for soft tissue conditioning using the dynamic compression technique（Buser，Chappuis，Bornstein，et al.，2013）. （LC - 09）

CP： The 8 - 0 suture，which had been previously exteriorized outside the chest wall and placed under the skin，was cleared of all debris from the skin and chest，and carefully taped to heavy metal picks.（LC - 19）

【T3T5T8】

P： The EAGeR trial（June 2007 through August 2012）included 1228 women aged 18 - 40 years who were attempting conception and had experienced one or two prior pregnancy losses，no more than two prior live births and no more than one elective termination or ectopic pregnancy and had regular menstrual cycles（21 - 42 days in length）.（LC - 01）

【T5】

S： The study protocol had been approved by the local ethical committee（StV Nr. 07/13）. （LC - 07）

B. 时态与语步

图 4.2.8 是该学科文章中三种占比较高的时态组合与语步的关系。如图所示，这三种组合中占比最高的前三个步骤存在较大的差异。T1 和 T1T3 两种组合中步骤占比较分散，最高的均为 M3.2。在 T3 组合中步骤占比最高的前三种也包括 M3.2，但是该步骤占比低于 M2.4，排在第二位。即使有些组合中同一个步骤占比排序完全一致，相同步骤在不同时态组合中数量和占比相差也较大。

此外，这三种时态组合中均包含了三个语步。就它们包含的步骤种类而言，T3 最高，包含了三个语步中所有步骤。其次为 T1T3，最低的为 T1，包含的步骤种类分别占所有步骤种类的 52% 和 40%。

总体来说，不同时态形式的句子与语步的联系存在一定的差异。时态与步骤关系紧密度与该时态在所有句子中的占比有关，同时也与该步骤在所有步骤中的占比有关，但并不是决定性的。

以下是按照四种类型句子给出的三种时态组合中占比最高的前三个步骤的例句，但是有些步骤中不包含所有类型的句子。由于 T1 和 T1T3 中步骤较分散，分别只给出占比较高的一种步骤例句。

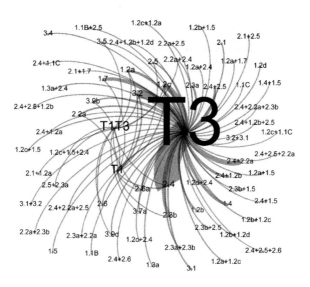

图4.2.8 时态与步骤关系网络图

【T1】

M 3. 2

S： The generalized estimating equation method accounts for the correlation between repeated measurements on the same patient. (LC – 05)

【T1T3】

M 3. 2

P： The primary outcome was analyzed using quantile regression because these methods provide a much more interpretable effect size than Cox proportional hazards regression (difference in medians versus hazard ratio, respectively). (LC – 05)

C： Categorical variables are presented as frequency and percentages and were compared using C_2 or Fisher exact test. (LC – 20)

【T3】

M 2. 4

S： Esophageal pressure, transpulmonary pressure, peak airway pressure, and flow were recorded continuously. (LC – 02)

P： Operative procedures were undertaken by 30 endodontic residents, who received calibration training on carious extracted teeth using both protocols. (LC – 06)

C： Finally, the patient was turned prone, and all measurements at both PEEP concentrations were repeated. (LC – 02)

CP: The inspired oxygen fraction was set to 1. 0, and preoxygenation lasted for at least 3 min or until the end-tidal oxygen concentration was greater than or equal to 90%. (LC – 04)

M 3. 2

S: Normality was assessed with the use of the Shapiro-Wilk test. (LC – 02)

P: Women who withdrew prior to pregnancy outcome ascertainment were not included in this analysis. (LC – 01)

C: One-way analysis of variance (ANOVA) was used to compare differences among groups, and statistical significance was assessed by the Tukey-Kramer post hoc test. (LC – 12)

CP: The number of potential associated factors included in the models were intentionally limited due to consideration of the number of events, and we selected those that were statistically significant in univariate analysis and also were believed to be most clinically relevant. (LC –20)

M 1. 2c

S: Transpulmonary pressure was calculated as peak airway pressure minus esophageal pressure. (LC – 02)

P: Women were randomized to receive 81 mg aspirin (LDA) daily or placebo, starting after bio-specimen collection at the enrollment visit, through up to six menstrual cycles of attempting pregnancy and until 36 weeks of pregnancy if pregnancy was achieved within six menstrual cycles. (LC – 01)

C: Airway pressure was measured at the endotracheal tube, esophageal pressure was measured using an esophageal balloon-catheter filled with 1. 0 ml air, and flow was measured with a Fleisch pneumotachograph (Hans Rudolph Inc. , USA) and later integrated to obtain volume change. (LC – 02)

CP: Then, the supernatant was removed and the cells were cultured for 12 – 14 days until they were confluent. (LC – 12)

（三）语态特征

A. 语态种类及组合

表4. 2.10 是该学科文章中使用的不同语态组合类型，不包含片段和有语法错误的句子。如表所示，该学科文章中均包含了这两种语态，同时还包含了这两种语态的组合形式。只包含 V2 的句子数量和占比最高，同时包含 V1 和 V2 的句子数量和占比最低。所有文章中均包含 V1 和 V2 同一种语态组合，但是有 3 篇文章中不包含 V1V2 组合，占所有文章的15%。同一种语态构成的句子中均包括了简单句、

复杂句、复合句和复合复杂句这四种类型。两种不同语态构成的句子中包括了除简单句以外的三种类型。

以下是按照四种类型句子给出的三种语态组合中的例句，但是有些语态组合中不包含所有类型的句子。

表 4.2.10 语态类型及组合

语态	V1	V1V2	V2
句数	144	65	656
占比	16.65%	7.51%	75.84%

【V1】

S: All participants received folic acid. (LC – 01)

P: We included preeclampsia, SGA and preterm birth as outcomes because preterm birth due to preeclampsia or placental insufficiency is also part of APS. (LC – 01)

C: We estimated the SD to be 2 percentage points and considered a 50% reduction in atelectasis size to be clinically significant. (LC – 04)

CP: We acknowledge that these categories overlap, but because they have different diagnostic strategies, we found it useful to analyze all of them. (LC – 01)

【V1V2】

P: The substantially negative transpulmonary pressure causes exhalation to the minimum air volume of the lung, at which time all the airways are collapsed and the alveoli are isolated from the pressure in the endotracheal tube. (LC – 02)

C: All participating centers obtained Institutional Board approval for the primary study and informed consent was obtained from all participants. (LC – 01)

CP: Odds ratios were calculated in some cases when the number of cases was too small; in some scenarios, no models could be estimated due to insufficient cases. (LC – 01)

【V2】

S: For this analysis, all enrolled women with data on aPL measured at the enrollment visit were included (n ¼ 1208). (LC – 01)

P: All computed tomography scans were assessed by the same radiologist, who was blinded to the group assignment and patient outcome. (LC – 04)

C: Potential study subjects were contacted by phone a few days before surgery and were given initial information about the study. (LC – 04)

CP： Patients were only enrolled after informed consent, but because the enrolled patients were temporarily incapacitated, they were all included after proxy consent by 2 independent physicians (a legal surrogate) according to Danish legislation. (LC – 03)

B. 语态与语步

图4.2.9是该学科文章中语态组合与语步的关系。如图所示，在这三种语态组合中，占比最高的前三个步骤相同，最高的均为 M2.4，在 V1 和 V1V2 中占比第二和第三的也完全一致，但 V2 中不同。即使不同语态组合中同一个步骤排序一致，但是该步骤数量和占比也不同。

就这三种组合中包含的语步种类而言，它们均包含了三个语步，但是它们包含的步骤种类在所有步骤中占比不同。V2 占比最高，包含了三个语步中所有步骤，其次是 V1，最低的是 V1V2，分别为88%和64%。

总体来说，语态与步骤关系紧密度与该语态在所有句子中的占比有关，同时也与该步骤在所有步骤中的占比有一定的关系。

以下是按照四种类型句子给出的三种语态组合中占比最高的前三个步骤的例句，但是有些步骤中不包含所有类型的句子。

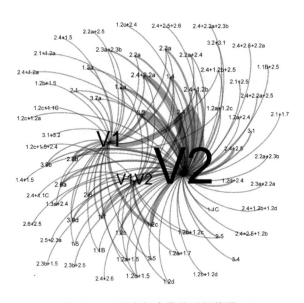

图4.2.9　语态与步骤关系网络图

【V1】

M 2. 4

S： Blood Bank research staff performed onsite randomization by envelope opening. (LC – 03)

P： We have therefore used a grading system, which is similar to that for allograft. (LC – 11)

C： The protocol default oral opioid was oxycodone (5 mg) /acetaminophen (325 mg), but varied according to patient preference/tolerance. (LC – 05)

M 1. 2c

S： All participants received folic acid. (LC – 01)

P： Children were eligible for inclusion if they were 2 or 3 but not yet 4 y old and caries (into dentine) free at baseline, including no history of fillings or extractions due to caries. (LC – 08)

M 3. 2

S： For both primary and secondary outcomes, we therefore used the Mann-Whitney U test for comparisons between groups. (LC – 04)

P： With an alpha error of 0. 05 and a power of 80%, we calculated that a sample size of 24 subjects would be sufficient. (LC – 04)

C： We estimated the SD to be 2 percentage points and considered a 50% reduction in atelectasis size to be clinically significant. (LC – 04)

【V1V2】

M 2. 4

P： After routine monitors were placed and oxygen was provided via nasal cannulae, patients received intravenous (IV) midazolam (2 – 5 mg), ketamine (10 – 20 mg), glycopyrrolate (0. 1mg), and propofol as needed. (LC – 05)

C： 29 Clinical staff caring for the patients in the transfusion phase were aware of the allocation, but the laboratory staff performing the biomarkers analyses and the statistician were blinded to the allocation. (LC – 03)

CP： The inspired oxygen fraction was set to 1. 0, and preoxygenation lasted for at least 3 min or until the end-tidal oxygen concentration was greater than or equal to 90%. (LC – 04)

M 1. 2c

P： Nondominant GGOs being followed were generally treated, by either surgical resection or stereotactic radiotherapy (SBRT), when they reached > 1 cm in size with any solid component, or > 1. 5 cm in size if entirely ground glass. (LC – 20)

C： Upon arrival at the day case unit, a normal spirometry result was assured, and we excluded patients with a peripheral arterial oxygen saturation level (Sp O2) less than 96% while breathing air and subjects with hemoglobin levels less than 10g/dl. (LC – 04)

CP： Then, the supernatant was removed and the cells were cultured for 12 – 14 days until they were confluent. (LC – 12)

M 3. 2

P: The primary outcome was analyzed using quantile regression because these methods provide a much more interpretable effect size than Cox proportional hazards regression (difference in medians versus hazard ratio, respectively). (LC – 05)

CP: Odds ratios were calculated in some cases when the number of cases was too small; in some scenarios, no models could be estimated due to insufficient cases. (LC – 01)

【V2】

M 2. 4

S: Free beta hCG was measured in these urine samples to enable more sensitive detection of very early pregnancy than possible with conventional urine pregnancy testing. (LC – 01)

P: Temgesic was administered postoperatively by the veterinarian any time pain-associated behavior of the mice was observed. (LC – 17)

C: Finally, the patient was turned prone, and all measurements at both PEEP concentrations were repeated. (LC – 02)

CP: The 8 – 0 suture, which had been previously exteriorized outside the chest wall and placed under the skin, was cleared of all debris from the skin and chest, and carefully taped to heavy metal picks. (LC – 19)

M 3. 2

S: Normality was assessed with the use of the Shapiro-Wilk test. (LC – 02)

P: A two-sided P value less than 0. 05 was considered significant unless Bonferroni adjustments were made. (LC – 04)

C: Patients being evaluable on the primary end point were included in the further masked per-protocol (PP) analyses of the primary, secondary, and safety outcome measures, and an abstract was written before unblinding of the allocation. (LC – 03)

M 1. 2c

S: Surgery was performed as a standard in deep hypothermic circulatory arrest. (LC – 03)

P: Patients who had not been seen within 6 months of data analysis (due to being beyond 2. 5 years after surgery) were contacted for telephone follow-up. (LC – 20)

C: Potential study subjects were contacted by phone a few days before surgery and were given initial information about the study. (LC – 04)

第三节　基础医学

本研究中使用的 20 篇基础医学实验类研究论文选自 11 种医学

领域国际知名期刊，用于分析的句子共计 783 句，约 18144 个单词。所选文章中有 95% 的文章为 2010 年后发表的论文，有 75% 的论文第一作者通信地址为英语国家或以英语为官方语言的国家。论文均遵循了 IMRD（C）的结构。实验方法部分篇幅在全文的占比总体较高，平均值为 70%，最小值为 43%，最大值为 83%，标准差为 0.095。

一　标题特征分析

图 4.3.1 和图 4.3.2 分别是所分析的论文实验方法部分大小标题词汇云图。如图所示，大标题中出现的词汇一共有 4 种，其中 method（s）共出现过 19 次，materials 共出现过 13 次。experimental 和 procedures 各出现过 1 次。主要使用的标题为 materials and methods，共出现过 13 次，其次是 methods，共出现过 5 次，也有使用单数 method 的情况，但只有一篇。所有文章中均包含了二级小标题，最多的有 13 个，最少的有 2 个。小标题中出现频次超过 5 次的主要有 8 个单词，analysis 共出现过 27 次，cell 出现过 17 次，statistics 出现过 16 次，treatment 出现过 9 次，study 出现过 8 次，culture 和 isolation 分别出现过 6 次。

图 4.3.1　一级大标题词汇云图

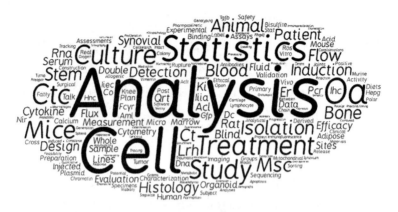

图 4.3.2　二级小标题词汇云图

综上所述，该领域论文方法部分均包含一级大标题和二级小标题。一级大标题与文章研究主题没有显著的相关性，二级小标题中词汇与研究所涉及的大的方面内容关系更密切。所有文章中均没有三级小标题。不同文章中包含的二级小标题数量存在一定的差异。

二　语步特征分析

本节主要研究论文实验方法部分写作的语步特征。分析发现，该学科论文这部分写作的总体语步框架可以分为三个大的语步，与本研究中涉及的其他几个学科相似，但是不同学科中各语步中包含的步骤种类存在一定的差异。本节各语步列表中只列出该学科论文中所出现的步骤。

（一）语步一特征

表 4.3.1 是语步一中所包含的步骤种类。如表所示，语步一中共包括 10 个步骤。表 4.3.2 是各篇文章语步一中各步骤在该语步中的占比情况。如表所示，各篇文章中均包含该语步，但该语步中各步骤在各篇文章中占比情况不一。此外，同一个步骤在不同文章中占比的情况也有所差异。以下是针对每个步骤占比情况的具体分析及实例。

表4.3.1　　　　　　　　　　**语步一各步骤列表**

M	语步一、实验准备		
1.1B	重述研究目的	1.3a	实验条件及注意事项
1.1C	交代实验时间/场所	1.4	分组变量标准评价系统
1.2a	样本来源/数量/特点	1.5	前人实验准备方法
1.2b	材料/数据/试剂来源/数量及特点	1.6	强调实验准备的合理性
1.2d	样本/材料/数据预处理或培养方法	1.7	符合伦理要求/注册信息

表4.3.2　　　　　　　　　　**语步一各步骤占比**

M	1.1B	1.1C	1.2a	1.2b	1.2d	1.3a	1.4	1.5	1.6	1.7
JC－01	—	—	27%	33%	27%	—	—	—	—	13%
JC－02	4%	—	8%	17%	61%	—	—	4%	4%	1%
JC－03	—	—	20%	40%	7%	20%	—	—	—	13%
JC－04	—	—	3%	41%	41%	—	—	3%	—	13%
JC－05	—	—	3%	21%	18%	18%	—	3%	26%	11%
JC－06	—	—	27%	20%	40%	—	—	—	—	13%
JC－07	—	—	14%	7%	29%	21%	—	14%	—	14%
JC－08	—	—	—	18%	29%	—	—	9%	—	44%
JC－09	—	—	2%	25%	16%	52%	—	5%	—	—
JC－10	—	—	19%	25%	25%	—	—	6%	13%	13%
JC－11	—	2%	2%	15%	7%	47%	—	15%	9%	2%
JC－12	—	—	40%	30%	20%	—	—	—	10%	—
JC－13	—	—	19%	29%	24%	10%	—	10%	—	10%
JC－14	—	10%	40%	—	—	—	20%	—	—	30%
JC－15	7%	4%	4%	—	4%	—	71%	—	—	11%
JC－16	—	—	33%	—	33%	17%	—	—	—	17%
JC－17	—	—	6%	—	72%	—	—	22%	—	—
JC－18	20%	—	20%	—	20%	—	—	—	—	40%
JC－19	5%	5%	25%	—	43%	—	9%	—	5%	9%
JC－20	8%	—	15%	—	—	—	46%	—	—	31%

M 1.1B 重述研究目的：所选文章中有 25% 的文章包含该步骤。在包含该步骤的文章中，该步骤在语步一中的占比最大值为 20%，最小值为 4%，平均值为 9%，标准差为 0.06。实例如下：

Part 2 sought to characterize the systemic trafficking and intraarticular migration of MSCs following ACL injury. (JC – 02)

The main objective was to assess the ability of Gr1234 and GrABC to predict an effect of chemotherapy based on baseline and follow-up values of CTC in 7.5 ml of blood. (JC – 15)

M 1.1C 交代实验时间/场所：所选文章中有 20% 的文章包含该步骤。在包含该步骤的文章中，该步骤在语步一中的占比最大值为 10%，最小值为 2%，平均值为 5%，标准差为 0.03。实例如下：

The study was conducted from May 2012 to July 2014 at 34 sites in the United States (US), Great Britain, and Russia. (JC – 14)

After oral and printed information, all patients gave written consent for enrolment in the study at the Department of Oncology, Lillebaelt Hospital, Vejle, Denmark. (JC – 15)

M 1.2a 样本来源/数量/特点：所选文章中有 95% 的文章包含该步骤。在包含该步骤的文章中，该步骤在语步一中的占比最大值为 40%，最小值为 2%，平均值为 17%，标准差为 0.12。实例如下：

Eighty male 129S6/SvEv mice (Taconic, Inc., Germantown, NY) were used since this is a common background strain for knock out (KO) generation, including the ADAMTS-4 and AD-AMTS- 5 KO mice. (JC – 01)

A total of 120 C57BL6J mice were obtained from Janvier. (JC – 03)

M 1.2b 材料/数据/试剂来源/数量及特点：所选文章中有 65% 的文章包含该步骤。在包含该步骤的文章中，该步骤在语步一中的占比最大值为 41%，最小值为 7%，平均值为 25%，标准差为 0.09。实例如下：

The fluorescent dyes 20, 70-dichlorodihydrofluorescein diacetate (H2DCFDA), propidium iodide (PI), Fura-2 AM, and JC-1 were purchased from Invitrogen (Carlsbad, CA, USA). (JC – 09)

Adherent tumor cells were detached by warm Trypsin-EDTA (0.25%) solution (Invitrogen, Carlsbad, CA). (JC – 11)

M 1.2d 样本/材料/数据预处理或培养方法：所选文章中有 90% 的文章包含该步骤。在包含该步骤的文章中，该步骤在语步一中的占比最大值为 72%，最小值为 4%，平均值为 29%，标准差为 0.18。实例如下：

All mice in a genotype were bred by brother-sister mating and raised at our mouse facility operating at constant temperature of 21℃ and on a 12-h light/dark cycle at high standards of sanitation. (JC – 06)

After procurement, all specimens were processed, and cells were immediately analyzed with flow cytometry. (JC – 13)

M 1.3a 实验条件及注意事项：所选文章中有 35% 的文章包含该步骤。在包含该步骤的文章中，该步骤在语步一中的占比最大值为 52%，最小值为 10%，平均值为 26%，标准差为 0.15。实例如下：

This rhGDF5 solution was then diluted to a final concentration of 0.5 mg/ml rhGDF5 in a 5mM glycine-HCl buffer containing 5% trehalose (W：V) at pH 3.0. (JC – 05)

FFA stock solutions were prepared by coupling free fatty acids with BSA. (JC – 09)

M 1.4 分组变量标准评价系统：所选文章中有 20% 的文章包含该步骤。在包含该步骤的文章中，该步骤在语步一中的占比最大值为 71%，最小值为 9%，平均值为 37%，标准差为 0.24。实例如下：

Patients were required to have one or more metastatic tumors measurable on CT scan per Response Evaluation Criteria in Solid Tumor (RECIST) v1.1. (JC – 14)

Patients were starting up in 1st-6th line of chemotherapy with or without HER2 targeted trastuzumab, bevacizumab or lapatinib therapy. Clinical evaluations were conducted in a standard manner and were blinded for CTC data. (JC – 15)

M 1.5 前人实验准备方法：所选文章中有 50% 的文章包含该步骤。在包含该步骤的文章中，该步骤在语步一中的占比最大值为 22%，最小值为 3%，平均值为 9%，标准差为 0.06。实例如下：

All cell lines were authenticated, and validated as unique using STR profiling and HLA genotyping every 6 months (24, 25). (JC – 11)

Samples were processed and analysed using the Epic CTC platform (Figure 1) as previously described [41] [43]. (JC – 17)

M 1.6 强调实验准备的合理性：所选文章中有 30% 的文章包含该步骤。在包含该步骤的文章中，该步骤在语步一中的占比最大值为 26%，最小值为 4%，平均值为 11%，标准差为 0.07。实例如下：

Rather than employing the broad the 0, 50% and 100% loss scaling outlined by Gerwin, Bendele, Glasson, and Carlson[21], a more sensitive range of loss approach was used in order to provide a more specific and detailed look at the depths of degeneration and/or repair. (JC – 05)

All experiments using cell lines were run in triplicate and reproduced at least in two independent experiments. (JC – 10)

M 1.7 符合伦理要求/注册信息：所选文章中有 85% 的文章包含该步骤。在包含该步骤的文章中，该步骤在语步一中的占比最大值为 44%，最小值为 1%，平均值为 17%，标准差为 0.12。实例如下：

All studies were performed following approval from the Wyeth Institutional Animal Care and

Use Committee. (JC – 01)

Written informed consent was obtained from all patients. (JC – 14)

　　综上所述，所分析的文章中均包含了该语步。在该语步中，涉及篇章数最高的步骤是 M1.2a，占所有文章的 95%；最低的是 M1.1C 和 M1.4，均占所有文章的 20%。各篇文章中，语步一各步骤涉及篇章数平均值为 10.3 篇，占所有文章的 52%，标准差为 6。在这些文章中涉及步骤种类最多的有 8 种，最低的只有 3 种，分别占语步一中所有步骤的 80% 和 30%，平均值为 5.15 种，占所有步骤的 52%，标准差为 1.39。不同文章中包含的步骤种类存在一定的差异，同一个步骤在不同文章中的占比也存在一定的差异。

　　（二）语步二特征

　　表4.3.3 是语步二中所包含的步骤种类。该语步共包括 7 种步骤。表4.3.4 是各篇文章语步二中各步骤在该语步中的占比情况。如表所示，所有文章中均包括了该语步，但该语步中各步骤占比情况不一。此外，同一个步骤在不同文章中使用的情况也存在差异。以下是针对每个步骤占比情况的具体分析及实例。

表4.3.3　　　　　　　　　　　语步二各步骤列表

M	语步二、变量测量			
2.1	概述变量测量设计		2.5	前人变量测量方法
2.2a	交代仪器/设备/工具/理论/方程/模型		2.6	强调变量测量方法的科学性
2.3a	定义变量		2.6a	实验/治疗效果评价
2.4	描述变量测量步骤			

表4.3.4　　　　　　　　　　　语步二各步骤占比

M	2.1	2.2a	2.3a	2.4	2.5	2.6	2.6a
JC – 01	—	3%	—	97%	—	—	—
JC – 02	—	6%	2%	88%	2%	—	1%
JC – 03	—	—	—	68%	9%	—	23%

续表

M	2.1	2.2a	2.3a	2.4	2.5	2.6	2.6a
JC－04	—	5%	2%	80%	10%	—	2%
JC－05	8%	—	—	92%	—	—	—
JC－06	—	7%	4%	58%	24%	4%	2%
JC－07	—	—	—	89%	11%	—	—
JC－08	—	5%	—	86%	10%	—	—
JC－09	—	12%	—	72%	11%	5%	—
JC－10	—	25%	—	58%	17%	—	—
JC－11	—	11%	—	71%	5%	—	13%
JC－12	—	28%	—	72%	—	—	—
JC－13	—	10%	—	77%	13%	—	—
JC－14	—	6%	19%	44%	8%	8%	14%
JC－15	10%	5%	—	30%	8%	—	48%
JC－16	—	15%	10%	55%	10%	—	10%
JC－17	—	9%	—	79%	—	12%	—
JC－18	—	3%	—	74%	12%	—	12%
JC－19	5%	—	5%	36%	14%	14%	27%
JC－20	14%	—	—	38%	2%	3%	43%

M 2.1 概述变量测量设计：所选文章中有20%的文章包含该步骤。在包含该步骤的文章中，该步骤在语步二中的占比最大值为14%，最小值为5%，平均值为9%，标准差为0.04。实例如下：

All surgery was performed under isoflurane anesthesia, and all efforts were made to minimize suffering with pre and post-operative analgesia. (JC－05)

The study consisted of two parts, each 24 weeks in duration with its own goals and randomization scheme. (JC－20)

M 2.2a 交代仪器/设备/工具/理论/方程/模型：所选文章中有75%的文章包含该步骤。在包含该步骤的文章中，该步骤在语步二中的占比最大值为28%，最小值为3%，平均值为10%，标准差为0.07。实例如下：

Briefly, animals were positioned prone on a materials testing system utilizing custom fixtures (Insight 5, MTS Systems, Eden Prairie, MN, USA). (JC－02)

Data were acquired using a BD FACSAria or Fortessa LSR flow cytometer and analyzed using

FlowJo software (Tree Star). (JC – 13)

M 2.3a 定义变量：所选文章中有 30% 的文章包含该步骤。在包含该步骤的文章中，该步骤在语步二中的占比最大值为 19%，最小值为 2%，平均值为 7%，标准差为 0.06。实例如下：

The OA score was defined as the product of the multiplication of these two scores. (JC – 04)

A dose-limiting toxicity (DLT) was defined as any treatment-emergent AE (TEAE) ≥ grade 3 occurring within the first 4 weeks of treatment considered to be PEGPH20 related. (JC – 14)

M 2.4 描述变量测量步骤：所选文章均包含该步骤。该步骤在语步二中的占比最大值为 97%，最小值为 30%，平均值为 68%，标准差为 0.19。实例如下：

Safety was assessed through regular physical examinations, clinical laboratory tests, 12-lead ECGs, and vital sign measurements. (JC – 19)

In Part 1, subjects were randomized to placebo, ABT-126 25 mg, ABT-126 50 mg, ABT-126 75 mg, or donepezil, identical in appearance. (JC – 20)

M 2.5 前人变量测量方法：所选文章中有 80% 的文章包含该步骤。在包含该步骤的文章中，该步骤在语步二中的占比最大值为 24%，最小值为 2%，平均值为 10%，标准差为 0.05。实例如下：

Collection of blood and immunofluorescent (IF) staining of CTC was performed using the Cell Search® system (Janssen Diagnostics, LLC), as previously reported [4, 26]. (JC – 16)

Additionally medical assessments including symptomatic progression and performance status as well as routine laboratory results like AP, LDH and PSA-values were taken into account with increasing levels indicating progression, similarly to Khoury et al. [11, 28, 29]. (JC – 18)

M 2.6 强调变量测量方法的科学性：所选文章中有 30% 的文章包含该步骤。在包含该步骤的文章中，该步骤在语步二中的占比最大值为 14%，最小值为 3%，平均值为 8%，标准差为 0.04。实例如下：

These enrichment patterns provide quantitative information on the relative fluxes through intracellular metabolic pathways. (JC – 09)

CTC enumeration (CTC/mL) was compared to that found for 18 healthy donor blood samples (two slides tested per sample), which also further addressed assay specificity. (JC – 17)

M 2.6a 实验/治疗效果评价：所选文章中有 55% 的文章包含该步骤。在包含该步骤的文章中，该步骤在语步二中的占比最大值为 48%，最小值为 1%，平均值为 18%，标准差为 0.15。实例如下：

Minimal score is 0, indicating no cartilage pathology whatsoever, whereas 30 is the maximum score, indicating highest grade (6) and stage (5). (JC – 03)

Subjects taking 70% of the study drug were considered compliant. (JC – 20)

综上所述，所分析的文章均包含语步二。在该语步中，涉及篇章数最高的步骤是 M2.4，最低的是 M2.1，分别占所有文章的100% 和20%，平均值为11.14 篇，占所有文章的56%，标准差为6.07。在这些文章中，涉及步骤种类最多的有6 种，最低的只有2种，分别占语步二中所有步骤的86% 和29%。平均值为3.9 种，占所有步骤的56%，标准差为1.41。不同文章中包含的步骤种类存在一定的差异，同一个步骤在不同文章中的占比也存在一定的差异。

（三）语步三特征

表4.3.5 是语步三中所包含的步骤种类。如表所示，该语步中共包括了5 个步骤。表4.3.6 是各篇文章语步三中各步骤在该语步中的占比情况。如表所示，有极少数文章中不包含该语步。在包含该步骤的文章中，该语步中各步骤占比情况不一。此外，同一个步骤在不同文章中的占比情况也有所差异。以下是针对每个步骤占比情况的具体分析及实例。

表4.3.5　　　　　　　　　　语步三各步骤列表

M	语步三、数据分析		
3.1	描述数据分析工具/符号	3.4	获取本研究数据/所研发软件途径
3.2	描述数据统计方法	3.5	分析实验结果
3.3	前人数据分析方法		

表4.3.6　　　　　　　　　　语步三各步骤占比

M	3.1	3.2	3.3	3.4	3.5
JC－01	33%	67%	—	—	—
JC－02	9%	73%	—	—	18%
JC－03	25%	75%	—	—	—
JC－04	17%	83%	—	—	—

续表

M	3.1	3.2	3.3	3.4	3.5
JC – 05	—	100%	—	—	—
JC – 06	33%	67%	—	—	—
JC – 07	—	—	—	—	—
JC – 08	—	75%	—	25%	—
JC – 09	—	100%	—	—	—
JC – 10	20%	60%	—	20%	—
JC – 11	50%	50%	—	—	—
JC – 12	—	90%	10%	—	—
JC – 13	33%	67%	—	—	—
JC – 14	67%	33%	—	—	—
JC – 15	50%	50%	—	—	—
JC – 16	7%	93%	—	—	—
JC – 17	—	—	—	—	—
JC – 18	4%	92%	4%	—	—
JC – 19	9%	91%	—	—	—
JC – 20	—	100%	—	—	—

M 3.1 描述数据分析工具/符号：所选文章中有65%的文章包含该步骤。在包含该步骤的文章中，该步骤在语步三中的占比最大值为67%，最小值为4%，平均值为27%，标准差为0.19。实例如下：

Statistical analysis was performed in SPSS（v22，IBM，Armonk，NY，USA）.（JC – 02）

Data were analyzed with SPSS 16.0（SPSS Inc.，Chicago，IL）.（JC – 04）

M 3.2 描述数据统计方法：所选文章中有90%的文章包含该步骤。在包含该步骤的文章中，该步骤在语步三中的占比最大值为100%，最小值为33%，平均值为76%，标准差为0.19。实例如下：

Normality and equal variance assumptions were assessed using the Shapiroe-Wilk test and Levene's test，respectively.（JC – 02）

Chi-square tests were used to analyze categorical data.（JC – 16）

M 3.3 前人数据分析方法：所选文章中只有两篇包含该步骤。在这两篇文章中，该步骤在语步三中的占比分别为 10% 和 4%。实例如下：

> For each metric, a lower boundary of the 95% confidence interval (CI) was calculated with no upper bound using the Clopper-Pearson method (29). (JC - 12)

> Categorical CTC-counts were dichotomized according to the established threshold of < 5 vs. ≥ 5 CTCs analogous to prognostic favorable and unfavorable CTC-counts described in the current literature and according to the FDA approved procedure [10]. (JC - 18)

M 3.4 获取本研究数据/所研发软件途径：所选文章中只有两篇包含该步骤。在这两篇文章中，该步骤在语步三中的占比分别为 25% 和 20%。实例如下：

> The accession number for the RNA-sequencing data reported in this paper is GenBank: GSE109982. (JC - 08)

> Numbers of mice or replicates for each group used in experiments are indicated in the figure legends. (JC - 10)

M 3.5 分析实验结果：所选文章中只有一篇包含该步骤。在该篇文章中，该步骤在语步三中的占比为 18%。实例如下：

> Collected serum was analyzed using the Proteome Profiler Rat Cytokine Array Kit (R & D Systems), which assesses the relative levels of 29 different cytokines and chemokines in a semiquantitative fashion using a membrane-based immunoassay[38]. Serum was also quantitatively assayed for SDF-1a concentration using ELISA (R & D Systems, Minneapolis, MN, USA). (JC - 02)

综上所述，在所分析的文章中有 90% 的文章包含了语步三。在这些文章中，涉及篇章数最高的步骤是 M3.2，最低的是 M3.5，分别占所有文章的 90% 和 5%。各篇文章中语步三各步骤涉及篇章数平均值为 7.2，占所有文章的 36%，标准差为 7.79。在包含该步骤的文章中，涉及步骤种类最多的有 3 种，最低的只有 1 种，分别占语步三中所有步骤的 60% 和 20%，平均值为 2 种，占所有步骤的 40%，标准差为 5.9。不同文章中包含的步骤种类存在一定的差异，同一个步骤在不同文章中的占比也存在一定的差异。

（四）语步占比及分布轨迹

图 4.3.3 是所分析各篇文章中三个语步总体占比。如图所示，所有文章均包含语步一和语步二，有 90% 的文章包含语步三。分别有 85% 的文章语步二占比最高，10% 的文章语步一占比最高，5% 的文章语步一和语步二占比相同，均高于语步三。在语步二占比最

高的文章中，有 60% 的文章语步一占比高于语步三，有 20% 的文章语步三高于语步一，另外有 5% 的文章这两个语步占比相同。在语步一占比最高的文章中，语步二占比均高于语步三。

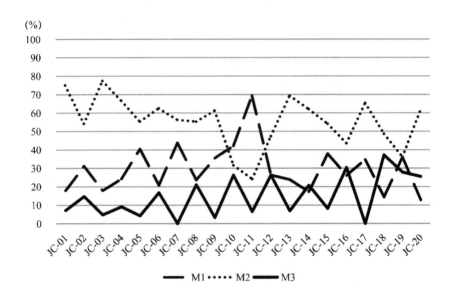

图 4.3.3　各篇文章中三个语步占比

就各步骤在所有语步中占比平均值来看，占比最高的前三个步骤依次为 M2.4、M3.2 和 M1.2d。占比最低的三个步骤分别是 M3.3、M3.4 和 M3.5。就步骤涉及的篇章数而言，所有文章中均包含 M2.4。涉及篇章数较高的还有 M1.2a、M1.2d 和 M3.2。就各篇文章中包含的步骤种类来看，包含步骤最多的文章有 15 种，最少的有 6 种，分别占所有步骤种类的 68% 和 27%。各篇文章中步骤种类平均值为 10.85 种，占所有步骤的 49%，标准差为 2.39。

图 4.3.4 至 4.3.6 为各篇文章的三个语步分布轨迹。如图所示，所有文章中均包含了语步一和语步二，有两篇文章不包含语步三。

在不包含语步三的两篇文章中语步二占比均略高于语步一，语步一主要分布在文章的前部、语步二之前，但是这两篇文章中均有少部分语步一分布在语步二中，两个语步有交叉。

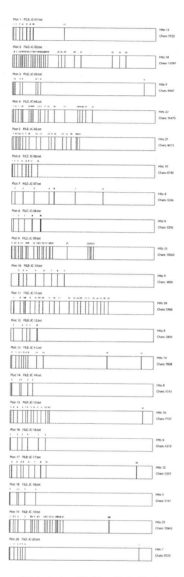

图4.3.4 语步一分布轨迹

在包含三个语步的文章中，语步二占比最高、分布也最广，语步一略高于语步三，语步三分布最集中。各篇文章中最前部均为语步一，但是有一半的文章中语步一中部分语句分布在文章的其他位置，主要分布在语步二中，其中有一篇文章中有一句出现在语步二后、语步三前。除两篇文章外，其他各篇文章中语步三均分布在文章的最后，与其他两个语步没有交叉。语步二主要分布在语步一和语步三之间，在一部分文章中与语步一有交叉，与语步三交叉的情况较少。

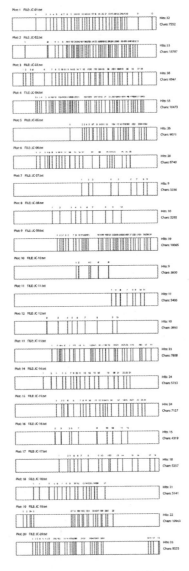

图 4.3.5　语步二分布轨迹

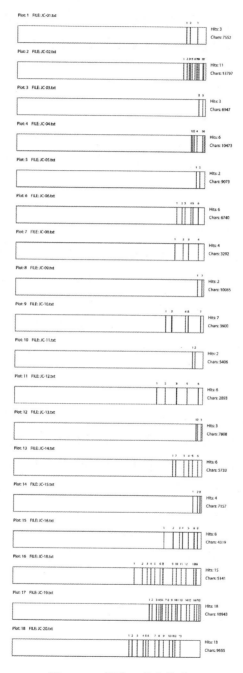

图 4.3.6 语步三分布轨迹

综上所述，同一学科不同文章中语步占比和分布轨迹既有相同之处，也存在一定的差异。所有文章中均出现了语步一和语步二，在绝大部分文章中语步二占比明显高于其他两个语步，语步一略高于语步三。就这三个语步在方法部分的分布而言，语步二分布最广，几乎覆盖了前部、中间及偏后的部位，语步一和语步三之间。语步一以文章最前和前部为主，语步三分布最集中，以文章最后为主。有一半的文章中语步一与语步二有交叉，语步三与其他语步之间基本上都没有交叉。

三　语言特征分析

本小节主要从句子、时态和语态三大方面分析实验方法部分的语言特征。针对句子的分析主要包含句子类型、四类主要句子长度分布及四类主要句子与语步之间的关系。针对时态的分析主要包含时态种类、不同时态组合及三种占比最高的时态组合与语步的关系。针对语态的分析主要包含语态种类、各语态组合与语步的关系。

（一）句子特征

A. 句子类型

表4.3.7是本学科文章中所包含的句子类型及各类句子占比。如表所示，简单句、复杂句、复合句及复合复杂句占所有句子的96.69%。片段和有语法错误的句子占所有句子的0.64%。其他为带有冒号、括号及i.e.的各类特殊句子。四类句子中简单句占比远高于其他三类句子，其次是复合句。其他两类句子占比均较低，其中复合复杂句最低。特殊类型句子形式多样，共有8种，其中NWS占比较高，其他的均较低。以下例句为特殊类型的句子。

表4.3.7　　　　　　　　　　　句类及占比

句类	句数	占比	句类	句数	占比
S	557	71.14%	NSC	2	0.26%
P	71	9.07%	NSP	1	0.13%

句类	句数	占比	句类	句数	占比
C	123	15.71%	NSS	1	0.13%
CP	6	0.77%	NWP	1	0.13%
BSP	1	0.13%	NWS	13	1.66%
BWAS	1	0.13%	F	1	0.13%
ISS	1	0.13%	R	4	0.51%

BSP：HER2 were evaluated using the Danish Breast Cancer Cooperative Group（DBCG）criteria（IHC = 0, 1, 2 or 3; if IHC = 2 FISH should be > 2.0 to confirm positive HER2 status）. (JC – 15)

BWAS：Data from repeated measurements of gene expression and data from animal study except for OA score were analyzed by oneway Analysis of Variance（ANOVA）followed by post hoc multiple comparison tests（Tukey's test when equal variance was assumed, or GameseHowell test when equal variance was not assumed）. (JC – 04)

ISS：Cultured cancer cell line cells（CLCs; COLO – 205）were spiked into whole blood specimens from healthy donors（HD）at varying concentrations ranging from six-300 CLCs/slide（six slides each of six, 12, 25, 50, 100, 300 CLCs/slide, and 24 additional slides were created for the 25 and 300 CLCs/slide dilution）. (JC – 17)

NSC：Figure S3, two separate patient cohorts were assessed in exploratory analyses: for（a）and（c）, patients with ≥5 total CTCs and ≥1 vimentin-positive or Ki67-positive CTC were compared with those patients with ≥5 total CTCs and no vimentin-positive or Ki67-positive CTC; for（b）and（d）, the 10 CTC-positive patients with the highest proportions of vimentin/Ki67-positive CTCs were compared with the 10 CTC-positive patients with the lowest proportions of vimentin/Ki67-positive CTCs. (JC – 16)

NSP：Data cutoff for survival estimates was March 1st, 2015: outcomes were censored if a patient had not died before this date. (JC – 16)

NSS：This was established using the CellSearch platform: in separate experiments, FITC- labelled anti-vimentin antibody（Santa-Cruz, 'vimentin cohort'）and anti-Ki67 antibody（BD Biosciences, 'Ki67 cohort'）were added to the free channel in the CellSearch system. (JC – 16)

NWP：To assess whether cartilage breakdown and turnover has been initiated 72 h post-injury, serum was assayed for six biomarkers of cartilage metabolism using enzyme-linked immunosorbent assays（ELISAs）: Cartilage Oligomeric Matrix Protein（COMP, MD Biosciences, St. Paul, MN,

USA）, Aggrecan Chrondroitin Sulfate 846 Epitope（CS-846, Ibex Pharmaceuticals Inc, Mont-Royal, QC, Canada）, C-terminal Telopeptide of Collagen II（CTxII, Nordic Biosciences, Herlev, Denmark）, Type II Collagen Cleavage Product（C2C, Ibex Pharmaceuticals Inc）, Type II Collagen Propeptides（CPII, Ibex Pharmaceuticals Inc）, and Types I and II Collagen Cleavage Neoepitope （C1, C2, Ibex Pharmaceuticals Inc）.（JC – 02）

NWS: The following grouping criteria were employed［12］: Group 1: Baseline C1 < 5 CTC/ 7. 5 ml and follow-up C3 < 5 CTC/7. 5 ml; Gr. 2: C1 $\geqslant$ 5/C3 < 5; Gr. 3: C1 < 5/C3 $\geqslant$ 5; Gr. 4: C1 $\geqslant$ 5/C3 $\geqslant$ 5.（JC – 15）

B. 句类与语步

图 4. 3. 7 是四种类型句子与语步的关系。如图所示，四类句子中占比最高的步骤均为 M2. 4。除复合复杂句外，其他三类句子中占比最高的前三个步骤均包含 M3. 2，但是占比排序不完全一致。由于四类句子在文章中占比不同，即使相同步骤在这四种句子中排序一致，数量和占比也不相同。复合复杂句中除 M2. 4 外，其他步骤占比均较低。

除复合复杂句外，其他三类句子均包含三个语步。简单句中包含了三个语步中所有步骤，复杂句和复合句中包含的步骤种类分别占三个语步中所有步骤种类的 77% 和 86%。复合复杂句只包含语步一和语步二，所包含的步骤种类占所有步骤种类的 27%。

总体来说，不同句子类型与步骤之间的关系存在异同，句子与步骤关系紧密度与该类句子在所有句子中的占比有关，同时也与该步骤在所有步骤中的占比有关，但是不完全成一一对应的关系，句类与步骤之间没有明显的相关性。

以下是四类句子中步骤占比最高的前三个步骤例句。由于复合复杂句中步骤较分散，只给出占比较高的一个步骤例句。

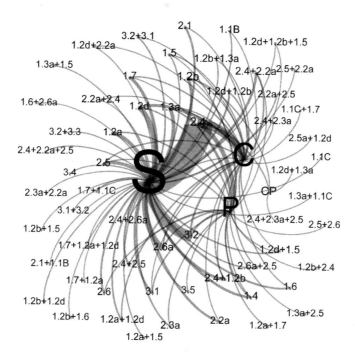

图 4.3.7　句类与步骤关系网络图

【S】

M 2. 4： In both parts, subjects were assigned to treatment using an interactive voice response/interactive Web-based system. (JC – 20)

M 3. 2： Analysis of variance (Model I ANOVA) and Tukeye Kramer methods for multiple comparisons, along with Student's t-test for pair-wise comparisons, were utilized to determine statistical significance amongst the experimental data. (JC – 09)

M 2. 6a： Treatment effect was evaluated according to the existing approach based on a cut-off of 5 CTC/7. 5ml blood and the new approach based on significant change value (SCV) limits. (JC – 15)

【P】

M 2. 4： Levels of intracellular ROS were assessed using the radical-sensitive dye H2DCFDA, which is oxidized to the fluorescent 2, 7-dicholorofluorescein (DCF) upon exposure to ROS. (JC – 09)

M 3. 2：All randomized subjects from Parts 1 and 2 who took 1 dose of study drug were combined and included in the intent-to-treat (ITT) and safety datasets. (JC – 20)

M 1. 3a：To monitor cellular apoptosis as a function of caspase 3 and 7 activities, we utilized the commercial Apo-ONE Homogenous Caspase 3/7 Assay kit that combines a lysis buffer with Z-DEVD-R110, a caspase-3/7 specific substrate. (JC – 09)

【C】

M 2. 4：Briefly, genomic DNA was denatured and bisulfite treated. (JC – 04)

M 1. 2d：All cells used in this work, with the exception of the mouse-derived RCAS-GFAP-tva/PDGFB cell culture, were patient-derived primary cultures and all specimens were verified by comparison of short tandem repeat (STR) analysis performed both immediately after isolation and periodically during the course of experimentation. (JC – 07)

M 3. 2：All p values were two sided and considered statistically significant at < 0. 05. (JC – 16)

【CP】

M 2. 4：Following blood collection, synovial fluid was aspirated from the right knee using a lavage procedure during which 200 mL of sterile PBS were injected into the anteromedial joint space using a 27-gauge needle, and ~ 100 mL of synovial fluid lavage was collected via a posteriorlyinserted 23-gauge needle. (JC – 02)

C. 句类与句长

表4.3.8 是四种类型句子长度占比情况。如表所示，各类句子长度分布在不同方面相似度不同。在长度分布占比方面，简单句中句子长度占比最高的是单词数介于 11—20 的句子，其次是介于 21—30 的句子。其他三类句子占比最高的均为单词数介于 21—30 的句子，但是这三类句子长度占比排在第二的各不相同。总体来说，前三类句子长度主要集中在 11— 40 之间，但是简单句以短句为主。

就各类句子覆盖范围而言，四种类型句子长度分布存在一定的差异。复杂句长度跨度最广，简单句和复合句相同，排在第二，复合复杂句跨度最小。

就句子长度最大值而言，复杂句最高，其他三类句子相近，其中复合句和复合复杂句同为最低。句子长度最小值简单句和复合句较接近，但是简单句最低，其他两类句子差异均较大，复合复杂句最高。如果不排除特殊类型句子，将每个公式算为一个单词的话，所有句子中最长的句子为 NWP，最短的为简单句。

　　以下是所有句子中最长的 NWP 例句和四类句子中最长和最短句子的例句。

表4.3.8　　　　　　　　　　四类句子长度分布

句长范围		1—10	11—20	21—30	31—40	41—50	51—60	61—70	71—80	81—90	MAX	MIX
S	句数	71	260	139	59	16	6	5	*	*	69	5
	占比	12.77%	46.76%	25.00%	10.61%	2.88%	1.08%	0.90%	*	*		
P	句数	*	14	27	15	9	3	1	1	1	88	14
	占比	*	19.72%	38.03%	21.13%	12.68%	4.23%	1.41%	1.41%	1.41%		
C	句数	2	40	45	23	10	1	1	*	*	62	8
	占比	1.64%	32.79%	36.89%	18.85%	8.20%	0.82%	0.82%	*	*		
CP	句数	*	*	3	1	1	*	1	*	*	62	21
	占比	*	*	50.00%	16.67%	16.67%	*	16.67%	*	*		

NWP［**Max：89**］To assess whether cartilage breakdown and turnover has been initiated 72 h post-injury, serum was assayed for six biomarkers of cartilage metabolism using enzyme-linked immunosorbent assays（ELISAs）: Cartilage Oligomeric Matrix Protein（COMP, MD Biosciences, St. Paul, MN, USA）, Aggrecan Chrondroitin Sulfate 846 Epitope（CS-846, Ibex Pharmaceuticals Inc, Mont-Royal, QC, Canada）, C-terminal Telopeptide of Collagen II（CTxII, Nordic Biosciences, Herlev, Denmark）, Type II Collagen Cleavage Product（C2C, Ibex Pharmaceuticals Inc）, Type II Collagen Propeptides（CPII, Ibex Pharmaceuticals Inc）, and Types I and II Collagen Cleavage Neo-epitope（C1, C2, Ibex Pharmaceuticals Inc）.（JC‑02）

S/［**Max：69**］The human GIST cell lines GIST-T1（KIT exon 11 mutant; Ref. 20）, HG129（also KIT exon 11 mutant; Ref. 21）, and GIST882（KIT exon 13 mutant; provided by Jonathan Fletcher［Department of Pathology, Brigham and Women's Hospital, Harvard Medical School, Boston, MA］）were maintained at 37℃ in 5% CO2 in RPMI1640 medium supplemented with 10% ﹨ FBS, 2 mmol/L l-glutamine, 50 U/mL penicillin-streptomycin, 0.1% 2-mercaptoethanol, and 10 mmol/L Hepes.（JC‑13）

S/［**Min：5**］Chips were run in duplicate.（JC‑10）

P/［**Max：88**］Each knee yielded 13‑16 slides for scoring by two blinded observers using a modified semi-quantitative grading scale 8, where 0 represented normal cartilage; 0.5: loss of Safranin-O with no structural lesions; 1: roughened articular surface and small fibrillations; 2: fibrillation below the superficial layer and some loss of lamina; 3: fibrillations extending to the calcified cartilage across less than 20% of the cartilage width; 5: fibrillation and erosions extending from 20 to 80% of the cartilage width; 6: cartilage erosion extending beyond 80% of the cartilage width. (JC – 01)

P/ [**Min: 13**] The efficacy-evaluable (EE) population included patients who received 1. 6 or 3. 0 μg/kg PEGPH20. (JC – 14)

C/ [**Max: 62**] In cycle 1 (8 weeks), PEGPH20 was administered i. v. twice weekly 24 hours prior to Gem during weeks 1 to 4 and once weekly 2 to 24 hours prior to Gem during weeks 5 to 7, followed by 1 week off; Gem (1, 000 mg/m2 i. v. ; Sun Pharmaceuticals) was administered once weekly during weeks 1 to 7 followed by 1 week off. (YXJ – 14)

C/ [**Min: 8**] Briefly, genomic DNA was denaturated and bisulfite treated. (JC – 04)

CP/ [**Max: 62**] Then the cells were dispersed, washed four times, and suspended in attachment media, which consisted of 20 mM glucose DMEM supplemented with 30 mg/L proline, 100 mg/L ornithine, 0. 544 mg/L ZnCl2, 0. 75 mg/L ZnSO4 $ 7H2O, 0. 2 mg/L CuSO4 $ 5H2O, 0. 25 mg/L MnSO4, 2 g/L bovine serum albumin (Sigma), 5 nM insulin, 100 nM dexamethasone, 100, 000 U penicillin, 100, 000 U streptomycin, and 2 mM glutamine. (JC – 09)

CP/ [**Min: 21**] The final dataset comprised 493 samples; 7 samples were excluded from the final analysis as they did not meet sample requirements. (JC – 12)

（二）时态特征

A. 时态种类及组合

表4.3.9是该学科论文中使用的时态类型及组合形式。如表所示，除去片段和有语法错误的句子，该学科文章中共出现了6种不同时态，其中T5没有单独使用，与其他时态共同出现在一个句子中。由不同时态构成的组合共有7种，均为两种时态组合。不同时态组合中包含T3的最多，其次为T1，其他时态在组合中占比均较低。

各种时态组合中，全部由一种时态构成的句子中占比最高的是T3，其次为T1。由不同时态构成的句子中占比最高的是由T1和T3两种不同时态构成的句子，其他相同或不同时态组合占比均较低。

以下是按照四种类型句子给出的相同时态和不同时态组合的例句，但不是所有时态组合中均包含这四类句子。

表 4.3.9　　　　　　　　　时态类型及组合

时态	T1	T2	T3	T8	T10	T1T2
句数	57	3	686	1	1	2
占比	7.33%	0.39%	88.17%	0.13%	0.13%	0.26%
时态	T1T3	T1T10	T2T3	T3T5	T3T8	T3T10
句数	19	1	2	2	1	3
占比	2.44%	0.13%	0.26%	0.26%	0.13%	0.39%

【T1】

S： This accumulation is accompanied by formation of dye aggregates shifting the fluorescence to the red (em: 590 nm) spectrum. (JC – 09)

P： Since the mouse knee is flexed during weight bearing, this results in greater stress on the posterior femur and central tibia, predominantly on the medial side. (JC – 01)

C： Aggregate in-text results are stated as mean [95% confidence interval], and error bars on all figures represent the 95% confidence interval. (JC – 02)

【T8】

S： Patients were starting up in 1st-6th line of chemotherapy with or without HER2 targeted trastuzumab, bevacizumab or lapatinib therapy. (JC – 15)

【T10】

S： Occasionally, application of one drop of epinephrine 1 : 1000 (AmVetTM, Neogen Corporation, Lexington, KY) would assist with recalcitrant bleeding. (JC – 01)

【T1T10】

C： Occasionally there is a small band running between the MMTL and LMTL, and only in that case would it be transected. (JC – 01)

【T1T2】

C： IL – 17 is a cytokine involved in numerous inflammatory conditions, and has also been linked to the subsequent expression of chemokines, such as CXCL1236. (JC – 02)

【T1T3】

P： One ml of each formulation was dispensed directly into vials for lyophilization to achieve the indicated treatment dosages when the lyophilized cake is resuspended in 1 ml of water for injection. (JC – 05)

C： In these cases, we used Tukey's post-hoc adjustments of standard errors in pair-wise comparisons of sham- and DMM-operated knees of WT and CCR5-/- mice, and report 95% confidence intervals for significant contrasts. (JC－06)

CP: Two different shRNAs were chosen from rat Nanog mRNA sequence, which target nucleotides 2254e2276 and 752e774, respectively, and another nonspecific shRNA was designed as control. (JC－04)

【T2】

S: Generation of Lrh－1 liver-specific knockout mice has been previously described. (JC－10)

【T2T3】

P: Any PEGPH20 treatment-related AE that resulted in drug interruption or reduction may have been considered a DLT at the Investigator's or Sponsor's discretion. (JC－14)

【T3】

S: For each phenotype, we performed analysis of variance using the factors genotype (CCR5-/-, WT) and procedure (sham, DMM) and the genotype-by-procedure interaction. (JC－06)

P: Livers of WT and LRH-1/mice fed with either chow or 2 weeks of the MCD diet (three per group) and pooled tissue from human liver wedge biopsies, which served as normal control samples in a previous study[17], were processed for chromatin immunoprecipitation (ChIP) experiments using the ChIP-IT High Sensitivity kit (Active Motif, Inc. , Carlsbad, CA) and an anti-LRH-1 antibody (R & D Systems, Abingdon, UK; #PP-H2325-00) according to the protocol. (JC－10)

C: CA19－9 values were monitored at baseline and every 4 weeks, and the best CA19－9 response was defined as the maximum percent decrease from baseline. (JC－14)

CP: When decalcification was complete, the knees were transected in the frontal plane at the level of the anterior cruciate ligament so the medial and lateral orientation was maintained and both halves were embedded in paraffin with the cut side on the face of the block. (JC－05)

【T3T10】

P: Medically stable subjects could enroll in the extension study if they completed the double-blind study. (JC－20)

C: In the existing 5 CTC cut-off approach presented by Cristofanilli and Hayes et al. [12], [13] a change from unfavourable CTC $\geqslant$ 5 at baseline to favourable CTC $<$ 5 at follow-up should improve survival and was expected to function as a marker for treatment response. (JC－15)

【T3T5】

P: Subjects who were currently receiving medication for AD or had taken such agents within 60 days of the first screening visit were excluded. (JC－20)

【T3T8】

P: The 1-sided test was chosen because ABT-126 was being studied to demonstrate improvement vs placebo. (JC－19)

B. 时态与语步

图 4.3.8 是该学科文章中三种占比较高的时态组合与语步的关系。如图所示，这三种时态组合中占比最高的步骤均为 M2.4。T1 和 T3 中占比排在第二位的相同，但是排在第三的不同。T1T3 组合中除 M2.4，其他步骤占比均很低。虽然在 T1 和 T3 中步骤占比最高的两个步骤排序一致，但是它们的数量和占比差异较大。

这三种时态组合形式中均包含了三个语步。就它们包含的步骤种类而言，T3 最高，包含了三个语步中所有步骤。其次为 T1 和 T1T3，包含的步骤种类分别占所有步骤种类的 73% 和 46%。

总体来说，不同时态形式的句子与语步的联系存在一定的差异，时态与步骤关系紧密度与该时态在所有句子中的占比有关，同时也与该步骤在所有步骤中的占比有关，但并不是决定性的。

以下是按照四种类型句子给出的三种时态组合中占比最高的前三个步骤的例句，但是有些步骤中不包含所有类型的句子。由于 T1T3 中步骤占比较分散也较低，在此只给出一个步骤的例句。

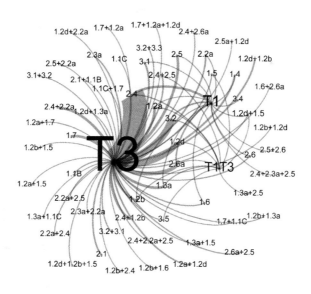

图 4.3.8　时态与步骤关系网络图

【T1】

M 2. 4

S： The data shown are expressed in normalized fluorescence units with excitation at 340/380 nm for 5 individual plates with 30 – 50 cells analyzed per plate. (JC – 09)

P： Sectioning in this manner provides simultaneous histological coverage of the anterior and posterior aspects of the central tibial plateau and the corresponding articulation of the femoral condyle across the weight bearing region where the most severe osteoarthritic lesions develop in this model. (JC – 05)

C： Upon exposure to active caspases, the DEVD peptide is cleaved and the molecule becomes fluorescent (ex/em, 485/30 nm). (JC – 09)

M 3. 2

S： We set the probability of significance of a factor at 0.05. (JC – 06)

C： F is the fundamental test statistic used in analysis of variance, and is calculated as the ratio of the mean squares of the factors (between group variation) and residual error (within group variation). (JC – 06)

M 2. 6a

S： The MCCB neurocognitive score contains all of the tests and domains of the MCCB composite score with the exception of social cognition. (JC – 19)

P： The SCV-limits in the difference plot determine if a difference between a CTC baseline and follow-up value is a significant increase, a significant decrease or an insignificant change. (JC – 15)

【T1 T3】

M 2. 4

P： Care was taken to identify and avoid the lateral meniscotibial ligament (LMTL), which is posterior and has fibers running in a similar direction [Figs. 1 and 3 (A)]. (JC – 01)

C： Primer sequences were designed on exon-exon transition of murine genes and can be found in Table I. (JC – 03)

【T3】

M 2. 4

S： ASCs (passage 2) were stimulated for 24 h with 10 ng/ml IFNg and IL-1b and 1 mg/ml recombinant murine S100A8. (JC – 03)

P： Control joints included no surgery and sham surgery in which the ligament was visualized but not transected. (JC – 01)

C： Rats were then randomized to a control group (Control) or noninvasive ACL rupture (Rupture) using a computer algorithm, n = 6 rats/group, and housed in individual cages in a 12h light-dark facility with unrestricted access to food and water. (JC – 02)

CP: When decalcification was complete, the knees were transected in the frontal plane at the level of the anterior cruciate ligament so the medial and lateral orientation was maintained and both halves were embedded in paraffin with the cut side on the face of the block. (JC – 05)

M 3.2

S: The association of CTC number with clinical characteristics and patient demographics were assessed using Fisher's exact test for dichotomous factors, and Mann-Whitney tests for continuous data. (JC – 16)

P: Safety analyses were performed on the safety data set, which included all subjects who received 1 dose of study drug. (JC – 19)

C: All p values were two sided and considered statistically significant at < 0.05. (JC – 16)

M 1.2d

S: One hour prior to anesthesia, rats were subcutaneously administered 5 mg/kg Carprofen, a non-steroidal, anti-inflammatory drug. (JC – 02)

P: All rats were allowed ad libitum cage activity until 72h post-procedure, at which point they were euthanized via CO_2 asphyxia. (JC – 02)

C: Anticholinergics were allowed during the study; however, they had to be at stable doses and were not to be taken within 12 hours prior to protocol-specific cognitive testing. (JC – 19)

（三）语态特征

A. 语态种类及组合

表4.3.10是该学科文章中使用的不同语步组合类型，不包含片段和有语法错误的句子。如表所示，该学科文章中两种语态均出现了，同时还包含了这两种语态的组合形式。只包含 V2 的句子数量和占比最高，同时包含 V1 和 V2 的句子数量和占比最低。所有文章中均包含了只使用 V2 的句子；有 19 篇文章中包含了由 V1 一种语态构成的句子，占所有文章的95%；有 18 篇文章中包含了由 V1 和 V2 两种语态构成的句子，占所有文章的90%。只包含 V1 一种语态的句子中均包括了简单句、复杂句和复合句这三种类型的句子。只包含 V2 一种语态的句子中包括了四种类型的句子。两种不同语态构成的句子中包括了除简单句以外的三种类型的句子。

以下是按照四种类型句子给出的三种语态组合中的例句，但是有些语态组合中不包含所有类型的句子。

表4.3.10 语态类型及组合

语态	V1	V1V2	V2
句数	129	58	591
占比	16.58%	7.46%	75.96%

【V1】

S: The medial meniscotibial ligament (MMTL) anchors the medial meniscus (MM) to the tibial plateau [Figs. 1 and 2 (B)]. (JC – 01)

P: Sectioning in this manner provides simultaneous histological coverage of the anterior and posterior aspects of the central tibial plateau and the corresponding articulation of the femoral condyle across the weight bearing region where the most severe osteoarthritic lesions develop in this model. (JC – 05)

C: All animals resumed weight bearing immediately postsurgery upon recovery from anesthesia and there was no evidence of excessive post-operative swelling indicative of joint infection. (JC – 05)

【V1V2】

P: First, palmitate or oleate was dissolved in pure ethanol at a concentration of 195 mM so that the final concentration of ethanol in our FFA stock solutions did not exceed 1.5% by volume. (JC – 09)

C: Occasionally there is a small band running between the MMTL and LMTL, and only in that case would it be transected. (JC – 01)

CP: When decalcification was complete, the knees were transected in the frontal plane at the level of the anterior cruciate ligament so the medial and lateral orientation was maintained and both halves were embedded in paraffin with the cut side on the face of the block. (JC – 05)

【V2】

S: The skin was closed by the application of tissue adhesive. (JC – 01)

P: Levels of intracellular ROS were assessed using the radical-sensitive dye H2DCFDA, which is oxidized to the fluorescent 2, 7-dicholorofluorescein (DCF) upon exposure to ROS. (JC – 09)

C: The sections were stained with toluidine blue and photomicrographs were taken using a Cool-SNAP™-Pro microscope camera. (JC – 05)

CP: Once a baseline was established, 1 mM thapsigargin was perfused across the dish to prevent ER calcium reuptake, and fluorescence was measured every 5s. (JC – 09)

B. 语态与语步

图4.3.9是该学科文章中语态组合与语步的关系。如图所示，这

三种组合中占比最高的前两个步骤完全一致，但 V1 中排在第三的步骤与其他两个不同，其他两个相同。即使不同语态组合中步骤占比排序相同，它们的数量及占比也均有差异。

就这三种组合中包含的语步种类而言，各组合中均包含了三个语步，但它们包含的步骤种类在所有步骤中占比不同。最高的是 V2，包含了三个语步中的所有步骤，其次是 V1，最低的是两种语态的组合，分别占所有步骤的91%和77%。

总体来说，语态与步骤关系紧密度与该语态在所有句子中的占比有关，同时也与该步骤在所有步骤中的占比有一定的关系。

以下是按照四种类型句子给出的三种语态组合中占比最高的前三个步骤的例句，但是有些步骤不包含所有类型的句子。

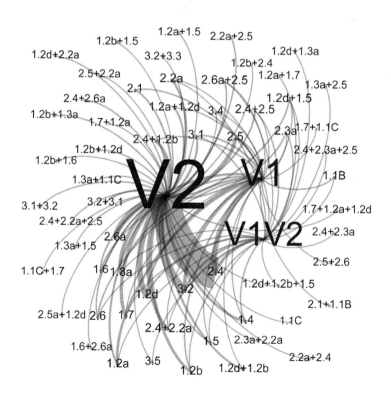

图 4.3.9　语态与步骤关系网络图

【V1】

M 2. 4

S：An attending veterinarian was on site or on call during the live phase of the study. （JC – 05）

P：Using pre-established decision rules that considered estimated effect sizes and their predictive probabilities of success as well as safety/tolerability for each dose group, an independent, unblinded efficacy data monitoring committee （DMC） used interim data to select the dose of ABT-126 for use in stage 2 of the study. （JC – 19）

C：All animals resumed weight bearing immediately postsurgery upon recovery from anesthesia and there was no evidence of excessive post-operative swelling indicative of joint infection. （JC – 05）

M 3. 2

S：The additional stage 2 sample size of 150 allowed the study to have 80% power to detect an effect size of 0. 30 for the change from baseline to final assessment in UPSA – 2ER total score when comparing the ABT – 126 50 mg dose group with placebo. （JC – 19）

P：The primary efficacy analysis used a likelihood based, mixed-effects model for repeated measures （MMRM） that included fixed, categorical effects for treatment, site, visit, and treatment-by-visit interaction, with continuous fixed covariates for baseline score and the baseline score-by-visit interaction. （JC – 20）

C：In these cases, we used Tukey's post-hoc adjustments of standard errors in pair-wise comparisons of sham- and DMM-operated knees of WT and CCR5-/- mice, and report 95% confidence intervals for significant contrasts. （JC – 06）

M 1. 2a

S：Participants were otherwise healthy based on their medical history, physical examination, vital signs, laboratory testing, and a 12-lead electrocardiogram （ECG）. （JC – 19）

P：Medically stable subjects could enroll in the extension study if they completed the double-blind study. （JC – 20）

【V1V2】

M 2. 4

P：The ACL is lateral to the posterior cruciate ligament （PCL）, which was only rarely visualized in our surgical approach, in the posterio-medial intercondylar region. （JC – 01）

C：Upon exposure to active caspases, the DEVD peptide is cleaved and the molecule becomes fluorescent （ex/em, 485/30 nm）. （JC – 09）

CP：When decalcification was complete, the knees were transected in the frontal plane at the level of the anterior cruciate ligament so the medial and lateral orientation was maintained and both halves were embedded in paraffin with the cut side on the face of the block. （JC – 05）

M 3. 2

P： All randomized subjects from Parts 1 and 2 who took 1 dose of study drug were combined and included in the intent-to-treat (ITT) and safety datasets. (JC – 20)

C： Aggregate in-text results are stated as mean [95% confidence interval], and error bars on all figures represent the 95% confidence interval. (JC – 02)

M 1. 2d

P： After 4h of incubation in the attachment media, the primary hepatocytes were switched to a maintenance media identical to the attachment media except it had a concentration of 1 nM (instead of 5 nM) insulin. (JC – 09)

C： Control rats received identical anesthesia and analgesia but were not subjected to any mechanical loading. (JC – 02)

【V2】

M 2. 4

S： In Part 1, subjects were randomized to placebo, ABT – 126 25 mg, ABT – 126 50 mg, ABT – 126 75 mg, or donepezil, identical in appearance. (JC – 20)

P： Levels of intracellular ROS were assessed using the radical-sensitive dye H2DCFDA, which is oxidized to the fluorescent 2, 7-dicholorofluorescein (DCF) upon exposure to ROS. (JC – 09)

C： The joint capsule immediately medial to the patellar tendon was incised with a#15 blade and the joint capsule opened with micro-iris scissors [Fig. 2 (A)]. (JC – 01)

CP： Once a baseline was established, 1 mM thapsigargin was perfused across the dish to prevent ER calcium reuptake, and fluorescence was measured every 5 s. (JC – 09)

M 3. 2

S： Efficacy analyses were conducted using the ITT dataset and safety analyses on the safety dataset unless otherwise noted. (JC – 20)

C： Data are presented as mean ± SEM and were analyzed using paired two-tailed Student's t test to determine significance. (JC – 08)

M 1. 2d

S： Nonsmoking status was confirmed with urine cotinine tests prior to and at several visits following randomization. (JC – 19)

P： All rats were allowed ad libitum cage activity until 72 h post-procedure, at which point they were euthanized via CO2 asphyxia. (JC – 02)

C： Offspring were housed with their mothers until weaning at 3-weeks of age, and then separated into sex-specific cages of 4e5 mice/cage with each cage individu- ally ventilated. (JC – 06)

第四节　海洋地球物理科学

海洋地球物理科学是研究地球被海水覆盖部分的物理性质及其与地球组成、构造关系的学科。传统实验方法是该学科主要实验方法之一。本研究共从 12 种国际学术期刊上选取了 20 篇传统实验类论文。这些文章基本上为 2010 年后发表的，第一作者通信地址基本上为英语国家。用于分析的句子总数为 656 句，单词总数约 16166 个，句子数量最多的论文有 85 句，最少的有 10 句，平均值为 32.8 句，标准差为 17.6。方法部分篇幅在全文的占比总体上不高，最大值为 16.7%，最小值为 3.08%，平均值为 8.11%，标准差为 0.038。分析发现，这些文章基本上均遵循了 IMRD（C）的结构，但是有一些文章在方法部分之前会对研究地点及该地点的气候单独说明。

一　标题特征分析

图 4.4.1 和图 4.4.2 分别为所选文章方法部分一级大标题和二级小标题词汇云图。如图所示，一级大标题中出现的词汇最多的是 method，在所有文章中共出现了 18 次，其次是 sample、materials 和 study。二级小标题中 sample 这一词的出现频率远远高于其他词汇，共出现过 12 次，而出现频次处于第二位的 analysis/analyses 共出现过 6 次，处于第三位的 preparation 和 isotope 分别出现过 4 次。二级小标题除 sample、analysis 和 preparation 外，基本上均与本学科具体研究内容相关。有十篇文章方法部分由两个平行部分构成，即有两个一级大标题，其中三篇文章中有二级小标题，其他文章中均没有。还有十篇文章中均只有一个一级大标题，其中有三篇文章没有二级小标题，另外七篇中最多的有 8 个二级小标题，最少的有 2 个。

图 4.4.1 一级大标题词汇云图

图 4.4.2 二级小标题词汇云图

综上所述，该领域有一半文章中实验方法部分的写作包含了两个部分。大部分文章中包含二级小标题。一级大标题与文章研究主题没有显著的相关性，但是一部分与学科有关。二级小标题中词汇与研究所涉及的具体问题关系更密切。此外，不同文章中包含的小标题数量存在一定的差异。

二 语步特征分析

本节研究该学科论文实验方法写作的语步特征。分析发现，该学科论文这部分写作的总体语步框架可以分为三个大的语步，与本研究中涉及的其他几个学科相似，但是不同学科各语步中包含的步骤种类存在一定的差异，本节各语步列表中只列出该学科论文中出现的步骤。

（一）语步一特征

表4.4.1是语步一中所包含的步骤种类。如表所示，语步一中共包括了9个步骤。表4.4.2是各篇文章语步一中各步骤在该语步中的占比情况。如表所示，各篇文章中均包括该语步，但该语步中各步骤在各篇文章中占比情况不一。此外，同一个步骤在不同文章中的占比情况也有所差异。以下是针对每个步骤占比情况的具体分析及实例。

表4.4.1　　　　　　　　　　语步一各步骤列表

M	语步一、实验准备		
1.1B	重述研究目的	1.2d	样本/材料/数据预处理或培养方法
1.1C	交代实验时间/场所	1.3a	实验条件及注意事项
1.2a	样本来源/数量/特点	1.5	前人实验准备方法
1.2b	材料/数据/试剂来源/数量及特点	1.6	强调实验准备的合理性
1.2c	样本/材料/数据选取方法		

表4.4.2　　　　　　　　　　语步一各步骤占比

M	1.1B	1.1C	1.2a	1.2b	1.2c	1.2d	1.3a	1.5	1.6
HY－01	—	36%	36%	9%		18%			
HY－02	29%	—	71%	—	—	—	—	—	—
HY－03	—	75%	14%	—	2%	9%			
HY－04	—	83%	5%	10%		2%			
HY－05	—	50%	—			25%		25%	
HY－06	—	4%	96%	—					
HY－07	5%	7%	64%			7%		17%	
HY－08	—	18%	52%			31%	—	—	—
HY－09	—	60%	14%	4%	2%			16%	4%
HY－10	—	62%	29%	7%					2%
HY－11	—	23%	53%			2%		2%	20%
HY－12	—	22%	56%						22%
HY－13	10%	—	30%			50%			10%

M	1.1B	1.1C	1.2a	1.2b	1.2c	1.2d	1.3a	1.5	1.6
HY-14	20%	5%	70%	—	—	—	—	5%	—
HY-15	—	9%	45%	45%	—	—	—	—	—
HY-16	—	65%	6%	—	10%	—	—	—	19%
HY-17	12%	14%	61%	—	—	6%	—	6%	—
HY-18	—	9%	17%	13%	4%	35%	13%	9%	—
HY-19	—	25%	2%	2%	36%	30%	—	5%	—
HY-20	—	—	50%	—	17%	17%	—	—	17%

M 1.1B 重述研究目的：所选文章中有 25% 的文章包含该步骤。在包含该步骤的文章中，该步骤在语步一中的占比最大值为 29%，最小值为 5%，平均值为 15%，标准差为 0.08。实例如下：

We examined the distributions of n-alkanes in the extractable lipids of a variety of bog plants to identify systematic variation in the abundance of n-alkanes of different carbon number. (HY-02)

To clarify the question of the presence of OH in naturally occurring corundum, samples from a variety of different localities were studied. (HY-13)

M 1.1C 交代实验时间/场所：所选文章中有 85% 的文章包含该步骤。在包含该步骤的文章中，该步骤在语步一中的占比最大值为 83%，最小值为 4%，平均值为 33%，标准差为 0.26。实例如下：

The study site（Lake Caco, Maranhao State, Brazil）is located about 80km from the Atlantic coast and close to the Equator（Fig. 1, and 21580S, 431250W and 120m above sea-level）. The local present-day climate is tropical humid with pronounced seasonality. （HY-03）

The Kirishima volcanic area（Fig. 1）has a surface area of approximately 471 km^2 with a maximum elevation of 1700m above sea level（m. a. s. l.）. It is composed of multiple volcanoes that have variously erupted over the past 0.3Ma（Imura, 1992; Sawamura and Matsui, 1957）. （HY-11）

M 1.2a 样本来源/数量/特点：所选文章中有 95% 的文章包含该步骤。在包含该步骤的文章中，该步骤在语步一中的占比最大值为 96%，最小值为 2%，平均值为 41%，标准差为 0.26。实例如下：

A sample of schist（NAZ15-01）was collected from the tailings pile of an excavation on West 76th St in Manhattan, New York City. It is a coarse grained muscovite-quartz-garnet schist that is similar in texture, mineralogy, and appearance to the large outcroppings of schist that occur in nearby Central Park. (HY – 07)

Benthic samples consisted of mixed species of benthic foraminifera. These were mostly infaunal genera including Globobulimina, Bulimina, Virgulina, and Uvigerina. (HY – 10)

M 1.2b 材料/数据/试剂来源/数量及特点：所选文章中有 35% 的文章包含该步骤。在包含该步骤的文章中，该步骤在语步一中的占比最大值为 45%，最小值为 2%，平均值为 13%，标准差为 0.14。实例如下：

The rainfall data of the Mohanpur has been obtained from the meteorological station at Indian Institute of Science Education and Research Kolkata (IISER – K). (HY – 01)

Graphite targets were prepared at the INSTAAR Laboratory for AMS Radiocarbon Preparation and Research (NSRL). (HY – 10)

M 1.2c 样本/材料/数据选取方法：所选文章中有 30% 的文章包含该步骤。在包含该步骤的文章中，该步骤在语步一中的占比最大值为 36%，最小值为 2%，平均值为 12%，标准差为 0.12。实例如下：

Two closely located cores, 5 and 32, from intermediate water depths of around 1.5 km were continuously sampled by Polyak at 1.5 – 2 – cm intervals for a detailed investigation. (HY – 16)

Approximately 0.5 ml of sample water was collected in a 1-ml syringe and passed through a 0.2-μm-pore-size filter, and 0.1 ml of filtrate was added to 0.9 ml of ferrozine reagent in the field. (HY – 19)

M 1.2d 样本/材料/数据预处理或培养方法：所选文章中有 60% 的文章包含该步骤。在包含该步骤的文章中，该步骤在语步一中的占比最大值为 50%，最小值为 2%，平均值为 19%，标准差为 0.14。实例如下：

The samples were carefully cleaned in water but most were not ground and polished. (HY – 13)

Mat samples were placed in either 15- or 50-ml plastic conical tubes, put in a cooler containing blue ice, and returned to the laboratory for processing. Samples for DNA extraction were frozen and returned to Bigelow Laboratory. (HY – 19)

M 1.3a 实验条件及注意事项：所选文章中只有一篇包含该步骤。在该篇文章中，该步骤在语步一中的占比为 13%。实例如下：

Briefly, the milling process begins with two large troughs milled from either side of the foil with high ion current (2700 pA). The second stage of milling is conducted at lower current, 350 pA, to a foil thickness of approximately 500 nm. (HY – 18)

M 1.5 前人实验准备方法：所选文章中有 40% 的文章包含该步骤。在包含该步骤的文章中，该步骤在语步一中的占比最大值为 25%，最小值为 2%，平均值为 11%，标准差为

0.07。实例如下:

> Both sampling procedure and techniques for the chemical analyses of cation and anion concentrations are described in more detail elsewhere (Gannoun et al., 2006; Vigier et al., 2006). (HY－05)

> Sample (PI－01) was collected from an exposure in an area mapped as pre-Illinoian Port Murray Formation tillite (Stone et al., 2002). (HY－07)

M 1.6 强调实验准备的合理性:所选文章中有 35% 的文章包含该步骤。在包含该步骤的文章中,该步骤在语步一中的占比最大值为 22%,最小值为 2%,平均值为 14%,标准差为 0.07。实例如下:

> This core is ideally situated: It is directly in the flow path of GNAIW if this water mass exits the North Atlantic. (HY－11)

> Several sites from the Indian Ocean only have a few centimeters (~15 cm) of Holocene sediments but omission of these data does not alter the general conclusions of this study. (HY－12)

综上所述,所分析的文章中均包含语步一。在该语步中,涉及篇章数最高的步骤是 M1.2a,最低的是 M1.3a,分别占所有文章的 95% 和 5%,平均值为 9.11 篇,占所有文章的 46%,标准差为 5.82。各篇文章中涉及步骤种类最多的有 7 种,最低的只有 2 种,分别占语步一中所有步骤的 78% 和 22%。各篇文章中包含的语步一各步骤种类的平均值为 4.1 种,占所有步骤的 46%,标准差为 1.29。不同文章中包含的步骤种类存在一定的差异,同一个步骤在不同文章中的占比也存在一定的差异。

(二)语步二特征

表 4.4.3 是语步二中所包含的步骤种类。该语步共包括 7 种步骤。表 4.4.4 是各篇文章语步二中各步骤在该语步中的占比情况。如表所示,除一篇文章外,其他各篇文章中均包括了该语步。但在包含该步骤的文章中,该语步中各步骤占比情况不一。此外,同一个步骤在不同文章中的占比情况也存在差异。以下是针对每个步骤占比情况的具体分析及实例。

表4.4.3 **语步二各步骤列表**

M	语步二、变量测量		
2.1	概述变量测量设计	2.4	描述变量测量步骤
2.2a	交代仪器/设备/工具/理论/方程/模型	2.5	前人变量测量方法
2.2b	实验参数设置	2.6	强调变量测量方法的科学性
2.3b	测试/获取相关变量		

表4.4.4 **语步二各步骤占比**

M	2.1	2.2a	2.2b	2.3b	2.4	2.5	2.6
HY–01	—	19%	3%	8%	61%	8%	—
HY–02	9%	26%	—	9%	57%	—	—
HY–03	—	19%	—	—	40%	15%	25%
HY–04	—	27%	—	20%	20%	7%	27%
HY–05	—	11%	—	—	48%	16%	25%
HY–06	—	18%	—	—	54%	28%	—
HY–07	—	10%	6%	—	70%	3%	11%
HY–08	—	14%	13%	—	63%	—	10%
HY–09	—	32%	5%	—	33%	4%	26%
HY–10	—	10%	—	—	80%	10%	—
HY–11	—	25%	—	—	38%	6%	31%
HY–12	—	12%	7%	—	61%	20%	—
HY–13	—	36%	28%	—	36%	—	—
HY–14	—	26%	13%	—	52%	9%	—
HY–15	—	21%	36%	18%	20%	5%	—
HY–16	—	—	—	—	—	—	—
HY–17	—	3%	3%	—	70%	—	23%
HY–18	—	25%	9%	—	60%	2%	4%
HY–19	3%	34%	—	—	50%	14%	—
HY–20	—	36%	—	—	32%	5%	27%

M 2.1 概述变量测量设计：所选文章中只有两篇文章包含该步骤。在这两篇文章中，该步骤在语步二中的占比分别为9%和3%。实例如下：

We used two complementary approaches. We examined the distributions of n-alkanes in the extractable lipids of a variety of bog plants to identify systematic variation in the abundance of n-alkanes of different carbon number. We then analyzed the abundance of n-alkanes in 107 peat samples, representing 3000 yr, from a 184 cm sediment core from Minden Bog, Michigan, USA. (HY－02)

All sequence processing was performed using mothur version 1. 34. 0, in accordance with a previously published methodology (17) (mothur. org/wiki/Schloss＿ SOP). (HY－19)

M 2.2a 交代仪器/设备/工具/理论/方程/模型：所选文章中有95%的文章包含该步骤。在包含该步骤的文章中，该步骤在语步二中的占比最大值为36%，最小值为3%，平均值为21%，标准差为0. 09。实例如下：

A Hewlett Packard 6890 GC interfaced to a Finnigan Delta + XL stable isotope spectrometer through high-temperature pyrolysis and combustion reactors were used for hydrogen and carbon isotopic analysis. （HY－03）

TEM investigations were performed with a TECNAI F20 XTWIN TEM operating at 200 kV with a field emis- sion gun electron source (Potsdam, Germany). The TEM is equipped with a Gatan TridiemTM filter, an EDX Gene- sisTM X-ray analyzer with ultra thin window and a Fish-ione high angle annular dark field detector. （HY－18）

M 2.2b 实验参数设置：所选文章中有一半的文章包含该步骤。在包含该步骤的文章中，该步骤在语步二中的占比最大值为36%，最小值为3%，平均值为12%，标准差为0. 1。实例如下：

Electron Probe Micro Analysis was performed at Caltech on a JEOL JXA- 8200 with an accelerating voltage of 15 kV and a defocused beam of 5 μm and 2. 5 nA or 10 μm and 10 nA to avoid alkali migration. （HY－15）

Spot size was approximately 1 nm, and acquisition time 60 s. （HY－18）

M 2.3b 测试/获取相关变量：所选文章中有20%的文章包含该步骤。在包含该步骤的文章中，该步骤在语步二中的占比最大值为20%，最小值为8%，平均值为14%，标准差为0. 05。实例如下：

We compared the n-alkane results with paleohydrological variation inferred form other proxies from the same core. （HY－02）

Isotopes measured are 24Mg, 47Ti, 52Cr, 57Fe, and 71 Ga. （HY－15）

M 2.4 描述变量测量步骤：所选文章中有95%的文章包含该步骤。在包含该步骤的文章中，该步骤在语步二中的占比最大值为80%，最小值为20%，平均值为50%，标准差为0. 16。实例如下：

Foraminiferal abundances were calculated per gram of dry sediment excluding large pebbles. (HY – 17)

To determine iron concentrations deeper within microbial iron mats, a prefilter step was included to eliminate thick mat precipitates that can rapidly clog syringes and filters. (HY – 19)

M 2.5 前人变量测量方法：所选文章中有75%的文章包含该步骤。在包含该步骤的文章中，该步骤在语步二中的占比最大值为28%，最小值为2%，平均值为10%，标准差为0.07。实例如下：

CO2 was reduced to graphite using an Fe catalyst in the presence of H2 (McNichol et al., 1992). (HY – 10)

Alignments were generated against a SILVA-based reference alignment (mothur. org/wiki/ Silva_ reference_ files), in accordance with previously published methods. (HY – 19)

M 2.6 强调变量测量方法的科学性：所选文章中有50%的文章包含该步骤。在包含该步骤的文章中，该步骤在语步二中的占比最大值为31%，最小值为4%，平均值为21%，标准差为0.09。实例如下：

This mixture was analysed every 6 injections and the standard deviation for these isotopic standards was on average less than ±4.5‰ during the course of this study. (HY –03)

All of these values are within error of the accepted values (Fisher et al., 2014a and sources cited above) and were also consistent with the long-term averages obtained using the same instrument. (HY –07)

综上所述，在所分析的文章中除一篇文章外，其他文章中均包含了语步二。在这些文章中，涉及篇章数最高的步骤是M2.2a和M2.4，占所有文章的95%，最低的是M2.1，为10%。各篇文章中语步二各步骤涉及篇章数平均值为11.3篇，占所有文章的56%，标准差为7.58。在包含该步骤的文章中，涉及步骤种类最多的有5种，最低的有3种，分别占语步二中所有步骤的71%和43%，平均值为4.16种，占所有步骤的59%，标准差为0.69。不同文章中包含的步骤种类存在一定的差异，同一个步骤在不同文章中的占比也存在一定的差异。

（三）语步三特征

表4.4.5是语步三中所包含的步骤种类。如表所示，该语步中共包括了8个步骤。表4.4.6是各篇文章语步三中各步骤在该语步中的占比情况。如表所示，部分文章中不包含该语步。在包含该步骤的文

章中，该语步中各步骤占比情况不一。此外，同一个步骤在不同文章中占比情况也有所差异。以下是针对每个步骤占比情况的具体分析及实例。

表4.4.5　　　　　　　　　　　语步三各步骤列表

M	语步三、数据分析		
3.1	描述数据分析工具/符号	3.5	分析实验结果
3.2	描述数据统计方法	3.7a	描述实验结果
3.3	前人数据分析方法	3.7c	突出实验结果的有效性
3.4	获取本研究数据/所研发软件途径	3.8	本研究不足之处

表4.4.6　　　　　　　　　　语步三各步骤占比

M	3.1	3.2	3.3	3.4	3.5	3.7a	3.7c	3.8
HY－01	—	—	—	—	—	—	—	—
HY－02	7%	93%	—	—	—	—	—	—
HY－03	17%	50%	—	—	—	—	33%	—
HY－04	11%	50%	17%	11%	—	11%	—	—
HY－05	—	—	—	—	—	29%	71%	—
HY－06	—	—	—	33%	—	33%	33%	—
HY－07	—	56%	2%	10%	14%	3%	3%	12%
HY－08	—	60%	—	20%	—	20%	—	—
HY－09	10%	70%	—	20%	—	—	—	—
HY－10	—	28%	17%	—	—	22%	11%	22%
HY－11	—	—	—	—	—	75%	25%	—
HY－12	—	83%	17%	—	—	—	—	—
HY－13	—	—	—	—	—	—	—	—
HY－14	—	33%	—	—	33%	—	33%	—
HY－15	—	—	—	—	—	—	—	—
HY－16	—	—	—	—	—	—	—	—
HY－17	—	—	—	—	—	—	—	—

续表

M	3.1	3.2	3.3	3.4	3.5	3.7a	3.7c	3.8
HY－18	—	73%	—	7%	13%	7%	—	—
HY－19	4%	86%	4%	7%	—	—	—	—
HY－20	—	—	—	—	—	—	—	—

M 3.1 描述数据分析工具/符号：所选文章中有25%的文章包含该步骤。在包含该步骤的文章中，该步骤在语步三中的占比最大值为17%，最小值为4%，平均值为10%，标准差为0.04。实例如下：

MATLAB 7.0.1.24704 software was used for the analyses and correlation coefficients were used for the cross products matrix. （HY－02）

To calculate the SI and the activity values, we used Phreeqc Interactive 3.0.2－7614 （USGS, USA） software and the LLNL_ AQUEOUS_ MODEL_ PARAMETERS （Lawrence Livermore National Laboratory, USA） mineral database. （HY－04）

M 3.2 描述数据统计方法：所选文章中有55%的文章包含该步骤。在包含该步骤的文章中，该步骤在语步三中的占比最大值为93%，最小值为28%，平均值为62%，标准差为0.2。实例如下：

MATLAB 7.0.1.24704 software was used for the analyses and correlation coefficients were used for the cross products matrix. （HY－02）

The quality of each spectral fit was evaluated quantitatively with the reduced chi square （vm2） and R-factor parameters. （HY－18）

M 3.3 前人数据分析方法：所选文章中有25%的文章包含该步骤。在包含该步骤的文章中，该步骤在语步三中的占比最大值为17%，最小值为2%，平均值为11%，标准差为0.07。实例如下：

The SI calculation and compilation of activity （stability） diagrams were done for May 2013 samples according to the work of Song et al. （2002） and Garrels and Christ （1965）, respectively. （HY－04）

We apply the GISP2 calendar age model （Meese et al., 1997） to RC27－14 and RC27－23 by correlating the $\delta15N$ records from the two sediment cores to the GISP2 $\delta18O$ record （Grootes and Stuiver, 1997）. （HY－10）

M 3.4 获取本研究数据/所研发软件途径：所选文章中有35%的文章包含该步骤。在包含该步骤的文章中，该步骤在语步三中的占比最大值为33%，最小值为7%，平均值为15%，标准差为0.09。实例如下：

Results from the standards analyzed during this session are provided in Electronic Appendix

B. （HY－07）

All pyrosequencing libraries were deposited at the European Nucleotide Archive under the study accession numbers PRJEB10276 and ERP011506.（HY－19）

M 3.5 分析实验结果：所选文章中只有三篇文章包含该步骤。在这三篇文章中，该步骤在语步三中的占比分别为33%、14%和13%。实例如下：

The Mud Tank standard was run 8 times, yielding a weighted mean 206Pb/238U age of 748 ± 13 Ma（2σ；MSWD = 8.9）and a weighted mean 207Pb/206Pb age of 577 ±40 Ma（2σ；MSWD = 1.3）.（HY－07）

The analytical uncertainties for all measured elements are estimated to be 15% at the 95% confidence level.（HY－14）

M 3.7a 描述实验结果：所选文章中有40%的文章包含该步骤。在包含该步骤的文章中，该步骤在语步三中的占比最大值为75%，最小值为3%，平均值为25%，标准差为0.21。实例如下：

Silicon isotope data are reported as deviations of 30Si/28Si and 29Si/28Si from the international standard NBS-28 in parts per thousand（the standard delta notation δ30Si and δ29Si, x = 30 or 29）as follows：The long-term reproducibility of over 300 measurements of the IRMM-018 standard was ±0.14‰（2σSD）for δ30Si values and ±0.10‰（2σSD）for δ29Si values（Reynolds et al.，2006b）.（HY－05）

Results from 4 analyses in sample 49677（677-ru1），8 analyses in sample 49688（688-ru1-4）are summarised in Table 1.（HY－08）

M 3.7c 突出实验结果的有效性：所选文章中有35%的文章包含该步骤。在包含该步骤的文章中，该步骤在语步三中的占比最大值为71%，最小值为3%，平均值为30%，标准差为0.2。实例如下：

Triplicate（for deuterium）and duplicate（for 13C）analyses of the samples resulted in an overall precision better than ±3‰（δD）and ±0.35‰（δ13C）for nC16，nC22 and nC30 fatty acid methyl esters.（HY－03）

The repeated analyses agree within the 95% confidence range of the population's SEM with earlier analyses，and thus demonstrate that the high level of precision reported in this study is real.（HY－05）

M 3.8 本研究不足之处：所选文章中只有两篇文章包含该步骤。在这两篇文章中，该步骤在语步三中的占比分别为22%和12%。实例如下：

However，at low 171Yb signals（e.g. < 0.01V），Cecil et al.（2011）have shown that it is not possible to accurately constrain ßYb. Further complicating the issue of accurately determining βYb is the fact that the NeptunePlus® has an interface pressure that is more than an order of magnitude lower than its predecessor instrument（Bouman et al.，2009）. The low interface pressure affects the accurate determination of ß factors, with the magnitude of the effect being highly sporadic, element specific, and partly dependent on the selection of the sample and skimmer cones as well as the composition of the carrier gas (Hu et al. , 2012). (HY‒07)

This error analysis does not include possible error in the GISP2 age model. (HY‒10)

综上所述，在所分析的文章中30%的文章不包含该语步。在包含该步骤的文章中，涉及篇章数最高的步骤是 M3.2，最低的是 M3.8，分别占所有文章的55%和10%。各篇文章中语步三中各步骤涉及篇章数平均值为6篇，占所有文章的30%，标准差为2.88。在包含语步三的文章中，涉及步骤种类最多的有7种，最低的只有2种，分别占语步三中所有步骤的88%和25%，平均值为3.42种，占所有步骤的43%，标准差为1.45。不同文章中包含的步骤种类存在一定的差异，同一个步骤在不同文章中的占比也存在一定的差异。

（四）语步占比分布轨迹

图4.4.3是所分析各篇文章中三个语步总体占比。如图所示，所有文章均包含了语步一，分别有95%和70%的文章包含了语步二和语步三。就各个语步占比而言，55%的文章语步二占比最高，40%的文章语步一占比最高，只有5%的文章语步三占比最高。在语步二占比最高的文章中，有30%的文章语步一占比高于语步三。在语步一占比最高的文章中，有一篇文章只包含语步一。在其他文章中，有五篇语步二占比高于语步三，两篇语步三占比高于语步二，分别占所有文章的25%和10%。在语步三占比最高的一篇文章中，语步一占比略高于语步二。

就各步骤在所有语步中占比平均值来看，占比最高的前三个步骤依次为 M2.4、M1.1c 和 M1.2a，占比最低的分别是 M2.1、M1.3a 和 M3.1。就步骤涉及的篇章数而言，最高的为 M1.2a、M2.2a 和 2.4M，有95%的文章包含这三个步骤。就各篇文章中包含的步骤种类来看，最多的有17种，占所有步骤种类的71%。最低的仅有4种，占所有步骤种类的17%。各篇文章中包含步骤种类的平均值为10.5，占所有步骤的44%，标准差为3.2。

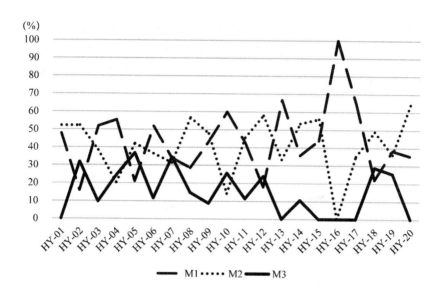

图 4.4.3　各篇文章中三个语步占比

图 4.4.4 至图 4.4.6 分别为语步一、语步二和语步三的分布轨迹。如图所示，所有文章中均包含了语步一，分别有十九篇文章中包含了语步二，十四篇文章中包含语步三。其中有一篇文章中只包含语步一。

在不包含语步三的六篇文章中，有一篇只包含语步一，在其他五篇文章中有两篇语步一占比最高，其他三篇语步二占比高于语步一。各篇文章的最前部均为语步一，有三篇文章语步一全部分布在语步二前，两个语步之间没有交叉，另外两篇文章中，语步一中少部分语句分散分布在了语步二中，两个语步之间有交叉。

在包含三个语步的 15 篇文章中，除有两篇语步一占比最高、分布最广外，其余均语步二占比最高，分布也较广。总体来说，文章的最前位置主要为语步一，但是在大部分文章语步一中部分语句也会分布在文章的其他位置、分散分布在语步二中，但是语步一还是以文章前部为主。除一篇文章中语步一全部分布在文章的最前部与其他语步没有交叉，其他各篇文章中语步一与语步二均有交叉，在极少数文章中与语步三也有交叉。语步三总体占比均最低，分布也较集中，主要分布在文章最后，少部分文章语步三中有少量语句会分散分布在语步二中。有近一半文章中语步三全部分布在文章的最后，与其他语步没有交叉。语步二主要分布在语步一后、语步三前，但是多数情况下语步二中部分语句会分布在文章较前的位置，出现在语步一中。部分文章中语步二与语步三之间也有交叉。极少情况下语步二中部分语句出现在文章的最后。

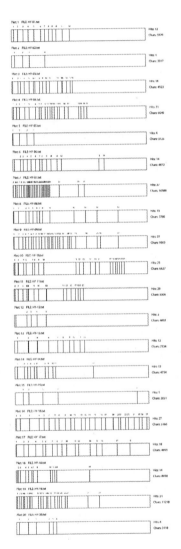

图 4.4.4　语步一分布轨迹

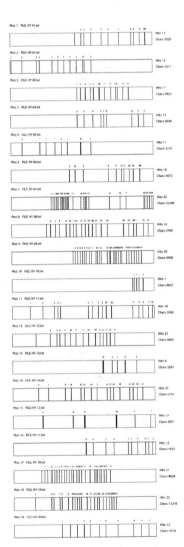

图 4.4.5　语步二分布轨迹

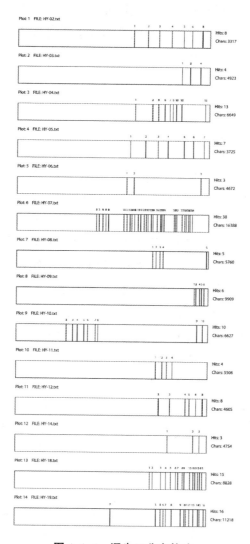

图4.4.6 语步三分布轨迹

综上所述，同一学科不同文章中语步占比和分布轨迹既有相同之处，同时也存在一定的差异。所有文章中均出现了语步一，但是在绝大部分文章中语步二占比明显高于其他两个语步。语步一总体占比高于语步三。就这三个语步在方法部分的分布而言，语步一以文章最前和前部为主，语步三则以文章后部及最后为主。语步二分布最广，主要分布在语步一和语步三之间。大部分文章语步一中部分语句会出现在语步二中，极少数情况下文章的最前面也会出现语步二，大部分文章中语步二与语步一有少量交叉。语步三相对较集中，部分文章语步三中少量语句也会分布在语步二中，语步三与语步一交叉的情况极少。三个语步均有交叉的情况。

三　语言特征分析

本小节主要分析论文实验方法部分的语言特征。主要从句子、时态和语态三个大的方面进行分析。针对句子的分析主要包含句子类型、四类主要句子长度分布及四类主要句子与语步之间的关系。针对时态的分析主要包含时态种类、不同时态组合及三种占比最高的时态组合与语步的关系。针对语态的分析主要包含语态种类及语态组合与语步的关系。

（一）句子特征

A. 句子类型

表 4.4.7 是本学科文章中所包含的句子类型及各类句子占比。如表所示，简单句、复杂句、复合句及复合复杂句占所有句子的98.02%。其他为带有冒号及括号的各类特殊句子。四类句子中简单句占比远高于其他三类句子，其次为复合句和复杂句，这两类句子占比非常接近。复合复杂句最低。特殊类型句子形式多样，共有 7 种，其中 NWS 占比较高，其他的均较低。以下例句为特殊类型的句子：

表 4.4.7　　　　　　　　　　　句类及占比

句类	句数	占比	句类	句数	占比
S	484	73.78%	NSC	1	0.15%
P	74	11.28%	NSCP	1	0.15%
C	73	11.13%	NSS	1	0.15%
CP	12	1.83%	NWC	1	0.15%
			NWAS	1	0.15%
BSS	1	0.15%	NWS	7	1.07%

BSS: The terrane comprises vesicular basalts, dolerites, and gabbros, with occasional rhyolites and leucogabbros (a representative selection of photomicrographs can be found in Supplementary Material 1). (HY – 06)

NSC: These fixed samples were used for doing direct total cell counts from mat samples using a previously described method (13), with the following modifications: the nucleic acid dye SYTO 13 (Invitrogen) was substituted for acridine orange, and fluorescent antibody slides (Gold Seal; Thermo Scientific) with circumscribed 1-cm circles were used in place of regular microscope slide. (HY – 19)

NSCP: These cores were selected for two primary reasons: they contain stratigraphic information that can be used to develop age models that are independent of 14C, and we expect that they would have been influenced by SAMW or AAIW during the deglaciation. (HY – 10)

NSS: The R-factor parameter represents the goodness of fit in terms of the point-by-point difference between the data and fit (Ravel, 2000): Eq. , Im [vth (Ri)] are the imaginary part, and Re [vdat (Ri)] and Re [vth (Ri)] the real part of the complex Fourier transformed data (vdat) and fit (vth). (HY – 18)

NWC: The zircon standards Plešovice, MudTank, R33, 91500, and Penglai (Li et al., 2010) were measured throughout this study, and the following short-term (e. g. during this study's Hf isotope analytical session) averages were obtained (where n = # of analyses): Plešovice: n = 55, 176Hf/177Hf = 0.282458 ±17 (2σ population standard deviations), εHf (present) = – 11.5 ±0.6; Mud Tank: n = 9, 176Hf/177Hf = 0.282492 ±27, εHf (present) = – 10.3 ± 0.9; R33: n = 15, 176Hf/177Hf = 0.282721 ±47, εHf (present) = – 2.5 ±1.7; Penglai: n = 8, 176Hf/177Hf = 0.282872 ±30, εHf (present) = + 3.1 ±1.0. (HY – 07)

NWAS: Full procedural blanks gave Sr, Nd, Hf and Pb concentrations of: Pb: 23.4 pg; Hf: 4 – 5 pg; Sr: 0.2 – 0.6 pg and Nd: 53 – 495 pg, which are negligible relative to sample concentrations. (HY – 06)

NWS: Our new measurements come from two sediment cores collected in the northern Arabian Sea near the coast of Oman: RC27 – 14 and RC27 – 23 (Table 1; Fig. 1). (HY – 10)

B. 句类与语步

图4.4.7是四种类型句子与语步的关系。如图所示，四类句子中占比最高的前三个步骤中均包含了M1.1C。另外，分别有三类句子中包含了M2.4或M1.2a，但是它们在这些句子中排序不完全一致。由于四类句子在文章中占比不同，即使相同步骤在这四类句子中排序一

致，数量和占比也不相同。

这四类句子均包含了三个语步，就各类句子包含的三个语步中步骤种类而言，简单句包含了三个语步中所有步骤，复杂句和复合句包含的步骤种类相同，均占三个语步中所有步骤种类的67%，复合复杂句包含的步骤种类最少，占比为42%。

总体来说，不同类型句子与步骤之间的关系存在异同，句子与步骤关系紧密度与该类句子在所有句子中的占比有关，同时也与该步骤在所有步骤中的占比有关，但是不完全成一一对应的关系，句类与步骤之间没有明显的相关性。

以下是四类句子中步骤占比最高的前三个步骤例句。由于复合复杂句中步骤较分散，在此只给出占比较高的两个步骤的例句。

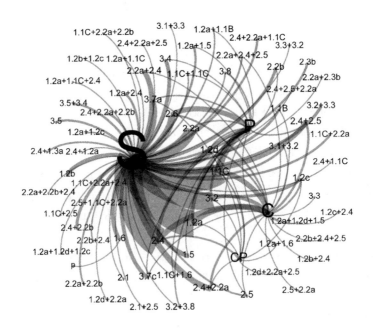

图4.4.7　句类与步骤关系网络图

【S】

M 2.4：Dried leaves were powdered for the determination of δ13Cvalue from the bulk tissues of modern plants and phytolith extraction. (HY – 01)

M 1. 2a： Mature plant leaves were collected in post-monsoon period during October to November. (HY – 01)

M 1. 1C： These characteristics are consistent with the description of the Losee Suite in Volkert (2012) and Volkert et al. (2010). (HY – 07)

【P】

M 1. 1C： It is composed of multiple volcanoes that have variously erupted over the past 0. 3Ma (Imura, 1992; Sawamura and Matsui, 1957). (HY – 04)

M 2. 6： Oppo and Horowitz [2000] therefore concluded that the two species used for δ13C measurements in this core are equivalent. (HY – 11)

M 1. 2a： It is a coarse grained muscovite-quartz-garnet schist that is similar in texture, mineralogy, and appearance to the large outcroppings of schist that occur in nearby Central Park. (HY – 07)

【C】

M 1. 2a： Each sample represented 1 cm of peat depth and each had a corresponding testate-amoeba assemblage, testate-amoeba-inferred water table depth and humification measurement. (HY – 02)

M 2. 4： The un-lithified nature of the tillite samples did not warrant crushing, so these samples were instead sieved directly under running water to liberate the heavy mineral fraction from the muddy matrix. (HY – 07)

M 1. 1C： The bedrocks of the studied catchments range between 0. 2 and 11. 2 Ma in age and the glacial cover varies in extent between 0 and 100% (Gannoun et al. , 2006). (HY – 05)

【CP】

M 2. 4： Leaves were digested with concentrated H_2SO_4 and heated in a hot plate for 12 to 48 h until the organicmatter was completely dissolved by the acid. (HY – 01)

M 1. 1C： The surface water of the Arctic Ocean receives the voluminous river runoff that keeps the salinity low and thus maintains the sea ice cover. (HY – 16)

C. 句类与句长

表 4. 4. 8 是四种类型句子长度占比情况。如表所示，各类句子之间在长度分布方面相似情况不同。在长度分布占比方面，简单句与其他三类句子差异较大。简单句中句子长度占比最高的是单词数介于 11—20 的句子，其次是介于 21—30 的句子。其他三类句子占比最高的均为单词数介于 21—30 的句子，复杂句和复合句占比排在第二的

为介于 31—40 的句子，而复合复杂句则为介于 41—50 的句子。就各类句子覆盖范围而言，复杂句跨度最广，复合复杂句最小。其他两类句子相同。

就句子长度最大值而言，复杂句和复合句较为接近，其中复杂句较高，其他两类句子同为最低。句子长度最小值也是复杂句和复合句较为接近，简单句最低，复合复杂句最长。如果不排除特殊类型句子，将每个公式算为一个单词的话，所有句子中最长的句子为 NWC，最短的为简单句。

以下是所有句子中最长的 NWC 例句和四类句子中最长和最短句子的例句。

表 4.4.8　　　　　　　　　四类句子长度分布

长范围		1—10	11—20	21—30	31—40	41—50	51—60	61—70	71—80	MAX	MIX
S	句数	37	186	173	66	20	2	*	*	53	4
S	占比	7.63%	38.35%	35.67%	13.64%	4.12%	0.41%	*	*		
P	句数	*	13	32	18	7	2	1	1	78	14
P	占比	*	17.81%	43.84%	24.32%	9.59%	2.74%	1.37%	1.37%		
C	句数	*	16	30	18	4	4	*	1	71	13
C	占比	*	22.22%	41.67%	24.66%	5.56%	5.56%	*	1.39%		
CP	句数	*	*	6	1	4	1	*	*	53	23
CP	占比	*	*	46.15%	8.33%	30.77%	7.69%	*	*		

NWC/ [**Max: 102**] The zircon standards Plešovice, MudTank, R33, 91500, and Penglai (Li et al., 2010) were measured throughout this study, and the following short-term (e.g. during this study's Hf isotope analytical session) averages were obtained (where n = # of analyses): Plešovice: n = 55, 176Hf/177Hf = 0.282458 ± 17 (2σ population standard deviations), εHf (present) = − 11.5 ± 0.6; Mud Tank: n = 9, 176Hf/177Hf = 0.282492 ± 27, εHf (present) = − 10.3 ± 0.9; R33: n = 15, 176Hf/177Hf = 0.282721 ± 47, εHf (present) = − 2.5 ± 1.7; Penglai: n = 8, 176Hf/177Hf = 0.282872 ± 30, εHf (present) = + 3.1 ± 1.0. (HY − 7)

S/ [**Max: 53**] On the shallow southern part of the Mendeleev Ridge and adjacent Chukchi Borderland (Chukchi Plateau and Northwind Ridge), sedimentation rates are higher than in the interior of the Amerasia Basin（Poore et al. , 1993；Phillips and Grantz, 1997）, probably because of sediment transport from the adjacent shelves and more frequent summer ice melt.（HY－16）

S/［**Min：4**］No aliquot was taken.（HY－02）

P/［**Max：78**］Changes in denitrification, aragonite preservation, organic geochemistry, and stable isotopes have also been interpreted to indicate increased presence of oxygen-rich SAMW/AAIW in the Arabian Sea during HS1 and the YD（e. g. , Böning and Bard, 2009；Jung et al. , 2009；Pichevin et al. , 2007；Schulte et al. , 1999）, consistent with records from the SW Pacific and Atlantic Oceans which suggest enhanced advection of AAIW during these intervals（Pahnke and Zahn, 2005；Pahnke et al. , 2008；Rickaby and Elderfield, 2005）.（HY－10）

P/［**Min：14**］Carracedo et al.（1998）proposed that the Canary Islands formed from an asthenospheric plume.（HY－09）

C/［**Max：71**］alphaMELTS（Smith and Asimow, 2005）was used for MELTS calculations（Ghiorso and Sack, 1995）performed for 1. 2 GPa at temperature intervals of 10℃ in the range of 700－1300℃ with the oxygen fugacity set at QFM＋1 log units to be within the estimated range of Frost and McCammon（2008）for the top of the upper mantle; however, changing this from QFM－1 to QFM＋1 does not produce significantly different results. (HY－15)

C/［**Min：13**］Foraminifera were then hydrolyzed using H_3PO_4, and the resultant CO_2 was purified cryogenically.（HY－10）

CP/［**Max：53**］For this purpose, the barrel end of a 10－ml plastic syringe was cut off, such that about 2. 5 cm of the barrel remained; this was filled loosely with glass wool, and a 100－$ m Nitex mesh was placed over the open end of the syringe barrel and held in place with a zip tie.（HY－19）

CP/［**Min：23**］The vast majority of elements are within 2 σ of certified values and those that are not in this range are not included.（HY－06）

（二）时态特征

A. 时态种类及组合

表4.4.9是该学科论文中使用的时态类型及组合形式。如表所示，该学科文章中共出现了8种不同时态，其中T4、T5和T14没有单独使用，与其他时态共同出现在一个句子中。由不同时态构成的组合共有10种，其中两种时态的组合共8种，三种时态组合的共2种。不同时态组合中包含T1的最多，其次为T3，分别占所有组合的67%和56%，其他时态在组合中占比均较低。各种时态组合中，全部由

一种时态构成的句子中占比最高的是 T3，其次为 T1。由不同时态构成的句子中占比最高的是由 T1 和 T3 两种不同时态构成的句子，其他相同或不同时态组合占比均较低。

以下是按照四种类型句子给出的相同时态和不同时态组合的例句，但不是所有时态组合中均包含这四类句子。此外，T1T3T6 组合只出现在特殊类型句子中，因此给出的是特殊类型句子。

表4.4.9　　　　　　　　时态类型及组合

时态	T1	T2	T3	T6	T10	T1T2	T1T3	T3T14
句数	199	13	395	1	1	7	31	1
占比	30.34%	1.98%	60.21%	0.15%	0.15%	1.07%	4.73%	0.15%
时态	T1T3T6	T1T3T10	T1T10	T1T4	T2T3	T2T6	T3T5	
句数	1	1	1	1	1	1	1	
占比	0.15%	0.15%	0.15%	0.15%	0.15%	0.15%	0.15%	

【T1】

S：The Gangetic Plain is mainly covered by alluvium deposited by the Ganges River system. (HY-01)

P：Modern vegetation that is governed by dune dynamics and topography ranges from littoral steppe vegetation "restinga" to sandy savanna "cerrado" with "restinga" species admixed (Ledru et al., 2001). (HY-03)

C：The dominant mafic minerals in these volcanic rocks are two pyroxenes (augite and hypersthene), and plagioclase is the dominant felsic mineral (Sawamura and Matsui, 1957). (HY-04)

CP：The vast majority of elements are within 2 σ of certified values and those that are not in this range are not included. (HY-06)

【T2】

S：The rainfall data of the Mohanpur has been obtained from the meteorological station at Indian Institute of Science Education and Research Kolkata (IISER-K). (HY-01)

C：We have observed some compaction in the first meter of sediment but the water-sediment interface has been preserved. (HY-03)

【T3】

S：Mature plant leaves were collected in post-monsoon period during October to November.

（HY－01）

P： Plants and extracted phytoliths collected from in and around Kanpurand Versa Ghat region, were analyzed at Indian Institute of Technology Kharagpur（IIT-KGP）, while Mohanpur vegetation and extractedphytoliths were measured at the stable isotope laboratory in IISER-K.（HY－01）

C： Each sample represented 1 cm of peat depth and each had a corresponding testate-amoeba assemblage, testate-amoeba-inferred water table depth and humification measurement.（HY－02）

CP： Leaves were digested with concentrated H_2SO_4 and heated in a hot plate for 12 to 48h until the organicmatter was completely dissolved by the acid.（HY－01）

【T6】

S： Lower sea level during the last glacial period would have substantially reduced or eliminated outflow from the marginal seas（Rohling and Zachariasse, 1996）, likely increasing the relative proportion of AAIW and SAMW in the Arabian Sea.（HY－10）

【T10】

S： Due to the low 176Lu/177Hf exhibited by all of the zircons, however, this uncertainty should be almost negligible.（HY－07）

【T1T2】

P： It is composed of multiple volcanoes that have variously erupted over the past 0.3Ma（Imura, 1992; Sawamura and Matsui, 1957）.（HY－04）

C： Other Crescent Formation samples, and the Siletz River Volcanics to the south, have undergone zeolite to prehnite-pumpellyite facies alteration and contain zeolite, calcite, pumpellyite and prehnite. （HY－06）

【T1T3】

P： The black and opaque solution was further reacted with 30% H_2O_2 which was added incrementally until the solution becomes clear and colorless indicating only silica remained in the system as organic matter was entirely oxidized.（HY－01）

C： All of these values are within error of the accepted values（Fisher et al., 2014a and sources cited above）and were also consistent with the long-term averages obtained using the same instrument. （HY－07）

CP： All the species in the analysis are common bog plants, but we assumed that a particular species produces a similar distribution of n-alkanes regardless of location.（HY－02）

【T3T14】

C： During the last glacial, water at this location consisted of at least one-third GNAIW but may have been entirely GNAIW（aged）［Oppo and Horowitz, 2000］.（HY－11）

【T1T3T6】

NSCP： These cores were selected for two primary reasons: they contain stratigraphic information that can be used to develop age models that are independent of 14C, and we expect that they would have been influenced by SAMW or AAIW during the deglaciation. （HY－10）

【T1T3T10】

P：However, this standard was not used to apply analytical session-specific normalization factors （e. g. a final offset of the mass bias- and interference-corrected 176Hf/177Hf and 178Hf/177Hf of the unknowns）because this correction would only result in a one εHf （present）unit （at most）adjustment of the unknowns and due to the fact that the values for Plešovice remain consistent within and across the sessions. （HY－07）

【T1T10】

CP：Furthermore, many of these crystals have internal flaws that would render them unsuitable for gemstone purposes, but have sufficient clear regions to be studied with our techniques. （HY－13）

【T1T4】

CP：Geological samples consist of multiple minerals of different densities and it is important to understand how such samples will react to exposure to the X-ray beam. （HY－09）

【T2T3】

P：The Si concentration of these snow samples was below detection limit of ICP-OES, although the average Si concentration for Icelandic precipitation has been estimated to be about 0. 5 μg/l SiO2 or 0. 23 ppb Si （Gislason et al. , 1996）, and thus a negligible contribution to the riverine Si concentrations that are N1 ppm. （HY－05）

【T2T6】

P：Using sample volumes instead of weights would have introduced more bias as sediment has partially dried out during storage. （HY－17）

【T3T5】

P：Background corrections, mass bias determinations, and isobaric interference corrections were applied for each cycle in the 60 cycle block, with a pre-screening of the block to remove cycles where the laser had passed through the zircon grain or penetrated an inclusion. （HY－07）

B. 时态与语步

图 4.4.8 是该学科文章中三种占比最高的时态组合与语步的关系。三个时态组合中占比最高的前三个步骤中均包含了 M1.2a，但是它们在各组合中的排序不完全一致。此外，分别有两组时态组合中包含了 M1.1C 和 M2.4，它们在不同组合中的排序不完全一致。即使同

一个步骤在不同时态组合中占比排序一致，相同步骤在不同时态组合中数量和占比也不相同。

此外，这三种时态组合形式中均包含了三个语步，就它们包含的步骤种类而言，T3 最高，包含了三个语步中所有步骤。其次为 T1 和 T1T3，包含的步骤种类分别占所有步骤种类的 88% 和 54%。

总体来说，不同时态形式的句子与语步的联系存在一定的差异，时态与步骤关系紧密度与该时态在所有句子中的占比有关，同时也与该步骤在所有步骤中的占比有关，但并不是决定性的。

以下是按照四种类型句子给出的三种时态组合中占比最高的前三个步骤的例句，但是有些步骤中不包含所有类型的句子。

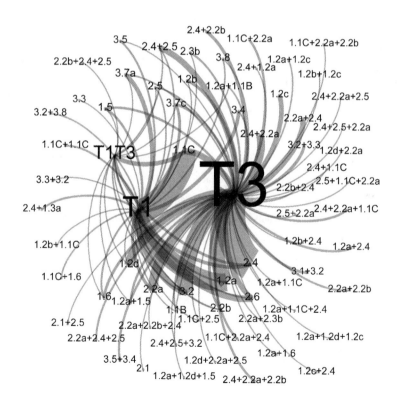

图 4.4.8 时态与步骤关系网络图

【T1】

M 1.1C

S： The Gangetic Plain is mainly covered by alluvium deposited by the Ganges River system. (HY – 01)

P： Basement rocks of this area consist of pelagic sedimentary rocks (sandstone and mudstone) of accretionary prism of the Paleogene Shimanto Group which are overlain by Quaternary volcanic rocks such as andesite and some alluvial deposits derived from the same Quaternary volcanic rocks (Iwahashi et al., 1999). (HY – 04)

C： The dominant mafic minerals in these volcanic rocks are two pyroxenes (augite and hypersthene), and plagioclase is the dominant felsic mineral (Sawamura and Matsui, 1957). (HY – 04)

CP： The surface water of the Arctic Ocean receives the voluminous river runoff that keeps the salinity low and thus maintains the sea ice cover. (HY – 16)

M 1.2a

S： Tree derived phytoliths are long in size and are not stable in soil environment. (HY – 01)

P： It is a coarse grained muscovite-quartz-garnet schist that is similar in texture, mineralogy, and appearance to the large outcroppings of schist that occur in nearby Central Park. (HY – 07)

C： Opaque minerals comprise between 10% and 20% of most samples and are particularly abundant in the Siletz River Volcanics (Roseburg). (HY – 06)

M 2.6

S： The X/Cl molar ratios for Mg, Na, K, Ca, Sr are 0.093, 0.9, 0.003, 0.02, 0.0002, respectively, typical of an oceanic origin (Gannoun et al., 2006). (HY – 05)

P： However, the attenuation curves for forsterite and enstatite are similar across the whole range of energies, which makes it very difficult to distinguish the two minerals. (HY – 09)

C： Clinopyroxene has a higher attenuation factor at low energies (50 keV) because of the high atomic number of Ca, and so clinopyroxene can be distinguished in CT images. (HY – 09)

【T1T3】

M 1.1C

P： They showed that the lithosphere is significantly thinned (i.e. 75 km) under the Limagne graben whilst the adjacent lithosphere-asthenosphere boundary is at a depth of N100 km. (HY – 09)

C： Modern sedimentation rates were estimated to be as low as 0.2 – 0.3 mm/kyr throughout the Amerasia Basin by ^{230}Th and pore water chemistry methods (Cranston, 1997; Huh et al., 1997); however, ^{14}C data from the Chukchi Borderland show up to two orders of magnitude higher sedimentation rates during the deglaciation and the Holocene (Darby et al., 1997). (HY – 16)

CP： The summer sea-ice margin was located south of the ridge in climatological data, but shifted to its northern edge in recent years, which makes the Northwind Ridge an area of choice for studying the history of sea ice in the western Arctic. (HY – 17)

M 2. 4

S: The black and opaque solution was further reacted with 30% H_2O_2 which was added incrementally until the solution becomes clear and colorless indicating only silica remained in the system as organic matter was entirely oxidized. (HY – 01)

C: The mass spectrum is deconvolved into Y, Hf and REE atomic and monoxide species and concentrations were determined relative to 30Si + with an assumed stoichiometric zircon value of 33. 00 wt% SiO_2. (HY – 14)

M 1. 2a

P: Samples did not include any Pyrgo spp. , which may yield anomalous 14C ages (Nadeau et al. , 2001). (HY – 10)

C: In an effort to include as many different species as possible, we included specimens collected from Europe as well as North America. (HY – 02)

【T3】

M 2. 4

S: Dried leaves were powdered for the determination of δ13Cvalue from the bulk tissues of modern plants and phytolith extraction. (HY – 01)

P: Once these initial steps were performed, the size-classified (b 250 μm) materials from each sample were panned in clean water to remove the bulk of the material. (HY – 07)

C: For these analyses, nitric acid was added to prevent precipitation and indium was added as an internal standard. (HY – 04)

CP: Leaves were digested with concentrated H_2SO_4 and heated in a hot plate for 12 to 48 h until the organic matter was completely dissolved by the acid. (HY – 01)

M 3. 2

S: We explored various ratios of n-alkanes extracted from both modern plants and peat and used principal components analysis (PCA) to identify patterns of variability within the distribution data for bothmodern and downcore samples. (HY – 02)

P: Once all of these corrections were performed, isotope ratios from each line were averaged together. (HY – 07)

C: Non-linear methods such as non-metric multidimensional scaling and correspondence analysis were also explored, and the dominant gradient of variability was similar among all methods. (HY – 02)

M 1. 2a

S: Mature plant leaves were collected in post-monsoon period during October to November.

（HY - 01）

P： In order to assess the precision of measurements on the AAS, three consistency standards were treated as samples in each of the six runs in which the data were generated. （HY - 11）

C： Each sample represented 1 cm of peat depth and each had a corresponding testate-amoeba assemblage, testate-amoeba-inferred water table depth and humification measurement. （HY - 02）

（三）语态特征

A. 语态种类及组合

表 4.4.10 是该学科文章中使用的不同语态组合类型，不包含片段和有语法错误的句子。如表所示，该学科文章中两种语态均出现了，同时还包含了这两种语态的组合形式。只包含 V2 的句子数量和占比最高，同时包含两种语态的句子数量和占比最低。所有文章中均包含了同一种语态构成的句子，但是只有 90% 的文章中包含由两种不同语态构成的句子。同一种语态构成的句子中均包括了简单句、复杂句、复合句和复合复杂句这四种类型的句子。两种不同语态构成的句子中包括了除简单句以外的三种类型的句子。

以下是按照四种类型句子给出的三种语态组合中的例句，但是有些语态组合中不包含所有类型的句子。

表 4.4.10　　　　　　　　　语态类型及组合

语态	V1	V1V2	V2
句数	220	48	388
占比	33.54%	7.32%	59.15%

【V1】

S： The study areas lie within the middle and lower reaches of the Gangetic Plain situated in the eastern part of India （Fig. 1）. （HY - 01）

P： It is a coarse grained muscovite-quartz-garnet schist that is similar in texture, mineralogy, and appearance to the large outcroppings of schist that occur in nearby Central Park. （HY - 07）

C： Each sample represented 1 cm of peat depth and each had a corresponding testate-amoeba assemblage, testate-amoeba-inferred water table depth and humification measurement. （HY - 02）

CP: All the species in the analysis are common bog plants, but we assumed that a particular species produces a similar distribution of n-alkanes regardless of location. (HY – 02)

【V1 V2】

P: The black and opaque solution was further reacted with 30% H_2O_2 which was added incrementally until the solution becomes clear and colorless indicating only silica remained in the system as organic matter was entirely oxidized. (HY – 01)

C: Non-linear methods such as non-metric multidimensional scaling and correspondence analysis were also explored, and the dominant gradient of variability was similar among all methods. (HY – 02)

CP: Generally, the morphology of the crystal made it possible to locate the c-axis and to use an orientation that placed the c-axis normal to the direction of the propagation of the infrared beam, but this was not accomplished with all samples. (HY – 13)

【V2】

S: The Gangetic Plain is mainly covered by alluvium deposited by the Ganges River system. (HY – 01)

P: Plants and extracted phytoliths collected from in and around Kanpurand Versa Ghat region, were analyzed at Indian Institute of TechnologyKharagpur (IIT-KGP), while Mohanpur vegetation and extractedphytoliths were measured at the stable isotope laboratory in IISER – K. (HY – 01)

C: For these analyses, nitric acid was added to prevent precipitation and indium was added as an internal standard. (HY – 04)

CP: Leaves were digested with concentrated H_2SO_4 and heated in a hot plate for 12 to 48 h until the organic matter was completely dissolved by the acid. (HY – 01)

B. 语态与语步

图 4.4.9 是该学科文章中语态组合与语步的关系。如图所示，这三种组合中占比最高的前三个步骤中均包含 M1.2a，但是该步骤在这三种语态组合中的占比排序不完全一致。此外，M1.1C、M2.4 和 M3.2 只分别涉及两种语态组合。各步骤在不同语态组合中的排序不完全一致。即使排序一致，同一个步骤在不同语态组合中的数量和占比也均存在差异。

就这三种组合中包含的步骤种类而言，它们均包含了三个语步，其中 V1 和 V2 这两种组合中包括了三个语步中的所有步骤。由两种不同语态构成的组合中所包含的步骤种类在所有步骤中占比最低，为63%。

总体来说，语态与步骤关系紧密度与该语态在所有句子中的占比有关，同时也与该步骤在所有步骤中的占比有一定的关系。

以下是按照四种类型句子给出的三种语态组合中占比最高的前三个步骤的例句，但是有些步骤不包含所有类型的句子。

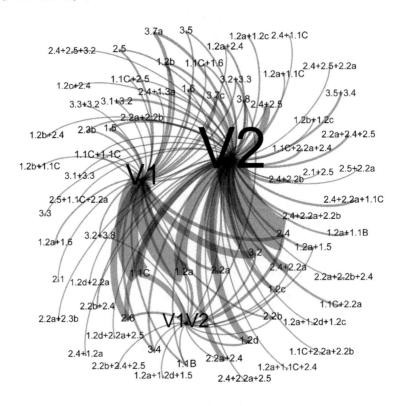

图4.4.9 语态与步骤关系网络图

【V1】

M 1.1C

S: Mendeleev Ridge is an elevated portion of the Arctic Ocean floor extending from the East Siberian shelf towards the North Pole (Fig. 1). (HY - 16)

P: Due to perennial sea ice cover, the productivity in the central Arctic Ocean is low, although recent studies estimate the amount of primary production as high as 15 g C/m2/yr, much higher than previously believed (Gosselin et al., 1997). (HY - 16)

C: The deep water of the Amerasia Basin is relatively warm （ $-0.5℃$ ） and may have a notably old age of almost 1000 years （Macdonald and Carmack, 1991）. （HY – 16）

CP: The surface water of the Arctic Ocean receives the voluminous river runoff that keeps the salinity low and thus maintains the sea ice cover. （HY – 16）

M 1. 2a

S: The mafic rocks consist mostly of plagioclase, clinopyroxene and Fe-Ti oxide. （HY – 06）

P: It is a coarse grained muscovite-quartz-garnet schist that is similar in texture, mineralogy, and appearance to the large outcroppings of schist that occur in nearby Central Park. （HY – 07）

C: Opaque minerals comprise between 10% and 20% of most samples and are particularly abundant in the Siletz River Volcanics （Roseburg）. （HY – 06）

CP: Geological samples consist of multiple minerals of different densities and it is important to understand how such samples will react to exposure to the X-ray beam. （HY – 09）

M 3. 2

S: In an effort to include as many different species as possible, we included specimens collected from Europe as well as North America. （HY – 02）

P: Zirakparvar et al. （2014） and Zirakparvar （2015） have shown that this overcorrection does not exist when ßYb $= 0.945$ × ßHf. （HY – 07）

C: However, the uncertainty on the initial value only reflects uncertainty in the present-day 176Hf/177Hf value and does not account for error in the 176Lu/177Hf or age-related uncertainty. （HY – 07）

CP: All the species in the analysis are common bog plants, but we assumed that a particular species produces a similar distribution of n-alkanes regardless of location. （HY – 02）

【V1 V2】

M 1. 1C

P: It is composed of multiple volcanoes that have variously erupted over the past 0. 3Ma （Imura, 1992; Sawamura and Matsui, 1957）. （HY – 04）

C: Modern sedimentation rates were estimated to be as low as 0. 2 – 0. 3 mm/kyr throughout the Amerasia Basin by ^{230}Th and pore water chemistry methods （Cranston, 1997; Huh et al. , 1997）; however, ^{14}C data from the Chukchi Borderland show up to two orders of magnitude higher sedimentation rates during the deglaciation and the Holocene （Darby et al. , 1997）. （HY – 16）

CP: The summer sea-ice margin was located south of the ridge in climatological data, but shifted to its northern edge in recent years, which makes the Northwind Ridge an area of choice for studying the history of sea ice in the western Arctic. （HY – 17）

M 2. 4

P: The black and opaque solution was further reacted with 30% H_2O_2 which was added incrementally until the solution becomes clear and colorless indicating only silica remained in the system as organic matter was entirely oxidized. (HY – 01)

C: Specifically, the foils examined were obtained from within the Fe-encrusted biofilm only, and are not transects through the biofilm and into the sulfides. (HY – 18)

CP: Samples collected during the later period of field work had iron measurements done for the first 3 days at TFS and then were placed in a cooler with blue ice and shipped to Bigelow Laboratory, where incubations were continued for an additional 4 days. (HY – 19)

M 1. 2a

C: We have observed some compaction in the first meter of sediment but the water-sediment interface has been preserved. (HY – 03)

【V2】

M 2. 4

S: Dried leaves were powdered for the determination of δ13C value from the bulk tissues of modern plants and phytolith extraction. (HY –01)

P: The riverine solute load has been corrected for airborne derived wet depositional input assuming all Cl – in the rivers is derived from precipitation with a known or estimated chemical composition (Stallard and Edmond, 1981). (HY – 05)

C: For these analyses, nitric acid was added to prevent precipitation and indium was added as an internal standard. (HY – 04)

CP: Leaves were digested with concentrated H_2SO_4 and heated in a hot plate for 12 to 48 h until the organicmatter was completely dissolved by the acid. (HY – 01)

M 3. 2

S: Leaves were initially cleaned with 1 N HCl and subsequently with distilled water through an ultrasonic bath for 15 min to remove sediments from surfaces of the leaves. (HY – 01)

P: Once all of these corrections were performed, isotope ratios from each line were averaged together. (HY – 07)

C: The anthropogenic CO_2 contribution was subtracted from DIC and preindustrial values including bottom water [B (OH) 4 –] / [HCO_3 –], [CO_3^{2-}], pH (total scale), and the saturation states (Ω) for calcite and aragonite were calculated using CO_2 sys. xls (Ver. 12) [26] with K1 and K_2 according to Mehrbach et al. [27] and KSO_4 according to Dickson [28] (Table A1). (HY – 12)

M 1. 2a

S: Mature plant leaves were collected in post-monsoon period during October to November. (HY – 01)

P: In order to assess the precision of measurements on the AAS, three consistency standards were treated as samples in each of the six runs in which the data were generated. (HY – 11)

C: A polished thick section of a Juan de Fuca chimney sulfide (collected from the seafloor on a previous Alvin dive 3468 – 5) was mounted on a glass slide, cut into square chips ($1 \times 1 \times 0.3$ cm, referred to as a "chip"), and incubated at the seafloor for 2 months along with other pure metal sulfides (Edwards et al. , 2003a). (HY – 18)

第五节　环境科学与工程

环境科学与工程是工科门类下的一个一级学科，该学科中包含多个二级学科。该学科中的市政工程主要涉及研究城市和工业给水工程、排水工程、水资源利用和固体废弃物处理与处置工程的规划、设计、施工、管理和运行。传统上的实验室实验或现场实验是市政工程中用到的主要实验方法。

本研究共从市政工程领域 11 种国际学术期刊中选取了 20 篇该领域传统实验类论文，主要涉及给水处理、污水处理及供水管网优化三大方向的研究。其中 80% 的文章为 2010 年后发表的论文，论文的第一作者通信地址均为英语国家或以英语为官方语言的国家。用于分析的句子共有 807 句，约 18837 个单词。句子数量最多的文章中有 67 句，最少的有 15 句，平均值为 40.35 句，标准差为 17.64。该学科论文方法部分均出现在引言后，即所分析的论文均遵循了 IMRD（C）的结构。此外，方法部分在正文中篇幅占比较低，最大值为 38%，最小值为 8%，平均值为 18%，标准差为 0.075，各篇总体差异不大。

一　标题特征分析

图 4.5.1 和图 4.5.2 分别是所分析论文实验方法部分的大小标题词汇云图。所有文章均包含一个一级大标题。如图所示，一级大标题中出现频率最高的是 method，共出现过 14 次，其次是 material，共出现过 11 次。而 experiment（al）和 setup 分别共出现过 5 次和 3 次。在所选文章中有十二篇均使用了 materials and methods 作为方法部分的大标题，还有三篇使用了 methods 作为标题。此外，experiment setup 共出现过 3 次，

experimental、experimental section 和 methodology 分别出现过 1 次。有 14 篇文章中使用了二级小标题，数量最多的有 10 个，最少的有 2 个。此外，有两篇文章中包含三级小标题。小标题中使用的词汇较分散，占比最高的为 membrane 和 nanoparticle；但是小标题中也会出现非专业性的词汇，如 sample、analysis、study、experiments、synthesis。

图 4.5.1　一级大标题词汇云图

图 4.5.2　二级小标题词汇云图

综上所述，该领域论文方法部分均包含一级大标题，大多数文章使用二级小标题，个别文章使用三级小标题。一级大标题与所研究的学科没有显著的相关性，二级小标题中出现频次较高的词汇与研究对象和研究手段关系更密切，三级小标题与所要测量的具体变量有关。此外，不同文章包含的小标题数量存在一定的差异。

二 语步特征分析

本节主要研究该学科论文实验方法写作的语步特征。分析发现该学科论文这部分写作的总体语步框架可以分为三个大的语步，与本研究中涉及的其他几个学科相似，但是不同学科各语步中包含的步骤种类存在一定的差异，本节各语步列表中只列出该学科论文中出现的步骤。

（一）语步一特征

表4.5.1是语步一中所包含的步骤种类。如表所示，语步一中共包括了9个步骤。表4.5.2是各篇文章语步一中各步骤在该语步中的占比情况。如表所示，所有文章中均包含语步一。但该语步中各步骤在各篇文章中占比情况不一。此外，同一个步骤在不同文章中的占比情况也有所差异。以下是针对每个步骤占比情况的具体分析及实例。

表4.5.1 　　　　　　　　　语步一各步骤列表

M			
	语步一、实验准备		
1.1B	重述研究目的	1.2d	样本/材料/数据预处理或培养方法
1.1C	交代实验时间/场所	1.3a	实验条件及注意事项
1.2a	样本来源/数量/特点	1.5	前人实验准备方法
1.2b	材料/数据/试剂来源/数量及特点	1.6	强调实验准备的合理性
1.2c	样本/材料/数据选取方法		

表4.5.2 　　　　　　　　　语步一各步骤占比

M	1.1B	1.1C	1.2a	1.2b	1.2c	1.2d	1.3a	1.5	1.6
SZ－01	—	—	—	43%	—	57%	—	—	—
SZ－02	—	—	—	—	100%	—	—	—	—
SZ－03	—	—	11%	—	56%	11%	—	22%	—
SZ－04	—	—	63%	—	13%	19%	—	6%	—
SZ－05	—	—	22%	1%	25%	47%	—	—	5%

续表

M	1.1B	1.1C	1.2a	1.2b	1.2c	1.2d	1.3a	1.5	1.6
SZ－06	—	—	—	50%	—	17%	33%	—	—
SZ－07	—	—	—	5%	46%	28%	5%	13%	3%
SZ－08	—	—	—	63%	13%	25%	—	—	—
SZ－09	—	29%	—	5%	62%	5%	—	—	—
SZ－10	22%	33%	—	—	22%	—	—	—	22%
SZ－11	26%	—	11%	—	—	—	58%	—	5%
SZ－12	—	13%	13%	25%	25%	13%	—	—	13%
SZ－13	—	—	—	—	100%	—	—	—	—
SZ－14	—	—	—	—	—	100%	—	—	—
SZ－15	—	33%	67%	—	—	—	—	—	—
SZ－16	—	—	—	43%	29%	24%	5%	—	—
SZ－17	—	—	5%	5%	53%	32%	5%	—	—
SZ－18	—	—	60%	—	—	40%	—	—	—
SZ－19	—	—	—	44%	31%	10%	—	5%	10%
SZ－20	—	—	—	52%	—	48%	—	—	—

M 1.1B 重述研究目的：所选文章中有两篇包含该步骤。在这两篇文章中，该步骤在语步一中的占比分别为26%和22%。实例如下：

A daily monitoring program of the Pinheiros and Tietê Rivers was carried out over 2.5 years. The objective was to provide information to a special study on the performance of a tentative flotation system to reduce contamination in the Pinheiros River. (SZ－10)

In this paper the results are examined in more detail. ⋯ Whilst the EA samples are not focused on particular storm events they are important because the results, recorded in a public register, are used to judge compliance and support prosecutions for infringements. (SZ－11)

M 1.1C 交代实验时间/场所：所选文章中有20%的文章包含该步骤。在包含该步骤的文章中，该步骤在语步一中的占比最大值为33%，最小值为13%，平均值为27%，标准差为0.09。实例如下：

The sampling location (sewer manhole 368092) is located on the campus grounds but is just upstream of wastewater discharges from the university facilities (Figure 1), which avoids fluctuations and atypical inputs caused by university generated activities. (SZ－09)

Experiments were performed in a 1.54-m-wide, 45-m-long, and 1.2-m-deep glass-sided flume and a 2.4-m-wide, 25-m-long, and 0.6-m-deep flume in the Fluid Mechanics Laboratory at the University of Auckland. (SZ－15)

M 1.2a 样本来源/数量/特点：所选文章中有40%的文章包含该步骤。在包含该步骤的文章中，该步骤在语步一中的占比最大值为67%，最小值为5%，平均值为31%，标准差为0.25。实例如下：

The sludge sample that served as the inoculum for this study was obtained from the Jefferson Peak Wastewater Treatment Plant, which consists of an oxic tank followed by an anoxic membrane reactor, from where mixed liquor is recycled back to the oxic tank. (SZ－04)

The facility in this study has been worked on previously [Marcoux et al. (2017)] and is located in the City of St-Jerome, Quebec, Canada and takes its water from the Du Nord River that flows south from the Laurentian Mountains. (SZ－05)

M 1.2b 材料/数据/试剂来源/数量及特点：所选文章中有55%的文章包含该步骤。在包含该步骤的文章中，该步骤在语步一中的占比最大值为63%，最小值为1%，平均值为30%，标准差为0.22。实例如下：

Sodium persulfate and hexachloroethane were purchased from Sigma Aldrich (St. Louis, MO). (SZ－06)

Sodium persulfate ($Na_2S_2O_8$, 99%) and ferrous heptahydrate sulfate ($FeSO_4 \cdot 7H_2O$, 99.5%) were procured from HiMedia Laboratories Pvt. Ltd. (SZ－08)

M 1.2c 样本/材料/数据选取方法：所选文章中有65%的文章包含该步骤。在包含该步骤的文章中，该步骤在语步一中的占比最大值为100%，最小值为13%，平均值为44%，标准差为0.28。实例如下：

Batch experiments (100 ml) were conducted in 160 ml hermetically-closed serum bottles inoculated with 1.43 g volatile solids (VS) l－1 of fresh Anammox sludge. (SZ－03)

Unregulated DBPs were measured at sampling points S3, S6, S8, S10, S12 and DW. Average travel time after the first chlorination points is also indicated for each point in Fig. 1. (SZ－05)

M 1.2d 样本/材料/数据预处理或培养方法：所选文章中有75%的文章包含该步骤。在包含该步骤的文章中，该步骤在语步一中的占比最大值为100%，最小值为5%，平均值为32%，标准差为0.24。实例如下：

Nitrite was fixed at 5.29 mM and total ammonia (TA) was supplemented at 4, 8 and 32 mM. (SZ－03)

The treatment plant (Fig. 1) consists of a slightly modified conventional treatment train. Potassium permanganate ($KMnO_4$) is used on the raw water as a pre-oxidant. (SZ－05)

M 1.3a 实验条件及注意事项：所选文章中有 25% 的文章包含该步骤。在包含该步骤的文章中，该步骤在语步一中的占比最大值为 58%，最小值为 5%，平均值为 21%，标准差为 0.21。实例如下：

All reactions were conducted at 20 ± 2oC. (SZ－06)

The water level was initially set at 5 cm below the bed surface but in the Spring of 1993 it was raised to about 5 cm above the bed surface, in line with the water levels on the adjacent tertiary treatment beds where problems were being experienced with reed growth. (SZ－11)

M 1.5 前人实验准备方法：所选文章中有 20% 的文章包含该步骤。在包含该步骤的文章中，该步骤在语步一中的占比最大值为 22%，最小值为 5%，平均值为 12%，标准差为 0.07。实例如下：

Nutrients were added as previously reported (Puyol et al. , 2013a). (SZ－03)

Use of sodium thiosulfate to quench the persulfate and stop the reaction as previously shown by Kambhu et al. (2012). (SZ－07)

M 1.6 强调实验准备的合理性：所选文章中有 30% 的文章包含该步骤。在包含该步骤的文章中，该步骤在语步一中的占比最大值为 22%，最小值为 3%，平均值为 10%，标准差为 0.06。实例如下：

Sodium sulphite was preferred to ammonium chloride because it does not interfere with UV measurement when dosed adequately, while ammonium chloride forms monochloramines that exhibit high UV absorbance, thus causing interference. (SZ－05)

This monitoring program was the largest water quality data collection program ever held in the Brazil, with over 200, 000 water quality lab analyses. (SZ－10)

综上所述，所分析的文章中均包含了语步一。在该语步中，涉及篇章数最高的步骤是 M1.2d，最低的是 M1.1B，分别占所有文章的 75% 和 10%，平均值为 7.6 篇，占所有文章的 38%，标准差为 4.5。在这些文章中涉及步骤种类最多的有 6 种，最低的只有 1 种，分别占语步一中所有步骤的 67% 和 11%，平均值为 3.4 种，占所有步骤的 38%，标准差为 1.6。不同文章中包含的步骤种类存在一定的差异，同一个步骤在不同文章中的占比也存在一定的差异。

（二）语步二特征

表 4.5.3 是语步二中所包含的步骤种类。该语步共包括 8 种步骤。表 4.5.4 是各篇文章语步二中各步骤在该语步中的占比情况。如表所示，所有文章均包括了该语步，但该语步中各步骤占比情况不

一。此外，同一个步骤在不同文章中的占比情况也存在差异。以下是针对每个步骤占比情况的具体分析及实例。

表 4.5.3　　　　　　　　　　**语步二各步骤列表**

M	语步二、变量测量		
2.1	概述变量测量设计	2.3b	测试/获取相关变量
2.2a	交代仪器/设备/工具/理论/方程/模型	2.4	描述变量测量步骤
2.2b	实验参数设置	2.5	前人变量测量方法
2.3a	定义变量	2.6	强调变量测量方法的科学性

表 4.5.4　　　　　　　　　　**语步二各步骤占比**

M	2.1	2.2a	2.2b	2.3a	2.3b	2.4	2.5	2.6
SZ – 01	—	13%	11%	—	1%	65%	10%	—
SZ – 02	7%	18%	4%	36%	7%	29%		
SZ – 03		36%	—	—	20%	33%	11%	
SZ – 04	—	28%	12%	—	8%	39%	3%	10%
SZ – 05		16%	19%		20%	27%	3%	14%
SZ – 06	—	30%	24%	—	2%	19%	13%	12%
SZ – 07	—	27%	3%	—		65%	3%	1%
SZ – 08	9%	37%	4%	—		41%	9%	—
SZ – 09	3%	24%	4%		3%	61%	3%	3%
SZ – 10	—	—	—	—	100%	—	—	—
SZ – 11	—		—	—	—	86%	—	14%
SZ – 12	30%	5%	—			65%	—	—
SZ – 13	—	26%	5%	—		49%	11%	9%
SZ – 14		52%	6%			42%	—	—
SZ – 15	4%	45%	13%	—		29%	2%	7%
SZ – 16	—	34%	1%	—		65%	—	—
SZ – 17	—	—	—	—		70%	10%	20%
SZ – 18	—	97%				3%	—	—

M	2.1	2.2a	2.2b	2.3a	2.3b	2.4	2.5	2.6
SZ－19	—	39%	2%	—	—	53%	6%	—
SZ－20	4%	8%	5%		—	83%	—	—

M 2.1 概述变量测量设计：所选文章中有30%的文章包含该步骤。在包含该步骤的文章中，该步骤在语步二中的占比最大值为30%，最小值为3%，平均值为9%，标准差为0.09。实例如下：

Experiments were conducted in 3 categories with either individual or binary or ternary activation techniques (with combinations of ultrasound, Fe2 + and UVC) for activation of persulfate. As base case for comparison of decolorization results, experiments were also conducted with individual technique of sonolysis, UVC treatment with mechanical stirring and persulfate treatment with mechanical stirring. (SZ－08)

The fate and behavior of nine biocides used for material protection of building envelopes was studied (Table 1). Paints and plasters of facades and roof waterproofing membranes for flat roofs (bitumen and plastic sheets) are considered as potential sources. Ongoing experiments cover different scales from laboratory, small-scale model systems to watershed level. (SZ－12)

M 2.2a 交代仪器/设备/工具/理论/方程/模型：所选文章中有85%的文章包含该步骤。在包含该步骤的文章中，该步骤在语步二中的占比最大值为97%，最小值为5%，平均值为31%，标准差为0.2。实例如下：

A digital PIV system (LaVision, Germany) was used to measure the velocity distributions in the scour hole. (SZ－13)

The eluents were evaporated using a N-Evap nitrogen evaporator (Thompson, Clear Brook, VA) to approximately 0.4 mL. (SZ－09)

M 2.2b 实验参数设置：所选文章中有70%的文章包含该步骤。在包含该步骤的文章中，该步骤在语步二中的占比最大值为24%，最小值为1%，平均值为8%，标准差为0.06。实例如下：

A constant potential of 0.8 V was applied for the anodic polymerization in a stirred N_2-gas saturated solution. (SZ－01)

Free-flow tests were run at gate openings of 0.0381, 0.0762, 0.1143, 0.1524, and 0.1905 m. (SZ－14)

M 2.3a 定义变量：所选文章中只有一篇包含该步骤。在该篇文章中，该步骤在语步二中的占比为36%。实例如下：

Both nitrification capacities were expressed in terms of suspended biomass concentration for the mixed liquor samples and media surface area for the media samples. (SZ – 02)

M 2.3b 测试/获取相关变量：所选文章中有40%的文章包含该步骤。在包含该步骤的文章中，该步骤在语步二中的占比最大值为100%，最小值为1%，平均值为20%，标准差为0.31。实例如下：

Ammonia was analysed using the salicylate method (Hach 10023) with the same spectro-photometer. (SZ – 05)

The concentration of the extracted DNA/RNA was measured using a Nanodrop spectropho-tometer (Nano-Drop Technologies, USA). (SZ – 04)

M 2.4 描述变量测量步骤：所选文章中有95%的文章包含该步骤。在包含该步骤的文章中，该步骤在语步二中的占比最大值为86%，最小值为3%，平均值为49%，标准差为0.22。实例如下：

Samples were then mixed on a vortex mixer and allowed to settle for 24 h in the dark before analyzing on a Packard 1900 TR liquid scintillation counter (LSC; Packard instrument Co, Downers Grove, IL). (SZ – 07)

After the model was installed in the recess boxes, the bed surface was compacted and leveled, and was filled with water gradually to avoid disturbing leveled sediments. (SZ – 15)

M 2.5 前人变量测量方法：所选文章中有60%的文章包含该步骤。在包含该步骤的文章中，该步骤在语步二中的占比最大值为13%，最小值为2%，平均值为7%，标准差为0.04。实例如下：

For UVC-activated persulfate treatment for decolorization, the pH of the reaction mixture was set at optimum value of 6.5, as reported by Gao et al. ［50］. (SZ – 08)

Gold nanoparticles were formed in situ on membranes using a modified method from Kumar et al. (2009). (SZ – 19)

M 2.6 强调变量测量方法的科学性：所选文章中有45%的文章包含该步骤。在包含该步骤的文章中，该步骤在语步二中的占比最大值为20%，最小值为1%，平均值为10%，标准差为0.06。实例如下：

A test of replicate extractions was performed to ensure reproducible yields from the DNA/RNA extractions. (SZ – 04)

However, in the present study, increasing skewness to the flow was inevitably accompanied-by a stronger shallowing effect, thereby complicating the mechanism of scour at complex piers. (SZ – 15)

综上所述，所分析的文章均包含语步二。在该语步中，涉及篇章数最高的步骤是 M2.4，最低的是 M2.3a，分别占所有文章的95%和

5%，平均值为10.75篇，占所有文章的54%，标准差为5.95。在这些文章中涉及步骤种类最多的有7种，最低的只有1种，分别占语步二中所有步骤的88%和13%，平均值为4.3种，占所有步骤的54%，标准差为1.66。不同文章包含的步骤种类存在一定的差异，同一个步骤在不同文章中的占比也存在一定的差异。

（三）语步三特征

表4.5.5是语步三中包含的步骤种类。如表所示，该语步中共包括了5个步骤。表4.5.6是各篇文章语步三中各步骤在该语步中的占比情况。如表所示，有一部分文章中不包含语步三。在包含该步骤的文章中，该语步中各步骤占比情况不一。此外，同一个步骤在不同文章中的占比情况也有所差异。以下是针对每个步骤占比情况的具体分析及实例。

表4.5.5　　　　　　　　　　语步三各步骤列表

M	语步三、数据分析		
3.1	描述数据分析工具/符号	3.4	获取本研究数据/所研发软件途径
3.2	描述数据统计方法	3.6	强调数据分析方法的合理性
3.3	前人数据分析方法		

表4.5.6　　　　　　　　　　语步三各步骤占比

M	3.1	3.2	3.3	3.4	3.6
SZ-01	—	—	—	—	—
SZ-02	—	—	—	—	—
SZ-03	—	—	50%	50%	—
SZ-04	—	100%	—	—	—
SZ-05	—	—	—	—	—
SZ-06	50%	25%	—	—	25%
SZ-07	—	—	—	—	—

M	3.1	3.2	3.3	3.4	3.6
SZ-08	—	100%	—	—	—
SZ-09	13%	88%	—	—	—
SZ-10	—	91%	5%	—	5%
SZ-11	9%	27%	—	—	64%
SZ-12	—	—	—	—	—
SZ-13	—	50%	—	—	50%
SZ-14	—	100%	—	—	—
SZ-15	—	—	—	—	—
SZ-16	—	—	—	—	—
SZ-17	12%	71%	2%	—	15%
SZ-18	—	—	—	—	—
SZ-19	50%	50%	—	—	—
SZ-20	—	50%	—	—	50%

M 3.1 描述数据分析工具/符号：所选文章中有 25% 的文章包含该步骤。在包含该步骤的文章中，该步骤在语步三中的占比最大值为 50%，最小值为 9%，平均值为 27%，标准差为 0.19。实例如下：

Stepwise regression was used for the selection of response surface model terms, with all terms in the final model significant at p < 0.05. Response surfaces representing first order rate constants for the loss of nitrobenzene and hexachloroethane were developed using Minitab 17® Statistical Software. (SZ-06)

The BSE images were analyzed using Image J64 software (NIH provided public domain Java image processing software). (SZ-19)

M 3.2 描述数据统计方法：所选文章中有 55% 的文章包含该步骤。在包含该步骤的文章中，该步骤在语步三中的占比最大值为 100%，最小值为 25%，平均值为 68%，标准差为 0.28。实例如下：

A melting curve analysis for the SYBR Green assay was prepared after amplification to distinguish the targeted PCR product from the non-targeted PCR product. (SZ-04)

For such markers, fluxes under dry weather conditions should be equal to fluxes under wetweather conditions（Eq. 1），where Cdry is the average marker concentration…and Qwet is the wet-weather sewage flow with RDII contribution.（SZ – 09）

M 3.3 前人数据分析方法：所选文章中有三篇文章包含该步骤。在这三篇文章中，该步骤在语步三中的占比分别为 50%、5% 和 2%。实例如下：

Fittings of data to each equation and statistical analyses were performed as reported in a previous work（Puyol et al., 2013b）.（SZ – 03）

To evaluate the wash loads a Pollutant Mass Distribution × Runoff Volume methodology, described by Gupta & Saul, was used.（SZ – 10）

M 3.4 获取本研究数据/所研发软件途径：所选文章中只有一篇文章包含该步骤。在该篇文章中，该步骤在语步三中的占比为 50%。实例如下：

Derivations of Eqs.（1 – 3）can be accessed in the supplementary information.（SZ – 03）

M 3.6 强调数据分析方法的合理性：所选文章中有 30% 的文章包含该步骤。在包含该步骤的文章中，该步骤在语步三中的占比最大值为 64%，最小值为 5%，平均值为 34%，标准差为 0.2。实例如下：

Although Stretton on Fosse was treated a special case, Severn Trent Water had been building combined storm and tertiary treatment reed beds since 1992.（SZ – 11）

In combination with the L1 regularization using rectified linear units（ReLU）further encourages sparsity in the network, which has several computational and representational advantages（Glorot et al., 2011）.（SZ – 17）

综上所述，在所分析的文章中有 40% 不包含语步三。在包含该步骤的文章中，该语步中涉及篇章数最高的步骤是 M3.2，最低的是 M3.4，分别占所有文章的 55% 和 5%。各篇文章中语步三各步骤涉及篇章数平均值为 5.2 篇，占所有文章的 26%，标准差为 3.77。在包含该步骤的文章中，涉及步骤种类最多的有 4 种，最低的只有 1 种，分别占语步三中所有步骤的 80% 和 20%，平均值为 2.17 种，占所有步骤的 43%，标准差为 0.94。不同文章中包含的步骤种类存在一定的差异，同一个步骤在不同文章中的占比也存在一定的差异。

（四）语步占比及轨迹

图 4.5.3 是所分析各篇文章中三个语步总体占比。如图所示，所有文章均包含语步一和语步二，有 40% 的文章不包含语步三。就各个语步占比而言，80% 的文章语步二占比最高，分别有 10% 的文章

语步一和语步三占比最高。在语步二占比最高的文章中，有70%的文章语步一占比高于语步三。有5%的文章这两个语步占比相同，还有5%的文章语步三占比高于语步一。在语步一占比最高的两篇文章中，其中一篇语步二占比高于语步三，另一篇则相反。

就各步骤在所有语步中占比平均值来看，占比最高的前三个步骤依次为M2.4、M2.2a和M1.2c。占比最低的分别是M3.4、M3.3和M2.3a。就各步骤涉及的篇章数而言，最高的也是M2.4，其次为M2.2a和M1.2d，分别占所有文章的95%、85%和75%。就各篇文章中包含的步骤种类来看，最多的有13种，占所有步骤种类的59%。最低的仅有4种，占所有步骤种类的18%。各篇文章中所包含步骤种类的平均值为9种，占所有步骤的41%，标准差为2.38。

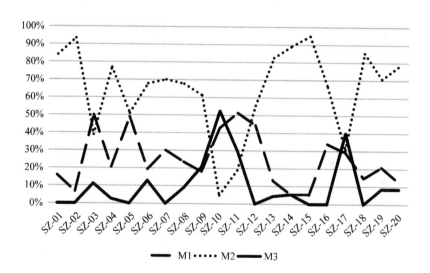

图4.5.3 各篇文章中三个语步占比

图4.5.4至图4.5.6分别为语步一、语步二和语步三的分布轨迹。如图所示，所有文章均包含了语步一和语步二，有八篇文章不包含语步三。

在不包含语步三的文章中，各篇文章中语步二占比均高于语步一，分布也较语步一广。有一半的文章最前部以语步一为主，同时语步一中部分语句也会分散分布在文章的其他位置，出现在语步二中。在另一半文章中，出现在文章最前的为语步二中部分语句，语步一主要分布在文章的前部、中间和后部。除一篇文章外，其他文章中语步一和语步二均有交叉。

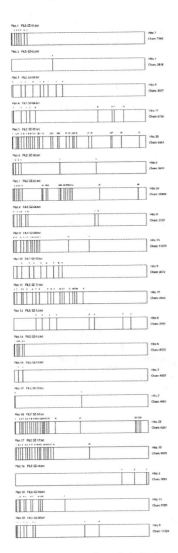

图 4.5.4　语步一分布轨迹

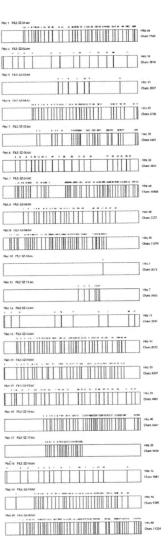

图 4.5.5　语步二分布轨迹

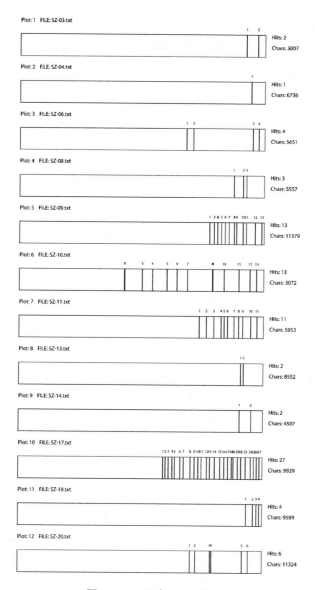

图 4.5.6　语步三分布轨迹

在包含三个语步的文章中，语步二占比均最高，分布也最广，语步一略高于语步三。各篇文章的最前部均为语步一，在其中三篇文章中语步一全部集中分布在语步二前，其他文章中均有少部分语步一分散分布在语步二中。除两篇文章最后为语步二外，其他各篇文章中分布在最后的均为语步三，其中有一篇文章中语步三与语步二有交叉，其他各篇中语步三与其他语步均没有交叉。语步二主要分布在语步一和语步三之间，在少数文章中有部分语句会出现在文章最前，在极少数文章中会出现在文章的最后。语步二与语步一交叉的情况较多，与语步三偶有交叉。

综上所述，同一学科不同文章中语步占比和分布轨迹既有相同之处，同时也存在一定的差异。所有文章中均出现了语步一和语步二，在绝大部分文章中语步二占比明显高于其他两个语步，语步一占比高于语步三。就这三个语步在方法部分的分布而言，语步二分布最广，几乎覆盖了方法部分的前部、中间及偏后的部位，语步一和语步三之间。语步一以文章最前和前部为主，语步三则以文章后部及最后为主。在绝大多数文章中语步二中会有少量语句与语步一有交叉，语步二与语步三交叉的情况少于语步一与语步二交叉的情况。语步一与语步三之间没有交叉。

三　语言特征分析

本小节主要分析论文实验方法写作部分的语言特征。主要从句子、时态和语态三个大的方面进行分析。针对句子的分析主要包含句子类型、四类主要句子长度分布及四类主要句子与语步之间的关系。针对时态的分析主要包含时态种类、不同时态组合及三种占比最高的时态组合与语步的关系。针对语态的分析主要包含语态种类、各语态组合与语步的关系。

（一）句子特征

A. 句子类型

表4.5.7是本学科20篇文章中所包含的句子类型及各类句子占比。如表所示，简单句、复杂句、复合句及复合复杂句占所有句子的97.39%。片段和有语法错误的句子占所有句子的0.37%。其他为带有冒号的各类特殊句子。四类句子中简单句占比远高于其他三类句子。复杂句和复合句占比非常接近，其中复杂句略高于复合句，复合复杂句最低。特殊类型句子形式多样，共有7种，其中NWS占比较高，其他的均较低。以下例句为特殊类型的句子。

表 4.5.7　　　　　　　　　　句类及占比

句类	句数	占比	句类	句数	占比
S	573	71.00%	NPW	1	0.12%
P	98	12.14%	NSW	1	0.12%
C	94	11.65%	NWAS	1	0.12%
CP	21	2.60%	NWC	1	0.12%
			NWS	10	1.24%
NWHP	1	0.12%	F	1	0.12%
NWHS	3	0.37%	R	2	0.25%

NWHP: Second, the scour development can be captured clearly while the scour hole can always be completely covered by the camera: Eq. 1 where U_e = average velocity at entry point; C_o = velocity coefficient, for which a value of 0.672 was proposed by Dey and Raikar (2007); g = gravitational acceleration; h_o = height of weir above tailwater surface; y_c = critical water depth upstream of weir; α = kinetic energy coefficient, which is approximately equal to 1.0 (Zhao et al., 2009); q = discharge per unit width; y_e = width of plunging jet at entry point; v = kinematic viscosity (= 1.007 × 10^{-6} m^2/s); and d_{50} = median particle diameter. (SZ – 13)

NWHS: The effects of pH and FA were simultaneously analyzed by a non-linear multiple regression procedure with two factors by plotting the NAA as a function of the pH and the TA concentration and fitting the data to the following surface equations: Eq. 1 where NAAmax is the maximum NAA, pHo is the optimum pH value, c is the standard deviation of the Gaussian distribution, K S-TA is the saturation constant for TA (mM TA), $\alpha 0$ is the unionized fraction factor FA/TA { $[\alpha 0 = 1/ [10 (9.1 - pH) + 1)]$ }, and Ki-FAKiFA is the inhibitory constant of FA to the Anammox process (mM FA). (SZ – 03)

NPW: Nonparametric test of the medians: the non-parametric tests do not require that data follow any specific distribution. (SZ – 10)

NSW: Significance test for comparing means: a null and an alternative hypothesis for a population parameter are defined. (SZ – 10)

NWAS: The flow field was illuminated by a double-cavity Nd: YAG laser (wavelength of 532 nm, power of 135 mJ per pulse, and pulse duration of 5 ns), which was manufactured by Litron (Rugby, United Kingdom). (SZ – 13)

NWC: Sample points A, B and C are marked in Fig 4 and they represent: A- before the RO inlet following the mixed bed in service cycle; B-RO reject for regeneration and C-waste stream following regeneration of the other mixed bed. (SZ – 18)

NWS: The first four MFCs test reactors contained: 1) AQDS immobilized with PVA particles (AQDS/PVA); 2) AQDS immobilized on the anode by electropolymerization (AQDS-anode); 3) a combination of both approaches, with immobilized AQDS on the PVA particles and with electropolymerization of AQDS on the anode (AQDS/PVA-anode); and 4) no AQDS addition. (SZ – 01)

B. 句类与语步

图 4.5.7 是四种类型句子与语步的关系。如图所示，四种类型句子中占比最高的前两个步骤完全一致，即最高的均为 M2.4，其次是 M2.2a，但是复合复杂句中 M2.2a 与 M3.2 占比相同。复杂句和复合复杂句中占比最高的三个步骤中均包含了 M3.2。其他两个步骤各类句子中均不相同。由于四类句子在文章中占比不同，即使相同步骤在这四类句子中排序一致，数量和占比也不相同。

这四类句子中均包含了三个语步，就各类句子包含的三个语步中步骤种类而言，简单句中包含了三个语步中所有步骤，复杂句、复合句、复合复杂句中包含的步骤种类分别占三个语步中所有步骤种类的 82%、68% 和 36%。

总体来说，不同句子类型与步骤之间的关系存在异同，句子与步骤关系紧密度与该类句子在所有句子中的占比有关，同时也与该步骤在所有步骤中的占比有关，但是不完全成一一对应的关系，句类与步骤之间没有明显的相关性。

以下是四类句子中步骤占比最高的前三个步骤例句。

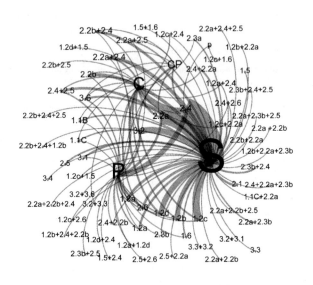

图 4.5.7 句类与步骤关系网络图

【S】

M 2. 4: The pyrrole monomer was purified two times by distillation prior to use. (SZ – 01)

M 2. 2a: A carbon brush was used as the working electrode, with a stainless steel mesh (50 × 50 mesh) counter electrode, and an Ag/AgCl reference electrode. (SZ – 01)

M 1. 2c: Batch experiments (100 ml) were conducted in 160 ml hermetically-closed serum bottles inoculated with 1. 43 g volatile solids (VS) l – 1 of fresh Anammox sludge. (SZ – 03)

【P】

M 2. 4: AQDS/PVA particles were initially equilibrated with a more concentrated RR2 solution (5 g L – 1) in order to ensure that particles added to the reactor did not appreciably deplete the soluble concentration of RR2. (SZ – 01)

M 2. 2a: Equation 1 implies simultaneous non-competitive inhibition by FA and pH limitation, whereas Eqs. (2, 3) indicate inhibition by FA or pH only, respectively. (SZ – 03)

M 3. 2: A positive value of synergy would mean that individual mechanisms of the two or three techniques reinforce each other's effect resulting in greater activation of persulfate anion that would result in higher sulfate radical generation leading to enhanced decolorization as compared to the sum total of decolorization obtained with the two individual techniques of persulfate activation. (SZ – 08)

【C】

M 2. 4: The electropolymerized electrodes were rinsed three times with distilled water and kept in distilled water saturated with N2 gas before use. (SZ – 01)

M 2. 2a: The first tank was filled with media at a 37% filling ratio, and the other two tanks were free of media. (SZ – 01)

M 1. 2d: Nitrite was fixed at 5. 29 mM and total ammonia (TA) was supplemented at 4, 8 and 32 mM. (SZ – 03)

【CP】

M 2. 4: Influent and effluent samples from both reactors were taken daily and analyzed immediately or stored in the refrigerator at 4℃ until they were analyzed. (SZ – 04)

M 2. 2a: The bed profile was uniform along the spanwise direction and was also quite even at any stage of the scourhole development (early, intermediate, or equilibrium), indicating that the flow inside the scour hole was two-dimensional (2D). (SZ – 13)

M 3. 2: Typically, the threshold (δ) for Huber loss is set to 1 and provides a loss function which is more robust and less sensitive to outliers. (SZ – 17)

C. 句类与句长：

表4.5.8是四类句子长度占比情况。如表所示，各类句子之间在长度分布方面相似情况不同。在长度分布占比方面，简单句与其他三类句子差异较大。简单句中句子长度占比最高的是单词数介于11—20的句子，其次是介于21—30的句子。其他三类句子占比最高的均为介于21—30的句子，复杂句和复合复杂句中占比第二的均为介于31—40的句子，复合句则为介于11—20的句子。就各类句子覆盖范围而言，简单句和复杂句长度跨度最广，复合复杂句跨度最小。但是简单句中短句占比高于复杂句。

就句子长度最大值而言，从高到低依次为复杂句、复合句、简单句和复合复杂句。但是复杂句和复合句较为接近，简单句和复合复杂句较为接近。句子长度最小值简单句最低，复合复杂句最高，其他两类句子相同，介于其中。如果不排除特殊类型句子，将每个公式算为一个单词的话，所有句子中最长的句子为NWHP，最短的为简单句。以下是所有句子中最长的NWHP例句和四类句子中最长和最短句子的例句。

表4.5.8　　　　　　　　四类句子长度分布

句长范围		1—10	11—20	21—30	31—40	41—50	51—60	61—70	MAX	MIX
S	句数	46	273	177	61	14	2	*	53	7
S	占比	8.03%	47.64%	30.89%	10.65%	2.44%	0.35%	*		
P	句数	*	21	37	26	8	4	2	63	12
P	占比	*	21.43%	37.76%	26.53%	8.16%	4.08%	2.04%		
C	句数	*	25	37	23	5	4	*	60	12
C	占比	*	26.60%	39.36%	24.47%	5.32%	4.26%	*		
CP	句数	*	*	8	7	6	*	*	50	25
CP	占比	*	*	38.10%	33.33%	28.57%	*	*		

NWHP/［**Max：102**］Second, the scour development can be captured clearly while the scour hole can always be completely covered by the camera Eq. 1 where U_e = average velocity at entry point; C_o = velocity coefficient, for which a value of 0. 672 was proposed by Dey and Raikar (2007); g = gravitational acceleration; h_o = height of weir above tailwater surface; y_c = critical water depth upstream of weir; α = kinetic energy coefficient, which is approximately equal to 1. 0 (Zhao et al. , 2009); q = discharge per unit width; y_e = width of plunging jet at entry point; v = kinematic viscosity (= 1. 007 × 10^{-6} m^2/s); and d_{50} = median particle diameter. (SZ – 13)

S/〔Max：53〕 Sampling locations were chosen to adequately characterize the impact of coagulation on natural organic matter (NOM) (RW, S1, S2, S4, S5) and to provide DBP concentrations after short and long reaction times in the reservoirs, before (S3, S6, S7, S8) and after (S9, S10, S11, S12, S13, DW) the addition of chlorine dioxide. (SZ – 05)

S/〔Min：7〕 Compounds were identified based on mass spectra. (SZ – 09)

P/〔Max：63〕 To pinpoint why the oxidant candles were not performing as well (i. e. , plateauing) after the 1st cycle, 2nd cycle persulfate candles were paired with a fresh Fe^0 candle (i. e. , a 1st cycle Fe^0 candle), a 2nd cycle Fe^0 candle that had its outer layer removed by scrapping and 2nd cycle Fe^0 candle that was chopped into smaller pieces to create more surface area. (SZ – 07)

P/〔Min：12〕 The anode solution was refreshed when the voltage decreased below 20 mV. (SZ – 01)

C/〔Max：60〕 Briefly, 10-fold serial dilutions of each sewage sample were made, and 20 mL of appropriate dilutions (usually the 10^{-6} and 10^{-5} dilutions for E. coli and the 10^{-4} and 10^{-3} dilutions for enterococci) were filtered through sterile $0. 45 - \mu m$ cellulose-ester membrane filters using vacuum filtration and placed on the modified mTEC agar plates (for E. coli) and the mEI agar plates (for enterococci). (SZ – 09)

C/〔Min：12〕 The bed was planted with P. austra/is and commissioned in September, 1992. (SZ – 11)

CP/〔Max：50〕 The wet-weather sewage flow (Qwet) can be expressed as the summation of a dry-weather average flow component (Qdry) and the RDII contribution (QRDII) (Eq. 2), and the ratio between QRDII and Qdry is defined as RRDII (Eq. 3), which is an indicator of the severity of RDII and sewer deterioration. (SZ – 09)

CP/〔Min：25〕 Typically, the threshold (δ) for Huber loss is set to 1 and provides a loss function which is more robust and less sensitive to outliers. (SZ – 17)

（二）时态特征

A. 时态种类及组合

表 4. 5. 9 是该学科论文中使用的时态类型及组合形式。如表所示，除去片段和有语法错误的句子，该学科文章中共出现了 8 种不同

的时态，其中 T7、T8 和 T11 没有单独使用，与其他时态共同出现在一个句子中。由不同时态构成的组合共有 9 种，均为两种时态组合，不同时态组合中包含 T3 的最多，其他时态在组合中占比均较低。

各种时态组合中，全部由一种时态构成的句子中占比最高的是 T3，其次为 T1。由不同时态构成的句子中占比最高的是由 T1 和 T3 两种不同时态构成的句子，其他相同或不同时态组合占比均较低。

以下是按照四种类型句子给出的相同时态和不同时态组合的例句，但不是所有时态组合中均包含这四类句子。

表 4.5.9　　　　　　　　时态类型及组合

时态	T1	T2	T3	T5	T10	T1T2	T1T3
句数	122	6	619	1	5	4	33
占比	15.16%	0.75%	76.89%	0.12%	0.62%	0.50%	4.10%
时态	T1T10	T2T3	T3T5	T3T7	T3T8	T3T10	T3T11
句数	2	2	5	1	2	1	2
占比	0.25%	0.25%	0.62%	0.12%	0.25%	0.12%	0.25%

【T1】

S： The results shown are based on duplicate reactors, with the results given as averages and standard deviations. (SZ – 01)

P： F Equation 1 implies simultaneous non-competitive inhibition by FA and pH limitation, whereas Eqs. (2, 3) indicate inhibition by FA or pH only, respectively. (SZ – 03)

C： Then the flow is set to a new discharge and the process repeated. (SZ – 14)

CP： The sampling location (sewer manhole 368092) is located on the campus grounds but is just upstream of wastewater discharges from the university facilities (Figure 1), which avoids fluctuations and atypical inputs caused by university generated activities. (SZ – 09)

【T2】

S： The analyses of regulated and unregulated DBPs has been described previously (Mercier Shanks et al., 2013). (SZ – 05)

C： The biocidal ingredients of all coatings and roof materials have been assessed and the initial biocides stock calculated. (SZ – 12)

【T3】

S: Polyvinyl alcohol (PVA, average molecular weight 89, 000 – 98, 000) and Reactive Red 2 (RR2, 40% purity) were purchased from Sigma-Aldrich. (SZ – 01)

P: The AQDS-PVA solution was then cooled at – 20℃ for 1 d to form a solid that was cut into squares (~1 to 2 mm^2 each) to produce particles containing the mediator. (SZ – 01)

C: A suspension of AQDS (10% w/v) was mixed with PVA (7% w/v) and heated to 80℃ to dissolve the PVA. (SZ – 01)

CP: Influent and effluent samples from both reactors were taken daily and analyzed immediately or stored in the refrigerator at 4℃ until they were analyzed. (SZ – 04)

【T5】

S: The other 20 sites had been commissioned or converted from stand alone storm or tertiary treatment beds at various dates up to June 1995. (SZ – 11)

【T10】

S: A sewage marker with stable flux should have a flux pattern reproducible each day and a limited secular variation within the study period. (SZ – 09)

【T1 T2】

P: Previous research has shown that this is within the optimum temperature range for the growth of anammox bacteria (Fernandez et al. , 2011). (SZ – 04)

C: Low-pressure membranes are also the more difficult polymeric membrane type to coat with nanoparticles due to larger pore size, and fewer demonstrations of nanoparticle coating of low-pressure water treatment membranes have been completed. (SZ – 19)

CP: The facility in this study has been worked on previously [Marcoux et al. (2017)] and is located in the City of St-Jerome, Quebec, Canada and takes its water from the Du Nord River that flows south from the Laurentian Mountains. (SZ – 05)

【T1 T3】

P: The sludge sample that served as the inoculum for this study was obtained from the Jefferson Peak Wastewater Treatment Plant, which consists of an oxic tank followed by an anoxic membrane reactor, from where mixed liquor is recycled back to the oxic tank. (SZ – 04)

C: Results from the triplicate reactions at each time point were averaged ; error bars represent the standard error of the mean. (SZ – 06)

CP: Hexachloroethane was used as a nucleophile t reductant probe because it has negligible reactivity with hydroxyl radical (k_{OH}. ≤ 1 × 10^6 M^{-1}s^{-1}) (Haag and Yao, 1992), but is reactive with superoxide and reductants (k_{O2}. = 400 M^{-1}s^{-1}) (Afanas'ev, 1989). (SZ – 06)

【T1 T10】

P: For such markers, fluxes under dry weather conditions should be equal to fluxes under wet weather conditions (Eq. 1) , where C_{dry} is the average marker concentration under dry-weather conditions, Qdry is the average sewage flow under dry-weather conditions, C_{wet} is the wetweather marker concentration under the influence of RDII, and Q_{wet} is the wet-weather sewage flow with RDII contribution. (SZ – 09)

【T2T3】

P：All network units, or nodes, contained a rectified linear activation function, which have shown to be both a better model of biological neurons with improved performance and sparsity. (SZ – 17)

C：The storms at the former have been described in Green et al. (1995) and Green and Martin (1996) and the storms at both were illustrated along with design details for both sites in Cooper et al. (1996) . (SZ – 11)

【T3T5】

C：The most recent of these, Shipston on Stour, had been commissioned in stages in 1997 and was not included in the data search and one site, Knightcote, had not been sampled by the EA. (SZ – 11)

P：To evaluate the possible toxic effects of RR2 and its reduction products, three consecutive experimental conditions were tested using the control lacking AQDS after it had been operated for 6 months. (SZ – 01)

【T3T7】

P：For one of the reactors, the sludge from the Jefferson Peak plant was mixed at a volumetric ratio of 1 : 0. 2 with anammox granules obtained from a treatment plant, which is being operated under anammox conditions in Austria. (SZ – 04)

【T3T8】

P：To pinpoint why the oxidant candles were not performing as well (i. e. , plateauing) after the 1st cycle, 2nd cycle persulfate candles were paired with a fresh Fe^0 candle (i. e. , a 1st cycle Fe^0 candle) , a 2nd cycle Fe^0 candle that had its outer layer removed by scrapping and 2nd cycle Fe^0 candle that was chopped into smaller pieces to create more surface area. (SZ – 07)

CP：The water level was initially set at 5cm below the bed surface but in the Spring of 1993 it was raised to about 5cm above the bed surface, in line with the water levels on the adjacent tertiary treatment beds where problems were being experienced with reed growth. (SZ – 11)

【T3T10】

P：The gate-lip seals were removed for the experiments so that we could make sure that we could properly model the phenomenon without the seals. (SZ – 14)

【T3T11】

P：In stage (ii) the medium was refreshed only one time with pre-acclimated bacteria from another MFC that had been running in fed batch mode for over 6 months. (SZ – 01)

B. 时态与语步

图 4.5.8 是该学科文章中三种占比较高的时态组合与语步的关系。如图所示，这三种组合中占比最高的前三个步骤中均包含了 M2.2a 和 M2.4，其他三个步骤均不相同。同一个步骤在这三种时态组合中排序不完全一致，即使排序一致，相同步骤在不同时态组合中数量和占比也不相同。此外，这三种时态组合形式中均包含了三个语步，就它们包含的步骤种类而言，T3 最高，其次为 T1 和 T1T3，它们所包含的步骤种类分别占所有步骤种类的 95%、86% 和 55%。

总体来说，不同时态形式的句子与语步的联系存在一定的差异，时态与步骤关系紧密度与该时态在所有句子中的占比有关，同时也与该步骤在所有步骤中的占比有关，但并不是决定性的。

以下是按照四种类型句子给出的三种时态组合中占比最高的前三个步骤的例句，但是有些步骤中不包含所有类型的句子。

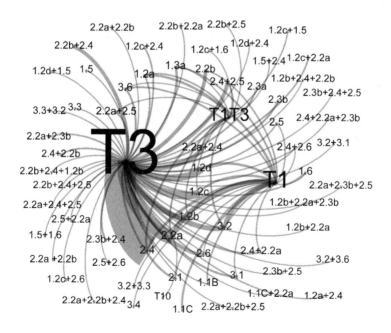

图 4.5.8　时态与步骤关系网络图

【T1】

M 2. 2a

S: A sketch of the experimental setup is provided in Figs. 1 (a and b). (SZ – 13)

P: Equation 1 implies simultaneous non-competitive inhibition by FA and pH limitation, whereas Eqs. (2, 3) indicate inhibition by FA or pH only, respectively. (SZ – 03)

C: Illustrations of the design and dimensions of Model A and Model B are shown in Figs. 1 (a – d); Figs. 1 (c and d) also show the flow field around thepiers. (SZ – 15)

CP: The trunnion-pin height is set at 0.366 m, and is placed 0.091 m upstream from the downstream end of the side walls, which, if scaled, is typical of SRP installations. (SZ – 14)

M 3. 2

S: Independently, RRDII can also be expressed as a function of sewage marker concentrations (Eq. 3). (SZ – 09)

P: The test gives information if two independent groups come from populations with the same median. (SZ – 10)

C: The decoder function receives the encoded vector as input and outputs the reconstructed input ($\hat{x}$) [i. e. $\hat{x} = g(z)$] (Fig. 1). (SZ – 17)

CP: The wet-weather sewage flow (Qwet) can be expressed as the summation of a dry-weather average flow component (Q_{dry}) and the RDII contribution (QRDII) (Eq. 2), and the ratio between QRDII and Q_{dry} is defined as RRDII (Eq. 3), which is an indicator of the severity of RDII and sewer deterioration. (SZ – 09)

M 2. 4

S: The results shown are based on duplicate reactors, with the results given as averages and standard deviations. (SZ – 01)

C: Then the flow is set to a new discharge and the process repeated. (SZ – 14)

【T1T3】

M 2. 4

P: The discharge limits were set at 25 mg 1^{-1} BOD$_5$. 45 mg J^{-1} TSS when flow is below the storm overflow threshold of 4.1 $1s^{-1}$ and 150 mg 1^{-1} TSS for flows exceeding this threshold. (SZ – 11)

CP: Once the flow stabilized, the water-level and velocity measurements were made, and discharge measurements were taken with an 30,000 L (8,000 gallon) weight tank system which is typically accurate to 0.1%. (SZ – 14)

M 2. 2a

P: The head-tank, flume and weigh-tank system has a capacity of 500 L/s, although this model was capable of handling only about 60 L/s. (SZ – 14)

CP: Fig. 5 shows the assembled system and Fig. S3 shows the photograph of the pilot testing floor in BGNDRF facility where the test was carried out. (SZ – 18)

M 1. 2a

P: The sludge sample that served as the inoculum for this study was obtained from the Jefferson Peak Wastewater Treatment Plant, which consists of an oxic tank followed by an anoxic membrane reactor, from where mixed liquor is recycled back to the oxic tank. (SZ – 04)

【T3】

M 2. 4

S: The pyrrole monomer was purified two times by distillation prior to use. (SZ – 01)

P: AQDS/PVA particles were initially equilibrated with a more concentrated RR2 solution (5 g L^{-1}) in order to ensure that particles added to the reactor did not appreciably deplete the soluble concentration of RR2. (SZ – 01)

C: The electropoly merized electrodes were rinsed three times with distilled water and kept in distilled water saturated with N_2 gas before use. (SZ – 01)

CP: Influent and effluent samples from both reactors were taken daily and analyzed immediately or stored in the refrigerator at 4℃ until they were analyzed. (SZ – 04)

M 2. 2a

S: A carbon brush was used as the working electrode, with a stainless steel mesh (50 × 50 mesh) counter electrode, and an Ag/AgCl reference electrode. (SZ – 01)

P: Each reactor had a volume of 2 l, which the membrane modules submerged in them. (SZ – 04)

C: The first tank was filled with media at a 37% filling ratio, and the other two tanks were free of media. (SZ – 02)

CP: The bed profile was uniform along the spanwise direction and was also quite even at any stage of the scourhole development (early, intermediate, or equilibrium), indicating that the flow inside the scour hole was two-dimensional (2D). (SZ – 13)

M 1. 2c

S: Experiments were carried out at 30 ± 0. 1℃ in an incubator shaker set at 3. 29 Newton to minimize the external diffusion contribution. (SZ – 03)

P: This resulted in a dataset with a large degree of variance in organic concentrations and characteristics that were all derived from common source water. (SZ – 17)

C: Mixed liquor samples were taken from each zone on a three times a week basis and analysed for BOD5soluble, CODsoluble, NH4 – N, NO2 – N and NO3 – N. (SZ – 02)

（三）语态特征

A. 语态种类及组合

表 4.5.10 是该学科文章中使用的不同语态组合类型，不包含片段和有语法错误的句子。如表所示，该学科文章中两种语态均出现了，同时还包含了这两种语态的组合形式。只包含 V2 的句子数量和占比最高，同时包含两种语态的句子数量和占比最低。所有文章中均包含了同一种语态构成的句子，但是只有 90% 的文章中包含由两种不同语态构成的句子。同一种语态构成的句子中均包括了简单句、复杂句、复合句和复合复杂句这四种类型的句子。两种不同语态构成的句子中包括了除简单句以外的三种类型的句子。

以下是按照四种类型句子给出的三种语态组合中的例句，但是有些语态组合中不包含所有类型的句子。

表 4.5.10　　　　　　语态类型及组合

语态	V1	V1V2	V2
句数	171	72	562
占比	21.24%	8.94%	69.81%

【V1】

S：All other chemicals were of reagent grade.（SZ - 01）

P：Previous research has shown that this is within the optimum temperature range for the growth of anammox bacteria（Fernandez et al., 2011）.（SZ - 04）

C：The injector and detector port temperatures were 200℃ and 250℃, respectively, the initial oven temperature was 60℃, the program rate was 30℃/min, and the final temperature was 180℃.（SZ - 06）

CP：The bed profile was uniform along the spanwise direction and was also quite even at any stage of the scourhole development（early, intermediate, or equilibrium）, indicating that the flow inside the scour hole was two-dimensional（2D）.（SZ - 13）

【V1V2】

P：AQDS/PVA particles were initially equilibrated with a more concentrated RR2 solution（5 g L^{-1}）in order to ensure that particles added to the reactor did not appreciably deplete the soluble concentration of RR2. (SZ – 01)

C: The first tank was filled with media at a 37% filling ratio, and the other two tanks were free of media. (SZ – 02)

CP: Hexachloroethane was used as a nucleophile t reductant probe because it has negligible reactivity with hydroxyl radical (k_{OH}. $\leqslant 1 \times 10^6$ M^{-1}s^{-1}) (Haag and Yao, 1992), but is reactive with superoxide and reductants (k_{O2}. = 400 M^{-1}s^{-1}) (Afanas/ev, 1989). (SZ – 06)

【V2】

S: Polyvinyl alcohol (PVA, average molecular weight 89, 000 – 98, 000) and Reactive Red 2 (RR2, 40% purity) were purchased from Sigma-Aldrich. (SZ – 01)

P: The AQDS-PVA solution was then cooled at – 20℃ for 1 d to form a solid that was cut into squares (~1 to 2 mm^2 each) to produce particles containing the mediator. (SZ – 01)

C: A suspension of AQDS (10% w/v) was mixed with PVA (7% w/v) and heated to 80℃ to dissolve the PVA. (SZ – 01)

CP: RR2 was then added to all MFCs at the same final concentration (0.3 mM), and the MFCs were again operated for several cycles until repeatable cycles of voltage were produced. (SZ – 01)

B. 语态与语步

图 4.5.9 是该学科文章中语态组合与语步的关系。如图所示，V1 和 V1V2 这两种语态组合中占比最高的前三个步骤完全相同，但是这三个步骤在这两种语态组合中的排序不完全一致。V2 语态组合中步骤占比最高的前两个也与 V1 和 V1V2 这两种组合相同，排序与 V1V2 相同，但是排在第三的步骤不同。即使相同步骤排序一致，在不同语态组合中数量和占比也不相同。

就这三种组合中包含的语步种类而言，它们均包含了三个语步，但是它们包含的步骤种类在所有步骤中占比不同。V2 占比最高，包含了三个语步中的所有步骤，其次为 V1，最低的是 V1V2，分别占所有步骤的 82% 和 77%。

总体来说，语态与步骤关系紧密度与该语态在所有句子中的占比有关，同时也与该步骤在所有步骤中的占比有一定的关系。

以下是按照四种类型句子给出的三种语态组合中占比最高的前三个步骤的例句，但是有些步骤中不包含所有类型的句子。

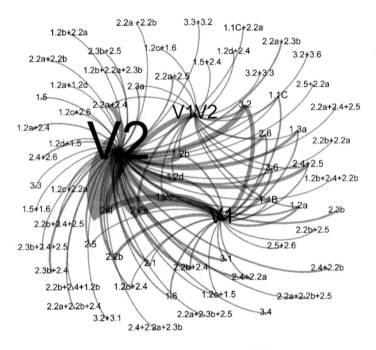

图 4.5.9 语态与步骤关系网络图

【V1】

M 2.2a

S: The media used was the AnoxKaldnes K1 media (AnoxKaldnes, Norway) with a 7.2mm length and a 9.1mm diameter leading to a total surface area of $800m^2 \cdot m^{-3}$ and a protected surface area of $500m^2 \cdot m^{-3}$. (SZ-02)

P: Equation 1 implies simultaneous non-competitive inhibition by FA and pH limitation, whereas Eqs. (2, 3) indicate inhibition by FA or pH only, respectively. (SZ-03)

C: The field of view was 280 × 210 mm; therefore, the spatial resolution for the present measurements was $2.8 \, mm^2$. (SZ-13)

CP: The bed profile was uniform along the spanwise direction and was also quite even at any stage of the scourhole development (early, intermediate, or equilibrium), indicating that the flow inside the scour hole was two-dimensional (2D). (SZ-13)

M 2.4

S: Stage (ii) consisted of addition of exoelectrogenic microorganisms to investigate the impact on recovery of current output. (SZ-01)

P: Comparative studies by our laboratory found that powdered persulfate lasted longer than ones made with un-ground persulfate. (SZ-07)

M 3. 2

S： The default significance level in statistical tests was P≤ 0.05 unless otherwise stated. (SZ – 09)

P： A positive value of synergy would mean that individual mechanisms of the two or three techniques reinforce each other's effect resulting in greater activation of persulfate anion that would result in higher sulfate radical generation leading to enhanced decolorization as compared to the sum total of decolorization obtained with the two individual techniques of persulfate activation. (SZ – 08)

C： The decoder function receives the encoded vector as input and outputs the reconstructed input ($\hat{x}$) (i. e. $\hat{x} = g(z)$) (Fig. 1). (SZ – 17)

CP： For several runs, we measured the pressure distribution within the jet and it was sufficiently hydrostatic, verifying that our single pressure readings were sufficient to define the contraction coefficient. (SZ – 14)

【V1 V2】

M 2. 4

P： AQDS/PVA particles were initially equilibrated with a more concentrated RR2 solution (5 g L^{-1}) in order to ensure that particles added to the reactor did not appreciably deplete the soluble concentration of RR2. (SZ – 01)

C： The concentration of nanoparticles deposited on the membrane was intended to be similar to the low loading from the AIDA-coated membranes; subsequent analysis (nanoparticle area by scanning electron microscopy) confirmed this. (SZ – 19)

CP： However, due to the disturbance of the plunging jet, it was noted that the water surface became wavy, which resulted in a nonunifrom distribution of laser light power and hence affected the quality of the particle images. (SZ – 13)

M 2. 2a

P： We used an anion exchange analytical column (Dionex IonPacTM AS11 – HC, RFICTM, 4250 mm) that was coupled with a guard column (Dionex IonPacTM AG11 – HC, RFICTM, 4 50 mm). (SZ – 07)

C： The first tank was filled with media at a 37% filling ratio, and the other two tanks were free of media. (SZ – 02)

CP： The trunnion-pin height is set at 0.366 m, and is placed 0.091 m upstream from the downstream end of the side walls, which, if scaled, is typical of SRP installations. (SZ – 14)

M 3. 2

P： Average marker flux differences and their 95% confidence intervals between the two dry-weather sampling periods, which flanks the wet-weather sampling periods, were calculated and plotted to indicate secular variations of marker fluxes. (SZ – 09)

CP: The wet-weather sewage flow (Q_{wet}) can be expressed as the summation of a dry-weather average flow component (Q_{dry}) and the RDII contribution (QRDII) (Eq. 2), and the ratio between QRDII and Q_{dry} is defined as RRDII (Eq. 3), which is an indicator of the severity of RDII and sewer deterioration. (SZ – 09)

【V2】

M 2.4

S: The pyrrole monomer was purified two times by distillation prior to use. (SZ – 01)

P: The electropolymerized electrodes were rinsed three times with distilled water and kept in distilled water saturated with N_2 gas before use. (SZ – 01)

C: These non-regulated DBPs were extracted using liquid extraction and were analysed with GC-ECD. (SZ – 05)

CP: Influent and effluent samples from both reactors were taken daily and analyzed immediately or stored in the refrigerator at 4℃ until they were analyzed. (SZ – 04)

M 2.2a

S: A carbon brush was used as the working electrode, with a stainless steel mesh (50 × 50 mesh) counter electrode, and an Ag/AgCl reference electrode. (SZ – 01)

P: The downstream water levels at Sections 2 and 3 were measured with the static side of a 5 mm-diameter Prandtl tube which was placed in the middle of the stream. (SZ – 13)

C: The particle images were recorded using a 14-bit charge-coupled device (CCD) camera with a resolution of 1, 600 × 1, 200 pixels and a sampling frequency of 14 Hz, and it was placed on one side of the channel, see Fig. 1 (a). (SZ – 13)

M 1.2d

S: The amount of AQDS was calculated from the total mass of AQDS-PVA obtained after cooling, with 2. 55 g of PVA-AQDS material containing 0. 5 g of AQDS, with these amounts of materials added to the solution of the MFCs. (SZ – 01)

P: The AQDS-PVA solution was then cooled at – 20℃ for 1 d to form a solid that was cut into squares (~1 to 2 mm^2 each) to produce particles containing the mediator. (SZ – 01)

C: The squares were mixed in H3BO3 (5% w/v) for 1 h to ensure crosslinking of the PVA, and then rinsed at least 3 times using distilled water. (SZ – 01)

第六节　化学学科

化学是一门以实验为基础的自然科学，化学作为一级学科包括无机化学、有机化学、物理化学和高分子化学。该学科研究手段主要为实验室研究。本研究主要分析该领域论文传统实验方法写作的体裁特征。

本研究共从该领域 15 种国际期刊中收集了 20 篇传统实验类实证性研究论文，用于分析的句子共有 573 句，约 12530 个单词。该部分包含句子最多的论文中有 72 句，最少的有 11 句，平均值为 28.65 句，标准差为 16.09。论文第一作者通信地址有 75% 为英语国家，论文均为 2010 年以后发表。

该学科实验方法部分在文章中出现的位置主要呈现出 3 种不同情况。有四篇论文的方法部分在 SI（Supplement Information）中，通常期刊中不刊登 SI，而是给出网址供读者查找。有九篇论文采用了 IMRD (C) 的结构，另外有七篇采用 IRD(C)M 的结构，即方法部分出现在正文的最后，这类文章中有 95% 没有独立的结尾部分（C）。方法部分在全文的篇幅占比最大值是 53.3%，最小值是 6.94%，平均值为 14.41%，标准差为 0.098，其中有 95% 的方法部分在全文中占比在 20% 以下。

一 标题特征分析

图 4.6.1 和图 4.6.2 分别是该学科论文方法部分大小标题中词汇使用情况。所选文章实验方法中均只包含一个部分，即一个一级大标题。大标题中主要使用到的词汇有 4 种，使用频率最高的为 experimental，共出现过 14 次；其次为 methods，共出现过 10 次，section 和 materials 分别出现过 6 次和 1 次。使用 experimental 单独作为标题的有四篇，与 methods 和 section 一起使用的分别为四篇和六篇，而单独使用 methods 为标题的有五篇，还有一篇标题使用了 materials and methods。所分析文章中六篇没有二级小标题，其他文章中二级小标题最多的有 8 个，最少的只有 1 个。各篇文章中均不包含三级小标题。二级小标题中出现频率最高的是 characterization，共出现了 15 次，其他较高的还有 material、synthesis、measurement、electrochemical 等。

图 4.6.1　一级大标题词汇云图

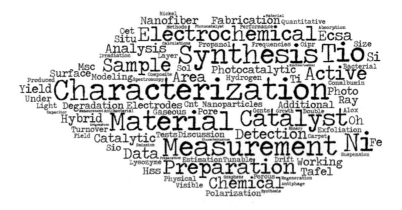

图 4.6.2　二级小标题词汇云图

综上所述，该领域论文方法部分均包含一级大标题，大部分文章同时包含二级小标题，各篇文章均不包含三级小标题。一级大标题与所研究的学科没有显著的相关性，二级小标题中词汇与研究对象和研究手段关系更密切。此外，不同文章包含的二级小标题数量存在一定的差异。

二　语步特征分析

本节主要研究论文实验方法写作的语步特征。分析发现该学科论文这部分写作的总体语步框架可以分为三个大的语步，与本研究中涉及的其他几个学科相似，但是不同学科中各语步中包含的步骤种类存在一定的差异。本节各语步列表中只列出该学科论文中出现的步骤。

（一）语步一特征

表4.6.1是语步一中所包含的步骤种类。如表所示，语步一中共包括了8个步骤。表4.6.2是各篇文章语步一中各步骤在该语步中的占比情况。如表所示，所有文章中均包括了该语步，但该语步中各步骤占比情况不一。此外，同一个步骤在不同文章中的占比情况也存在差异。以下是针对每个步骤占比情况的具体分析及实例。

表4.6.1 语步一各步骤列表

M	语步一、实验准备		
1.1C	交代实验时间/场所	1.2d	样本/材料/数据预处理或培养方法
1.2a	样本来源/数量/特点	1.3a	实验条件及注意事项
1.2b	材料/数据/试剂来源/数量及特点	1.5	前人实验准备方法
1.2c	样本/材料/数据选取方法	1.6	强调实验准备的合理性

表4.6.2 语步一各步骤占比

M	1.1C	1.2a	1.2b	1.2c	1.2d	1.3a	1.5	1.6
HX-01	—	14%	—	—	68%	14%	—	5%
HX-02	—	—	11%	—	57%	29%	—	4%
HX-03	—	—	—	—	65%	30%	5%	—
HX-04	—	—	21%	—	—	—	79%	—
HX-05	—	50%	—	—	50%	—	—	—
HX-06	—	—	—	100%	—	—	—	—
HX-07	—	16%	—	5%	5%	74%	—	—
HX-08	—	—	36%	45%	—	18%	—	—
HX-09	100%	—	—	—	—	—	—	—
HX-10	—	—	—	—	100%	—	—	—
HX-11	—	7%	33%	—	—	47%	13%	—

M	1.1C	1.2a	1.2b	1.2c	1.2d	1.3a	1.5	1.6
HX－12	—	—	59%	6%	—	35%	—	—
HX－13	—	—	—	—	—	25%	75%	—
HX－14	—	—	9%	5%	18%	68%	—	—
HX－15	—	14%	5%	—	62%	10%	—	10%
HX－16	—	—	—	15%	—	69%	15%	—
HX－17	—	29%	43%	—	—	14%	14%	—
HX－18	—	—	50%	—	50%	—	—	—
HX－19	—	17%	58%	—	—	—	25%	—
HX－20	—	13%	75%	—	—	—	13%	—

M 1.1C 交代实验时间/场所：所选文章中只有一篇包含该步骤。在该篇文章中，该步骤在语步一中的占比为 100%。实例如下：

In situ Ti K-edge XAS measurement were performed at beamline X18A at the National Syn-chrotron Light Source (NSLS) of the Brookhaven National Laboratory (BNL) using a Si (111) double-crystal monochromator, detuned to 40% of its original maximum intensity to eliminate high-order harmonics. (HX－09)

M 1.2a 样本来源/数量/特点：所选文章中有 40% 的文章包含该步骤。在包含该步骤的文章中，该步骤在语步一中的占比最大值为 50%，最小值为 7%，平均值为 19%，标准差为 0.13。实例如下：

Bulk mineral MoS_2 was purchased from SPI Supplies. (HX－01)

The anatase TiO_2 (101) sample employed in these studies is a natural mineral crystal ($5x5x1mm^3$) that was cleaned by repeated cycles of Ne ion sputtering and annealing in vacuum at 920 K. (HX－05)

M 1.2b 材料/数据/试剂来源/数量及特点：所选文章中有 55% 的文章包含该步骤。在包含该步骤的文章中，该步骤在语步一中的占比最大值为 75%，最小值为 5%，平均值为 36%，标准差为 0.22。实例如下：

Two-part epoxy [HYSOL 9460] was purchased from McMaster-Carr, and Nafion was pur-chased from FuelCellStore.com. (HX－02)

AgNWs were synthesized following the polyol reduction method described by Korte et al., using polyvinylpyrrolidone (PVP) and ethylene glycol as comediators. (HX－04)

M 1. 2c 样本/材料/数据选取方法：所选文章中有30%的文章包含该步骤。在包含该步骤的文章中，该步骤在语步一中的占比最大值为100%，最小值为5%，平均值为29%，标准差为0. 35。实例如下：

A rutile TiO_2（110）（1×1）single-crystal（MaTecK）sample was prepared by successive cycles of argon ion sputtering and annealing to 1000 K.（HX－06）

The TEM samples were prepared by deposition of the flakes from an isopropanol suspension on a lacey-200 mesh carbon-coated copper grid.（HX－08）

M 1. 2d 样本/材料/数据预处理或培养方法：所选文章中有45%的文章包含该步骤。在包含该步骤的文章中，该步骤在语步一中的占比最大值为100%，最小值为5%，平均值为53%，标准差为0. 26。实例如下：

Some microflake MoS_2 was further prepared by grinding it with a mortar and pestle in an attempt to make smaller flakes.（HX－01）

Starting at 220℃, the solution exhibited a stark color change and turned black. After holding the solution at 320℃ for 2 h, the reaction was cooled slowly by turning off the heating mantle until the solution reached 200℃.（HX－02）

M 1. 3a 实验条件及注意事项：所选文章中有60%的文章包含该步骤。在包含该步骤的文章中，该步骤在语步一中的占比最大值为74%，最小值为10%，平均值为36%，标准差为0. 22。实例如下：

The double layer capacitances were obtained as the follows: As-received, ～4. 14μF cm^{-2}; 700℃ annealed sample, ～0. 47μF cm^{-2}; 800℃ annealed sample, ～2. 95μF cm^{-2}; 900℃ annealed sample, ～2. 83μF cm^{-2}.（HX－01）

Because this procedure involves the high-temperature decomposition of a phosphine that can liberate phosphorus, this reaction should be considered as highly corrosive and flammable, and therefore should only be carried out by appropriately trained personnel using rigorously air-free conditions.（HX－02）

M 1. 5 前人实验准备方法：所选文章中有40%的文章包含该步骤。在包含该步骤的文章中，该步骤在语步一中的占比最大值为79%，最小值为5%，平均值为30%，标准差为0. 28。实例如下：

The G-Cu foil was grown based on our previously published method, and the GNR and CF were purchased from Merck EMD and Fuel Cells Etc. Inc.（XH－19）

AgNWs were synthesized following the polyol reduction method described by Korte et al., using polyvinylpyrrolidone（PVP）and ethylene glycol as comediators.[41]（HX－04）

M 1. 6 强调实验准备的合理性：所选文章中只有三篇文章包含该步骤。在这三篇文章中，该步骤在语步一中的占比分别为10%、4%和5%。实例如下：

After drying off the DMF solvent（about 5min）, repeat the suspension casting again. All samples termed as-received MoS$_2$ (bulk and microflake film) or as-ground (ground microflake film) underwent a 250℃ forming gas anneal for 3 hrs to clean the surface and remove any remaining DMF solvent. This temperature has essentially no effect on MoS$_2$. (HX – 01)

It is one of the best-studied bacteriophages, and extensive genetic and biochemical studies have been performed so far. Furthermore, Qβ is often used for evaluation of antiphage performance with photocatalysis. Therefore, we determined to use bacteriophage Qβ in our experiment. (HX – 15)

综上所述，所分析的文章中均包含语步一。在该语步中，涉及篇章数最高的步骤是 M1.3a，最低的是 M1.1C，分别占所有文章的 60% 和 5%，平均值为 7.25 篇，占所有文章的 36%，标准差为 3.77。在这些文章中涉及步骤种类最多的有 5 种，最低的只有 1 种，分别占语步一中所有步骤的 63% 和 13%，平均值为 2.9 种，占所有步骤的 36%，标准差为 1.17。不同文章中包含的步骤种类存在一定的差异，同一个步骤在不同文章中的占比也存在一定的差异。

（二）语步二特征

表 4.6.3 是语步二中所包含的步骤种类。该语步共包括了 7 种步骤。表 4.6.4 是各篇文章语步二中各步骤在该语步中的占比情况。如表所示，所有文章中均包括了该语步，但该语步中各步骤占比情况不一。此外，同一个步骤在不同文章中的占比情况也存在差异。以下是针对每个步骤占比情况的具体分析及实例。

表 4.6.3   **语步二各步骤列表**

M	语步二、变量测量		
2.1	概述变量测量设计	2.6	强调变量测量方法的科学性
2.2a	交代仪器/设备/工具/理论/方程/模型	2.6c	说明文字符号指代内容
2.4	描述变量测量步骤	2.7	对比实验
2.5	前人变量测量方法		

表 4.6.4　　　　　　　　　　语步二各步骤占比

M	2.1	2.2a	2.4	2.5	2.6	2.6c	2.7
HX – 01	—	51%	49%	—	—	—	—
HX – 02	6%	45%	45%	—	3%	—	—
HX – 03	—	78%	22%	—	—	—	—
HX – 04	—	100%	—	—	—	—	—
HX – 05	—	14%	86%	—	—	—	—
HX – 06	—	60%	40%	—	—	—	—
HX – 07	—	100%	—	—	—	—	—
HX – 08	—	32%	68%	—	—	—	—
HX – 09	41%	3%	56%	—	—	—	—
HX – 10	44%	44%	11%	—	—	—	—
HX – 11	—	24%	66%	—	3%	7%	—
HX – 12	9%	16%	69%	2%	2%	2%	—
HX – 13	18%	12%	64%	6%	—	—	—
HX – 14	16%	—	78%	2%	—	4%	—
HX – 15	8%	4%	71%	—	4%	13%	—
HX – 16	—	15%	85%	—	—	—	—
HX – 17	—	67%	33%	—	—	—	—
HX – 18	—	14%	86%	—	—	—	—
HX – 19	—	23%	75%	—	—	—	3%
HX – 20	—	54%	44%	2%	—	—	—

M 2.1 概述变量测量设计：所选文章中有 35% 的文章包含该步骤。在包含该步骤的文章中，该步骤在语步二中的占比最大值为 44%，最小值为 6%，平均值为 21%，标准差为 0.15。实例如下：

The synthesis of TiO_2@HSS was carried out according to previously described methods. (HX – 12)

A tetraethylorthosilicate $[Si(OEt)_4]$ and titanium isopropoxide $[Ti(OiPr)_4]$ based composite sols were prepared using various $Ti(OiPr)_4$ molar ratios. (HX – 13)

M 2.2a 交代仪器/设备/工具/理论/方程/模型：所选文章中有 95% 的文章包含该步骤。在包含该步骤的文章中，该步骤在语步二中的占比最大值为 100%，最小值为 3%，平均值为 40%，标准差为 0.3。实例如下：

The alkaline electrochemical measurements were performed in a single-compartment three electrode cell with Ti foil working electrodes, a Hg/HgO reference electrode, and a nickel mesh counter electrode. (HX - 02)

A scanning electron microscope, (SEM, Zeiss Supra 50VP, Germany) was used to obtain high-magnification images of the treated powders. (HX - 08)

M 2.4 描述变量测量步骤：所选文章中有 90% 的文章包含该步骤。在包含该步骤的文章中，该步骤在语步二中的占比最大值为 86%，最小值为 11%，平均值为 58%，标准差为 0.21。实例如下：

Ag paint was then used to fasten the foils to a polyvinylchloride PVC-coated Cu wire that had been threaded through a 6 mm diameter glass capillary. All surfaces except the Ni_2P-decorated side of the titanium electrode were then insulated from the solution by application of two-part epoxy. (HX - 02)

The annealing was performed at 750℃ for 3 min. After annealing, the carbon source was introduced and the growth time depended on the carpet growth height that was sought. (HX - 16)

M 2.5 前人变量测量方法：所选文章中有 20% 的文章包含该步骤。在包含该步骤的文章中，该步骤在语步二中的占比最大值为 6%，最小值为 2%，平均值为 3%，标准差为 0.02。实例如下：

The synthesis of TiO_2@HSS was carried out according to previously described methods. (HX - 12)

The synthetic details of this "mixed" sol solution is described in the references by Cornelius et al. . (HX - 13)

M 2.6 强调变量测量方法的科学性：所选文章中有 20% 的文章包含该步骤。在包含该步骤的文章中，该步骤在语步二中的占比最大值为 4%，最小值为 2%，平均值为 3%，标准差为 0.01。实例如下：

A constant value for the real hydrogen electrode (RHE) potential was maintained by continually bubbling the solution with ~1 atm of research-grade H_2 (g). (HX - 02)

The intrinsically rough and porous morphology of paper surface could provide good adhesion to MXene films with thicknesses in the range of $\approx 100 - 150 \mu m$ and mass loading of ≈ 1 mg cm^{-2}. (HX - 11)

M 2.6C 说明文字符号指代内容：所选文章中有 20% 的文章包含该步骤。在包含该步骤的文章中，该步骤在语步二中的占比最大值为 13%，最小值为 2%，平均值为 6%，标准差为 0.04。实例如下：

The collected MXene powder was dried and stored in a vacuum desiccator to avoid unwanted air oxidation and referred to as HF-etched MXene in this manuscript. (HX – 11)

These calcined samples will be referred as CHMx, where x is the Mg/Al molar ratio：2，3，5. (HX – 14)

M 2.7 对比实验：所选文章中只有一篇包含该步骤。在该篇文章中，该步骤在语步二中的占比为3%。实例如下：

Control experiments were done with e-beam evaporation of 1 nm of Fe, followed by 3 nm of Al_2O_3 over G-Cu substrate[3]. (HX – 19)

综上所述，所分析的文章中均包含语步二。在该语步中，涉及篇章数最高的步骤是 M2.2a，最低的是 M2.7，分别占所有文章的95%和5%，平均值为8.14篇，占所有文章的41%，标准差为7.29。这些文章中涉及步骤种类最多的有6种，最低的只有1种，分别占语步二中所有步骤的86%和14%，平均值为2.85种，占所有步骤的41%，标准差为1.31。不同文章中包含的步骤种类存在一定的差异，同一个步骤在不同文章中的占比也存在一定的差异。

（三）语步三特征

表4.6.5是语步三中所包含的步骤种类。如表所示，该语步中共包括了5个步骤。表4.6.6是各篇文章语步三中各步骤在该语步中的占比情况。如表所示，有一部分文章不包含该语步。在包含该步骤的文章中，该语步中各步骤占比情况不一。此外，同一个步骤在不同文章中的占比情况也有所差异。以下是针对每个步骤占比情况的具体分析及实例。

表4.6.5　　　　　　　　　　**语步三各步骤列表**

M	语步三、数据分析		
3.2	描述数据统计方法	3.7a	描述实验结果
3.4	获取本研究数据/所研发软件途径	3.9c	描述应用
3.5	分析实验结果		

表 4.6.6　　　　　　　　　语步三各步骤占比

M	3.2	3.4	3.5	3.7a	3.9c
HX－01	80%	—	—	20%	
HX－02			69%	31%	
HX－03	—	—	—	100%	
HX－04				—	—
HX－05	33%	—	33%	33%	
HX－06	—	—	—	100%	
HX－07	—	—	—	100%	
HX－08	100%	—	—	—	—
HX－09	—	100%			
HX－10	100%	—	—	—	—
HX－11	—	—	—	—	
HX－12	100%				
HX－13	—	—	43%	—	57%
HX－14	50%		50%		
HX－15	50%	—	—	—	50%
HX－16	14%			86%	
HX－17	—	—	50%	50%	
HX－18		—		—	—
HX－19	—	—	—	100%	
HX－20	50%	—	—	50%	—

M 3.2 描述数据统计方法：所选文章中有 45% 的文章包含该步骤。在包含该步骤的文章中，该步骤在语步三中的占比最大值为 100%，最小值为 14%，平均值为 64%，标准差为 0.3。实例如下：

The relative active surface areas are obtained from the relative values of the above double layer capacitances. (HX－01)

The photocatalytic activity toward 2-propanol degradation and the formation rate of CO_2 (described as kpro and R_{CO_2}, respectively) were calculated by assuming pseudo-first-order reaction kinetics. (HX－12)

M 3.4 获取本研究数据/所研发软件途径：所选文章中只有一篇包含该步骤。在该篇文章中，该步骤在语步三中的占比为 100%。实例如下：

Detailed information on sample and electrode preparation, electrochemical measurements can be found in the Supporting Information. (HX－09)

M 3.5 分析实验结果：所选文章中有25%的文章包含该步骤。在包含该步骤的文章中，该步骤在语步三中的占比最大值为69%，最小值为33%，平均值为49%，标准差为0.12。实例如下：

The b constant was kept the same for the forward and reverse rate, which implies that the symmetry factor α for the reaction barrier is equal to 0.5 for both catalysts. (HX－02)

A small fraction (＜0.6%) of these impurities could not be completely removed even after repeated (＞20) sputter/anneal cleaning cycles. (HX－05)

M 3.7a 描述实验结果：所选文章中有50%的文章包含该步骤。在包含该步骤的文章中，该步骤在语步三中的占比最大值为100%，最小值为20%，平均值为67%，标准差为0.32。实例如下：

Typically, a 10-min growth produced a CNT forest with a height of ~35 μm. (HX－17)

Typically, a 10-min growth period will yield carpet with a height of B60 mm. (HX－16)

M 3.9C 描述应用：所选文章中有两篇包含该步骤。在这两篇文章中，该步骤在语步三中的占比分别为50%和57%。实例如下：

The compositionally designed Si(OEt)$_4$ and Ti(OiPr)$_4$ based sols were generated in attempt to control homogeneity and optical clarity. These controlled sols were used to create nanoparticles, nanofibers, coatings, and monolithic structures as shown in Fig. 2. (HX－13)

For reference, 5 mg of a TiO$_2$ photocatalyst (Aeroxide P－25, Evonik) was used for testing inactivation of phage or bacteria in suspensions (50 mL) under UV light irradiation (0.12 mW/cm2). (HX－15)

综上所述，在所分析的文章中有15%的文章不包含语步三。在包含该步骤的文章中，涉及篇章数最高的步骤是M3.7a，占所有文章的50%；最低的为M3.4，占所有文章的5%。各篇文章中语步三各步骤涉及篇章数平均值为4.67篇，占所有文章的23%，标准差为4.03。在包含该步骤的文章中，涉及步骤种类最多的有3种，最低的只有1种，分别占语步三中所有步骤的50%和17%，平均值为1.65种，占所有步骤的27%，标准差为0.7。不同文章中包含的步骤种类存在一定的差异，同一个步骤在不同文章中占比也存在一定的差异。

（四）语步占比及轨迹

图4.6.3是所分析各篇文章中三个语步的总体占比。如图所示，所有文章中均包含了语步一和语步二，85%的文章包含了语步三。就

各个语步占比而言，85%的文章语步二占比最高，15%的文章语步一占比最高。在语步二占比最高的文章中，有 13 篇语步一占比高于语步三，有四篇语步三占比高于语步一。

就各步骤在所有语步中占比平均值来看，占比最高的前三个步骤依次为 M2.4、M2.2a 和 M1.2d。占比最低是 M1.1C。此外，M1.3b、M2.7、M2.8 和 M3.4 占比也均较低。就各步骤涉及的篇章数而言，最高的为 M2.2a，其次为 M2.4，分别占所有文章的 95% 和 90%。就各篇文章中包含的步骤种类来看，最多的有 12 种，占所有步骤种类的 57%。最低的仅有 3 种，占所有步骤种类的 14%。各篇文章中包含步骤种类的平均值为 7.1 种，占所有步骤的 34%，标准差为 2.31。

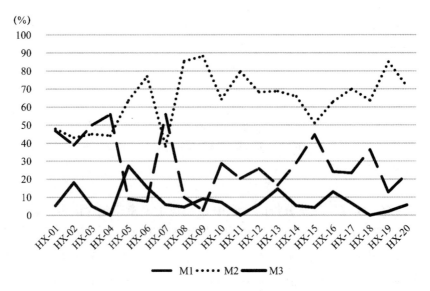

图 4.6.3　各篇文章中三个语步占比

图 4.6.4 至图 4.6.6 分别为语步一、语步二和语步三的分布轨迹。如图所示，所分析的文章中均包含了语步一和语步二，有三篇文章不包含语步三。

在不包含语步三的文章中，有一篇语步一占比高于语步二，其他两篇正好相反。这三篇文章的最前均为语步一，但是其中一篇文章语步一分布较分散，有大部分句子分散分布在语步二中。另外两篇文章中语步一均集中分布在语步二前，两个语步之间没有交叉。绝大部分文章最前以语步一为主，但有部分文章中分布在最前的为语步二中部分语句。此外，各篇文章中语步一分布均较分散，有一部分语句分布在文章的其他位置、语步二中。语步三分布也较分散，文章的前部、中间及后部均有分布。多篇文章中三个语步均有交叉。

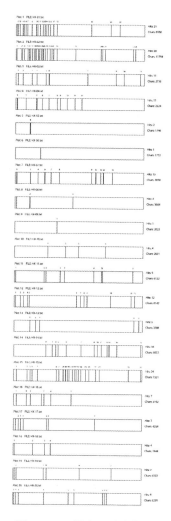

图 4.6.4　语步一分布轨迹

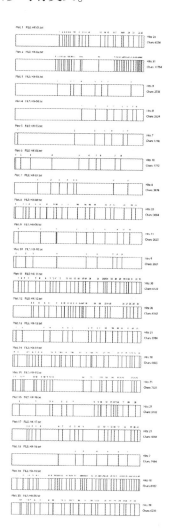

图 4.6.5　语步二分布轨迹

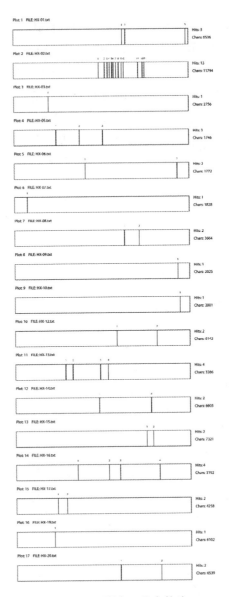

图4.6.6 语步三分布轨迹

综上所述，同一学科不同文章中语步占比和分布轨迹既有相同之处，同时也存在一定的差异。所有文章中均出现了语步一和语步二，在绝大部分文章中语步二占比明显高于其他两个语步，语步三占比最低。就这三个语步分布而言，语步二分布最广，几乎覆盖了方法部分的前部、中间及偏后的部位。语步一以文章最前和前部为主，但大部分文章中分布较为分散，有部分语句同时分布在文章的其他位置。语步三分布也较分散，极少数文章中分布在文章的最后，大部分文章中分散分布在文章的多个位置。三个语步交叉的情况较多。

三 语言特征分析

本小节主要分析论文实验方法部分的语言特征。主要从句子、时态和语态三个大的方面进行分析。针对句子的分析主要包含句子类型、四类主要句子长度分布及四类主要句子与语步之间的关系。针对时态的分析主要包含时态种类、不同时态组合及三种占比最高的时态组合与语步的关系。针对语态的分析主要包含语态种类及各语态组合与语步的关系。

（一）句子特征

A. 句子类型

表4.6.7是本学科20篇文章中所包含的句子类型及各类句子占比。如表所示，简单句、复杂句、复合句及复合复杂句占所有句子的98.43%，片段占所有句子的0.17%，其他为带有冒号的各类特殊句子。四类句子中简单句占比远高于其他三类句子，其次是复合句。其他两类句子占比均较低，其中复合复杂句最低。特殊类型句子共有5种，占比均较低，其中 NWS 占比略高。以下例句为特殊类型的句子。

表4.6.7　　　　　　　　　　　　句类及占比

句类	句数	占比	句类	句数	占比
S	443	77.31%	NSC	1	0.17%
P	46	8.03%	NWC	1	0.17%
C	69	12.04%	NWP	1	0.17%
CP	6	1.05%	NWS	4	0.70%
BWHC	1	0.17%	F	1	0.17%

BWHC: The Tafel equation (= b * log j + a, where is overpotential, j is the current density, b is the Tafel slope, and a is the Tafel constant) was applied to make Tafel plots of Log (j) and the Tafel slope, b, was obtained. (HX - 01)

NSC: Survival rate of pathogens in a mixed suspension of phage and bacteria was also examined as follows: photocatalyst (150 mg) was added to sterilized water (45 mL) and sonicated for 5 min, and then the solutions of phage and bacteria were added. (HX - 15)

NWC: The isolated powder was re-suspended using 1 : 3 (v : v) hexanes : ethanol and then was centrifuged again. (HX - 02)

NWP: The initial $Ti(OiPr)_4$ molar concentration within $Si(OEt)_4$ was x that was varied to create the following compositions: x = 0.1, 0.25, 0.5, 0.75, 0.9, and 1. (HX - 13)

NWS: The double layer capacitances were obtained as the follows: As-received, ~ 4.14F cm^{-2}; 700℃ annealed sample, ~ 0.47F cm^{-2}; 800℃ annealed sample, ~ 2.95F cm^{-2}; 900℃ annealed sample, ~ 2.83F cm^{-2}. (HX - 01)

B. 句类与语步

图 4.6.7 是四类句子与语步的关系。如图所示，除复合复杂句外，其他三类句子中包含的占比最高的前三个步骤均相同，其中简单句和复杂句中三个步骤排序完全一致，与复合句不同。复合复杂句中步骤占比均很低，分布也较分散，最高的为 M2.4，与其他三类句子一致。此外，由于四种句子在文章中占比不同，即使相同步骤在这四种句子中排序一致，数量和占比也不相同。

这四种类型句子中均包含了三个语步，就各类句子包含的三个语步中步骤种类而言，简单句中包含了四个语步中所有步骤，复杂句、复合句、复合复杂句包含的步骤种类分别占三个语步中所有步骤种类的 48%、57% 和 17%。

总体来说，不同句子类型与步骤之间的关系存在异同，句子与步骤关系紧密度与该类句子在所有句子中的占比有关，同时也与该步骤在所有步骤中的占比有关，但是不完全成一一对应的关系，句类与步骤之间没有明显的相关性。

以下是四类句子中步骤占比最高的前三个步骤例句。由于复合复杂句中步骤较分散，在此只给出占比较高的一个步骤例句。

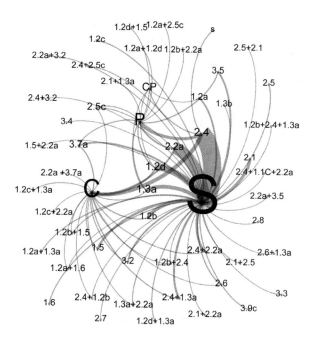

图 4.6.7　句类与步骤关系网络图

【S】

M 2. 4： N_2 was then flown over the headspace of the electrolyte during the measurements. (HX − 01)

M 2. 2a： Cyclic voltammetry was used at two different scan rates to obtain the data for the Tafel plots (5 mV/sec) and polarization curves (50 mV s^{-1}). (HX − 01)

M 1. 2d： Ni(acac)$_2$ (250 mg, 0. 98 mmol) was added to a 50-mL three-necked, round bottom flask containing a borosilicate stir bar. (HX − 02)

【P】

M 2. 4： A designed inorganic sol solution was placed in a syringe pump that was set at a constant feeding rate of 0. 5 mL/h. (HX − 13)

M 2. 2a： The XRD patterns were taken on a Rigaku SmartLab S4 system which is capable of measuring both grazing incidence and normal XRD patterns. (HX − 01)

M 1. 2d： After holding the solution at 320℃ for 2h, the reaction was cooled slowly by turning off the heating mantle until the solution reached 200℃. (HX − 02)

【C】

M 2. 4： Diffuse reflectance spectra were obtained on a UV-visible spectrometer (Jasco V-670)；

reflection data were converted into absorbance values by the Kubelka-Munk formula. (HX – 15)

M 1.2d: The resulting powder was re-suspended in hexanes and centrifuged one final time, and the supernatant was discarded. (HX – 02)

M 2.2a: Brunauer-Emmett-Teller (BET) surface area measurements were performed using a Micromeretics ASAP 2020 at liquid nitrogen temperatures, and the data were analyzed using the ASAP 2020 software version 3.04 (2007). (HX – 02)

【CP】

M 2.4: After the system was cooled to room temperature (RT), the NPs were precipitated by adding methanol, and the mixture was centrifuged at 4000rpm for 6min. (HX – 19)

C. 句类与句长

表4.6.8是四类句子长度占比情况。如表所示，各类句子在长度分布方面相似情况不同。在长度分布占比方面，简单句与其他三类句子差异较大。简单句中句子长度占比最高的是单词数介于11—20的句子，其次是介于21—30的句子。复杂句和复合句占比最高的均为介于21—30的句子，但是这两类句子中长度占比排在第二的有所不同。复合复杂句中介于21—30和介于31—40的句子占比相同。

就各类句子覆盖范围而言，简单句长度跨度最广，其次是复合复杂句，复杂句跨度最小。就句子长度最大值而言，从高到低依次为简单句、复合复杂句、复合句和复杂句，其中复杂句和复合句较接近。句子长度最小值简单句最低，复合复杂句最高，其他两类句子较接近，其中复杂句略高于复合句。如果不排除特殊类型句子，将每个公式算为一个单词的话，所有句子中最长和最短的句子均为简单句。

以下是四类句子中最长和最短句子的例句。

表4.6.8 四类句子长度分布

句长范围		1—10	11—20	21—30	31—40	41—50	51—60	61—70	71—80	MAX	MIX
S	句数	55	208	131	33	11	2	1	1	78	6
	占比	12.44%	47.06%	29.64%	7.47%	2.49%	0.45%	0.23%	0.23%		
P	句数	*	9	22	12	3	*	*	*	48	12
	占比	*	19.57%	47.83%	26.09%	6.52%	*	*	*		

句长范围		1—10	11—20	21—30	31—40	41—50	51—60	61—70	71—80	MAX	MIX
C	句数	1	17	25	15	11	*	*	*	51	10
	占比	1.45%	24.64%	36.23%	21.74%	15.94%	*	*	*		
CP	句数	*	1	2	2	*	*	1	*	65	20
	占比	*	16.67%	33.33%	33.33%	*	*	16.67%	*		

S/［**Max：78**］Solid-state NMR experiments were performed at room temperature on a Wide Bore 400 MHz 9.4 T Bruker Avance III HD NMR spectrometer equipped with a 4 mm HXY triple-resonance MAS probe (in double resonance mode) for 13C and 15N and with a 4 mm HX MAS probe for 109Ag or on a Wide Bore 850 MHz 20 T Bruker Avance II NMR spectrometer equipped with a 3.2 mm HXY triple-resonance MAS probe (in double resonance mode) for 13C. (HX – 07)

S/［**Min：6**］This material is called ground microflake. (HX – 01)

P/［**Max：44**］Exposed Ti atoms located on the bottom and top of the remaining Ti_3C_2 layers were saturated by OH (Figure 1b) or F groups, followed by full geometry optimization until all components of the residual forces became less than $0.01eV\text{Å}^{-1}$. (HX – 08)

P/［**Min：12**］The growth time depended on the CNT forest height that was sought. (HX – 17)

C/［**Max：49**］Ni_2P electrodes gave measured gas yields of $3.98 \pm 0.03mL(n = 4)$, and Pt electrodes also gave measured gas yields of $3.98 \pm 0.03mL(n = 3)$, as compared to the theoretical gas yield of 3.74 mL for passage of 30 coulombs of charge at 1 atm and 20℃ ambient conditions. (HX – 02)

C/［**Min：10**］All chemicals were analytical grade and used without further purification (HX – 19)

CP/［**Max：65**］Subsequently, the mixture of 13.4 mmol of TEOS and 2 mmol of APTES was added to the solution and vigorously stirred for 5 min in order to fabricate the silica shell around the O/W microemulsions, which was then aged for 2 h at room temperature under static conditions and left to age for another 24 h at 80℃ to form the rigid silica network. (HX – 12)

CP/［**Min：20**］After annealing, the carbon source was introduced and the growth time depended on the carpet growth height that was sought. (HX – 16)

（二）时态特征

A. 时态种类及占比

表4.6.9是该学科论文中使用的时态类型及组合形式。如表所示，除去片段，该学科文章中共出现了6种不同时态，其中T5没有单独使用，与其他时态共同出现在一个句子中。由不同时态构成的组

合共有 5 种，均为两种时态组合。不同时态组合中包含 T3 和 T1 的最多，均占所有组合的 60%，其他时态在组合中占比均较低。

各种时态组合中，全部由一种时态构成的句子中占比最高的是 T3，其次为 T1。由不同时态构成的句子中，占比最高的是由 T1 和 T3 两种不同时态构成的句子，其他相同或不同时态组合占比均较低。

以下是按照四种类型句子给出的相同时态和不同时态组合的例句，但不是所有时态组合中均包含这四类句子。

表 4.6.9　　　　　　　　　　时态类型及组合

时态	T1	T2	T3	T4	T10
句数	48	1	492	4	4
占比	8.39%	0.17%	86.01%	0.70%	0.70%
时态	T1T2	T1T3	T1T10	T3T5	T3T10
句数	1	15	4	2	1
占比	0.17%	2.62%	0.70%	0.35%	0.17%

【T1】

S：A detailed description of the experimental methods is presented in the SI. (HX－05)

P：The sample is denoted as STO：Rh (x%), where x refers to the Rh doping percentage. (HX－15)

C：The exfoliation goes fast, and the solution turns completely dark after a few seconds. (HX－03)

CP：Qβ is easier to utilize in experimental systems than other phages because Qβ is quite simple and is the smallest of the known phages; it has capsids with T = 3 icosahedral morphology without an envelope. (HX－15)

【T2】

S：Saturated calomel electrode (Pine Research Instrumentation) and graphite rod (Sigma Aldrich) have been used as reference and counter electrodes, respectively. (HX－03)

【T3】

S：The electrolyte was constantly stirred at 750RPM with a magnetic, Teflon coated, stir bar. (HX－01)

P：A designed inorganic sol solution was placed in a syringe pump that was set at a constant feeding rate of 0. 5 mL/h. (HX – 13)

C: Both powders were mixed to ensure homogeneity and then heated at 300℃ under argon. (HX – 03)

CP: After irradiation, serial dilutions of the phage were mixed with bacteria and plated in a double-agar-layer plaque assay, while serial dilutions of the bacterial suspension were plated to nutrient agar. (HX – 15)

【T4】

S: Typically, a 10-min growth will yield a carpet with a height of B120mm. (HX – 16)

【T10】

S: However, a Tafel fit would be similarly suitable for overpotentials > 15 – 20 mV. (HX – 02)

【T1T2】

C: It is one of the best-studied bacteriophages, and extensive genetic and biochemical studies have been performed so far. (HX – 15)

【T1T3】

P: However, the actual solution pH was altered due to the addition of metal alkoxide and isopropanol, which makes its measurement using a conductivity meter unreliable. (HX – 13)

C: The exchange current density was calculated from the Tafel plot and is also shown in Table S1. (HX – 01)

【T1T10】

P: If the rate determining step in HER is one of the above reactions, the Tafel slope should be close to either ~ 120 mV decade-1, ~ 40 mV decade-1, or ~ 30 mV decade-1 for the Volmer, the Heyrovsky, or the Tafel reaction respectively. (HX – 01)

C: According to the above considerations, the rate determining step for the as-received bulk MoS_2 is suggested to be the Volmer reaction (Tafel slope ~ 150 mV decade-1) and the annealed bulk MoS_2 samples could possibly be the Heyrovsky reaction (Tafel slope ~ 60 mV decade-1). (HX – 01)

CP: Because this procedure involves the high-temperature decomposition of a phosphine that can liberate phosphorus, this reaction should be considered as highly corrosive and flammable, and therefore should only be carried out by appropriately trained personnel using rigorously air-free conditions. (HX – 02)

【T3T5】

P: Ag paint was then used to fasten the foils to a polyvinylchloride PVC-coated Cu wire that had been threaded through a 6 mm diameter glass capillary. (HX – 02)

【T3T10】

P: Bulk mineral MoS_2 samples needed to be mounted before they could be used as electrodes. (HX – 01)

B. 时态与语步

图4.6.8是该学科文章中三种占比最高的时态组合与语步的关系。如图所示，三种时态组合中占比最高的前两个步骤均相同，T1和T1T3组合中这两个步骤排序完全一致，但是T3中正好相反。占比最高的第三个步骤均不同。即使各组合中步骤的排序完全一致，同一个步骤在不同时态组合中的数量和占比也均不同。

此外，这三种时态组合形式中均包含了三个语步，就它们包含的步骤种类而言，T3最高，其次为T1和T1T3，所包含的步骤种类分别占所有步骤种类的91%、70%和39%。

总体来说，不同时态形式的句子与语步的联系存在一定的差异，时态与步骤关系紧密度与该时态在所有句子中的占比有关，同时也与该步骤在所有步骤中的占比有关，但并不是决定性的。

以下是按照四种类型句子给出的三种时态组合中占比最高的前三个步骤的例句，但是有些步骤中不包含所有类型的句子。

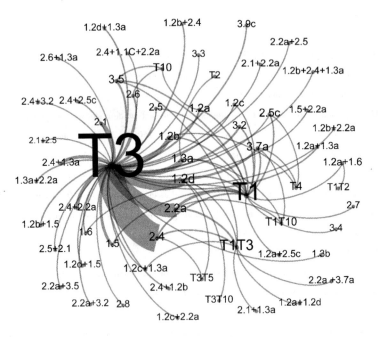

图4.6.8　时态与步骤关系网络图

【T1】

M 2. 2a

S： One is a low-temperature bath cryostat machine (LT STM) operated at 78 K with a base pressure of 3×10^{-11} mbar. (HX – 06)

P： The exchange current density (j_0) is also an important parameter which indicates the inherent catalytic activity of the material. (HX – 01)

C： This calculation takes into account the light-matter interaction in the reactor and considers all optical events (absorbance, transmittance, and reflectance) occurring in the catalyst-reactor system [31]. (HX – 20)

M 2. 4

S： At this stage, the surface of the TiO_2 NPs is decorated with OA by forming Ti-oleic acid moieties to give an oleophilic surface, allowing them to be uniformly dispersed in OA. (HX – 12)

P： In the simulations, molecules adsorbing on empty sites are immobilized, while the molecules adsorbing on top of already covered sites are allowed to diffuse randomly along the row until an empty site is found. (HX – 05)

M 3. 7a

S： Figure S3 shows the polarization data for four Ni_2P on Ti electrodes and one Pt electrode, along with a Butler-Volmer electrochemical kinetic model of the form. (HX – 02)

P： As evidenced by XPS [Figure S1, Supporting Information (SI)] and large area STM images (Figure S2, SI), our sample contains a small amount of impurities (i. e., Cr, Sb) that segregate from the bulk during vacuum annealing. (HX – 05)

C： The exfoliation goes fast, and the solution turns completely dark after a few seconds. (HX – 03)

【TTT3】

M 2. 2a

P： The XRD patterns were taken on a Rigaku SmartLab S4 system which is capable of measuring both grazing incidence and normal XRD patterns. (HX – 01)

M 2. 4

P： Theoretical surface area values were obtained by assuming that a 0. 5nm shell represents the surface of a solid 20nm particle. (HX – 02)

M 3. 5

P： The b constant was kept the same for the forward and reverse rate, which implies that the symmetry factor α for the reaction barrier is equal to 0. 5 for both catalysts. (HX – 02)

【T3】

M 2. 4

S： The electrolyte was constantly stirred at 750RPM with a magnetic, Teflon coated, stir bar. (HX－01)

P： In the LT-STM, Au was deposited onto as-prepared TiO_2 (110) at room temperature using a Au rod wrapped around a tungsten filament, which was resistively heated to induce Au sublimation. (HX－06)

C： The catalysts were activated before the reaction at 500℃ and were transferred immediately over the methanol to be used in the reaction to avoid contact with ambient water and CO_2. (HX－14)

CP： After the system was cooled to room temperature (RT), the NPs were precipitated by adding methanol, and the mixture was centrifuged at 4000rpm for 6min. (HX－19)

M 2. 2a

S： The experiments were performed in an ultrahigh vacuum (UHV) system equipped with Omicron low-temperature scanning tunneling microscope (LT-STM). (HX－05)

P： Transmission electron microscopy (TEM) images were collected using a JEOL 1200 EX-II microscope that was operated at an accelerating voltage of 80kV. (HX－02)

C： Brunauer-Emmett-Teller (BET) surface area measurements were performed using a using a Micromeretics ASAP 2020 at liquid nitrogen temperatures, and the data were analyzed using the ASAP 2020 software version 3. 04 (2007). (HX－02)

M 1. 2d

S： After 3 days, the black powder was immerged in water with a ratio of 1 mg/mL of water. (HX－03)

P： Phage was incubated in soft agar medium containing bacteria at 37℃ for 16h, whereas bacteria were incubated in nutrient broth liquid medium at 37℃ for 16h. (HX－15)

C： Both powders were mixed to ensure homogeneity and then heated at 300℃ under argon. (HX－03)

CP： After irradiation, serial dilutions of the phage were mixed with bacteria and plated in a double-agar-layer plaque assay, while serial dilutions of the bacterial suspension were plated to nutrient agar. (HX－15)

（三）语态特征

A. 语态种类及组合

表4.6.10是该学科文章中使用的不同语态组合类型，不包含片段和有语法错误的句子。如表所示，该学科文章中两种语态均有出

现，同时还包含了这两种语态的组合形式。只包含 V2 的句子数量和占比最高，同时包含两种语态的句子数量和占比最低。所有文章中均包含了由 V2 一种语态构成的句子，但是由 V1 一种语态构成的句子和由两种不同语态构成的句子分别只涉及 85% 和 75% 的文章。同一种语态构成的句子中均包括了简单句、复杂句、复合句和复合复杂句这四种类型的句子。两种不同语态构成的句子中包括了除简单句以外的三种类型的句子。

以下是按照四种类型句子给出的三种语态组合中的例句，但是有些语态组合中不包含所有类型的句子。

表 4. 6. 10 　　　　　　　　　语态类型及组合

语态	V1	V1V2	V2
句数	70	39	463
占比	12. 24%	6. 82%	80. 94%

【V1】

S: The collecting angle was between 100 and 267 mrad. (HX – 04)

P: The Ni_2P data showed an inconsistent deviation from linear Tafel behavior that also did not match the Butler-Volmer model at overpotentials below about 50 mV. (HX – 02)

C: The exfoliation goes fast, and the solution turns completely dark after a few seconds. (HX – 03)

CP: $Q\beta$ is easier to utilize in experimental systems than other phages because $Q\beta$ is quite simple and is the smallest of the known phages; it has capsids with T = 3 icosahedral morphology without an envelope. (HX – 15)

【V1V2】

P: The XRD patterns were taken on a Rigaku SmartLab S4 system which is capable of measuring both grazing incidence and normal XRD patterns. (HX – 01)

C: This approach produced uniform AgNWs with lengths of several microns and diameters of 63 ± 10 nm; the NWs were washed with acetone and water and dried under vacuum at 60℃. (HX – 04)

CP: After annealing, the carbon source was introduced and the growth time depended on the carpet growth height that was sought. (HX – 16)

【V2】

S：Electrical measurements were carried out at room temperature using a Keithley 4200 – SCS. (HX – 04)

P：Turnover frequencies were estimated per surface atom (both Ni and P) , rather than per hydrogen binding site, because the hydrogen binding sites are not explicitly known. (HX – 02)

C：The exchange current density was calculated from the Tafel plot and is also shown in Table S1. (HX – 01)

CP：After the system was cooled to room temperature (RT) , the NPs were precipitated by adding methanol, and the mixture was centrifuged at 4000 rpm for 6 min. (HX – 19)

B. 语态与语步

图 4.6.9 是该学科文章中三种不同语态组合与语步的关系。如图所示，三个语态组合中占比最高的前两个步骤均相同，其中 V2 和 V1V2 中这两个步骤排序相同，但是 V1 中排序恰巧相反。占比排在第三的步骤在各语态组合中均不同。即使各组合中步骤的排序完全一致，同一个步骤在不同语态组合中的数量和占比也均不同。

就这三种语态组合中包含的语步种类而言，它们全部包含了三个语步，但是其包含的步骤种类在所有步骤中占比不同。V2 包含了所有步骤，其他两个语态组合中步骤种类相同，均占所有步骤的61%。

总体来说，语态与步骤关系紧密度与该语态在所有句子中的占比有关，同时也与该步骤在所有步骤中的占比有一定的关系。

以下是按照四种类型句子给出的三种语态组合中占比最高的前三个步骤的例句，但是有些步骤中不包含所有类型的句子。

【V1】

M 2.2a

S：The collecting angle was between 100 and 267 mrad. (HX – 03)

P：If the rate determining step in HER is one of the above reactions, the Tafel slope should be close to either ~120 mV decade^{-1}, ~40 mV decade^{-1}, or ~30 mV decade^{-1} for the Volmer, the Heyrovsky, or the Tafel reaction respectively. (HX – 01)

C：This calculation takes into account the light-matter interaction in the reactor and considers all optical events (absorbance, transmittance, and reflectance) occurring in the catalyst-reactor system [31]. (HX – 20)

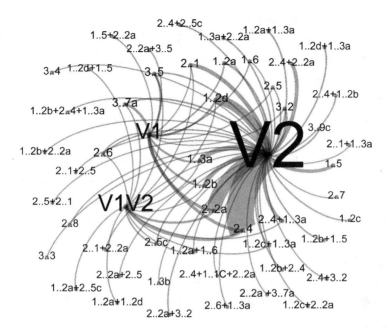

图 4.6.9 语态与步骤关系网络图

M 2.4

S： We employed electrochemical impedance spectroscopy, using a Biologic SP-300 potentiostat, at open circuit potential scanning frequencies from 10Hz to ~0.05Hz. (HX-01)

M 3.7a

S： There were no significant differences in Au coverage or dispersion seen in STM images recorded at 78 and 300 K. (HX-06)

P： As evidenced by XPS [Figure S1, Supporting Information (SI)] and large area STM images (Figure S2, SI), our sample contains a small amount of impurities (i.e., Cr, Sb) that segregate from the bulk during vacuum annealing. (HX-05)

C： The exfoliation goes fast, and the solution turns completely dark after a few seconds. (HX-03)

【V1V2】

M 2.4

P： Selected samples were repeatedly rinsed with distilled water until a test with silver nitrate did not detect chlorine ions at the solution. (HX-20)

C： The masses of Al (acac) 3 to prepare different Al：Fe ratios ranged from 0.01 to 0.28g;

all the other reagents remained the same, control experiments were performed with synthesis of only Fe (acac) 3 or Al (acac) 3. (HX – 19)

CP: After annealing, the carbon source was introduced and the growth time depended on the carpet growth height that was sought. (HX – 16)

M 2. 2a

P: The XRD patterns were taken on a Rigaku SmartLab S4 system which is capable of measuring both grazing incidence and normal XRD patterns. (HX – 01)

C: According to the above considerations, the rate determining step for the as-received bulk MoS_2 is suggested to be the Volmer reaction (Tafel slope ~ 150 mV decade^{-1}) and the annealed bulk MoS_2 samples could possibly be the Heyrovsky reaction (Tafel slope ~ 60 mV decade^{-1}). (HX – 01)

M 2. 5c

P: The sample is denoted as g-STO: Rh (y%), Sb (y%), where y refers to the Rh and Sb doping percentages. (HX – 15)

C: The Ti_3C_2 MXene prepared by this method contained intercalated Li ions and was referred to as clay-like MXene in the remaining part of this manuscript. (HX – 11)

【V2】

M 2. 4

S: The electrolyte was initially sparged with N_2 bubbling for more than 10 mins to remove oxygen. (HX – 01)

P: Turnover frequencies were estimated per surface atom (both Ni and P), rather than per hydrogen binding site, because the hydrogen binding sites are not explicitly known. (HX – 02)

C: The resulting suspension was washed several times with deionized water and filtered over mixed cellulose ester filter paper. (HX – 11)

CP: After the system was cooled to room temperature (RT), the NPs were precipitated by adding methanol, and the mixture was centrifuged at 4000 rpm for 6 min. (HX – 19)

M 2. 2a

S: Simulated XRD patterns were produced by the CrystalMaker/CrystalDiffract software package. (HX – 02)

P: Transmission electron microscopy (TEM) images were collected using a JEOL 1200 EX – II microscope that was operated at an accelerating voltage of 80 kV. (HX – 02)

C: Brunauer-Emmett-Teller (BET) surface area measurements were performed using a using a Micromeretics ASAP 2020 at liquid nitrogen temperatures, and the data were analyzed using the ASAP 2020 software version 3. 04 (2007). (HX – 02)

M 1. 2d

S: Prior to sealing the flask, 1-octadecene (4. 5 mL, 14. 1 mmol), oleylamine (6. 4 mL, 19. 5 mmol), and tri-n-octylphosphine (2 mL, 4. 4 mmol) were added to the vessel. (HX－02)

P: Ag paint was then used to fasten the foils to a polyvinylchloride PVC-coated Cu wire that had been threaded through a 6mm diameter glass capillary. (HX－02)

C: Both powders were mixed to ensure homogeneity and then heated at 300℃ under argon. (HX－03)

CP: After irradiation, serial dilutions of the phage were mixed with bacteria and plated in a double-agar-layer plaque assay, while serial dilutions of the bacterial suspension were plated to nutrient agar. (HX－15)

第七节 材料工程与科学

材料工程与科学主要研究材料组成、结构、工艺、性质和使用性能之间的相互关系。传统实验室实验是该学科主要实验方法。本研究共从该领域 14 种国际期刊中选取了 20 篇传统实验类论文。除一篇文章外，其他文章第一作者的通信地址均为英语国家或以英语为官方语言的国家。

本研究主要分析各篇文章实验方法的写作特征，用于分析的句子共计 543 句，单词共计 12023 个。句子数量最多的论文中有 39 句，最少的有 13 句，各篇平均值为 26. 85 句，标准差为 7. 82。方法部分在全文的占比平均值为 17%，最大值为 39%，最小值仅为 7%，标准差为 0. 098。该部分出现在文章中的位置呈现出 3 种情况：有七篇文章遵循了 IRD(C)M 结构，七篇遵循了 IMRD(C)结构，六篇文章的方法部分出现在补充材料中。

一 标题特征分析

图 4. 7. 1 和图 4. 7. 2 分别是方法部分大小标题中词汇使用情况。所选文章实验方法部分均只包含一个一级大标题。大标题中出现频率最高的词是 experimental，共出现过 13 次，其次是 section 和 methods，分别出现了 8 次和 5 次。有八篇文章中使用的标题是 experimental section，分别有四篇文章中使用的是 experimental details 和 materials and methods。除七篇文章外，其他各篇均使用了二级小标题，最多的有 5 个，最少的有 2 个。小标题中词汇分布比较分散，出现次数最高的是 characterization，共 7 次，其次是 preparation，共 6 次。此外，material 和 synthesis 均出现过 5 次。

图 4.7.1 一级大标题词汇云图

图 4.7.2 二级小标题词汇云图

综上所述，该领域论文方法部分均包含一个一级大标题，大部分文章中同时包含二级小标题，各篇文章中均不包含三级小标题。一级大标题与所研究的学科没有显著的相关性，二级小标题中词汇与研究对象和研究手段关系更密切。此外，不同文章中包含的二级小标题数量存在一定的差异。

二　语步特征分析

本节主要研究实验方法写作的语步特征。分析发现该学科这部分写作的总体框架可以分为三个大的语步，与本研究中涉及的其他几个学科相似，但是不同学科中各语步中包含的步骤种类存在一定的差异，本节各语步列表中只列出该学科论文中出现的步骤。

（一）语步一特征

表4.7.1是语步一中所包含的步骤种类。如表所示，语步一中共包括7个步骤。表4.7.2是各篇文章语步一中各步骤在该语步中的占比情况。如表所示，各篇文章均包含该语步，但在包含该步骤的文章中，该语步中各步骤在各篇文章中占比情况不一。此外，同一个步骤在不同文章中占比情况也有所差异。以下是针对每个步骤占比情况的具体分析及实例。

表4.7.1　　　　　　　　语步一各步骤列表

M	语步一、实验准备		
1.2a	样本来源/数量/特点	1.3a	实验条件及注意事项
1.2b	材料/数据/试剂来源/数量及特点	1.3b	样本/材料/数据局限性
1.2c	样本/材料/数据选取方法	1.5	前人实验准备方法
1.2d	样本/材料/数据预处理或培养方法		

表4.7.2　　　　　　　　语步一各步骤占比

M	1.2a	1.2b	1.2c	1.2d	1.3a	1.3b	1.5
CL－01	—	17%	25%	29%	29%	—	—
CL－02	9%	39%	—	22%	26%	—	4%
CL－03	—	23%	—	50%	18%	9%	—
CL－04	—	67%	—	17%	17%	—	—

续表

M	1.2a	1.2b	1.2c	1.2d	1.3a	1.3b	1.5
CL - 05	4%	13%	4%	29%	50%	—	—
CL - 06	—	25%	—	25%	25%	—	25%
CL - 07	43%	—	—	14%	43%	—	—
CL - 08	25%	—	—	—	75%	—	—
CL - 09	100%	—	—	—	—	—	—
CL - 10	100%	—	—	—	—	—	—
CL - 11	—	15%	—	46%	38%	—	—
CL - 12	—	21%	—	13%	61%	—	5%
CL - 13	—	29%	—	14%	29%	—	29%
CL - 14	—	100%	—	—	—	—	—
CL - 15	—	100%	—	—	—	—	—
CL - 16	100%	—	—	—	—	—	—
CL - 17	—	60%	—	40%	—	—	—
CL - 18	—	100%	—	—	—	—	—
CL - 19	7%	14%	—	43%	21%	—	14%
CL - 20	20%	23%	—	34%	23%	—	—

M 1.2a 样本来源/数量/特点：所选文章中有45%的文章包含该步骤。在包含该步骤的文章中，该步骤在语步一中的占比最大值为100%，最小值为4%，平均值为45%，标准差为0.4。实例如下：

The electrode was composed of 95 wt% active material, 3 wt% polyvinylidene fluoride binder, and 2 wt% Super P carbon black. (CL - 07)

The P2-type K0.6CoO$_2$ was synthesized using a solid-state method. (CL - 10)

M 1.2b 材料/数据/试剂来源/数量及特点：所选文章中有75%的文章包含该步骤。在包含该步骤的文章中，该步骤在语步一中的占比最大值为100%，最小值为13%，平均值为43%，标准差为0.32。实例如下：

Polystyrene microspheres of 470 nm were purchased from Polybead (cat. no. 07763, amino-functionalized). (CL - 02)

Cyclopore polycarbonate membranes, with 5 m diameter conical-shaped micropores, were purchased from Whatman (Catalog No 7060 - 2511; Maidstone, U. K.). (CL - 04)

M 1.2c 样本/材料/数据选取方法：所选文章中只有两篇包含该步骤。在这两篇文章中，该步骤在语步一中的占比分别为25%和4%。实例如下：

> Peptides were cleaved from the resin in trifluoroacetic acid（Acros Organics）with a triiso-propylsilane scavenger（Sigma-Aldrich）and H_2O at 90：5：5 vol% under agitation for 2h. （CL－01）

> The preparation and characterization of SBM, SBV, SBT and TVB triblock terpolymers were reported in detail previously. （CL－05）

M 1.2d 样本/材料/数据预处理或培养方法：所选文章中有65%的文章包含该步骤。在包含该步骤的文章中，该步骤在语步一中的占比最大值为50%，最小值为13%，平均值为29%，标准差为0.12。实例如下：

> Fmoc deprotections were performed with 20% morpholine in DMF（Merck-Millipore）, followed by Cl-HOBt（AGTC Bioproducts, 0.5 M in DMF）and DIC（AGTC Bioproducts, 1 M in DMF）activated couplings of each amino acid（AGTC Bioproducts）. （CL－01）

> All specimens were stored in a desiccant chamber except when being tested or examined. （CL－12）

M 1.3a 实验条件及注意事项：所选文章中有65%的文章包含该步骤。在包含该步骤的文章中，该步骤在语步一中的占比最大值为75%，最小值为17%，平均值为35%，标准差为0.17。实例如下：

> Before BETmeasurements, the samples were undertaken vacuum degassing at 150℃ for 3h. （CL－08）

> Table 2 shows experimental conditions and variables that were used to create a fretting map. （CL－12）

M 1.3b 样本/材料/数据局限性：所选文章中只有一篇包含该步骤。在该篇文章中，该步骤在语步一中的占比为9%。实例如下：

> These dimensions are based on the manufacturers specifications and could potentially vary, and so are the estimates of the pore loading calculations. （CL－03）

M 1.5 前人实验准备方法：所选文章中有25%的文章包含该步骤。在包含该步骤的文章中，该步骤在语步一中的占比最大值为29%，最小值为4%，平均值为15%，标准差为0.1。实例如下：

> The synthetic procedure for growing microrods was adapted from previous reports. （CL－02）

> Detailed experimental conditions and the procedure employed for depositing MAO coating are given elsewhere [6]. （CL－19）

综上所述，所分析的文章均包含语步一。在该语步中，涉及篇章数最高的步骤是 M1.2b，最低的是 M1.3b，分别占所有文章的 75%

和 5%，平均值为 8.29 篇，占所有文章的 41%，标准差为 5.68。在这些文章中涉及步骤种类最多的有 5 种，最低的只有 1 种，分别占语步一中所有步骤的 71% 和 14%，平均值为 2.9 种，占所有步骤的41%，标准差为 1.52。不同文章中包含的步骤种类存在一定的差异，同一个步骤在不同文章中的占比也存在一定的差异。

（二）语步二特征

表 4.7.3 是所分析的该学科文章语步二中包含的步骤种类。该语步共包括 10 种步骤。表 4.7.4 是各篇文章语步二中各步骤在该语步中的占比情况。如表所示，所有文章中均包括该语步，但该语步中各步骤占比情况不一。此外，同一个步骤在不同文章中使用的占比也存在差异。以下是针对每个步骤占比情况的具体分析及实例。

表 4.7.3　　　　　　　　　　语步二各步骤列表

M	语步二、变量测量		
2.1	概述变量测量设计	2.4	描述变量测量步骤
2.2a	交代仪器/设备/工具/理论/方程/模型	2.5	前人变量测量方法
2.2b	实验参数设置	2.6	强调变量测量方法的科学性
2.3a	定义变量	2.6b	介绍实验原理
2.3b	测试/获取相关变量	2.8	试样后处理

表 4.7.4　　　　　　　　　　语步二各步骤占比

M	2.1	2.2a	2.2b	2.3a	2.3b	2.4	2.5	2.6	2.6b	2.8
CL-01	25%	—	—	25%	—	50%	—	—		
CL-02	—	36%	45%	9%	—	—	9%	—		
CL-03	9%	9%	30%	4%	—	48%	—	—		
CL-04	5%	21%	42%	—	16%	—	—	—	17%	
CL-05	—	45%	18%	—	—	18%	—	18%		
CL-06	—	27%	21%	—	—	42%	9%	—		
CL-07	12%	24%	6%	—	—	47%	—	12%		

M	2.1	2.2a	2.2b	2.3a	2.3b	2.4	2.5	2.6	2.6b	2.8
CL-08	18%	47%	24%	—	—	12%	—	—	—	—
CL-09	—	32%	29%	—	—	32%	6%	—	—	—
CL-10	—	40%	33%	—	—	27%	—	—	—	—
CL-11	—	86%	—	—	—	14%	—	—	—	—
CL-12	—	56%	—	25%	—	13%	—	—	—	—
CL-13	—	46%	—	—	—	46%	4%	—	—	—
CL-14	—	16%	23%	—	—	61%	—	—	—	—
CL-15	8%	31%	17%	—	—	44%	—	—	—	—
CL-16	7%	18%	24%	—	—	51%	—	—	—	—
CL-17	—	64%	5%	—	—	13%	11%	7%	—	—
CL-18	—	63%	5%	—	—	28%	—	—	—	—
CL-19	—	88%	6%	6%	—	—	—	—	—	—
CL-20	—	39%	—	48%	6%	—	—	—	—	6%

M 2.1 概述变量测量设计：所选文章中有 35% 的文章包含该步骤。在包含该步骤的文章中，该步骤在语步二中的占比最大值为 25%，最小值为 5%，平均值为 12%，标准差为 0.07。实例如下：

All electrochemical measurements were performed on a typical three-electrode testing system assisted with rotation equipment（ALS, Japan）at room temperature.（CL-08）

PZT sols were prepared from Sigma-Aldrich precursors.（CL-16）

M 2.2a 交代仪器/设备/工具/理论/方程/模型：所选文章中有 95% 的文章包含该步骤。在包含该步骤的文章中，该步骤在语步二中的占比最大值为 88%，最小值为 9%，平均值为 41%，标准差为 0.21。实例如下：

For all materials studied in this investigation, we estimate the absolute value of specific heat, CE（T, E）by adding the computed zero-field values of the excesss pecific heatΔCE（T, E）from eqn（3）to the lattice or hard-mode contributions taken from the experimental values.（CL-17）

Plain fatigue and fretting fatigue tests were conducted using MTS 810 servo-hydraulic testing machine on uncoated and coated specimens at room temperature with a stress ratio of 0.1 at different cyclic stress levels.（CL-19）

M 2.2b 实验参数设置：所选文章中有 75% 的文章包含该步骤。在包含该步骤的文章中，该步骤在语步二中的占比最大值为 45%，最小为 5%，平均值为 22%，标准差为 0.12。实例如下：

A PCI – 5412 arbitrary waveform (National Instruments，Austin，TX) was used to create a single 10 ms long US pulse at 2.25 MHz. (CL – 03)

The potential was systematically cycled between + 0.4 and – 1.4 V vs. Ag/AgCl at frequencies of 5 kHz. (CL – 06)

M 2.3a 定义变量：所选文章中有 30% 的文章包含该步骤。在包含该步骤的文章中，该步骤在语步二中的占比最大值为 48%，最小值为 4%，平均值为 20%，标准差为 0.15。实例如下：

Pit depth is defined as the maximum depth of pits formed by fretting fatigue damage. (CL – 12)

The initial discontinuity state (IDS) is defined as "the initial (intrinsic) population of discontinuities that are in a structure made of a given material as it was manufactured in a given geometric form" [10]. (CL – 20)

M 2.3b 测试/获取相关变量：所选文章中只有两篇包含该步骤。在这两篇文章中，该步骤在语步二中的占比分别为 16% 和 6%。实例如下：

The Bjerknes forces are normally divided into two basic types：primary Bjerknes forces and secondary Bjerknes forces. (CL – 04)

Residual life fatigue testing was performed on the specimens using in situ fatigue test equipment in lab air. (CL – 20)

M 2.4 描述变量测量步骤：所选文章中有 80% 的文章包含该步骤。在包含该步骤的文章中，该步骤在语步二中的占比最大值为 61%，最小值为 12%，平均值为 34%，标准差为 0.16。实例如下：

The dried film was roll-pressed and cut into round disks of 15 mm diameter. Sodium metal foil was used as the negative electrodes. (CL – 09)

The arithmetic height (Ra) of 2D surface roughness profiles in longitudinal direction was measured around the hole of the plates for uncoated and coated specimens. (CL – 13)

M 2.5 前人变量测量方法：所选文章中有 25% 的文章包含该步骤。在包含该步骤的文章中，该步骤在语步二中的占比最大值为 11%，最小值为 4%，平均值为 8%，标准差为 0.02。实例如下：

The in situ cell used for lab X-ray consists of single-sided beryllium window，as used in previous work. (CL – 09)

The free energy potentials are supplemented by experimental "hard-mode" contributions to heat capacity determined experimentally[see description below and Ref. 36]. (CL – 17)

M 2.6 强调变量测量方法的科学性：所选文章中有三篇包含该步骤。在这三篇文章中，该步骤在语步二中的占比分别为18%、12%和7%。实例如下：

Apparent hydrodynamic radii were calculated according to the Stokes-Einstein equation. All CONTIN plots are intensity-weighted. (CL – 05)

The capacitive current was corrected by means of measuring a LSV in a N2 saturated 0.1M KOH. And all potential here is calibrated using the method described in our precious report[3] and converted to R. H. E value by adding 0.926V to measured potential. (CL5 – 07)

M 2.6b 介绍实验原理：所选文章中只有一篇包含该步骤。在该篇文章中，该步骤在语步二中的占比为17%。实例如下：

The interference between different standing acoustic waves establishes a differential pressure field in the fluid; acoustic radiation forces drive gas bubbles to nodes or antinodes in the acoustic pressure field. The acoustic radiation forces on gas bubbles are normally referred to as Bjerknes forces. (CL – 04)

M 2.8 试样后处理：所选文章中只有一篇包含该步骤。在该篇文章中，该步骤在语步二中的占比为6%。实例如下：

The specimens were cleaned in the acetone in an ultrasonic cleaner for a minimum of 30min after failure for 100% fretting fatigue specimens or when a certain damage level was reached. (CL – 20)

综上所述，所分析的文章均包含语步二。在该语步中，涉及篇章数最高的步骤是 M2.2a，占所有文章的 95%，最低的是 M2.6b 和 M2.8，均占所有文章的 5%。各篇文章中语步二各步骤涉及篇章数平均值为 7.5 篇，占所有文章的 38%，标准差为 6.7。在这些文章中涉及步骤种类最多的有 5 种，最低的有 2 种，分别占语步二中所有步骤的 50% 和 20%，平均值为 3.75 种，占所有步骤的 38%，标准差为 0.85。不同文章中包含的步骤种类存在一定的差异，同一个步骤在不同文章中的占比也存在一定的差异。

（三）语步三特征

表4.7.5 是语步三中所包含的步骤种类。如表所示，该语步中共包括 7 个步骤。表4.7.6 是各篇文章语步三中各步骤在该语步中的占比情况。如表所示，有一部分文章不包含该语步。在包含该步骤的文章中，该语步中各步骤占比情况不一。此外，同一个步骤在不同文章中的占比情况也有所差异。以下是针对每个步骤占比情况的具体分析及实例。

表4.7.5　　　　　　　　　　　**语步三各步骤列表**

M	语步三、数据分析		
3.1	描述数据分析工具/符号	3.7a	描述实验结果
3.2	描述数据统计方法	3.7b	预估的实验结果
3.5	分析实验结果	3.7d	对预估结果的解释
3.6	强调数据分析方法的合理性		

表4.7.6　　　　　　　　　　　**语步三各步骤占比**

M	3.1	3.2	3.5	3.6	3.7a	3.7b	3.7d
CL－01	—	100%	—	—	—	—	—
CL－02	—	—	—	100%	—	—	—
CL－03	—	—	—	—	—	—	—
CL－04	—	—	33%	—	67%	—	—
CL－05	—	—	—	—	—	—	—
CL－06	—	—	—	—	—	—	—
CL－07	—	—	—	—	—	—	—
CL－08	50%	50%	—	—	—	—	—
CL－09	—	100%	—	—	—	—	—
CL－10	—	—	—	—	—	—	—
CL－11	—	—	—	—	—	—	—
CL－12	—	—	60%	—	—	20%	20%
CL－13	—	—	—	—	100%	—	—
CL－14	—	—	—	—	—	—	—
CL－15	—	—	—	—	—	—	—
CL－16	—	—	—	—	—	—	—
CL－17	—	—	—	—	—	—	—
CL－18	—	—	71%	—	29%	—	—
CL－19	—	—	—	—	—	—	—
CL－20	—	—	—	—	—	—	—

M 3.1 描述数据分析工具/符号：所选文章中只有一篇包含该步骤。在该篇文章中，该步骤在语步三中的占比为50%。实例如下：

Koutecky-Levich（K-L）equation was used for analyzing the kinetical process of ORR.（CL – 08）

M 3.2 描述数据统计方法：所选文章中有三篇包含该步骤。在这三篇文章中，该步骤在语步三中的占比分别为100%、50%和100%。实例如下：

Data were weighted by estimated uncertainties in both quantities（SI supporting discussion and Table S5）.（CL – 01）

The obtained diffraction data were normalized against a vanadium rod and background subtracted.（CL – 09）

M 3.5 分析实验结果：所选文章中有三篇包含该步骤。在这三篇文章中，该步骤在语步三中的占比分别为33%、60%和71%。实例如下：

Presented in Fig. S1 is the DSC data of a P（VDF-TrFE）68/32 mol% copolymer. Two peaks are observed. The one at temperatures near 100℃ is the F-P transition and at 150℃ is the melting transition... As expected, for a ferroelectric relaxor, there is no heat capacity peak in the temperature range of dielectric constant peak（16 – 18, 25）.（CL – 18）

This resulted in fretting damage on both the pad and fatigue specimen.（CL – 12）

M 3.6 强调数据分析方法的合理性：所选文章中只有一篇包含该步骤。在该篇文章中，该步骤在语步三中的占比为100%。实例如下：

Further data analysis was done in Microsoft Excel 2010. Rod speed was calculated by dividing the displacement of the rod center between two frames by the time interval（0.033 s），then taking the average of the speed over the selected tracking period.（CL – 02）

M 3.7a 描述实验结果：所选文章中有三篇包含该步骤。在这三篇文章中，该步骤在语步三中的占比分别为100%、29%和67%。实例如下：

Fatigue life results are shown in Figure 2a in the form of S-N curves.（CL – 13）

From equations 3 and 5, we find that applied transducer potentials have a direct influence on the resulting Bjerknes forces. When the applied potential is increasing, the primary Bjerknes forces and the secondary Bjerknes forces also become larger. （CL – 04）

M 3.7b 预估的实验结果：所选文章中只有一篇包含该步骤。在该篇文章中，该步骤在语步三中的占比为20%。实例如下：

The actual slip at the contact may be different from the measured displacement due to elastic accommodation of the testing apparatus and the specimen.（CL – 12）

M 3.7d 对预估结果的解释：所选文章中只有一篇包含该步骤。在该篇文章中，该步骤在语步三中的占比为20%。实例如下：

Strain induced by specimen fatigue produced a small amplitude oscillatory motion between the fatigue specimen and the fretting pad. (CL－12)

综上所述，所分析的文章中只有40%的文章包含语步三。在这些文章中，语步三的7个步骤中有3个步骤分别涉及3篇文章，有4个步骤分别只涉及1篇文章，分别占所有文章的15%和5%。各步骤涉及篇章数平均值为1.86篇，占所有文章的9%，标准差为1.07。在这些文章中涉及步骤种类最多的有3种，最低的只有1种，分别占语步三中所有步骤的43%和14%，平均值为1.63种，占所有步骤的23%，标准差为0.74。不同文章中包含的步骤种类存在一定的差异，同一个步骤在不同文章中的占比也存在一定的差异。

（四）语步占比及轨迹

图4.7.3是所分析各篇文章中三个语步总体占比。如图所示，所有文章均包含了语步一和语步二，只有40%的文章包含语步三。就各个语步占比而言，有75%的文章语步二占比最高，25%的文章语步一占比最高。在语步二占比最高的文章中，有12篇文章语步一占比高于语步三，占所有文章的60%。在语步一占比最高的文章中，除一篇文章语步二与语步三占比相同外，其他各篇文章语步二均高于语步三。

就各步骤在所有语步中占比平均值来看，占比最高的前三个步骤依次为M2.2a、M2.4、M2.2b。有5个步骤占比相同，均最低，分别为M1.3b、M2.8、M3.1、M3.7b和M3.7d。就各步骤涉及的篇章数而言，最高的为M2.2a，占所有文章的95%，最低的有7个步骤，均只涉及一篇，分别占所有文章的5%，这些步骤分别为M1.3b、M2.5d、M2.8、M3.1、M3.6、M3.7b和M3.7d。就各篇文章中包含的步骤种类来看，最多的有10种，占所有步骤种类的42%，最低的仅有4种，占所有步骤种类的17%。各篇文章中包含步骤种类的平均值为7.25种，占所有步骤的30%，标准差为1.89。

图4.7.4至图4.7.6为三个语步的分布轨迹，如图所示，所有文章中均包含语步一和语步二，只有八篇文章包含语步三。

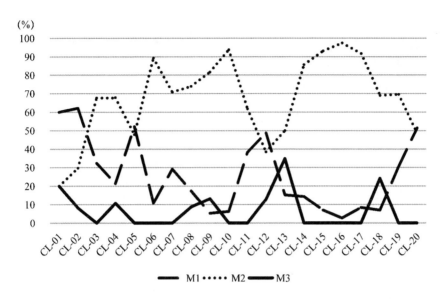

图 4.7.3 各篇文章中三个语步占比

在不包含语步三的文章中，除一篇文章外，其他各篇文章中语步二占比均最高，分布也最广。除三篇文章外，文章最前部以语步一为主，其中有两篇语步一全部分布在文章的最前，与语步二没有交叉，其余几篇中语步一中部分语句会同时分布在文章的其他位置、语步二中。

在包含三个语步的文章中，绝大多数文章中语步二占比最高，语步三最低。文章最前部也是以语步一为主，只有两篇文章第一句话为语步二。大部分文章中语步一的部分语句会同时分布在文章的其他位置。语步三相对比较集中，近一半的文章中语步三主要分布在文章的最后，但是也有部分文章中语步三分布在了文章的中间及偏前的位置。绝大部分文章中语步二主要集中分布在语步一后、语步三前，但是有较多的文章中语步二有部分语句也会分布在文章的最前或最后。

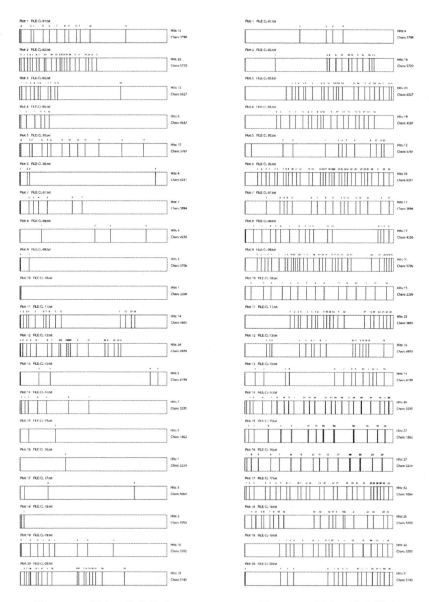

图 4.7.4　语步一分布轨迹　　　　图 4.7.5　语步二分布轨迹

　　综上所述，同一学科不同文章中语步占比和分布轨迹既有相同之处，同时也存在一定的差异。所有文章中均出现了语步一和语步二，一半以上文章中不包含语步三。绝大部分文章中语步二占比明显高于

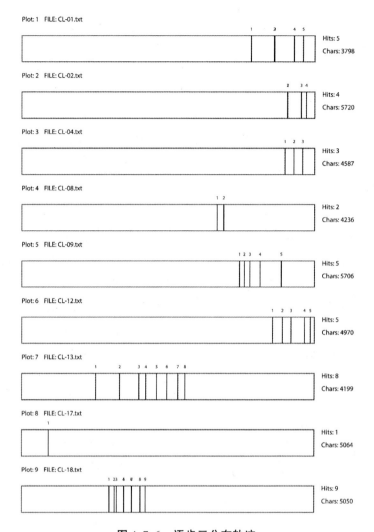

图4.7.6　语步三分布轨迹

其他两个语步，语步三最低，分布最集中。就这三个语步在方法部分的分布而言，语步二分布最广，几乎覆盖了方法部分的前部、中间及偏后的位置、语步一和语步三之间。语步一以文章最前和前部为主，语步三则以文章后部及最后为主，但在有些文章中也会分布在文章中间偏前的位置。大多数文章中语步二与语步一、语步三均有交叉，尤其是与语步二之间。

三 语言特征分析

本小节主要从句子、时态和语态三大方面分析实验方法写作的语言特征。针对句子的分析主要包含句子类型、四类主要句子长度分布及四类主要句子与语步之间的关系。针对时态的分析主要包含时态种类、不同时态组合及三种占比较高的时态组合与语步的关系。针对语态的分析主要包含语态种类、各语态组合与语步的关系。

（一）句子特征

A. 句子类型

表4.7.7是本学科20篇文章中所包含的句子类型及各类句子占比。如表所示，简单句、复杂句、复合句及复合复杂句占所有句子的95.40%。有语法错误的句子占所有句子的1.66%。其他为带有冒号及 i. e. 的各类特殊句子。四类句子中简单句占比远高于其他三类句子，其次是复合句。其他两类句子占比均较低，其中复合复杂句最低。特殊类型句子形式多样，共有6种，其中 NWS 和 NWHS 占比较高，其他均较低。以下例句为特殊类型的句子。

表4.7.7 句类及占比

句类	句数	占比	句类	句数	占比
S	406	74.77%	BCS	1	0.18%
P	47	8.66%	BSS	1	0.18%
C	62	11.42%	NWHP	2	0.37%
CP	3	0.55%	NWHS	5	0.92%
NWS	6	1.10%	R	9	1.66%
ISF	1	0.18%			

ISF：A background corresponding to the random chance of observing two origami structures in close proximity (i. e. , when their peptide-functionalized ends are within 8nm of each other; see main text) was subtracted. (CL – 01)

BCS：However, in the experiment results reported in this paper, the spin cast films are very thin (most of the data were taken at films of less than 1 μm thickness) and their electrode area A will not change with temperature very much due to the low thermal expansion coefficient of the glass substrate, compared with polymer films. (CL – 18)

BSS: To improve the performance of PSCs, mesoporous TiO$_2$ layers were dipped in a 2 M of inorganic acid (HCl, HBr, or HI) solution for several hours, followed by ethanol rinsing and O$_2$ plasma treatment (unless otherwise specified, all the TiO$_2$ layers, regardless of acid treatment or not, were processed by plasma exposure). (CL – 06)

NWHP: For the normal ferroelectric copolymer of P (VDF-TrFE) 55/45 mol%, since the F-P transition is continuous, the free energy can be written as: Eq. where G$_0$ is the free energy of paraelectric phase, β and ξ are phenomenological parameters, Tc is the Curie temperature. (CL – 18)

NWHS: Mass transfer corrections using Levich equation were performed to investigate kinetic current of electrocatalyst: Eq. Where imeasured is the measured ORR limiting current density, ik is the kinetic current density, and id is the limiting current density. (CL – 07)

NWS: The Bjerknes forces are normally divided into two basic types: primary Bjerknes forces and secondary Bjerknes forces. (CL – 04)

B. 句类与语步

图 4.7.7 是四种类型句子与语步的关系。如图所示，四类句子中除复合复杂句外，占比最高的前三个步骤中均包含了 M2.4，但是该步骤在这三类句子中排序均不相同。此外，分别有两类句子中包含了 M2.2a 和 M2.2b，但是它们的排序不完全一致。其他步骤均不相同。即使相同步骤在这四类句子中排序一致，同一个步骤在不同句类中数量和占比也不相同。所有文章中共有三句复合复杂句，分别涉及 4 种不同步骤，其中 2 个步骤同时出现在一句中。

这四种类型句子中均包含了三个语步，就各类句子中包含的三个语步步骤种类而言，简单句中最多，其次依次为复合句、复杂句和复合复杂句，包含的步骤种类分别占三个语步中所有步骤种类的 92%、64%、60% 和 20%。

总体来说，不同句子类型与步骤之间的关系存在异同，句子与步骤关系紧密度与该类句子在所有句子中的占比有关，同时也与该步骤在所有步骤中的占比有关，但是不完全成一一对应的关系，句类与步骤之间没有明显的相关性。

以下是四类句子中步骤占比最高的前三个步骤例句。复合复杂句中各步骤及步骤组合均只出现过一次。

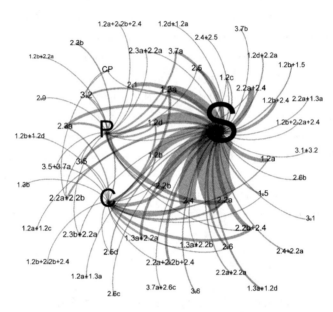

图 4.7.7　句类与步骤关系网络图

【S】

M 2.2a：Electrochemical characterization was conducted using potentiostat（Biologic VMP3）.（CL – 07）

M 2.4：This solution was further analyzed using an UV-vis equipment（Shimadzu UV-2450, Japan）to explore the decontamination efficiency by the microdose.（CL – 03）

M 2.2b：A custom-designed LabVIEW 8.2 program was utilized to initiate the US pulses.（CL – 03）

【P】

M 2.2a：The transducer was submerged in a water tank while a Petri dish containing the sample was positioned at the water surface, placing the sample in both the focal zone of the optics and the US transducer.（CL – 03）

M 2.3a：Pitting is confined to a point or small area that takes the form of small cavities.（CL – 12）

M 2.4：This mixture was brought to a light boil for about 5 min or until the agar solubilized under periodic stirring.（CL – 03）

【C】

M 2. 4: The solution was then poured into Petri dishes and then solidified at room temperature. (CL – 03)

M 2. 2b: For penetration depth studies, the tattoo patch was placed on top of the skin phantom and activated using high-intensity focused ultrasound pulses. (CL – 03)

M 1. 3a: After the electrodeposition step the membrane was thoroughly rinsed with DI water and dried, and usually one-half of the membrane was soaked sequentially in 1 : 1 v/v HNO3 and 0. 5 M NaOH to dissolve the silver and the alumina membrane, respectively. (CL – 02)

【CP】

M 1. 3a: Note that at the potential to deposit polypyrrole, silver is oxidized and dissolved, and therefore in this case a short gold plug was plated in the membrane instead of silver sacrificial layer. (CL – 02)

M 3. 2: During the refinement, d_0 and dfc were fixed to the values refined from Si standard while dfa was allowed to vary to account for the sample displacement and absorption induced diffraction peak shifts. (CL – 09)

M 2. 2a + 2. 2b: The transducer was connected to a function generator that outputted sine waves (5062 Tabor Electronics, Israel), and the signal was amplified if necessary by a dual differential wide band 100 MHz amplifier (9250 Tabor Electronics, Israel). (CL – 02)

C. 句类与句长

表4.7.8是四种类型句子长度占比情况。如表所示，各类句子之间在长度分布方面相似情况不同。在长度分布占比方面，简单句和复合句相似，占比最高的均为单词数介于11—20的句子，其次为介于21—30的句子，但是简单句中短句占比较复合句多。复杂句正好相反，介于21—30的句子占比高于11—20的句子。复合复杂句只有3句，全部介于31—40个单词数。就各类句子覆盖范围而言，简单句和复杂句相同，跨度均最广，复合句略低，复合复杂句最小。

就句子长度最大值而言，复合句最大，复合复杂句最小，复杂句略高于简单句。句子长度最小值简单句最低，复合复杂句最高，复杂句和复合句较为接近，其中复合句略高于复杂句。总体来说，复合复杂句在最大值和最小值方面与其他三类句子差异较显著。如果不排除特殊类型句子，将每个公式算为一个单词的话，所有句子中最长的句子为 NWHS，最短的为简单句。

以下是所有句子中最长的 NWHS 例句和四类句子中最长和最短句子的例句。

表 4.7.8　　　　　　　　　　四类句子长度分布

句长范围		1—10	11—20	21—30	31—40	41—50	51—60	MAX	MIX
S	句数	45	188	114	45	13	1	50	4
	占比	11.08%	46.31%	28.08%	11.08%	3.20%	0.25%		
P	句数	1	15	17	10	3	1	55	10
	占比	2.13%	31.91%	36.17%	21.28%	6.38%	2.13%		
C	句数	*	27	21	10	3	1	60	13
	占比	*	43.55%	33.87%	16.13%	4.84%	1.61%		
CP	句数	*	*	*	3	*	*	36	32
	占比	*	*	*	100.00%	*	*		

NWHS/［**Max：88**］The electron transferred as well as the production of hydrogen peroxide during ORR was calculated by the following calculations: Eq. , where j was the measured current density, j_K and j_L were the kinetic and diffusion – limiting current densities, ω was the rotation speed (rpm), F is the Faraday constant (96485 C/mol), n was the transferred electron numbers, C_0 was the bulk concentration of O_2 in 0.1 M KOH ($1.21 \times 10^{-3} mol/L$), D_0 was the diffusion coefficient of O_2 ($1.9 \times 10^{-5} cm^2/s$), and ν was the kinematic viscosity ($0.01 cm^2/s$). (CL – 08)

S/［**Max：50**］Fatigue test specimens (8 mm thickness, 10 mm gauge width and 65 mm gauge length) and bridge type flat fretting pads (pad foot length of 10 mm, foot width of 2 mm, foot depth of 1.5 mm and pad span of 30 mm) were fabricated from the heat treated material. (CL – 11)

S/［**Min：4**］Two peaks are observed. (CL – 18)

P/［**Max：55**］The skin conformation and mechanical stability tests of the tattoo patch were performed without any cargo loaded, to comply with the protocols approved by the institutional review board (IRB) of the University of California, San Diego, which requires to pose "no greater than minimal risk" to the prescreened subjects who were recruited for the investigation. (CL – 03)

P/［**Min：10**］These experiments were performed until fracture of the specimen occurred. (CL – 12)

C/［**Max：60**］Next, a 30 μL droplet of gel solution composed of 75% gelatin (at 80 mg mL –

1) and a 25% of a perfluorononane emulsion diluted to 1% from original solution prepared, following the protocol in Soto et al. ; it was placed on top of the membrane and left for 20min, to infiltrate by gravity into the interior of the pores. (CL – 03)

C/ 〔Min：13〕 The obtained diffraction data were normalized against a vanadium rod and background subtracted. (CL – 09)

CP/ 〔Max：36〕 The transducer was connected to a function generator that outputted sine waves (5062 Tabor Electronics, Israel), and the signal was amplified if necessary by a dual differential wide band 100 MHz amplifier (9250 Tabor Electronics, Israel). (CL – 02)

CP/ 〔Min：32〕 Note that at the potential to deposit polypyrrole, silver is oxidized and dissolved, and therefore in this case a short gold plug was plated in the membrane instead of silver sacrificial layer. (CL – 02)

（二）时态特征

A. 时态种类及组合

表 4.7.9 是该学科论文中使用的时态类型及组合形式。如表所示，除有语法错误的句子，该学科文章中共出现了 7 种不同时态，其中 T4、T7 和 T5 没有单独使用，与其他时态共同出现在一个句子中。由不同时态构成的组合共有 8 种，均为两种时态组合。不同时态组合中包含 T1 和 T3 的最多，均占所有组合的 50%，其他时态在组合中占比均较低。

各种时态组合中，全部由一种时态构成的句子中占比最高的是 T3，其次为 T1。由不同时态构成的句子中占比最高的是由 T1 和 T3 两种不同时态构成的句子，其他相同或不同时态组合占比均较低。

以下是按照四种类型句子给出的相同时态和不同时态组合的例句，但不是所有时态组合中均包含这四类句子。此外，T1T3T4 组合只涉及一句特殊句类，四种类型的句子均没有涉及，因此只给出其所在的特殊类型句子。

表 4.7.9 时态类型及组合

时态	T1	T2	T3	T10	T1T2	T1T3
句数	82	2	423	1	1	18
占比	15.33%	0.37%	79.07%	0.19%	0.19%	3.36%

时态	T1T3T4	T1T7	T1T10	T2T3	T3T5	T3T10
句数	1	1	2	2	1	1
占比	0.19%	0.19%	0.37%	0.37%	0.19%	0.19%

【T1】

S：All CONTIN plots are intensity-weighted. (CL – 05)

P：Higher US power thus leads to higher Bejerkns forces and thus a faster bubble immigration and aggregation process, which leads to further deceleration on the speed of microengines. (CL – 04)

C：The resulting solution contains 0.1 M phosphate and 0.15 M NaCl, and has a pH value of 7.2. (CL – 02)

【T2】

S：This study has benefited from a substantial series of test data from prior experimental results, detailed extensively in Ref. 25 and 37 – 41. (CL – 17)

【T3】

S：Polythymidine extensions (in most cases T4) were added to staple strands at the ends of each origami, except at the handle positions, to minimize nonspecific helix-stacking interactions between o-rigamis. (CL – 01)

P：The dissociation constant was estimated as the gradient of a linear fit to these data which was constrained to pass through the origin (0, 0). (CL – 01)

C：The equilibrium concentration of each species was assumed to be proportional to the number counted and was estimated from counted numbers of each assembled complex and the total monomer concentrations (summed over all assemblies). (CL – 01)

CP：The transducer was connected to a function generator that outputted sine waves (5062 Tabor Electronics, Israel), and the signal was amplified if necessary by a dual differential wide band 100 MHz amplifier (9250 Tabor Electronics, Israel). (CL – 02)

【T10】

S：Thus, the Maxwell equation $\left(\dfrac{\partial D}{\partial T}\right)_E = \left(\dfrac{\partial S}{\partial E}\right)_T$, as normally used in ceramics for samples under constant mechanical stress condition, should be replaced by Eq. . (CL – 18)

【T1T2】

P：For ferroelectric polymers, especially PVDF, it has been shown that the secondary pyroelectric effect measured under mechanical stress free condition can be in the range of 25% to 50% of the measured pyroelectric coefficient. (CL – 18)

【T1 T3】

P： The skin conformation and mechanical stability tests of the tattoo patch were performed without any cargo loaded, to comply with the protocols approved by the institutional review board (IRB) of the University of California, San Diego, which requires to pose "no greater than minimal risk" to the prescreened subjects who were recruited for the investigation. (CL – 03)

C： The specimens used were dog bone in shape and have an orientation with the longitudinal axis in the L-T direction with a thickness of 1.6 mm, with the fretting pad a flat of 6.35mm in width and 8.9mm in length. (CL – 12)

CP： Note that at the potential to deposit polypyrrole, silver is oxidized and dissolved, and therefore in this case a short gold plug was plated in the membrane instead of silver sacrificial layer. (CL – 02)

【T1 T3 T4】

BCS： However, in the experiment results reported in this paper, the spin cast films are very thin (most of the data were taken at films of less than 1 μm thickness) and their electrode area A will not change with temperature very much due to the low thermal expansion coefficient of the glass substrate, compared with polymer films. (CL – 18)

【T1 T7】

P： When the applied potential is increasing, the primary Bjerknes forces and the secondary Bjerknes forces also become larger. (CL – 04)

【T1 T10】

C： These dimensions are based on the manufacturers specifications and could potentially vary, and so are the estimates of the pore loading calculations. (CL – 03)

【T2 T3】

P： For direct EC measurements, a high-resolution calorimeter with small modifications to the experimental setup has been utilized to measure a sample temperature variation due to the EC when an external field was applied. (CL – 17)

C： DART-PFM was carried out on Asylum Cypher ES, and the conductive AFM tip has averaged spring constant ~5 N/m. (CL – 15)

【T3 T5】

P： Sols were spin-coated at 3000 rpm for 30 s onto Pt (111) /TiOx/SiO2/Si (100) substrates that had been rinsed with acetone and propanol. (CL – 16)

【T3 T10】

P： The results showed that, at high and moderate cyclic load levels (maximum remote stresses, Smax > 130 MPa), the higher clamping force could increase the fatigue life in both the uncoated and coated joints because of the more compressive stresses around the hole. (CL – 13)

B. 时态与语步

图 4.7.8 是该学科文章中三种占比最高的时态组合与语步的关系。如图所示，这三种时态组合中占比最高的前三个步骤存在较大的差异，只有 M2.2a 为各组合共有，但是该步骤在不同时态组合中排序不完全一致，其他步骤均不相同。即使相同步骤在不同时态组合中排序一致，同一个步骤在不同时态组合中的数量和占比也不相同。

此外，这三种时态组合中均包含了三个语步，就它们包含的步骤种类而言，T3 最高，其次为 T1 和 T1T3，这三种时态组合中包含的步骤种类分别占所有步骤种类的 88%、64% 和 28%。

总体来说，不同时态形式的句子与语步的联系存在一定的差异，时态与步骤关系紧密度与该时态在所有句子中的占比有关，同时也与该步骤在所有步骤中的占比有关，但并不是决定性的。

以下是按照四种类型句子给出的三种时态组合中占比最高的前三个步骤的例句，但是有些步骤中不包含所有类型的句子。

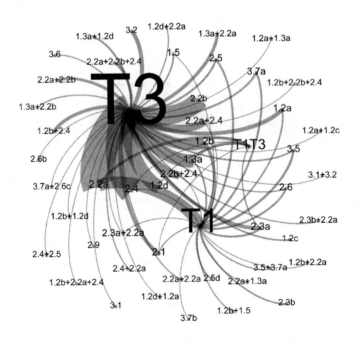

图 4.7.8　时态与步骤关系网络图

【T1】

M 2. 2a

S: A schematic diagram of the fretting fatigue test setup is shown in Fig. 1. (CL – 11)

P: The IDS is a geometric and material characteristic that is a function of composition, microstructure, phases and phase morphology, as well as the manufacturing process used to create the material. (CL – 20)

M 1. 2b

S: The 7075 aluminum alloy is a high strength commercial wrought aluminum alloy used mainly in aircraft applications. (CL – 12)

M 3. 5

S: Two peaks are observed. (CL – 18)

P: Higher US power thus leads to higher Bejerkns forces and thus a faster bubble immigration and aggregation process, which leads to further deceleration on the speed of microengines. (CL – 04)

C: The one at temperatures near $100\,^{\circ}\!C$ is the F – P transition and at $150\,^{\circ}\!C$ is the melting transition. (CL – 18)

【T1 T3】

M 1. 3a

P: Some or all of these handles were substituted with dummy handles, nucleotide extensions that are noncomplementary to the peptide-oligonucleotide conjugates, when origamis functionalized with 2, 1, or 0 peptides were produced. (CL – 01)

C: The specimens used were dog bone in shape and have an orientation with the longitudinal axis in the L – T direction with a thickness of 1. 6mm, with the fretting pad a flat of 6. 35mm in width and 8. 9mm in length. (CL – 12)

CP: Note that at the potential to deposit polypyrrole, silver is oxidized and dissolved, and therefore in this case a short gold plug was plated in the membrane instead of silver sacrificial layer. (CL – 02)

M 2. 2a

P: The piezoelectric transducer which produces the ultrasound waves (Physik Instrumente PZT ring 0. 5mm thickness, 10mm outside diameter by 5mm center hole diameter) was attached to the bottom center of the glass slide. (CL – 04)

M 2. 3a

P: The initial discontinuity state (IDS) is defined as "the initial (intrinsic) population of discontinuities that are in a structure made of a given material as it was manufactured in a given geometric form" [10]. (CL – 20)

【T3】

M 2. 2a

S: The ultrasonic experiments were carried out in a cell similar to that described previously.

（CL－04）

P: The transducer was submerged in a water tank while a Petri dish containing the sample was positioned at the water surface, placing the sample in both the focal zone of the optics and the US transducer. (CL－03)

C: The homemade in situ cell had a Be window and was galvanostatically cycled using a Solartron 1287 potentiostat. (CL－10)

M 2.4

S: After complete adsorption of methyl paraoxon solution by phantom, a 6.25 mm (¼ in.) patch in diameter over a previously contaminated agarose skin phantom was placed. (CL－03)

P: This mixture was brought to a light boil for about 5 min or until the agar solubilized under periodic stirring. (CL－03)

C: The solution was then poured into Petri dishes and then solidified at room temperature. (CL－03)

M 2.2b

S: Videos of the metal rods were captured at 30 frames per second. (CL－02)

P: After natural cooling, the temperature was held at 200℃ before the samples were collected to prevent contamination from moisture in the air. (CL－10)

C: The patch was placed on top of the skin-mimicking phantom for 5min and then removed. (CL－03)

（三）语步特征

A. 语态种类及组合

表 4.7.10 是该学科文章中使用的不同语态组合类型，不包含有语法错误的句子。如表所示，该学科文章中两种语态均有出现，同时还包含了这两种语态的组合形式。只包含 V2 的句子数量和占比最高，同时包含两种不同语态的句子数量和占比最低。所有文章均包含由 V2 一种语态构成的句子，但是只有 75% 的文章包含由 V1 一种语态构成的句子，有 70% 的文章包含同时由两种语态构成的句子。由 V1 一种语态构成的句子中不包含复合复杂句，由 V2 一种语态构成的句子中包含了简单句、复杂句和复合句这三种类型的句子。两种不同语态构成的句子中包含了除简单句以外的三种类型的句子。

以下是按照四种类型句子给出的三种语态组合的例句，但是有些语态组合中不包含所有类型的句子。

表4.7.10　　　　　　　　语态类型及组合

语态	V1	V1V2	V2
句数	82	36	417
占比	15.33%	6.73%	77.94%

【V1】

S： The resulting film thickness was in the range of 0.4μm to 2μm. (CL－18)

P： From equations 3 and 5, we find that applied transducer potentials have a direct influence on the resulting Bjerknes forces. (CL－04)

C： The resulting solution contains 0.1 M phosphate and 0.15 M NaCl, and has a pH value of 7.2. (CL－02)

【V1V2】

P： After that the wires were sonicated and washed in DI water several times until the pH was neutral. (CL－02)

C： All chemicals were analytical-grade reagents and were used as received without any further purification. (CL－04)

CP： Note that at the potential to deposit polypyrrole, silver is oxidized and dissolved, and therefore in this case a short gold plug was plated in the membrane instead of silver sacrificial layer. (CL－02)

【V2】

S： DNA origamis A and B were designed using caDNAno. (CL－01)

P： The transducer was submerged in a water tank while a Petri dish containing the sample was positioned at the water surface, placing the sample in both the focal zone of the optics and the US transducer. (CL－03)

C： The cleavage mixtures were then filtered to remove the resin, and the volume was reduced to <5mL by a flow of nitrogen before precipitation of the crude peptides by addition of cold diethyl ether. (CL－01)

B. 语态与语步

图4.7.9是该学科文章中三种语态组合与语步的关系。如图所示，这三种组合中占比最高的前三个步骤中只有第一个相同，其他两个均不同。即使同一个步骤在不同语态组合中排序一致，该步骤在不同语态组合中的数量和占比也不同。

就这三种组合中包含的语步种类而言，它们均包含了三个语步，但是它们包含的步骤种类在所有步骤中占比不同。V2 最高，其次为 V1，最低的是 V1V2，占比分别为 88%、68% 和 52%。

总体来说，语态与步骤关系紧密度与该语态在所有句子中的占比有关，同时也与该步骤在所有步骤中的占比有一定的关系。

以下是按照四种类型句子给出的三种语态组合中占比最高的前三个步骤的例句，但是有些步骤中不包含所有类型的句子。

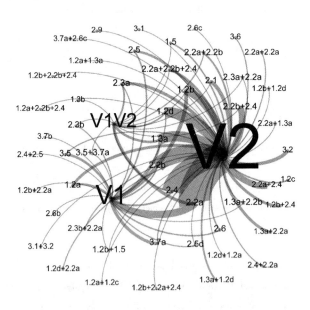

图 4.7.9　语态与步骤关系网络图

【V1】

M 2.2a

S：The relative slip values reported in the present study are macroscopic or global relative slip values.（CL–11）

P：The IDS is a geometric and material characteristic that is a function of composition, microstructure, phases and phase morphology, as well as the manufacturing process used to create the material.（CL–20）

C：Thus, the experimentally measured pyroelectric coefficient is $\left(\dfrac{\partial D}{\partial T}\right)_E$ and the Maxwell relation used should be $\left(\dfrac{\partial D}{\partial T}\right)_E = \left(\dfrac{\partial S}{\partial E}\right)_T$.（CL–18）

M 1. 2b

S： The material used for this study was 7075 – T6 aluminum alloy. (CL – 12)

M 3. 7a

S： However, the higher torque caused less number of cycles to failure under Smax = 80 MPa. (CL – 13)

P： Under Smax = 220 MPa, the higher tightening torque (8 Nm) increased the fatigue life, although coatings did not considerably influence the life. (CL – 13)

【V1V2】

M 2. 2a

P： The piezoelectric transducer which produces the ultrasound waves (Physik Instrumente PZT ring 0. 5mm thickness, 10mm outside diameter by 5mm center hole diameter) was attached to the bottom center of the glass slide. (CL – 04)

C： The proving ring had strain gauges pasted on opposite sides (two on the inner surface and two on the outer surface) and it was calibrated. (CL – 11)

M 1. 3a

P： Table 3 shows experimental conditions for the procedures that were performed to characterize the fretting damage for various different axial stress levels and normal pressure. (CL – 12)

C： The displacement amplitude varied from approximately 50 to 128m and normal force was varied from approximately 100 to 550 N. (CL – 12)

CP： Note that at the potential to deposit polypyrrole, silver is oxidized and dissolved, and therefore in this case a short gold plug was plated in the membrane instead of silver sacrificial layer. (CL – 02)

M 2. 3a

P： The numbers (N) of monomers (An, Bn) and of dimers (An：Bn, An：An, Bn：Bn) and higher multimers, in which the proximity of the peptide-functionalized ends was consistent with the formation of a peptide-bound complex, were counted. (CL – 01)

【V2】

M 2. 2a

S： An Olympus BX60 M optical microscope and a commercial video capturing bundle (Dazzle Video Creator Plus) were used for observing the particles and recording videos. (CL – 02)

P： For direct EC measurements, a high-resolution calorimeter with small modifications to the experimental setup has been utilized to measure a sample temperature variation due to the EC when an external field was applied. (CL – 17)

C： The contact surfaces of the uncoated pads were polished using silicon carbide emery papers and cleaned with ace tone prior to each test. (CL – 19)

M 2. 4

S：500 mg agarose（MCB reagents, Germany）was dissolved in 50mL deionized（DI）distilled water at 100℃, with continuous magnetic stirring（500 rpm）to prepare a 1% w/v agarose skin mimicking phantom.（CL – 03）

P：The solution was mixed and stirred vigorously at 110℃ until a dry powder was obtained.（CL – 07）

C：After first charging the cell up to 4. 6V at 0. 05℃, the cell was disassembled and cathode electrode was washed several times by NMP and ethanol.（CL – 07）

M 2. 2b

S：Videos of the metal rods were captured at 30 frames per second.（CL – 02）

P：After natural cooling, the temperature was held at 200℃ before the samples were collected to prevent contamination from moisture in the air.（CL – 10）

C：The values at 1. 16 V were used in the corresponding linear fitting and the fitted slopes were used for the ECSA comparison.（CL – 08）

第八节　土木工程与科学

土木工程与科学是一门基础研究和工程应用研究相结合的学科，其研究领域主要可分为隧道工程、桥梁工程、道路工程、建筑工程和铁道工程五个方面。研究手段主要有现场实验、室内实验、数值模拟和理论推导。但是无论采用实验以外的何种研究手段，其结果还是需要室内实验或者现场实验来验证。该研究主要分析传统实验方法部分的体裁特征。

本研究共从该领域19种国际知名期刊上选取了26篇论文，其中用于分析的句子共有1063句，约24346个单词。该部分包括句子最多的论文中有67句，最少的有17句，平均值为40. 85句，标准差为13. 43。所选文章均于2010年后发表，有62%的论文第一作者通信地址为英语国家。该类论文基本上均遵循了IMRD（C）的结构。方法部分在论文中占比总体较低，最大值为32%，最小值为7%，平均值为16%，标准差为0. 06。

一　标题特征分析

图4. 8. 1和图4. 8. 2分别是该学科论文方法部分大小标题中词

汇使用情况。所选文章实验方法部分均只包含一个部分，即一个一级大标题。大标题中，experimental 出现的次数最高，共 14 次，但是该单词通常与 procedures、design and methods、research 和 studies 连用，不单独使用。排在第二位的是 method，共出现了 6 次。其他词汇使用的频率均较低。所分析文章中四篇没有二级小标题，约占所有文章的15%，其他文章中均包含二级小标题，最多的有 7 个，最少的只有 2 个。小标题中出现的词汇频率最高的是 test，共 23 次，其次是 setup 和 instrumentation，分别为 11 次和 10 次，与这些词搭配最多的词是 setup。

图 4.8.1 一级大标题词汇云图

图 4.8.2 二级大标题词汇云图

综上所述，该领域论文方法部分均包含一级大标题，大部分文章中同时包含二级小标题。一级大标题与所研究的学科没有显著的相关性，二级小标题中词汇与研究手段关系更密切。此外，不同文章中包含的二级小标题数量存在一定的差异。

二 语步特征分析

本节主要研究论文实验方法写作的语步特征。分析发现，该学科论文这部分写作的总体框架可以分为三个大的语步，与本研究中涉及的其他几个学科相似，但是不同学科中各语步包含的步骤种类存在一定的差异。本节各语步列表中只列出该学科论文中出现的步骤。

（一）语步一特征

表4.8.1是语步一中所包含的步骤种类。如表所示，语步一中共包含12个步骤。表4.8.2是各篇文章语步一中各步骤在该语步中的占比情况。如表所示，所有文章均包含该语步，但该语步中各步骤在各篇文章中占比情况不一。此外，同一个步骤在不同文章中的占比情况也有所差异。以下是针对每个步骤占比情况的具体分析及实例。

表4.8.1　　　　　　　　语步一各步骤列表

M	语步一、实验准备		
1.1A	文章概述	1.2d	样本/材料/数据预处理或培养方法
1.1B	重述研究目的	1.3a	实验条件及注意事项
1.1C	交代实验时间/场所	1.3b	样本/材料/数据局限性
1.2a	样本来源/数量/特点	1.4	分组变量标准评价系统
1.2b	材料/数据/试剂来源/数量及特点	1.5	前人实验准备方法
1.2c	样本/材料/数据选取方法	1.6	强调实验准备的合理性

表 4.8.2　　　　　　　　　　　语步一各步骤占比

M	1.1A	1.1B	1.1C	1.2a	1.2b	1.2c	1.2d	1.3a	1.3b	1.4	1.5	1.6
TM－01	—	—	4%	67%	—	—	30%	—	—	—	—	—
TM－02	—	100%	—	—	—	—	—	—	—	—	—	—
TM－03	—	—	—	10%	10%	—	60%	—	—	—	—	20%
TM－04	—	—	—	8%	8%	58%	—	8%	8%	—	—	8%
TM－05	—	—	—	82%	—	10%	—	8%	—	—	—	—
TM－06	—	—	—	57%	7%	—	36%	—	—	—	—	—
TM－07	—	—	—	—	100%	—	—	—	—	—	—	—
TM－08	5%	14%	—	9%	18%	32%	23%	—	—	—	—	—
TM－09	5%	5%	—	32%	32%	21%	—	5%	—	—	—	—
TM－10	7%	—	—	10%	5%	52%	12%	1%	—	—	—	12%
TM－11	—	—	—	—	—	—	—	100%	—	—	—	—
TM－12	—	9%	35%	26%	—	—	—	13%	—	—	—	17%
TM－13	—	—	—	75%	—	—	7%	—	—	—	14%	4%
TM－14	—	—	—	—	71%	—	14%	14%	—	—	—	—
TM－15	—	4%	—	55%	2%	—	—	11%	—	—	—	29%
TM－16	—	—	—	14%	41%	—	39%	—	—	—	7%	—
TM－17	—	9%	—	18%	24%	—	34%	—	—	—	3%	12%
TM－18	—	—	4%	52%	11%	—	13%	—	—	15%	—	6%
TM－19	—	—	—	45%	40%	—	7%	3%	—	—	2%	3%
TM－20	—	—	—	60%	—	—	40%	—	—	—	—	—
TM－21	—	—	12%	—	—	—	—	53%	—	—	—	35%
TM－22	—	4%	—	42%	—	—	38%	—	—	—	—	15%
TM－23	—	4%	—	50%	6%	—	7%	2%	—	—	13%	17%
TM－24	—	—	—	24%	18%	—	18%	—	12%	—	29%	—
TM－25	—	2%	—	21%	17%	—	45%	3%	3%	—	6%	3%
TM－26	—	—	—	24%	8%	—	56%	4%	—	8%	—	—

M 1.1A 文章概述：所选文章中有三篇包含该步骤。在这三篇文章中，该步骤在语步一中的占比分别为 7%、5% 和 5%。实例如下：

This section describes three types of wrinkles observed in the liner, the preparation process of ring test samples from exhumed lined cast iron pipes, test setup, instrumentation, test procedure, and the three parameters investigated. (TM - 09)

The following sections provide details of the experimental program in terms of preparation and testing of various types of test specimens. (TM - 10)

M 1.1B 重述研究目的：所选文章中有 35% 的文章包含该步骤。在包含该步骤的文章中，该步骤在语步一中的占比最大值为 100%，最小值为 2%，平均值为 17%，标准差为 0.3。实例如下：

The purpose of thrust load testing is to evaluate the tensile splitting stresses and thrust induced by tunnel boring machines (TBMs) during the construction phase. (TM - 08)

The experimental specimens are designed to investigate the effect of concrete cover on the pure torsional capacity of RC members. (TM - 15)

M 1.1C 交代实验时间/场所：所选文章中有 15% 的文章包含该步骤。在包含该步骤的文章中，该步骤在语步一中的占比最大值为 35%、最小值为 4%，平均值为 13%，标准差为 0.13。实例如下：

Experimental work was conducted at the University of California, San Diego (UCSD) Powell Labs. (TM - 01)

Portland (45°N, 122°W) experiences a temperate oceanic climate typified by warm, dry summers and mild, damp winters. (TM - 12)

M 1.2a 样本来源/数量/特点：所选文章中有 81% 的文章包含该步骤。在包含该步骤的文章中，该步骤在语步一中的占比最大值为 82%，最小值为 8%，平均值为 37%，标准差为 0.23。实例如下：

All specimens were of the same height and specified material strengths and were designed with low-transverse reinforcement. (TM - 01)

The samples include two cylindrical blocks of 101.6mm diameter and 50.8mm height. (TM - 05)

M 1.2b 材料/数据/试剂来源/数量及特点：所选文章中有 65% 的文章包含该步骤。在包含该步骤的文章中，该步骤在语步一中的占比最大值为 100%，最小值为 2%，平均值为 25%，标准差为 0.25。实例如下：

To obtain first-order constraints on the spatio-temporal evolution of the landslide over the last decade, we use a series of high- and very-high-resolution images from Planet (Planet Team, 2018), Pléiades (CNES) and Spot (Spot World Heritage) satellite constellations, complemented with the images available via Google Earth® and Bing MapsTM. (TM - 07)

The total thickness of the liner, including the two plain woven polyester jackets, was approximately 4.5mm. (TM - 09)

M 1.2c 样本/材料/数据选取方法：所选文章中有 19% 的文章包含该步骤。在包含该步骤的文章中，该步骤在语步一中的占比最大值为58%，最小值为10%，平均值为35%，标准差为0.18。实例如下：

Cores with a diameter of 100 mm（3.94 in）were cut through the full depth of 235mm（9.25 in）of the segments.（TM－08）

To obtain the ring samples, the lined cast iron pipes were cut into shorter sections with lengths of about 250mm.（TM－09）

M 1.2d 样本/材料/数据预处理或培养方法：所选文章中有58%的文章包含该步骤。在包含该步骤的文章中，该步骤在语步一中的占比最大值为60%，最小值为7%，平均值为27%，标准差为0.17。实例如下：

To identify and abbreviate name of samples, C, has been used for clay, S, for sand, G, for geogrid, and the number used before S, indicates the thickness of sand layer encapsulating the geogrid in centimeters.（TM－16）

All the walls were reinforced with two layers of vertical reinforcements, which limited out-of-plane displacement and increased the stability when the walls were under inelastic strains [30].（TM－17）

M 1.3a 实验条件及注意事项：所选文章中有54%的文章包含该步骤。在包含该步骤的文章中，该步骤在语步一中的占比最大值为100%，最小值为1%，平均值为21%，标准差为0.27。实例如下：

All the tests conducted under monotonic loading conditions were stroke controlled and were performed at a loading rate of 5mm/min using the Zwick/Roell machine.（TM－09）

Three acceleration time histories were employed in these dynamic tests.（TM－22）

M 1.3b 样本/材料/数据局限性：所选文章中只有三篇包含该步骤。在这三篇文章中，该步骤在语步一中的占比分别为12%、8%和3%。实例如下：

Sample disturbance was not quantified. Bulk soil samples were also obtained from these depths.（TM－04）

No formation of main shear failure plain or relative strength gain was evidenced, that could be attributed to significant scale effects.（TM－25）

M 1.4 分组变量标准评价系统：所选文章中只有三篇包含该步骤。在这三篇文章中，该步骤在语步一中的占比分别为15%、8%和8%。实例如下：

The first group（group A）corresponds to the beams with an ultimate strength higher than the capacity of the hydraulic jack（around 900kN）.（TM－18）

Each beam was given a proper code in order to identify all the features：T-fck, cube（compressive strength）-size（S, M or L）-shear reinforcement（N = none, s = stirrups）-fibers（N-none, F = fibers）.（TM－26）

M 1.5 前人实验准备方法：所选文章中有27%的文章包含该步骤。在包含该步骤的文章中，该步骤在语步一中的占比最大值为29%，最小值为2%，平均值为11%，标准差为0.09。实例如下：

> The present test series includes 13 square footings planned as a systematic addition to the previous research projects of Ricker/Hegger [8, 9, 10, 11]. (TM – 13)

> In accordance to Khedkar and Mandal (2009), and in order to reduce rigidity effects of the frontal face of the box to some extent, a 1.0cm thick geo-foam sheet was placed on the inner face of the front wall. (TM – 16)

M 1.6 强调实验准备的合理性：所选文章中有50%的文章包含该步骤。在包含该步骤的文章中，该步骤在语步一中的占比最大值为35%，最小值为3%，平均值为14%，标准差为0.1。实例如下：

> Flat uniaxial test specimens cannot be prepared from the exhumed cured liner to determine the constitutive characteristics in the hoop direction since the liner is curved. (TM – 10)

> These geocell products, referred as novel polymeric alloy (NPA) geocells, have a lower thermal expansion coefficient and creep reduction factor, and higher tensile stiffness and strength than HDPE geocells. (TM – 19)

　　综上所述，所分析的文章均包含语步一。在该语步中，涉及篇章数最高的步骤是M1.2a，占所有文章的81%，最低的有3个，分别是M1.1A、M1.3b和M1.4，均占所有文章的12%。各步骤涉及篇章数平均值为9.5篇，占所有文章的37%，标准差为6.28。这些文章中涉及步骤种类最多的有8种，最低的只有1种，分别占语步一中所有步骤的67%和8%，平均值为4.38种，占所有步骤的37%，标准差为1.94。不同文章中包含的步骤种类存在一定的差异，同一个步骤在不同文章中的占比也存在一定的差异。

　　（二）语步二特征

　　表4.8.3是语步二中所包含的步骤种类。该语步共包括9个步骤。表4.8.4是各篇文章语步二中各步骤在该语步中的占比情况。如表所示，所有文章均包括该语步，但该语步中各步骤占比情况不一。此外，同一个步骤在不同文章中的占比情况也存在差异。以下是针对每个步骤占比情况的具体分析及实例。

表4.8.3　　　　　　　　　**语步二各步骤列表**

M	语步二、变量测量		
2.1	概述变量测量设计	2.3c	测量变量的原因
2.2a	交代仪器/设备/工具/理论/方程/模型	2.4	描述变量测量步骤
2.2b	实验参数设置	2.5	前人变量测量方法
2.3a	定义变量	2.6	强调变量测量方法的科学性
2.3b	测试/获取相关变量		

表4.8.4　　　　　　　　　**语步二各步骤占比**

M	2.1	2.2a	2.2b	2.3a	2.3b	2.3c	2.4	2.5	2.6
TM－01	3%	58%	—	—	6%	9%	24%	—	—
TM－02	4%	56%	4%	—	—	—	24%	4%	8%
TM－03	—	8%	6%	4%	10%	4%	42%	2%	25%
TM－04	—	35%	10%	—	10%	—	38%	—	8%
TM－05	—	33%	13%	—	—	—	49%	—	5%
TM－06	4%	15%	4%	20%	15%	4%	9%	15%	15%
TM－07	—	67%	17%	—	—	—	17%	—	—
TM－08	—	56%	15%	—	—	—	29%	—	—
TM－09	—	33%	33%	4%	—	—	26%	4%	—
TM－10	27%	67%	7%	—	—	—	—	—	—
TM－11	13%	84%	—	—	—	—	3%	—	—
TM－12	15%	74%	7%	—	—	—	4%	—	—
TM－13	5%	21%	5%	—	21%	—	42%	5%	—
TM－14	12%	46%	—	8%	—	—	35%	—	—
TM－15	—	9%	23%	32%	14%	5%	14%	5%	—
TM－16	—	45%	9%	—	18%	—	27%	—	—
TM－17	9%	65%	9%	—	—	—	14%	2%	—
TM－18	4%	42%	8%	21%	10%	—	8%	—	6%
TM－19	—	41%	—	—	3%	—	56%	—	—
TM－20	12%	33%	—	—	10%	—	20%	20%	4%
TM－21	14%	54%	22%	5%	—	—	—	—	5%

M	2.1	2.2a	2.2b	2.3a	2.3b	2.3c	2.4	2.5	2.6
TM – 22	11%	39%	—	—	13%	—	32%	—	5%
TM – 23	—	53%	28%	10%	5%	—	5%	—	—
TM – 24	—	84%	—	5%	9%	2%	—	—	—
TM – 25	—	11%	11%	—	29%	4%	29%	4%	14%
TM – 26	44%	44%	—	—	11%	—	—	—	—

M 2.1 概述变量测量设计：所选文章中有 54% 的文章包含该步骤。在包含该步骤的文章中，该步骤在语步二中的占比最大值为 44%，最小值为 3%，平均值为 13%，标准差为 0.11。实例如下：

Hardness, fracture toughness, and elastic modulus were measured using depth-sensing indentation experiments (Broz et al., 2006). (TM – 06)

A total of seven test configurations were investigated. Four tests that capture the range of response in this experimental program are summarized in Table 4. (TM – 20)

M 2.2a 交代仪器/设备/工具/理论/方程/模型：所选文章均包含该步骤。该步骤在语步二中的占比最大值为 84%，最小值为 8%，平均值为 45%，标准差为 0.21。实例如下：

The loading system had a 150mm diameter air cylinder with a maximum air pressure of 900kPa. (TM – 19)

The schematic of the impact testing machine is illustrated in Fig. 3. The core of the test rig is the free-fall hammer that can be dropped from a maximum height of 6m, or equivalent to the drop velocity up to about 10m/s. (TM – 24)

M 2.2b 实验参数设置：所选文章中有 69% 的文章包含该步骤。在包含该步骤的文章中，该步骤在语步二中的占比最大值为 33%，最小值为 4%，平均值为 13%，标准差为 0.08。实例如下：

The load was applied under displacement control at a rate of 25mm/min. (TM – 02)

Four high-strength rods were used to apply 50-kip (178-kN) axial load on each column corresponding to an axial load index (ALI) of 0.065. (TM – 23)

M 2.3a 定义变量：所选文章中有 35% 的文章包含该步骤。在包含该步骤的文章中，该步骤在语步二中的占比最大值为 32%，最小值为 4%，平均值为 12%，标准差为 0.09。实例如下：

In each set, for similar transverse rebar, longitudinal rebar and concrete grade, the only variable was the concrete cover. (TM – 15)

ALI is defined as the ratio of the axial load to the product of the specified compressive strength of concrete and gross cross section area of the column. (TM – 23)

M 2. 3b 测试/获取相关变量：所选文章中有58%的文章包含该步骤。在包含该步骤的文章中，该步骤在语步二中的占比最大值为29%，最小值为3%，平均值为12%，标准差为0. 06。实例如下：

To ensure uniform sample preparations, density and moisture content determinations using a ring sampler were randomly carried out. (TM – 16)

The effect of the mode of loading was also examined, as some specimens were loaded to failure by monotonic compressive loads, while others were subjected to compression cycles of load-un-load-reload. (TM – 25)

M 2. 3c 测量变量的原因：所选文章中有23%的文章包含该步骤。在包含该步骤的文章中，该步骤在语步二中的占比最大值为9%，最小值为2%，平均值为5%，标准差为0. 02。实例如下：

The principal objective in defining the loading protocol was to replicate the deflected shape observed in field tests. (TM – 01)

Collisions between these fast moving outermost grains will be most likely to contribute to the measure of acoustic energy. (TM – 03)

M 2. 4 描述变量测量步骤：所选文章中有81%的文章包含该步骤。在包含该步骤的文章中，该步骤在语步二中的占比最大值为56%，最小值为4%，平均值为26%，标准差为0. 14。实例如下：

All hydraulic jacks were linked to the same oil circuit and applied the same load independent of the displacement. (TM – 13)

The second testing phase consisted of an incremental dynamic testing procedure with the Gr-1 accelerograms, which could be considered a realistic excitation for a wall located at the ground floor of a building. (TM – 22)

M 2. 5 前人变量测量方法：所选文章中有38%的文章包含该步骤。在包含该步骤的文章中，该步骤在语步二中的占比最大值为20%，最小值为2%，平均值为6%，标准差为0. 06。实例如下：

Fig. 5 shows the placement of selected instrumentation for the WUF-B and the RBS test specimens used in this paper. The reader is referred to Sadek et al. (2010) for further details. (TM – 02)

We tested samples using a TA Instruments AR2000ex torsional rheometer to measure volume changes in granular samples as they were sheared while maintaining constant pressure (Fig. 1), after the design used by van der Elst et al. [12] and Lu et al. [33]. (TM – 03)

M 2.6 强调变量测量方法的科学性：所选文章中有38%的文章包含该步骤。在包含该步骤的文章中，该步骤在语步二中的占比最大值为25%，最小值为4%，平均值为10%，标准差为0.06。实例如下：

Figures 3（b）and 4（b）show this reversibility and repeatability for sample height and acoustic energy, respectively. (TM－03)

The footing arrangement allowed the vertical and horizontal load measurements at the wall boundaries to be fully decoupled. (TM－20)

综上所述，所分析的文章均包含语步二。在该语步中，涉及篇章数最高的步骤是M2.2a，最低的是M2.3c，分别占所有文章的100%和23%。各步骤涉及篇章数平均值为14.33篇，占所有文章的55%，标准差为6.43。在这些文章中涉及步骤种类最多的有9种，最低的只有3种，分别占语步二中所有步骤的89%和33%，平均值为4.96种，占所有步骤的55%，标准差为1.66。不同文章中包含的步骤种类存在一定的差异，同一个步骤在不同文章中的占比也存在一定的差异。

（三）语步三特征

表4.8.5是语步三中所包含的步骤种类。如表所示，该语步中共包括6个步骤。表4.8.6是各篇文章语步三中各步骤在该语步中的占比情况。如表所示，绝大部分文章中不包含该语步。在包含该步骤的文章中，该语步中各步骤占比情况不一。此外，同一个步骤在不同文章中的占比情况也有所差异。以下是针对每个步骤占比情况的具体分析及实例。

表4.8.5　　　　　　　　　　　**语步三各步骤列表**

M	语步三、数据分析		
3.2	描述数据统计方法	3.6	强调数据分析方法的合理性
3.3	前人数据分析方法	3.7a	描述实验结果
3.5	分析实验结果	3.8	本研究不足之处

表 4.8.6 语步三各步骤占比

M	3.2	3.3	3.5	3.6	3.7a	3.8
TM－01	—	—	—	—	—	—
TM－02	—	—	—	—	—	—
TM－03	56%	—	11%	—	11%	22%
TM－04	100%	—	—	—	—	—
TM－05	—	—	—	—	—	—
TM－06	65%	5%	20%	10%	—	—
TM－07	50%	18%	18%	5%	—	9%
TM－08	—	—	—	—	—	—
TM－09	—	—	—	—	—	—
TM－10	—	—	—	—	—	—
TM－11	—	—	—	—	—	—
TM－12	—	—	—	—	—	—
TM－13	—	—	—	—	—	—
TM－14	—	—	—	—	—	—
TM－15	—	—	—	—	—	—
TM－16	—	—	—	—	—	—
TM－17	—	—	—	—	—	—
TM－18	—	—	—	—	—	—
TM－19	—	—	—	—	—	—
TM－20	—	—	100%	—	—	—
TM－21	—	—	—	—	—	—
TM－22	—	—	—	—	—	—
TM－23	—	—	—	—	—	—
TM－24	—	—	—	—	—	—
TM－25	—	—	—	—	—	—

M 3.2 描述数据统计方法：所选文章中有 16% 的文章包含该步骤。在包含该步骤的文章中，该步骤在语步三中的占比最大值为 100%，最小值为 50%，平均值为 68%，标准差为 0.19。实例如下：

Measured steady-state heights (h) shown in Fig. 3 (b) were zeroed to the sample height during the first 100 rad/s velocity step, and then 0.33 grain diameter was added to all height measurements in order to show h. (TM – 03)

Displacement data were averaged to provide one displacement dataset after the two cable displacement transducers were installed on January 10, 2007. (TM – 04)

M 3.3 前人数据分析方法：所选文章中只有两篇包含该步骤。在这两篇文章中，该步骤在语步三中的占比分别为18%和5%。实例如下：

Comparing results between the different minerals as a function of material properties, we rely on the error estimates provided by Broz et al. (2006) shown in Table 1. (TM – 06)

Similar confrontation is made with earthquake catalogues for theregion (Delvaux et al., 2017; Oth et al., 2017; USGS, 2018). (TM – 07)

M 3.5 分析实验结果：所选文章中有16%的文章包含该步骤。在包含该步骤的文章中，该步骤在语步三中的占比最大值为100%，最小值为11%，平均值为37%，标准差为0.36。实例如下：

For these experiments, the stress is controlled but the volume is not, and each experiment is begun with more sand in the sample cylinder than will ultimately be integrated into the shear zone. (TM – 03)

TMPA-RT was validated for the region and proved to match fairly well rainfall trends; though one has to keep in mind for further interpretation that average rainfall underestimations are in the order of 40% (Monsieurs et al., 2018b). (TM – 07)

M 3.6 强调数据分析方法的合理性：所选文章中只有两篇包含该步骤。在这两篇文章中，该步骤在语步三中的占比分别为10%和5%。实例如下：

Normalizing by NS is the best way to take grain size into account and compare the average acoustic energy produced per grain. (TM – 06)

The information collected on the Orth mosaic and DSM was further cross-checked with detailed field observations (in May 2015, Nov. 2016, May 2017, Oct. 2017 and May 2018). (TM – 07)

M 3.7a 描述实验结果：所选文章中只有一篇包含该步骤。在该篇文章中，该步骤在语步三中的占比为11%。实例如下：

Therefore we find h relative to the low velocity, steady-state critical sample height (h_0). (TM – 03)

M 3.8 本研究不足之处：所选文章中只有两篇包含该步骤。在这两篇文章中，该步骤在语步三中的占比分别为22%和9%。实例如下：

Absolute shear zone thickness measurements do not have sufficient precision because the base of the shear zone is not well determined. (TM – 03)

Many of those were ploughed closely before the acquisition of UAV images, potentially hiding some of the ground surface fissures related to internal deformation of the landslide body. (TM – 07)

综上所述，所分析的文章中只有19%的文章包含语步三。在这些文章中，语步三中涉及篇章数最高的步骤有两个，分别是 M3.2 和 M3.5，均占所有文章的16%，最低的是 M3.7a，占所有文章的4%，各步骤涉及篇章数平均值为2.5篇，占所有文章的10%，标准差为1.22。在包含该步骤的文章中，涉及步骤种类最多的有5种，最低的只有1种，分别占语步三中所有步骤的83%和17%，平均值为3种，占所有步骤的50%，标准差为1.87。不同文章中包含的步骤种类存在一定的差异，同一个步骤在不同文章中的占比也存在一定的差异。

（四）语步占比及轨迹

图4.8.3是所分析各篇文章中三个语步总体占比。如图所示，所有文章均包含语步一和语步二，仅有19%的文章包含语步三。就各个语步占比而言，50%的文章语步二占比最高，46%的文章语步一占比最高，另外4%的文章语步三占比最高。在语步二占比最高的文章中，有12篇语步一占比高于语步三。就各步骤在所有语步中占比平均值来看，占比最高的前三个步骤依次为 M2.2a、M1.2a 和 M2.4，占比最低的分别是 M3.7a、M3.6 和 M3.3。就各步骤涉及的篇章数而言，最高的为 M2.2a，所有文章均包含该步骤。最低的是 M3.7a，只出现在一篇文章中，占所有文章的4%。就各篇文章中包含的步骤种类来看，最多的有16种，占所有步骤种类的59%。最低的仅有4种，占所有步骤种类的15%。各篇文章中包含步骤种类的平均值为9.9种，占所有步骤的37%，标准差为2.87。

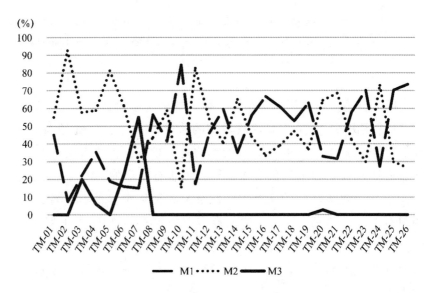

图 4.8.3　各篇文章中三个语步占比

图 4.8.4 至图 4.8.6 是各篇文章中三个语步的分布轨迹。如图所示，所有文章均包含语步一和语步二，只有五篇文章包含语步三。

在不包含语步三的文章中，有 57% 的文章语步一占比高于语步二。绝大多数文章前部主要为语步一，但是有部分文章语步一分布较广，同时分布在文章的中间及偏后的位置，有极少数文章还会分布在最后。语步二在大部分文章中分布较广，主要分布在中间及后部，但是在有些文章中也会分布在语步一前。多数文章中这两个语步有交叉。

在包含三个语步的文章中，语步三总体分布低于其他两个语步，主要集中分布在后部，有个别文章中语步三分布较广，与语步二有交叉。三个语步中存在交叉情况较多的为语步一和语步二。

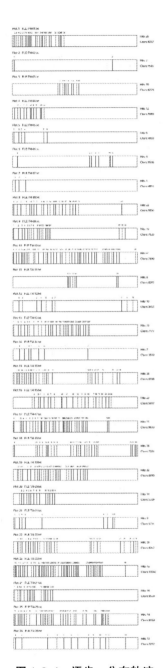

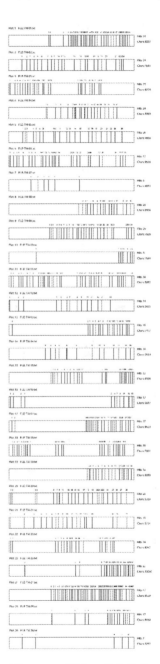

图 4.8.4 语步一分布轨迹　　　图 4.8.5 语步二分布轨迹

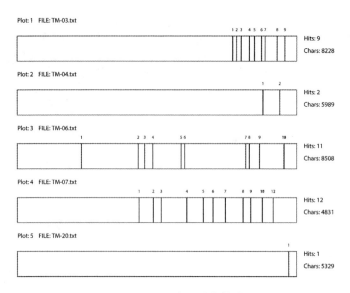

图 4.8.6　语步三分布轨迹

　　综上所述，同一学科不同文章中语步占比和分布轨迹既有相同之处，同时也存在一定的差异。所有文章中均出现了语步一和语步二，包含语步三的文章较少。语步一占比高的文章数量略高于语步二占比高的文章，语步三占比最低。就三个语步在方法部分的分布而言，语步二分布总体比语步一广，大部分文章中语步三分布最集中。文章最前部以语步一为主，部分文章中也会出现语步二。在语步一占比较高的文章中，部分语句还会分布在文章的中间、后部等位置，在极少数文章中会分布在最后。绝大多数文章中语步二分布较广，主要分布在语步一后、语步三前，但是会有少部分语句出现在语步一和语步三中。语步三分布最集中，以文章的后部为主，但是在极少数文章中会分布在中间。极少数文章中三个语步均没有交叉，大多数文章中语步一与语步二有交叉，语步二与语步三交叉的情况较少，三个语步均有交叉的情况极少。

三　语言特征分析

　　本小节主要分析实验方法部分的语言特征。主要从句子、时态和语态三个大的方面进行分析。针对句子的分析主要包含句子类型、四类主要句子长度分布及四类主要句子与语步之间的关系。针对时态的分析主要包含时态种类、不同时态组合及三种占比最高的时态组合与语步的关系。针对语态的分析主要包含语态种类及各语态组合与语步的关系。

（一）句子特征

A. 句子类型

表4.8.7是本学科文章中所包含的句子类型及各类句子占比。如表所示，简单句、复杂句、复合句及复合复杂句占所有句子的96.52%。有1句为片段，有10句有语法错误，其他为带有冒号、括号及 i.e. 的各类特殊句子。四类句子中简单句占比远高于其他三类句子，其次是复杂句。其他两类句子占比均较低，其中复合复杂句最低。特殊类型句子形式多样，共有11种，其中 NWS 占比较高，其他的均较低。以下例句为特殊类型的句子。

表4.8.7 句类及占比

句类	句数	占比	句类	句数	占比
S	758	71.31%	IPS	1	0.09%
P	163	15.33%	ISS	1	0.09%
C	86	8.09%	NSC	1	0.09%
CP	19	1.79%	NSP	1	0.09%
BCPF	1	0.09%	NWHS	5	0.47%
BPC	1	0.09%	NWS	11	1.04%
BSF	2	0.19%			
BPS	1	0.09%	F	1	0.09%
BSS	1	0.09%	R	10	0.94%

BCPF: A spring system was used to provide the axial force (see Fig. 3d) on the CS wall and ensure that the increase in axial force at collapse (when the wall height is maximum), computed considering a rigid body failure mechanism, was less than 5% higher than the initial static force. (TM – 22)

BPC: Piezometer readings were corrected for elevation (calibrated at sea level) and temperature, while displacement data were corrected to determine actual landslide displacement (the cable displacement transducers were oriented at acute angles to the direction of landslide displacement; these angles changed continuously during landslide movement). (TM – 04)

BSF: The accelerations were captured by using the Dytran Series 3200B accelerometers [8] with the peak amplitude of up to 10, 000g (where g is the Earth's gravitational acceleration or about 9. 81 m/s2). (TM – 24)

BPS: Once the load was applied, the actuators were held in place to provide vertical fixity (during a blast event inertial effects render the boundary conditions fixed despite the flexibility of the adjoining structural elements). (TM – 01)

BSS: Additional vertical transducers were installed on the 2nd and 33th brick layers of the inner wall in order to detect significant rotations with respect to the 1st and 34th brick layers, respectively (the number of layers is indicated in Fig. 2). (TM – 22)

IPS: It was also found that varying the number of rubber mat layers can mimic any track supporting bed, e. g. 2 – 3 layers of such could replicate a stiffness of the hard track bed. (TM – 24)

ISS: Also, comparison among specimens having the same rigidity of confining material is feasible (e. g. one or three layers of carbon sheet have similar rigidity as three or nine layers of glass sheet correspondingly). (TM – 25)

NSC: Hereafter the measures recorded by instruments used during the dynamic tests are represented with the following symbols: dDHi is the displacement measured by the laser sensors ith expressed in mm; aAFi is the component of the acceleration along the transversal direction measured by the accelerometer ith. (TM – 21)

NSP: The high strength concretes were made with the addition ofdifferent mineral admixtures: fly ash was added to the concretewith the characteristic strength of 75 MPa, while microsilica was added to the mix with the strength of 90 MPa. (TM – 26)

NWHS: Based on the energy and the impulse consumption, as well as the longitudinal wave propagation's theory in a long solid bar, the dynamic Young's modulus (Edyn) and the dynamic tensile strength (ft, dyn) are derived as follows (Millon et al., 2013; Ruiz-Ripoll et al., 2015; Thoma et al., 2012): Eq., where Δupb is the pull-back velocity measured during the experiment, ρ is the density of the tested material, and CLm is the longitudinal wave speed of the tested material. (TM – 11)

NWS: Six strips were applied longitudinally: three on the loaded face and three on the opposite face. (TM – 01)

B. 句类与语步

图 4.8.7 是四种类型句子与步骤的关系。如图所示，除了复合复

杂句外，其他三类句子中占比最高的前三个步骤相同，排在第一的均为 M2.2a，在简单句和复合句中其他两个步骤排序一致，而在复杂句中正好相反。复合复杂句中步骤占比较分散，有两个步骤占比稍高，与复杂句一致。即使相同步骤在不同句类中排序一致，该步骤在不同句类中数量和占比也不相同。

这四类句子中均包含了三个语步，就各类句子中包含的三个语步中步骤种类而言，简单句中包含了三个语步中所有步骤，复杂句、复合句、复合复杂句中包含的步骤种类分别占三个语步中所有步骤种类的 85%、52% 和 48%。

总体来说，不同句子类型与步骤之间的关系存在异同，句子与步骤关系紧密度与该类句子在所有句子中的占比有关，同时也与该步骤在所有步骤中的占比有关，但是不完全成一一对应的关系，句类与步骤之间没有明显的相关性。

以下是四类句子中步骤占比最高的前三个步骤例句。由于复合复杂句中步骤较分散，只给出占比最高的两个步骤例句。

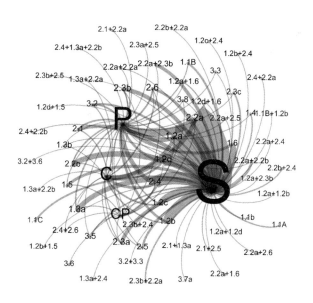

图 4.8.7　句类与步骤关系网络图

【S】

M 2. 2a：A 19-mm-diameter steel rotor fits inside a glass jacket with approximately $10\mu m$ clearance between the rotor edge and the jacket (Fig. 1). (TM – 03)

M 1. 2a：The borehole required 9 days to complete. (TM – 04)

M 2. 4：Lateral load was applied quasistatically with the center actuator in displacement control and the other two actuators matching the force in the center actuator, resulting in a uniform load on the column. (TM – 01)

【P】

M 2. 2a：Since the positions of the gauges are known, the time difference between them easily leads to the determination of the wave velocity, assuming a steady motion. (TM – 11)

M 2. 4：We also installed coaxial cable in our borehole to detect the depth of shear displacement, assuming that shear displacement would result in cable breakage at that depth. (TM – 04)

M 1. 2a：The test matrix in Table 1 summarizes the parameters that were varied across tests. (TM – 01)

【C】

M 2. 2a：This stress pulse propagates through the bar and reaches the specimen (see Fig. 1). (TM – 11)

M 1. 2a：Nine RC column specimens were tested and an additional one was used to develop the loading protocol. (TM – 01)

M 2. 4：Instrument readings were made hourly and downloaded to a portable computer on a periodic basis. (TM – 04)

【CP】

M 2. 2a：Some authors have used this technique for the characterization of some rocks, like granite (Dai et al. , 2010b), but as commented in that paper, the use of BD for dynamic characterization of tensile properties using the SHB device must be taken carefully, since the application of the quasi-static equation has not yet been deeply validated. (TM – 11)

M 2. 4：Rotor height, shear strain rate, and axial force were recorded at 1 Hz sampling frequency, and the first 30 s of each velocity step was ignored during analysis so that only steady-state data were used in evaluation. (TM – 03)

C. 句类与句长

表4.8.8 是四种类型句子长度占比情况。如表所示，各类句子在长度分布方面相似情况不同。在长度分布占比方面，简单句中句子长度占比最高的是单词数介于 11—20 的句子，其次是介于 21—30 的句

子。复杂句和复合句中占比最高的均为介于 21—30 的句子，但是这两类句子中占比排在第二的有所不同，分别为介于 31—40 和介于 11—20 的句子。复合复杂句中占比最高的为介于 31—40 的句子，其次为介于 21—30 的句子。就各类句子覆盖范围而言，简单句和复杂句最广，但是简单句中短句占比高于复杂句。复合句覆盖范围略低于这两类句子，复合复杂句最低。

就句子长度最大值而言，简单句和复杂句相似，均高于其他两类句子。复合句和复合复杂句相似。其中复杂句略高于简单句，复合句略高于复合复杂句。句子长度最小值简单句最低，复合复杂句最高，其他两类句子相似，介于其中。复合复杂句与其他三类差异较大。如果不排除特殊类型句子，将每个公式算为一个单词的话，所有句子中最长的句子为 NWHS，最短的为简单句。

以下是所有句子中最长的 NWHS 例句和四类句子中最长和最短句子的例句。

表 4.8.8　　　　　　　　　四类句子长度分布

句长范围		1—10	11—20	21—30	31—40	41—50	51—60	71—80	MAX	MIX
S	句数	67	359	228	73	22	7	1	72	5
	占比	8.85%	47.42%	30.12%	9.64%	2.91%	0.92%	0.13%		
P	句数	1	38	71	40	10	2	*	59	10
	占比	0.62%	23.46%	43.83%	24.69%	6.17%	1.23%	*		
C	句数	1	27	37	15	3	4	*	57	9
	占比	1.15%	31.03%	42.53%	17.24%	3.45%	4.60%	*		
CP	句数	*	*	7	9	3	1	*	55	21
	占比	*	*	35.00%	45.00%	15.00%	5.00%	*		

NWHS \ ［Max：78］ Based on the energy and the impulse consumption, as well as the longitudinal wave propagation's theory in a long solid bar, the dynamic Young's modulus (Edyn) and the dynamic tensile strength (ft, dyn) are derived as follows (Millon et al., 2013; Ruiz-Ripoll et al., 2015; Thoma et al., 2012): Eq., where Δupb is the pull-back velocity measured during the experiment, ρ is the density of the tested material, and CLm is the longitudinal wave speed of the tested material. (TM - 11)

S ** [Max：72**] The main design levels were obtained by scaling factors of about 20% for the probability of occurrence equal to 63% in 50 years (corresponding to the immediate occupancy design level), 50% for the probability of occurrence equal to 10% in 50 years (corresponding to the life safety design level), and 75% for the probability of occurrence equal to 2% in 50 years (corresponding to the near collapse design level), as shown in Fig. 12b. (TM - 21)

S ** [Min：5**] Sample disturbance was not quantified. (TM - 04)

P ** [Max：59**] In order to evaluate the dynamic properties (fundamental vibration period and damping ratio), white - noise tests were carried out on both bare structure and complete construction, whereas earthquake tests were conducted on complete construction in order to evaluate the seismic performance by applying with different scaling factors a selected natural ground motion (AQV) recorded during the 2009 Aquila (Central Italy) earthquake. (TM - 21)

P ** [Min：10**] Shattuck Hall was selected because it has a terrace courtyard. (TM - 12)

C ** [Max：57**] The test setup (Fig. 1) was designed to replicate the loading and in situ boundary conditions experienced by an RC moment frame column during blast loading; in a real building, the column is preloaded by gravity loads, its ends are fixed because of inertia, and the blast load is applied laterally over the face of the column. (TM - 01)

C ** [Min：9**] Nine specimens were unconfined and were used as reference. (TM - 25)

CP ** [Max：55**] Some authors have used this technique for the characterization of some rocks, like granite (Dai et al., 2010b), but as commented in that paper, the use of BD for dynamic characterization of tensile properties using the SHB device must be taken carefully, since the application of the quasi-static equation has not yet been deeply validated. (TM - 11)

CP ** [Min：21**] The columns were cast after the footing was set and finally, the cap beam was cast on top of the columns. (TM - 23)

（二）时态特征

A. 时态种类及组合

表 4.8.9 是该学科论文中使用的时态类型及组合形式。如表所示，除去片段和有语法错误的句子，该学科文章中共出现了 7 种不同时态，其中 T5 没有单独使用，与其他时态共同出现在一个句子中。由不同时态构成的组合共有 12 种，其中两种时态组合共 9 种，三种时态组合共 3 种。不同时态组合中包含 T3 的最多，其次依次为 T1 和 T10，分别占所有组合的 67%、50% 和 42%，其他时态在组合中占比

均较低。

　　各种时态组合中，全部由一种时态构成的句子中占比最高的是 T3，其次为 T1。由不同时态构成的句子中占比最高的是 T1 和 T3 的组合，其他相同或不同时态组合占比均较低。

　　以下是按照四种类型句子给出的相同时态和不同时态组合的例句，但不是所有时态组合中均包含四类句子。

表 4.8.9　　　　　　　　　　时态类型及组合

时态	T1	T2	T3	T4	T8	T10	T1T2	T1T3	T1T3T8
句数	329	10	624	3	1	4	8	44	1
占比	31.27%	0.95%	59.32%	0.29%	0.10%	0.38%	0.76%	4.18%	0.10%
时态	T1T3T10	T1T4	T1T10	T2T3	T2T10	T3T5	T3T8	T3T5T10	T3T10
句数	2	3	3	1	1	2	1	1	14
占比	0.19%	0.29%	0.29%	0.10%	0.10%	0.19%	0.10%	0.10%	1.33%

【T1】

S: This includes specimens exhumed from the field pipes and those fabricated in the laboratory, along with specimens of the individual components of the liner. (TM – 10)

P: Velocity profiles measured using particle image velocimetry (Thielicke & Stamhuis, 2014) show that different driving velocities all converge toward zero at approximately five grain diameter depth (Figure 1). (TM – 06)

C: This stress pulse propagates through the bar and reaches the specimen (see Fig.1). (TM – 11)

CP: The core of the test rig is the free-fall hammer that can be dropped from a maximum height of 6m, or equivalent to the drop velocity up to about 10m/s. (TM – 24)

【T2】

S: According to Unified Soil Classification System (USCS), clay has been classified as CL (clay with low plasticity) and sand as SW (well-graded sand). (TM – 16)

C: This program has been extensively validated and widely used for studying the effect of climate change [48, 49] and the impact of natural elements on a microclimate [47, 50, 51]. (TM – 12)

【T3】

S: Cold-drawn hooked-end steel fibers (60mm [2. 36 in] long and 0. 75mm [0. 030 in] in diameter) having ultimate tensile strength greater than 1050 MPa (152. 30 ksi) were added at a rate of 1. 5% by mixture volume. (TM – 08)

P: However, the cored samples, drilled from the sleepers, were taken for a confirmation test, as per the Australian Standard AS1012. 14 [6], given that the average compressive strength at the test age of about 2 years was 80 MPa. (TM – 24)

C: Measured steady-state heights (h) shown in Fig. 3 (b) were zeroed to the sample height during the first 100 rad/s velocity step, and then 0. 33 grain diameter was added to all height measurements in order to show h. (TM – 03)

CP: For these experiments, friction between the grains and the sample cylinder during shear results in a shear rate that decreases with depth, and thus, the true local inertial number decreases with depth. (TM – 06)

【T4】

S: This pressure will define the speed of the striker, and consequently, the strain rate obtained during the experiment. (TM – 11)

【T8】

S: In that case, the axial force was likely changing during the motion due to a general redistribution of axial forces in the building as well as to the partial restrained uplift of the wall induced by the floor. (TM – 22)

【T10】

S: The difference in the impedances between the input bar and the specimen should be as low as possible to generate a possibly high wave transmission by the specimen. (TM – 11)

【T1T2】

P: Fig. 2 shows the extruded HDPE geogrid that has been used as reinforcement. (TM – 16)

C: To identify and abbreviate name of samples, C, has been used for clay, S, for sand, G, for geogrid, and the number used before S, indicates the thickness of sand layer encapsulating the geogrid in centimeters. (TM – 16)

CP: Some authors have used this technique for the characterization of some rocks, like granite (Dai et al. , 2010b), but as commented in that paper, the use of BD for dynamic characterization of tensile properties using the SHB device must be taken carefully, since the application of the quasi-static equation has not yet been deeply validated. (TM – 11)

【T1T3】

P: With pressure constant, grains were sheared by the overlying rotor at nine steady state velocities between 50 and 300rad/s, which corresponds to linear velocities along the outer circumference of

0. 5 – 3m/s, with 60s at each discrete velocity step. （TM – 06）

C：Test – day strength differs between tests because of different time spans between construction and testing; the same concrete mix was specified in all cases and similar behavior is expected for all specimens. (TM – 01)

CP：TMPA-RT was validated for the region and proved to match fairly well rainfall trends; though one has to keep in mind for further interpretation that average rainfall underestimations are in the order of 40% (Monsieurs et al. , 2018b). (TM – 07)

【T1T3T8】

CP：Data were recorded at steady state for a given velocity, and results are reversible, meaning the rotor height did not change for a given velocity step whether the overall velocity ramp direction was moving from slow to fast or from fast to slow. （TM – 03）

【T1T4】

P：The alternative method specifies that, when the support is subjected to an increase in static load from 50kN to 60kN at a railseat, it shall allow a vertical displacement between 0. 1mm and 0. 5mm (inclusive). (TM – 24)

CP：For these experiments, the stress is controlled but the volume is not, and each experiment is begun with more sand in the sample cylinder than will ultimately be integrated into the shear zone. （TM – 03）

【T1T10】

P：The tendency of the test rig efficiency, which is gently decreased as the drop height increases, could then be established. (TM – 24)

C：For these minerals, hardness and elastic moduli are sufficiently separated in scale that even allowing for small differences in the chemical composition of the minerals used in the study and scalings should be consistent. (TM – 06)

【T2T3】

C：A fine grained soil marketed as kaolinite and used in pottery industry, has been used as the clay soil and natural sand was selected as the granular material. (TM – 16)

【T2T10】

P：Moreover, since very limited research has studied the cyclic behavior of PCTL segments, this study should contribute knowledge on the seismic behavior of PCTL segments. （TM – 08）

【T3T5】

P：The moving time frames were captured when the mark on the impactor had fully passed by an adjacent mark on the reference column. （TM – 24）

【T3T8】

P：A fully reversed cyclic displacement-controlled load was applied quasi-static to the top of the walls as shown in Fig. 1 while the wall was being subjected to a constant axial load throughout the test. (TM – 17)

【T3T5T10】

P: It had been believed that the high strength prestressing wires were of high quality and the strength would not change during time. (TM – 24)

【T3T10】

P: It was decided to gage the strength at 5% drift ratio because this drift would be associated with significant nonlinearity in both columns while not being close to the drift capacity of the columns. (TM – 23)

C: Three drop tests were done at each drop height and the average drop velocity could be obtained. (TM – 24)

【T1T3T10】

CP: Recent work by Sadeghian and Fam [15] indicates an embedment length of 0.7 times column diameter might be sufficient, but this length was not investigated in the current study. (TM – 23)

B. 时态与语步

图 4.8.8 是该学科文章中三种占比最高的时态组合与三个语步中各步骤的关系。如图所示，就这三种组合中占比最高的前三个步骤而言，除了 T1 中占比第三的步骤外，其他步骤均相同，排序也一致，其中 T3 中排在第二和第三的两个步骤占比相同。即使不同时态组合中步骤排序一致，同一个步骤在不同时态组合中的数量和占比也不相同。

此外，这三种时态组合形式中均包含了三个语步，就它们包含的步骤种类而言，T1 最高，其次为 T3 和 T1T3，所包含的步骤种类分别占所有步骤种类的 93%、89% 和 74%。

总体来说，不同时态形式的句子与语步的联系存在一定的差异，时态与步骤关系紧密度与该时态在所有句子中的占比有关，同时也与该步骤在所有步骤中的占比有关，但并不是决定性的。

以下是按照四种类型句子给出的三种时态组合中占比最高的前三个步骤的例句，但是有些步骤中不包含所有类型的句子。

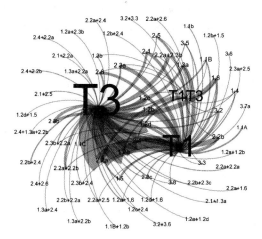

图 4.8.8 时态与步骤关系网络图

【T1】

M2. 2a

S： The Split-Hopkinson-Bar is a test facility for the accomplishment of dynamic characterizations under well-defined conditions. (TM – 11)

P： As the study is focused on the specific failure of the openings, lateral supports are used to avoid the global lateral buckling of the tested beams. (TM – 18)

C： In case of a lower impedance of the specimen compared to the bar a certain portion of the pulse is transmitted by the specimen, and the rest reflects on the surface and runs back in the input bar as inverse stress pulse. (TM – 11)

CP： For these experiments, friction between the grains and the sample cylinder during shear results in a shear rate that decreases with depth, and thus, the true local inertial number decreases with depth. (TM – 06)

M1. 2a

S： The dimensions and shape of the prestressed concrete sleeper specimens are shown in Table 1. (TM – 24)

P： The critical section where the pure torsional moment acts has a length of 1. 1m. (TM – 15)

C： Fig. 5 shows the beam with high opening (depth of 300 mm) and no stiffeners and Fig. 6 shows the case of small opening (depth of 200mm). (TM – 18)

M1. 2b

S： Segments are skewed at their ends rather than straight edges. (TM – 08)

P：So, considering a modulus of elasticity of 210GPa, the corresponding elastic strain is taken equal to1440μm/m which is used as a reference value for the analysis of the strain gauge values. (TM – 18)

C：The three most common patterns of wrinkles found in those samples are shown in Figs. 1 (a – c), and these are identified as sample types SW, IW, and LW, respectively. (TM – 09)

【T1T3】

M2. 2a

P：Although the extensometer has a robust construction and an impact-resistant measuring system, its arms were unclamped from the coupons at specified loads prior to failure, except when testing the resin coupons. (TM – 10)

C：The distance marks on the impactor and a reference column were identically scaled to be 100mm long. (TM – 24)

M1. 2a

P：The test matrix in Table 1 summarizes the parameters that were varied across tests. (TM – 01)

C：Test-day strength differs between tests because of different time spans between construction and testing; the same concrete mix was specified in all cases and similar behavior is expected for all specimens. (TM – 01)

M2. 4

P：The type of geomembrane GC1 was selected, because it is used in the manufacture of geocell mattresses (Indraratna et al., 2015). (TM – 14)

C：As a check on the input base acceleration frequency analysis of the entire measured accelerogram was carried out and this analysis is shown in Fig. 8. (TM – 20)

【T3】

M2. 2a

S：The displacement of the lower box was controlled by an electric motor with a set of gears. (TM – 14)

P：The load stub at the top of the column was restrained by a link system that provided moment and lateral fixity while allowing unrestrained vertical motion. (TM – 01)

C：The potentiometers were mounted directly on the aluminum bulkhead and the cores passed through a 20 – mm-diameter opening through the bulkhead and the geofoam buffer to aluminum plates inserted flush with the buffer surface (Fig. 4). (TM – 20)

CP：A predetermined amount of granular material was placed inside the shear box and compacted in several layers to achieve the desired density that was representative of field conditions (ρ = 2100 kg/m3). (TM – 14)

M1. 2a

S： Reinforcement was provided as described in Table 2. (TM – 01)

P： The test model consisted of a concrete footing, two 14in. (356mm) diameter, 59.5in. (1511mm) long columns with center-to-center distance of 84in. (2134mm), and a cap beam that was built in two pieces. (TM – 23)

C： Each wall was 1m in height and each seismic buffer was 150mm thick. (TM – 20)

CP： The columns were cast after the footing was set and finally, the cap beam was cast on top of the columns. (TM – 23)

M2. 4

S： With the axial force controlled at 1 N, rotor height was measured at logarithmically spaced velocity steps between 25 and 300rad/s. (TM – 03)

P： Shearing continued during these experiments until a maximum horizontal strain (εh) of 10% was reached. (TM – 14)

C： The acceleration record was stepped in 0.05g increments and each amplitude increment was held for 5s. (TM – 20)

CP： Acoustic energy decreased with the number of conditioning steps as the sample settled into a repeatable orientation, and acoustic energy was repeatable and reversible for the final three steady-state stepped velocity ramps [see Fig. 4 (b)]. (TM – 03)

（三）语态特征

A. 语态种类及组合

表4.8.10是该学科文章中使用的不同语态组合类型，其中不包含片段和有语法错误的句子。如表所示，该学科文章中两种语态均有出现，同时还包含了这两种语态的组合形式。只包含 V2 的句子数量和占比最高，同时包含两种语态的句子数量和占比最低。所有文章中均包含由同一种语态构成的句子，但是有一篇文章不包含由两种不同时态构成的句子。同一种语态构成的句子中均包括了简单句、复杂句、复合句和复合复杂句这四类句子。两种不同语态构成的句子中包括了除简单句以外的三种类型的句子。

以下是按照四种类型句子给出的三种语态组合中的例句，但是有些语态组合中不包含所有类型的句子。

表 4. 8. 10　　　　　　　　　　**语态类型及组合**

语态	V1	V1V2	V2
句数	339	112	601
占比	32. 22%	10. 65%	57. 13%

【V1】

S： The specimens varied primarily in cross-sectional dimensions and the thickness of the carbon fiber-reinforced polymer (CFRP) wrap. (TM－01)

P： The inner and outer jackets are essentially the same, except that the inner jacket has a non-structural polyurethane elastomer layer bonded to its inner surface which is suitable for potable water. (TM－10)

C： The effective weight of the mass rig (Fig. 6) was 100kip (445kN) and corresponded to the total axial load on the columns. (TM－23)

CP： For these experiments, friction between the grains and the sample cylinder during shear results in a shear rate that decreases with depth, and thus, the true local inertial number decreases with depth. (TM－06)

【V1V2】

P： Energy is normalized by NS because collisions between the fastest moving grains closest to the accelerometer placement contribute the most to the measured acousic energy of the system. (TM－06)

C： All tests were performed at 23℃ ±1℃ (room temperature), and the rate of loading for each test was 5mm/min. (TM－10)

CP： Acceleration is assumed to be linearly related to displacement at any given frequency because the glass sample cylinder is assumed to be elastic; therefore, wave amplitude squared gives a relative measurement of acoustic energy. (TM－06)

【V2】

S： Cross-section dimensions are given in Table 1. (TM－01)

P： The glass jacket is epoxied to a flat aluminum plate, which is attached to a temperature-controlled Peltier plate, set to 25℃. (TM－03)

C： To establish confidence in the validity of this technique to represent the behavior in the hoop direction, additional coupons representing the longitudinal direction were fabricated using the same technique and were used to compare the behavior in the longitudinal direction with that observed from the coupons cut from the exhumed liner (those discussed in the previous subsection). (TM－10)

CP： The columns were cast after the footing was set and finally, the cap beam was cast on top of the columns. (TM－23)

B. 语态与语步

图 4.8.9 是该学科文章中三种语态组合与各步骤的关系。如图所示，这三个语态组合中占比最高的前三个步骤中均包含 M2.2a 和 M1.2a。此外，还有两组中包含 M2.4，但是它们的排序不完全一致。即使不同语态组合中步骤排序一致，同一个步骤在不同语态组合中数量和占比也不相同。

就这三种组合中包含的语步种类而言，它们均包含三个语步，但是所包含的步骤种类在所有步骤中占比不同。V1 和 V2 占比最高，均为 96%，V1V2 最低，为 70%。

总体来说，语态与步骤关系紧密度与该语态在所有句子中的占比有关，同时也与该步骤在所有步骤中的占比有一定的关系。

以下是按照四种类型句子给出的三种语态组合中占比最高的前三个步骤的例句，但是有些步骤中不包含所有类型的句子。

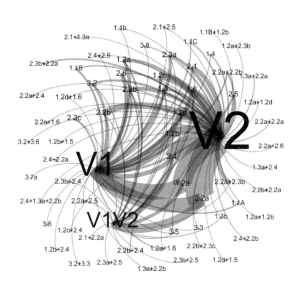

图 4.8.9　语态与步骤关系网络图

【V1】

M 1.2a

S：Figure 5 shows a picture of the finished coupon, with the 50mm long tabs installed at each end. (TM – 10)

P: Phase 2 (scale 2) focused on three courtyards on the campus which were either bare, green or with a water pond. (TM – 12)

C: All specimens were 3276mm tall and had 38mm of cover concrete to the edge of the stirrups. (TM – 01)

M 2.2a

S: This is a tabletop test machine with a maximum load capacity of 20kN. (TM – 10)

P: This program is a prognostic model based on the fundamental laws of fluid dynamics and thermodynamics that can simulate exchange processes of heat and vapor at the ground surface and at walls, flows around and between buildings. (TM – 12)

C: The effective weight of the mass rig (Fig. 6) was 100kip (445kN) and corresponded to the total axial load on the columns. (TM – 23)

M 1.2b

S: The experimental program considered three types of concrete designed for a compressive strength fck, at 28 days, of approximately 40, 75 and 90 MPa. (TM – 26)

P: We bored a hole 3.4 m from the strike-slip fault that marks the left margin of the landslide and about 4 m from the inside edge of the flank ridge (Figs. 3 and 4). (TM – 04)

C: The outer diameter of the liner was 155mm and the mean thickness was 4.7mm, varying from a minimum of 4.51mm to a maximum of 4.81mm. (TM – 10)

M 1.2d

S: The tabs consisted of glass fiber woven fabric, Tyfo SHE-51A, impregnated by Tyfo S Epoxy resin. (TM – 10)

P: The most important data in this table are the hoop and the beam bending strength that are 23ksi (159 MPa) and 34ksi (234 MPa), respectively. (TM – 23)

C: The average yielding strength of the longitudinal reinforcement was 522 MPa and that of transversal reinforcement was 533 MPa. (TM – 26)

【V1V2】

M 2.2a

P: Although the extensometer has a robust construction and an impact-resistant measuring system, its arms were unclamped from the coupons at specified loads prior to failure, except when testing the resin coupons. (TM – 10)

C: In case of a lower impedance of the specimen compared to the bar a certain portion of the pulse is transmitted by the specimen, and the rest reflects on the surface and runs back in the input bar as inverse stress pulse. (TM – 11)

CP: Some authors have used this technique for the characterization of some rocks, like granite

（Dai et al. , 2010b）, but as commented in that paper, the use of BD for dynamic characterization of tensile properties using the SHB device must be taken carefully, since the application of the quasi-static equation has not yet been deeply validated. (TM – 11)

M 2. 4

P: Tests were terminated when pullout failure occurred, geogrid was damaged, or a frontal displacement of 9cm was reached. (TM – 16)

CP: Density and average aspect ratio were measured in the lab, and grains were seived into the same grain size range, as shown in Table 1, with the exception of corundum, which arrived presieved from the industrial abrasives company Panadyne, Inc. (TM – 06)

M 1. 2a

P: All specimens had the same longitudinal reinforcement B450C (2 Φ 6）, while in the beams with shear reinforcement, 2 Φ 8 were used as compression steel. (TM – 26)

C: Three rebar specimens were tested; the average yield stress was 462MPa and the average ultimate stress was 627MPa. (TM – 01)

【V2】

M 2. 2a

S: ENVI-met is generally used with a typical spatial resolution of 0. 5e10 m in space and 10s in time. (TM – 12)

P: Although perfect fixity was sought, this support was, in reality, only partially fixed. (TM – 01)

C: The tie rods were not overtightened and a significant gap was maintained between the column and the tie rods to avoid applying any significant artificial confinement. (TM – 01)

M 1. 2a

S: The dimensions and shape of the prestressed concrete sleeper specimens are shown in Table 1. (TM – 24)

P: The typical full-scale prestressed concrete sleepers, which are often used in broad gauge tracks, were selected for these tests. (TM – 24)

C: In total, 14 and 7 coupons were prepared from the outer jacket in the longitudinal and transverse directions, respectively, and 7 coupons were prepared from the inner jacket in each direction, longitudinal and transverse. (TM – 10)

CP: The columns were cast after the footing was set and finally, the cap beam was cast on top of the columns. (TM – 23)

M 2. 4

S: Acceleration amplitude is recorded in volts (Av) at 200kHz sampling frequency. (TM – 03)

P: The loading was then continued until the experimental yield load Q_y and corresponding top wall displacement Δ_y were determined. (TM – 17)

C: For the confined geocell sections, the sand was placed into the box and compacted to 70% relative density in three layers, 50mm each for the first two layers and 20mm for the top layer. (TM – 19)

CP: Rotor height, shear strain rate, and axial force were recorded at 1 Hz sampling frequency, and the first 30s of each velocity step was ignored during analysis so that only steady-state data were used in evaluation. (TM – 03)

第九节　外国语言学及应用语言学

语音学是外国语言学及应用语言学主要研究对象之一，语音学主要研究语音的产生、传导和接收，以及言语的声音、语音的描述和分类、单词和连音等。传统实验室研究方法为该领域最主要的研究方法，本研究主要分析该领域实证性论文传统实验方法写作部分的体裁特征。

本研究共从 12 种国际知名语言学期刊上选取了 20 篇语音研究方面的论文，其中用于分析的句子共有 1199 句，约 27086 个单词。该部分包含句子最多的论文中有 137 句，最少的有 18 句，平均值为 59.95 句，标准差为 29.57。其中有 70% 的论文于 2010 年后发表。有 80% 文章的第一作者通信地址为英语国家。这些文章基本上均采用了 IMRD(C)的结构，方法部分在论文中占比各语篇之间存在一定的差异，但是总体上占比不高，最大值为 43%，最小值为 6%，平均值为 21%，标准差为 0.08。

一　标题特征分析

图 4.9.1 和图 4.9.2 分别是该学科实验方法部分大小标题词汇云图。有一篇文章中实验方法包括两个平行的部分，即有两个一级大标题，其他各篇文章均只包含一个一级大标题。大标题中共出现了 3 种不同的词汇，其中 method（s）使用频率最高，共出现过 18 次，其次是 materials，共出现过 13 次。所有的文章中均包含了二级小标题，最多的有 7 个，最少的有 3 个。二级小标题中出现频率最高的单词为

procedure，共出现过 18 次，其次分别为 analysis 和 participants，均出现过 13 次。出现频率较高的还有 stimuli，共出现过 12 次。所分析的文章均为语音学研究论文，在语音实验中会涉及发音人，有时也会强调发音材料，因此小标题中 participants 和 stimuli 出现频率较高。此外，有四篇文章包含三级小标题，最多的有 5 个，最少的有 2 个。

图 4.9.1　一级大标题词汇云图

图 4.9.2　二级小标题词汇云图

综上所述，该领域论文方法部分均包含一级大标题和二级小标题，少数文章中还包含三级小标题。一级大标题与所研究的学科没有显著的相关性，二级小标题中词汇与研究对象和研究手段关系更密切，三级小标题与具体研究问题关系最密切。此外，不同文章中包含的二级或三级小标题数量存在一定的差异。

二　语步特征分析

本节主要研究论文实验方法写作的语步特征。分析发现，这部分写作的总体框架可以分为三个大的语步，与本研究中涉及的其他几个学科相似，但是不同学科各语步中包含的步骤种类存在一定的差异，本节各语步列表中只列出该学科论文中出现的步骤。

（一）语步一特征

表4.9.1是语步一中所包含的步骤种类。如表所示，语步一中共包括了14个步骤。表4.9.2是各篇文章语步一中各步骤在该语步中的占比情况。如表所示，所有文章均包含该语步，但该语步中各步骤在各篇文章中占比情况不一。此外，同一个步骤在不同文章中的占比情况也有所差异。以下是针对每个步骤占比情况的具体分析及实例。

表4.9.1　　　　　　　　　　语步一各步骤列表

M		语步一、实验准备	
1.1B	重述研究目的	1.2d	样本/材料/数据预处理或培养方法
1.1C	交代实验时间/场所	1.3a	实验条件及注意事项
1.1D	被试者来源/数量/特征	1.3b	样本/材料/数据局限性
1.1E	被试者招募方法	1.5	前人实验准备方法
1.2a	样本来源/数量/特点	1.6	强调实验准备的合理性
1.2b	材料/数据/试剂来源/数量及特点	1.7	符合伦理要求/注册信息
1.2c	样本/材料/数据选取方法	1.8	付给参与者的薪酬

表4.9.2　　　　　　　　　　语步一各步骤占比

M	1.1B	1.1C	1.1D	1.1E	1.2a	1.2b	1.2c	1.2d	1.3a	1.3b	1.5	1.6	1.7	1.8
YY-01	—	5%	36%	—	12%	18%	—	18%	—	—	—	—	—	12%
YY-02	—	5%	29%	—	29%	—	14%	—	14%	—	—	—	—	10%
YY-03	—	—	22%	11%	11%	22%	—	33%	—	—	—	—	—	—
YY-04	—	—	10%	—	—	10%	40%	40%	—	—	—	—	—	—
YY-05	—	3%	9%	—	—	44%	9%	19%	—	9%	—	3%	—	3%
YY-06	25%	—	13%	—	13%	—	6%	13%	13%	—	—	19%	—	—
YY-07	—	—	16%	—	—	35%	—	25%	—	—	—	16%	8%	—
YY-08	3%	—	47%	17%	—	11%	—	—	—	3%	—	11%	6%	3%
YY-09	—	—	59%	12%	12%	12%	—	—	6%	—	—	—	—	—
YY-10	—	25%	42%	—	—	—	—	—	17%	—	—	—	—	17%
YY-11	—	—	12%	—	—	65%	9%	3%	—	2%	—	3%	—	6%
YY-12	—	—	4%	2%	—	8%	8%	29%	12%	—	4%	33%	—	—
YY-13	—	—	12%	24%	—	9%	—	35%	—	—	3%	18%	—	—
YY-14	—	—	34%	—	—	19%	—	—	—	—	—	44%	—	3%
YY-15	—	—	8%	—	5%	27%	2%	16%	21%	—	2%	11%	8%	—
YY-16	2%	—	7%	2%	—	55%	9%	3%	3%	—	3%	13%	—	2%
YY-17	—	—	8%	12%	—	37%	16%	—	22%	—	—	4%	—	—
YY-18	—	—	38%	7%	—	31%	—	12%	4%	—	—	5%	5%	—
YY-19	—	2%	7%	14%	—	21%	9%	5%	30%	—	2%	5%	5%	—
YY-20	—	7%	67%	—	—	7%	—	—	—	—	7%	—	—	13%

M 1.1B 重述研究目的：所选文章中只有三篇包含该步骤。在这三篇文章中，该步骤在语步一中的占比分别为25%、3%和2%。实例如下：

As noted previously, virtually nothing is known about acoustic differences between different populations of speakers. For this reason, in this initial study we opted to control for possible systematic differences between populations by studying a homogeneous group, so that we would be able to unambiguously attribute acoustic differences to within- or between-speaker factors, without the added complication of differences between populations. (YY-06)

One of the goals of Experiment 1 was to examine voice quality, by measuring the difference in amplitude between the first and second harmonics (H2－H1) of the glottal waveform. (YY-

08）

M 1.1C 交代实验时间/场所：所选文章中有30%的文章包含该步骤。在包含该步骤的文章中，该步骤在语步一中的占比最大值为25%，最小值为2%，平均值为8%，标准差为0.08。实例如下：

The two elicitation sessions（2012 and 2015）were recorded in training rooms of the Benishangul-Gumuz Ministry of Education in Asosa, Ethiopia during Komo literacy workshops.（YY – 05）

The recordings were conducted indoors at various sited throughout the city of Santiago, including participants' homes（n = 12）and a soundproof booth at a local university（n = 8）.（YY – 10）

M 1.1D 被试者来源/数量/特征：所选文章均包含该步骤。该步骤在语步一中的占比最大值为67%，最小值为4%，平均值为24%，标准差为0.18。实例如下：

Twenty talkers（ten females and ten males）aged between 19 and 34 were recruited from the University of California, Berkeley and the University of Kansas, Lawrence communities.（YY – 01）

Twenty speakers（ten females and ten males）were recruited from the Cornell University student population.（YY – 02）

M 1.1E 被试者招募方法：所选文章中有40%的文章包含该步骤。在包含该步骤的文章中，该步骤在语步一中的占比最大值为24%，最小值为2%，平均值为11%，标准差为0.07。实例如下：

Talkers were recruited from a variety of locations, both from the University of Minnesota, and from the St. Paul/Minneapolis metropolitan area.（YY – 08）

Adults were recruited through the author's personal network in Songyuan, China, and children were recruited and tested in the No. 2 Daycare Center in Songyuan.（YY – 09）

M 1.2a 样本来源/数量/特点：所选文章中有30%的文章包含该步骤。在包含该步骤的文章中，该步骤在语步一中的占比最大值为29%，最小值为5%，平均值为14%，标准差为0.07。实例如下：

The final consonant was always/p/.（YY – 02）

In all, each subject produced four consonants × five vowels × five exemplars of each for a total of 100 tokens.（YY – 03）

M 1.2b 材料/数据/试剂来源/数量及特点：所选文章中有80%的文章包含该步骤。在包含该步骤的文章中，该步骤在语步一中的占比最大值为65%，最小值为7%，平均值为26%，标准差为0.17。实例如下：

Items were written as follows: "afa," "atha," "asa," "asha," "ava," "adha," "aza," and "azha."（YY – 01）

Stimuli consisted of the four voiceless fricatives of English [f θ s ʃ] followed by the five vowels [i e a o u]. (YY – 03)

M 1. 2c 样本/材料/数据选取方法：所选文章中有55%的文章包含该步骤。在包含该步骤的文章中，该步骤在语步一中的占比最大值为22%，最小值为2%，平均值为11%，标准差为0. 05。实例如下：

All recordings were sampled at 22kHz (16-bit quantization, 11-kHz low-pass filter) on a Sun SPARCstation 5. (YY – 02)

Each syllable was printed on a notecard in orthographic form (e. g. , see, fee). (YY – 03)

M 1. 2d 样本/材料/数据预处理或培养方法：所选文章中有55%的文章包含该步骤。在包含该步骤的文章中，该步骤在语步一中的占比最大值为40%，最小值为3%，平均值为17%，标准差为0. 12。实例如下：

Each syllable was identified from the BLISS waveform display, excised from the master recordings, and saved as an audio file. Peak amplitude was normalized across the audio files. (YY – 04)

We split the [c-a] and [ba] syllables into a frication portion and a vocalic portion, and generated one continuum for each one of those portions by mixing the signals at different levels of amplitude. (YY – 12)

M 1. 3a 实验条件及注意事项：所选文章中有65%的文章包含该步骤。在包含该步骤的文章中，该步骤在语步一中的占比最大值为40%，最小值为3%，平均值为18%，标准差为0. 11。实例如下：

The recordings were made in a double-wall sound booth (IAC) with a professional microphone (Shure SM81 – LC). The microphone was connected through a preamplifier and analog-to-digital converter (Sound Devices USBPre Microphone Interface) to a personal computer. (YY – 04)

Data was collected in a quiet room with an ophthalmic examination chair and ultrasound machine. All the sound files were recorded at 48kHz and later resampled to 44. 1kHz. (YY – 07)

M 1. 3b 样本/材料/数据局限性：所选文章中只有两篇包含该步骤。在这两篇文章中，该步骤在语步一中的占比分别为9%和3%。实例如下：

As evident in the cross-tabulation, the data were unbalanced, partly as a function of the data being collected initially for other purposes. (YY – 05)

The H2 – H1 measure has the potential to be affected by F1 resonance, particularly for high vowels (which have low F1 frequencies) spoken by people with high f0. (YY – 08)

M 1. 5 前人实验准备方法：所选文章中有35%的文章包含该步骤。在包含该步骤的文章中，该步骤在语步一中的占比最大值为7%，最小值为2%，平均值为3%，标准差为0. 02。实例如下：

Following Wellmann et al. (2012), the stimuli consisted of a sequence of three coordina-ted, in this case French, names. (YY – 19)

All other procedural details are as in the previous reports (Best and Strange, 1992, Hallé et al., 1999). (YY – 20)

M 1.6 强调实验准备的合理性：所选文章中有 65% 的文章包含该步骤。在包含该步骤的文章中，该步骤在语步一中的占比最大值为 44%，最小值为 3%，平均值为 14%，标准差为 0.12。实例如下：

For this reason, in this initial study we opted to control for possible systematic differences between populations by studying a homogeneous group, so that we would be able to unambigu-ously attribute acoustic differences to within- or between-speaker factors, without the added com-plication of differences between populations. (YY – 06)

Since the experimenter's production only focused on the tones for the target words and not on the choice of sibilants, it is highly unlikely that the experimenter's production changed or biased their choices of sibilant fricatives. (YY – 07)

M 1.7 符合伦理要求/注册信息：所选文章中有 25% 的文章包含该步骤。在包含该步骤的文章中，该步骤在语步一中的占比最大值为 8%，最小值为 5%，平均值为 6%，标准差为 0.01。实例如下：

All participants signed written consent forms prior to data collection. The study was conduc-ted in accordance with ethical guidelines approved by the University of British Columbia. (YY – 07)

They were then given the opportunity to withdraw their consent and have their data de-stroyed. None opted to do so. (YY – 08)

M 1.8 付给参与者的薪酬：所选文章中有 45% 的文章包含该步骤。在包含该步骤的文章中，该步骤在语步一中的占比最大值为 17%，最小值为 2%，平均值为 8%，标准差为 0.05。实例如下：

They volunteered for the experiment without monetary compensation. (YY – 01)

In exchange for participating, the speakers were compensated for their time at a rate typical for local language consultants and equivalent to about 1 hour of work at the average hourly wage in the area. (YY – 05)

综上所述，所分析的文章均包含语步一。在该语步中，涉及篇章数最高的步骤是 M1.1D，最低的是 M1.3b，分别占所有文章的 100% 和 10%。各步骤涉及篇章数平均值为 9.29 篇，占所有文章的 46%，标准差为 5.06。在这些文章中涉及步骤种类最多的有 10 种，最低的只有 4 种，分别占语步一中所有步骤的 71% 和 29%，平均值为 6.5 种，占所有步骤的 46%，标准差为 1.88。不同文章中包含的步骤种类存在一定的差异，同一个步骤在不同文章中的占比也存在一定的差异。

（二）语步二特征

表 4.9.3 是语步二中所包含的步骤种类。该语步共包括 9 种步骤。表 4.9.4 是各篇文章语步二中各步骤在该语步中的占比情况。如表所示，所有文章中均包括该语步，但该语步中各步骤占比情况不一。此外，同一个步骤在不同文章中的占比情况也存在差异。以下是针对每个步骤占比情况的具体分析及实例。

表 4.9.3 语步二各步骤列表

M	语步二、变量测量		
2.1	概述变量测量设计	2.3d	概述变量
2.2a	交代仪器/设备/工具/理论/方程/模型	2.4	描述变量测量步骤
2.2b	实验参数设置	2.5	前人变量测量方法
2.3a	定义变量	2.6	强调变量测量方法的科学性
2.3c	测量变量的原因		

表 4.9.4 语步二各步骤占比

M	2.1	2.2a	2.2b	2.3a	2.3c	2.3d	2.4	2.5	2.6
YY－01	7%	1%	—	—	7%	7%	66%	4%	7%
YY－02	—	20%	20%	53%	—	—	—	7%	—
YY－03	—	—	—	—	—	—	100%	—	—
YY－04	—	50%	—	—	—	—	50%	—	—
YY－05	36%	4%	—	—	—	—	61%	—	—
YY－06	100%	—	—	—	—	—	—	—	—
YY－07	—	17%	7%	—	—	—	55%	3%	17%
YY－08	—	4%	3%	—	—	—	93%	—	—
YY－09	—	12%	6%	—	—	—	71%	12%	—

M	2.1	2.2a	2.2b	2.3a	2.3c	2.3d	2.4	2.5	2.6
YY－10	67%	33%	—	—	—	—	—	—	—
YY－11	7%	7%	—	—	—	—	87%	—	—
YY－12	15%	3%	—	5%	—	—	67%	—	10%
YY－13	—	9%	—	—	—	—	91%	—	—
YY－14	57%	—	—	—	—	—	43%	—	—
YY－15	25%	5%	4%	—	—	—	61%	2%	4%
YY－16	33%	2%	—	—	—	—	61%	—	4%
YY－17	29%	15%	—	2%	—	—	51%	3%	—
YY－18	—	11%	—	—	—	—	89%	—	—
YY－19	2%	1%	2%	—	—	—	88%	2%	5%
YY－20	43%	10%	—	—	—	—	38%	10%	—

M 2.1 概述变量测量设计：所选文章中有 60% 的文章包含该步骤。在包含该步骤的文章中，该步骤在语步二中的占比最大值为 100%，最小值为 2%，平均值为 35%，标准差为 0.27。实例如下：

The design of this experiment is shown schematically in Figure 3. There were two blocks of the experiment. In both blocks, listeners were informed that they would hear consonant-vowel syllables taken from words that were supposed to start with "s" or "th". (YY－16)

The experiment had two phases: habituation and testing (the methodology for the experiment is diagrammed in Fig. 4). (YY－17)

M 2.2a 交代仪器/设备/工具/理论/方程/模型：所选文章中有 85% 的文章包含该步骤。在包含该步骤的文章中，该步骤在语步二中的占比最大值为 50%，最小值为 1%，平均值为 12%，标准差为 0.12。实例如下：

Recordings for both sessions were made with a Shure Beta 54 headset microphone connected to a Zoom H4n portable digital recorder. (YY－05)

VoiceSauce uses a function called STRAIGHT (Kawahara et al., 1999) to obtain fundamental frequency measures and Snack (Sjölander, 2004) to estimate the frequencies and bandwidths of the first through the fourth formants, and these estimates are used to correct the harmonic amplitudes using the correction algorithm by Iseli, Shue, and Alwan (2007). (YY－10)

M 2.2b 实验参数设置：所选文章中有 30% 的文章包含该步骤。在包含该步骤的文章中，该步骤在语步二中的占比最大值为 20%，最小值为 2%，平均值为 7%，标准差为 0.06。实例如下：

Fricative segmentation involved the simultaneous consultation of waveform and wideband spectrogram. (YY – 02)

All the sound files were recorded at 48kHz and later resampled to 44.1kHz. (YY – 07)

M 2.3a 定义变量：所选文章中有三篇包含该步骤。在这三篇文章中，该步骤在语步二中的占比分别为53%、5%和2%。实例如下：

Fricative onset was defined as the point at which high-frequency energy first appeared on the spectrogram and/or the point at which the number of zero crossings rapidly increased. (YY – 02)

Finally, an important factor in infant studies is the naturalness of the stimuli. Given that differences in length, amplitude, and pitch had been equated prior to this manipulation, there were no artifacts, and the interpolation resulted in stimuli that sounded extremely natural. (YY – 12)

M 2.3c 测量变量的原因：所选文章中只有一篇包含该步骤。在该篇文章中，该步骤在语步二中的占比为7%。实例如下：

These repeated productions served as clear speech in acoustic analyses. (YY – 01)

M 2.3d 概述变量：所选文章中只有一篇包含该步骤。在该篇文章中，该步骤在语步二中的占比为7%。实例如下：

Spectral measures included the discrete Fourier transform (DFT) spectral peak frequency (1), the first four spectral moments (M1 – M4; 2 – 5), F2 onset transitions (6), spectral slopes below (7) and above (8) peak frequencies, and the average fundamental frequency (f0) of adjacent vowels (9). (YY – 01)

M 2.4 描述变量测量步骤：所选文章中有85%的文章包含该步骤。在包含该步骤的文章中，该步骤在语步二中的占比最大值为100%，最小值为38%，平均值为69%，标准差为0.18。实例如下：

Test trials began with the green light at the front flashing. When the infant oriented towards this light, it was extinguished and one of the red side lights began flashing. (YY – 12)

At test, they heard both types of sequences. Infants were randomly assigned to a familiarization condition, with 20 infants per age group and condition. (YY – 19)

M 2.5 前人变量测量方法：所选文章中有40%的文章包含该步骤。在包含该步骤的文章中，该步骤在语步二中的占比最大值为12%，最小值为2%，平均值为5%，标准差为0.03。实例如下：

The test procedure was similar to what is described in Li (2012). (YY – 09)

The test phase continued until the infant habituated again (following Best and McRoberts, 2003; Best et al., 1988; Best et al., 1995). (YY – 17)

M 2.6 强调变量测量方法的科学性：所选文章中有30%的文章包含该步骤。在包含该步骤的文章中，该步骤在语步二中的占比最大值为17%，最小值为4%，平均值为8%，标准差为 0.05。实例如下：

> Speakers were not explicitly instructed or coached on stress type or placement since this might have created a bias toward one style or the other or caused speakers to imitate the experimenter instead of producing clear speech modifications spontaneously. (YY – 01)

> This procedure helps with adjusting the probe to an appropriate position, as the drinking movement determines the trace of the palate (Epstein & Stone, 2005). (YY – 07)

综上所述，所分析的文章均包含语步二。在该语步中，涉及篇章数最高的步骤有两个，分别是 M2.2a 和 M2.4，均占所有文章的85%；最低的也有两个，分别是 M2.3c 和 M2.3d，均占所有文章的5%。各步骤涉及篇章数平均值为7.89篇，占所有文章的39%，标准差为6.21。在这些文章中涉及步骤种类最多的有7种，最低的只有1种，分别占语步二中所有步骤的78%和11%，平均值为3.55种，占所有步骤的39%，标准差为1.73。不同文章中包含的步骤种类存在一定的差异，同一个步骤在不同文章中的占比也存在一定的差异。

（三）语步三特征

表4.9.5是语步三中所包含的步骤种类。如表所示，该语步中共包括10个步骤。表4.9.6是各篇文章语步三中各步骤在该语步中的占比情况。如表所示，有一部分文章不包含该语步。在包含该步骤的文章中，该语步中各步骤占比情况不一。此外，同一个步骤在不同文章中的占比情况也有所差异。以下是针对每个步骤占比情况的具体分析及实例。

表4.9.5　　　　　　　　　　语步三各步骤列表

M			
	语步三、数据分析		
3.1	描述数据分析工具/符号	3.5	分析实验结果
3.2	描述数据统计方法	3.6	强调数据分析方法的合理性
3.2a	数据处理步骤	3.7a	描述实验结果
3.2b	概述数据类型	3.7b	预估的实验结果
3.3	前人数据分析方法	3.9a	解释实验数据与模型/理论的偏差

表4.9.6　　　　　　　　　　　语步三各步骤占比

M	3.1	3.2	3.2a	3.2b	3.3	3.5	3.6	3.7a	3.7b	3.9a
YY–01	3%	19%	35%	19%	4%	—	20%	—	—	—
YY–02	—	—	74%	3%	9%	—	14%	—	—	—
YY–03	—	—	17%	—	—	—	7%	66%	—	10%
YY–04	13%	5%	51%	3%	4%	10%	13%	—	3%	—
YY–05	7%	56%	9%	13%	4%	—	10%	—	—	—
YY–06	2%	25%	44%	10%	2%	—	17%	—	—	—
YY–07	8%	33%	44%	6%	—	—	6%	3%	—	—
YY–08	4%	7%	58%	14%	10%	—	7%	—	—	—
YY–09	14%	32%	36%	18%	—	—	—	—	—	—
YY–10	8%	15%	36%	16%	10%	—	16%	—	—	—
YY–11	—	—	—	—	—	—	—	—	—	—
YY–12	—	—	—	100%	—	—	—	—	—	—
YY–13	—	—	—	—	—	—	—	—	—	—
YY–14	—	—	—	—	—	—	—	—	—	—
YY–15	9%	20%	54%	5%	9%	—	4%	—	—	—
YY–16	—	—	78%	—	—	—	22%	—	—	—
YY–17	—	—	—	—	—	—	—	—	—	—
YY–18	—	25%	—	13%	—	63%	—	—	—	—
YY–19	3%	83%	—	—	—	—	13%	—	—	—
YY–20	—	—	—	—	—	—	—	—	—	—

M 3.1 描述数据分析工具/符号：所选文章中有一半的文章包含该步骤。在包含该步骤的文章中，该步骤在语步三中的占比最大值为14%，最小值为2%，平均值为7%，标准差为0.04。实例如下：

Acoustic analysis was conducted with BLISS and MATLAB (MathWorks). (YY–04)

The analyses were conducted in R using the lme4 and lmerTest packages. (YY–7)

M 3.2 描述数据统计方法：所选文章中有55%的文章包含该步骤。在包含该步骤的文章中，该步骤在语步三中的占比最大值为83%，最小值为5%，平均值为29%，标准差为0.22。实例如下：

Unless noted otherwise, an ANOVA was conducted for each acoustic measure with place of articulation (f, s, x, and sh) as a within subject factor, speaker gender (female and male) as a between-subject factors, and speakers as a random factor. (YY–04)

Predictor contrasts were deviation-coded, allowing for an ANOVA-style interpretation of main effects and interactions (see Singmann & Kellen, forthcoming). (YY – 05)

M 3. 2a 数据处理步骤：所选文章中有 60% 的文章包含该步骤。在包含该步骤的文章中，该步骤在语步三中的占比最大值为 78%，最小值为 9%，平均值为 45%，标准差为 0. 19。实例如下：

Each production was high-pass filtered at 300Hz using a second order Butterworth filter to minimize voicing and other low frequency perturbations that might obscure zero-crossings resulting from the turbulent source. (YY – 01)

Fast Fourier transforms (FFTs) were conducted with a 40-ms full Hamming window at three locations: onset, middle, and offset of the fricative. (YY – 04)

M 3. 2b 概述数据类型：所选文章中有 60% 的文章包含该步骤。在包含该步骤的文章中，该步骤在语步三中的占比最大值为 100%，最小值为 3%，平均值为 18%，标准差为 0. 25。实例如下：

The acoustic analysis considered 14 spectral, amplitudinal, and duration parameters that previous studies indicate may work in combination with signal fricative contrasts. (YY – 01)

Spectral peak is defined here as the highest amplitude peak of the FFT spectrum. (YY – 02)

M 3. 3 前人数据分析方法：所选文章中有 40% 的文章包含该步骤。在包含该步骤的文章中，该步骤在语步三中的占比最大值为 10%，最小值为 2%，平均值为 6%，标准差为 0. 03。实例如下：

Following the psychoacoustic model of voice quality described in Kreiman et al. (2014), acoustic parameters included fundamental frequency (F0); the first four formant frequencies (F1, F2, F3, F4), the relative amplitudes of the first and second harmonics (H1* – H2*) and the second and fourth harmonics (H2* – H4*); and the spectral slopes from the fourth harmonic to the harmonic nearest 2kHz in frequency (H4* – H2kHz*) and from the harmonic nearest 2kHz to the harmonic nearest 5kHz in frequency (H2kHz* – H5kHz). (YY – 06)

As in previous research (Pierrehumbert et al. , 2004), these were expressed in Bark units (Zwicker & Ternhardt, 1980). (YY – 08)

M 3. 5 分析实验结果：所选文章中只有两篇包含该步骤。在这两篇文章中，该步骤在语步三中的占比分别为 63% 和 10%。实例如下：

The differences among fricatives in this measure can be predicted from the front cavity resonance excited by the noise source. (YY – 04)

The intraclass correlation coefficients for intra-listener and inter-listener reliability were 93. 7% and 92. 4%, respectively. (YY – 18)

M 3. 6 强调数据分析方法的合理性：所选文章中有 60% 的文章包含该步骤。在包含该步骤的文章中，该步骤在语步三中的占比最大值为22%，最小值为4%，平均值为12%，标准差为0.06。实例如下：

> We found that good identification was achieved by (1) normalizing the log of this envelope to the range [−1, 1] and (2) taking the single continuous region closest to the center of the production for which the resulting sequence was above zero corresponding to the fricative. (YY−01)

> This larger window size yields better resolution in the frequency domain, at the expense of resolution in the temporal domain. (YY−02)

M 3.7a 描述实验结果：所选文章中只有两篇包含该步骤。在这两篇文章中，该步骤在语步三中的占比分别为66%和3%。实例如下：

> For all speakers [s] and [š] are longer in duration than [f] and [θ], with smaller differences occurring between [s] and [š] and between [f] and [θ]. (YY−03)

> Notably, higher coefficients of variation were consistently found for the first and the last four data points for all speakers and across all vowel contexts. (YY−07)

M 3.7b 预估的实验结果：所选文章中只有一篇包含该步骤。在该篇文章中，该步骤在语步三中的占比为3%。实例如下：

> Therefore, one would expect non-sibilant fricatives to have lower normalized amplitude than sibilant fricatives. (YY−04)

M 3.9a 解释实验数据与模型/理论的偏差：所选文章中只有一篇包含该步骤。在这篇文章中，该步骤在语步三中的占比为10%。实例如下：

> Our data contradict those of Klatt (ms.) who found that [f] had the shortest noise duration of the four voiceless fricatives and that [s š θ] did not differ in duration among each other. (YY−03)

综上所述，所分析的文章中25%的文章不包含语步三。在包含该步骤的文章中，该语步中涉及篇章数最高的步骤有3个，分别是M3.2a、M3.2b和M3.6，均占所有文章的60%；最低的有2个，分别是M3.7b和M3.9a，均占所有文章的5%，平均值为7.1篇，占所有文章的36%，标准差为5。在这些文章中涉及步骤种类最多的有8种，最低的只有1种，分别占语步三中所有步骤的80%和10%，平均值为4.73种，占所有步骤的47%，标准差为1.91。不同文章中包含的步骤种类存在一定的差异，同一个步骤在不同文章中的占比也存在一定的差异。

（四）语步占比及轨迹

图 4.9.3 是所分析各篇文章中三个语步总体占比。如图所示，所有文章均包含语步一和语步二，75% 的文章包含语步三。就各个语步占比而言，分别有 30% 和 55% 的文章语步一和语步三占比最高，15% 的文章语步二占比最高。在语步三占比最高的文章中，有八篇文章语步一占比高于语步二，另外有一篇文章这两个步骤占比相同。在语步一占比最高的文章中，语步二占比均高于语步三。语步二占比最高的文章中均不包含语步三。

就各步骤在所有语步中占比平均值来看，占比最高的前三个步骤依次为 M2.4、M3.2a 和 M1.2b。占比最低的分别是 M3.7b、M2.3c 和 M2.3d。就各步骤涉及的篇章数而言，所有文章中均包含 M1.1D，另外有 85% 的文章中包含 M2.2a 和 M2.4；最低的有四个步骤，分别是 M2.3c、M2.3d、M3.7b 和 M3.9a，只有一篇文章同时包含这几个步骤，占所有文章的 5%。就各篇文章中包含的步骤种类来看，最多的有 19 种，占所有步骤种类的 58%。最低的仅有 6 种，占所有步骤种类的 18%。各篇文章中包含步骤种类的平均值为 13.6 种，占所有步骤种类的 41%，标准差为 3.95。

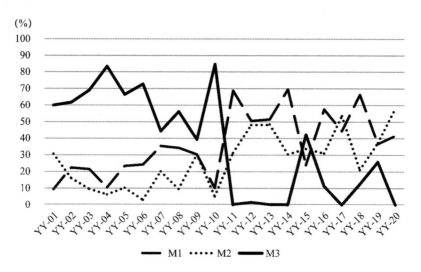

图 4.9.3　各篇文章中三个语步占比

　　图 4.9.4 至图 4.9.6 分别为语步一、语步二和语步三的分布轨迹。如图所示，所分析的 20 篇文章中均包含语步一和语步二，有五篇文章中不包含语步三。

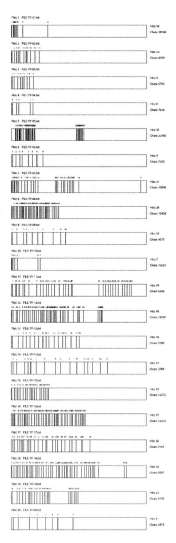

图 4.9.4　语步一分布轨迹

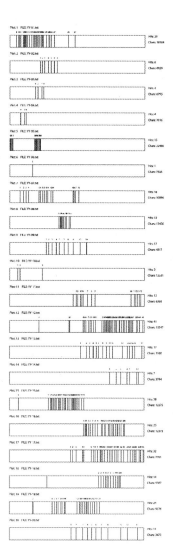

图 4.9.5　语步二分布轨迹

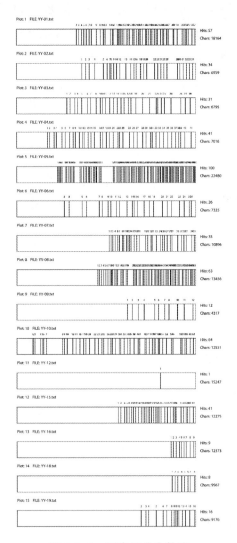

图4.9.6 语步三分布轨迹

在不包含语步三的文章中，有一半以上文章语步一占比高于语步二，语步一分布也较广。各篇文章的最前部分均为语步一，语步一主要分布在文章的前部及中间偏后的位置，语步二主要分布在语步一后，但是在少数文章中语步一和语步二有交叉。

在包含三个语步的文章中，有大部分语步三占比最高，分布也最广，其他两个语步占比均较低，覆盖范围也较窄。各篇文章中语步一主要分布在文章的前部，少数文章中部分语句也会分布在文章的中间及偏后的位置。语步二主要分布在语步一后、语步三前，也有少部分文章语步二中部分语句分布在语步一前。除在一篇只包含一句语步三的文章中，语步三分布在语步二中，其他各篇文章中语步三均分布在语步二后，两个语步之间没有交叉。但是大部分文章中语步一和语步二之间有交叉。

综上所述，同一学科不同文章中语步占比和分布轨迹既有相同之处，同时也存在一定的差异。所有文章均出现了语步一和语步二。大多数文章中语步三占比最高，分布最广，同时也较集中。语步一以文章最前和前部为主，语步二主要分布在语步一后、语步三前，但是少部分文章语步二中部分语句也会分布在语步一前，在极少数情况下分布在文章的最后。大部分文章中语步一与语步二有交叉，语步三与语步一之间没有交叉，与语步二交叉的情况也极少。

三 语言特征分析

本小节主要分析该领域论文实验方法写作的语言特征。主要从句子、时态和语态三个大的方面进行分析。针对句子的分析主要包含句子类型、四类主要句子长度分布及四类主要句子与语步之间的关系。针对时态的分析主要包含时态种类、不同时态组合及三种占比最高的时态组合与语步的关系。针对语态的分析主要包含语态种类及各语态组合与语步的关系。

（一）句子特征

A. 句子类型

表4.9.7是本学科20篇文章中所包含的句子类型及各类句子占比。如表所示，简单句、复杂句、复合句及复合复杂句占所有句子的97.33%。有语法错误的句子占所有句子的0.42%，其他为带有冒号及i.e.的各类特殊句子。四类句子中简单句占比远高于其他三类句子，其次是复杂句。其他两类句子占比均较低，其中复合复杂句最

低。特殊类型句子形式多样，共有 15 种，其中 NWS 占比较高，其他的均较低。以下例句为特殊类型的句子。

表 4.9.7 　　　　　　　　　　句类及占比

句类	句数	占比	句类	句数	占比
S	757	63. 14%	PPC	1	0. 08%
P	264	22. 02%	NCPF	1	0. 08%
C	107	8. 92%	NPS	1	0. 08%
CP	39	3. 25%	NSC	1	0. 08%
BCS	1	0. 08%	NSP	1	0. 08%
BPFW	1	0. 08%	NSS	1	0. 08%
BSP	1	0. 08%	NWC	1	0. 08%
IPP	1	0. 08%	NWP	4	0. 33%
IPS	1	0. 08%	NWS	13	1. 08%
ISP	1	0. 08%	R	5	0. 42%

BCS： All participants were native Putonghua speakers (therefore the possibly of dialectal influence was eliminated) and received primary palatoplasty earlier than three years of age. (YY – 18)

IPP： If the confidence interval of standardized beta includes zero, we conclude that there is no reason to reject the null hypothesis, that is, we conclude that the results indicate no difference between conditions. (YY – 19)

IPS： For example, /s/-/ʃ/distances were considered (1) between productions of/s/that were produced specifically in response to a "misidentification" as/ʃ/ (we will represent this with the notation s丨ʃ) and/ʃ/productions produced after identification as/s/ (ʃ丨s), (2) between clear/s/productions that were produced in response to misidentifications of sounds other than/ʃ/ (represented s丨~ʃ) and ʃ丨~s productions, and (3) initial conversational productions of the two sounds (s丨ø, ʃ丨ø). (YY – 01)

ISP： Members of each AB comparison were made by pairing each stimulus with the next stimulus one or two steps apart along the continuum, i. e. 140 – 130ms is a one-step pair while 140 – 120ms is a twostep pair. (YY – 11)

PPC： To investigate leftward 〔+ATR〕 spreading, we chose verb roots with the non-high vowels/a, e, ɔ/— these were underlyingly 〔-ATR〕 and served as potential harmony targets — and elicited verb agreement suffixes whose vowels varied in 〔ATR〕 value (/-a/1SG for 〔-ATR〕 and/-i-p'/

DDø-3SG. F for [+ ATR]). (YY – 05)

NCPF: Each model included a random effect of participant in which each participant contributed their own random intercept in order to account for production idiosyncrasies at the participant level, and all models included an interaction between the following segment predictor and the variable of interest: whether each vowel originated from a singular word (termed a singular vowel), a plural word with the final/s/deleted (termed a plural vowel), or a monomorphemic/s/-final word with the/s/deleted (termed a monomorphemic vowel). (YY – 10)

NPS: The top node indicates that the initial split was based on F1: target vowels with normalized F1 values less than 0. 1 were more likely to be in [+ ATR] contexts. (YY – 05)

NSC: Familiarization condition was counterbalanced: one group of infants heard no-boundary sequences, and the other heard with-boundary sequences. (YY – 19)

NSP: For vowels with higher F1 values, periodicity played a further role: vowels with low CPP tended to be in [+ ATR] contexts while those high on the measure were likely to be in [ATR] contexts. (YY – 05)

NSS: The other three pairs spanned the same distance in terms of interpolation steps: we call these natural, mid, and unnatural. (YY – 12)

NWC: For example, /i/tokens outnumbered/ɔ/by more than a 2: 1 margin, speaker K1 was relatively overrepresented, and there were several missing cells: only four speakers provided/u/tokens, with K17 providing little else. (YY – 05)

NWP: A background questionnaire confirmed that each subject met the following selection criteria: no history of hearing loss, native Danish, native Danish-speaking parents, and limited immersion in languages other than Danish (<8 months living in a foreign language environment). (YY – 20)

NWS: She read the sequences in two different prosodic groupings as indicated by different bracketing as below: no boundary: [Loulou et Manou et Nina] With boundary: [Loulou et Manou] [et Nina]. (YY – 19)

B. 句类与语步

图 4.9.7 是四种类型句子与三个语步中各步骤的关系。如图所示，这四类句子中占比最高的三个步骤中均包含了 M2.4 和 M3.2，但是这两个步骤在各类句子中排序不完全一致。还有一个步骤各类句子中均不相同。此外，由于四类句子在文章中占比不同，即使相同步骤在这四种句子中排序一致，同一个步骤在不同句类中的数量和占比也均不相同。

　　这四类句子中均包含了三个语步，就各类句子中包含的三个语步中步骤种类而言，占比最高的是简单句，其他依次为复杂句、复合句和复合复杂句，它们所包含的步骤种类分别占三个语步中所有步骤种类的97%、85%、64%和42%。

　　总体来说，不同句子类型与步骤之间的关系存在异同，句子与步骤关系紧密度与该类句子在所有句子中的占比有关，同时也与该步骤在所有步骤中的占比有关，但是不完全成——对应的关系，句类与步骤之间没有明显的相关性。

　　以下是四类句子中步骤占比最高的前三个步骤例句。

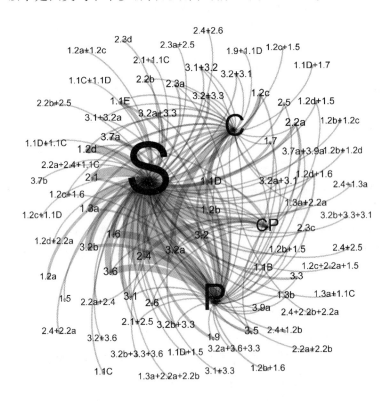

图4.9.7　句类与步骤关系网络图

【S】

M 3.2a：The epochs of interest comprised a pre-stimulus baseline of 100ms and a following 900ms window. (YY－15)

M 2. 4：Each trial began with a red light flashing on the monitor to attract the infant's attention. (YY – 17)

M 1. 2b：Stimuli consisted of the four voiceless fricatives of English [f θ s š] followed by the five vowels [i e a o u]. (YY – 03)

【P】

M 2. 4：The experimenter was unaware of the point at which the infant reached the habituation criterion. (YY – 17)

M 3. 2a：Trials with artifacts were rejected if any of the artifact detection algorithms exceeded threshold of 20pT. (YY – 15)

M 1. 6：Since the experimenter's production only focused on the tones for the target words and not on the choice of sibilants, it is highly unlikely that the experimenter's production changed or biased their choices of sibilant fricatives. (YY – 07)

【C】

M 3. 2a：A low-frequency slope (dB/kHz) was derived from the spectral values below this peak, and a high-frequency slope was derived from the peak to 15kHz. (YY – 01)

M 1. 1D：Of the cleft participants, five had unilateral cleft lip and palate and nine had bilateral cleft lip and palate. (YY – 18)

M 2. 4：One word was the target of the speaker's production, and the other was a contrast, and they were randomly associated with the left and right screen sides. (YY – 18)

【CP】

M 2. 4：If the infant looked away for two seconds, the trial ended and a new trial began. (YY – 17)

M 3. 2：The results were first generated in the Cartesian coordinate system and later converted into polar coordinates, which were fitted through smoothing spline analysis of variance (SS-ANOVA) with a 95% confidence interval (dashed-lined ribbons in the following figures) around the predicted fit (solid lines in the following figures) (Davidson, 2006; Gu, 2002; Mielke, 2015). (YY – 07)

M 3. 2a：The production was then converted into a time series in which each sample was labeled as either differing in sign from the previous sample [1] or not [0], and a zero-crossing envelope was created by lowpass filtering this series at 30 Hz. (YY – 01)

C. 句类与句长

表 4.9.8 是四种类型句子长度占比情况。如表所示，各类句子之间在长度分布方面相似情况不同。在长度分布占比方面，简单句与其他三类差异较大。简单句中句子长度占比最高的是单词数介于 11—

20 的句子，其次是介于 21—30 的句子。其他三类句子占比最高的均为介于 21—30 的句子，但是这三类句子中占比第二的有所不同，复合复杂句为介于 31—40 的句子，其他两类则为介于 11—20 的句子。就各类句子覆盖范围而言，复杂句和简单句跨度最广，但是简单句中没有介于 61—70 的句子。其他两类句子相同，但是复合复杂句中单词数介于 31—60 的句子占比高于复合句。

就句子长度最大值而言，简单句和复杂句相似，均高于其他两类句子，其中复杂句略高于简单句。另两类句子较为相似，其中复合句略高于复合复杂句。句子长度最小值简单句最低，复合复杂句最高。另两类句子较为接近，其中复合句略高于复杂句。如果不排除特殊类型句子，将每个公式算为一个单词的话，所有句子中最长的句子为 NCPF，最短的为简单句。

以下是所有句子中最长的 NCPF 例句和四类句子中最长和最短句子的例句。

表 4. 9. 8 　　　　　　　　　　四类句子长度分布

句长范围		1—10	11—20	21—30	31—40	41—50	51—60	61—70	71—80	MAX	MIX
S	句数	131	381	162	60	15	7	*	1	75	3
	占比	17.31%	50.33%	21.40%	7.93%	1.98%	0.92%	*	0.13%		
P	句数	2	67	103	55	22	8	4	2	76	10
	占比	0.76%	25.48%	39.16%	20.91%	8.37%	3.04%	1.52%	0.76%		
C	句数	*	34	41	22	5	4	*	*	60	11
	占比	*	32.08%	38.68%	20.75%	4.72%	3.77%	*	*		
CP	句数	*	2	14	11	8	3	*	*	57	16
	占比	*	5.26%	36.84%	28.95%	21.05%	7.89%	*	*		

NCPF \ ［**Max：81**］Each model included a random effect of participant in which each participant contributed their own random intercept in order to account for production idiosyncrasies at the participant level, and all models included an interaction between the following segment predictor and the variable of interest： whether each vowel originated from a singular word (termed a singular vowel), a plural word with the final/s/deleted (termed a plural vowel), or a monomorphemic/s/-final word with the/s/deleted (termed a monomorphemic vowel). (YY – 10)

S ** 〔Max：75**〕 Following the psychoacoustic model of voice quality described in Kreiman et al. (2014), acoustic parameters included fundamental frequency (F0); the first four formant frequencies (F1, F2, F3, F4), the relative amplitudes of the first and second harmonics (H1* – H2*) and the second and fourth harmonics (H2* – H4*); and the spectral slopes from the fourth harmonic to the harmonic nearest 2kHz in frequency (H4* – H2kHz*) and from the harmonic nearest 2kHz to the harmonic nearest 5kHz in frequency (H2kHz* – H5kHz). (YY – 06)

S ** 〔Min：3**〕 Outliers were hand-measured. (YY – 16)

P ** 〔Max：76**〕 To check that these stimuli were not more unnatural than others used in previous literature, the 2 endpoints of our stimuli (f0v0 and f9v9) and those of Maye et al.'s (2008) coronal series (d1 – 100, and t1 + 21) were played to 8 naive listeners of mixed language backgrounds (2 Italian, 2 Russian, 2 French, 2 English), who were asked to rate the 4 stimuli in naturalness/unnaturalness on a scale from 1 (very unnatural) to 9 (very natural). (YY – 12)

P ** 〔Min：10**〕 Subjects were told that they should respond on every trial. (YY – 11)

C ** 〔Max：60**〕 Ensemble averaging across tokens within a given speaker/fricative/style condition was used to reduce error in spectral estimates; each spectrum X (f) considered below, then, represents an average of 5 – 20 (depending on the comparison; see Sec. II E for analysis details) │ DFT│2 values at frequencies of 50 – 15 000 Hz (the frequency response of the microphone) in 1 Hz increments. (YY – 01)

C ** 〔Min：11**〕 This window of data was extracted, and its spectrum was calculated. (YY – 08)

CP ** 〔Max：57**〕 In each AXB discrimination test, triads of stimuli were presented in which the first and third item were separated by three steps along a 10-step continuum, and the middle item matched the first or third item; all possible 3-step pairings were presented an equal number of times, in all four possible triad orders (AAB, ABB, BAA, BBA). (YY – C20)

CP ** 〔Min：16**〕 If the infant looked away for two seconds, the trial ended and a new trial began. (YY – 17)

（二）时态特征

A. 时态种类及占比

表4.9.9是该学科论文中使用的时态类型及组合形式。如表所示，除去有语法错误的句子，该学科文章中共出现了9种不同时态，其中T6、T8和T11没有单独使用，与其他时态共同出现在一个句子

中。由不同时态构成的组合共有 18 种，其中两种时态组合共 11 种，三种时态组合共 5 种，四种时态组合共 2 种。不同时态组合中包含 T3 的最多，其次为 T1，分别占所有组合的 74% 和 58%，其他时态在组合中占比均较低。

各种时态组合中，全部由一种时态构成的句子中占比最高的是 T3，其次为 T1。由不同时态构成的句子中占比最高的是 T1 和 T3 组合，其他相同或不同时态组合占比均较低。

以下是按照四种类型句子给出的相同时态和不同时态组合的例句，但不是所有时态组合中均包含这四类句子。

表 4.9.9　　　　　　　　　　时态类型及组合

时态	T1	T2	T3	T4	T5	T10	T1T2	T1T2T3
句数	134	6	923	3	3	6	5	2
占比	11.22%	0.50%	77.30%	0.25%	0.25%	0.50%	0.42%	0.17%
时态	T1T3	T1T3T4	T1T3T4T10	T1T3T5	T1T3T5T10	T1T3T10	T1T4	T1T8
句数	52	1	1	1	1	3	3	1
占比	4.36%	0.08%	0.08%	0.08%	0.08%	0.25%	0.25%	0.08%
时态	T1T10	T2T3	T3T4	T3T5	T3T5T11	T3T6	T3T8	T3T10
句数	1	4	1	12	1	2	3	25
占比	0.08%	0.34%	0.08%	1.01%	0.08%	0.17%	0.25%	2.09%

【T1】

S: For space reasons, henceforth we use the notation M1 – 4 to refer to the normalized mean, SD, skewness, and kurtosis values. (YY – 01)

P: For example, in (6a) the suffix consists of a neutral [-ATR] context vowel, whereas in (6b) it contains a [+ ATR] trigger expected to affect to root. (YY – 05)

C: [s] and [š] can be clearly distinguished by the distribution of spectral peaks; major peaks for [s] fall in a higher frequency range (3.8 – 8 ~ 5kHz) than for [s] (2.3 – 7kHz). (YY – 03)

CP: This condition represents a perceptual baseline, since infants are exposed to the same sounds but there is no mode in frequency to shape their perceptual space. (YY – 12)

【T2】

S: The perceptual relevance of the relative amplitude difference has been demonstrated by Hedrick and Ohde (1993) and Stevens (1985). (YY–04)

【T3】

S: Men and women differed significantly in age (Mwomen ¼ 29 years, SDwomen ¼ 7: 2 years; Mmen ¼ 24: 5, SDmen ¼ 4: 5 years; tð42T¼ 3: 5, po0: 01). (YY–08)

P: These patterns appeared to be maintained across the three time windows, although high frequency peaks tended to appear more often at the mid-point measures. (YY–10)

C: These values were calculated for individual vowels, and the average f0 range was calculated based on the averages for each vowel. (YY–08)

CP: Efforts were made to ensure that the participants' homes were as quiet as possible in order to facilitate comparison with the data from the soundproof booth, such as asking participants to close doors and windows, and speech that was recorded with background noise was not included in this analysis. (YY–10)

【T4】

S: Hence, the results sections will focus on effects involving familiarity. (YY–19)

【T5】

S: None of the subjects had ever heard any synthetic speech before the experiment. (YY–11)

C: Eleven participants had not spent any time in an English-speaking environment; the other seven had been exposed to native English for a mean period of 4. 3 months (range: 1–7 months). (YY–20)

【T10】

S: Therefore, one would expect non-sibilant fricatives to have lower normalized amplitude than sibilant fricatives. (YY–04)

【T1T2】

P: In particular, this interpolation method produces intermediate tokens that essentially have doubled formants, one from each signal. (YY–12)

【T1T2T3】

P: This measure was included because previous research has shown that the f0 of a vowel in a fricative-vowel sequence influences whether listeners judge the fricative as/s/or/θ/ (Munson & Coyne, 2010). (YY–16)

【T1T3】

P: Nonwords were used to elicit a sufficient number of responses for target/θ/, which has a low type frequency in English. (YY–16)

C: Pause represents segments in utterance-final prosodic position, and the interviews were also coded for major breaks (a level 4 break in the Spanish ToBI system [Beckman et al. , 2002; Face & Prieto, 2007; Estebas Vilaplana & Prieto, 2009]) . (YY – 10)

CP: The difference in the duration of tokens of the two words was statistically significant (p = 0. 04) because the fricative portion of the aspirated affricates is necessarily longer than that of unaspirated affricates (Harris, Bell-Berti, & Raphael, 1995, p. 161) ; no other significant differences were found. (YY – 17)

【T1T3T4】

P: The fact that the Dutch listeners were also able to speak English only works against our hypothesis by minimizing the chances that language-specific effects will be found. (YY – 14)

【T1T3T4T10】

CP: They were also told that whenever they repeated a word, the duck would climb up one rung of the ladder, and if they help the duck to climb all the way up to the top of the ladder, they will win the game. (YY – 09)

【T1T3T5】

P: A few measures that had been previously employed but either yielded inconsistent, contradictory, or unreliable results for these contrasts (e. g. , F2 range, F3 transition, and locus equations) or are not yet fully understood with respect to fricative production and perception [i. e. , fricative noise modulation and "dynamic amplitude" —e. g. , see Jackson and Shadle (2000) , Jesus and Shadle (2002) , Pincas and Jackson (2006) , Shadle and Mair (1996)] were not considered. (YY – 01)

【T1T3T5T10】

P: The sibilant fricatives were chosen for this investigation because their production is closely related to popular-culture stereotypes of G/B men's speech (e. g. , Sedaris, 2001) , and because previous research had suggested that they might differ between G/B and heterosexual men (Linville, 1998) . (YY – 08)

【T1T3T10】

P: Familiarization time in seconds was included because it varies per infant as a result of their orientation behavior during familiarization, and might influence infants' orientation to familiar and novel trials during the test [e. g. , long familiarization can flip a familiarity preference to a novelty preference (Hunter & Ames, 1988)]. (YY – 19)

【T1T4】

C: The output of the VoiceSauce measures may be "chunked" into as many as 9 subsegments; using this option will average the data in each of 9 chunks using a certain number of glottal periods. (YY – 10)

CP: Formants that are sufficiently close will be perceptually integrated (the center-of-gravity effect; see e. g, Chistovich & Lublinskaja, 1979; Delattre, Liberman, Cooper, & Gerstman, 1952;

Xu, Jacewicz, Feth, & Krisnamurthy, 2004); specifically, listeners perceive a weighted average when formants are within 3 – 3. 5 Bark. (YY – 12)

【T1T8】

BPFW: Briefly, if infants were responding to acoustic distance between the two tokens being presented in a trial, looking times to the long trials ought to be maximal (if infants exhibited a preference for distinct tokens) or minimal (if they preferred similar-sounding tokens), given that these two tokens span the largest distance (both in interpolation steps and in acoustic terms). (YY – 12)

【T1T10】

P: In contrast with the N1, which is commonly modeled by one generator per hemisphere (e. g. , Näätänen and Alho, 1995a; Näätänen and Picton, 1987), the MMN is standardly assumed to have at least two different sources per hemisphere, an assumption that would be violated by a single-dipole analysis (Alho, 1995; Näätänen and Alho, 1995b). (YY – 15)

【T2T3】

P: We chose a total 10 measures that have been found to correlate with production and perception of phonation contrasts (i. e. which distinguish between breathy, modal and/or creaky vowels or else contribute to tonal or consonantal contrasts) in a number of languages, including ! Xoo, Arabic, Chong, Fuzhou, Gujarati, Hmong, Ju | 'hoansi, Khmer, Mazatec, Tamang, Yi, and Zapotec (Al-Tamimi, 2017; Avelino, 2010; Blankenship, 2002; DiCanio, 2009; Esposito, 2006; Garellek & Keating, 2011; Garellek, Esposito, Keating, & Kreiman, 2013; Keating, Esposito, Garellek, Khan, & Kuang, 2011; Ladefoged & Antoñanzas-Barroso, 1985; Miller, 2007; Thati, Bollepalli, Bhaskararao, & Yegnanarayana, 2012; Wayland & Jongman, 2003). (YY – 05)

【T3T4】

P: We tested the possibility that even bilingual speakers with a fairly high level of attainment in their second language will show effects of native language in speech perception. (YY – 14)

【T3T5】

P: It was assumed that formant values had been mistracked if they were greater than 2 standard deviations away from the mean values reported by Munson and Solomon (2004), who studied speakers of the same dialect as those in this study. (YY – 08)

C: All participants had been born and raised in Santiago and used Spanish as their primary language, and none had lived outside Santiago for more than 1 year. (YY – 10)

CP: Given that differences in length, amplitude, and pitch had been equated prior to this manipulation, there were no artifacts, and the interpolation resulted in stimuli that sounded extremely natural. (YY – 12)

【T3T5T11】

P: In both blocks, listeners did not know which rating they would be providing (consonant goodness, vowel category, gender typicality) until after the stimulus had finished playing. (YY – 16)

【T3T6】

P: This minimized the extent to which differences in regional dialect might have affected results. (YY – 08)

【T3T8】

P: When the experimenter judged that the infant was looking at the screen, a key was pressed to deliver the visual stimulus, a black and white checkerboard, to the testing-room monitor. (YY – 17)

C: Articipants were lying in supine position and wore non-magnetic Etymonics in-ear headphones (ETYMOTIC Research Inc., Elk Grove Village, IL). (YY – 15)

【T3T10】

P: To the extent that a predictor contributed to the tree model, scrambling its values should decrease accuracy. (YY – 05)

CP: Participants were told that they would hear 'ba' or 'da' and were instructed to report which of the two sounds they heard. (YY – 13)

B. 时态与语步

图 4.9.8 是该学科文章中三种占比最高的时态组合与语步的关系。如图所示，这三种组合中占比最高的前三个步骤存在较大的差异，分别有两个组合中包含了 M3.6 和 M3.2a，其他步骤均不相同。M3.2a 在两个组合中排序相同，M3.6 在两个组合中排序不同。即使相同步骤在不同时态组合中排序一致，同一个步骤在不同时态组合中的数量和占比也不同。

此外，这三种时态组合形式中均包含三个语步，就所包含的步骤种类而言，T3 最高，其次为 T1 和 T1T3，所包含的步骤种类分别占所有步骤种类的 97%、67% 和 45%。

总体来说，不同时态形式的句子与语步的联系存在一定的差异，时态与步骤关系紧密度与该时态在所有句子中的占比有关，同时也与该步骤在所有步骤中的占比有关，但并不是决定性的。

以下是按照四种类型句子给出的三种时态组合中占比最高的前三个步骤的例句，但是有些步骤中不包含所有类型的句子。

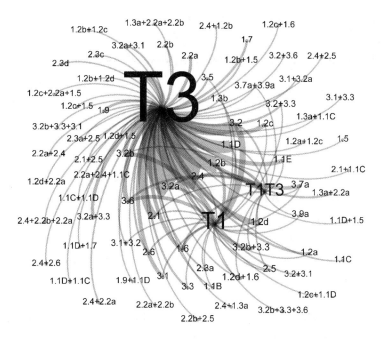

图 4.9.8 时态与步骤关系网络图

【T1】

M 3. 2

S： Polynomial regressions are used to predict the first spectral moments from their position in the fricative. (YY – 08)

P： Once such a split is found, the process repeats for each subregion until further partitioning no longer significantly reduces entropy. (YY – 05)

C： The tree is then evaluated on the remaining observations, the out-of-bag sample, and a measure of accuracy is obtained by comparing the predicted to the observed classifications. (YY – 05)

M 3. 2b

S： Normalized amplitude provides information about the relative strength of the noise source and the glottal source during fricative and vowel production. (YY – 04)

P： The first eight measures in Table 2 are based on amplitude differences between pairs of harmonics, where H1 is the fundamental, H2 and H4 are the second and fourth harmonics, and A1, A2, A3 correspond to the harmonics nearest in frequency to F1, F2 and F3 spectral peaks, respectively. (YY – 05)

C： Voice Sauce can output many measures, but of interest to the present investigation are those of vowel duration, vowel quality (F1 and F2), and H1 – H2. (YY – 10)

M 3. 6

S： The overall ranking of frication duration in the present study is similar to that reported by You (1979). (YY – 03)

P： Because modal phonation is generally more periodic than breathy voice, it is often associated with higher CPP and HNR values. (YY – 05)

【T1T3】

M 3. 6

P： A previous comparison of spectral properties of fricatives as measured at onset, midpoint, and offset of the frication noise showed that these properties are relatively stable throughout the noise portion, with high-frequency peaks more likely to emerge in the middle and end of the noise (Behrens and Blumstein, 1988a). (YY – 02)

C： Voice Sauce measures HNR at three frequency bands; for this study, we opted to investigate periodicity between 0 and 500 Hz. (YY – 05)

M 3. 2a

P： This also excluded /i/- and /u/-final words, infrequent in Spanish overall, since many of these words do not have an overt singular-versus-plural contrast on the noun itself (cf. la tesis " the thesis" and el virus " the virus," singular, vs. las tesis " the theses" and los virus " the viruses," plural). (YY – 10)

C： Ensemble averaging across tokens within a given speaker /fricative/style condition was used to reduce error in spectral estimates; each spectrum X (f) considered below, then, represents an average of 5 – 20 (depending on the comparison; see Sec. II E for analysis details) | DFT | 2 values at frequencies of 50 – 15000 Hz (the frequency response of the microphone) in 1 Hz increments. (YY – 01)

M 1. 6

P： The first author (a native speaker of American English) was recorded saying multiple instances of the 18 disyllabic sequences that result from placing each of the six fricatives into the three vowel environments. (YY – 14)

【T3】

M 2. 4

S： Listeners had 5 s to respond with a button press, rating the pair on a 5-point scale from " very similar" (1) to " very different" (5). (YY – 14)

P： The session began with four practice trials after which listeners were given a chance to ask questions about the task before proceeding to the test trials. (YY – 14)

C： One word was the target of the speaker's production, and the other was a contrast, and they were randomly associated with the left and right screen sides. (YY – 18)

CP: During the actual experiment, the sound stimuli were presented twice, and the listener was asked to move the cursor on the bar to a point that best represented what he or she heard. (YY – 18)

M 3. 2a

S: First, Praat was used to determine the f0 at the midpoint of the vowel. (YY – 08)

P: Formant values were hand-measured if they appeared to have been mistracked by the LPC algorithm. (YY – 08)

C: For each vowel, the software performed measurements at 1 millisecond intervals and returned the average value. (YY – 05)

CP: In Figure 3, singular/pjesa/ < pieza > "roomfem sg." was produced, and again, the [a] vowel was segmented at the offset of a continuous F2, though some breathy voicing occurred following this offset. (YY – 10)

M 1. 2b

S: Stimuli consisted of the four voiceless fricatives of English [f θ s š] followed by the five vowels [i e a o u]. (YY – 03)

P: There were nine possible one-step comparisons (with stimula having a difference of 10ms) and eight two-step comparisons (with stimuli having a difference of 20ms) which produced 17 AB pairs. (YY – 11)

C: Speech samples were audio-recorded using Audacity (version 2. 0. 0) [18], and sampled into. wav files at 44. 1 kHz. (YY – 18)

（三）语态特征

A. 语态种类及组合

表 4. 9. 10 是该学科文章中使用的不同语态组合类型，其中不包含有语法错误的句子。如表所示，该学科文章中两种语态均有出现，同时还包含了这两种语态的组合形式。只包含 V2 的句子数量和占比最高，其次是由 V1 构成的句子，包含两种不同语态的句子数量和占比最低。所有文章中均包含这三种形式语态组合。同一种语态构成的句子中均包括了简单句、复杂句、复合句和复合复杂句这四种类型的句子。两种不同语态构成的句子中包括了除简单句以外的其他三种类型的句子。

以下是按照四种类型句子给出的三种语态组合中的例句，但是有些语态组合中不包含所有类型的句子。

表 4. 9. 10　　　　　　　　　　语态类型及组合

语态	V1	V1 V2	V2
句数	448	187	559
占比	37. 52%	15. 66%	46. 82%

【V1】

S：The subject read all syllables in citation form five times in a random order. (YY – 03)

P：Statistical analyses revealed that across the three speakers, [s] and [s] are always of greater amplitude than [f] and [θ]. (YY – 03)

C：To ensure agreement, the two coders jointly segmented the first speaker and spot-checked each other on approximately 10% of the remaining files. (YY – 05)

CP：In the present study, the algorithm began by considering the best binary split in each of the acoustic correlates and selects the one that results in the most homogeneous subregions with respect to responses (in this case, the probability of [+ ATR] as the context feature value). (YY – 05)

【V1 V2】

P：LPC spectra were computed to examine if their peaks matched those of the FFT spectra. (YY – 02)

C：[s] and [š] can be clearly distinguished by the distribution of spectral peaks; major peaks for [s] fall in a higher frequency range (3. 8 – 8 ~ 5kHz) than for [s] (2. 3 – 7kHz). (YY – 03)

CP：These tokens were added when normalizing the vowel space and duration measures (see below), but are not included in Table 3, which only lists the targets analyzed in the study. (YY – 05)

【V2】

S：Then, for each sentence production, a smoothing window of 50ms (10 observations) was used to calculate moving averages and moving coefficients of variation for the 13 variables during that sentence. (YY – 06)

P：All of the ultrasound images and their corresponding acoustics were analyzed, except for one trial in which the intended Tone 1 was incorrectly produced as Tone 4. (YY – 07)

C：Task order was randomized, and equal numbers of participants were assigned to the different task orders. (YY – 08)

CP：The results were first generated in the Cartesian coordinate system and later converted into polar coordinates, which were fitted through smoothing spline analysis of variance (SS – ANOVA) with a 95% confidence interval (dashed – lined ribbons in the following figures) around the predicted fit (solid lines in the following figures) (Davidson, 2006; Gu, 2002; Mielke, 2015). (YY – 07)

B. 语态与语步

图4.9.9是该学科文章中三种语态组合与语步的关系。如图所示，这三种语态组合中占比最高的前三个步骤中均包含 M2.4，但是排序不完全一致。另外，分别有两种组合中包含 M3.2 和 M3.2a，但是排序也不完全一致。即使相同步骤在不同语态组合中排序一致，同一个步骤在不同语态组合中的数量和占比也不同。

就这三种语态组合中包含的语步种类而言，各组合中均包含了三个语步，但是它们包含的步骤种类在所有步骤中占比不同。V1 占比最高，其次为 V2 和 V1V2，分别占所有步骤的97%、88%和79%。

总体来说，语态与步骤关系紧密度与该语态在所有句子中的占比有关，同时也与该步骤在所有步骤中的占比有一定的关系。

以下是按照四种类型句子给出的三种语态组合中占比最高的前三个步骤的例句，但是有些步骤中不包含所有类型的句子。

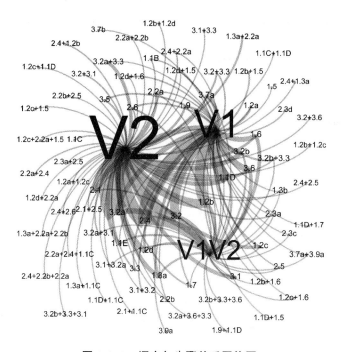

图4.9.9　语态与步骤关系网络图

【V1】

M 2. 4

S： Through the familiarization phase, the infant becomes more "familiar" with one type of stimulus. (YY－19)

P： Each sound file played until completion, or until the infant looked away for longer than 2s. (YY－19)

C： Infants across conditions heard the same total number of tokens (a total of 176 syllables; total presentation time was 157s), and the same selection of tokens, but the frequency of specific tokens varied across the two distribution conditions, as represented in Fig. 5. (YY－12)

CP： On each trial, the experimenter announced the right answer ('same' or 'different') and, after the pair presentation, asked whether the participant agreed. (YY－13)

M 1. 1D

S： None had a significant delay in academic performance as reported by their parents/grandparents. (YY－18)

P： The subjects were eight students, four males and four females, who reported no past history of hearing disorder. (YY－11)

C： All participants tested had normal hearing and had passed a hearing screening test using otoacoustic emissions at 2000, 3000, 4000, and 5000 Hz. (YY－09)

CP： These participants were college undergraduate students who received partial course credit for their participation in the experiment, and none of them reported any past or present speech or hearing disorders. (YY－14)

M 1. 2b

S： Table 3 shows the vowel and fricative durations of the stimuli. (YY－14)

P： For the MEG experiment, we selected four sound positions that evenly spanned the category boundary determined by the behavioral tests. (YY－15)

C： All sound files had the same duration of 25. 34 s and contained the same number of tokens. (YY－19)

【V1V2】

M 2. 4

P： Children were instructed to play a computer game by listening to what word the computer says first and then repeat the word back into the microphone. (YY－09)

C： In the identification task, participants heard sounds from the [ʃi-si] continuum and were instructed to classify the fricative portion as either [ʃ] or [s] by means of button presses. (YY－15)

CP： In each AXB discrimination test, triads of stimuli were presented in which the first and third item were separated by three steps along a 10-step continuum, and the middle item matched the first or third item; all possible 3-step pairings were presented an equal number of times, in all four possible triad orders (AAB, ABB, BAA, BBA) . (YY-20)

M 3. 2a

P: Period doubling, which is not included in the original psychoacoustic model but is common in the speech of UCLA students, was measured as the amplitude ratio between subharmonics and harmonics (SHR; Sun, 2002). (YY-06)

C: All acoustic analyses were done automatically in Praat using custom-written scripts; all of these made reference to these labels. (YY-08)

CP: While the probe used for image capturing covers a 180° curve, the probe did not fully contact the submental surface, and only the contact area was captured in the images. (YY-07)

M 3. 2

P: As moderate correlations were expected between variables, we employed an oblique rotation to create the simplest possible factor structure for our data (Cattell, 1978; Thurstone, 1947). (YY-06)

C: The initial, maximal models also contained by-speaker slopes for the interaction (see Barr, Levy, Scheepers, & Tily, 2013); however, these did not contribute to fit and were removed following the procedure described in Bates, Kliegl, Vasishth, and Baayen (2015). (YY-05)

CP: Model comparison was conducted via the anova function in R, and main effects are only reported when the model testing revealed that interactions were not significant, and the interactions were subsequently removed to obtain the best fit model. (YY-10)

【V2】

M 3. 2a

S: Of these, 605 tokens were verified by hand. (YY-10)

P: This average was taken over the eight vowel types rather than the 32 word types so that the overall average formant values were not unduly influenced by the preponderance of low front vowels in the stimulus set. (YY-08)

C: As with average F1 and F2, these values were calculated for individual vowels, and the average values were used to calculate each talker's overall f0. (YY-08)

CP: The production was then converted into a time series in which each sample was labeled as either differing in sign from the previous sample [1] or not [0], and a zero-crossing envelope was created by lowpass filtering this series at 30 Hz. (YY-01)

M 2. 4

S: Tokens were sampled at a 20kHz sampling rate with a 9.0kHz low-pass filter setting and a 10-bit quantization. (YY-03)

P: The stimuli were pseudo-randomized on the condition (no condition more than two times in a row) and the side from which the sound files were presented (no side more than two times in a row), with a different randomization per infant. (YY – 19)

C: In the first block of trials, the value of the unvarying portion was set to one place of articulation (e. g., retroflex), and in the second block of trials the value was set to the other place (e. g., alveolopalatal). (YY – 12)

M 3. 2

S: In this model, infants' orientation times in seconds were predicted by familiarity (novel versus familiar type), familiarization condition (familiarization with no-boundary versus with-boundary stimuli) and age (6 versus 8 months), taking into account covariance of the familiarization time in seconds (scaled) and trial order (centered), interacting with familiarity. (YY – 19)

P: Once a tree is grown and evaluated, the values of one of the predictors are scrambled (conditional on the other predictors), breaking that predictor's association with the response variable. (YY – 05)

C: The tree is then evaluated on the remaining observations, the out-of-bag sample, and a measure of accuracy is obtained by comparing the predicted to the observed classifications. (YY – 05)

CP: The results were first generated in the Cartesian coordinate system and later converted into polar coordinates, which were fitted through smoothing spline analysis of variance (SS-ANOVA) with a 95% confidence interval (dashed-lined ribbons in the following figures) around the predicted fit (solid lines in the following figures) (Davidson, 2006; Gu, 2002; Mielke, 2015). (YY – 07)

第十节　学科间对比分析

本节主要对比分析本章前九个小节所涉及的各学科论文中传统实验方法写作的体裁特征。对比分析所涉及内容与第三章第三小节一致。

一　篇幅占比

在所分析的各学科论文中，除了生物科学、化学和材料科学这三个学科外，其他学科文章的结构都遵循了 IMRD(C)格式。在 20 篇生物科学论文中，有九篇论文中实验方法部分出现在了正文的最后，即采用的是 IRD(C)M 格式，有两篇论文中该部分出现在了附录中。在

20 篇化学学科论文中,有七篇采用了 IRD(C)M 的结构,有四篇在补充材料（SI）中；此外,补充材料不是在论文后面与论文一起发表,而是单独出现在给定的网站上。材料科学 20 篇论文中也有七篇采用了 IRDM 的结构,还有六篇与化学学科一样,实验方法部分单独出现在了 SI 中。

就论文中实验方法写作部分总体篇幅占比而言,在所分析各学科论文中,无论是临床医学还是基础医学论文中,该部分在正文中的平均占比均远高于其他学科,最低的是海洋科学。单个语篇中占比最大值也是医学最高,其次是化学,海洋科学最低。占比最小值也是医学最高,生物和海洋最低,其他几个学科也很低。此外,各学科各篇论文实验方法部分占比差异均不大,其中海洋科学最小,其次是土木。

二 标题特征

在一级大标题词汇的使用上各学科具有较高的一致性,各学科中均使用了 method (s) 这个单词,除化学和材料科学外,该单词在其他学科标题中使用频率也最高。在化学和材料这两个学科大标题中使用频率最高的是 experimental,该单词在化学和材料两个学科中分别出现了 14 次和 13 次。在这两个学科中 method 出现频率都很高,在化学中出现了 10 次,排在第二,在材料中出现了 5 次,排在第三。此外,materials 这个单词虽然出现频率不是特别高,但是它在所分析的各学科文章中均有出现。

小标题词汇的使用上各学科之间差异较明显,各学科小标题中词汇没有一个为所研究的九个学科中半数以上学科共有的。大部分词汇都与学科研究内容相关,但是各学科中还是会出现一些学科性不强的词汇,如 preparation 在材料、化学和海洋学科中均占有一定的比例；analysis 在医学、语言学和市政工程中出现的次数也较高。对比基础医学和临床医学文章,可以发现这两类文章小标题词汇使用的相似度明显高于它们与其他学科的相似度。

就大小标题数而言,生物和海洋学科部分文章中实验方法由两个或三个平行部分构成，即有不止一个一级大标题，而其他各学科只有一个一级大标题。生物、基础医学和语言学实验方法部分均包含了二级小标题，在其他学科论文中均有少部分文章不包含二级小标题，其中海洋学科不包含二级小标题的文章最多，而该学科包含两个一级大标题的文章也最多，占所选文章的一半。在包含二级小标题的文章中，同一个学科文章中二级小标题数量存在一定的差异。生物和市政两个学科中分别有一到两篇文章中包含少量三级小标题。

总体来看，不同学科实验方法部分大标题中使用的单词差异不大，但是在小标题方面不同学科存在较大的差异，而同一学科不同方向的论文之间虽然存在差异，但是学科内差异小于学科间的差异。此外，有少部分学科部分论文中会包含两到三个一级大标题，有三个学科所选论文中均使用二级小标题，其他学科中有少部分文章不包含二级小标题。有极少数学科中较少的文章中会使用三级小标题。同一学科论文中小标题数量存在一定的差异。

三 语步特征

本小节主要讨论各学科论文中三个语步在以下三个方面的异同：第一，不同语步中包含的步骤种类；第二，各步骤涉及的篇章数量；第三，各语步中不同步骤占比。步骤占比中，平均值和标准差只涉及包含该步骤的文章。分别用" ＊ "代表该步骤只涉及一篇文章，用"—"表示文章中不涉及该步骤。

A. 语步一

表 4.10.1 是各学科语步一中各步骤涉及篇章数及在所分析的文章中的占比。如表所示，语言学中语步一涉及的步骤种类最多，最少的是生物和材料两个学科。就各步骤涉及的文章在各自学科所有文章的占比而言，各学科存在一定的差异。各学科均包含的步骤有四个。有四个步骤只涉及一个学科，其中三个为语言学专有，一个为土木专有。

表 4.10.1　　　　各学科语步一中各步骤涉及篇章数及占比

M	SW	LC	JC	HY	SZ	HX	CL	TM	YY
	篇数—占比	篇数—占比	篇数—占比	篇数—占比	篇数—占比	篇数—占比	篇数—占比	篇数—占比	篇数—占比
1.1A	—	—	—	—	—	—	—	3%—12%	—
1.1B	—	1%—5%	5%—25%	5%—25%	2%—10%	—	—	9%—35%	3%—15%
1.1C	—	4%—20%	4%—20%	17%—85%	4%—20%	1%—5%	—	4%—15%	6%—30%
1.1D	—	—	—	—	—	—	—	—	20%—100%
1.1E	—	—	—	—	—	—	—	—	8%—40%
1.2a	18%—90%	15%—75%	19%—95%	19%—95%	8%—40%	8%—40%	9%—45%	21%—81%	6%—30%
1.2b	2%—10%	8%—40%	13%—65%	7%—35%	11%—55%	11%—55%	15%—75%	17%—65%	16%—80%
1.2c	—	17%—85%	—	6%—30%	13%—65%	6%—30%	2%—10%	5%—19%	11%—55%
1.2d	16%—80%	4%—20%	18%—90%	12%—60%	15%—75%	9%—45%	13%—65%	15%—58%	11%—55%
1.3a	—	4%—20%	7%—35%	1%—5%	5%—25%	12%—60%	13%—65%	14%—54%	13%—65%
1.3b	3%—15%		—	—	—	—	1%—5%	3%—12%	2%—10%
1.4	—	7%—35%	4%—20%	—	—	—	—	3%—12%	—
1.5	8%—40%	8%—40%	10%—50%	8%—40%	4%—20%	8%—40%	5%—25%	7%—27%	7%—35%
1.6	1%—5%	—	6%—30%	7%—35%	6%—30%	3%—15%	—	13%—50%	13%—65%
1.7	8%—40%	16%—80%	17%—85%	—	—	—	—	—	5%—25%
1.8	—	—	—	—	—	—	—	—	9%—45%

表4.10.2至表4.10.5是各学科语步一中各步骤在该语步中占比最大值、最小值、平均值和标准差。其中平均值和标准差为包含该步骤的文章，不包含该步骤的文章不计入其中。如表所示，M1.2a和M1.2d最大值总体均较高，但是语言学中这两个步骤最大值相对较低，在生物中这两个步骤占比均最高。在市政和化学中M1.2c和M1.2d最大值最高。除生物外，M1.2b最大值总体也较高。不同学科中各步骤最小值差异不大。平均值情况与最大值相似。标准差学科间差异小于学科内步骤间差异。总体来说，同一学科不同步骤及不同学科同一步骤在这四个方面均存在差异。

表4.10.2　　　　　　各学科语步一中各步骤占比最大值

M	MAX（%）								
	SW	LC	JC	HY	SZ	HX	CL	TM	YY
1.1A	—								
1.1B	—	10	20	29	26	—	—	100	25
1.1C	—	11	10	83	33	100		35	25
1.1D	—	—	—	—	—	—		—	67
1.1E									24
1.2a	100	63	40	96	67	50	100	82	29
1.2b	27	82	41	45	63	75	100	100	65
1.2c	—	81	—	36	100	100	25	58	22
1.2d	100	56	72	50	100	100	50	60	40
1.3a	—	13	52	13	58	74	75	100	40
1.3b	9	—	—	—	—	—	9	13	9
1.4	—	65	71	—	—	—	—	15	—
1.5	20	17	22	25	22	79	29	29	7
1.6	1	—	26	22	22	10	—	35	44
1.7	40	64	44						8
1.8	—	—	—	—	—	—	—	—	17

表 4.10.3　　　　　各学科语步一中各步骤占比最小值

M	MIN（%）								
	SW	LC	JC	HY	SZ	HX	CL	TM	YY
1.1A	—	—	—	—	—	—	—	—	—
1.1B	—	10	4	5	22	—	—	2	2
1.1C	—	4	2	4	13	100	—	4	2
1.1D	—	—	—	—	—	—	—	—	4
1.1E	—	—	—	—	—	—	—	—	2
1.2a	17	3	2	2	5	7	4	8	5
1.2b	25	11	7	2	1	5	13	2	7
1.2c	—	12	—	2	13	5	4	10	2
1.2d	13	5	4	2	5	5	13	7	3
1.3a	—	6	10	13	5	10	17	1	3
1.3b	6	—	—	—	—	—	9	3	3
1.4	—	3	9	—	—	—	—	8	—
1.5	2	4	3	2	5	5	4	2	2
1.6	1	—	4	2	3	4	—	3	3
1.7	3	5	1	—	—	—	—	—	5
1.8	—	—	—	—	—	—	—	—	2

表 4.10.4　　　　　各学科语步一中各步骤占比平均值

M	MEAN（%）								
	SW	LC	JC	HY	SZ	HX	CL	TM	YY
1.1A	—	—	—	—	—	—	—	—	—
1.1B	—	10	9	15	24	—	—	17	10
1.1C	—	8	5	33	27	100	—	13	8
1.1D	—	—	—	—	—	—	—	—	24
1.1E	—	—	—	—	—	—	—	—	11
1.2a	58	21	17	41	31	20	45	37	14

续表

M	MEAN（%）								
	SW	LC	JC	HY	SZ	HX	CL	TM	YY
1.2b	26	34	25	13	31	36	43	25	26
1.2c	—	41	—	12	44	29	15	35	11
1.2d	36	19	29	19	32	53	29	27	17
1.3a	—	9	26	13	21	36	35	21	18
1.3b	7	—	—	—	—	—	9	8	6
1.4	—	31	37	—	—	—	—	10	—
1.5	9	10	9	11	12	30	15	11	3
1.6	1	—	11	14	10	6	—	14	14
1.7	16	17	17	—	—	—	—	—	6
1.8	—	—	—	—	—	—	—	—	8

表4.10.5　　　　各学科语步一中各步骤占比标准差

M	SD								
	SW	LC	JC	HY	SZ	HX	CL	TM	YY
1.1A	—	—	—	—	—	—	—	—	—
1.1B	—	*	0.06	0.08	0.02	—	—	0.3	0.11
1.1C	—	0.03	0.03	0.26	0.09	*	—	0.13	0.08
1.1D	—	—	—	—	—	—	—	—	0.18
1.1E	—	—	—	—	—	—	—	—	0.07
1.2a	0.22	0.17	0.12	0.26	0.25	0.13	0.4	0.23	0.07
1.2b	0.01	0.22	0.09	0.14	0.22	0.22	0.32	0.25	0.17
1.2c	—	0.19	—	0.12	0.28	0.35	0.1	0.18	0.05
1.2d	0.25	0.22	0.18	0.14	0.24	0.26	0.12	0.17	0.12
1.3a	—	0.03	0.15	*	0.21	0.22	0.17	0.27	0.11
1.3b	0.01	—	—	—	—	—	*	0.04	0.03
1.4	—	0.2	0.24	—	—	—	—	0.03	—
1.5	0.06	0.05	0.06	0.07	0.07	0.28	0.1	0.09	0.02

M	SD								
	SW	LC	JC	HY	SZ	HX	CL	TM	YY
1.6	*	—	0.07	0.07	0.07	0.03	—	0.1	0.12
1.7	0.13	0.13	0.12	—	—	—	—	—	0.01
1.8	—	—	—	—	—	—	—	—	0.05

B. 语步二

表4.10.6是各学科语步二中各步骤涉及篇章数及在所分析文章中的占比。如表所示，材料学科语步二涉及的步骤种类最多，最少的是生物。各个学科共有的步骤有五种。就各步骤涉及的文章在各自学科所有文章中占比而言，各学科存在一定的差异，但是总体来说，各学科 M2.2a 和 M2.4 涉及篇章数较高。

表4.10.6　　**各学科语步二中各步骤涉及篇章数及占比**

M	SW	LC	JC	HY	SZ	HX	CL	TM	YY
	篇数—占比	篇数—占比	篇数—占比	篇数—占比	篇数—占比	篇数—占比	篇数—占比	篇数—占比	篇数—占比
2.1	4%—20%	7%—35%	4%—20%	2%—10%	6%—30%	7%—35%	7%—35%	14%—54%	12%—60%
2.2a	12%—60%	15%—75%	15%—75%	19%—95%	17%—85%	19%—95%	19%—95%	26%—100%	17%—85%
2.2b				10%—50%	14%—70%		15%—75%	18%—69%	6%—30%
2.3a	5%—25%	6%—30%	6%—30%		1%—5%		6%—30%	9%—35%	3%—15%
2.3b		10%—50%		4%—20%	8%—40%		2%—10%	15%—58%	
2.3c								6%—23%	1%—5%
2.3d									1%—5%
2.4	20%—100%	20%—100%	20%—100%	19%—95%	19%—95%	18%—90%	16%—80%	21%—81%	17%—85%

续表

M	SW 篇数— 占比	LC 篇数— 占比	JC 篇数— 占比	HY 篇数— 占比	SZ 篇数— 占比	HX 篇数— 占比	CL 篇数— 占比	TM 篇数— 占比	YY 篇数— 占比
2.5	16%— 80%	14%— 70%	16%— 80%	15%— 75%	12%— 60%	4%— 20%	5%— 25%	10%— 38%	8%— 40%
2.6	5%— 25%	4%— 20%	6%— 30%	10%— 50%	9%— 45%	4%— 20%	3%— 15%	10%— 38%	6%— 30%
2.6a	—	2%— 10%	11%— 55%	—	—	—	—	—	—
2.6b	—	—	—	—	—	—	1%— 5%	—	—
2.6c	—	—	—	—	—	4%— 20%	—	—	—
2.7	—	—	—	—	—	1%— 5%	—	—	—
2.8	—	—	—	—	—	—	1% —5%	—	—

　　表4.10.7至表4.10.10是各学科语步二中各步骤在该语步中占比最大值、最小值、平均值和标准差。其中平均值和标准差为包含该步骤的文章，不包含该步骤的文章不计入其中。如表所示，各学科中M2.4的最大值、最小值和平均值占比均较高。M2.2a最大值和平均值总体上也较高，仅次于M2.4，但该步骤最小值较低。语言学中M2.1和M2.4最大值均最高。M2.5和M2.6标准差较其他步骤略低。总体来说，同一学科不同步骤及不同学科同一步骤在这四个方面均存在差异。

表4.10.7　　　　　　**各学科语步二中各步骤占比最大值**

M	MAX（%）								
	SW	LC	JC	HY	SZ	HX	CL	TM	YY
2.1	3	10	14	9	30	44	25	44	100
2.2a	13	32	28	36	97	100	88	84	50
2.2b	—	—	—	36	24	—	45	33	20
2.3a	11	70	19	—	36	—	48	32	53
2.3b	—	52	—	20	100	—	16	29	—
2.3c	—	—	—	—	—	—	—	9	7

M	MAX（%）								
	SW	LC	JC	HY	SZ	HX	CL	TM	YY
2.3d	—	—	—	—	—	—	—	—	7
2.4	98	94	97	80	86	86	61	56	100
2.5	15	23	24	28	13	6	11	20	12
2.6	14	12	14	31	20	4	18	25	17
2.6a	—	31	48	—	—	—	—	—	—
2.6b	—	—	—	—	—	—	16	—	—
2.6c	—	—	—	—	—	13	—	—	—
2.7	—	—	—	—	—	3	—	—	—
2.8	—	—	—	—	—	—	6	—	—

表4.10.8　　　　各学科语步二中各步骤占比最小值

M	MIN（%）								
	SW	LC	JC	HY	SZ	HX	CL	TM	YY
2.1	1	1	5	3	3	6	5	3	2
2.2a	1	3	3	3	5	3	9	8	1
2.2b	—	—	—	3	1	—	5	4	2
2.3a	2	2	2	—	36	—	4	4	2
2.3b	—	1	—	8	1	—	6	3	—
2.3c	—	—	—	—	—	—	—	2	7
2.3d	—	—	—	—	—	—	—	—	7
2.4	77	18	30	20	3	11	12	4	38
2.5	1	2	2	2	2	2	4	2	2
2.6	2	1	3	4	1	2	7	4	4
2.6a	—	12	1	—	—	—	—	—	—
2.6b	—	—	—	—	—	—	16	—	—
2.6c	—	—	—	—	—	2	—	—	—
2.7	—	—	—	—	—	3	—	—	—
2.8	—	—	—	—	—	—	6	—	—

表 4.10.9　　　　　　各学科语步二中各步骤占比平均值

M	MEAN（%）								
	SW	LC	JC	HY	SZ	HX	CL	TM	YY
2.1	2	5	9	6	9	21	12	13	35
2.2a	5	11	10	21	31	40	42	45	12
2.2b	—	—	—	12	8	—	22	13	7
2.3a	7	21	7	—	36	—	20	12	20
2.3b	—	20	—	14	20	—	11	12	—
2.3c	—	—	—	—	—	—	—	5	7
2.3d	—	—	—	—	—	—	—	—	7
2.4	89	66	68	50	49	58	34	26	69
2.5	5	7	10	10	7	3	8	6	5
2.6	6	6	8	21	10	3	12	10	8
2.6a	—	22	18	—	—	—	—	—	—
2.6b	—	—	—	—	—	—	16	—	—
2.6c	—	—	—	—	—	6	—	—	—
2.7	—	—	—	—	—	3	—	—	—
2.8	—	—	—	—	—	—	6	—	—

表 4.10.10　　　　　各学科语步二中各步骤占比标准差

M	SD								
	SW	LC	JC	HY	SZ	HX	CL	TM	YY
2.1	0.01	0.03	0.04	0.03	0.09	0.15	0.07	0.11	0.27
2.2a	0.03	0.07	0.07	0.09	0.2	0.3	0.22	0.21	0.12
2.2b	—	—	—	0.1	0.06	—	0.12	0.08	0.06
2.3a	0.04	0.23	0.06	—	*	—	0.15	0.09	0.24
2.3b	—	0.2	—	0.05	0.31	—	0.05	0.06	—
2.3c	—	—	—	—	—	—	—	0.02	*
2.3d	—	—	—	—	—	—	—	—	*
2.4	0.07	0.23	0.19	0.16	0.22	0.21	0.16	0.14	0.18
2.5	0.04	0.06	0.05	0.07	0.04	0.02	0.02	0.06	0.03
2.6	0.04	0.05	0.04	0.09	0.06	0.01	0.04	0.06	0.05
2.6a	—	0.1	0.15	—	—	—	—	—	—

M	SD								
	SW	LC	JC	HY	SZ	HX	CL	TM	YY
2.6b	—	—	—	—	—	—	*	—	—
2.6c	—	—	—	—	—	0.04	—	—	—
2.7	—	—	—	—	—	*	—	—	—
2.8	—	—	—	—	—	—	*	—	—

C. 语步三

表 4.10.11 是各学科语步三中各步骤涉及篇章数及在所分析的文章中的占比。如表所示，语言学中语步三涉及的步骤种类最多，最少的是生物。各学科共有的步骤只有 M3.2 一种。但是半数以上学科中均包含了 M3.1、M3.3、M3.4、M3.5 和 M3.7a。就各步骤涉及的文章在各自学科所有文章中占比而言，各学科存在一定的差异。总体上 M3.2 涉及篇章数占比较高。

表 4.10.11 **各学科语步三中各步骤篇章数及占比**

M	SW	LC	JC	HY	SZ	HX	CL	TM	YY
	篇数—占比	篇数—占比	篇数—占比	篇数—占比	篇数—占比	篇数—占比	篇数—占比	篇数—占比	篇数—占比
3.1	10%—50%	9%—45%	13%—65%	5%—25%	5%—25%	—	1%—5%	—	10%—50%
3.2	14%—70%	16%—80%	18%—90%	11%—55%	11%—55%	9%—45%	3%—15%	4%—15%	11%—55%
3.2a	—	—	—	—	—	—	—	—	12%—60%
3.2b	—	—	—	—	—	—	—	—	12%—60%
3.3	4%—20%	—	2%—10%	5%—25%	3%—15%	—	—	2%—8%	8%—40%
3.4	4%—20%	1%—5%	2%—10%	7%—35%	1%—5%	1%—5%	—	—	—
3.5	—	2%—10%	1%—5%	3%—15%	—	5%—25%	3%—15%	4%—15%	2%—10%
3.6	—	—	—	—	6%—30%	—	1%—5%	2%—8%	12%—60%

M	SW 篇数—占比	LC 篇数—占比	JC 篇数—占比	HY 篇数—占比	SZ 篇数—占比	HX 篇数—占比	CL 篇数—占比	TM 篇数—占比	YY 篇数—占比
3.7a	—	1%—5%	—	8%—40%		10%—50%	3%—15%	1%—4%	2%—10%
3.7b	—	—	—	—		—	1%—5%	—	1%—5%
3.7c	—	—	—	7%—35%		—	—	—	—
3.7d	—	—	—	—		—	1%—5%	—	—
3.8	—	—	—	2%—10%		—	—	2%—8%	—
3.9a	—	—	—	—		—	—	—	1%—5%
3.9b	—	3%—15%	—	—		—	—	—	—
3.9c	—	—	—	—		2%—10%	—	—	—
3.9d	—	2%—10%	—	—		—	—	—	—

表4.10.12至表4.10.15是各学科语步三中各步骤在该语步中占比最大值、最小值、平均值和标准差。其中平均值和标准差为包含该步骤的文章，不包含该步骤的文章不计入其中。如表所示，各学科均包含了M3.2，除了海洋学和语言学，该步骤在其他学科中的最大值均为100%，该步骤平均值总体也较高。其他步骤最大值各学科间差异较大。学科间最小值和平均值差异也较大。标准差总体差异不大。

表4.10.12　　　　　各学科语步三中各步骤占比最大值

M	MAX（%）								
	SW	LC	JC	HY	SZ	HX	CL	TM	YY
3.1	50	25	67	17	50	—	50	—	14
3.2	100	100	100	93	100	100	100	100	83
3.2a	—	—	—	—	—	—	—	—	78

续表

M	MAX（%）								
	SW	LC	JC	HY	SZ	HX	CL	TM	YY
3.2b	—	—	—	—	—	—	—	—	100
3.3	25	—	10	17	50	—	—	18	10
3.4	100	100	25	33	50	100	—	—	—
3.5	—	10	18	33	—	69	71	100	63
3.6	—	—	—	—	64	—	100	10	22
3.7a	—	33	—	75	—	100	100	11	66
3.7b	—	—	—	—	—	—	20	—	3
3.7c	—	—	—	71	—	—	—	—	—
3.7d	—	—	—	—	—	—	20	—	—
3.8	—	—	—	22	—	—	—	22	—
3.9a	—	—	—	—	—	—	—	—	10
3.9b	—	67	—	—	—	—	—	—	—
3.9c	—	—	—	—	—	—	50	—	—
3.9d	—	33	—	—	—	—	—	—	—

表 4.10.13　　**各学科语步三中各步骤占比最小值**

M	MIN（%）								
	SW	LC	JC	HY	SZ	HX	CL	TM	YY
3.1	13	4	4	4	9	—	50	—	2
3.2	36	53	33	28	25	14	50	50	5
3.2a	—	—	—	—	—	—	—	—	9
3.2b	—	—	—	—	—	—	—	—	3
3.3	3	—	4	2	2	—	—	5	2
3.4	25	100	20	7	50	100	—	—	—
3.5	—	7	18	13	—	33	33	11	10
3.6	—	—	—	—	5	—	100	5	4
3.7a	—	33	—	3	—	20	29	11	3
3.7b	—	—	—	—	—	—	20	—	3
3.7c	—	—	—	3	—	—	—	—	—
3.7d	—	—	—	—	—	—	20	—	—

续表

M	MIN（%）								
	SW	LC	JC	HY	SZ	HX	CL	TM	YY
3.8	—	—	—	12	—	—	—	9	—
3.9a	—	—	—	—	—	—	—	—	10
3.9b	—	10	—	—	—	—	—	—	—
3.9c	—	—	—	—	—	44	—	—	—
3.9d	—	21	—	—	—	—	—	—	—

表 4.10.14　　　**各学科语步三中各步骤占比平均值**

M	MEAN（%）								
	SW	LC	JC	HY	SZ	HX	CL	TM	YY
3.1	30	11	27	10	27	—	50	—	7
3.2	68	88	76	62	68	64	83	68	29
3.2a	—	—	—	—	—	—	—	—	45
3.2b	—	—	—	—	—	—	—	—	18
3.3	13	—	7	11	19	—	—	12	6
3.4	49	100	23	15	50	100	—	—	—
3.5	—	8	18	20	—	47	55	37	36
3.6	—	—	—	—	35	—	100	7	12
3.7a	—	33	—	25	—	67	65	11	34
3.7b	—	—	—	—	—	—	20	—	3
3.7c	—	—	—	30	—	—	—	—	—
3.7d	—	—	—	—	—	—	20	—	—
3.8	—	—	—	17	—	—	—	16	—
3.9a	—	—	—	—	—	—	—	—	10
3.9b	—	33	—	—	—	—	—	—	—
3.9c	—	—	—	—	—	47	—	—	—
3.9d	—	27	—	—	—	—	—	—	—

表4.10.15 　　　　　各学科语步三中各步骤占比标准差

M	SD								
	SW	LC	JC	HY	SZ	HX	CL	TM	YY
3.1	0.14	0.06	0.19	0.04	0.19	—	*	—	0.04
3.2	0.22	0.16	0.19	0.2	0.28	0.3	0.24	0.19	0.22
3.2a	—	—	—	—	—	—	—	—	0.19
3.2b	—	—	—	—	—	—	—	—	0.25
3.3	0.08	—	0.03	0.07	0.22	—	—	0.07	0.03
3.4	0.3	*	0.03	0.09	*	*	—	—	—
3.5	—	0.02	*	0.09	—	0.13	0.16	0.36	0.26
3.6	—	—	—	—	0.21	—	*	0.03	0.06
3.7a	—	*	—	0.21	—	0.32	0.29	*	0.31
3.7b	—	—	—	—	—	—	*	—	*
3.7c	—	—	—	0.2	—	—	—	—	—
3.7d	—	—	—	—	—	—	*	—	—
3.8	—	—	—	0.05	—	—	—	0.07	—
3.9a	—	—	—	—	—	—	—	—	*
3.9b	—	0.25	—	—	—	—	—	—	—
3.9c	—	—	—	—	—	0.03	—	—	—
3.9d	—	0.06	—	—	—	—	—	—	—

D. 语步及步骤占比

表4.10.16 为各学科三个语步中占比最高的文章占所有文章的百分比及各学科中各步骤在所有步骤中占比最高的前三个步骤。表中"*"代表在生物和基础医学这两个学科中分别有5%的文章语步一和语步二占比最高且相同。此外，临床中有5%的文章语步二和语步三占比相同且最高。如表所示，除了语言学外，各学科中绝大多数文章语步二占比均最高，其次为语步一。语言学多数文章中语步三占比最高，其次是语步一，语步二最低。在海洋和土木学文章中语步一和语步二较接近。另外，在生物和基础医学中分别有一篇文章语步一和语步二占比相同，高于语步三，在临床医学中有一篇文章语步二和语步三占比相

同。各学科中占比最高的前三个步骤中均包含 M2.4，但是该步骤在各学科中的排序不完全一致。即使排序一致，同一个步骤在不同学科中的占比也不相同。基础医学和临床医学同为医学学科，占比最高的前两个步骤一致，但是第三个不同。各学科占比最低的步骤均不相同。

表 4.10.16　　　　　各学科语步占比分布及高占比步骤

学科	占比最高语步			占比最高前三个步骤		
	M1	M2	M3	第一	第二	第三
SW	5%	90%	*	2.4	1.2a	1.2d
LC	5%	80%	10%	2.4	3.2	1.2c
JC	10%	85%	*	2.4	3.2	1.2d
HY	40%	55%	5%	2.4	1.1c	1.2a
SZ	10%	80%	10%	2.4	2.2a	1.2c
HX	15%	85%	—	2.4	2.2a	1.2d
CL	25%	75%		2.2a	2.4	2.2b
TM	46%	50%	4%	2.2a	1.2a	2.4
YY	30%	15%	55%	2.4	3.2a	1.2b

E. 三个语步分布轨迹

在只包含语步一和语步二的文章中，土木学和语言学两个学科有一半以上的文章中语步一占比高于语步二，分布也较广，其他学科正好相反。各学科少部分文章语步一全部集中分布在语步二前，但是在大部分文章中，文章的最前均以语步一为主，但是多数文章语步一中部分语句同时也会分布在文章中前部、中部和后部，出现在语步二中，与语步二有交叉。海洋学科的多数文章中这两个语步没有交叉。土木学科极少数论文语步一中部分语句同时也出现在了文章的最后、语步二后。

在包含三个语步的文章中，语步二分布均最广，其次是语步一，语步三分布最集中。语步一主要集中在方法部分的前部，语步三主要集中分布在文章的最后，语步二主要分布在语步一和语步三之间，但是各学科均有较多的文章语步一中有少量语句分布在文章其他位置、语步二中。语步一与语步二有交叉。各学科中语步三主要集中分布在文章的最后，在临床医学和语言学中语步三均集中分布在文章的最后，与其他语步没有交叉。其他各学科的大部分文章中语步三分布在语步二后，与其他两个语步之间没有交叉，少部分文章语步一中部分语句也会分布在文章中间及偏后的位置、语步二中。化学学科有较多的文章中三个语步均有交叉，生物学科中极少数情况三个语步有交叉，其他各学科未发现三个语步同时交叉的情况。

四　语言特征

本小节主要对比分析各学科论文在句子结构、时态和语态三个方面的语言特征。具体内容与第三章第三节相同。

（一）句子特征

A. 句类及占比

表 4.10.17 是各学科四类句子在所有句子中占比、特殊句子种类及占比最高的三类特殊句子。如表所示，各学科中简单句、复杂句、复合句和复合复杂句这四种类型的句子占比均较高。四类句子中简单句占比均远高于其他三类句子，占比最低的是复合复杂句。大部分学科中复合句占比略高于复杂句，海洋、市政、土木和语言学这四个学科刚好相反。在简单句中各学科占比差异较小，最高的是化学，最低的是语言学。在复杂句中最高的是语言学，最低的是临床医学。在复合句中最高的是基础医学，临床医学与基础医学几乎没有区别，最低的是土木，语言学与土木非常接近。在复合复杂句中最高的是语言学，最低的是材料。

就特殊类型句子而言，各学科特殊类型句子中均包含带冒号的句子，大部分学科中包含带 i. e. 的句子，少部分学科中包含带有括号和破折号的句子。特殊类型句子种类最高的是语言学，最低的是临床医学，除语言学和土木学科，其他各学科差异较小。占比最高的特殊句类各学科均相同，但是占比第二和第三的存在一定的差异。表中"＊"表示该学科文章中其他特殊句类占比差异较小，均很低。

表4.10.17 各学科句类及占比

学科	S	P	C	CP	特殊句类			
					种类	第一	第二	第三
SW	75.59%	8.07%	12.67%	0.61%	6	NWS	NWBSS	NWC
LC	68.86%	12.56%	15.18%	1.45%	4	NWS	NWC	*
JC	71.14%	9.07%	15.71%	0.77%	9	NWS	NSC	*
HY	73.78%	11.28%	11.13%	1.83%	7	NWS	*	*
SZ	71.00%	12.14%	11.65%	2.60%	7	NWS	NWHS	*
HX	77.31%	8.03%	12.04%	1.05%	5	NWS	*	*
CL	74.77%	8.66%	11.42%	0.55%	6	NWS	NWHS	NWHP
TM	71.31%	15.33%	8.09%	1.79%	11	NWS	NWHS	BSF
YY	63.14%	22.02%	8.92%	3.25%	15	NWS	NWP	*

B. 句类与语步

表4.10.18是各学科中四类句子与步骤之间的关系。"种类比"一栏表示各类句子中出现的步骤种类在该学科所有步骤种类中的占比。右边三栏为各类句子中占比最高的前三个步骤。单元格中用加号连接的两个步骤为同时出现在一句中的步骤组合，单元格中 * 表示有多个步骤占比相同，但均较低。

如表所示，除了生物学科，其他各学科四类句子中包含步骤种类占比最高的均为简单句，最低的均为复合复杂句。在生物学科中步骤占比最高的是复合句，占比最低的也是复合复杂句。其他两类句子存在一定的学科性差异，临床医学和基础医学四类句子中步骤种类占比一致。

就四类句子中出现的占比最高的前三个步骤而言，在简单句中各学科论文中均包含了 M2.4，在多数学科中占比均最高，其中临床和基础医学一致。涉及学科较多的还有 M2.2a，共涉及四个学科。复杂句和复合句中情况与简单句类似。在复合复杂句中除材料学科外，其他各学科均包含 M2.4，其中土木学科中该步骤排在第二，其他各学科中均排在第一。

表4.10.18　　　　　**各学科四类句子与高占比步骤**

句类	学科	种类比	第一	第二	第三
S	SW	94%	2.4	1.2a	3.2
	LC	100%	2.4	3.2	1.2c
	JC	100%	2.4	3.2	2.6a
	HY	100%	2.4	1.2a	1.1C
	SZ	100%	2.4	2.2a	1.2c
	HX	100%	2.4	2.2a	1.2d
	CL	92%	2.2a	2.4	2.2b
	TM	100%	2.2a	1.2a	2.4
	YY	97%	3.2a	2.4	1.2b
P	SW	71%	2.4	1.2a	*
	LC	64%	2.4	3.2	1.2c
	JC	77%	2.4	3.2	1.3a
	HY	67%	1.1C	2.6	1.2a
	SZ	82%	2.4	2.2a	3.2
	HX	48%	2.4	2.2a	1.2d
	CL	60%	2.2a	2.3a	2.4
	TM	85%	2.2a	2.4	1.2a
	YY	85%	2.4	3.2a	1.6
C	SW	100%	2.4	1.2d	1.2a
	LC	68%	2.4	1.2c	1.7
	JC	86%	2.4	1.2d	3.2
	HY	67%	1.2a	2.4	1.1C
	SZ	68%	2.4	2.2a	1.2d
	HX	57%	2.4	1.2d	2.2a
	CL	64%	2.4	2.2b	1.3a
	TM	52%	2.2a	1.2a	2.4
	YY	64%	3.2a	1.1D	2.4

句类	学科	种类比	第一	第二	第三
CP	SW	6%	2.4	*	*
	LC	36%	2.4	*	*
	JC	27%	2.4	*	*
	HY	42%	2.4	1.1C	*
	SZ	36%	2.4	2.2a	3.2
	HX	17%	2.4	*	*
	CL	20%	1.3a	3.2	2.2a + 2.2b
	TM	48%	2.2a	2.4	*
	YY	42%	2.4	3.2	3.2a

C. 句类与句长

表4.10.19是各学科中四类句子长度分布占比及句长最大值和最小值。如表所示，总体来说，各学科中四类句子长度分布较为相似。但就同一类句子长度分布而言，各学科之间既有共性，也存在一定的差异。

就简单句而言，各学科中句长占比从高到低排序具有较高的一致性，但是句长介于1—10和31—40的句子占比存在一定的学科性差异。总体来说，这两类句子占比较为接近。各学科句子最大值存在较大的差异，其中临床医学最高，海洋、市政和材料三个学科较接近，也最低；其他几个学科较为接近、居中。各学科句子最小值差异较小。就句长覆盖广度而言，临床医学与其他学科差异较大，覆盖最广。

就复杂句而言，各学科中句长占比从高到低排序具有较高的一致性，但是有少部分学科介于11—20的句子占比略高于介于31—40的句子，但是临床和基础两个医学学科也有差异。总体来说，这两类句子占比较接近。句长最大值中，基础医学最高，其次是临床医学，化学最低。总体来说，不同学科存在一定的差异，但有些学科之间差异较小，有些学科之间差异较明显。各学科句长最小值差异均不明显。就句长覆盖广度而言，临床医学、基础医学和语言学均较广，但临床和基础医学中没有介于1—10的句子。覆盖范围最小的是化学。

表4.10.19　各学科四类句子长度分布

句类	学科	句长范围											MAX	MIX
		1—10	11—20	21—30	31—40	41—50	51—60	61—70	71—80	81—90	91—100	111—120		
S	SW	17.30%	45.00%	24.86%	9.05%	3.11%	0.54%	0.14%	*	*	*	*	62	5
	LC	13.92%	45.63%	26.05%	8.25%	3.24%	1.29%	0.65%	0.32%	*	0.49%	0.16%	111	4
	JC	12.77%	46.76%	25.00%	10.61%	2.88%	1.08%	0.90%	*	*	*	*	69	5
	HY	7.63%	38.35%	35.67%	13.64%	4.12%	0.41%	*	*	*	*	*	53	4
	SZ	8.03%	47.64%	30.89%	10.65%	2.44%	0.35%	*	*	*	*	*	53	7
	HX	12.44%	47.06%	29.64%	7.47%	2.49%	0.45%	0.23%	0.23%	*	*	*	78	6
	CL	11.08%	46.31%	28.08%	11.08%	3.20%	0.25%	*	*	*	*	*	50	4
	TM	8.85%	47.42%	30.12%	9.64%	2.91%	0.92%	*	0.13%	*	*	*	72	5
	YY	17.31%	50.33%	21.40%	7.93%	1.98%	0.92%	*	0.13%	*	*	*	75	3
P	SW	*	28.57%	33.77%	24.36%	7.79%	2.60%	3.90%	*	*	*	*	70	11
	LC	*	24.66%	36.99%	21.92%	9.59%	4.11%	*	*	2.74%	*	*	82	11
	JC	*	19.72%	38.03%	21.13%	12.68%	4.23%	1.41%	1.41%	1.41%	*	*	88	14
	HY	*	17.81%	43.84%	24.32%	9.59%	2.74%	1.37%	1.37%	*	*	*	78	14
	SZ	*	21.43%	37.76%	26.53%	8.16%	4.08%	2.04%	*	*	*	*	63	12
	HX	*	19.57%	47.83%	26.09%	6.52%	*	*	*	*	*	*	48	12
	CL	2.13%	31.91%	36.17%	21.28%	6.38%	2.13%	*	*	*	*	*	55	10
	TM	0.62%	23.46%	43.83%	24.69%	6.17%	1.23%	*	*	*	*	*	59	10
	YY	0.76%	25.48%	39.16%	20.91%	8.37%	3.04%	1.52%	0.76%	*	*	*	76	10

续表

句类	学科	句长范围											MAX	MIX
		1—10	11—20	21—30	31—40	41—50	51—60	61—70	71—80	81—90	91—100	111—120		
C	SW	2.40%	26.40%	44.80%	16.94%	4.80%	2.40%	*	0.80%	0.80%	*	*	88	7
	LC	1.47%	25.74%	42.65%	17.65%	10.29%	2.21%	*	*	*	*	*	58	9
	JC	1.64%	32.79%	36.89%	18.85%	8.20%	0.82%	0.82%	*	*	*	*	62	8
	HY	*	22.22%	41.67%	24.66%	5.56%	5.56%	*	1.39%	*	*	*	71	13
	SZ	*	26.60%	39.36%	24.47%	5.32%	4.26%	*	*	*	*	*	60	12
	HX	1.45%	24.64%	36.23%	21.74%	15.94%	*	*	*	*	*	*	51	10
	CL	*	43.55%	33.87%	16.13%	4.84%	1.61%	*	*	*	*	*	60	13
	TM	1.15%	31.03%	42.53%	17.24%	3.45%	4.60%	*	*	*	*	*	57	9
	YY	*	32.08%	38.68%	20.75%	4.72%	3.77%	*	*	*	*	*	60	11
CP	SW	*	16.67%	66.67%	*	16.67%	*	*	*	*	*	*	48	14
	LC	*	7.69%	38.46%	23.08%	30.77%	*	*	*	*	*	*	49	17
	JC	*	*	50.00%	16.67%	16.67%	*	16.67%	*	*	*	*	62	21
	HY	*	*	46.15%	8.33%	30.77%	7.69%	*	*	*	*	*	53	23
	SZ	*	*	38.10%	33.33%	28.57%	*	*	*	*	*	*	50	25
	HX	*	16.67%	33.33%	33.33%	*	*	16.67%	*	*	*	*	65	20
	CL	*	*	*	100.00%	*	*	*	*	*	*	*	36	32
	TM	*	*	35.00%	45.00%	15.00%	5.00%	*	*	*	*	*	55	21
	YY	*	5.26%	36.84%	28.95%	21.05%	7.89%	*	*	*	*	*	57	16

就复合句而言，除材料学科外，其他学科句长占比从高到低排序具有较高的一致性。材料学科中占比最高的是句长介于 11—20 的句子，其次是介于 21—30 的句子，其他学科情况恰好相反。此外，化学学科中句长介于 31—40 的句子占比略高于介于 21—30 的句子。就句长最大值而言，最高的是生物，最低的是化学，不同学科存在一定的差异，但是有些学科之间差异较小，有些学科之间差异较明显。句长最小值生物最低，海洋最高，有些学科差异较小，有些学科之间差异较明显。就句长覆盖广度而言，生物最广，各学科主要集中在 11—40 之间，总体差异不大。

就复合复杂句而言，与前面三类句子相比学科间差异较大。就句长占比而言，化学介于 21—30 和介于 31—40 的句子占比相同，土木介于 31—40 的句子占比高于介于 21—30 的句子，材料均为介于 31—40 的句子，其他各学科占比最高的均为介于 21—30 的句子，除了生物学科中不包含介于 31—40 的句子外，占比第二的均为介于 31—40 的句子。就句子长度最大值和最小值而言，各学科均存在一定的差异，最大值中化学最高，材料最低，最小值中材料最高，生物最低。就句长覆盖广度而言，化学最广，但是化学论文中不包含介于 41—60 的句子，覆盖广度最低的是材料学科，均集中在 31—40 范围内。

（二）时态特征

A. 时态及组合

表 4.10.20 至表 4.10.22 为各学科中不同时态组合类型及占比。如表所示，各学科中包含时态种类较为接近，其中最高的有 8 种，为市政和语言学，最低的有 6 种，为基础和临床医学及化学，但有些时态不单独使用，而是与其他时态共同出现在同一个语句中。各学科均包含的时态有 4 种，分别为 T1、T2、T3 和 T10。就不同时态组合种类而言，学科差异较大。由两种时态构成的组合最多的为语言学，共有 12 种，最低的共有 4 种，为生物和临床医学。由三种时态构成的组合中最多的有 5 种，有三个学科和基础医学不包含该类组合。语言学中还包含了 2 种由四种不同时态构成的组合。就构成不同时态组合

的时态类型而言，除海洋中由 T1 构成的组合最多，化学中 T1 和 T3 相同；其他各学科中最多的均为由 T3 构成的组合。

就各时态组合占比而言，由同一种时态构成的组合中，占比最高的均为 T3，其次是 T1，其他均较低。但是临床医学文章中 T3 占比最高，生物和基础医学也较高，与临床医学差异不显著。最低的是土木和海洋。在只包含 T1 的组合中，各学科差异较明显，其中最高的是土木，其次是海洋；最低的是临床医学，其次是生物。各学科中，由不同时态构成的组合中占比最高的均为 T1T3 组合，同时该组合占比也高于其他由相同或不同时态构成的组合。

表 4.10.20　　　　　**各学科相同时态组合及占比**

学科	时态组合							
	T1	T2	T3	T4	T5	T6	T8	T10
SW	5.04%	0.21%	91.26%	*	*	*	*	0.41%
LC	2.66%	0.58%	92.60%	*	0.58%	*	*	0.12%
JC	7.33%	0.39%	88.17%	*	*	*	0.13%	0.13%
HY	30.34%	1.98%	60.21%	*	*	0.15%	*	0.15%
SZ	15.16%	0.75%	76.89%	*	0.12%	*	*	0.62%
HX	8.39%	0.17%	86.01%	0.70%	*	*	*	0.70%
CL	15.33%	0.37%	79.07%	*	*	*	*	0.19%
TM	31.27%	0.95%	59.32%	0.29%	*	*	0.10%	0.38%
YY	11.22%	0.50%	77.30%	0.25%	0.25%	*	*	0.50%

表 4.10.21　　　　　**各学科两种时态组合及占比**

学科	时态组合							
	T1T2	T1T3	T1T4	T1T7	T1T8	T1T10	T2T3	T2T6	T2T10
SW	*	2.16%	*	*	*	*	*	*	*
LC	0.23%	1.73%	*	*	*	*	*	*	*
JC	0.26%	2.44%	*	*	*	0.13%	0.26%	*	*

续表

学科	时态组合								
	T1T2	T1T3	T1T4	T1T7	T1T8	T1T10	T2T3	T2T6	T2T10
HY	1.07%	4.73%	0.15%	*	*	0.15%	0.15%	0.15%	*
SZ	0.50%	4.10%	*	*	*	0.25%	0.25%	*	*
HX	0.17%	2.62%	*	*	*	0.70%	*	*	*
CL	0.19%	3.36%	*	0.19%	*	0.37%	0.37%	*	*
TM	0.76%	4.18%	0.29%	*	*	0.29%	0.10%	*	0.10%
YY	0.42%	4.36%	0.25%	*	0.08%	0.08%	0.34%	*	*

学科	T3T4	T3T5	T3T6	T3T7	T3T8	T3T10	T3T11	T3T14	
SW	0.10%	0.10%	*	*	*	0.62%	*	*	
LC	*	0.81%	*	*	*	0.46%	*	*	
JC	*	0.26%	*	*	0.13%	0.39%	*	*	
HY	*	0.15%	*	*	*	*	*	0.15%	
SZ	*	0.62%	*	0.12%	0.25%	0.12%	0.25%	*	
HX	*	0.35%	*	*	*	0.17%	*	*	
CL	*	0.19%	*	*	*	0.19%	*	*	
TM	*	0.19%	*	*	0.10%	1.33%	*	*	
YY	0.08%	1.01%	0.17%	*	0.25%	2.09%	*	*	

表 4.10.22 **各学科三种及以上时态组合及占比**

学科	时态组合					
	T1T2T3	T1T3T4	T1T3T5	T1T3T6	T1T3T8	T3T5T8
SW	*	*	*	0.10%	*	*
LC	0.12%	*	*	*	*	0.12%
JC	*	*	*	*	*	*
HY	*	*	*	0.15%	*	*
SZ	*	*	*	*	*	*
HX	*	*	*	*	*	*
CL	*	0.19%	*	*	*	*
TM	*	*	*	*	0.10%	*
YY	0.17%	0.08%	0.08%	*	*	*

续表

学科	时态组合					T3T5T8
学科	T1T2T3	T1T3T4	T1T3T5	T1T3T6	T1T3T8	
	T3T5T10	T3T5T11	T1T3T10	T1T3T4T10	T1T3T5T10	
SW	*		*	*	*	
LC	*	*	*	*	*	
JC	*	*	*	*	*	
HY	*	*	0.15%	*	*	
SZ	*	*	*	*	*	
HX	*	*	*	*	*	
CL	*	*	*	*	*	
TM	0.10%	*	0.19%	*	*	
YY	*	0.08%	0.25%	0.08%	0.08%	

B. 时态与语步

表4.10.23是各学科中三种主要时态组合与步骤之间的关系。"时态"一栏表示同一个句子中出现的时态组合形式。"种类比"一栏表示该时态组合形式中出现的步骤种类在该学科所有步骤种类中的占比。*表示该学科中其他步骤占比均较低。右边三栏为各学科时态组合中占比最高的前三个步骤。

如表所示，除土木学科外，其他各学科中步骤占比最高的均为T3组合，其次为T1组合，最低的为T1T3组合。土木学科中T1组合步骤占比略高于T3。T1组合中占比最高的是土木，其次是海洋，最低的是临床医学和生物。T3组合中，生物、临床医学、基础医学和海洋中均包含了所有步骤，最低的为材料和土木。T1T3组合中，最高的是土木，最低的是化学和生物。

就各学科时态组合中占比最高的前三个步骤而言，T1组合中没有一个步骤为所有学科共有，其中涉及学科最多的为M2.4和M2.2a。T3组合中各学科均包含M2.4，但是该步骤在各学科中排序不完全一致。涉及学科较多的步骤还有M2.2a。在T1T3组合中也没有一个步骤为各学科共有，涉及学科较多的步骤为M2.4，其次是M2.2a。

表4.10.23　　**各学科三种类型时态组合与高占比步骤**

时态	学科	语步			
		种类比	第一	第二	第三
T1	SW	41%	2.4	1.2a	3.4
	LC	40%	3.2	*	*
	JC	73%	2.4	3.2	2.6a
	HY	88%	1.1C	1.2a	2.6
	SZ	86%	2.2a	3.2	2.4
	HX	70%	2.2a	2.4	3.7a
	CL	64%	2.2a	1.2b	3.5
	TM	93%	2.2a	1.2a	1.2b
	YY	67%	3.2	3.2b	3.6
T3	SW	100%	2.4	1.2a	1.2d
	LC	100%	2.4	3.2	1.2c
	JC	100%	2.4	3.2	1.2d
	HY	100%	2.4	3.2	1.2a
	SZ	95%	2.4	2.2a	1.2c
	HX	91%	2.4	2.2a	1.2d
	CL	88%	2.2a	2.4	2.2b
	TM	89%	2.2a	1.2a	2.4
	YY	97%	2.4	3.2a	1.2b
T1T3	SW	41%	2.4	*	*
	LC	52%	3.2	*	*
	JC	46%	2.4	*	*
	HY	54%	1.1C	2.4	1.2a
	SZ	55%	2.4	2.2a	1.2a
	HX	39%	2.2a	2.4	3.5
	CL	28%	1.3a	2.2a	2.3a
	TM	74%	2.2a	1.2a	2.4
	YY	45%	3.6	3.2a	1.6

（三）语态特征

表4.10.24是各学科中不同语态组合占比。"语态"一栏表示同一个句子中出现的语态组合形式。"种类比"表示该语态组合中出现的步骤种类在该学科所有步骤种类中的占比。最右边三栏分别是该语态组合中占比最高的前三个步骤。＊表示该学科中其他步骤占比均较低。如表所示，不同学科中均包含三种语态组合。其中全部V2为被动语态构成的句子占比远高于其他两类句子，占比最低的均为由两种不同语态构成的组合。V2组合在生物、临床医学、基础医学、市政、化学和材料中占比均较高，其中化学中最高，其他三个学科相对较低，最低的为语言学。V1组合在海洋、土木和语言学三个学科中占比较高，其中最高的为语言学，其他几个学科较为接近，最低的为化学。V1V2组合中，语言学明显高于其他各学科，其次为土木，最低的为生物，其他各学科较为接近。

表4.10.24　　　　　　　各学科语态组合与步骤

语态	学科	组合占比	语步		
			种类比	第一	第二	第三
V1	SW	17.49%	88%	2.4	1.2a	1.2d
	LC	16.65%	88%	2.4	1.2c	3.2
	JC	16.58%	91%	2.4	3.2	1.2a
	HY	33.54%	100%	1.1C	1.2a	3.2
	SZ	21.24%	82%	2.2a	2.4	3.2
	HX	12.24%	61%	2.2a	2.4	3.7a
	CL	15.33%	68%	2.2a	1.2b	3.7a
	TM	32.22%	96%	1.2a	2.2a	1.2b/1.2d
	YY	37.52%	97%	2.4	1.1D	1.2b

语态	学科	组合占比	语步			
			种类比	第一	第二	第三
V2	SW	78.70%	100%	2.4	1.2a	3.2
	LC	75.84%	100%	2.4	3.2	1.2c
	JC	75.96%	100%	2.4	3.2	1.2d
	HY	59.15%	100%	2.4	3.2	1.2a
	SZ	69.81%	100%	2.4	2.2a	1.2d
	HX	80.94%	100%	2.4	2.2a	1.2d
	CL	77.94%	88%	2.2a	2.4	2.2b
	TM	57.13%	96%	2.2a	1.2a	2.4
	YY	46.82%	88%	3.2a	2.4	3.2
V1V2	SW	3.81%	53%	2.4	*	*
	LC	7.51%	64%	2.4	1.2c	3.2
	JC	7.46%	77%	2.4	3.2	1.2d
	HY	7.32%	63%	1.1C	2.4	1.2a
	SZ	8.94%	77%	2.4	2.2a	3.2
	HX	6.82%	61%	2.4	2.2a	2.5c
	CL	6.73%	52%	2.2a	1.3a	2.3a
	TM	10.65%	70%	2.2a	2.4	1.2a
	YY	15.66%	79%	2.4	3.2a	3.2

就三种语态组合涉及步骤种类而言，除土木和语言学外，各学科中 V2 组合形式中涉及的步骤种类占比均最高，其次是 V1 组合。土木学科这两种组合中步骤种类占比相同，语言学刚好相反。V1V2 组合中语言学占比最高，其次是基础医学和市政，占比最低的是材料和生物。

就三种组合中占比最高的前三个步骤而言，V1 中没有一个步骤为所有学科共有，其中涉及学科最多的为 M2.4，其次是 M2.2a 和 M3.2。在 V2 中所有学科均包含了 M2.4，其次依次为 M3.2 和 M2.2a。在 V1V2 中除材料外，其他各学科中均包含 M2.4，涉及学科较多的还有 M2.2a。即使不同学科中包含的步骤相同，排序也不完全一致。即使在步骤排序相同的学科中，该步骤数量及占比也不相同。

第五章 建模实验写作特征

随着计算机技术的发展，实验的手段也发生了变化，特别是在理工科领域，传统上主要采取实验室或现场实体实验手段，但是有些实验受到现实条件的影响，难以进行实体实验，数学建模不仅可以弥补这一缺陷，同时还具有成本低这一特点，可重复次数高，适用于试件尺寸巨大、传统实验无法实现的情况。目前有越来越多的学科已经将数学建模作为了主要的研究手段。

分析发现，建模类论文方法部分的写作特征与传统类实体实验及问卷调查在语步特征方面存在较大的差异。本研究结合 Swales 的语步理论，对多个学科论文建模实验部分进行了细致分析，发现建模实验写作可以划分为"问题陈述""模型研发""模型验证或应用"和"模型有效性验证"四个大的语步，同时每个语步中又包含数量不等的步骤。

语步一、问题陈述：描述问题；章节介绍；工程概况；研究背景；前人研究的不足；问题解决难点；创建新模型目的及必要性；承接下文。

语步二、模型研发：介绍模型；模型及相关元素（描述公式/理论/方程/模块；参数/变量/指标特点及关系；模型假设/限制条件；事实描述；推理描述）；构建模型（模型结构；实施步骤及最终结构；模型算法/优化；强调模型的科学性）；模型预期结果（输出格式描述；运行结果；结果分析；模型使用环境）；与前人研究的关系（模型理论基础及原理；相似之处及改进方面；前人使用的工具变量）。

语步三、模型验证或应用：实验目的；实验所需设备/软件；介绍数据源；模型应用流程概括；实验费用；实验场地；模型运行时设置（模型组件；工作特征/参数；输入输出的设置；模型使用方法的目的）；用于测试/评价的指标；数据收集及取样技术（来源；特征；取样技术；数据存放位置；取样目的；监测情况）；概述研究结果；结果分析。

语步四、模型有效性验证：强调验证的必要性；实验验证（实验条件和程序；使用获得的数据验证模型；现场实验按规范确定参数；验证实验的局限性）；有效性验证分析（对比实验与建模结果；评价模型使用的评价指标；评价有效性检验结果；强调有效性查验的合理性；该模型的优点；该模型的局限性；模型对比；模型比较结果分析）；不同学科要求检验的范式（稳健性检验；灵敏度分析；异质性分析；论证工具变量的有效性）；基于建立的模型案例研究描述。

本研究共从管理科学与工程、电子信息工程、交通运输工程、车辆工程和软件工程五个不同学科 79 种国际期刊上选取了 116 篇文章，主要用于分析各学科论文中建模实验写作的体裁特征。

第一节　管理科学与工程

管理科学与工程是一门复杂的学科，综合运用系统科学、管理科学、数学、经济和行为科学及工程等方法，结合信息技术研究解决社会、经济、工程等方面的管理。数学建模是该学科主要研究手段之一，通过建立数学模型，以及利用数学方法来研究管理系统的结构、运行机制和改进方法。

本节主要分析该领域论文建模实验写作的体裁特征。共从 17 种该领域国际期刊上选取了 24 篇建模类学术论文，用于分析的句子共3067 句，71119 个单词，句子数量最多的文章共有 280 句，最少的为54 句，平均值为 127.79 句，标准差为 65.06。所选文章中有 58% 的论文为近十年发表的，92% 的论文的第一作者通信地址为英语国家或以英语为官方语言的国家。各篇文章中建模方法在论文中的篇幅占比平均值为 47%，最大值为 85%，最小值为 13%，总体占比较高，有近 46% 的文章中方法部分占比超过 50%。

一　标题特征分析

该学科建模类论文实验方法的写作一般会分成几个平行部分，各部分还会进一步细分，因此通常会包含不止一个一级大标题。在所分析的文章中有 85% 的文章包含了一个以上大标题，最多的有五个，最少的有两个。图 5.1.1 是所分析文章建模实验部分大标题词汇云图。如图所示，大标题中 model 出现次数最高，共出现了 12 次，其次是 data 和 problem，分别出现了 7 次和 6 次，其他出现次数较高的还有 formulation 和 methodology 等。所分析的文章中有 60% 的文章没有二级小标题，其他文章中使用二级小标题数量最多的有五个，最少的有两个。图 5.1.2 是小标题词汇云图。如图所示，出现次数最高的词汇也是 model，共出现了 10 次，其次是 data 和 result，均出现了 6 次，此外，variable、system 也出现了 5 次。对比以下两个图还可以发现，在大小标题中出现频次最高的两个词均是 model 和 data，但是这两个词在大标题中出现的频率略高于小标题。

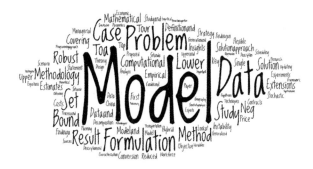

图 5.1.1　一级大标题词汇云图

图 5.1.2　二级小标题词汇云图

综上所述，该学科建模实验方法写作中大部分文章包含了不止一个一级大标题，但是使用二级小标题的文章占比较低。大小标题中还共同拥有其他一些词汇，但是在频次和占比方面会存在一定差异。大小标题中词汇与建模实验所涉及的问题关系均比较紧密，但有些文章大标题中少部分词汇与学科和实验手段关系不甚紧密。

二　语步特征分析

本节主要分析建模实验方法写作的语步特征。分析发现该部分总体语步框架与本研究分析的其他四个学科一致，均可分成四个大的语步，但是该学科四个语步包含的步骤类型与其他学科存在一定的差异。本节各语步列表中只列出所分析的该学科论文中出现的步骤。

（一）语步一特征

表 5.1.1 是所分析的本学科论文语步一中所包含的步骤种类。如表所示，该语步中共包括 6 个步骤。表 5.1.2 是各篇文章语步一中各步骤在该语步中的占比情况。如表所示，绝大部分文章中包含该语步。在包含该语步的文章中，各步骤占比情况不一。此外，同一个步骤在不同文章中占比情况也存在差异。以下是针对每个步骤占比情况的具体分析及实例。

表 5.1.1　　　　　　　　　　　语步一各步骤列表

M	语步一、问题陈述		
1.1	描述问题	1.3	问题解决难点
1.1a	章节介绍	1.4	创建新模型目的及必要性
1.2	前人研究的不足	1.5	承接下文

表 5.1.2　　　　　　　　　　语步一各步骤占比

M	1.1	1.1a	1.2	1.3	1.4	1.5
GL－01	20%	—	—	60%	20%	—
GL－02	13%	88%	—	—	—	—
GL－03	—	—	—	—	—	—

M	1. 1	1. 1a	1. 2	1. 3	1. 4	1. 5
GL－04	—	—	—	—	—	—
GL－05	11%	—	56%	—	33%	—
GL－06	56%	—	20%	—	24%	—
GL－07	100%	—	—	—	—	—
GL－08	—	—	—	—	—	—
GL－09	—	—	—	—	—	100%
GL－10	76%	—	—	5%	20%	—
GL－11	—	—	—	50%	50%	—
GL－12	53%	20%	7%	—	20%	—
GL－13	23%	—	—	27%	50%	—
GL－14	24%	—	—	6%	71%	—
GL－15	—	—	—	—	100%	—
GL－16	—	—	67%	17%	17%	—
GL－17	4%	—	74%	13%	9%	—
GL－18	79%	—	10%	—	10%	—
GL－19	—	—	—	—	100%	—
GL－20	67%	—	33%	—	—	—
GL－21	67%	—	33%	—	—	—
GL－22	31%	15%	—	4%	35%	15%
GL－23	46%	—	29%	21%	4%	—
GL－24	—	—	—	—	—	—

M 1.1 描述问题: 所选文章中有 63% 的文章包含该步骤。在包含该步骤的文章中，该步骤在语步一中的占比最大值为 100%，最小值为 4%，平均值为 45%，标准差为 0.28。实例如下:

All agent requirements, labor law constraints, and agent contract restrictions must be fulfilled. At this stage of the planning procedure, it is also possible to assign individual agents to specific flights. However, due to changes in the underlying information (e. g. , changing flight schedules and employee availability), a replanning is necessary one or two days before the day of operation. (GL－06)

SFA has also been used in energy efficiency evaluation. Managi et al. (2006) used SFA to examine the impact of changes in technology on the exploration of oil and gas, and Farsi et al. (2007) used it to study the cost efficiency of the Swiss gas distribution companies. (GL－18)

M 1.1a 章节介绍: 所选文章中有三篇包含该步骤。在这三篇文章中，该步骤在语步一中的占比分别为88%、15%和20%。实例如下：

This section presents our computational experience in solving model MSWN using a combined sample average approximation (SAA) algorithm proposed in Section 3. (GL-12)

This section presents the data and describes the econometric methods. (GL-02)

M 1.2 前人研究的不足：所选文章中有38%的文章包含该步骤。在包含该步骤的文章中，该步骤在语步一中的占比最大值为74%，最小值为7%，平均值为37%，标准差为0.23。实例如下：

Dickey et al. (1991, p. 65) note that 'cointegrating vectors can be thought of as representing constraints that an economic system imposes on the movement of the variables in the system in the long-run.' Thus, the more the number of cointegrating vectors, the more stable the system will be. (GL-17)

Extending the discussion of Jacobs and Bechtold (1993), the considered planning system allows for the following scheduling flexibility types with respect to employee contracts: (i) Shift-length flexibility: Each shift has a minimal length of 3 h and must end after 10 h. (GL-06)

M 1.3 问题解决难点：所选文章中有38%的文章包含该步骤。在包含该步骤的文章中，该步骤在语步一中的占比最大值为60%，最小值为4%，平均值为22%，标准差为0.19。实例如下：

The major concern with this specification is that finance is not assigned to parishes at random. (GL-01)

Even if sufficient data are available to generate credible scenarios, considering many of them for both demands and returns will create computational challenges. (GL-13)

M 1.4 创建新模型目的及必要性：所选文章中有63%的文章包含该步骤。在包含该步骤的文章中，该步骤在语步一中的占比最大值为100%，最小值为4%，平均值为37%，标准差为0.3。实例如下：

We now turn to characterizing the sources of this instability. A better accounting of the underlying sources of instability can inform theory and policy alike. (GL-15)

The flexible contracts of the service provider have no guaranteed amount of paid working hours per week or per month, but an integration of such constraints in our model is possible. (GL-06)

M 1.5 承接下文：所选文章中只有两篇包含该步骤，在其中一篇文章中该步骤是语步一中唯一一个步骤，在另一篇文章中该步骤在语步一中占比为15%。实例如下：

Results obtained for each of the three solution methods discussed in this section will be presented and compared in the following section. (GL-09)

Before turning to our main empirical exercise, we provide a brief overview of China's current economic geography. (GL-22)

综上所述，在所分析的文章中有83%的文章包含语步一。在包含该步骤的文章中，涉及文章数最多的步骤为M1.1和M1.4，均为15篇，占所有文章的63%，最少的为M1.5，仅有两篇，占所有文章的8%。各篇文章中包含的语步一中步骤种类最高的有4种，最低的只有1种，分别占该语步中所有步骤的83%和16%。各篇文章语步一中各步骤种类的平均值为2.65种，占该语步中所有步骤的17%，标准差为1.14。不同文章中包含的步骤种类存在一定的差异，同一个步骤在不同文章中占比也存在一定的差异。各个步骤在不同文章中占比平均值最高的是M1.5，最低的是M1.3，分别为58%和22%，各步骤平均值为40%，标准差为11.76。

（二）语步二特征

表5.1.3是语步二中所包含的步骤种类。如表所示，语步二共包含5个大的步骤，其中步骤2.2又细分为5个小的步骤，步骤2.3又细分为3个小的步骤，步骤2.4和步骤2.5又分别细分为2个和3个小的步骤。语步二中共有14种不同步骤。表5.1.4是不同文章语步二中各步骤在该语步中的占比情况。所有文章均包括该语步，但是该语步中各步骤占比情况不一。此外，同一个步骤在不同文章中的占比情况也有所差异。以下是针对每个步骤占比情况的具体分析及实例。

表5.1.3　　　　　　　　　　语步二各步骤列表

M			语步二、模型研发
2.1	介绍模型	2.3b	实施步骤及最终结构
2.2	模型及相关元素	2.3c	模型算法/优化
2.2a	描述公式/理论/方程/模块	2.4	模型预期结果
2.2b	参数/变量/指标特点及关系	2.4a	输出格式描写
2.2c	模型假设/限制条件	2.4b	运行结果
2.2d	事实描述	2.5	与前人研究的关系
2.2e	推理描述	2.5a	模型理论基础及原理
2.3	构建模型	2.5b	相似之处及改进方面
2.3a	模型结构	2.5c	前人使用的工具变量

表5.1.4 语步二各步骤占比

M	2.1	2.2a	2.2b	2.2c	2.2d	2.2e	2.3a	2.3b	2.3c	2.4a	2.4b	2.5a	2.5b	2.5c
GL-01	—	24%	41%	29%	—	—	6%	—	—	—	—	—	—	—
GL-02	—	9%	91%	—	—	—	—	—	—	—	—	—	—	—
GL-03	—	—	92%	2%	—	—	4%	—	—	—	—	—	—	2%
GL-04	—	17%	57%	26%	—	—	—	—	—	—	—	—	—	—
GL-05	—	—	70%	—	—	—	—	—	—	—	—	—	30%	—
GL-06	24%	26%	15%	—	—	—	35%	—	—	—	—	—	—	—
GL-07	23%	61%	—	—	—	—	10%	—	—	—	2%	4%	—	—
GL-08	2%	—	—	—	—	—	14%	39%	32%	—	—	14%	—	—
GL-09	1%	—	12%	—	—	—	—	18%	69%	—	—	—	—	—
GL-10	10%	4%	1%	8%	—	—	38%	—	39%	—	—	0%	—	—
GL-11	17%	—	4%	1%	—	—	33%	8%	33%	—	—	3%	—	—
GL-12	5%	—	37%	1%	—	—	15%	—	39%	—	—	4%	—	—
GL-13	7%	1%	1%	2%	—	—	51%	—	39%	—	—	0%	—	—
GL-14	1%	1%	6%	10%	—	—	27%	—	55%	—	—	—	—	—

续表

M	2.1	2.2a	2.2b	2.2c	2.2d	2.2e	2.3a	2.3b	2.3c	2.4a	2.4b	2.5a	2.5b	2.5c
GL-15	1%	4%	65%	—	—	—	10%	10%	7%	2%	—	—	—	—
GL-16	7%	3%	31%	7%	—	—	—	—	—	28%	3%	14%	7%	—
GL-17	—	18%	73%	—	—	—	—	—	—	—	9%	—	—	—
GL-18	—	8%	9%	6%	—	—	16%	15%	—	—	1%	40%	4%	—
GL-19	4%	12%	4%	—	—	—	9%	37%	—	—	—	17%	17%	—
GL-20	3%	16%	38%	13%	—	—	2%	—	5%	1%	14%	3%	7%	—
GL-21	—	—	51%	11%	3%	2%	3%	6%	6%	—	6%	13%	1%	—
GL-22	—	7%	29%	17%	5%	—	1%	4%	2%	—	4%	15%	15%	—
GL-23	1%	4%	25%	4%	7%	—	2%	3%	2%	—	28%	18%	6%	—
GL-24	—	—	31%	3%	18%	5%	3%	6%	6%	—	13%	13%	3%	—

M 2.1 介绍模型：所选文章中有58%的文章包含该步骤。在包含该步骤的文章中，该步骤在语步二中的占比最大值为24%，最小值为1%，平均值为7%，标准差为0.08。实例如下：

This formulation can be used for the shift scheduling, the days-off scheduling, and the tour scheduling problem [see Morris and Showalter (1983)]. (GL – 06)

Protection and through-flight arcs are handled in a similar fashion. The original arc is split into the number of legs covered by the original arc plus two new arcs. (GL – 07)

M 2.2a 描述公式/理论/方程/模块：所选文章中有63%的文章包含该步骤。在包含该步骤的文章中，该步骤在语步二中的占比最大值为61%，最小值为1%，平均值为14%，标准差为0.15。实例如下：

The smooth partial adjustment in Eq. (4) may only approximate an individual firm's actual adjustments. (GL – 04)

To achieve this end, we use the following notation: a single shift type j with start period s_j and last working period f_j is described by the shift parameters a_{ij} with Eq. (GL – 06)

M 2.2b 参数/变量/指标特点及关系：所选文章中有92%的文章包含该步骤。在包含该步骤的文章中，该步骤在语步二中的占比最大值为92%，最小值为1%，平均值为36%，标准差为0.28。实例如下：

A higher MB is generally taken as a sign of more attractive future growth options, which a firm tends to protect by limiting its leverage. (GL – 04)

A5 represents the set of arcs that directly connect chipping terminals J with bio-refineries S; A6 represents the set of arcs joining pelletizing terminals K with multi-modal facilities; A7 represents the set of arcs between multi-modal facilities and bio-refineries S; A8 represents the set of arcs connecting bio-refineries S with blending facilities; and finally A9 represents the set of arcs that connect blending facilities $\mathscr{F}$ with bio-fuel customers G. (GL – 12)

M 2.2c 模型假设/限制条件：所选文章中有63%的文章包含该步骤。在包含该步骤的文章中，该步骤在语步二中的占比最大值为29%，最小值为1%，平均值为9%，标准差为0.09。实例如下：

Note that our addition of a non-tradable service sector, housing, has no consequences when labor does not move between regions. (GL – 22)

The following assumptions are considered to formulate the problem under investigation: Both MCs and BMs are capacitated. (GL – 10)

M 2.2d 事实描述：所选文章中有17%的文章包含该步骤。在包含该步骤的文章中，该步骤在语步二中的占比最大值为18%，最小值为3%，平均值为8%，标准差为0.06。实例如下：

Like the El train lines, four interstate highways radiate from the Chicago Loop. The convenience of living near a highway, however, may be outweighed by the accompanying noise, pollution, and traffic congestion. Particularly for inner-city residents, who are less likely to travel short distance in town by car, proximity to an interstate is a strong disamenity that is likely to discourage renovation activity. (GL – 23)

As already mentioned in Section 4, doubts have been raised on the reliability of non-Census year data. (GL – 22)

M 2.2e 推理描述：所选文章中只有两篇包含该步骤。在这两篇文章中，该步骤在语步二中的占比分别为5%和2%。实例如下：

When on the other hand, people are able to move around, the equilibrium distribution of people will change [except in the (very) unlikely case that real wages are initially already equalized], with people moving towards places offering higher real wages. Whether or not this will result in more or less agglomeration, is a priori not clear. (GL – 22)

Inferences do not change when we use first differences. (GL – 24)

M 2.3a 模型结构：所选文章中有75%的文章包含该步骤。在包含该步骤的文章中，该步骤在语步二中的占比最大值为51%，最小值为1%，平均值为16%，标准差为0.15。实例如下：

In an Online Appendix, we introduce a simple model that connects financial frictions to structural transformation and growth. (GL – 01)

Eq. (9) ensures that, at most, one shift per day can be assigned to one employee. The number of employees assigned has to meet the requirement r td for each time period t and each day d as stated in Eq. (10). (GL – 06)

M 2.3b 实施步骤及最终结构：所选文章中有42%的文章包含该步骤。在包含该步骤的文章中，该步骤在语步二中的占比最大值为39%，最小值为3%，平均值为15%，标准差为0.13。实例如下：

As mentioned previously, each tour column within the model belongs to or is owned by an individual employee. Constraint (2.2) ensures that exactly one of the possible tours for each employee is selected by the model. (GL – 09)

An initial subproblem is obtained by selecting a certain number of columns with smallest reduced costs. At each iteration, the current subproblem is solved. (GL – 08)

M 2.3c 模型算法/优化：所选文章中有54%的文章包含该步骤。在包含该步骤的文章中，该步骤在语步二中的占比最大值为69%，最小值为2%，平均值为26%，标准差为0.22。实例如下：

In the longest path algorithm, if two or more partial paths arrive at the same node, then the paths with the smallest length will be ignored. This is illustrated in figure 4 where path 1 would be selected due to its higher (partial) reduced cost. (GL – 09)

A cycle in our graph G represents a pairing if and only if it consists of exactly one return arc. The cycles need not be disjoint because we allow deadheading. (GL – 08)

M 2.4a 输出格式描写：所选文章中有13%的文章包含该步骤。在包含该步骤的文章中，该步骤在语步二中的占比最大值为28%，最小值为1%，平均值为10%，标准差为0.12。实例如下：

According to standard gravity models (e. g., Eaton and Kortum, 2002; Anderson and van Wincoop, 2003; Chaney, 2008), Product Destination effects are driven by changing incomes in destinations, changes in expenditure shares across products within destinations, and "pure" demand factors-but also by variation in Source Product factors (e. g., variation in industry competitiveness and policies across industries within source countries). (GL – 15)

If R is small (< 100), then the country is able to achieve greater stability by exporting larger amounts of the major commodity, rather than diversifying its exports to larger number of commodities. (GL – 16)

M 2.4b 运行结果：所选文章中有38%的文章包含该步骤。在包含该步骤的文章中，该步骤在语步二中的占比最大值为28%，最小值为1%，平均值为9%，标准差为0.08。实例如下：

This observation points to the need to examine fluctuations in the major export on an individual country basis or should cross-country analysis be employed, differences in the stability of the major exports be accounted for. (GL – 16)

Despite our best identification efforts, we note at this point the potential for unobservable factors to influence the results, for example, issues around the on-the-ground implementation of the policy, external and internal economic and political influences. (GL – 21)

M 2.5a 模型理论基础及原理：所选文章中有58%的文章包含该步骤。在包含该步骤的文章中，该步骤在语步二中的占比最大值为40%，最小值为0%，平均值为11%，标准差为0.1。实例如下：

This model is derived from the work of Yan and his co-authors (Yan and Yang, 1996; Yan and Young, 1996; Yan and Lin, 1997; Yan and Tu, 1997), and solves the aircraft recovery problem for multiple fleets with the objective of maximizing a modified "profit" function over the flight schedule during the recovery period. (GL – 07)

In the first step of our framework, we measure innovation efficiency using the multi-directional efficiency analysis (MEA) model (Asmild et al., 2003; Bogetoft & Hougaard, 1999), which builds on the framework of data envelopment analysis (DEA). (GL – 19)

M 2.5b 相似之处及改进方面：所选文章中有38%的文章包含该步骤。在包含该步骤的文章中，该步骤在语步二中的占比最大值为30%，最小值为1%，平均值为10%，标准差为 0.09。实例如下：

The main differences between our model and Rajan and Zingales (1998) setup are twofold.
(GL‑05)

In extending this model, we rely heavily on Helms (2003) by following the general deriva-
tion and notation as used therein. (GL‑20)

M 2.5c 前人使用的工具变量：所选文章中只有一篇包含该步骤。在该篇文章中，该步骤在语步二中的占比为 2%。实例如下：

While a number of studies in the urban economics literature use historical data as a source of
exogenous variation (BaumSnow, 2007; Duranton & Turner, 2012; Duranton et al., 2014),
this empirical approach is novel in the entrepreneurship and innovation literature. (GL‑03)

综上所述，所有文章均包含语步二。在语步二各步骤中，涉及文章数最多的为 M2.2b，共 22 篇，占所有文章的 92%，最少的为 M2.5c，共 1 篇，占所有文章的 4%。各步骤涉及文章平均数为 10.64篇，占所有文章的 44%，标准差为 6.36。各篇文章中包含步骤最多的有 11 种，最少的仅有 2 种，分别占所有步骤的 79% 和 14%。各篇文章语步二中各步骤种类平均值为 6.21 种，占语步二中所有步骤的44%，标准差为 2.72。不同文章中包含的步骤种类存在一定的差异，同一个步骤在不同文章中的占比也存在一定的差异。各个步骤在不同文章中占比平均值最高的是 M2.2b，最低的是 M2.5c，分别为 36% 和2%，各步骤平均值为 13%，标准差为 8.89。

（三）语步三特征

表 5.1.5 是语步三中所包含的步骤种类。如表所示，语步三共包含 8 个大的步骤，其中步骤 3.2 又包含 2 个小的步骤，步骤 3.4 又包含 4 个小的步骤。该语步中共有 12 种不同步骤。表 5.1.6 是不同文章语步三中各步骤在该语步中的占比情况。有少数文章中不包含语步三。在包含该步骤的文章中，该语步中各步骤占比情况不一。此外，同一个步骤在不同文章中占比情况也有所差异。以下是针对每个步骤占比情况的具体分析及实例。

表 5.1.5　　　　　　　　　　**语步三各步骤列表**

M	语步三、模型验证或应用		
3.1A	实验目的	3.3	用于测试/评价的指标
3.1a	实验所需设备/软件	3.4	数据收集及取样技术
3.1d	实验费用	3.4a	来源
3.1e	实验场地	3.4b	特征
3.2	模型运行时设置	3.4c	取样技术
3.2a	模型组件	3.4d	数据存放位置
3.2b	工作特征/参数	3.5	概述研究结果

表 5.1.6　　　　　　　　　　**语步三各步骤占比**

M	3.1A	3.1a	3.1d	3.1e	3.2a	3.2b	3.3	3.4a	3.4b	3.4c	3.4d	3.5
GL－01	—	—	—	—	—	—	—	—	—	—	—	100%
GL－02	—	—	—	—	—	—	—	86%	—	14%	—	—
GL－03	—	—	—	—	—	—	—	55%	—	—	—	45%
GL－04	—	17%	—	—	—	—	—	83%	—	—	—	—
GL－05	—	—	—	—	—	—	—	48%	—	—	—	52%
GL－06	—	5%	—	—	—	—	10%	38%	—	—	—	48%
GL－07	—	—	—	—	—	—	13%	87%	—	—	—	—
GL－08	—	—	—	—	—	—	3%	97%	—	—	—	—
GL－09	7%	—	—	—	—	—	7%	87%	—	—	—	—
GL－10	—	25%	—	—	—	—	25%	—	50%	—	—	—
GL－11	—	—	—	—	—	—	100%	—	—	—	—	—
GL－12	—	4%	2%	2%	—	2%	—	42%	47%	—	—	—
GL－13												
GL－14	—	33%	33%	—	—	33%	—	—	—	—	—	—
GL－15	—	—	—	—	—	—	—	—	—	—	—	—

续表

M	3.1A	3.1a	3.1d	3.1e	3.2a	3.2b	3.3	3.4a	3.4b	3.4c	3.4d	3.5
GL-16	—	—	—	—	—	—	—	50%	25%	25%	—	—
GL-17	—	—	—	—	—	—	—	—	—	—	—	—
GL-18	—	—	—	—	—	—	—	26%	11%	63%	—	—
GL-19	—	—	—	—	—	—	—	—	—	—	—	—
GL-20	—	—	—	—	1%	—	1%	7%	56%	16%	—	18%
GL-21	—	—	—	—	—	—	—	8%	65%	27%	—	—
GL-22	—	—	—	—	7%	11%	1%	11%	54%	6%	—	9%
GL-23	—	6%	—	—	—	—	6%	12%	39%	6%	—	30%
GL-24	—	—	—	—	15%	10%	5%	28%	33%	5%	—	5%

M 3.1A 实验目的：所选文章中只有一篇包含该步骤。在该篇文章中，该步骤在语步三中的占比为7%。实例如下：

We aim to solve a number of test problems varying in size and difficulty. (GL-09)

M 3.1a 实验所需设备/软件：所选文章中有25%的文章包含该步骤。在包含该步骤的文章中，该步骤在语步三中的占比最大值为33%，最小值为4%，平均值为15%，标准差为0.11。实例如下：

A regression specification used to test for tradeoff leverage behavior must permit each firm's target debt ratio to vary over time, and must recognize that deviations from target leverage are not necessarily offset quickly. (GL-04)

Our proposed mathematical model and solution algorithm are coded in python 2.7 on a desktop with Intel Core i7 3.6 GHz processor and 16.0 GB RAM. (GL-12)

3.1d 实验费用：所选文章中只有两篇文章包含该步骤。在这两篇文章中，该步骤在语步三中的占比分别为33%和2%。实例如下：

All costs are calculated based on 2016 dollars value. (GL-12)

The maximum budget was set at \$100,000. (GL-14)

3.1e 实验场地：所选文章中只有一篇包含该步骤。在该篇文章中，该步骤在语步三中的占比为2%。实例如下：

We have chosen the state of Mississippi as a testing ground for the case study. (GL-12)

M 3.2a 模型组件：所选文章中只有三篇包含该步骤。在这三篇文章中，该步骤在语步三中的占比分别为15%、7%和1%。实例如下：

For tractability, the variables have been categorized into three major categories: property, location, and neighborhood demographic. (GL – 20)

We use all estimates discussed in this section as inputs to a simulation analysis based on the complete NEG model. (GL – 22)

M 3.2b 工作特征/参数：所选文章中有17%的文章包含该步骤。在包含该步骤的文章中，该步骤在语步三中的占比最大值为33%，最小值为2%，平均值为14%，标准差为0.12。实例如下：

The robustness parameters η and λ that were introduced to the model were set at 0.75 and 0.25, respectively. (GL – 14)

The running parameter is the margin of a left-wing majority in state parliament; the RD threshold is set at more than 50% of all seats in the state parliament. (GL – 24)

M 3.3 用于测试/评价的指标：所选文章中有25%的文章包含该步骤。在包含该步骤的文章中，该步骤在语步三中的占比最大值为26%，最小值为1%，平均值为11%，标准差为0.11。实例如下：

The five commonly used metrics in the evolutionary multi-objective optimization literature are: (1) quality metric (QM), (2) convergence metric (CM), (3) divergence metric (DM), (4) spacing metric (SM), and (5) mean ideal distance (MID) metric, which represent both quantitative and qualitative comparisons with MOEAs (see Deb, 2001 for further information). (GL – 10)

We derive four measures: (1) hospitals per capita, (2) hospital beds per capita, (3) beds per hospital (approximating state-average hospital size) and (4) capital expenditure per capita in 2014 prices. (GL – 24)

M 3.4a 来源：所选文章中有54%的文章包含该步骤。在包含该步骤的文章中，该步骤在语步三中的占比最大值为100%，最小值为3%，平均值为23%，标准差为0.26。实例如下：

All inputs and outputs of DEA were obtained from the World Input & Output Database1 (WIOD), a consistent data set that enables the calculation of a consistent year-to-year time series. (GL – 18)

Agricultural residue data are based on the USDA National Agricultural Statistics Service (NASS). (GL – 11)

M 3.4b 特征：所选文章中有67%的文章包含该步骤。在包含该步骤的文章中，该步骤在语步三中的占比最大值为97%，最小值为25%，平均值为60%，标准差为0.21。实例如下：

All of these variables are winsorized at the 1st and 99th percentiles to avoid the influence of extreme observations. (GL – 04)

For the given schedule, 49% of the flights have IAH as their origin or destination, 35%

have EWR as their origin or destination and 14% have CLE as their origin or destination. (GL – 07)

M 3.4c 取样技术：所选文章中有29%的文章包含该步骤。在包含该步骤的文章中，该步骤在语步三中的占比最大值为50%，最小值为5%，平均值为19%，标准差为0.15。实例如下：

In order to examine the contribution of the major export commodity to total instability of export earnings, the total export for each country is decomposed in receipts from the major commodity and from the minor commodities (total export receipts minus receipts from the major export). (GL – 16)

After deleting observations with missing or inconsistent values for important variables and observations with addresses that could not be geocoded or matched with the addresses in the renovation data set, the final sample consists of 435, 534 buildings with unique addresses. (GL – 23)

M 3.4d 数据存放位置：所选文章中只有一篇包含该步骤。在该篇文章中，该步骤在语步三中的占比为14%。实例如下：

In the Internet Appendix (an Internet Appendix for this article is available online in the "Supplements and Datasets" section at http：//www. afajof. org/supplements. asp) we present the deregulation dates. (GL – 02)

M 3.5 概述研究结果：所选文章中有33%的文章包含该步骤。在包含该步骤的文章中，该步骤在语步三中的占比最大值为100%，最小值为5%，平均值为38%，标准差为0.29。实例如下：

Along the transitional path to a high level of balanced growth, the economy is characterized by a structural transformation that is accelerated by access to financial services. (GL – 01)

Table 2 summarizes the results of all three cases. The aggregated demand and the assigned working hours are shown. The utilization provides the relationship between the required and the scheduled working hours. (GL – 06)

综上所述，有20篇文章中包括语步三，约占所分析文章的83%。在包含语步三的文章中，涉及文章数最多的步骤为M3.4b，共涉及所有文章的67%。有三个步骤只涉及一篇文章，分别是M3.1A、M3.1e和M3.4d，均占所有文章的4%。各篇文章中包含步骤种类最多的有7种，最少的只有1种，分别占所有步骤的58%和8%。各篇文章中包含步骤种类的平均值为3.4种，占该语步中所有步骤的28%，标准差为1.93。不同文章中包含的步骤种类存在一定的差异，同一个步骤在不同文章中的占比也存在一定的差异。各个步骤在不同文章中占比平均值最高的是 M3.4b，为 60%，最低的是 M3.1e，为 2%，各步骤平均值为 19%，标准差为 15.79。

（四）语步四特征

表 5.1.7 是语步四中各步骤列表。如表所示，语步四共包括 5 个大的步骤，其中步骤 4.2 又包含 2 个小的步骤，步骤 4.3 又包含 8 个小的步骤，步骤 4.4 又包含 4 个小的步骤。语步四共包含 16 种不同步骤。表 5.1.8 是不同文章语步四中各步骤在该语步中的占比情况。如表所示，有一小部分文章中不包含该语步。在包含该步骤的文章中，该语步中各步骤占比情况不一。此外，同一个步骤在不同文章中的占比情况也有所差异。以下是针对每个步骤占比情况的具体分析及实例。

表 5.1.7 　　　　　　　　　　　**语步四各步骤列表**

M	语步四、模型有效性验证		
4.1	强调验证的必要性	4.3f	该模型的局限性
4.2	实验验证	4.3g	模型对比
4.2a	实验条件和程序	4.3h	模型比较结果分析
4.2b	使用获得的数据验证模型	4.4	不同学科要求检验的范式
4.3	有效性验证分析	4.4a	稳健性检验
4.3a	对比实验与建模结果	4.4b	灵敏度分析
4.3b	评价模型使用的评价指标	4.4c	异质性分析
4.3c	评价有效性检验结果	4.4d	论证工具变量的有效性
4.3d	强调有效性检验的合理性	4.5	基于建立的模型案例研究描述
4.3e	该模型的优点		

表5.1.8 语步四各步骤占比

M	4.1	4.2a	4.2b	4.3a	4.3b	4.3c	4.3d	4.3e	4.3f	4.3g	4.3h	4.4a	4.4b	4.4c	4.4d	4.5
GL-01	—	—	—	—	—	—	—	—	—	—	—	—	—	—	100%	—
GL-02	—	—	—	—	—	—	—	—	—	—	—	—	—	—	—	—
GL-03	—	—	—	—	—	—	—	—	—	—	—	100%	—	—	—	—
GL-04	—	—	—	—	—	—	—	—	—	—	—	—	—	—	—	—
GL-05	—	—	—	—	—	—	—	—	—	—	—	100%	—	—	—	—
GL-06	—	—	—	—	—	—	—	—	—	—	—	—	100%	—	—	—
GL-07	—	—	—	—	—	—	—	—	—	—	—	—	—	—	—	—
GL-08	—	—	—	—	—	—	—	—	—	—	—	—	—	—	—	—
GL-09	—	—	—	—	—	—	—	—	—	—	—	—	—	—	—	—
GL-10	4%	—	—	15%	—	—	—	—	—	—	—	37%	—	—	—	45%
GL-11	—	—	62%	—	—	—	—	—	—	—	—	30%	—	—	—	8%
GL-12	—	—	—	—	1%	87%	—	—	—	—	—	12%	—	—	—	—
GL-13	3%	—	—	—	—	97%	—	—	—	—	—	—	—	—	—	—
GL-14	—	—	—	—	—	10%	—	—	—	2%	19%	38%	—	—	—	31%

续表

M	4.1	4.2a	4.2b	4.3a	4.3b	4.3c	4.3d	4.3e	4.3f	4.3g	4.3h	4.4a	4.4b	4.4c	4.4d	4.5
GL-15	—	1%	—	11%	16%	57%	—	—	—	—	—	4%	—	11%	—	—
GL-16	—	—	59%	24%	—	—	—	18%	—	—	—	—	—	—	—	—
GL-17	—	8%	16%	—	7%	44%	19%	4%	2%	—	—	—	—	—	—	—
GL-18	—	—	—	—	—	—	—	—	—	—	—	—	—	—	—	—
GL-19	—	—	—	—	—	—	—	—	—	—	—	100%	—	—	—	—
GL-20	—	50%	—	50%	—	—	—	—	—	—	—	7%	—	—	—	—
GL-21	13%	20%	7%	13%	—	20%	7%	—	13%	—	—	8%	—	—	—	—
GL-22	—	23%	—	8%	23%	—	—	—	38%	—	—	—	—	—	—	—
GL-23	—	—	—	—	—	—	—	—	—	—	—	—	—	—	—	—
GL-24	—	—	—	25%	—	25%	13%	—	13%	—	—	25%	—	—	—	—

M 4.1 强调验证的必要性：所选文章中只有三篇包含该步骤。在这三篇文章中，该步骤在语步四中的占比分别为13%、4%和3%。实例如下：

While the policy was launched in 2003, actions on the ground may have taken time to implement, resulting in lagged outcomes. (GL – 21)

In this section, applicability of the formulated model and the developed solution approach are validated. (GL – 10)

M 4.2a 实验条件和程序：所选文章中有21%的文章包含该步骤。在包含该步骤的文章中，该步骤在语步四中的占比最大值为50%，最小值为1%，平均值为21%，标准差为0.17。实例如下：

Second, we include a proxy for human capital as a higher educated workforce is likely to be more productive (see also Hering and Poncet, 2010b; Breinlich, 2006 and Bosker and Garretsen, forthcoming). (GL – 22)

Our analysis is stratified by gender, the ethnic 'marker' of religion in NI (Catholic and Pro-testant; explained in greater detail in the supplemental data online) and educational attainment (low qualifications -accomplished mandatory secondary education or lower). (GL – 21)

M 4.2b 使用获得的数据验证模型：所选文章中有17%的文章包含该步骤。在包含该步骤的文章中，该步骤在语步四中的占比最大值为62%，最小值为7%，平均值为36%，标准差为0.25。实例如下：

In the baseline scenario, we consider four discrete demand scenarios of 300, 400, 600, and 700 MGY with equal probabilities. (GL – 11)

Using the 5 percent critical values from Ostenvald-Lenum (1992) we observe that in some cases the h-max and h-trace statistics give conflicting results. (GL – 17)

M 4.3a 对比实验与建模结果：所选文章中有29%的文章包含该步骤。在包含该步骤的文章中，该步骤在语步四中的占比最大值为50%，最小值为8%，平均值为21%，标准差为0.13。实例如下：

As the results show, the NFs of the MSDV dominate those of other algorithms. (GL – 10)

This variable is discontinuous at the 10% significance level at the left-wing seat margin threshold. However, when we use conventional instead of robust standard errors (data not shown), the coefficient does not turn out to be significant. (GL – 24)

M 4.3b 评价模型使用的评价指标：所选文章中有17%的文章包含该步骤。在包含该步骤的文章中，该步骤在语步四中的占比最大值为23%，最小值为1%，平均值为12%，标准差为0.08。实例如下：

We observe that export instability, XI, is significant in all the countries, except Morocco, but income terms of trade instability is significant in all the countries. (GL – 17)

We perform a similar analysis while allowing either initial or end years to change. (GL – 15)

M 4. 3c 评价有效性检验结果：所选文章中有29%的文章包含该步骤。在包含该步骤的文章中，该步骤在语步四中的占比最大值为97%，最小值为10%，平均值为49%，标准差为0. 31。实例如下：

As expected, we observe from Figs. 6 and 7 that for each level of variability, the magnitude of reduction in profit increases while the constraint violation probability decreases with as the uncertainty budget increases. (GL – 13)

In the case of sufficient supply, since the model is always able to collect additional supply, the inventory level decreases to zero at the end of the forecast cycle. (GL – 14)

M 4. 3d 强调有效性检验的合理性：所选文章中只有三篇包含该步骤。在这三篇文章中，该步骤在语步四中的占比分别为19%、13%和7%。实例如下：

Thus, interpretations of the difference-in-difference coefficient on household income may be viewed with caution. (GL – 21)

Looking at the above results one must also note that causality runs both ways in a number of countries. That is, external instability influences internal variables such as output, investment, and the ability to import and, in turn, the latter variables also cause the former. (GL – 17)

M 4. 3e 该模型的优点：所选文章中只有两篇包含该步骤。在这两篇文章中，该步骤在语步四中的占比分别为18%和4%。实例如下：

The implication of line 1, the results for the whole sample, is similar to the results reported in the studies cited earlier where small or no association are reported between commodity concentration and instability. (GL – 16)

In summary, the results concerning the impact on export instability and income terms of trade instability on growth and investment seem to be consistent with those found in many of the recent studies cited earlier. (GL – 17)

M 4. 3f 该模型的局限性：所选文章中有17%的文章包含该步骤。在包含该步骤的文章中，该步骤在语步四中的占比最大值为38%，最小值为2%，平均值为17%，标准差为0. 13。实例如下：

However, our results also indicate that significant reverse causality also occurs; that is, changes internal to these economies have causal impacts on external trading relationships. (GL – 17)

In the long-run, the location of workers and production is not given; market access is endogenous (the hallmark of NEG). (GL – 22)

M 4. 3g 模型对比：所选文章中只有一篇包含该步骤。该步骤在语步四中的占比为2%。实例如下：

Fig. 10 demonstrates the different model behavior for the two supply scenarios. (GL – 14)

M 4. 3h 模型比较结果分析：所选文章中只有一篇包含该步骤。在该篇文章中，该步骤在语步四中的占比为19%。实例如下：

> In the first scenario, (a), the model does not import any units from neighboring districts since the available supply is adequate to satisfy the demand. (GL-14)

M 4.4a 稳健性检验：所选文章中有46%的文章包含该步骤。在包含该步骤的文章中，该步骤在语步四中的占比最大值为100%，最小值为4%，平均值为42%，标准差为0.37。实例如下：

> For robustness, we also apply the same method as in Rajan and Zingales (1998) to financial data on US firms from Compustat to estimate external dependence figures for the period 1980 to 1999. (GL-05)

> As a robustness check we use a multi-layer perceptron (MLP), which is treated as a performance benchmark to evaluate whether PLS can approximate the underlying data model adequately. (GL-19)

M 4.4b 灵敏度分析：所选文章中只有一篇包含该步骤。该步骤也是该篇文章语步四中唯一一个步骤。实例如下：

> Fig. 6 shows the number of excess hours for the optimal solution of Case I for different numbers of employees E and for different bounds on number of allowed workdays. For each range for the number of allowed workdays, the minimum number of excess hours can be reached for multiple numbers of employees E. (GL-06)

M 4.4c 异质性分析：所选文章中只有一篇包含该步骤。在该篇文章中，该步骤在语步四中的占比为11%。实例如下：

> It is particularly telling that these results are broadly similar for countries with high, medium and low total export growth, and across different regions and levels of development, as illustrated in Table 5 for top 20 export flows, although there are some important differences too. Africa has higher overall variation in export growth than Europe. (GL-15)

M 4.4d 论证工具变量的有效性：所选文章中只有一篇包含该步骤。该步骤也是该篇文章语步四中唯一一个步骤。实例如下：

> There are two useful characteristics of the organization of this early postal network: First, the roads were laid principally for State purposes; and, second, the post towns along those roads were spaced according to the need to change horses. (GL-01)

M 4.5 基于建立的模型案例研究描述：所选文章中只有三篇包含该步骤。在这三篇文章中，该步骤在语步四中的占比分别为45%、31%和8%。实例如下：

> Founded in 1979, Sari Blood Donation Center (SBDC) is one of the main blood donation centers in Mazandaran province, Iran. Statistics in the year 2014 reveal that approximately 85% of donation attempts were successful (in terms of acceptable age of donors, density of the certain concentrations, etc.), which resulted in collecting more than 135, 000 units of donated blood.

Although the amount of collected blood sufficiently met the total demand, some critical issues still exist. (GL – 10)

In this section, we consider a real case study to demonstrate several aspects of the proposed supply chain modeling approach. We consider the case of Jordan, a country with 13 districts, and the goal is to design a robust blood supply chain that minimizes the effects of disasters for a set of given disruption scenarios. (GL – 14)

综上所述，所分析的文章中有70%的文章包含该语步。在包含该步骤的文章中，涉及篇章数最多的步骤为 M4.4a，共 11 篇，占所有文章的46%，有 5 个步骤只涉及一篇文章，分别是 M4.3g、M4.3h、M4.4b、M4.4c 和 M4.4d。各步骤涉及篇章数平均值为 3.63 篇，占所有文章的15%，标准差为2.8。不同文章中包含的步骤种类最多的有 8 种，最少的只有 1 种，分别占语步四中所有步骤的50%和6%。各篇文章中步骤种类的平均值为 2.41 种，占该语步中所有步骤的15%，标准差为2.46。不同文章中包含的步骤种类存在一定的差异，同一个步骤在不同文章中的占比也存在一定的差异。各步骤在不同文章中占比平均值最高的是 M4.4b 和 M4.4d，均为100%，最低的是 M4.3g，为2%，各步骤平均值为31%，标准差为29.93。

（五）语步占比及轨迹

图5.1.3是所分析各篇文章中四个语步的总体占比，如图所示，所有文章均包含语步二，分别有82%、67%和55%的文章包含了语步一、语步三和语步四。就四个语步占比而言，在88%的文章语步二占比最高，其次是语步三，语步一和语步四占比均较低。

从各步骤在所有语步中占比平均值来看，占比最高的三个步骤依次是 M2.2b、M2.3c 和 M2.2a，分别为 14.05%、11.33% 和 7.66%。占比最低的仅有 0.03%，它们分别是 M1.5、M2.5c、M3.1A、M3.4d 和 M4.3g 这五个步骤。

就各步骤涉及的篇章数而言，涉及篇章数最多的步骤也是占比最高的，即 M2.2b，共有 30 篇文章包含该步骤。包含 M2.3c 和 M2.2a 的文章分别有 14 篇和 22 篇。有 23 篇文章包含 M2.3a，该步骤占比

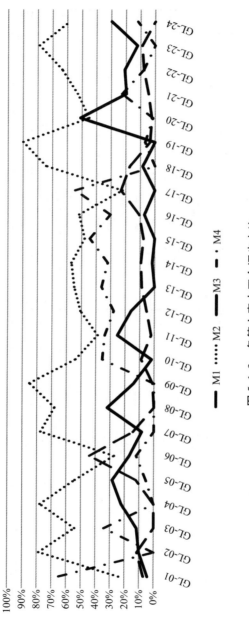

图 5.1.3 各篇文章中四个语步占比

虽然不是前三位，但是位居第四，占比为 7.4%。有 9 个步骤只出现在一篇文章中，分别为 M1.5、M2.5c、M3A、M3.4d、M4.3g、M4.3h、M4.4b、M4.4c 和 M4.4d。这些步骤的占比也较低。总体来说，占比高的步骤涉及的篇章数较多，占比低的步骤涉及的篇章数也较少，但是不存在完全一一对应的关系。

就各篇文章中包含的步骤种类来看，最高的文章中共包含 28 种，占所有步骤的 61%，最低的文章中共包含 4 种，占所有步骤的 9%；平均值为 12 种，标准差为 5.96。

表 5.1.9 是各篇文章中包含的语步种类。如表所示，在所分析的 24 篇文章中共有五种语步组合，包含四个语步的文章共有 11 篇，包含三个语步的文章共有 11 篇，有两篇文章包含两个语步，它们在所有文章中的占比分别为 46%、46% 和 8%。

表 5.1.9　　　　　　　　　　　语步组合

学科	M1234	M123	M124	M234	M23
GL－01	√				
GL－02		√			
GL－03				√	
GL－04					√
GL－05	√				
GL－06	√				
GL－07		√			
GL－08					√
GL－09		√			
GL－10	√				
GL－11	√				
GL－12	√				
GL－13			√		
GL－14	√				
GL－15			√		

学科	M1234	M123	M124	M234	M23
GL－16	√				
GL－17			√		
GL－18		√			
GL－19			√		
GL－20	√				
GL－21	√				
GL－22	√				
GL－23		√			
GL－24				√	

图 5.1.4 至图 5.1.7 为四个语步在不同文章中的分布轨迹。在包含四个语步的文章中，语步二分布最广也最密集，语步一和语步三分布较窄，极少数文章中这两个语步分布也较广；大部分文章中语步四分布也较广，但低于语步二。四个语步基本上从前向后依次分布，文章最前以语步一为主，但有些文章中语步一部分语句也会出现在文章的前部及中间偏前的位置，只有一篇文章中语步一同时出现在了文章的第二句、中间、偏后及最后四个位置，还有一篇文章中语步一有一句出现在了文章偏后的位置。语步二主要分布在语步一后、语步三前，但是有两篇文章中语步二部分语句出现在了文章的最前。语步三以文章中间偏后的位置为主，但是在四篇文章中该语步分布较特殊：一篇文章中该语步出现在了文章较前的位置；一篇文章中同时出现在了文章的最前、中间偏前及后部；一篇文章中同时出现在了文章的前部及中间及最后，该篇文章中语步三占比较高，分布也较广，接近语步二；还有一篇文章中同时分布在了文章的最前、中间偏前及后部，其中以前部为主。语步四主要分布在文章的最后，少数文章中语步四部分语句会出现在文章的中间。在大多数文章中不同语步之间存在不同情况的交叉。主要是语步一和语步二之间；其次是语步二与语步三之间，语步三与语步四之间，极少数文章中四个语步均有交叉。

　　该学科有五篇文章同时包含前三个语步。就语步占比及分布密集程度而言，语步二占比最高，分布也最广、最密集，语步一和语步二在不同文章中存在一定的差异，但是总体来说占比均较低，在大多数文章中分布较集中。就各语步分布轨迹而言，语步一主要集中在文章的前部，有一篇文章中分布在最后，有一篇在中间。语步二主要分布在语步一后，但是有一篇文章最前出现了语步二中部分语句。语步三在大多数文章中主要分散分布在语步二中，以文章的前部和中间为主，只有一篇文章中集中分布在文章的最后、语步二后面；还有一篇文章中集中分布在文章中间偏前的位置、语步二中。就三个语步之间交叉情况而言，各篇文章中语步二与语步三均有交叉，有两篇文章中三个语步均有交叉，其他文章中语步一与另外两个语步均无交叉。

　　该学科中有四篇文章同时包含了语步一、语步二和语步四。除一篇文章外，语步二占比最高，分布也最广，较密集；有一篇文章中语步四占比最高，其他文章中语步四占比低于语步二，但是高于语步一，分布相对比较集中；语步一占比最低，分布也较分散。语步一主要分布在文章的前部和中间靠前的部位。语步二主要分布在文章的前60％—90％范围。语步四在两篇文章中全部集中在文章的最后，在另外两篇文章中主要集中在文章的中间及后部。两篇文章中语步一和语步二有交叉，另外两篇中三个语步之间均有交叉。

　　有两篇文章同时包含语步二、语步三和语步四。其中一篇文章中语步二占比最高，分布也最广，其次是语步四，各语步之间没有交叉，按照语步二、语步四、语步三顺序分布。在另一篇文章中，语步二和语步三占比均较高，分布也较广，出现在文章最前面的是语步三，文章的后部以语步四为主，但是三个语步均有交叉。

　　有两篇文章只包含语步二和语步三。语步二占比均高于语步三。两篇文章中两个语步分布存在一定差异。在其中一篇文章中语步二全部分布在语步三前，两个语步之间没有交叉。在另一篇文章中有少部分语步三分布在文章的最前面，大部分均集中分布在语步二中、文章中间偏后的位置。

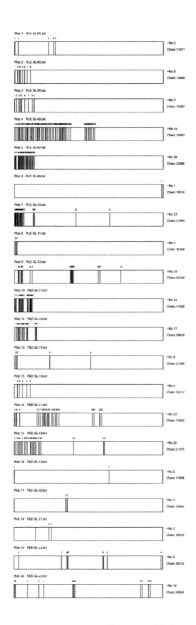

图 5.1.4　语步一分布轨迹

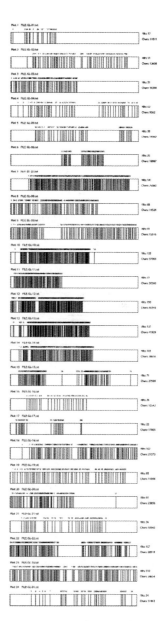

图 5.1.5　语步二分布轨迹

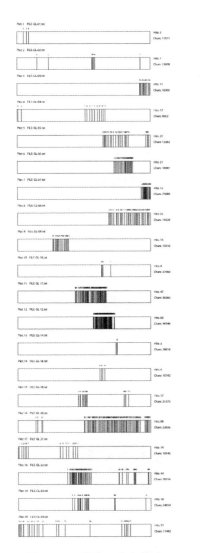

图 5.1.6　语步三分布轨迹

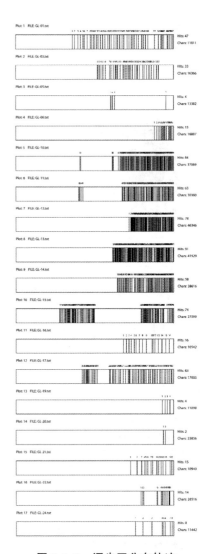

图 5.1.7　语步四分布轨迹

综上所述，同一学科不同文章中语步占比和分布轨迹既有相同之处，同时也存在一定的差异。所有文章均包含语步二，该语步在多数文章中占比最高，分布最广。语步三的整体占比略高于语步一和语步四，语步三和语步四分布相对比较集中。在包含四个语步的文章中，文章最前以语步一为主，最后以语步四为主，中间依次为语步二和语步三。四个语步中,语步二分布较广,与多个语步有交叉,尤其是与语步一和语步三有交叉。个别文章中四个语步均有交叉。在不包含语步一的文章中,文章前部以语步二为主,语步二分布较广,语步四主要分布在文章最后,语步三介于语步二和语步四中间,但是个别文章中语步三也会分布在文章的前部。

三 语言特征分析

本小节主要分析建模实验写作部分的语言特征。主要从句子结构、时态和语态三个大的方面进行分析。针对句子结构的分析主要包含句子类型、四类主要句子长度分布及句子类型与语步之间的关系。针对时态的分析主要包含时态种类、不同时态组合及时态与语步的关系。针对语态的分析主要包含语态种类、不同语态组合及语态与语步的关系。

（一）句子特征

A. 句类

表 5.1.10 是本学科中所包含的句子类型及各类句子占比。如表所示,简单句、复杂句、复合句及复合复杂句占所有句子的94.19%,分别有 4 句为片段和有语法错误的句子,占所有句子的0.26%,其他带有冒号、括号、破折号及 i.e. 的各类特殊句子占所有句子的5.54%。在四类主要句子中,简单句占比明显高于其他三类,其次是复杂句,其他两类句子占比均很低,其中复合句略高于复合复杂句。特殊类型句子形式多样,共 32 种,其中占比较高的依次为 NWS、NWHS 及 BSS。以下例句为特殊类型的句子。

表 5.1.10   句类及占比

句类	句数	占比	句类	句数	占比
S	1560	50.86%	BPS	14	0.46%
P	1047	34.14%	BCS	4	0.13%
C	219	7.14%	BCPS	2	0.07%

句类	句数	占比	句类	句数	占比
CP	63	2.05%	BCPF	2	0.07%
NCS	1	0.03%	BPF	12	0.39%
NPC	1	0.03%	BPP	1	0.03%
NPS	1	0.03%	BSF	6	0.20%
NSP	1	0.03%	BSP	1	0.03%
NSS	4	0.13%	BSS	20	0.65%
NWAS	2	0.07%	IPS	1	0.03%
NWC	2	0.07%	ISBFF	1	0.03%
NWHC	3	0.10%	ISS	2	0.07%
NWHP	4	0.13%	ISWH	1	0.03%
NWHS	28	0.91%	PCS	1	0.03%
NWHWW	1	0.03%	PPC	1	0.03%
NWP	9	0.29%	PSW	1	0.03%
NWS	40	1.30%	NSWHIWH	1	0.03%
NWABPF	1	0.03%	F	4	0.13%
NWBSF	1	0.03%	R	4	0.13%

NCS: There is some variation across subsamples, but the broad message is similar: variation in export growth is driven by all dimensions. (GL – 15)

NPC: The algorithm is terminated when at least one of the following criteria is met: (a) the optimality gap (i. e. , $Y = |UB\text{-}LB| / UB \times 100\%$) falls below a threshold value $Y = 0.01$; or (b) the maximum time limit timemax = 36, 000. 0 (in CPU seconds) is reached; or (c) the maximum number of iteration itermax = 100 is reached. (GL – 12)

NPS: This helps understanding why specializations are so unstable: they may be driven by demand effects coming from many different sources. (GL – 15)

NSP: Our findings confirm those by earlier NEG based wage studies for China: we find strong evidence that market access plays an important role in explaining the observed wage differences between Chinese prefecture cities. (GL – 22)

NSS: Our data set covers a large subset of these Prefecture cities for the period 1999 – 2005: 264 of the 283 cities are included. (GL – 22)

NWAS: In particular, we consider: a dummy that indicates the presence of a Domesday village within 5 km of the parish centroid; distance to 1670 waterways, existing ports and the coast; average slope (in percent); a dummy that indicates access to coal; average agro-climatically attainable yield (in tons per hectare) for the four dominant crops according to the 1801 agricultural census: barley, oats, rye, and wheat; and the agricultural land classification for England and Wales. (GL-01)

NWC: We estimate fixed effects and evaluate the sources of export growth twice: Once for top 20 exports (defined as being in the top 20 category either in 1998 or in 2010, or in both), and for all exports. (GL-15)

NWHC: The J-factor is a strictly increasing transformation and can be written as: Eq. , where $\Phi-1$ is the inverse of the standard normal distribution function and Fs is the distribution function for the extreme value distribution. (GL-20)

NWHP: The most widely used measure of commodity concentration is the Gini-Hirschman coefficient which defines the degree of concentration in a country's exports as: Eq. where X_{jt} is the value of exports of commodity j in year t and Xt is total export receipts in that year. (GL-16)

NWHS: Specifically, we estimate the following basic model in Rajan and Zingales (1998) [model (1)] for our sample of countries: Eq. where $RVAGR\ ij$ is the real growth in value added of sector j in country i, [3] a_i is a country fixed effect for country i, μ_j is an industry fixed effect for industry j, $SHAREij$ is the share of sector j in the total value added of country i, FDi is the development of the financial system of country i, and EDj is the external dependence ratio of sector j, following Rajan and Zingales (1998) as described above. (GL-05)

NWHWW: Therefore, the regression: Eq. where I, C, and G are instability index for total exports, proportional contribution statistic (equation 5), and concentration index (equation 1) is estimated for three sets of samples: (1) the whole sample of 29 countries; (2) a sample of 17 countries for which R > 100; and (3) the remaining 12 countries for which R < 100. (GL-16)

NWP: As Duranton et al. (2014) reported, the motivations for these expeditions were very different: searching for gold, establishing fur trading territories, finding emigration routes to Oregon, or expanding the U. S. territory toward the Pacific Ocean. (GL-03)

NWS: Besides providing information on the means of the inequality indicators and their minimum and maximum values, we also present three types of standard deviations of the natural logarithms of the inequality indexes: cross-state, within-state, and within state-year. (GL-02)

NWABPF: From the figure it is obvious that bio-fuel demand shortage U is much higher in the base case MSW recycling scenario [when recycling of MSW rate is set equal to 34.3% (United States Environmental Protection Agency, 2015)] and it becomes worst during the winter: December to February (t = 8-10) when neither corn-stover nor forest residues are available. (GL-12)

NWBSF: For these reasons, it is difficult to predict the signs of the coefficients of four demographic variables: BLACK and OTHERMIN (the percentages of the population in each block who are black or non-black, non-Hispanic minorities, respectively）；FOREIGN（the percentage of the population in each blockgroup born outside the United States）；and MFI（median family income in each blockgroup）.（GL - 23）

BPS：In addition, initial testing showed that the LP relaxation of this formulation provided very poor upper bounds which, in turn, led to very long branch and bound runtimes（some scenarios were stopped after 10 h）.（GL - 07）

BCS：As a result, we see post towns lined up as string of pearls and a Heblich and Trew Banking and Industrialization 1765 distribution of distances（see Figure 3）between the post towns shows a peak at around 24 km（about 15 miles）.（GL - 01）

BCPS：In order to see the behavior of the objective functions at their extreme points, we first assume that only the first objective function is important to the DM, and the model is thus transformed into a single-objective one（we name this model as（i））.（GL - 10）

BCPF：Most rehabilitation of vacant buildings is probably not gentrification-based, but a positive coefficient is expected for VACANT（the dummy variable indicating whether the building is vacant）because ceteris paribus, unoccupied buildings tend to be in poorer condition, and because it is easier to undertake large-scale rehabilitation projects in the absence of residents.（GL - 23）

BPF：As income growth occurs and commuting costs vary, mode-switching may occur differentially across income groups（e. g. , the rich adopting streetcars while the poor continue to walk to work）.（GL - 23）

BPP：We omit from Table 4 the covariance terms, which account for a negligible amount of overall variation（see Appendix for how small their contribution is）.（GL - 15）

BSF：To address this issue, we include in our regressions a number of direct controls for the geography of the region（e. g. , the share of MSA land that overlays an aquifer, MSA elevation range, an index of terrain ruggedness, heating and cooling degree days）.（GL - 03）

BSP：From the Statistical Yearbook of the Chinese Bureau of Statistics we obtain the Cobb-Douglas share of labor in agriculture production as the share of wages in total agricultural value added, h = 0. 879（the high value indicates that agricultural production is（still）relatively labor intensive in China）.（GL - 22）

BSS：In the Internet Appendix（an Internet Appendix for this article is available online in the "Supplements and Datasets" section at http：//www. afajof. org/supplements. asp）we present the deregulation dates.（GL - 02）

IPS：On the other hand, if R is large（> 100, i. e. , earnings from the major commodity are highly volatile）, commodity concentration leads to instability and diversification of export offers prospect of lower export earnings instability.（GL - 16）

ISBFF：Second, we estimate the model for crisis countries only, that is, for countries that are listed in Caprio and Klingebiel (2002) as having experienced a banking crisis (and for which we have data). (GL – 05)

ISS：The estimated value for r implies a market access (MA) coefficient [$1/\sigma$, see (5)] of about 0. 17：that is, a 1% increase in a city's market access is associated with a wage increase of 0. 17% . (GL – 22)

ISWH：Thus, in an alternative specification of model (1), we use the difference in real growth in value added between the crisis period and the pre-crisis period as a dependent variable, that is, DRVAGRij ¼ ai t mj t b1 SHAREij t b2 FDi EDj t ij, (2) where DRVAGR ij is the difference in real growth in value added of sector j in country i between the crisis period and the pre-crisis period. (GL – 05)

PCS：Wave 1 (2001) is therefore the reference year, and investigating parallel trends is attempted by examining the statistical significance of the interaction between wave 2 and NR status-this should not be significant for the parallel trends assumption to hold. (GL – 21)

PPC：As can be seen from table 2, the results of lines 1 and 3 are quite similar—in both cases the coefficient of G is not significant and C and G account for about 20% of the variation in instability indices. (GL – 16)

PSW：For cross-sector differences, the contribution of a sector's gross value added to the total gross value of a country (VAIND), the energy mix (EM), the share of fossil fuels in total gross energy consumption (FF), the real fixed capital stock to gross value added (CVA), the real fixed capital stock to number of employees (CEMP), and the productivity (PROD) —defined as the gross value added divided by the total hours worked by employees—were used. (GL – 18)

NSWHIWH：In this case, the model is transformed as follows：公式 where n denotes a node on the scenario tree, and $\rho(n)$ is the occurrence probability of node n (i. e. $\sum_{n \in \Lambda} \rho(n) = 1$, where set$\Lambda$ shows a branch of the scenario tree involving node$n$). (GL – 10)

B. 句类与语步

图 5.1.8 是四种句子类型与语步的关系，如图所示，在所有步骤中 M2. 2b 与四种类型句子关系最密切。在简单句和复杂句中占比排在第二和第三的分别为 M2. 3c 和 M2. 3a。复合句中分别为 M3. 4b 和 M2. 3c。复合复杂句中则分别为 M4. 3c 和 M2. 4b。由于复合句和复合复杂句数量较少，与它们相关联的语步数量和类型远低于前两类句子。

这四类句子中均包含了四个语步。就各类句子包含的四个语步中步骤种类而言，简单句、复杂句、复合句、复合复杂句中包含的步骤种类分别占四个语步中所有步骤种类的94%、92%、73%和38%。

　　总体来说，不同句子类型与步骤之间的关系存在异同，句子与步骤关系紧密度与该类句子在所有句子中的占比有关，同时也与该步骤在所有步骤中的占比有关，但是不完全成一一对应的关系，句类与步骤之间没有明显的相关性。

　　以下是四类句子中步骤占比最高的前三个步骤例句。

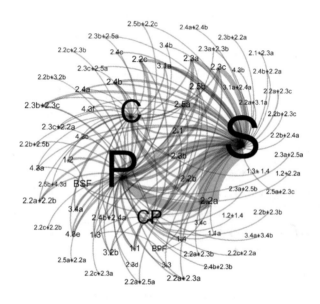

图 5.1.8　句类与步骤关系网络图

【S】

M 2.2b：Each employee is placed in an equity group with others having the same core skills. （GL-09）

M 2.3c：In general, given a fractional optimal solution x to （P_{CRM}）, there may be many follow-on pairs of flight segments. （GL-08）

M 2.3a：We denote by P CRM the LP relaxation of IP CRM. （GL-08）

【P】

M 2.2b：The index parameter *ntours* represents the total number of possible tours for all employees, which is dependent on the skills and availability of the employees for the fortnightly rostering period. （GL-09）

M 2. 3c: Since model instances typically contain several million columns, each technique will involve strategies designed to manage both memory and solution time issues related to such large models. (GL – 09)

M 2. 3a: Note that the integrality of the variables s_l and v_k are implied and hence need not be imposed. (GL – 08)

【C】

M 2. 2b: The index parameter *nstaff* represents the total number of employees to be rostered, and the index parameter *ngroups* represents the number of different equity groups. (GL – 09)

M 3. 4b: However, the number of constraints is low and therefore is of lesser importance compared to the number of variables. (GL – 09)

M 2. 3c: These newly created sets of columns are added to the model and the original source columns are removed. (GL – 09)

【CP】

M 2. 2b: A vector of ones is denoted by 1, and ε is a small positive constant that allows the solution procedure to give first priority to the optimisation of θ_i. (GL – 18)

M 4. 3c: Thus, with increase in manufacturing cost, the expected coverage of returns increases and, since the remanufactured products are not sufficient to meet the demand, the expected coverage of demand decreases. (GL – 13)

M 2. 4b: This observation points to the need to examine fluctuations in the major export on an individual country basis or should cross-country analysis be employed, differences in the stability of the major exports be accounted for. (GL – 16)

C. 句类与句长

表 5.1.11 是四类句子长度占比情况。如表所示，简单句中句子长度占比最高的是单词数介于 11—20 的句子，其次是介于 21—30 的句子。复杂句和复合句占比最高的均为介于 21—30 的句子，其次均为介于 11—20 的句子，单词数介于 31—40 的句子占比略低于介于 11—20 的句子；复合复杂句中占比最高的则是单词数介于 31—40 的句子，其次是介于 21—30 的句子，介于 11—20 的句子占比明显低于介于 41—50 的句子。就四类句子长度覆盖范围而言，复合复杂句最小，其他三类句子相同。四类句子长度最大值均较接近，最小值简单句最低，复合复杂句最高，其中复合句与复杂句较接近。

如果不排除特殊句子类型，将每个公式算为一个单词的话，所有句子中最长的句子为 NWHS，共有 98 个单词，最短的句子为简单句，共有 5 个单词。

综上所述，四种类型句子中，复杂句和复合句长度具有较大的相似性。简单句中短句较其他三类句子占比高，复合复杂句中长句较其他三类句子占比略高。四类句子中简单句和复合复杂句差异最大，但是总体来说，各类句子中句长以介于 11—20、21—30 和 21—40 的为主。

以下是所有句子中最长的 NWHS 例句及四类句子中最长和最短句子的例句。

表 5.1.11　　　　　　　　　　句长分布

句长范围		1—10	11—20	21—30	31—40	41—50	51—60	61—70	MAX	MIX
S	句数	206	847	360	111	24	7	5	69	5
	占比	13.21%	54.29%	23.08%	7.12%	1.54%	0.45%	0.32%		
P	句数	14	291	445	222	54	19	2	63	8
	占比	1.34%	27.79%	42.50%	21.20%	5.16%	1.81%	0.19%		
C	句数	1	57	97	42	17	3	2	62	10
	占比	0.46%	26.03%	44.29%	19.18%	7.76%	1.37%	0.91%		
CP	句数	*	4	21	27	7	2	2	70	16
	占比	*	6.35%	33.33%	42.86%	11.11%	3.17%	3.17%		

NWHS/［**Max：98**］：Specifically, we estimate the following basic model in Rajan and Zingales (1998)［model (1)］for our sample of countries：Eq. , where $RVAGR\ ij$ is the real growth in value added of sector j in country i^3, α_i is a country fixed effect for country i, μ_j is an industry fixed effect for industry j, $SHARE_{ij}$ is the share of sector j in the total value added of country i, FD_i is the development of the financial system of country i, and ED_j is the external dependence ratio of sector j, following Rajan and Zingales (1998) as described above. (JT‑05)

S/［**Max：69**］：To improve the slow convergence of BD, acceleration techniques such as generation of valid inequalities, disaggregation of Benders cuts (Dogan & Goetschalckx, 1999), Pareto-optimal cut generation scheme (Magnanti and Wong, 1981；Papadakos, 2008), covering cut bundle strategy (Saharidis et al. , 2010), local branching (Rei et al. , 2009), generation of maximal non-dominated cuts（Sherali & Lunday, 2013）, and dynamically updated near-maximal Benders cuts（Oliveira et al. , 2014）have been proposed.（GL－13）

S/［**Min：5**］：Each model is an MIP. （GL－07）

P/［**Max：63**］：We can always find an initial primal solution by including all pairings with reduced cost close to zero, and adding columns with slack variables K_l representing cancellation of flight segment l if none of the selected pairings covers flight segment l and v_k representing deadheading the crew k to its crew base when no suitable extension to its disrupted pairing is found.（GL－08）

P/［**Min：8**］：This changes when labor moves freely between regions.（GL－22）

C/［**Max：62**］：In doing so, we first present the results of a number of randomly generated problem instances in different sizes to show the validity of our results as well as demonstrating the performance of the introduced solution algorithm compared to Multi-Objective Imperialist Competitive Algorithm（MOICA）and Non Dominated Sorting Genetic Algorithm（NSGA-II）, and then focus on our case study in the next subsection.（GL－10）

C/［**Min：10**］：The BSPs are scenario-specific and connected by the first-stage variables.（GL－13）

CP/［**Max：70**］：Data on the average wage of workers in the urban part of each prefecture city, and data on the total wage of employees are available, but following Hering and Poncet（2010b）who argue that the available prefectural city wage data do not sufficiently reflect wages in the private sector, we did not use either of these two wage measures as our main dependent variable, opting for gdp per capita instead.（GL－22）

CP/［**Min：16**］：Wheaton［33］empirically tests this assumption and finds that the two income elasticities are very similar.（GL－23）

（二）时态特征

A. 时态种类及组合

表 5.1.12 是该学科论文中使用的时态类型及组合形式。如表所示，除去片段和有语法错误的句子，共出现了 11 种时态，其中 T6、T8、T11 和 T14 没有单独使用。由不同时态构成的组合共有 22 种。在不同时态构成的组合中包含 T1 的组合最多，其次是 T3，分别占所有组合的 62% 和 38%。只包含 T1 一种时态的句子占比最高，其次为由 T3 一种时态组成的句子，占比第三的为 T1 和 T3 两种不同时态构成的句子，其他相同或不同时态组合占比均较低。

以下是按照四种类型句子给出的相同时态和不同时态组合的例句，但不是所有时态组合中均包含四类句子。

表5.1.12　时态类型及组合

时态	T1	T2	T3	T4	T5	T7	T10	T1T2	T1T3	T1T4	T1T6	T1T7	T1T8	T1T10	T1T3T1
句数	2522	38	149	37	1	3	36	41	86	51	1	20	2	54	1
占比	82.26%	1.24%	4.86%	1.21%	0.03%	0.10%	1.17%	1.34%	2.80%	1.66%	0.03%	0.65%	0.07%	1.76%	0.03%
时态	T1T2T3	T1T2T4	T1T3T4	T1T3T10	T1T4T11	T1T11	T2T3	T5T14	T3T5T6	T3T8	T3T10	T4T7	T4T10	T5T6	
句数	1	1	1	3	1	1	3	1	1	2	6	1	1	1	
占比	0.03%	0.03%	0.03%	0.10%	0.03%	0.03%	0.10%	0.03%	0.03%	0.07%	0.20%	0.03%	0.03%	0.03%	

【T1】

S: This theoretical connection from the level of financial services to the change in manufacturing employment motivates our baseline regression model. (GL – 01)

P: The focus of this paper is on whether access to banks affects growth via the structural transformation of the economy. (GL – 01)

C: In the context of our first difference estimation, these fixed effects pick up trends on the level of 570 registration districts; on average, a registration district nests 26 parishes. (GL – 01)

CP: The Gini coefficient equals zero if everyone receives the same income, and equals one if a single individual receives all of the economy's income. (GL – 02)

【T2】

S: The number of function calls-NFC (Črepinšek, Liu, & Mernik, 2012) has been considered as the stopping criterion in the proposed MSDV. (GL – 10)

C: In recent years, VNS has increasingly gained lots of attention and a large number of successful applications have been reported (Hansen & Mladenović, 2001). (GL – 10)

CP: In this network, path 1 has visited 2 nodes prior to reaching the current node, whereas path 2 has visited none, and therefore has had less opportunity to accumulate a large positive partial reduced cost. (GL – 09)

【T3】

S: In some numerical experiments, we were not able to solve the stochastic model directly using commercial solvers. (GL – 11)

P: Post towns were attractive locations for banks because they facilitated communication with London and because the roads were guarded and thus safe to transport gold and money between the financial market in London and local country banks. (GL – 01)

C: The network of post towns spanned a total of 395 post towns toward the end of the 18th century (Robertson 1961) and it was likely selective and established for economic reasons. (GL – 01)

CP: Aircraft was the top export in 1998 but fell to a rank of #143 in 2010, while the related category of aircraft parts fell from #7 to #40. (GL – 15)

【T4】

S: With this in mind, we will now turn to the basic estimation results. (GL – 01)

P: While the LP solution will give a lower bound on the optimal solution, this solution will not in general be integer. (GL – 09)

C: For instance, a 100% increase in recycling rate (68.6%) will increase the production of bio-fuel by 15.28% and thus drop the unit delivery cost of bio-fuel from \$4.19/gallon to \$3.64/

gallon. (GL – 12)

【T5】

S: By the time of Elizabeth I, the post network had developed to connect 85 post towns to London, as depicted in Figure 2. (GL – 01)

【T7】

S: Donation (D) is commonly taking place via bloodmobiles (BMs) or directly at the main (fixed) centers (MCs). (GL – 10)

【T10】

S: This would result in an incorrect measure of initial access to finance. (GL – 01)

【T1T2】

P: All products, which are transported to hospitals and/or transshipped between MCs at period t must be equal to the sum of blood components produced in the previous periods which have not exceeded their shelf lives and transported in the same period. (GL – 10)

C: The existing feedstock annual yields and location data are adopted from the Western Government Association (WGA) report (Parker et al. , 2007) and have been aggregated at county or city centroids in GIS. (GL – 11)

CP: Patent citations identify prior knowledge on which a patent builds, and prior literature (starting with Pakes & Griliches, 1980) has often employed the number of forward-citations received by a patent as an indirect measure of patent value. (GL – 03)

【T1T3】

P: However, the origin of this post town network goes back to the six "Great Roads" of the Elizabethan post network (Robinson, 1948), which was laid for State purposes. (GL – 01)

C: At that time, the U. S. economy was smaller and more agricultural than the one of the 1980s, and this substantially reduces the concern of correlation between railroads in 1898 and technology shocks in the 1980s. (GL – 03)

CP: As discussed in Duranton and Turner (2012) and Duranton et al. (2014), railroads were developed mainly to transport grain, livestock, and lumber, and it is unlikely that such a flow of agricultural commodities was correlated to innovation activity in the 1980s. (GL – 03)

【T1T4】

P: As we will discuss now, this provides an exogenous source of variation. (GL – 01)

C: Ground arcs (1i) are required only to be nonnegative but will be integral in any feasible solution as previously explained. (GL – 07)

CP：If the fluctuations of the major commodity and the minor commodity from their trends are in opposite directions（p < 0; i. e. offsetting fluctuations）, then total export shows relatively smaller fluctuations and the instability index, I, will have a smaller value.（GL－16）

【T1T6】

P：In a second test, we assess more broadly the balance of pre-existing differences that might have affected the location choice of Elizabethan post towns.（GL－01）

【T1T7】

P：We are examining the change in supply chain network performance if there is an improvement in biomass to bio-fuel conversion rate.（GL－12）

【T1T8】

P：As discussed in the previous section, we further believe that the instrument is a relevant predictor for finance access, because country banks were relying on the guarded roads to transport gold and money to and from the financial market in London.（GL－01）

【T1T10】

P：Fig. 8 shows the impact that improvements on conversion rate would have on production level and cost.（GL－12）

C：The actual investment cost would vary by location; however, in this study we use a common fixed cost for a reasonable approximation.（GL－12）

CP：We choose to use PLS over alternative suitable candidates, as it can estimate different sensitivities for each input-output combination and, therefore, allows us to evaluate whether investments in certain innovation inputs would find greater response in Knowledge & Technology outputs or Creative Outputs.（GL－19）

【T1T11】

CP：We address a concern that we could be exaggerating instability; perhaps there is just a lot of measurement error, such as misclassification of products over time.（GL－15）

【T2T3】

P：Although the amount of products sufficed to meet the total demand, significant waiting times of recipients at the hospitals, and ignoring the priority level of recipients have highly decreased the customer satisfaction level.（GL－10）

【T5T14】

P：If there had been more sunshine on election day, a narrow right-wing majority may have swung to a left-wing majority.（GL－24）

【T3T10】

P：Policy-makers hoped that efforts to revitalize intervention areas economically would lead to an improvement in the economic status of residents of assisted areas. (GL – 21)

【T3T8】

P：Respondents were asked how they were managing financially at the time of interview. (GL – 21)

【T4T7】

C：With labor completely immobile between regions, we will see firms moving to places offering better profit prospects, but people are, by definition, not moving around. (GL – 22)

【T4T10】

P：However, if p > 0 (the deviations from their trends of the major and minor exports move in phases rather than offsetting each other), the fluctuations of total export earnings would be large and I, the in stability index, will have a large value. (GL – 16)

【T5T6】

P：If a generalized network code had been available, it would have needed to be much faster than the standard dual or barrier algorithms to have made this formulation attractive. (GL – 07)

【T1T2T3】

P：The latter type of location was selected because studies have shown that the tendency to donate blood is directly correlated to an individual's educational level (Pule et al., 2014). (GL – 14)

【T1T3T14】

P：Since we measure financial employment at 1817, it may be the case that some parishes where we observe finance employment may have just established these services while other parishes established services just after. (GL – 01)

【T1T2T4】

CP：During the last decade, the oscillations in fuel price have dramatically influenced transportation costs and it is quite likely that this uncertainty on fuel price will be sustained (Pishvaee, Jolai, & Razmi, 2009). (GL – 13)

【T1T3T4】

P：These numerical experiments revealed that the selection of γ is crucial, which will affect the solution efficiency and the quality of the final results. (GL – 11)

【T1T3T10】

P：If balance were required at the subfleet level, demand points would appear on each individual network just as the supply points do（Fig. 5）.（GL – 07）

CP: On one hand, due to being an exclusive firm, these spare parts would appeal only to their customers who bought the computers from this company before, so there is not much competition in the target market.（GL – 13）

【T1T4T11】

P: Goods that show a fall in more than one country（such as computers or integrated circuits, all falling in the US, Germany and Japan）or a rise（printing machinery in Germany and Japan）could be reflecting worldwide product trends, a possibility that our analysis below will allow us to address.（GL – 15）

【T3T5T6】

P: Artificial control groups were fashioned to provide an understanding of the counterfactual of what would have occurred in NRAs had NR not been implemented.（GL – 21）

B. 时态与语步

图 5.1.9 是文章中各种时态及组合与语步的关系。如图所示，三种占比较高的时态组合与 M2.2b 联系均最紧密。T1 中占比第二和第三的步骤分别是 M2.3c 和 M2.3a；T3 和 T1T3 中占比第二的步骤分别是 M3.4b 和 M2.5a，占比排在第三的步骤均是 M4.4d。虽然 M2.2b 在这三种时态组合中占比均最高，但由于 T1 占比远高于 T3 和 T1T3，在 T1 中 M2.2b 数量远高于该步骤在其他两种时态组合中的数量。此外，这三种时态组合形式中均包含了四个语步，就它们包含的步骤种类数量而言，T1、T3 和 T1T3 中包含的步骤种类分别占四个语步中所有步骤种类的 96%、50% 和 42%。

总体来说，不同时态形式的句子与步骤的联系存在一定的差异，时态与步骤关系紧密度与该时态在所有句子中的占比有关，同时也与该步骤在所有步骤中的占比有关，但并不是决定性的。

以下是按照四类句子给出的三种时态组合中占比最高的前三个步骤的例句，但是有些步骤中不包含所有类型的句子。

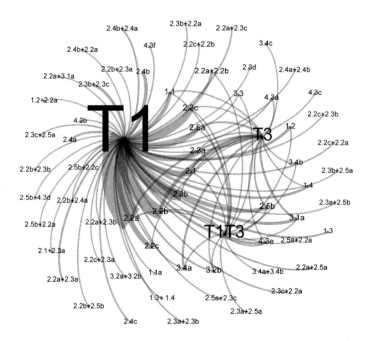

图 5.1.9　时态与步骤关系网络图

【T1】

M 2. 2b

S： We have data for 50 states and the District of Columbia. (GL – 02)

P： Information on the distribution of income comes from the March Supplement of the Current Population Survey (CPS), which is an annual survey of about 60, 000 households across the United States. (GL – 02)

C： We follow Agrawal et al. (2014) in constructing our sample and begin with the set of 268 metropolitan statistical areas (MSAs) defined in 1993 by the U. S. Office of Management and Budget and the set of six one-digit technology classes described in Hall, Jaffe, and Trajtenberg (2001). (GL – 03)

CP： The Gini coefficient equals zero if everyone receives the same income, and equals one if a single individual receives all of the economy's income. (GL – 02)

M 2. 3c

S： Instead, we apply Latin hypercube sampling (LHS) introduced by Olsson, Sandberg, and Dahlblom (2003). (GL – 13)

P： To generate the scenario tree for $|T|$ periods, suppose that in each period the error terms are generated using LHS. (GL – 13)

C: MCS often requires a large sample size to approximate an input distribution, but LHS is designed to accurately approximate the input distribution through sampling in fewer iterations compared with MCS. (GL – 13)

CP: Because our formulation possesses complete recourse, the BSP is feasible for the given values of first-stage variables, and an optimality cut (OC) may be deduced from an optimal solution to the dual of the sub-problem (DSP). (GL – 13)

M 2. 3a

S: The third and fourth terms account for ferry and subfleet imbalance costs. (GL – 07)

P: Eq. (1d), the flight cover constraint, assures that at most one arc associated with a particular flight receives flow. (GL – 07)

C: In fact, Eqs. (17), (19) are valid for those periods smaller than the product shelf life and Eqs. (18), (20) are valid for those periods greater than or equal to products' shelf lives. (GL – 10)

CP: Deadhead flight legs of different equipment types need not be included in the model because no additional crew is required to serve such flights, and the cost of deadheading is already added to the total cost of a pairing. (GL – 08)

【T3】

M 2. 2b

S: "Oils petroleum, bituminous, distillates, except crude" rose from #25 in 1998 to #1 in 2010. (GL – 15)

P: Parts for office machines fell from #5 to #15, while "Medicaments, therapeutic, prophylactic use, in dosage" rose from #26 to #7. (GL – 15)

C: For example, in Tanzania (Fig. 4 – A), the top 3 exports in 1998 were nuts, coffee, and fish; these 3 shifted down to be #6, #7, and #8 in 2010. (GL – 15)

CP: Manganese had the same kind of increase in Ghana as it did in Tanzania, going from $ 17 million to $ 119 million from 1998 to 2010, but Ghana's top destination for this product was Ukraine instead of China. (GL – 15)

M 3. 4b

S: The first wave of the NIHPS achieved a sample of approximately 3500 individuals from 2000 households. (GL – 21)

P: A second control group that contained respondents living in the 25% most deprived SOAs that were not NRA SOAs was distinguished as our analogous control narrow (ACN) group. (GL – 21)

M 4. 4d

S: In the wake of the Hundred Years' War, and given ongoing conflicts both within and outwith the British Isles, there was, in the 16th century, a growing need to improve and control information flows. (GL – 01)

P：The changing of horses took place in post towns that were ordered along these post roads. (GL – 01)

C：The suspicion accorded to privately organized means of correspondence and the growing demand for secure state communication across the realm led Henry VIII to choose Henry Tuke in 1514 to be the first Master of the Posts. (GL – 01)

【T1 T3】

M 2. 2b

P：Consistent with the literature on branch deregulation, we drop Delaware and South Dakota because the structure of their banking systems was heavily affected by laws that made them centers for the credit card industry. (GL – 02)

M2. 5a

P：They found that the results can be biased if undesirable outputs are excluded from the analysis (Watanabe and Tanaka, 2007; Zhou and Ang, 2008; Sueyoshi and Goto, 2011; Mandal and Madheswaran, 2011; Wu et al. , 2012; Riccardi et al. , 2012; Ramli and Munisamy, 2013; He et al. , 2013). (GL – 18)

M 4. 4d

P：Our instrument builds on the insight that out of 150 towns that had a country bank in 1791 (see Figure 2), 130 were a post town (Dawes and Ward-Perkins 2000). (GL – 01)

（三）语态特征

A. 语态种类及组合

表 5. 1. 13 是该学科文章中使用的语态种类及不同语态组合类型。如表所示，该学科文章中两种语态均有出现，同时还包含了这两种语态的组合形式。只包含 V1 的句子数量和占比远高于其他两种类型的句子，只包含 V2 的句子数量和占比略高于包含两种不同语态的句子。所有文章中均有这三种形式语态组合。同一种语态构成的句子中均包括了简单句、复杂句、复合句和复合复杂句这四种类型的句子。两种不同语态构成的句子中包括了除简单句以外的三种类型的句子。

以下是按照四种类型句子给出的三种语态组合中的例句，但是有些语态组合中不包含所有类型的句子。

表 5. 1. 13 语态类型及组合

语态	V1	V1 V2	V2
句数	1950	497	619
占比	63. 60%	16. 21%	20. 19%

【V1】

S： This theoretical connection from the level of financial services to the change in manufacturing employment motivates our baseline regression model. (GL – 01)

C： In the context of our first difference estimation, these fixed effects pick up trends on the level of 570 registration districts; on average, a registration district nests 26 parishes. (GL – 01)

P： The focus of this paper is on whether access to banks affects growth via the structural transformation of the economy. (GL – 01)

CP： Thus, with increase in manufacturing cost, the expected coverage of returns increases and, since the remanufactured products are not sufficient to meet the demand, the expected coverage of demand decreases. (GL – 13)

【V2】

S： First, the Gini coefficient of income distribution is derived from the Lorenz curve. (GL – 02)

C： Decisions about training and changes in the personnel level are based on the expected flight-schedule and the contracts made with the airlines. (GL – 06)

P： The decisions are based on the employees' availability and the current demand, which is determined by the current information about the flight schedule and the approximated number of passengers. (GL – 06)

CP： In the first-stage, strategic decisions such as locations and capacities of facilities as well as distribution base-stock levels are determined as the here-and-now decisions that should be made before realization of any uncertain parameters, and in the second-stage operational decisions such as network flows are made after realization of uncertain parameters. (GL – 13)

【V1 V2】

C： Many of the highways planned in 1947 were ultimately built, and the correlation between log 1983 interstate highway kilometers and log 1947 planned highway kilometers is 0. 62. (GL – 03)

P： We exclude patents that cannot be attributed to an MSA (due to incomplete address information or a location outside an MSA) and patents assigned to universities and hospitals. (GL – 03)

CP： In the case where the value of the upper bound equals the lower bound, then the algorithm terminates as the upper and lower bounds are equal and consequently an optimal solution has been reached. (GL – 14)

B. 语态与语步

图 5.1.10 是该学科文章中两个语态及组合与语步的关系。如图所示，三种语态组合形式中语步占比最高的前三个步骤中均包含 M2.2b 和 M2.3c，但是这两个步骤在 V1 中排名与 V2 和 V1V2 不同。V1 和 V1V2 中均包含了 M2.3a，但是排名也不相同。虽然三种语态组合中占比最高的前三个步骤中均包含了 M2.2b 和 M2.3c，但由于这三种语态在文章中占比不同，这两个步骤在这三种语态组合中的数量和占比也不相同。此外，这三种语态组合形式中均包含了四个语步，就它们包含的步骤种类而言，V1、V2 和 V1V2 各组合中包含的步骤种类分别占四个语步中所有步骤种类的 96%、83% 和 79%。总体来说，语态与步骤关系紧密度与该语态在所有句子中的占比有关，同时也与该步骤在所有步骤中的占比有关。

以下是按照四种类型句子给出的三种语态组合中占比最高的前三个步骤的例句，但是有些步骤中不包含所有类型的句子。

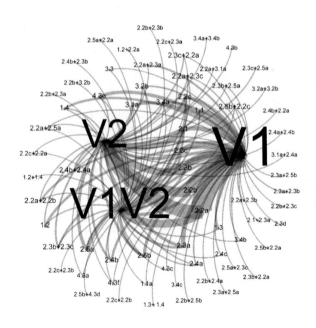

图 5.1.10　语态与步骤关系网络图

【V1】

M 2. 2b

S： We obtain information on U. S. patenting activity and on the affiliation and location of patenting inventors in a region from the U. S. Patent and Trademark Office (USPTO) data. (GL – 03)

P： Although this presents a significant limitation to these data, the innovation literature has shown that technologies with greater impact on social welfare and economic growth are more likely to be patented (Pakes & Griliches, 1980). (GL – 03)

C： For each city, we identify its centroid geographic coordinates from the U. S. Geological Survey and calculate distances between cities using the great circle method as in Singh and Marx (2013). (GL – 03)

CP： Patent citations identify prior knowledge on which a patent builds, and prior literature (starting with Pakes & Griliches, 1980) has often employed the number of forward-citations received by a patent as an indirect measure of patent value. (GL – 03)

M 2. 3a

S： Constraints (2) – (4) ensure capacity restrictions for manufacturing/remanufacturing, distribution and collection centers, respectively. (GL – 13)

P： Constraints (5) guarantee that the capacity of each distribution center is at least equal to its base-stock level. (GL – 13)

C： In the HRSP, we relax these constraints and penalize their violation in the objective function. (GL – 13)

M 2. 3c

S： This approach first uses Column Generation to solve the associated LP, starting with a small subset of columns for each employee. (GL – 09)

P： We now discuss the use of Branch and Price, which in principle achieves an optimal solution. (GL – 09)

C： Node ø is the source node for the network, and node T is the sink node. (GL – 09)

CP： Neither of the two previous methods could guarantee optimal solutions or provide any clear indication of how close solutions were to optimal. (GL – 09)

【V2】

M 2. 3c

S： To solve the proposed multi-period MINLP problem under data uncertainty, a multi-stage stochastic programming (MSSP) approach is applied in this section. (GL – 10)

P： Despite the two-stage stochastic programming (TSSP) approach which is merely adopted in single-period environments, MSSP approach was introduced to deal with the stochastic data in a dynamic (i. e. , multi-period) environment. (GL – 10)

C： The individuals are then ranked and the non-dominated ones are archived by applying the fuzzy dominance sorting（Kundu et al. , 2011）.（GL – 10）

M 2. 2b

S： From the renovation costs recorded in these permits, three dependent variables are defined.（GL – 23）

P： If multiple permits were issued for the same building, the expenditures were summed.（GL – 23）

C： Finally, regions are allowed to differ in their production efficiency, c_i , yet firms within the same region are assumed to be similar.（GL – 22）

M 2. 2a

S： Finally, the output equation in detailed form for model（3）is written as FFF.（GL – 17）

P： In order to calculate the queue waiting time of arrived products in hospitals, Eqs.（3）are presented, in which Athpn and Bthpn are calculated as Eqs.（4）,（5）, respectively（Zahiri, Tavakkoli-Moghaddam, Mohammadi, & Jula, 2014）.（GL – 10）

C： Incentive values are determined through experimentation and can be adjusted to obtain favorable solution characteristics in terms of the number of cancellations, number of delays, and the amount of deviation to the original aircraft routings.（GL – 07）

【V1 V2】

M 2. 3c

P： An advantage of using the ε-constraint method is that the number of efficient solutions can be easily controlled, as opposed to other methods（Mavrotas, 2009）.（GL – 14）

C： It is not feasible in reality to have unlimited supply from neighboring districts and therefore H^s_{mlt} is capped at 10% of the demand in that location.（GL – 14）

CP： In the case where the value of the upper bound equals the lower bound, then the algorithm terminates as the upper and lower bounds are equal and consequently an optimal solution has been reached.（GL – 14）

M 2. 2b

P： We exclude patents that cannot be attributed to an MSA（due to incomplete address information or a location outside an MSA）and patents assigned to universities and hospitals.（GL – 03）

C： The variables x_l select the best tour for each employee and the variables u_{ijk} are used to determine the level of understaffing in the roster.（GL – 09）

CP： Burchfield et al.（2006）show that the spatial structure of a region is strongly shaped by the availability of groundwater, so we exploit the share of each MSA's land that overlays an aquifer.（GL – 03）

M 2. 3a

P: Eq. (27) shows that a hospital or an MC can be assigned to a specified MC in each period, only if there is a route passed by the hospital or MC and originated from that specified MC. (GL – 10)

C: Ground arcs (1i) are required only to be nonnegative but will be integral in any feasible solution as previously explained. (GL – 07)

第二节　电子信息工程

电子信息工程是一门应用计算机等现代化技术进行电子信息控制和信息处理的学科，该领域包含多个二级学科，各学科实验手段有所差异，有的学科以传统实验为主，有的学科以建模仿真实验为主。

本节主要研究电子信息工程领域论文中建模实验方法写作的体裁特征。共从 15 种该领域国际知名期刊上选取 20 篇建模类研究论文，用于分析的句子共有 1510 句，约 34897 个单词。句子数量最多的文章共有 133 句，最少的为 15 句，平均值为 75.7 句，标准差为 31.95。所选取的论文均于 2015 年后发表，有 85% 的论文第一作者通信地址为英语国家或以英语为官方语言的国家。就论文方法部分在文章中篇幅占比情况来说，有一篇文章正文不包含方法部分，该部分出现在补充材料中，占正文的 9%；其他文章中该部分在正文中占比均值为 35%，最大值为 83%，最小值为 8%，标准差为 0.18。占比最小的文章正文篇幅约为 75 页，方法部分篇幅约为 6 页。总体来说，建模实验方法部分在正文中的占比在不同文章中存在一定差异。

一　标题特征分析

该学科建模类论文实验方法的写作有少部分会分成几个平行部分，各部分还会进一步细分，因此通常会包含不止一个一级大标题。所分析的文章中有一篇包含了三个一级大标题，一篇包含了两个一级大标题。图 5.2.1 和图 5.2.2 分别是所分析文章建模实验方法部分大小标题词汇云图。如图所示，大标题中使用最多的是 method，共出现过 6 次，其次是 imitation、learning 和 problem，均出现了 3 次。有三

篇文章不包含二级小标题，其他文章包含二级小标题数量最多的有
10 个，最少的有 2 个。小标题中使用最多的是 learning，共出现过 8
次，其次是 network，共出现过 5 次。其他出现频次较高的词汇还有
model、imitation、embedded、maintenance 和 algorithm。

图 5.2.1　一级大标题词汇云图

图 5.2.2　二级小标题词汇云图

综上所述，该学科建模实验方法的写作均包含一级大标题，少部
分文章包含多个一级大标题。大部分文章还包含二级小标题，不同文
章中的二级小标题数量存在差异。大小标题中会出现一些相同的单
词，但是它们在大小标题中出现的频次和排名存在差异。大标题中有
些词汇与学科和实验手段关系不紧密，小标题中词汇与建模实验所涉
及的问题关系更紧密。

二 语步特征分析

本节主要分析建模实验方法写作的语步特征。分析发现该部分总体语步框架与本研究分析的其他四个学科一致，即均包含四个大的语步，但是该学科四个语步包含的步骤类型与其他学科存在一定的差异，本节各语步列表中只列出所分析的该学科论文中出现的步骤。

（一）语步一特征

表 5.2.1 是语步一中所包含的步骤种类。如表所示，该语步共包括 6 个步骤。表 5.2.2 是各篇文章语步一中各步骤在该语步中的占比情况。如表所示，有 90% 的文章包括了该语步。在包含该步骤的文章中，该语步中各步骤占比情况不一。此外，同一个步骤在不同文章中的占比情况也存在差异。以下是针对每个步骤占比情况的具体分析及实例。

表 5.2.1　　　　　　　　　　语步一各步骤列表

M	语步一、问题陈述		
1.1	描述问题	1.3	问题解决难点
1.1a	章节介绍	1.4	创建新模型目的及必要性
1.2	前人研究的不足	1.5	承接下文

表 5.2.2　　　　　　　　　　语步一各步骤占比

M	1.1	1.1a	1.2	1.3	1.4	1.5
DX-01	—	—	14%	—	29%	57%
DX-02	—	7%	27%	—	27%	40%
DX-03	33%	7%	7%	7%	13%	33%
DX-04	24%	—	12%	6%	53%	6%
DX-05	33%	—	25%	—	33%	8%
DX-06	—	—	—	—	100%	—
DX-07	—	—	—	—	—	—

M	1. 1	1. 1a	1. 2	1. 3	1. 4	1. 5
DX－08	—	—	—	—	—	—
DX－09	—	—	—	—	—	100%
DX－10	—	—	—	—	73%	27%
DX－11	—	—	—	—	100%	—
DX－12	—	25%	—	—	25%	50%
DX－13	—	—	—	—	100%	—
DX－14	51%	—	23%	9%	17%	—
DX－15	88%	—	—	—	12%	—
DX－16	100%	—	—	—	—	—
DX－17	45%	—	43%	11%	2%	—
DX－18	57%	—	38%	—	4%	—
DX－19	70%	—	—	—	30%	—
DX－20	67%	—	—	—	33%	—

M 1.1 描述问题： 所选文章中有50%的文章包含该步骤。在包含该步骤的文章中，该步骤在语步一中的占比最大值为100%，最小值为24%，平均值为57%，标准差为0.24。实例如下：

Due to factors such as distance, occlusion, object's relative pose, and non-uniform sampling, the LiDAR point cloud is sparse and has highly variable point density throughout the space. Therefore, after grouping, a voxelwill contain a variable number of points. An illustration isshown in Figure 2, where Voxel-1 has significantly morepoints than Voxel-2 and Voxel-4, while Voxel-3 contains nopoint. (DX－03)

As discussed earlier, it is common that a point set comes with nonuniform density in different areas. Such non-uniformity introduces a significant challenge for point set feature learning. (DX－04)

M 1.1a 章节介绍： 所选文章中只有三篇包含该步骤。在这三篇文章中，该步骤在语步一中的占比最高为25%，其他两篇均为7%。实例如下：

In this section, we describe our PointFusion model, which performs 3D bounding box regression from a 2D imagecrop and a corresponding 3D point cloud that is typically produced by lidar sensors (see Fig. 1). (DX－02)

In this section we explain the architecture of VoxelNet, the loss function used for training, and an efficient algorithmto implement the network. (DX - 03)

M 1.2 前人研究的不足：所选文章中有40%的文章包含该步骤。在包含该步骤的文章中，该步骤在语步一中的占比最大值为43%，最小值为7%，平均值为23%，标准差为0.12。实例如下：

Existing methods for detecting branching structure usually involve some manual manipulations (Supplementary Section S4). This is highly undesirable, since for structure learning prior information (e. g. the existence of branches and the number of branches) is generally unavailable. (DX - 14)

A major drawback of the global fusion network is that the variance of the regression target $x\_\ i$ is directly dependent on the particular scenario. (DX - 02)

M 1.3 问题解决难点：所选文章中有20%的文章包含该步骤。在包含该步骤的文章中，该步骤在语步一中的占比最大值为11%，最小值为6%，平均值为8%，标准差为0.02。实例如下：

However, survival time is a poor indicator of cancer development, and multiple confounding factors (e. g. treatment regimens, patient compliance and even lifestyles) could significantly impact patient survival. It is difficult, if not impossible, to include unknown confounding factors into a computational model. (DX - 14)

Directly processing all the points not only imposes increased memory/efficiency burdens on the computing platform, but also highly variable point density throughout the space might bias the detection. (DX - 03)

M 1.4 创建新模型目的及必要性：所选文章中有80%的文章包含该步骤。在包含该步骤的文章中，该步骤在语步一中的占比最大值为100%，最小值为2%，平均值为41%，标准差为0.33。实例如下：

In our new dimensionality reduction setting, we aim to learn a set of points and an intrinsic structure, both of which reside in a reduced space. (DX - 17)

Ideally, we want to inspect as closely as possible into a point set to capture finest details in densely sampled regions. (DX - 04)

M 1.5 承接下文：所选文章中有40%的文章包含该步骤。在包含该步骤的文章中，该步骤在语步一中的占比最大值为100%，最小值为6%，平均值为40%，标准差为0.28。实例如下：

Details of the 2D detection network, VoxelNet, and the proposed fusion techniques are described in the following subsections. (DX - 01)

Below, we go into the details of our point cloud and fusion sub-components. (DX - 02)

综上所述，所分析的文章中有90%的文章包含该语步。在包含该步骤的文章中，涉及文章数最多的步骤是 M1.4，最少的是 M1.1a，分别占所有文章的80%和15%。各步骤涉及篇章数平均值为8.2篇，占所有文章的41%，标准差为4.67。各篇文章中包含的步骤种类最多的有6种，最少的只有1种，分别占该语步中所有步骤的100%和17%。各篇文章语步一中各步骤种类的平均值为2.7种，占该语步中所有步骤的45%，标准差为1.53。不同文章中该语步包含的步骤种类存在一定的差异，同一步骤在不同文章中的占比也存在一定的差异，各步骤占比平均值最高的是 M1.1，为57%，最低的是 M1.3，为8%。各步骤在不同文章中占比平均值之间的标准差为18.82。

（二）语步二特征

表5.2.3是语步二中所包含的步骤种类。如表所示，语步二共包括5个大的步骤，其中步骤 M2.2 和 M2.3 分别包含3个小的步骤，步骤 M2.4 和 M2.5 分别包含2个小的步骤。语步二中共有11种不同步骤。表5.2.4是各篇文章语步二中各步骤在该语步中的占比情况。如表所示，所有文章均包括该语步，但是该语步中不同步骤占比情况不一，同一个步骤在不同文章中的占比情况也有所差异。以下是针对每个步骤占比情况的具体分析及实例。

表5.2.3　　　　　　　　　　　语步二各步骤列表

M	语步二、模型研发		
2.1	介绍模型	2.3c	模型算法/优化
2.2	模型及相关元素	2.4	模型预期结果
2.2a	描述公式/理论/方程/模块	2.4a	输出格式描写
2.2b	参数/变量/指标特点及关系	2.4b	运行结果
2.2c	模型假设/限制条件	2.5	与前人研究的关系
2.3	构建模型	2.5a	模型理论基础及原理
2.3a	模型结构	2.5b	相似之处及改进方面
2.3b	实施步骤及最终结构		

表 5.2.4　　　　　　　　　　语步二各步骤占比

M	2.1	2.2a	2.2b	2.2c	2.3a	2.3b	2.3c	2.4a	2.4b	2.5a	2.5b
DX-01	6%	47%	30%	—	3%	—	—	—	—	—	14%
DX-02	8%	18%	26%	—	—	6%	8%	2%	—	14%	18%
DX-03	3%	5%	46%	—	7%	19%	5%	—	7%	2%	7%
DX-04	10%	6%	18%	—	8%	24%	—	—	15%	11%	8%
DX-05	25%	—	12%	—	37%	—	9%	—	7%	—	10%
DX-06	10%	—	7%	—	42%	—	41%	—	—	—	—
DX-07	—	—	—	—	—	32%	43%	—	25%	—	—
DX-08	—	—	35%	—	—	—	50%	—	8%	8%	
DX-09	—	—	11%	—	—	—	87%	—	—	3%	
DX-10	21%	12%	—	—	14%	21%	33%	—	—	—	—
DX-11	4%	—	—	—	32%	—	60%	4%	—	—	—
DX-12	8%	38%	18%	—	16%	8%	—	—	—	4%	8%
DX-13	—	—	7%	3%	5%	3%	16%	5%	8%	10%	42%
DX-14	1%	28%	18%	7%	6%	26%	13%	1%	—	—	—
DX-15	1%	18%	22%	3%	7%	37%	8%	2%	—	1%	1%
DX-16	—	—	25%	7%	2%	51%	15%	—	—	—	—
DX-17	—	45%	15%	13%	3%	19%	6%	—	—	—	—
DX-18	5%	30%	9%	3%	18%	33%	2%	—	—	—	—
DX-19	—	4%	19%	21%	3%	22%	6%	—	—	7%	16%
DX-20	3%	—	13%	21%	5%	11%	18%	—	3%	8%	18%

M 2.1 介绍模型：所选文章中有 65% 的文章包含该步骤。在包含该步骤的文章中，该步骤在语步二中的占比最大值为 25%，最小值为 1%，平均值为 8%，标准差为 0.07。实例如下：

A typical cycle of the change of the "Just-for-Peak" buffer inventory in one production horizon is illustrated in Fig. 3. The "Just-for-Peak" inventory is built during off-peak periods and the demand reduction is implemented during peak periods. (DX-20)

In this paper we propose a multi-task multi-sensor fusion model for the task of 3D object detection. We refer the reader to Figure 2 for an illustration of the model architecture. Our approach has the following highlights. First, we design a ···As a result, the whole model can be learned end-to-end by exploiting a multi-task loss. (DX – 05)

M 2. 2a 描述公式/理论/方程/模块：所选文章中有 55% 的文章包含该步骤。在包含该步骤的文章中，该步骤在语步二中的占比最大值为 47%，最小值为 4%，平均值为 23%，标准差为 0. 15。实例如下：

Finally, by using the constructed principal tree as a backbone, we combined the principal tree and the detected clusters to construct a cancer progression model and extracted disease progression paths. (DX – 14)

VoxelFusion：In contrast to PointFusion that combines features at an earlier stage, VoxelFusion employs a relatively later fusion strategy where the features from the RGB image are appended at the voxel level. (DX – 01)

M 2. 2b 参数/变量/指标特点及关系：所选文章中有 85% 的文章包含该步骤。在包含该步骤的文章中，该步骤在语步二中的占比最大值为 46%，最小值为 7%，平均值为 20%，标准差为 0. 1。实例如下：

In all of our experiments, we set margin = 0. 1, though in practice we found a wide range of values between 0. 01 < margin < 1. 0 that would work. (DX – 08)

Let a_i be the assumed linear accumulation rate for "Just-for-Peak" inventory built up in J_i during the off-peak periods without the impact on system throughput the production horizon. (DX – 20)

M 2. 2c 模型假设/限制条件：所选文章中有 40% 的文章包含该步骤。在包含该步骤的文章中，该步骤在语步二中的占比最大值为 21%，最小值为 3%，平均值为 10%，标准差为 0. 08。实例如下：

Two transition times and their energy costs must be considered in this model; the elapsed time when switching from shut down to processing (i. e. , turning on) and the reverse (i. e. , turning off). (DX – 19)

Note that the deterministic pricing system for the end-use customers is used for calculating the electricity bill cost in this research since in many unregulated markets, customers do not pay based on stochastic real-time price (Wikipedia, 2013). (CD – 20)

M 2. 3a 模型结构：所选文章中有 80% 的文章包含该步骤。在包含该步骤的文章中，该步骤在语步二中的占比最大值为 42%，最小值为 2%，平均值为 13%，标准差为 0. 13。实例如下：

The backbone network follows atwo-stream architecture [13] to process multi-sensor data. Specifically, for the image stream we use the pre-trained Res Net-18 [10] until the fourth convolutional block. (DX – 05)

In this type of architecture, GRU has an update and rest gates. Both gates enable GRU to pass the information forward over many time windows for a better predication or classification.

（DX－12）

M 2.3b 实施步骤及最终结构：所选文章中有70%的文章包含该步骤。在包含该步骤的文章中，该步骤在语步二中的占比最大值为51%，最小值为3%，平均值为22%，标准差为0.13。实例如下：

The results of the 1000 runs were then aggregated into a consensus matrix that gave a visual representation of the frequency of two samples being grouped into the same cluster. （DX－14）

We represent the discriminator, D, using a multi-layer perceptron with parameters 0 that takes as input a state transition and outputs a value between 0 and 1. （DX－07）

M 2.3c 模型算法/优化：所选文章中有85%的文章包含该步骤。在包含该步骤的文章中，该步骤在语步二中的占比最大值为87%，最小值为2%，平均值为25%，标准差为0.23。实例如下：

The tracking image of the marker was obtained using the following algorithm. （DX－11）

We now introduce our task embedding, which can be used independently in other fields, such as image classification, and so we keep this section general. （DX－08）

M 2.4a 输出格式描写：所选文章中有25%的文章包含该步骤。在包含该步骤的文章中，该步骤在语步二中的占比最大值为5%，最小值为1%，平均值为3%，标准差为0.01。实例如下：

As such, we integrated the results of subtyping methods developed in the past decade into one computational framework. （DX－14）

We therefore explored orthogonal means of measuring accuracy of each program's ordering based on the neuron simulation data（Supplementary Note）. （DX－15）

M 2.4b 运行结果：所选文章中有25%的文章包含该步骤。在包含该步骤的文章中，该步骤在语步二中的占比最大值为15%，最小值为3%，平均值为8%，标准差为0.04。实例如下：

After the voxel input buffer is constructed, the stacked VFE only involves point level and voxel level dense operations which can be computed on a GPU in parallel. （DX－03）

As shown in Fig. 3 （a）, a simple but effective way to capture multiscale patterns is to apply grouping layers with different scales followed by according Point Nets to extract features of each scale. Features at different scales are concatenated to form a multi-scalefeature. （DX－04）

M 2.5a 模型理论基础及原理：所选文章中有50%的文章包含该步骤。在包含该步骤的文章中，该步骤在语步二中的占比最大值为25%，最小值为1%，平均值为9%，标准差为0.07。实例如下：

Goldberg （1989）provided the fundamentals for genetic algorithms. Moreover, Sivanandam and Deepa （2007）have discussed the concepts of genetic algorithms in detail including pertinent information for understanding the optimization process and explanations for the various operators involved in genetic algorithms. (DX – 19)

In the case of imitation from observation, however, the demonstrations that the agent receives are limited to the expert's state-only trajectories. (DX – 07)

M 2.5b 相似之处及改进方面：所选文章中有 60% 的文章包含该步骤。在包含该步骤的文章中，该步骤在语步二中的占比最大值为 42%，最小值为 1%，平均值为 12%，标准差为 0.1。实例如下：

GRU can be considered as an LSTM unite but with no output gate. Both GRU and LSTM have a similar architecture and achieve excellent accuracies. (DX – 12)

We have extended the gene types available in the library to consider a subset of integers and to consider the feasibility of using the phenotype duringits generation because both characteristics that were required by our problem are of standard functionality. (DX – 19)

综上所述，所有文章均包含语步二。在该语步中涉及文章数最多的步骤是 M2.2b 和 M2.3c，均为 17 篇，占所有文章的 85%，最少的是 M2.4a 和 M2.4b，均为 5 篇，占所有文章的 25%。各步骤涉及篇章数平均值为 11.6 篇，占所有文章的 58%，标准差为 4.34。各篇文章中包含的步骤种类最多的有 10 种，最少的为 3 种，分别占该语步中所有步骤的 91% 和 27%。各篇文章中包含步骤种类平均值为 6.4 种，占比为 58%，标准差为 2.19。不同文章中该语步包含的步骤种类存在一定的差异，同一步骤在不同文章中的占比也存在一定的差异。各步骤占比均值最高的是 M2.3c，最低的是 M2.4a，分别为 25% 和 3%。各步骤在不同文章中占比平均值之间的标准差为 7.35。

（三）语步三特征

表 5.2.5 是语步三中所包含的步骤种类。如表所示，语步三中共包括 4 个大的步骤，其中步骤 M3.2 又包含 4 个小的步骤，步骤 M3.4 又包含 3 个小的步骤。该语步中共有 9 个不同步骤。表 5.2.6 是不同文章语步三中各步骤在该语步中的占比情况。如表所示，大部分文章不包括该语步。在包含该步骤的文章中，该语步中各步骤占比情况不一；此外，同一个步骤在不同文章中的占比情况也有所差异。以下是针对每个步骤占比情况的具体分析及实例。

表 5.2.5　　　　　　　　　　　　**语步三各步骤列表**

M	语步三、模型验证或应用		
3.1a	实验所需设备/软件	3.2d	模型使用方法的目的
3.1c	模型应用流程概括	3.4	数据收集及取样技术
3.2	模型运行时设置	3.4a	来源
3.2a	模型组件	3.4b	特征
3.2b	工作特征/参数	3.4c	取样技术
3.2c	输入输出的设置		

表 5.2.6　　　　　　　　　　　　**语步三各步骤占比**

M	3.1a	3.1c	3.2a	3.2b	3.2c	3.2d	3.4a	3.4b	3.4c
DX－01	—	—	—	—	—	—	—	—	—
DX－02	—	—	—	—	—	—	—	—	—
DX－03	—	—	—	—	—	—	—	—	—
DX－04	—	—	—	—	—	—	—	—	—
DX－05	—	—	—	—	—	—	—	—	—
DX－06	—	—	—	—	—	—	—	—	—
DX－07	—	—	—	—	—	—	—	—	—
DX－08	—	—	—	—	—	—	—	—	—
DX－09	—	—	—	—	—	100%	—	—	—
DX－10	—	—	—	67%	—	—	—	—	33%
DX－11	—	100%	—	—	—	—	—	—	—
DX－12	4%	—	9%	24%	15%	4%	26%	4%	13%
DX－13	38%	—	—	63%	—	—	—	—	—
DX－14	—	—	—	—	—	—	—	80%	20%
DX－15	—	—	—	—	—	—	—	—	—
DX－16	—	—	—	—	—	—	—	—	—
DX－17	—	—	—	—	—	—	—	—	—
DX－18	—	—	—	—	—	—	—	—	—
DX－19	14%	—	14%	71%	—	—	—	—	—
DX－20	83%	—	8%	8%	—	—	—	—	—

M 3.1a 实验所需设备/软件：所选文章中有20％的文章包含该步骤。在包含该步骤的文章中，该步骤在语步三中的占比最大值为83％，最小值为4％，平均值为35％，标准差为0.3。实例如下：

Commercial software packages are mature and convenient for this kind of problem solving (Bussieck and Pruessner, 2003). (DX – 20)

For capturing the input data to the framework, a set of wearable body sensors are placed on the patients to record the multimodal raw data of their activities' signals. (DX – 12)

M 3.1c 模型应用流程概括：所选文章中只有一篇包含该步骤。在该篇文章中，该步骤在语步三中的占比为100％。实例如下：

We used CNNs to estimate the forceps posture from the tracking image of the marker. (DX – 11)

M 3.2a 模型组件：所选文章中有三篇包含该步骤。在这三篇文章中，该步骤在语步三中的占比分别为14％、9％和8％。实例如下：

The basic settings of the machines in this manufacturing system, including cycle time, mean time between failures (MTBF), mean time to repair (MTTR), and rated power are recorded in Table 1. (DX – 20)

The first component contains the reshaping phase, which processes the signals as channels; every channel represents a class of activity. (DX – 12)

M 3.2b 工作特征/参数：所选文章中有25％的文章包含该步骤。在包含该步骤的文章中，该步骤在语步三中的占比最大值为71％，最小值为8％，平均值为47％，标准差为0.25。实例如下：

We can also consider time-contrastive models trained on 14 single-view video as shown in Fig 3. In this case, the positive frame is randomly selected within a certain range of the anchor. (DX – 10)

Table 2 shows the number of periods of time required to switch between the machine's states (i. e., transition time). (DX – 19)

M 3.2c 输入输出的设置：所选文章中只有一篇包含该步骤。在该篇文章中，该步骤在语步三中的占比为15％。实例如下：

The input of the model is a sequence of raw data coming from multiple sensors and the output is the activity name or activity code. (DX – 12)

M 3.2d 模型使用方法的目的：所选文章中只有一篇包含该步骤。在该篇文章中，该步骤在语步三中的占比为4％。实例如下：

The goal for dropout here is to avoid the overfitting issue by ignoring some random neurons in the training phase (10% in our model). (DX – 12)

M 3.4a 来源：所选文章中有两篇包含该步骤。在这两篇文章中，该步骤在语步三中的占比分别为100%和26%。实例如下：

> To ensure sufficient signal for discrimination between expert and non-expert, we collect third-person demonstrations in the expert domain from both an expert and from a non-expert. (DX – 09)

> The dataset used in our study is a mobile health (MHEALTH) benchmarked dataset [31]. It was collected from ten subjects by using body motion and vital signs recordings of SHIMMER2 wearable sensors. (DX – 12)

M 3.4b 特征： 所选文章中有两篇包含该步骤。在这两篇文章中，该步骤在语步三中的占比分别为80%和4%。实例如下：

> Such dataset collected multimodal body sensing can be utilized for various arrhythmias checking, heart monitoring, or even analyzing the effects of exercise on the ECG. (DX – 12)

> Data sets Molecular profile data from 27 studies was assembled into a database comprised of 8996 breast tumor tissues and 285 normal breast tissues (Supplementary Table S1). (DX – 14)

M 3.4c 取样技术： 所选文章中有三篇包含该步骤。在这三篇文章中，该步骤在语步三中的占比分别为33%、20%和13%。实例如下：

> Multi-view data collection is simple and can be captured with just two operators equipped with smartphones, as shown in Fig 2. (DX – 10)

> The progression modeling analysis was primarily performed on the METABRIC (17) and TCGA RNA-sEq. (12) data sets, which are the two largest single breast cancer data sets collected to date, containing 2133 and 1176 tumor samples, respectively. (DX – 14)

综上所述，所选文章中有40%的文章包括该语步。在包含该步骤的文章中，涉及文章数最多的步骤为M3.2b，共五篇，占所有文章的25%，有3个步骤只涉及一篇文章，分别为 M3.1c、M3.2c 和 M3.2d，占所有文章的5%。各步骤涉及篇章数平均值为2.44篇，占所有文章的12%，标准差为1.42。各篇文章中涉及的步骤种类最高的有8种，最低的只有1种，分别占所有步骤的89%和11%。在包含该步骤的文章中，各篇文章涉及的步骤种类平均值为2.75种，占该语步中所有步骤的31%，标准差为2.25。不同文章中包含的步骤种类存在一定的差异，同一步骤在不同文章中的占比也存在一定的差异。各步骤占比平均值最高的是 M3.1c，为100%，最低的是 M3.2d，为4%。各步骤在不同文章中占比平均值之间的标准差为30.2。

（四）语步四特征

表 5.2.7 是语步四所包含的步骤种类。如表所示，语步四共包含 4 个大的步骤，其中步骤 M4.2 又包含 2 个小的步骤，步骤 M4.3 又含 4 个小的步骤。该语步中共有 8 种不同步骤。表 5.2.8 是不同文章各步骤在该语步中的占比情况。如表所示，有一半文章不包括该语步。在包含该步骤的文章中，该语步中各步骤占比情况不一；此外，同一个步骤在不同文章中的占比情况也有所差异。以下是针对每个步骤占比情况的具体分析及实例。

表 5.2.7　　　　　　　　　　语步四各步骤列表

M	语步四、模型有效性验证		
4.1	强调验证的必要性	4.3c	评价有效性检验结果
4.2	实验验证	4.3d	强调有效性查验的合理性
4.2a	实验条件和程序	4.3e	该建模的优点
4.2b	使用获得的数据验证模型	4.4	不同学科要求检验的范式
4.3	有效性验证分析	4.4a	稳健性检验
4.3b	评价模型使用的评价指标		

表 5.2.8　　　　　　　　　　语步四各步骤占比

M	4.1	4.2a	4.2b	4.3b	4.3c	4.3d	4.3e	4.4a
DX - 01	—	—	—	—	—	—	—	—
DX - 02	—	—	—	—	—	—	—	—
DX - 03	—	—	—	—	—	—	—	—
DX - 04	—	—	—	—	—	—	—	—
DX - 05	—	—	—	—	—	—	—	—
DX - 06	—	—	—	—	—	—	—	—
DX - 07	—	—	—	—	—	—	—	—
DX - 08	—	57%	—	—	43%	—	—	—

M	4.1	4.2a	4.2b	4.3b	4.3c	4.3d	4.3e	4.4a
DX – 09	—	—	—	—	—	—	—	—
DX – 10	—	—	—	—	100%	—	—	—
DX – 11	—	—	—	—	—	—	100%	—
DX – 12	—	—	—	—	—	—	—	—
DX – 13	—	—	—	—	—	—	100%	—
DX – 14	—	—	—	—	11%	—	89%	—
DX – 15	—	—	50%	33%	—	—	17%	—
DX – 16	—	—	—	—	—	—	—	—
DX – 17	—	—	—	—	—	—	100%	—
DX – 18	9%	—	—	—	23%	—	50%	18%
DX – 19	—	49%	—	—	—	16%	18%	16%
DX – 20	—	—	33%	27%	40%	—	—	—

M 4.1 强调验证的必要性：所选文章中只有一篇包含该步骤。在该篇文章中，该步骤在语步四中的占比为 9%。实例如下：

In addition to learning the global structure, powering the diffusion operator has the effect of low-pass filtering the data such that the main pathways in it are emphasized and small noise dimensions are diminished, thus achieving the denoising objective of our method as well. (DX – 18)

M 4.2a 实验条件和程序：所选文章中只有两篇包含该步骤。在该篇文章中，在这两篇文章中，该步骤在语步四中的占比分别为 57% 和 49%。实例如下：

In real life, energy prices are more expensive in the morning and afternoon. Thus, this case seeks to test whether the GA solution provides the proper strategy to minimize energy costs, for example, by avoiding processing the jobs in the morning and at other peak times. The production schedule in Fig. 3 shows that different strategies have been adopted. Thus, the machine will remain in shutdown status for the first three periods (i. e. , P1, P2, and P3) because the energy prices during these periods are high. (DX – 19)

Input to the task-embedding network consists of (width, height, 3 x notatipn), where 3 represents the RGB channels. For all of our experiments, we found that we only need to take the first and last frame of an example trajectory notation for computing the task embedding and so discarded intermediate frames, resulting in an input of (width, height, 6). (DX – 08)

M 4.2b 使用获得的数据验证模型：所选文章中只有一篇包含该步骤。在该篇文章中，该步骤在语步四中的占比为33%。实例如下：

The information about the peak and off-peak periods is assumed and illustrated in Table 3. The demand reduction requirement is set to be about 13% of the full load of the production system, as shown in Table 3. It is based on the estimation of the reduction potential of peak power demand due to the effective load management programs by Faruqui et al. (2007). In addition, the electricity rates from the actual bill of our industrial partner are shown in Table 4. (DX – 20)

M 4.3b 评价模型使用的评价指标：所选文章中只有两篇包含该步骤。在这两篇文章中，该步骤在语步四中的占比分别为50%和27%。实例如下：

The average expression values of the genes that were found to bifurcate were used to calculate the lineage score for both the Olsson et al. and Paul et al. data sets (Supplementary Note). (DX – 15)

Fig 5 shows the buffer accumulation curve of buffer 1, buffer 2, and buffer 3 (Note that the accumulation rates of buffer 4, buffer 5 and buffer 6 are so small that they can be ignored). (DX – 20)

M 4.3c 评价有效性检验结果：所选文章中有30%的文章包含该步骤。在包含该步骤的文章中，该步骤在语步四中的占比最大值为100%，最小值为11%，平均值为38%，标准差为0.29。实例如下：

However contrary to time-contrastive and self-regression signals, the human supervision is very noisy and expensive to collect. We use it to benchmark our approach in Sec. IV-C and show that large quantities of cheap supervision can effectively be mixed with small amounts of expensive supervision. (DX – 10)

Additionally, this figure demonstrates that in the case of a full circle (i. e., with no end points or boundary conditions), our potential embedding (PHATE) yields the same representation as diffusion maps. (DX – 18)

M 4.3d 强调有效性查验的合理性：所选文章中只有一篇包含该步骤。在该篇文章中，该步骤在语步四中的占比为16%。实例如下：

Although the model seeks to minimize energy consumption costs for machine production, the computation time for running the solution is also an important issue. Because in real life the model could be running during working hours, the results would be achieved quickly and accurately. Thus, a comparison between the GA and an analytical solution is required to validate the reliability and scalability of both solutions. (DX – 19)

M 4.3e 该建模的优点：所选文章中有35%的文章包含该步骤。在包含该步骤的文章中，该步骤在语步四中的占比最大值为100%，最小值为17%，平均值为68%，标准差为0.36。实例如下：

> On performing the aforementioned processing, the influence of the variation in the distance between the endoscope and the forceps can be reduced, and a similar image can be obtained from the forceps posture. (DX – 11)

> Unlike SimplePPT, this method learns the graph by formulating the optimization as a linear programming problem. (DX – 15)

M 4.4a 稳健性检验：所选文章中只有两篇包含该步骤。在这两篇文章中，该步骤在语步四中的占比分别为18%和16%。实例如下：

> Robust：PHATE produces a robust embedding in the sense that the revealed boundaries and the intersections of progressions within the data are insensitive to user configurations of the algorithm. (DX – 18)

> In addition to the economic effect, adopting such strategies has a positive environmental effect. In fact, DSM objectives involve environmental issues such as reducing carbon emissions (Luo et al., 2010). (DX – 19)

综上所述，所分析的文章中有一半文章包含语步四。在包含该步骤的文章中，涉及文章最多的步骤是M4.3e，占所有文章的35%，有三个步骤只涉及一篇文章，分别是M4.1、M4.2b和M4.3d，均占所有文章的5%。各步骤涉及篇章数平均值为2.75篇，占所有文章的14%，标准差为2.38。不同文章中包含的步骤种类最多的有4种，占所有步骤的50%，最少的只有1种，占所有步骤的13%，各篇文章中步骤种类平均数为2.2种，占该语步中所有步骤的28%，标准差为1.22。不同文章中包含的步骤种类存在一定的差异，同一步骤在不同文章中的占比也存在一定的差异，各步骤占比平均值最高的是M4.3e，为68%，最低的是M4.1，为9%。各步骤在不同文章中占比平均值之间的标准差为21.75。

（五）语步占比及轨迹

图5.2.3是所分析各篇文章中四个语步的总体占比。如图所示，所有文章均包含语步二，有90%的文章包含语步一，但是包含语步三和语步四的文章占比较低，分别为40%和50%。就四个语步占比而言，在所有文章中占比最高的均为语步二，有一篇文章只包含语步二。

就各步骤在所有语步中占比平均值来看，占比最高的前三个步骤分别为 M2.3c、M2.2b 和 M2.3b。有三个步骤占比相同，在所有步骤中占比最低，分别为 M3.1c、M3.2d 和 M4.1。

就各步骤涉及的篇章数而言，最多的为 17 篇，占所有文章的 85%，分别是 M2.3c 和 M2.2b，这两个步骤也是占比平均值最高的两个步骤。最少的仅一篇，占所有文章的 5%，共有 6 个步骤，分别是 M3.1c、M3.2c、M3.2d、M4.1、M4.2b 和 M4.3d。

就各篇文章中包含的步骤种类来看，包含步骤最多的有 18 种，占所有步骤的 53%，有一篇；最少的有 3 种，占所有步骤的 9%，也有一篇。各篇文章中包含步骤种类的平均值为 11.05 种，占所有步骤的 33%，标准差为 4.64。

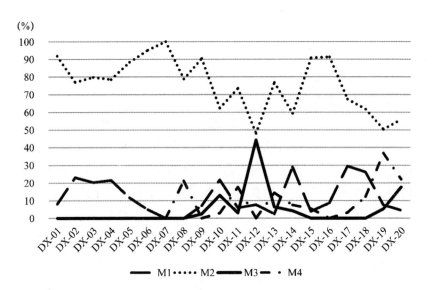

图 5.2.3　各篇文章中四个语步占比

表 5.2.9 是所分析文章中语步组合情况。如表所示，20 篇文章中共出现了六种语步组合，其中 30% 的文章包含了四个语步，25% 的文章包含了三个语步，包含两个语步的文章占比最高，为 40%，其中以语步一和语步二组合为主，只有一篇文章仅包含语步二一个语步。

表5.2.9　　　　　　　　　　语步组合

学科	M1234	M123	M124	M12	M24	M2
DX – 01				√		
DX – 02				√		
DX – 03				√		
DX – 04				√		
DX – 05				√		
DX – 06				√		
DX – 07						√
DX – 08					√	
DX – 09		√				
DX – 10	√					
DX – 11	√					
DX – 12		√				
DX – 13	√					
DX – 14	√					
DX – 15			√			
DX – 16				√		
DX – 17			√			
DX – 18			√			
DX – 19	√					
DX – 20	√					

　　图5.2.4至图5.2.7分别为不同文章中四个语步分布轨迹。如图所示，在包含四个语步的文章中，语步二分布最广也最密集，除一篇文章中语步一分布较广、较分散外，其他三个语步分布均较窄。在大部分文章中语步一主要集中分布在文章的最前及中间偏前的位置，但是有一篇文章语步一中部分语句出现在了文章偏后的位置，还有一篇文章该语步占比较高，分布较广，几乎贯穿了整个方法部分，但是该

篇文章中最前的句子为语步二，最后的句子也是语步二，语步二分布也较广，这两个语步交叉分布在整篇文章中。部分文章中语步二分布在语步一和语步三之间，还有部分文章语步二分布在文章的最前到较后的位置，极少数文章语步二分布在最后。语步三主要集中分布在中间偏后的位置，但是有一篇文章全部分布在最前，还有一篇文章分布在了中间偏前的位置。除了一篇文章，语步四主要集中分布在文章的最后。有两篇文章中四个语步按照语步一、语步二、语步三和语步四的顺序依次分布，语步之间没有交叉，其他各篇文章均存在语步交叉现象。交叉最多的是语步二与语步一，其次是语步二与语步三；有极少数文章中语步一、语步二和语步三之间均有交叉。除一篇文章中语步四与语步一和语步二有交叉外，其他文章中语步四与另外三个语步均没有交叉。

有两篇文章同时包含前三个语步。就语步占比及分布密集程度及分布轨迹而言，语步二占比最高，分布也最广、最密集。两篇文章中语步二分布轨迹存在一定的差异，在一篇文章中语步二几乎覆盖了各部分，其他两个语步均分布在其中。另一篇文章中，语步二主要集中分布在前四分之一到四分之三的位置。语步一占比较低，分布较集中，主要分布在文章的前部。两篇文章中语步三差异较大，其中一篇只包含一个语句，分布在文章较后的位置；另一篇占比仅略低于语步二，集中分布在文章较前和最后两处。就各语步之间交叉情况而言，一篇文章中语步一和语步三主要集中分布在语步二中，即语步二与这两个语步分别有交叉；另一篇文章中三个语步均有交叉。

有三篇文章同时包含了语步一、语步二和语步四。语步二占比最高，分布最广、最集中；在两篇文章中语步二几乎覆盖了文章的前百分之九十，在另一篇文章中覆盖了文章的后百分之七十，但是语步二中同时也包含其他两个语步；三篇文章中语步一占比均高于语步四，但是语步一和语步四分布均较分散。语步一主要分布在文章前部，语步四以后部为主，三个语步之间均有交叉。

有七篇文章同时包含语步一和语步二。各篇文章中语步二占比均

图 5.2.4　语步一分布轨迹

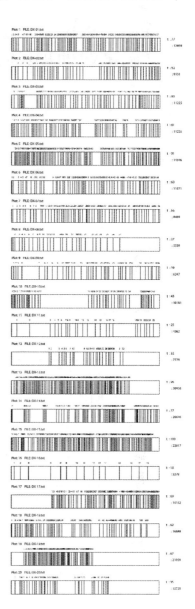

图 5.2.5　语步二分布轨迹

高于语步一，分布也最广、最集中。总体来说，语步一主要分布在文章的前部，语步二中大部分语句分布在语步一后，但是在四篇文章中部分语步二分布在文章最前部，两个语步之间均有交叉。

有一篇文章只包含语步二和语步四。该篇文章中语步二占比较语步四高，分布也较语步四广。两个语步分布均较集中，语步二全部分布在语步四前，两个语步没有交叉。

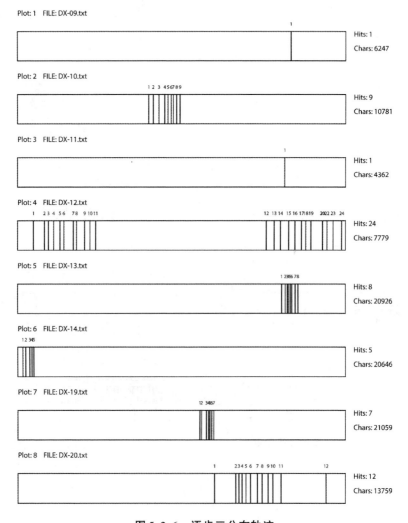

图 5.2.6　语步三分布轨迹

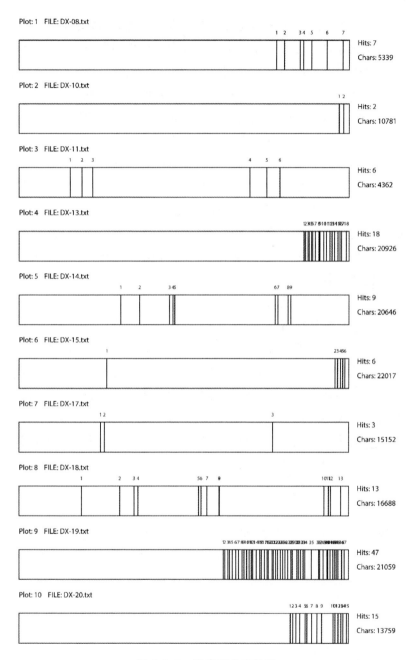

图 5.2.7　语步四分布轨迹

综上所述，同一学科不同文章中语步占比和分布轨迹既有相同之处，同时也存在一定的差异。所有文章中均出现了语步二，该语步在各篇文章中的占比均明显高于其他三个语步。语步一涉及的文章数也较高，略低于语步二；语步三和语步四涉及的文章数均较低。这三个语步在所出现的文章中占比均较低。就四个语步的分布而言，语步二分布最广，几乎覆盖了方法部分的前、中和后三个部位，但是中部较为集中。语步一分布较分散，但是主要集中在前部。语步三以后部居多，通常出现在语步四前。语步四分布较为集中，主要分布在最后。但是在个别文章中语步三也会出现在最前部。此外，四个语步分布均可能出现交叉，尤其是语步一和语步二之间，其次是语步二与语步三之间，语步一与语步三交叉的情况较少，语步四总体来说与其他语步交叉占比情况较少。

三　语言特征分析

本小节主要分析所选学科论文中建模实验写作中使用到的语言特征。主要从句子结构、时态和语态三个大的方面进行分析。针对句子结构的分析主要包含句子类型、四类主要句子长度分布及句子类型与语步之间的关系。针对时态的分析主要包含时态种类、不同时态组合及时态与语步的关系。针对语态的分析主要包含语态种类、不同语态组合及语态与语步的关系。

（一）句子特征

A. 句类

表 5.2.10 是本学科 20 篇文章中所包含的句子类型及各类句子占比。如表所示，简单句、复杂句、复合句及复合复杂句占所有句子的 93.38%，片段和有语法错误的句子占 0.86%，其他带有冒号、括号及 i.e. 的各类特殊句子占所有句子的 5.83%。四类句子中简单句占比远高于其他三类句子，其次是复杂句，其他两类句子占比均较低，其中复合句占比略高于复合复杂句。特殊类型句子形式多样，共有 25 种，其中 NWHS 和 NWS 占比较高，其他的均较低。以下例句为特殊类型的句子：

表 5. 2. 10　　　　　　　　　　句类及占比

句类	句数	占比	句类	句数	占比
S	872	57. 75%	NPF	1	0. 07%
P	407	26. 95%	BCP	1	0. 07%
C	96	6. 36%	BPS	5	0. 33%
CP	35	2. 32%	BSS	3	0. 20%
NCS	1	0. 07%	BPF	3	0. 20%
NSC	1	0. 07%	BPC	1	0. 07%
NSCIW	1	0. 07%	BSP	1	0. 07%
NSS	1	0. 07%	IPF	1	0. 07%
NWAS	6	0. 40%	IPP	2	0. 13%
NWC	1	0. 07%	ISF	2	0. 13%
NWHC	1	0. 07%	ISP	1	0. 07%
NWHP	4	0. 26%	ISS	1	0. 07%
NWHS	31	2. 05%	ISNWHS	1	0. 07%
NWS	13	0. 86%			
NPS	1	0. 07%	F	6	0. 40%
NPP	1	0. 07%	R	9	0. 60%

NSC：It generalizes any 3D shapes with N reference points, and it works well with our spatial anchorscheme：we can predict the spatial offsets instead of the absolute locations of the corners. (DX − 02)

NSC：PointNet has many desirable properties：it processes the raw points directly without lossy operations like voxelization or projection, and it scales linearly with the number of input points. (DX − 02)

NSCIW：We choose the VoxelNet architecture as the base 3D detection network for two main reasons：(ⅰ) it consumes raw point clouds and removes the need for hand − crafted features and (ⅱ) it provides a natural and effective interface for combining image features at different granualities in 3D space, i. e. , points and voxels. (DX − 01)

NSS：Corresponding example trajectories consist of a series of observations and actions：Eq. and we define each task to be a set of such examples, Eq. . (DX − 08)

NWAS：The production planning would thus be accomplished in two stages：first at the facility level, for example, to define the number of jobs to be processed and the second phase at the machine level to define when each job will be processed. (DX − 19)

NWC： Each image contains 76×101 RGB pixels, so the pixel space has a dimensionality of 23, 028, but the intrinsic structure has only one degree of freedom: the angle of rotation. (DX – 17)

NWHC： For notional simplicity, we denoted $fG(z_N)$ as θ_n, and solved the following optimization problem: Eq. where p_{ij} is the probability of assigning sample x_i to projection point θ_j, $\sigma \geq 0$ is a parameter for soft assignment using the negative entropy regularization (38), and $\{w_{ij}\}$ are constrained to be a feasible solution of a minimum spanning tree where the cost of an edge is computed as the squared Euclidean distance between two projection points. (DX – 14)

NWHP： We then calculated the absolute lag-1 autocorrelation r, which is defined as following: Eq. , where φ_i represents the gene expression at time stamp i, and μ is the mean expression across the pseudotime series for that gene. (DX – 15)

NWHS： The lossfunction with the global fusion network is then: where x_ iare the ground-truth box corners, x_i are the predicted corner locations and Lstn is the spatial transformation regularization loss introduced in [23] to enforce theorthogonality of the learned spatial transform matrix. (DX – 02)

NWS： In this section, we describe another approach for using TCNs: direct imitation of human pose. (DX – 10)

NPS： In the following proposition we use the convex conjugate concept which is defined as follows: for a function notation, the convex conjugate notation is defined as notation. (DX – 07)

NPP： Another way to understand the strong training signal that TCNs provide is to recognize the two constraints being simultaneously imposed on the model: along the view axis in Fig. 1 the model learns to explain what is common between images that look different, while along the temporal axis it learns to explain what is different between similar-looking images. (DX – 10)

NPF： From the analysis, it is possible to conclude that the most interesting application of this algorithm is in one of the following cases: 1) When the variances in energy prices during production shifts are high and demand is reduced as much as possible during the highest energy price periods. 2) When the energy consumption of the machine is high during its states and transition. 3) When the non-production times of a machine during a shift are high. (DX – 19)

BCP： Thus, the machine will be switched to shutdown status and begin processing jobs again at period 21 (this indicates that the machine will be in "turning on" transition during periods 19 and 20). (DX – 19)

BPS： We have shown by demonstration in Figure S1 that all of the steps of PHATE, including the potential transform and MDS, are necessary, as diffusion maps, tSNE on diffusion maps, and MDS on diffusion maps fail to provide an adequate visualization in several benchmark test cases with known ground truth (even when using the same customizedα-decaying kernel we developed for PHATE). (DX – 18)

BSS： Similar to ROIAlign [9], we extract bilinear interpolated feature into a n Å ~ n regular gridfor the BEV ROI (in practice we use n = 5). (DX – 09)

BPF: RGE simultaneously learns a principal graph that represents the cell trajectory, as well as a function that maps points on the trajectory (which is embedded in low dimensions) back to the original high-dimensional space. (DX – 15)

BPC: Like SimplePPT, DDRTree learns a latent point for each cell, along with a linear projection function Eq. , where Eq. is a matrix with columns that form an orthogonal basis $\{w_1, \cdots, w_d\}$ (D is the dimension of feature genes, and d is the dimension of latent space). (DX – 15)

BSP: The basic settings of the machines in this manufacturing system, including cycle time, mean time between failures (MTBF), mean time to repair (MTTR), and rated power are recorded in Table 1 (Note that the cycle time, MTBF, and MTTR are the real data from our industrial partner, while the rated power is assumed.). (DX – 20)

IPF: After the discriminator update, we perform trust region policy optimization (TRPO) to improve the policy using a reward function that encourages state transitions that yield small outputs from the discriminator (i. e. , those that appear to be from the demonstrator). (DX – 07)

IPP: The reason is that the mapping from notation to notation is not injective, i. e. , there could be one or multiple notation that corresponds to the same notation. (DX – 07)

ISF: The power reduction during the peak periods has to be greater than or equal to the demand reduction requirement, that is, where Psaving is the power reduction requirement during the peak periods. (DX – 20)

ISP: We cast this problem as one of behavioral cloning, i. e. , given a set of state-action tuples notation, the problem of learning an imitation policy becomes that of finding the parameter notation for which notation best matches this set of provided state-action pairs (Algorithm 1, Line 12). (DX – 06)

ISS: We find this parameter using maximum-likelihood estimation, i. e. , we seek notation as + Eq. . (DX – 06)

ISNWHS: We formulate this problem as one of maximum-likelihood estimation, i. e. , we seek notation as Eq. where notation is the conditional distribution over actions induced by notation given a specific state transition. (DX – 06)

B. 句类与语步

图 5.2.8 是四种类型句子与语步的关系。如图所示，除了复合复杂句外，其他三类句子中占比最高的前三个步骤均为 M2.3c、M2.2b 和 M2.3b，但是这三个步骤在这三类句子中占比排序不完全一致。复合复杂句中占比最高的前三个只给出 M2.3c 这一种，因为该步骤是

唯一一个占比较高的占比步骤，其他各步骤占比均较低，而且差异不大。此外，由于四类句子在文章中占比不同，即使同一步骤在这四类句子中排序一致，数量和占比也不相同。

这四类句子中均包含了四个语步，就各类句子包含的四个语步中步骤种类而言，简单句中包含了四个语步中所有步骤，复杂句、复合句、复合复杂句中包含的步骤种类分别占四个语步中所有步骤种类的72%、59%和44%。

总体来说，不同句子类型与步骤之间的关系存在异同，句子与步骤关系紧密度与该类句子在所有句子中的占比有关，同时也与该步骤在所有步骤中的占比有关，但是不完全成——对应的关系，句类与步骤之间没有明显的相关性。

以下是四类句子中步骤占比最高的前三个步骤例句。由于复合复杂句中步骤较分散，只给出占比较高的一个步骤例句。

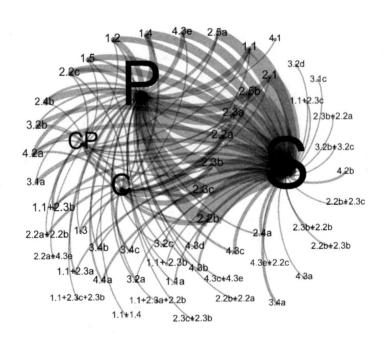

图 5.2.8　句类与步骤关系网络图

【S】

M 2. 3b：The network has three blocks of fully convolutional layers.（DX – 03）

M 2. 2b：We define each voxel of size v_D , v_H , and v_W accordingly.（DX – 03）

M 2. 3c：GPUs are optimized for processing dense tensor structures.（DX – 03）

【P】

M 2. 3c：We devised a method that converts the point cloud into a dense tensorstructure where stacked VFE operations can be processed in parallel across points and voxels.（DX – 03）

M 2. 2b：When the size across the M -dimensions are the same, we use a scalar to represent the size e. g. $\kappa for k = (\kappa, \kappa, \kappa)$.（DX – 03）

M 2. 3b：For each point in the point cloud, we check if the corresponding voxel already exists.（DX – 03）

【C】

M 2. 3c：In contrast, the depth completion task provides dense depth estimation per image pixel, and therefore can be used as "pseudo" LiDAR points to find dense pixel correspondence between multi-sensor feature maps.（DX – 05）

M 2. 3b：This action leads to a new state, and we feed both this state transition and the entire set of expert state transitions to the discriminator.（DX – 07）

M 2. 2b：The linear layer learns a matrixof size $c_{in} \times (c_{out}/2)$, and the point-wise concatenation yields the output of dimension c_{out} .（DX – 03）

【CP】

M 2. 3c：Because we seek an agent-specific inverse dynamics model as described in Section 3, we extract the agent-specific part of the states in notation and store them as notation, and their associated actions, notation（Algorithm 1, Lines 5 – 8）.（DX – 06）

C. 句类与句长

表 5. 2. 11 是四类句子长度占比情况。如表所示，不同类型句子在长度分布上存在一定的差异。简单句中句子长度占比最高的是单词数介于 11—20 的句子，其次是介于 21—30 的句子。复杂句和复合句占比最高的均为介于 21—30 的句子，其次均为介于 31—40 的句子。复合复杂句中占比最高的则是单词数介于 31—40 的句子，其次是介于 21—30 的句子，但是这两类长度的句子占比差异较小。就四类句子覆盖范围而言，简单句最广，其他三类相同。但是这三类句子覆盖范围不同，复杂句和复合句在 11—60 之间，而复合复杂句则在 21—70 之间。

就句子长度最大值和最小值而言，这四类句子长度最大值均很接近；句子长度最小值简单句最低，复合复杂句最高，其他两类居中，差异较小。如果不排除特殊类型句子，将每个公式算为一个单词的话，所有句子中最长的句子为 NWAS，共有 77 个单词，最短的是简单句，共有 5 个单词。

综上所述，四种类型句子长度分布在不同方面相似度不同。就占比而言，复杂句和复合句长度具有较大的相似性，简单句中短句较其他三类句子占比高，复合复杂句中长句较其他三类句子占比略高。就覆盖范围来说，复杂句和复合句相同，其他两类句子均不相同。就句子长度最大值和最小值而言，四类句子最大值差异均不明显，复杂句和复合句最小值较接近，其他两类差异较大。

以下是所有句子中最长的 NWAS 例句及四类句子中最长和最短句子的例句。

表 5.2.11　　　　　　　　　　　句长分布

句长范围		1—10	11—20	21—30	31—40	41—50	51—60	61—70	MAX	MIX
S	句数	128	444	216	71	11	1	1	67	5
	占比	14.68%	50.92%	24.77%	8.14%	1.26%	0.11%	0.11%		
P	句数	*	81	192	101	27	6	*	60	11
	占比	*	19.90%	47.17%	24.82%	6.63%	1.47%	*		
C	句数	*	21	44	25	2	4	*	60	13
	占比	*	21.88%	45.83%	26.04%	2.08%	4.17%	*		
CP	句数	*	*	11	12	7	3	2	61	23
	占比	*	*	31.43%	34.29%	20.00%	8.57%	5.71%		

NWAS/［**Max: 77**］: PHATE preserves and emphasizes the global and local structure of the data: 1. a localized affinity that is chained via diffusion to form global affinities through the intrinsic geometry of the data, 2. denoises the data by low-pass filtering through diffusion, 3. provides a distance that accounts for local and global relationships in the data and has robust boundary conditions for purposes of visualization, and 4. captures the data in low dimensions, using MDS, for visualization.

（DX－18）

S/［**Max：67**］For the pseudotime of cell i from a branching biological process s with branches given by b_x as Eq. , we can calculate its pseudotime recursively by adding the pseudotime of its parent cell on the MST of the projection points（closest cell on the same branch）with the Euclidean distance, Eq. between current cell and the parent on the MST, by setting the root cell as pseudotime 0.（DX – 15）

S/［**Min：5**］Then, we fixed and estimated.（DX – 14）

P/［**Max：60**］To learn a graph that describes the overall structure of the observed data, RGE aims to position the latent points such that their image under the function f_G（i. e. , their corresponding positions in the high-dimensional space）will be close to the input data while also ensuring that neighbor points on the low-dimensional principal graph are 'neighbors' in the input dimension.（DX – 15）

P/［**Min：11**］These ideas motivate our dense fusion network, which is described below.（DX – 02）

C/［**Max：60**］To calculate the accuracy of pseudotime and branch assignment of the simulation（neuron/astrogenesis）and the Paul et al. [10] data set, the reference ordering corresponded to the real simulation, and branch assignments were based on manual assessment（see Supplementary Note）or the pseudotime and branch（or cell type suggested from the original study[18]）from the marker-based ordering（see next section）.（DX – 15）

C/［**Min：13**］However, in most cases local transitions are noisy and global transitions are nonlinear.（DX – 18）

CP/［**Max：61**］Specifically, if a point to which multiple samples were mapped is a leaf vertex, we extended the principal curve by using polynomial curve fitting, and if a point was an inner point of the principal curve, we locally interpolated the curve and re-projected the samples onto an affine line determined by the inner point and its nearest point on the curve.（DX – 14）

CP/［**Min：23**］First, DDRTree does not assume that the graph resides in the input space, and it can reduce its dimensionality while learning the trajectory.（DX – 15）

（二）时态特征

A. 时态种类及组合

表 5.2.12 是该学科论文中使用的时态类型及组合形式。如表所示，除去片段和有语法错误的句子，共出现了 6 种不同时态，其中 T7 没有单独使用，而是与其他时态共同出现在一个句子中。由不同时态构成的组合共有 10 种，其中两种时态组合共 7 种，三种时态组

合的共 3 种。不同时态组合中包含 T1 的最多，其次为 T3 和 T2，分别占所有组合的 80%、50% 和 30%，其他时态在组合中占比均较低。

各种时态组合中，全部由一种时态构成的句子中占比最高的是 T1，其次为 T3。由不同时态构成的句子中占比最高的是由 T1 和 T3 两种不同时态构成的句子，其他相同或不同时态组合占比均较低。

以下是按照四种类型句子给出的相同时态和不同时态组合的例句，但不是所有时态组合中均包含这四类句子。

表 5.2.12 时态类型及组合

时态	T1	T2	T3	T4	T10	T1T2	T1T2T3	T3T10
句数	1254	15	123	10	8	13	1	1
占比	83.54%	1.00%	8.19%	0.67%	0.53%	0.87%	0.07%	0.07%
时态	T1T3	T1T3T7	T1T4	T1T4T7	T1T7	T1T10	T2T3	
句数	35	1	19	1	9	10	1	
占比	2.33%	0.07%	1.27%	0.07%	0.60%	0.67%	0.07%	

【T1】

S： In order to fuse information from RGB and point cloud data, we first extract features from the last convolutional layer of a 2D detection network. (DX – 01)

P： In this particular problem, the sequence of jobs is fixed for this machine because the jobs are established as components of the global production schedule for the factory. (DX – 19)

C： First, the necessary sets, parameters and variables are introduced; then the model itself is presented (constraints and objective function). (DX – 19)

CP： In IRL, both states and actions are available and the goal is to find a cost function that on average has a smaller value for the trajectories generated by the expert policy compared to the ones generated by any other policy. (DX – 07)

【T3】

S： In addition to the dot-product similarity and hinge rank loss, we also tried other distances and losses. (DX – 08)

P： A mutation data analysis was performed on the TCGA mutation data, which cataloged 54013 non-silent mutations in 13870 genes in 958 breast tumor samples. (DX – 14)

C： The bioinformatics pipeline was extensively tested on both simulation and cancer data sets and compared against existing approaches. (DX – 14)

CP： One such distance and loss was the squared Euclidean distance used in, but we found that this did not work as well for our case. (DX – 08)

【T2】

S： In the past two decades, a dozen methods have been developed for principal curve fitting (35, 36). (DX – 14)

【T4】

S： The identical process will be implemented after processing the 3rd job. (DX – 19)

C： The machine will be in "turning off" transition during period 8, will remain in shutdown status for three periods (P9, P10, and P11), and will utilize periods 12 and 13 for "turning on" the machine. (DX – 19)

【T10】

S： For example, it could be included as an extension of a manufacturing resource planning system (MRPII) to minimize the energy consumption costs of a machine by considering the changes in energy prices. (DX – 19)

【T1T3】

P： However, we found that the STN is not able to fully correct these biases. (DX – 02)

CP： We experimented with a number of fusion functions and found that a concatenation of the two vectors, followed by applying a number of fullyconnected layers, results in optimal performance. (DX – 02)

【T1T2】

P： Here, we propose to use an existing 2D detection framework which has shown excellent performance on various tasks [21], [10], [7]. (DX – 01)

【T1T10】

P： If we consider using an RL method to find a state – transition occupancy measure under notation, (5) can be rewritten as Formula (8) which would now output the desired state – transition occupancy measure notation. (DX – 07)

C： However, survival time is a poor indicator of cancer development, and multiple confounding factors (e. g. treatment regimens, patient compliance and even lifestyles) could significantly impact patient survival. (DX – 14)

CP： In contrast to metric learning systems for classification, which would use some sort of nearest neighbour test to find the matching class, here the embedding is relayed to the control network and both networks are trained jointly. (DX – 08)

【T1T4】

P： When the machine is in a processing status, a fixed number of periods will elapse until the machine is actually shut down (i. e. , turned off) . (DX – 19)

C：The "turning on" transition requires two periods (P4 and P5) ; then after processing the first three jobs, the machine will stop processing for six periods (i. e. , P15, P16, P17, P18, P19, P20) . (DX – 19)

CP：If these two conditions are not met, the idle cost will be calculated (i. e. the machine remains idle) ; otherwise, the energy consumption cost to turn the machine off/on will be calculated. (DX – 19)

【T1T7】

P：Here notation is a hyperparameter that determines the trade-off made between the objectives that are competing over DF. (DX – 09)

【T2T3】

CP：Several methods have been proposed to address the issue (20, 21) , but our numerical analysis showed that existing methods did not perform well (Supplementary Section S4) . (DX – 14)

【T1T2T3】

P：We have extended the gene types available in the library to consider a subset of integers and to consider the feasibility of using the phenotype duringits generation because both characteristics that were required by our problem are of standard functionality. (DX – 19)

【T1T3T7】

P：For example, if a pointmass is attempting to move to a target location and starts far away from its goal state, it can be difficult to judge if the policy itself is bad or the initialization was simply unlucky. (DX – 09)

【T3T10】

P：In all of our experiments, we set margin = 0. 1, though in practice we found a wide range of values between 0. 01 < margin < 1. 0 that would work. (DX – 08)

【T1T4T7】

CP：Note we also want to optimize over DF, the feature extractor, but it feeds both into Dr and into Dd, which are competing (hidden under notation) , which we will address now. (DX – 09)

B. 时态与语步

图 5.2.9 是该学科文章中三种占比较高的时态组合与语步的关系。如图所示，在这三种组合中占比最高的前三个步骤中均包含了 M2.3c，但是该步骤在三种时态组合中排序不完全一致。T1 和 T1T3 中均包含了 M2.2a，但是该步骤在 T1 中排在第三位，在 T1T3 中排在第一位。T1

和 T3 中均包含了 M2.2b,但是该步骤在 T1 中排在第一位,在 T3 中排在第二位。虽然三种时态组合中占比最高的前三个步骤中均包含了 M2.3c,但由于 T1 占比远高于 T3 和 T1T3,在 T1 中 M2.3c 数量及占比远高于该步骤在其他两种时态组合中的数量和占比。

此外,这三种时态组合形式中均包含了四个语步,就它们包含的步骤种类数量而言,T1、T3 和 T1T3 中包含的步骤种类分别占四个语步中所有步骤种类的 41%、65% 和 41%。

总体来说,不同时态形式的句子与语步的联系存在一定的差异,时态与步骤关系紧密度与该时态在所有句子中的占比有关,同时也与该步骤在所有步骤中的占比有关,但并不是决定性的。

以下是按照四种类型句子给出的三种时态组合中占比最高的前三个步骤的例句,但是有些步骤中不包含所有类型的句子。

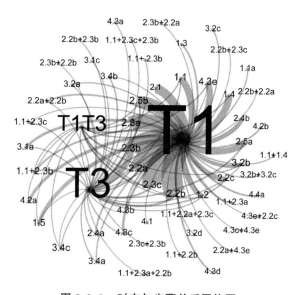

图 5.2.9　时态与步骤关系网络图

【T1】

M 2.2b

S: We use four sets of anchors with sizes {4, 8, 16, 32} and three aspect ratios {0.5, 1, 2} on the conv5 layer. (DX-01)

P: As defined, this supervised scoring function focuses the network on learning to predict the spatial offsets from points that are inside the target bounding box. (DX – 02)

C: Features extracted from conv5 layer of the pre-trained 2D detection network have a dimensionality of 512, and they are reduced to 128D and 64D using two FC layers, each followed by a BN and a ReLU non-linearity. (DX – 01)

CP: Anchors are labeled as positive if the intersection-overunion (IoU) with the ground truth boxes is greater than 0. 7, and the anchors are labeled as negative if the IoU is less than 0. 3. (DX – 01)

M 2. 3c

S: At the end we propose a practical implementation of the algorithm. (DX – 07)

P: We now introduce a proposition which is the foundation of our algorithm. (DX – 07)

C: In the rest of this section, we prove this proposition and then by choosing a specific regularizer, we present our algorithm. (DX – 07)

CP: To prove the proposition, we first define another problem, notation, and argue that it outputs a state-transition occupancy measure which is the same as notation induced by notation. (DX – 07)

M 2. 2a

S: We use the network as described in [43]. (DX – 01)

P: VFE is a feature learning network that aims to encode raw point clouds at the individual voxel level. (DX – 01)

C: All non-empty voxels are encoded in the same way and they share the same set of parameters in FCN. (DX – 01)

CP: Let $\{ x_1 , \cdots , x_N \}$ be a sample data set and $X_n \in R^D$ be the n th sample with D features, and assume that the tree structure to be learned lies in a latent space $Z \subset R^d$ with $d \ll D$. (DX – 14)

【T3】

M 2. 3b

S: The two steps were iterated until convergence. (DX – 14)

P: The results of the 1000 runs were then aggregated into a consensus matrix that gave a visual representation of the frequency of two samples being grouped into the same cluster. (DX – 14)

C: By following the same procedure, the centroids of the clusters were mapped onto the principal curve, and an undirected graph was constructed. (DX – 14)

M 2. 2b

S: In this study, we used the projection of the mean of the normal samples as the root vertex to represent the origin of cancer progression. (DX – 14)

P: After all the samples were projected onto the principal curve, the progression paths were extracted from the curve by finding the shortest path from a designated root vertex to all the leaf vertices of the principal curve. (DX – 14)

CP: One such distance and loss was the squared Euclidean distance used in, but we found that this did not work as well for our case. (DX – 08)

M 2. 3c

S: For the purpose of this study, the K-means method (42) was used. (DX – 14)

【T1T3】

M 2. 2a

P: We used an undirected graph $g = (\nu\varepsilon) = (\nu, \varepsilon)$ to represent the structure, where $\nu = \{v_1, \cdots, v_N\}$ is a set of vertices and E is a set of edges connecting the vertices. (DX – 14)

CP: We experimented with a number of fusion functions and found that a concatenation of the two vectors, followed by applying a number of fully connected layers, results in optimal performance. (DX – 02)

M 2. 3c

P: A blue marker was selected because the red component of the organ is dominant in vivo. (DX – 11)

CP: Specifically, if a point to which multiple samples were mapped is a leaf vertex, we extended the principal curve by using polynomial curve fitting, and if a point was an inner point of the principal curve, we locally interpolated the curve and re-projected the samples onto an affine line determined by the inner point and its nearest point on the curve. (DX – 14)

M 4. 3e

P: We also found that the performance of our principal tree construction method is largely insensitive to a specific choice of the parameters, which makes parameter tuning and hence the implementation of our method easy, even for researchers outside of the machine learning community. (DX – 14)

（三）语态特征

A. 语态种类及组合

表5.2.13是该学科文章中使用的不同语态组合类型，不包含片段和有语法错误的句子。如表所示，该学科文章中两种语态均出现了，同时还包含了这两种语态的组合形式。只包含 V1 的句子数量和占比远高于其他两种类型的句子，只包含 V2 的句子数量和占比略高于包含两种不同语态的句子。所有文章中均包含这三种形式语态组合。同一种语态构成的句子中均包含了简单句、复杂句、复合句和复合复杂句这四种类型的句子。两种不同语态构成的句子中包含了除简

单句以外的三种类型的句子。

以下是按照四种类型句子给出的三种语态组合中的例句，但是有些语态组合中不包含所有类型的句子。

表 5.2.13　　　　　　　　语态类型及组合

语态	V1	V1V2	V2
句数	975	193	333
占比	64.96%	12.86%	22.19%

【V1】

S：A 2D Detection Network Compared to LiDAR point clouds, RGB images capture richer color and texture information. (DX – 01)

P：Specifically, we employ the Faster-RCNN framework [31] which consists of a region proposal network (RPN) and a region classification network (RCN). (DX – 01)

C：It processes the rawpoints directly without lossy operations like voxelization orprojection, and it scales linearly with the number of inputpoints. (DX – 02)

CP：Because we seek an agent-specific inverse dynamics model as described in Section 3, we extract the agent-specific part of the states in notation and store them as notation, and their associated actions, notation (Algorithm 1, Lines 5 – 8). (DX – 06)

【V1V2】

P：Once these actions have been inferred, the agent performs imitation learning via a modified version of behavioral cloning (Figure 1). (DX – 06)

C：Multi-view data collection is simple and can be captured with just two operators equipped with smartphones, as shown in Fig 2. (DX – 10)

CP：We are motivated by the fact that humans have access to a large amount of prior experience about themselves, and so we aim to also provide an autonomous agent with this same prior knowledge. (DX – 06)

【V2】

S：GPUs are optimized for processing dense tensor structures. (DX – 03)

P：Before our method was applied to breast cancer data, it was intensively tested on synthetic data (Supplementary Section S2.5). (DX – 14)

C：Based on the type of fusion described earlier (PointFusion or VoxelFusion), either points or voxels are projected onto the image and the corresponding features are concatenated with point features or voxel features respectively. (DX – 01)

  CP：Moreover, edge weights $\{bi, j\}$ are not computed from data before learning; instead, they are learned from data by using distances between data points in the intrinsic space, which will be further clarified in Section 3. (DX – 17)

  B. 语态与语步

  图 5.2.10 是该学科文章中三种语态组合与语步的关系。如图所示，三种语态组合形式中语步占比最高的前三个步骤中均包含 M2.2b、M2.3b 和 M2.3c，但是它们在各语态组合中的排名完全不同。由于这三种语态在文章中的占比不同，这三个步骤在这三种语态组合中的数量和占比也不相同。此外，这三种语态组合形式中均包含了四个语步。就它们包含的步骤种类数量而言，V1、V2 和 V1V2 中包含的步骤种类分别占四个语步中所有步骤种类的 97%、91% 和 71%。总体来说，语态与步骤关系紧密度与该语态在所有句子中的占比有关，同时也与该步骤在所有步骤中的占比有一定的关系。

  以下是按照四种类型句子给出的三种语态组合中占比最高的前三个步骤的例句，但是有些步骤中不包含所有类型的句子。

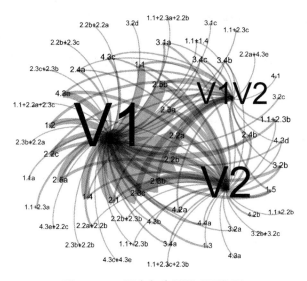

图 5.2.10　语态与步骤关系网络图

【V1】

M 2. 2b

S： These are different ways to implement the reversed graph embedding framework outlined above. (DX – 15)

P： We let b_{ij} denote the weight of edge (ν_i , ν_j) , which represents the connectivity between z_i and z_j . (DX – 15)

C： In addition, there may be noise in certain elements of z_i , and a natural idea is to estimate the edge weights by tolerating these errors. (DX – 15)

CP： The graph $g = (\nu, \varepsilon)$ contains a set of vertexes $\nu = \{\nu_1, \cdots, \nu_N\}$ and a set of weighted, undirected edges ε , where each ν_i corresponds to latent point z_i , so the graph also resides in the latent, low-dimensional space. (DX – 15)

M 2. 3c

S： Overloading notation, we will refer to the classifier as Dr going forward. (DX – 09)

P： For example, if a pointmass is attempting to move to a target location and starts far away from its goal state, it can be difficult to judge if the policy itself is bad or the initialization was simply unlucky. (DX – 09)

C： In third-person learning, observations are more typically available rather than direct state access, so going forward we will work with observations notation instead of states notation as representing the expert traces. (DX – 09)

CP： Note we also want to optimize over D_F , the feature extractor, but it feeds both into D_R and into D_D , which are competing (hidden under σ) , which we will address now. (DX – 09)

M 2. 3b

S： DDRTree returns a principal tree of the centroids of cell clusters in low dimension. (DX – 15)

C： In effect, the algorithm acts as soft K-means clustering on points Z, and it jointly learns a graph on the K-cluster centers. (DX – 15)

P： Second, it also does not require that there be one node in the graph per data point, which greatly accelerates the algorithm and reduces its memory footprint. (DX – 15)

CP： First, DDRTree does not assume that the graph resides in the input space, and it can reduce its dimensionality while learning the trajectory. (DX – 15)

【V2】

M 2. 3c

S： To identify a valid solving procedure, metaheuristics techniques may be considered. (DX – 19)

P： Because the shop floor scheduling problem is considered to be an NP (Non-deterministic

Polynomial time) hard-complete problem (Garey and Johnson, 1979), the formulated problem in Section 3 cannot be solved in real life using analytical algorithms such as integer programming in a useful time frame. (DX – 19)

C: The standard deviation is also learned for each dimension, but it is computed independently of the state transitions. (DX – 06)

M 2. 3b

S: For each point, these are concatenated with the global PointNet feature and the image feature resultingin an $n \times 3136$ input tensor. (DX – 02)

P: This lookup operation is done efficiently in $O(1)$ using a hash table where the voxel coordinate is used as the hash key. (DX – 03)

C: By following the same procedure, the centroids of the clusters were mapped onto the principal curve, and an undirected graph was constructed. (DX – 14)

M 2. 2b

S: The optimal number of clusters was estimated by using gap statistic (43). (DX – 14)

P: After all the samples were projected onto the principal curve, the progression paths were extracted from the curve by finding the shortest path from a designated root vertex to all the leaf vertices of the principal curve. (DX – 14)

【V1V2】

M 2. 3c

P: When the distance between the endoscope and the forceps changes, different tracking images are generated because the size of the projected marker on the image is different, even if the forceps posture remains the same. (DX – 11)

C: The image input of the CNN needs should have the same size; however, due to the uneven size of the trimmed images, they are resized to 500×500 pixels. (DX – 11)

CP: However, as we discussed in the previous section, in imitation from observation, we are primarily concerned with the effect of the policy on the environment so this situation is acceptable. (DX – 07)

M 2. 2b

P: The voxel-wise feature is obtained by transforming the output of VFE- n into $\mathbb{R}^C$ via FCN and applying element-wise Maxpool where C is the dimension of thevoxel-wise feature, as shown in Figure 2. (DX – 03)

C: Features extracted from conv5 layer of the pre-trained 2D detection network have a dimensionality of 512, and they are reduced to 128D and 64D using two FC layers, each followed by a BN and a ReLU non-linearity. (DX – 01)

CP: Anchors are labeled as positive if the intersection-overunion (IoU) with the ground truth boxes is greater than 0.7, and the anchors are labeled as negative if the IoU is less than 0.3. (DX – 01)

M 2.3b

P: The results of the 1000 runs were then aggregated into a consensus matrix that gave a visual representation of the frequency of two samples being grouped into the same cluster. (DX – 14)

C: Furthermore, function g (**W**, **Z**, **B**) is lower – bounded by 0, and then by Monotone Convergence Theorem, there exists $g^* \geq 0$, such that $\{g^*\}$ converges to g^* (DX – 17)

CP: If the voxel is not initialized, we initialize a new voxel, store its coordinate in the voxel coordinate buffer, and insert the point tothis voxel location. (DX – 03)

第三节　交通运输工程

交通运输工程为一级学科。该领域实验方法主要分为现场实验以及建模仿真实验等。其中建模仿真实验方法主要用于初步验证算法与模型，批量生成建模数据以验证模型有效性及优化模型，是道路交通研究中必不可少的一环。

本研究共从24种该领域国际期刊选取了36篇建模实验类论文，共计3382句、81785个单词。所选的文章中有75%的论文为2010年后发表的，有一半以上的论文第一作者通信地址为英语国家或以英语为官方语言的国家。方法部分在正文部分的总体占比平均值为51%，最大值为96%，最小值为15%，标准差为0.24。在占比为96%的文章中正文只包括引言、建模和结尾三个部分。这些文章建模实验方法的部分占比呈现出三种情况，有19篇在50%以上，30%以下的有八篇，介于30%—50%的有九篇。这主要是由于这些文章属于不同研究方向，研究内容和目的有所不同。

一　标题特征分析

该学科建模实验方法的写作一般会分成若干个平行部分，即包含不止一个一级大标题。本研究所选文章中有50%的文章使用了一个以上一级大标题，其中最多的有5个，最少的有2个。图5.3.1

是一级大标题词汇云图。如图所示，大标题中出现次数最多的单词是 model，共出现过 36 次，其次是 development，共出现过 6 次。排在第三位的分别是 mathematical、soil、response、proposed 和 formulation，均出现过 5 次。所选文章中除五篇不包含二级小标题（占所选文章的14%）外，其他文章均包含二级小标题，其中数量最多的有 10 个。图 5.3.2 是二级小标题词汇云图，小标题中出现次数最高的单词和大标题中一样，也是 model 这个单词，一共出现了 38 次，其次是 soil，共出现过 10 次。其他出现较多的还有 grout、algorithm、train 等单词。

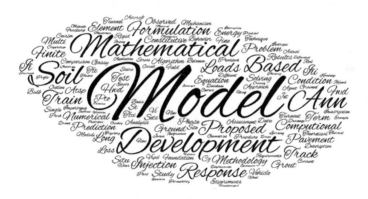

图 5.3.1 一级大标题词汇云图

图 5.3.2 二级小标题词汇云图

综上所述，该学科建模实验方法的写作均包含一级大标题，一半文章中会有多个一级大标题，大部分文章中还包含二级小标题，不同文章数量存在差异。大小标题中会出现一些相同的单词，但是它们在大小标题中使用的频次和排名存在差异。大标题中有些词汇与学科和实验手段关系不紧密，小标题中词汇与建模实验所涉及的问题关系更紧密。

二　语步特征分析

本节主要分析建模实验方法写作的语步特征。分析发现该部分写作的总体语步框架与本研究分析的其他四个学科一致，即均可分成四个大的语步，但是该学科四个语步包含的步骤种类与其他学科存在一定的差异，本节各语步列表中只列出该学科论文中出现的步骤。

（一）语步一特征

表5.3.1是语步一中所包含的步骤种类。如表所示，该语步中共包括了8个步骤。表5.3.2是各篇文章语步一中各步骤在该语步中的占比情况。如表所示，有部分文章中包含语步一，在包含该步骤的文章中，该语步中各步骤占比情况不一。此外，同一个步骤在不同文章中的占比情况也存在差异。以下是针对每个步骤占比情况的具体分析及实例。

表 5.3.1　　　　　　　　　　语步一各步骤列表

M	语步一、问题陈述		
1.1	描述问题	1.2	前人研究的不足
1.1a	章节介绍	1.3	问题解决难点
1.1b	工程概况	1.4	创建新模型目的及必要性
1.1c	研究背景	1.5	承接下文

表5.3.2　　　　　　　　　语步一各步骤占比

M	1.1	1.1a	1.1b	1.1c	1.2	1.3	1.4	1.5
JT－01	50%	—	—	—	—	17%	25%	8%
JT－02	38%	—	—	—	43%	10%	10%	—
JT－03	41%	—	—	22%	—	7%	30%	—
JT－04	100%	—	—	—	—	—	—	—
JT－05	100%	—	—	—	—	—	—	—
JT－06	82%	—	—	—	14%	5%	—	—
JT－07	100%	—	—	—	—	—	—	—
JT－08	18%	—	50%	—	5%	5%	23%	—
JT－09	—	—	—	—	—	—	—	—
JT－10	56%	—	—	18%	3%	—	23%	—
JT－11	97%	—	—	3%	—	—	—	—
JT－12	—	—	—	—	—	—	—	100%
JT－13	40%	60%	—	—	—	—	—	—
JT－14	—	—	—	—	100%	—	—	—
JT－15	—	—	—	—	—	—	—	—
JT－16	—	—	—	—	—	—	—	—
JT－17	67%	33%	—	—	—	—	—	—
JT－18	100%	—	—	—	—	—	—	—
JT－19	—	—	—	—	—	—	100%	—
JT－20	—	—	—	—	—	—	—	—
JT－21	100%	—	—	—	—	—	—	—
JT－22	—	—	—	—	—	—	—	—
JT－23	—	—	—	—	—	—	—	—
JT－24	100%	—	—	—	—	—	—	—
JT－25	—	—	—	—	44%	22%	11%	22%
JT－26	—	—	—	—	100%	—	—	—
JT－27	—	—	—	—	33%	—	67%	—
JT－28	—	—	—	—	—	—	100%	—
JT－29	33%	—	—	—	—	—	33%	33%
JT－30	14%	—	—	—	—	—	86%	—

续表

M	1.1	1.1a	1.1b	1.1c	1.2	1.3	1.4	1.5
JT－31	50%	—	—	—	—	—	50%	—
JT－32	—	—	—	—	—	—	—	—
JT－33	—	—	—	—	—	—	—	—
JT－34	—	—	—	—	—	—	—	—
JT－35	—	—	—	—	—	—	—	—
JT－36	100%	—	—	—	—	—	—	—

M 1.1 描述问题：所选文章中有 53% 的文章包含该步骤。在包含该步骤的文章中，该步骤在语步一中的占比最大值为 100%，最小值为 14%，平均值为 68%，标准差为 0.31。实例如下：

The purpose of compensation grouting usually is to control surface deformations to avoid damage to buildings. Building damage is commonly classified into six categories, from negligible to very severe according to visual assessment [25] or by simple elastic analysis assuming the structure to be a deep beam [26]. These categories of damage can be linked to direct measurements of building movements to allow assessment to take place during tunneling operation. In many cases, however, these calculations are completed before the start of the project to estimate values of vertical displacement at certain points in the structure that would lead to excessive damage. These calculated displacement values may then be treated as settlement limits that should not be exceeded during construction. One example of this approach occurred in the Jubilee Line project where a limit of 25 mm was applied to all rail structures [27]. Alternatively, it may be of greater importance to check levels of differential settlement (i. e. relative movement measured between two points). A common dimensionless measurement of differential settlement is deflection ratio DR Eq. , where $\triangle$ is the maximum vertical deflection measured between two points a distance L apart (see Figure 7). However, it seems that in practice, reported practical procedures in which compensation grouting is used to limit deflection ratio are less common than those to limit discrete values of settlement. (JT－06)

M 1.1a 章节介绍：所选文章中仅有两篇包含该步骤。在这两篇文章中，该步骤在语步一中的占比分别为 60% 和 33%。实例如下：

We first introduce the problem settings and formulate the basic model that addresses perfectly inelastic demand. Then, we analyze the properties (e. g. , existence) of Nash equilibrium solution for two special cases. Moreover, we extend the model by further incorporating demand elasticity. （JT-13）

This section is dedicated to the presentation of our computational experiments and their numerical results. In particular, we have carried out a total of 750 experiments. （JT-17）

M 1. 1b 工程概况：所选文章中仅有一篇包含该步骤。在该篇文章中，该步骤在语步一中的占比为50%。实例如下：

Detailed descriptions of the St James's Park instrumented site and the tunnel excavations beneath are given in Nyren（1998）；a brief summary is given in this section. St Jame's Park is one of the greenfield instrumented sites along the JLE route and is situated between Westminster and Green Park Stations. The alignment of the tunnels and locations of the instruments in plan and elevation views, together with the soil profile interpreted from boreholes near the instrumented section, are shown in Fig. 1. The twin tunnels are referred to as the westbound and the eastbound, with their axes located at approximately 31 m and 20. 5 m below the ground surface respectively. The tunnels were excavated using a 4. 2 m long open-face tunnel boring machine（TBM）with a backhoe excavator that has a 1. 9 m reach when fully extended. They are supported by a 200 mm thick expanded precast concrete lining, which was erected near the end of trailing fingers, with a standard assembly to achieve an external diameter of 4. 85 m（see Fig. 2）. Measurement of ground response was divided into five distinct periods（Nyren, 1998）, as summarised in Table 1.（JT-08）

M 1. 1c 研究背景：所选文章中有三篇包含该步骤。在这三篇文章中，该步骤在语步一中的占比分别为22%、18%和3%。实例如下：

ANNs have for a long time been successfully used in solving pavement engineering problems. ANNs are useful in modeling pavement systems because they have few of the limitations of conventional techniques such as normality, linearity, and variable independence. Moreover, ANNs can capture complex linear and nonlinear relationships between dependent and independent variables in a small fraction of time. （JT-03）

Time windows are the primary mechanism by which the SATS scheduling problem is most efficiently characterised. $\cdots$ These parameters represent the pair earliest^{entry} i, k, latest$^{entry}_{i,k}$, and earliest$^{exit}_{i,k}$, latest$^{exit}_{i,k}$. They are introduced to impose the following: Eq. . （JT-10）

M 1. 2 前人研究的不足：所选文章中有22%的文章包含该步骤。在包含该步骤的文章中，该步骤在语步一中的占比最大值为100%，最小值为3%，平均值为43%，标准差为0. 36。实例如下：

However, these FEM programs may have limitations to develop a factorial design of the J-integral.（JT-02）

The errors arise from the integration of the error of LAGRANGE-interpolation（see Bierbaum, 2001；Richter and Wick, 2012；T\xF6rnig, 1990）.（JT-25）

M 1.3 问题解决难点：所选文章中有 17% 的文章包含该步骤。在包含该步骤的文章中，该步骤在语步一中的占比最大值为 22%，最小值为 5%，平均值为 11%，标准差为 0.07。实例如下：

Although preliminary studies have also been carried out on compensation grouting beneath a surface structure (see Reference [11]) these studies have served principally to demonstrate that, for the case where a building is present, the problem of controlling the grout injection process becomes substantially more difficult than is the case for the greenfield site. (JT – 06)

However, the previous section has revealed that the transversal tensile stress induced damage only contributes to the longitudinal non-wheel path cracking. The longitudinal wheel path cracking and transverse cracking are associated with the shear stress at the tire edge and the longitudinal tensile stress on the asphalt surface, respectively. (JT – 01)

M 1.4 创建新模型目的及必要性：所选文章中有 33% 的文章包含该步骤。在包含该步骤的文章中，该步骤在语步一中的占比最大值为 100%，最小值为 10%，平均值为 46%，标准差为 0.32。实例如下：

The convex signal control model is introduced and embedded in this DTA framework to find the optimal route choices and signal settings that minimize the network total travel time. (JT – 30)

In this study, in order to demonstrate an efficient approach to applying the two-fluid model parameters in the development of stochastic catastrophe models, we will focus on establishing the statistical relationship between the two-fluid model parameters and the total crash rate. (JT – 29)

M 1.5 承接下文：所选文章中有 11% 的文章包含该步骤。在包含该步骤的文章中，该步骤在语步一中的占比最大值为 100%，最小值为 8%，平均值为 41%，标准差为 0.35。实例如下：

In the following section, the developed TDC initiation model will be used to predict the cracking initiation life for the six selected sections from the NCAT Test Track. (JT – 01)

This model has been tested with various scenarios, and computational results are presented and discussed in the next sections. (TJ – 12)

综上所述，大部分的文章都包含语步一。在包含该步骤的文章中，涉及文章数量最多的步骤为 M1.1，有 53% 的文章中包含了该步骤，最少的为 M1.1b，仅涉及一篇文章，在所有文章中占比不到 3%，各步骤涉及的文章数平均值为 6.9 篇，占所有文章的 19%，标准差为 6.06。各篇文章中包含步骤种类最多的有 5 种，占该语步中所有步骤的 63%，最少的为 1 种。各篇文章中步骤种类平均值为 2.1

种，占该语步中所有步骤的 26%，标准差为 1.31。不同文章中包含的步骤种类存在一定的差异，同一步骤在不同文章中的占比也存在一定的差异。各步骤占比平均值最高的是 M1.1，为 68%，最低的是 M1.3，为 11%，各步骤占比平均值为 40%，标准差为 18.88。

（二）语步二特征

表 5.3.3 是语步二中所包含的步骤种类。如表所示，语步二共包括 5 个大的步骤，其中步骤 M2.2 和 M2.3 分别包含 3 个小的步骤，步骤 M2.4 和 M2.5 分别包含 4 个和 2 个小的步骤。语步二中共有 13 种不同步骤。表 5.3.4 是各篇文章语步二中各步骤在该语步中的占比情况。如表所示，所有文章均包括该语步，但是该语步中不同步骤占比情况不一，同一个步骤在不同文章中占比情况也有所差异。以下是针对每个步骤占比情况的具体分析及实例。

表 5.3.3　　　　　　　　　**语步二各步骤列表**

M	语步二、模型研发		
2.1	介绍模型	2.4	模型预期结果
2.2	模型及相关元素	2.4a	输出格式描述
2.2a	描述公式/理论/方程/模块	2.4b	运行结果
2.2b	参数/变量/指标特点及关系	2.4c	结果分析
2.2c	模型假设/限制条件	2.4d	模型使用环境
2.3	构建模型	2.5	与前人研究的关系
2.3a	模型结构	2.5a	模型理论基础及原理
2.3b	实施步骤及最终结构	2.5b	相似之处及改进方面
2.3c	模型算法/优化		

表 5.3.4　　　　　　　　　**语步二各步骤占比**

M	2.1	2.2a	2.2b	2.2c	2.3a	2.3b	2.3c	2.4a	2.4b	2.4c	2.4d	2.5a	2.5b
JT－01	9%	13%	38%	13%	9%	—	—	—	—	—	—	16%	3%
JT－02	—	17%	30%	22%	2%	—	7%	4%	2%	—	—	14%	2%
JT－03	16%	11%	19%	18%	—	—	3%	5%	—	—	—	16%	11%

M	2.1	2.2a	2.2b	2.2c	2.3a	2.3b	2.3c	2.4a	2.4b	2.4c	2.4d	2.5a	2.5b
JT－04	—	13%	31%	35%	—	4%	3%	—	—	—	—	6%	7%
JT－05	—	29%	29%	21%	—	1%	8%	—	—	—	—	13%	
JT－06	—	27%	14%	7%	6%	17%	6%	—	—	—	—	20%	3%
JT－07	—	38%	18%	13%	1%	—	1%	1%	10%	—	—	18%	0%
JT－08	—	20%	19%	15%	—	17%	2%	1%	—	—	—	25%	1%
JT－09	4%	—	56%	14%	12%	2%	—	—	—	—	—	—	11%
JT－10	14%	11%	36%	5%	—	1%	—	—	—	—	—	12%	21%
JT－11	9%	22%	36%	8%	—	11%	—	—	—	—	—	4%	11%
JT－12	35%	—	18%	13%	—	—	—	35%	—	—	—	—	—
JT－13	—	—	48%	36%	—	4%	—	—	—	7%	—	5%	—
JT－14	4%	—	5%	—	6%	25%	13%	4%	36%	—	—	5%	1%
JT－15	23%	—	24%	6%	—	14%	1%	9%	4%	—	—	12%	6%
JT－16	—	27%	13%	—	4%	20%	18%	4%	—	—	—	15%	—
JT－17	11%	16%	3%	15%	—	36%	11%	—	—	—	—	2%	5%
JT－18	14%	3%	17%	14%	—	19%	6%	3%	6%	—	—	11%	8%
JT－19	5%	34%	23%	3%	19%	16%	—	—	—	—	—	—	—
JT－20	27%	13%	7%	—	—	53%	—	—	—	—	—	—	—
JT－21	1%	40%	—	—	1%	57%	—	—	—	—	—	—	—
JT－22	—	15%	3%	—	3%	79%	—	—	—	—	—	—	—
JT－23	—	46%	7%	4%	—	43%	—	—	—	—	—	—	—
JT－24	—	26%	18%	18%	3%	9%	7%	—	5%	—	—	11%	3%
JT－25	—	20%	25%	9%	15%	4%	2%	—	—	—	—	25%	—
JT－26	—	11%	19%	3%	9%	23%	4%	3%	—	—	—	29%	—
JT－27	—	24%	29%	16%	14%	2%	6%	—	—	—	2%	1%	5%
JT－28	—	11%	16%	23%	20%	20%	4%	1%	5%	—	—	—	—
JT－29	—	21%	—	12%	3%	12%	—	12%	—	—	—	41%	—
JT－30	4%	20%	32%	23%	3%	—	5%	—	3%	—	—	3%	8%
JT－31	9%	36%	23%	15%	4%	6%	4%	—	4%	—	—	—	—
JT－32	9%	23%	9%	3%	11%	26%	3%	—	17%	—	—	—	—
JT－33	3%	49%	38%	2%	—	—	—	—	—	—	—	8%	—

M	2.1	2.2a	2.2b	2.2c	2.3a	2.3b	2.3c	2.4a	2.4b	2.4c	2.4d	2.5a	2.5b
JT-34	4%	—	46%	21%	—	—	—	—	4%	—	4%	11%	11%
JT-35	10%	23%	23%	4%	—	2%	—	—	17%	—	—	15%	6%
JT-36	5%	22%	30%	19%	2%	—	2%	—	—	—	—	7%	14%

M 2.1 介绍模型：所选文章中有56%的文章包含该步骤。在包含该步骤的文章中，该步骤在语步二中的占比最大值为35%，最小值为1%，平均值为11%，标准差为0.09。实例如下：

Synchronization in multi-agent reinforcement generates a complex set of presentations achieved from the different agents' actions. A portion of good performing agent groups (i.e. a general form) is shared among the different agents via a specific form (Q_i) [22]. (JT-32)

In Sections 3.4 and 3.5, we propose several removal and insertion heuristics to be used inside the ALNS framework. Before testing the proposed algorithm on the set of instances, we use a subset of instances in order to determine the removal and insertion heuristics that are used inside the ALNS framework. (JT-15)

M 2.2a 描述公式/理论/方程/模块：所选文章中有83%的文章包含该步骤。在包含该步骤的文章中，该步骤在语步二中的占比最大值为49%，最小值为3%，平均值为23%，标准差为0.11。实例如下：

A solution to this energy minimization optimization problem is sought subject to the satisfaction of three constraints: the arrival time at the meeting point, train B's total journey time between stations s_1 and s_f, and the avoidance of interactions between trains or trains and the signaling system. (JT-28)

A schematic representation of Equations (1) and (2) is given in Fig. 1. (JT-19)

M 2.2b 参数/变量/指标特点及关系：所选文章中有94%的文章包含该步骤。在包含该步骤的文章中，该步骤在语步二中的占比最大值为56%，最小值为3%，平均值为23%，标准差为0.13。实例如下：

Table 2 presents assumptions for heavy and various light resource technologies. A capacity of 100 pieces is assumed for the delivery van. (JT-16)

The proportional constant is termed the seepage coefficient, K_T, and is equivalent to $k_{l/tlaw}$, where k_l and t_l are the permeability and thickness of the tunnel lining respectively. Additionally, no flow is allowed across the tunnel boundary when u_w is negative (i.e. water is not supplied from inside the tunnel). (JT-8)

M 2.2c 模型假设/限制条件：所选文章中有86%的文章包含该步骤。在包含该步骤的文章中，该步骤在语步二中的占比最大值为36%，最小值为2%，平均值为14%，标准差为0.09。实例如下：

A dependence of N（s）on s will be maintained for the sake of generality. Although some dependence of K on s is also likely, a constant value has been adopted to ensure that the elastic part of the model is conservative.（JT - 19）

A stiffer surface modulus due to the effects of aging and inverse temperature gradient produces a larger value of k. The modulus gradient parameters n and k were taken into account in the FEM and ANN models, which are discussed in the subsequent section.（JT - 2）

M 2. 3a 模型结构：所选文章中有56%的文章包含该步骤。在包含该步骤的文章中，该步骤在语步二中的占比最大值为20%，最小值为1%，平均值为7%，标准差为0.06。实例如下：

If both points, 1 and 3, belong to the same yield curve in a（p, s）stress plane［Fig. 2（b）］, a relationship between the generic yield stress, p and the saturated value po* can now be obtained by relating the specific volumes at points 1 and 3 through a virtual path which involves an initial unloading, at constant suction, from p_o to po*, and a subsequent reduction in suction, from s to zero, at constant stress（p_o*）. The sample, initially at point 1（p, s）follows the path 1 - 2 - 3［Figs. 2（a）and 2（b）］. The following identity may be established $v_1 + \Delta v_p + \Delta v_s = v_3$（3）where the different quantities are indicated in Fig. 2（a）.（JT - 19）

Additionally, since flap load or driving torque will depend on both pressure and flap pump displacement, the controller may need to implement a separate low-bandwidth pressure control loop as well as a wide-band loop to modulate the effective flap pump displacement.（JT - 27）

M 2. 3b 实施步骤及最终结构：所选文章中有69%的文章包含该步骤。在包含该步骤的文章中，该步骤在语步二中的占比最大值为79%，最小值为1%，平均值为20%，标准差为0.2。实例如下：

A flow chart for the settlement control algorithm is given in Figure 6. Since it is difficult to reduce the pressure to the level so that the Settlement Control Parameter exactly meets the specified Target Level, the user also specifies a tolerance e: Grouting is stopped when the observed SCP satisfies: $TA - \varepsilon \leqslant SCP \leqslant TA + \varepsilon$.（JT - 06）

Dyna Model: The coordination in the dyna method is gained as: each acts perceived by agent produces a reinforcement value（ + or - ）, that is the summation of all together expertise depends on rewards to all agents to action and achieved in the states.（JT - 32）

M 2. 3c 模型算法/优化：所选文章中有64%的文章包含该步骤。在包含该步骤的文章中，该步骤在语步二中的占比最大值为18%，最小值为1%，平均值为6%，标准差为0.04。实例如下：

Dwell time, however, is defined separately from the machine processing time because of additional complexities that arise when a train's length exceeds the current section. This is because additional occupation time is required on the previous section over and above the planned sectional running time. Dwell times are not just incorporated as additional node weights; they are utilised as additional time lag. A graphical demonstration of time lags and additional time lags in a distance versus time line chart is shown in Fig. 1. (JT – 11)

By adopting equation (22) the erosion process can be integrated along with time and treated as a moving front problem. (JT – 05)

M 2.4a 如：输出格式描述：所选文章中有33%的文章包含该步骤。在包含该步骤的文章中，该步骤在语步二中的占比最大值为35%，最小值为1%，平均值为7%，标准差为0.09。实例如下：

Detailed specifications for the heavy and light resource are summarized in Table 1. (JT – 16)

Waiting time variables are calculated in Constraints (9) as follows: Each pair ðei; ejP2L represents two stops at the same station and in the same direction, with ei scheduled before ej. For each pair ðei; ejP2L, variable WTeiej models the waiting time of passengers between scheduled stops ei and ej. (JT – 12)

M 2.4b 运行结果：所选文章中有33%的文章包含该步骤。在包含该步骤的文章中，该步骤在语步二中的占比最大值为36%，最小值为2%，平均值为9%，标准差为0.09。实例如下：

In Fig. 5, it is seen that the limiting pressure increases with depth. Additionally, the depth determines whether the limiting pressure is governed by puph or pex-df. (JT – 07)

When comparing the results of the two start heuristics, it can be seen that neither BF nor FF outperforms the other one for all neighborhoods. ⋯ However, the differences between the start heuristics are comparatively small compared to the differences between the neighborhoods. (JT – 14)

M 2.4c 结果分析：所选文章中只有一篇包含该步骤。在该篇文章中，该步骤在语步二中的占比为7%。实例如下：

It should be noted that the model (12) presented in Section 2.1 assumes perfectly inelastic demand, which may not always be the case in real-world operations. For example, if there are very few bikes in a neighborhood, travelers might have to switch to alternative transportation modes such as public transit. On the contrary, if travelers have extremely easy access to bikes near their origins, more demand may be induced. Hence, it is important to investigate the potential impacts of elastic demand. In so doing, each type of demand is assumed to be a function of travelers' access time to the nearest bike near their origins. (JT – 13)

M 2.4d 模型使用环境：所选文章中只有两篇包含该步骤。在这两篇文章中，该步骤在语步二中的占比分别为 4% 和 2%。实例如下：

> The modelling method described could be applied at any location, and to any mix of rail traffic, but this paper is based on vehicles using the UK East Coast Main Line. (JT – 34)

> This model is equally applicable to all control options. (JT – 27)

M 2.5a 模型理论基础及原理： 所选文章中有 72% 的文章包含该步骤。在包含该步骤的文章中，该步骤在语步二中的占比最大值为 41%，最小值为 1%，平均值为 13%，标准差为 0.09。实例如下：

> A detailed literature review has been undertaken on the deterioration mechanisms in the wheel-rail interface with focus on wear prediction [11]. (JT – 35)

> According to Daganzo and Ouyang (2019), the expected shortest distance to nq, t, i + n – q, t, i random points in a region of area Ai is proportional to Ai nq, t, i + n – q, t, i. (JT – 13)

M 2.5b 相似之处及改进方面： 所选文章中有 56% 的文章包含该步骤。在包含该步骤的文章中，该步骤在语步二中的占比最大值为 21%，最小值为 0%，平均值为 7%，标准差为 0.05。实例如下：

> An existing schedule is improved using a simulated annealing approach. Our simulated annealing approach is quite conventional in structure; a more complex variant was unnecessary but could be investigated as a source of future research. (JT – 10)

> In this study, two different RCF damage models were used as input for the crack propagation model. In both models, the contact area is considered to be elliptic and divided into cell elements. The first model is based on shakedown theory[11] and originally was developed to predict RCF on wheels. (JT – 36)

综上所述，所有文章均包含语步二。该语步中各步骤涉及的篇章数最多的是 M2.2b，共有 34 篇，占所有文章的 94%，最少的是 M2.4c，只涉及一篇文章。各步骤涉及篇章数平均值为 19.7 篇，占所有文章的 55%，标准差为 10.4。不同文章中包含的步骤种类最多的有 10 种，占所有步骤的 77%，最少的共有 4 种，占所有步骤的 31%。各篇文章中包含的步骤种类平均值为 7.11 种，占所有步骤的 55%，标准差为 1.72。不同文章中包含的步骤种类不一，同一个步骤在不同文章中的占比也存在一定的差异。不同文章中各步骤占比平均值最高的是 M2.2a 和 M2.2b，均为 23%，最低的是 M2.4d，为 3%，各步骤占比平均值为 11%，标准差为 6.74。

（三）语步三特征

表5.3.5是语步三中所包含的步骤种类。如表所示，语步三中共包括5个大的步骤，其中M3.2又包含2个小的步骤，M3.4包含5个小的步骤。该语步中共有10个不同步骤。表5.3.6是不同文章语步三中各步骤在该语步中的占比情况。如表所示，有部分文章不包含该语步。在包含该步骤的文章中，该语步中各步骤占比情况不一。此外，同一个步骤在不同文章中的占比情况也有所差异。以下是针对每个步骤占比情况的具体分析及实例。

表5.3.5 语步三各步骤列表

M	语步三、模型验证或应用		
3.1a	实验所需设备/软件	3.4a	来源
3.2	模型运行时的设置	3.4b	特征
3.2a	模型组件	3.4c	取样技术
3.2b	工作特征/参数	3.4f	取样目的
3.3	用于测试/评价的指标	3.4g	监测情况
3.4	数据收集及取样技术	3.6	结果分析

表5.3.6 语步三各步骤占比

M	3.1a	3.2a	3.2b	3.3	3.4a	3.4b	3.4c	3.4f	3.4g	3.6
JT-01	—	—	—	—	—	—	—	—	—	—
JT-02	—	—	—	—	15%	—	—	—	—	85%
JT-03	18%	—	26%	34%	—	16%	—	5%	—	—
JT-04	3%	—	75%	3%	2%	—	7%	—	10%	—
JT-05	6%	24%	59%	12%	—	—	—	—	—	—
JT-06	—	—	100%	—	—	—	—	—	—	—
JT-07	—	—	50%	—	50%	—	—	—	—	—
JT-08	27%	—	73%	—	—	—	—	—	—	—
JT-09	—	—	—	—	—	—	—	—	—	—
JT-10	—	—	—	—	—	—	—	—	—	—

续表

M	3.1a	3.2a	3.2b	3.3	3.4a	3.4b	3.4c	3.4f	3.4g	3.6
JT－11	—	—	—	—	—	—	—	—	—	—
JT－12	—	—	—	—	—	—	—	—	—	—
JT－13	—	—	—	—	—	—	—	—	—	—
JT－14	100%	—	—	—	—	—	—	—	—	—
JT－15	3%	16%	52%	29%	—	—	—	—	—	—
JT－16	8%	17%	75%	—	—	—	—	—	—	—
JT－17	30%	10%	50%	10%	—	—	—	—	—	—
JT－18	—	33%	67%	—	—	—	—	—	—	—
JT－19	—	—	—	—	—	—	—	—	—	—
JT－20	25%	—	25%	42%	8%	—	—	—	—	—
JT－21	—	—	—	—	—	—	—	—	—	—
JT－22	—	—	—	—	—	—	—	—	—	—
JT－23	—	—	—	—	—	—	—	—	—	—
JT－24	38%	—	54%	8%	—	—	—	—	—	—
JT－25	—	—	—	—	—	—	—	—	—	—
JT－26	37%	11%	37%	—	5%	—	11%	—	—	—
JT－27	—	—	—	—	—	—	—	—	—	—
JT－28	—	—	—	—	—	—	—	—	—	—
JT－29	—	—	—	100%	—	—	—	—	—	—
JT－30	—	13%	63%	25%	—	—	—	—	—	—
JT－31	—	—	100%	—	—	—	—	—	—	—
JT－32	—	29%	47%	24%	—	—	—	—	—	—
JT－33	—	—	—	100%	—	—	—	—	—	—
JT－34	—	6%	94%	—	—	—	—	—	—	—
JT－35	—	—	100%	—	—	—	—	—	—	—
JT－36	1%	—	53%	10%	6%	29%	1%	—	—	—

M 3.1a 实验所需设备/软件：所选文章中有33%的文章包含该步骤。在包含该步骤的文章中，该步骤在语步三中的占比最大值为100%，最小值为1%，平均值为25%，标准差为0.26。实例如下：

All algorithms were implemented in C + + . To solve the matching problem MIN-WPRCM by network flow techniques, the network simplex algorithm implemented in the LEMON library [Dezso et al. (2011)] (version 1. 3. 1) was used. (JT – 14)

All analyses presented in this paper were performed using the soil-fluid coupled 3D finite element (FE) method with the commercial finite element package ABAQUSTM. (JT – 08)

M 3. 2a 模型组件：所选文章中有 25% 的文章包含该步骤。在包含该步骤的文章中，该步骤在语步三中的占比最大值为 33%，最小值为 6%，平均值为 18%，标准差为 0.09。实例如下：

In the tables that follow, for each heuristic, the numbers on the left-hand side of the column headed "Average solution values and CPU time" are the total schedule time, total distance and total waiting time, respectively, of the best of several runs using different parameter values and initialization criteria, averaged over the respective problem set. (JT – 18)

In the study, traffic lights control actions can be categorized into 3 types: no change in signal duration, increasing signal duration, reducing signal duration. (JT – 32)

M 3. 2b 工作特征/参数：所选文章中有 53% 的文章包含该步骤。在包含该步骤的文章中，该步骤在语步三中的占比最大值为 100%，最小值为 25%，平均值为 63%，标准差为 0.23。实例如下：

The total schedule time is the sum of the total travel time, total service time, and total waiting time, respectively. The numbers on the right-hand side of this column are the number of routes of the best solution and the total CPU time for the different runs, averaged over the respective problem set. (JT – 18)

The constraints are then removed and the corresponding forces simultaneously applied, without any change in the stress-state of the surrounding soil. (JT – 04)

M 3. 3 用于测试/评价的指标：所选文章中有 33% 的文章包含该步骤。在包含该步骤的文章中，该步骤在语步三中的占比最大值为 100%，最小值为 3%，平均值为 33%，标准差为 0.32。实例如下：

This analysis is performed to tune the proposed algorithm. We only use the 20 instances with n = 80 customers. A summary of these experiments is reported in Table 2. (JT – 15)

Table 1 shows the input parameters for the model prediction and Fig. 1 presents the gassy soil model predictions as well as the experimental results from Test 18. (JT – 20)

M 3. 4a 来源：所选文章中有 17% 的文章包含该步骤。在包含该步骤的文章中，该步骤在语步三中的占比最大值为 50%，最小值为 2%，平均值为 14%，标准差为 0.16。实例如下：

DeltaRail (DeltaRail Group Limited, Utrecht, the Netherlands) (currently Plurel) has performed extensive field measurements in a railway curve located in the Netherlands (Bunnik) with a radius of 2455 m. (JT – 36)

The relaxation modulus was converted from the dynamic modulus master curve obtained from the LTPP database using the Prony series model. (JT – 02)

M 3.4b 特征：所选文章中只有两篇包含该步骤。在这两篇文章中，该步骤在语步三中的占比分别为29%和16%。实例如下：

Similar to the previous procedure, a synthetic database comprised of 500 samples was developed for various slab and pavement foundation sublayer thicknesses and moduli values. (JT – 03)

Three train types with the highest average daily tonnages were chosen to be modelled as multi-body systems: two passenger trains (interregiomaterieel (IRM) and intercitymaterieel (ICM)) and one freight train with Y25 bogies. (JT – 36)

M 3.4c 取样技术：所选文章中只有三篇包含该步骤。在这三篇文章中，该步骤在语步三中的占比分别为7%、11%和1%。实例如下：

However, due to time constraints, this limited the number of valid laps for both the baseline dry and 'system on' to three for each condition set. (JT – 26)

In these tests, the rail hardness, rail profile, surface crack length and crack depth were measured by DeltaRail, 15, 16 at the request of ProRail. (JT – 36)

M 3.4f 取样目的：所选文章中只有一篇包含该步骤。在该篇文章中，该步骤在语步三中的占比为5%。实例如下：

The objective is to back calculate the elastic modulus values for the pavement layers. (JT – 03)

M 3.4g 监测情况：在所选文章中只有一篇包含该步骤。在该篇文章中，该步骤在语步三中的占比为10%。实例如下：

A portion about 150 m long of the third line of the Milan Underground was monitored during the various phases of its construction and surface movements were recorded by means of ordinary surveying methods. In addition, three sections of the tunnel were monitored, each with two Trivec instruments (sliding micrometers which act at the same time as extensometer and inclinometer, so that displacements in the three mutually orthogonal directions can be measured). (JT – 04)

M 3.6 结果分析：所选文章中只有一篇包含该步骤。在该篇文章中，该步骤在语步三中的占比为85%。实例如下：

Sensitivity analysis was conducted to evaluate the influences of the input variables on the thermal J-integral based on the FEM results. As shown in Fig. 5 (a), when the thickness of asphalt layer increased, the J-integral decreased. When the thickness of asphalt layer was larger than 200 mm, the J-integral decreased as the thermal crack depth became greater than half of the asphalt layer thickness. (JT – 02)

综上所述，有64%的文章包含语步三。在包含语步三的文章中，涉及文章数最高的是M3.2b，共有19篇，占所有文章的53%，有3个步骤只涉及一篇文章。各步骤涉及篇章数平均值为6篇，占所有文章的17%，标准差为6.18。各篇文章中包含的步骤种类最多的有6种，最少的仅有1种，分别占所有步骤的60%和9%，平均值为2.87种，占该语步中所有步骤的26%，标准差为1.63。不同文章中包含的步骤种类存在一定的差异，同一种步骤在不同文章中的占比也存在一定的差异。各篇文章中不同步骤占比平均值最高的是M3.6，为85%，最低的是M3.4f，为5%，各步骤占比平均值为26%，标准差为25.73。

（四）语步四特征

表5.3.7是语步四中所包含的步骤种类。如表所示，语步四中共包括3个大的步骤，其中M4.2包含4个小的步骤，M4.3包含6个小的步骤，M4.4中包含1个小的步骤。该语步中共有11种不同步骤。表5.3.8是不同文章语步四中各步骤在该语步中的占比情况。如表所示，有一半以上文章不包括该语步。在包含该步骤的文章中，该语步中各步骤占比情况不一。此外，同一个步骤在不同文章中的占比情况也有所差异。以下是针对每个步骤占比情况的具体分析及实例。

表5.3.7 语步四各步骤列表

M	语步四、模型有效性验证		
4.2	实验验证	4.3b	评价模型使用的评价指标
4.2a	实验条件和程序	4.3c	评价有效性检验结果
4.2b	使用获得的数据验证模型	4.3d	强调有效性查验的合理性
4.2c	现场实验按规范确定参数	4.3e	该模型的优点
4.2d	验证实验的局限性	4.3f	该模型的局限性
4.3	有效性验证分析	4.4	不同学科要求检验的范式
4.3a	对比实验与建模结果	4.4a	稳健性检验

表5.3.8 　　　　　　　　语步四各步骤占比

M	4.2a	4.2b	4.2c	4.2d	4.3a	4.3b	4.3c	4.3d	4.3e	4.3f	4.4a
JT-01	—	—	—	—	—	—	—	—	—	—	—
JT-02	—	50%	—	—	50%	—	—	—	—	—	—
JT-03	—	—	—	—	—	—	—	—	100%	—	—
JT-04	9%	—	7%	6%	58%	—	9%	9%	3%	—	—
JT-05	—	—	—	—	89%	—	11%	—	—	—	—
JT-06	—	—	—	—	82%	—	2%	2%	6%	8%	—
JT-07	—	—	—	—	18%	2%	12%	52%	—	2%	14%
JT-08	11%	—	—	—	79%	2%	7%	—	—	1%	—
JT-09	—	—	—	—	—	—	—	—	—	—	—
JT-10	—	—	—	—	—	—	—	—	—	—	—
JT-11	—	—	—	—	—	—	—	—	—	—	—
JT-12	—	—	—	—	—	—	—	—	—	—	—
JT-13	—	—	—	—	—	—	—	—	—	—	—
JT-14	—	—	—	—	37%	11%	—	—	42%	11%	—
JT-15	18%	1%	—	—	12%	4%	43%	—	22%	—	—
JT-16	11%	—	—	—	—	—	39%	—	50%	—	—
JT-17	—	—	—	—	—	—	—	—	100%	—	—
JT-18	25%	—	—	—	12%	6%	29%	—	17%	12%	—
JT-19	—	—	—	—	—	—	—	—	—	—	—
JT-20	—	—	—	—	38%	—	63%	—	—	—	—
JT-21	—	—	—	—	—	—	—	—	—	—	—
JT-22	—	—	—	—	—	—	—	—	—	—	—
JT-23	—	—	—	—	—	—	—	—	—	—	—
JT-24	—	—	—	—	14%	—	50%	21%	—	14%	—
JT-25	100%	—	—	—	—	—	—	—	—	—	—
JT-26	52%	7%	—	—	—	30%	11%	—	—	—	—
JT-27	—	—	—	—	—	—	—	—	—	—	—
JT-28	—	—	—	—	—	—	—	—	—	—	—
JT-29	—	—	—	—	3%	6%	65%	6%	6%	13%	—
JT-30	—	—	—	—	—	21%	47%	11%	21%	—	—
JT-31	—	100%	—	—	—	—	—	—	—	—	—
JT-32	44%	33%	—	—	—	11%	—	—	11%	—	—
JT-33	—	—	—	—	—	—	—	—	—	—	—

续表

M	4.2a	4.2b	4.2c	4.2d	4.3a	4.3b	4.3c	4.3d	4.3e	4.3f	4.4a
JT-34	—	—	—	—	—	—	—	—	—	—	—
JT-35	—	—	—	—	—	—	—	—	—	—	—
JT-36	—	—	—	—	100%	—	—	—	—	—	—

M 4.2a 实验条件和程序：所选文章中有 22% 的文章包含该步骤。在包含该步骤的文章中，该步骤在语步四中的占比最大值为 100%，最小值为 9%，平均值为 34%，标准差为 0.29。实例如下：

The extensometer measurements recorded after the eastbound tunnel excavation are presented in Fig. 6 (a). A ground movement mechanism similar to that in the rest period was observed: slight swelling above the tunnel crown, which corresponds well with the rise in pore pressures above the tunnel, and consolidation at the sides of the tunnel due to the decrease in pore pressures, as shown in Figs. 4 (b) and 4 (c) respectively. (JT-08)

Most of the heuristics presented are parameterized. It is thus of interest to know whether there are any relationships between the parameter values and the initialization criteria that produced the best solution values, and the corresponding problem structures. Given our computational results, we will focus on the heuristic I. (JT-18)

M 4.2b 使用获得的数据验证模型：所选文章中有 14% 的文章包含该步骤。在包含该步骤的文章中，该步骤在语步四中的占比最大值为 100%，最小值为 1%，平均值为 38%，标准差为 0.35。实例如下：

As such, the experimental data comprises of a purely longitudinal creepage scenario, while the simulation data shows only the longitudinal component of a simulation containing longitudinal, lateral and spin creepages. (JT-26)

In the work, the agent makes signal control decisions under diverse traffic circumstances and returns an action sequence, so that by the actions the road traffic jamming to display are the least amount. (JT-32)

M 4.2c 现场实验按规范确定参数：所选文章中只有一篇包含该步骤。在该篇文章中，该步骤在语步三中的占比为 7%。实例如下：

In correspondence with the three instrumented sections (a typical one is sketched in Fig. 1), six boreholes were drilled close to the tunnel walls. SPT tests were conducted every 2 m depth. The ground consists of alternate layers of sand and gravel with some intercalations of sandy silt layers. The SPT blow number is high everywhere and often refusal to penetration is encountered. The density of the soil is therefore high. (JT-04)

M 4.2d 验证实验的局限性：所选文章中只有一篇包含该步骤。在该篇文章中，该步骤在语步四中的占比为6%。实例如下：

In order to evaluate the undisturbed stiffness of the natural soil, a series of pressuremeter tests were also conducted. The high density and coarse granularity of the soil prevented the use of self-boring instruments. ⋯ Unfortunately, the disturb once caused by the borehole excavation and pressuremeter insertion prevented a correct evaluation of the coefficient of earth pressure at rest, K0. (M3 – 76) (JT – 04)

M 4.3a 对比实验与建模结果：所选文章中有36%的文章包含该步骤。在包含该步骤的文章中，该步骤在语步四中的占比最大值为100%，最小值为3%，平均值为45%，标准差为0.32。实例如下：

The different curves in each plot refer to different injection velocities v_0 (from 180 to 380 m/s) and to different vs/m ratios (from 0.0015 to 0.005). The effect of different nozzle diameters can be observed by comparing Fig. 11 (a) and Fig. 11 (b). (JT – 05)

Since large instances usually require more iterations to obtain high-quality results, we compare the ALNS algorithm behavior with 5000 and 10,000 iterations on mid-80 instances. ⋯ ALNS can provide best-known solutions for the 20 mid-80 instances in the benchmark. (JT – 15)

M 4.3b 评价模型使用的评价指标：所选文章中有25%的文章包含该步骤。在包含该步骤的文章中，该步骤在语步四中的占比最大值为30%，最小值为2%，平均值为10%，标准差为0.09。实例如下：

Three arterials (Arterial Nos. 1, 6, and 7) show positive values. These arterials are positioned inside or very close to the inverse- V shape area (the bifurcation set) in the 2D projection of the cusp catastrophe surface (see Fig. 4). (JT – 29)

In A-J first, traffic splits equally into two paths (Fig. 3) while major traffic travels on the longer path R-A-J-S in R-J first (Fig. 4). (JT-30)

M 4.3c 评价有效性检验结果：所选文章中有36%的文章包含该步骤。在包含该步骤的文章中，该步骤在语步四中的占比最大值为65%，最小值为2%，平均值为30%，标准差为0.22。实例如下：

A maximum error of 0.2% has been found for all energy and time calculations. (JT – 24)

Average solution gaps for the VRPMS are 31%, 32% and 27% for the 10, 15 and 20 customer size instances respectively, while computation times for running the MIP and the GA are drastically different. (JT – 16)

M 4.3d 强调有效性查验的合理性：所选文章中有17%的文章包含该步骤。在包含该步骤的文章中，该步骤在语步四中的占比最大值为52%，最小值为2%，平均值为17%，标准差为0.17。实例如下：

Unrealistic heave is predicted in fact by the numerical analysis. ⋯ Actually, the unloading of the lower part of the tunnel is associated to a stiffness which is larger than that characterizing the loading prior to failure. (JT－04)

As seen in Fig. 5, all the predicted limiting pressures are within the range of the reported real ones. (M3－79)(JT－07)

M 4.3e 该模型的优点：所选文章中有31%的文章包含该步骤。在包含该步骤的文章中，该步骤在语步四中的占比最大值为100%，最小值为3%，平均值为34%，标准差为0.34。实例如下：

This implies that, for the given time limits, the MIN-based solvers work rather well on larger instances and are able to reduce the total costs faster than the HGS-CARP solver, although the latter may outperform the MIN-based solvers for larger time limits. (JT－14)

In contrast, our proposed framework provides both the optimal green splits and the exact traffic patterns associating with a particular order of phases. (M3－102)(JT－30)

M 4.3f 该模型的局限性：所选文章中有19%的文章包含该步骤。在包含该步骤的文章中，该步骤在语步四中的占比最大值为14%，最小值为1%，平均值为9%，标准差为0.05。实例如下：

An arterial that performs like a high- speed highway, especially when traffic concentration or demand is low, may not be the most desirable arterial from the point of view of safety. There may be tradeoffs between the operational performance and the safety performance of arterials that could result in a poorer than anticipated overall performance particularly when the traffic concentration is very low. This idea could be further explored in future studies. (JT－29)

This would increase considerably the complexity of the control algorithm used to determine the optimum grout pressures, however, and is beyond the scope of the current paper. (JT－06)

M 4.4a 稳健性检验：所选文章中只有一篇包含该步骤。在该篇文章中，该步骤在语步四中的占比为14%。实例如下：

A sensitivity study was undertaken to provide insight into the significance of the individual model parameters such as the angle of internal friction, void ratio, modulus of deformation, and drilling radius. The individual parameter is changed by 65% with respect to its reference value and the effect is evaluated on the limiting pressure. The reference values considered are those of soil B－4 in Table 1. The results, shown in Fig10, indicate that the limiting pressure increases with the increase in angle of internal friction and modulus of deformation, while it decreases with the increase in void ratio and drilling radius. The results also indicate that the angle of internal friction is the most significant parameter affecting the limiting pressure. On the other hand, the variation in drilling radius has almost no effect on the limiting pressure. This effect of the drilling radius agrees with the observations of Graf (1992). (JT－07)

综上所述，有58%的文章包含语步四。在包含该步骤的文章中，涉及篇章数最多的是M4.3a和M4.3c，均有13篇，占所有文章的36%。有三个步骤只涉及一篇，分别是M4.2c、M4.2d和4.4a。各篇文章中涉及篇章数平均值为6.82篇，占所有文章的19%。各篇文章中包含的步骤种类最多的有7种，最少的只有1种，分别占该语步中所有步骤的64%和9%。各篇文章中包含的步骤种类平均值为3.57种，占所有步骤的32%，标准差为2.01。不同文章中包含的步骤种类存在一定的差异，同一个步骤在不同文章中的占比也存在一定的差异，各步骤在各篇文章中占比平均值最高的是M4.3a，为45%，最低的是M4.2d，为6%，各步骤占比平均值为22%，标准差为14.21。

（五）语步占比及轨迹

图5.3.3是所分析各篇文章中四个语步的总体占比。如图所示，各篇文章均包含语步二，超过60%的文章包含了其他三个语步。有约83%的文章语步二占比最高，有三篇文章只包含语步二，占所分析文章的8%。有一篇文章语步三占比最高，占所有文章的3%，有五篇文章语步四占比最高，占所有文章的14%。

就各步骤在所有语步中占比平均值来看，占比最高的三个步骤依次为M2.2b（14.72%）、M2.2a（13.12%）和M2.2c（7.93%）。占比最低的为M3.4f，仅有0.03%，其次为M2.4d、M3.4c和M3.4e，均为0.06%。

语步占比最高的三个步骤也是涉及篇章数最多的，但占比和篇章数之间并不存在完全一一对应的关系。这三个步骤涉及的篇章数分别为43篇、30篇和30篇。有9个步骤只涉及一篇文章，但是占比最低的四个步骤并不均是涉及篇章数最低的步骤。

就各篇文章中包含的步骤种类来看，在包含步骤种类最多的文章中有21种不同步骤，在包含步骤最少的文章中有4种。各篇文章包含步骤种类的平均值为12.58种，标准差为5.14。

表5.3.9是所分析文章中语步组合情况，如表所示，所分析文章中共出现了六种不同语步组合，包含四个语步、三个语步和二个语步的文章分别占所有文章的44%、14%和33%，有三篇文章只包含语步二一个语步，占所有文章的8%。

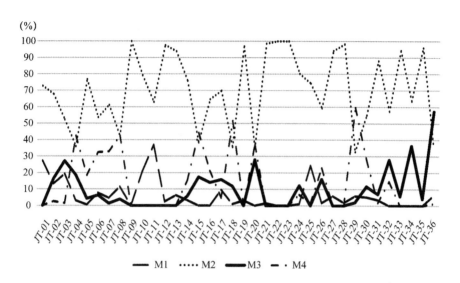

图 5.3.3 各篇文章中四个语步占比

表 5.3.9　　　　　　　　　　　语步组合

学科	M1234	M124	M234	M12	M23	M2
JT－01				√		
JT－02	√					
JT－03	√					
JT－04	√					
JT－05	√					
JT－06	√					
JT－07	√					
JT－08	√					
JT－09						√
JT－10				√		
JT－11				√		
JT－12				√		
JT－13				√		
JT－14	√					
JT－15			√			

续表

学科	M1234	M124	M234	M12	M23	M2
JT－16			√			
JT－17	√					
JT－18	√					
JT－19				√		
JT－20			√			
JT－21				√		
JT－22						√
JT－23						√
JT－24	√					
JT－25		√				
JT－26	√					
JT－27				√		
JT－28				√		
JT－29	√					
JT－30	√					
JT－31	√					
JT－32			√			
JT－33					√	
JT－34					√	
JT－35					√	
JT－36	√					

图5.3.4至图5.3.7分别为四个语步在不同文章中的分布轨迹。如图所示，在包含四个语步的文章中，除一篇文章中语步三占比最高、分布最广最密集外，其他文章中分布最广最密集的均为语步二。大多数文章中语步四分布比语步一和语步三广且密。总体来说，语步一分布还是以文章最前为主，少部分文章中会有部分语步一出现在文章中间偏前及中间的位置，还有个别文章中语步一会分布在文章的后部。语步二主要集中分布在语步一和语步三之间，但是有将近三分之一的文章中会出现在文章最前，还有极少数文章出现在最后。语步三主要分布在文章中间

偏后的位置，但是有少数文章中也会有部分语步三分布在文章最前或前部。文章最后部位以语步四为主，语步四前以语步三为主，但是在极少数文章中语步四也会出现在语步三之前、语步二中。各篇文章中不同语步之间均存在不同程度的交叉，少部分文章中四个语步之间均有交叉，其他文章中语步二与语步一交叉较多，其次是语步二与语步三之间，极少数文章中语步四与其他三个语步之间分别有交叉。

该学科中只有一篇文章中同时包含语步一、语步二和语步四。语步一和语步二分布均较广，但是语步二密度远高于语步一，语步一和语步二有交叉。在该篇文章中语步四只有一处，且与语步二共同出现在一句话中。

有四篇文章同时包含语步二、语步三和语步四。其中两篇文章中语步二占比最高，分布最广、最集中；另一篇文章中语步四占比最高，分布最广、最集中；还有一篇文章中语步二和语步四相似。除一篇文章中语步三占比高于语步四外，其他各篇文章中语步三占比均最低，分布较分散。各篇文章中三个语步均有交叉，但是文章前部主要以语步二为主，最后主要以语步四为主，语步三主要以中间偏后的位置为主。

有九篇文章同时包含语步一和语步二。各篇文章中语步二占比均高于语步一，分布也最广、最集中；有三篇文章中只有一句为语步一，其他各篇中语步一分布较分散。不同文章中语步一分布存在一定的差异，但是大部分文章的前部、中间及后部均有语步一分布，少数文章中也会有部分语步一分布在文章最前或最后。在大部分文章中语步二几乎覆盖了文章各个部位，语步一分散分布在语步二中。

有三篇文章中只包含语步二和语步三。语步二总体占比均高于语步三，分布也比语步三广和集中。语步三在各篇文章中占比存在一定的差异，在其中两篇中占比均很低，在另一篇中较高。在两篇文章中语步三分散分布在语步二中，在其中一篇中分布在文章较前的位置，还有一篇中分布在文章较后的位置。在语步三占比较高的文章中，语步分布较广，主要分布在文章五分之一以后的位置。三篇文章中两个语步均有交叉。

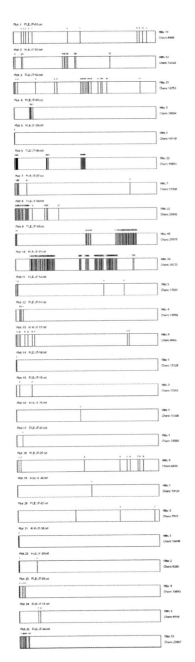

图 5.3.4　语步一分布轨迹

图 5.3.5　语步二分布轨迹

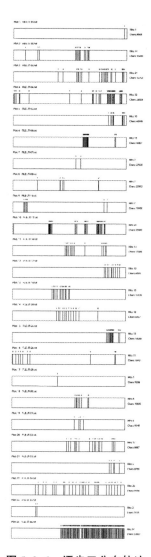

图 5.3.6　语步三分布轨迹

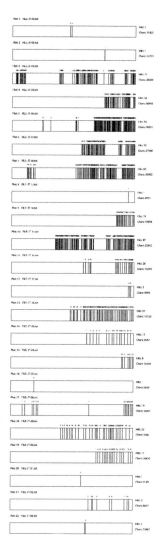

图 5.3.7　语步四分布轨迹

综上所述，同一学科不同文章中语步占比和分布轨迹既有相同之处，同时也存在一定的差异。所有文章中均出现了语步二。虽然不同文章中存在一定差异，但在绝大多数文章中语步二在四个语步中总体占比最高。其他三个语步中占比从高到低依次为语步一、语步三和语步四，但是总体差异不大。

就四个语步分布而言，总体来说，文章最前部以语步一为主，语步二主要集中分布在语步一和语步三之间，最后部位以语步四为主。但是文章最前也会出现语步二，语步二与语步一和语步三均有交叉，其中与语步一交叉情况较多，语步四与其他三个语步交叉的情况较少。

三　语言特征分析

本小节主要分析所选学科论文中建模实验方法写作中使用到的语言特征。主要从句子结构、时态和语态三个大的方面进行分析。针对句子结构的分析主要包含句子类型、四类主要句子长度分布及句子类型与语步之间的关系。针对时态的分析主要包含时态种类、不同时态组合及时态与语步的关系。针对语态的分析主要包含语态种类、不同语态组合及语态与语步的关系。

（一）句子特征

A. 句类

表5.3.10是本学科文章中所包含的句子类型及各类句子占比。如表所示，简单句、复杂句、复合句及复合复杂句占所有句子的93.53%，片段和有语法错误的句子占所有句子的0.50%，其他带有冒号、括号及 i.e. 的各类特殊句子占所有句子的5.97%。四类句子中简单句占比远高于其他三类句子，其次是复杂句，其他两类句子占比均较低，其中复合句占比略高于复合复杂句。特殊类型句子形式多样，共38种，其中占比较高的依次为 NWHS、NWS 及 NWHP。以下例句为特殊类型的句子：

表5.3.10　　　　　　　　　句类及占比

句类	句数	占比	句类	句数	占比
S	1788	52.34%	PSS	1	0.03%
P	1094	32.03%	BCPF	2	0.06%
C	220	6.44%	BCPS	1	0.03%
CP	93	2.72%	BCS	1	0.03%

句类	句数	占比	句类	句数	占比
ICS	1	0.03%	BPF	4	0.12%
IPC	1	0.03%	BSF	4	0.12%
IPWH	2	0.06%	BPFS	1	0.03%
IPS	5	0.15%	BPS	2	0.06%
ISCP	1	0.03%	BSS	2	0.06%
ISP	3	0.09%	IBSWS	1	0.03%
ISS	7	0.20%	ICPS	1	0.03%
NSP	1	0.03%	INPC	1	0.03%
NSS	2	0.06%	IPWA	2	0.06%
NWAS	7	0.20%	ISF	3	0.09%
NWC	1	0.03%	NPC	1	0.03%
NWHC	2	0.06%	NPCP	1	0.03%
NWHP	19	0.56%	NPP	2	0.06%
NWHS	65	1.90%	NSC	1	0.03%
NWHW	1	0.03%	NSCP	1	0.03%
NWP	5	0.15%	SP	1	0.03%
NWS	47	1.38%	F	5	0.15%
PPP	1	0.03%	R	12	0.35%

ICS: Constraint (5) limits each heavy resource to only one tour; (6) and (7) ensure each customer is serviced only once by either a heavy or light; (8) and (9) ensure lights launch and return to the same heavy; and (10) and (11) restrict the lights to directly launch from or return to the depot (i. e. lights must be carried by the heavy resources in and out of the depot). (JT – 16)

IPC: Moreover, the demand from zone $i \in N$ to zone $j \in N$ in time period $t \in T$, denoted as $\lambda_{i,j,t}$, is assumed to be a random variable that follows a finitely supported distribution, i. e., the set of demand realizations, denoted by $|\kappa|$, is a finite set and each realization $\kappa \in \kappa$ happens with a probability p_k. (JT – 13)

IPWH: They are also called virtual links as they have infinite flow capacity and storage, i. e., by setting these parameters $|Qa, Va, Wa| \rightarrow \infty$ for any $a \in AR \cup AS$ where AR and AS are the sets of source and sink links respectively. (JT – 30)

IPS: Another advantage of the routing flexibility approach is that the contents of the passing loop are explicitly known, i. e. there is a sequence for each track. (JT – 11)

ISCP: A simple method to solve the new equilibrium is to perform a two-dimensional search for the equilibrium fleet size tuple while using (12) as a subroutine, i. e. , we consider that m_q and m_{-q} are selected from a finite set of values, denoted by M, and then for each combination of (m_q, m_{-q}), we obtain a pair of equilibrium profits, ($\pi_q^e(m_q, m_{-q}), \pi_{-q}^e(m_q, m_{-q})$) by solving problem (12). (JT – 13)

ISP: The alternative graph model however may treat the processing time as a variable, i. e. the train speed may be selected as long as it does not exceed some maximum amount. (JT – 10)

ISS: The Vehicle Routing Problem with Drones (VRPD) looks for minimizing the maximum completion time, i. e. , the time required to serveall customers using the trucks and the drones such that, by the end of missionall trucks (carrying drones as well) must be at the depot [7, 12]. (JT – 17)

NSP: We follow the scheme proposed by Fran 8 lo汤水il. (2016): small moves are applied when a new solution has just been accepted, while large moves are applied when no new solution has been accepted in the most recent iterations. (JT – 15)

NSS: As for the injection phase, various possibilities were examined for the mechanical parameters of the improved soil: uniform distribution of the cohesion and shear modulus was considered first. (JT – 04)

NWAS: The procedure for modelling grout injection, in outline, is as follows: (a) The initial assignment of high shear and normal stiffness to the grout elements to tie together the gap into which grout will flow. (JT – 06)

NWC: The heuristics are composed of several components; in particular, they have two main stages: an initialization step and an improving (optimization) phase. (JT – 17)

NWHC: This is defined as the ratio between the volume of grout in the column and the volume of injected grout, and is estimated by assuming a homogeneous composition of Soilcrete and spoil and a nil volume of air in the Soilcrete (公式), where Dav is the mean value of the column along with depth. (JT – 05)

NWHP: The healing ability of asphalt mixture is related to the asphalt stiffness and fracture energy, which is presented in Eq. (6), where T is the healing factor at aging time t, T is the normalized asphalt stiffness, F is the initial fracture energy of asphalt, and Ch is a calibration factor. (JT – 01)

NWHS: The viscoelastic thermal stress was computed with Eq. (2) by the Boltzmann superposition principle: 公式 where E is the relaxation modulus of asphalt mixture at time t; s is the thermal strain at time s; s is the integral variable. (JT – 02)

NWHW: The wear number: Eq. where Fcx and Fcy are respectively the creep forces (N) at longitudinal and lateral directions, x and y are the corresponding creepages. (JT – 35)

NWP: Because the damage was severe at position 8 in the curve, this section was sub-divided into three parts: 8A, 8B and 8C. (JT – 36)

NWS: Based on the identified critical pavement responses, the load induced damage is divided into two categories: (1) tensile stress induced damage, and (2) shear stress induced damage. (JT – 02)

PPP: The second special case assumes that, in addition to CLocal $q = 0$, both companies make myopic decisions by only focusing on one-stage payoffs-this case could happen in the real world, for example, when the demand is difficult to forecast. (JT – 13)

PSS: The steering of the bogie is disregarded in the presented model—a constant yaw angle is assumed. (JT – 33)

BCPF: The arc weights in essence project backwards from these later nodes and takes into account the processing requirements that occur between $(o_{i,k}, o_{i,k^*})$ and $(o_{i',k'}, o_{i',k^*})$ respectively (where k^* is different in each). (JT – 10)

BCPS: The method is of order one, which means the global discretisation error (the difference between solution and approximated value summed over all steps) grows linear with Dt, so big pitches lead to big errors. (JT – 25)

BCS: To represent grinding the model considers only the crack size reduction through rail surface removal, and does not take account of other effects of grinding such as re-location of the contact patch across the rail head, or change in contact pressure as a result of any change in rail profile (these will be considered in future versions of the model). (JT – 34)

BPF: Grouting is started if the maximum settlement exceeds the Trigger Level and continues until either the maximum settlement reaches the lower Target Level (which coincides with the Trigger Level) or the minimum settlement (equal to the maximum heave) reaches the upper Target Level. (JT – 06)

BSF: In addition, three sections of the tunnel were monitored, each with two Trivec instruments (sliding micrometers which act at the same time as extensometer and inclinometer, so that displacements in the three mutually orthogonal directions can be measured). (JT – 04)

BPFS: Note that, our model tends to split a signal cycle in time (as it happens in practice) by separating the phases in each cycle while the approximation applies green split to flow capacity without considering the phase ordering (therefore there is no explicit constraints to avoid the crossover of traffic in the solution of approximation). (JT – 30)

BPS: Because each phase is preserved at least 25% of the cycle time (even there is no traffic), letting phase A-J performs first is the best option for traffic on link R-J to fully use the remaining time in the first cycle (time 0 to 60, Fig. 3). (JT – 30)

BSS: The geographical data are randomly generated by a random uniform distribution (denote the corresponding problem sets by R1 and R2), clustered (denote the corresponding problem sets by C1 and C2), and semiclustered (denote the corresponding problem sets by RC1 and RC2). (JT – 18)

IBSWS: AVG is the mean of the absolute values of the observed deflection ratios, i. e. Eq., with

NDFL the number of the deflection ratios defined by the user (NDFL would be four for the example shown in Figure 8). (JT – 06)

ICPS：The soil behaviour is elastic if the subloading surface is contracting (i. e. R is reducing), and is elastoplastic if the subloading surface is expanding (i. e. R is increasing). (JT – 08)

INPC：As expected, it decreases when the injection time t^* is increased: that is, it decreases with the number of nozzles and increases with the monitor withdrawal speed. (JT – 05)

IPWA：The secondary parameter, *maxExpr* , represents the maximum number of express trains that could possibly come within hTrack minutes of the first local train (i. e. the local train that departs at time 0) on any portion of the main track. (JT – 09)

ISF：Another compound move does the opposite (i. e. makes trains pass or overtake each other). (JT – 10)

NPC：Based on these observations, it is assumed that the injection process comprises the following two mechanisms: (1) the growing grout bulb is analogous to a spherical cavity expanding in the soil mass; and (2) the ground surface upheave is associated with a conical shearing failure above the grout bulb. (JT – 07)

NPCP：In this study, we assume the rebalancing operations are performed at two levels: (i) on the local level, extra bikes within a surplus zone are clustered to the zone center through local pickups (i. e. , getting ready to be shipped out), or incoming bikes to a deficit zone are evenly distributed from the zone center through local deliveries; and (ii) on the zonal level, interzonal shipments need to be made between each pair of zone centers such that the surplus and deficit of each zone can be cleared. (JT – 13)

NPP：Although other permeability profiles were examined by Wongsaroj (2005), these two profiles were the extreme cases: profile 1 is a 'simplified' permeability model case, whereas profile 2 is a more realistic 'refined' permeability model case. (JT – 08)

NSC：This choice is made to have a comparison fair: we remove two optimization components, but we allow alarge number of iterations. (JT – 15)

NSCP：The right-hand side of Eq. (1) represents two different conditions: (i) when the total supply of bikes from both companies is no greater than the total amount of demand at zone $\in N$ in time period $t \in T$, i. e. , Eq. , all the available bikes at zone i can be utilized and thus the probability can be computed as the ratio of the number of bikes deployed by company q to the total number of travelers, i. e. , Eq. ; otherwise, (ii) when the total supply of bikes is no less than the total demand, the uniformly distributed travelers at zone i would be shared by both companies, and the probability for company q to serve a certain traveler is assumed to be bounded by Eq. , which obviously also depends on the number of bikes that company -q allocates to zone i in time period t . (JT – 13)

SP：Table 1 shows a summary of the natural wear rates for each of the traffic types, it being assumed that these rates remain constant throughout the simulation, and that in mixed traffic cases there is no wear rate variation attributable to interaction between traffic types. (JT – 34)

B. 句类与语步

图 5.3.8 是四类句子与语步的关系。如图所示，在四类句子中占比最高的前三个步骤中均包含了 M2.2b，但是该步骤在这四类句子中占比排序不完全一致。在复合复杂句中 M2.2b 占比与其他两个步骤相等，但是在其他三类句子中该步骤均排在第一位。除复合句外，其他三类句子中均包含了 M2.2a，同样的，该步骤在这三类句子中占比排序也不完全一致。由于四类句子在文章中占比不同，即使相同步骤在这四类句子中排序一致，数量和占比也不相同。

这四类句子中均包含了四个语步。就各类句子包含的四个语步中步骤种类而言，简单句中包含了四个语步中所有步骤，复杂句、复合句、复合复杂句中包含的步骤种类分别占四个语步中所有步骤种类的91%、74%和53%。

总体来说，不同句子类型与步骤之间的关系存在异同，句子与步骤关系紧密度与该类句子在所有句子中的占比有关，同时也与该步骤在所有步骤中的占比有关，但是不完全成一一对应的关系，句类与步骤之间没有明显的相关性。

以下是四类句子中步骤占比最高的前三个步骤的例句。

【S】

M 2.2b：Three ANN models were constructed to account for the effect of different CTEs (1E – 5, 2E – 5, and 3E – 5) of base layer. (JT – 02)

M 2.2a：The cumulative thermal cracking growth with pavement depth was calculated using Eq. (1). (JT – 02)

M 2.3b：The most important step is the simulation of the effects of the injection of the cement mixes. (JT – 04)

【P】

M 2.2b：The computed thermal stress was one of the inputs in the ANN models, which is detailed in the next section. (JT – 02)

M 2.2a：In the FEM computation, due to the symmetry of the pavement structure and themal stress, only half of the structure was constructed, which significantly reduced the computation time. (JT – 02)

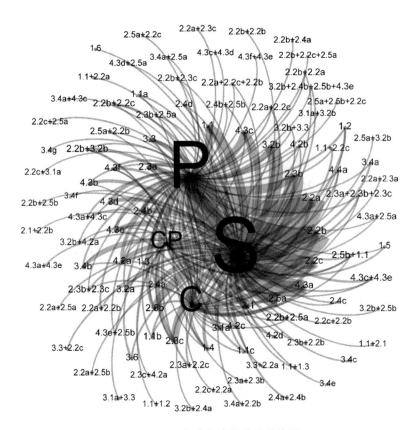

图 5.3.8 句类与步骤关系网络图

M 4. 3a： It seems clear, however, that the part just above the arch is moved upwards considerably, while movements of the adjacent zones are much smaller, as predicted by the numerical analysis. (JT – 04)

【C】

M 2. 2b： D The binary variables Y_{st} indicate the sequence of trains on the main line; they help to enforce the headway restrictions on the main line. (JT – 09)

M 2. 2c： Moreover, thin layer elements were applied to model the layer contact conditions, and a fully bounded condition was assumed in this study. (JT – 02)

M 1. 1： Thermal cracking of asphalt pavements can be simulated in some widely-used commercial FEM programs (e. g ABAQUS), and the thermally induced J-integral can also be calculated. (JT – 02)

【CP】

M 2. 2a： The back-propagation technique was adopted in the ANN models; it is a supervised learning method, in which the difference between the calculated output and target output were reduced in each backward iteration until the required performance was satisfied. (JT – 02)

M 2. 2c: The base layer modulus and asphalt layer modulus were assumed to be 600 and 4000 MPa in Fig 5 (c), respectively, and base layer thickness was shown to have much less effect compared to the asphalt layer thickness, which was mainly due to the location of the thermal crack and small base modulus compared to the asphalt layer modulus. (JT – 02)

M 2. 2b: Similarly, the value of a will depend on whether or not ' claquage' is formed and will be different from point to point. (JT – 04)

C. 句类与句长

表 5. 3. 11 是四类句子中句长占比情况。如表所示，简单句中句子长度占比最高的是单词数介于 11—20 的句子，其次是介于 21—30 的句子。复杂句和复合句占比最高的均为介于 21—30 的句子，其次均为介于 11—20 的句子，单词数介于 31— 40 的句子占比略低于介于 11—20 的句子。复合复杂句中占比最高的则是单词数介于 31— 40 和 21—30 的句子，这两类句长的句子只相差一个句子，没有显著性差异，其次是介于 41—50 的句子。就四类句子覆盖范围而言，复杂句和复合复杂句最广，复合句最小，简单句介于其间。就句子长度最大值和最小值而言，四类句子长度最大值简单句和复合句较为接近，复杂句和复合复杂句较为接近。最小值简单句最低，复杂句略高于简单句，复合句和复合复杂句相近，高于其他两类句子。

如果不排除特殊类型句子及有语法错误的句子，将每个公式算为一个单词的话，所有句子中最长的句子为带有冒号的句子，共有 170 个单词，最短的句子为简单句，共有 5 个单词。但是这个最长的句子有语法错误，在"which"前不应该使用分号，而应该改为逗号。

综上所述，四种类型句子中，复杂句和复合句长度具有较大的相似性，简单句中短句较其他三类句子占比高，复合复杂句中长句较其他三类占比略高，四类句子中简单句和复合复杂句差异最大。

以下是所有句子中最长的句子（有语法错误）及四类句子中最长和最短句子的例句。

表 5.3.11　　　　　　　　句长分布

句长范围		1—10	11—20	21—30	31—40	41—50	51—60	61—70	71—80	MAX	MIN
S	句数	240	895	505	118	25	5	*	*	59	4
	占比	13.42%	50.06%	28.24%	6.60%	1.40%	0.28%	*	*		
P	句数	12	272	462	234	82	19	10	2	77	6
	占比	1.10%	24.89%	42.27%	21.41%	7.50%	1.74%	0.91%	0.18%		
C	句数	*	61	99	48	12	1	*	*	53	11
	占比	*	27.60%	44.80%	21.72%	5.43%	0.45%	*	*		
CP	句数	1	3	32	33	16	7	*	1	75	10
	占比	1.08%	3.23%	34.41%	35.48%	17.20%	7.53%	*	1.08%		

R/ ［**Max：170**］: The J-integral was calculated with Eq. （7） in the ANN models, and the transfer functions for the output layer and hidden layers were the pure linear function and log-sigmodal functions, respectively; which are presented in Eqs （8） – （10）. Eq., where i, j and k are the subscripts for the input layer, first hidden layer and second hidden layer, respectively; m, n and q are the numbers of inputs (i. e. 9), nodes in the first hidden layer (i. e. 60) and the nodes in the second hidden layer (i. e. 60), respectively; A_0, A_{hj} and A_{hk} are the transfer functions for the output layer (i. e, pure-linear), the first hidden layer (i. e, log-sigmoid); and the second hidden layer (i. e, log-sigmoid); W_{ij}^{1h}, W_{jk}^{2h} and W_k^0 are the weight factors for the first hidden layer, the second hidden layer and the output layer; b_j^{1h}, b_k^{2h} and b_0 are the bias factors for the first hidden layer, second hidden layer and the output layer; P_i is the input variables, J is the output of J-integral. （JT – 02）

S/ ［**Max：59**］: Ceylan et al. and Ceylan demonstrated the success of ANN-based surrogate response models in computing lateral and longitudinal tensile stresses as well as deflections at the bottom of jointed concrete airfield pavements as a function of type, level, and location of an applied gear load, slab thickness, slab modulus, subgrade support, pavement temperature gradient, load-transfer efficiencies, and so on. （JT – 03）

S/ ［**Min: 4**］: Its dimension is J/m^2. （JT – 33）

P/ ［**Max: 77**］: If both points, 1 and 3, belong to the same yield curve in a (p, s) stress plane （Fig. 2 （b））, a relationship between the generic yield stress, p_o and the saturated value p_o^* can now be obtained by relating the specific volumes at points 1 and 3 through a virtual path which involves an initial unloading, at constant suction, from p_o to p_o^*, and a subsequent reduction in suction, from s to zero, at constant stress （p_o^*）. （JT – 19）

P/ ［**Min：6**］：If no solution is found, end. (JT - 28)

C/ ［**Max：53**］：The conventional procedure for assessing the likely damage, outlined for example by Mair et al. ［28］, considers the part of the building in the sagging region of the settlement trough separately from the part in the hogging region and is based on the definition of a sagging (DRs) and hogging (*DRh*) deflection ratio ［Figure 7 (a)］. (JT - 06)

C/ ［**Min：11**］：Both are the same distance and have a fixed velocity limit. (JT - 24)

CP/ ［**Max：75**］：When a stress state moves from point A at net mean stress (p) and matric suction ［$s_o(p)$］ to a new point C at suction ［$s_o(0)$］ and zero net mean stress ($p = 0$) along the yield curve under an isotropic stress state, the stress path from A to C follows the elastic stress path ABC and the change in specific volume (Δv) can be calculated based on two elastic stiffness parameters κ and κ_s as follows. (JT - 21)

CP/ ［**Min：10**］：Moves that cause cycles are recorded and not made again. (JT - 10)

（二）时态特征

A. 时态种类及组合

表 5. 3. 12 是该学科论文中使用的时态类型及组合形式。如表所示，除去片段和有语法错误的句子，该学科文章中共出现了 7 种不同时态。由不同时态构成的组合共有 17 种。不同时态组合中包含 T1 和 T3 的最多，均占所有组合的 58%，其次为 T2，占 26%，其他时态在组合中占比均较低。各种时态组合中，全部由 T1 构成的句子占比最高，其次为全部由 T3 构成的句子，第三位是由 T1 和 T3 两种不同时态构成的句子，其他相同或不同时态组合占比均较低。

以下是按照四种类型句子给出的各时态组合的例句，但是有些时态组合中不包含所有类型的句子。

表 5. 3. 12　　　　　　　　　**时态类型及组合**

时态	T1	T2	T3	T4	T7	T8	T10	T1T2	T1T2T3	T1T3	T1T3T4	T3T10
句数	2455	58	415	30	7	1	33	54	2	164	3	11
占比	72.02%	1.70%	12.17%	0.88%	0.21%	0.03%	0.97%	1.58%	0.06%	4.81%	0.09%	0.32%

时态	T1T3T10	T1T4	T1T7	T1T8	T1T10	T2T3	T2T4	T2T7	T3T4	T3T7	T3T8	T4T10
句数	4	65	21	1	70	5	1	1	1	2	2	1
占比	0.12%	1.91%	0.62%	0.03%	2.05%	0.15%	0.03%	0.03%	0.03%	0.06%	0.06%	0.03%

【T1】

S： In this study, the TDC initiation model follows an energy-based cracking initiation framework developed by Roque et al. and Dinegdae et al. (JT – 01)

P： In their approach, the transversal tensile stress is considered as the critical response to TDC, which is computed by a two-dimensional linear elastic program. (JT – 01)

C： In this model, all the materials are assumed linear elastic, and each interface is fully bonded. (JT – 01)

CP： It is common in pavement performance prediction that the exact relationships are difficult to determine among various input variables and output variable, and accurate performance using the conventional regression models cannot be achieved due to the large number of variables and potential nonlinear interactions between them. (JT – 02)

【T2】

S： ANNs have for a long time been successfully used in solving pavement engineering problems. (JT – 03)

P： However, the results of calculation have been shown to be independent of the value of such distance as well as of the parameter ξ, which has thus been fixed constant and set equal to 0. 5. (JT – 05)

C： The product of spin moment and spin creepage has not been considered in the calculations and has been assumed to be small. (JT – 35)

【T3】

S： Similar to the Pavement ME Design, regression equations were adopted in this study to predict A and n due to the use of LTPP data. (JT – 02)

P： The thermal J-integral DJ was determined to be sensitive to crack location, pavement structure, asphalt layer material properties and environmental conditions, which was computed by the FEM discussed in the next section. (JT – 02)

C： The nodal temperature was based on the surface temperature drop and the material thermal diffusivity was automatically determined. (JT – 02)

CP： The base layer modulus and asphalt layer modulus were assumed to be 600 and 4000 MPa in Fig 5 (c), respectively, and base layer thickness was shown to have much less effect compared to the asphalt layer thickness, which was mainly due to the location of the thermal crack and small base modulus compared to the asphalt layer modulus. (JT – 02)

【T4】

S： And these expertise base reinforcements will afterward supply to the agents. (JT – 32)

【T7】

S： Therefore the impact surface on the borehole face is continuously moving during treatment. (JT – 05)

CP: When the soil above the grout is being lifted, little compaction is taking place and the shear surface is being loosened (Graf 1992). (JT – 07)

【T8】

S: Above this consolidation zone (i. e. at a depth less than $20 - 25$ m below the ground surface in this case), the soil was settling as a rigid body. (JT – 08)

【T10】

S: In order to reasonably simulate the ground movements during the long-term consolidation in the field, the computed changes in pore pressure should have similar values to those observed in the field. (JT – 08)

C: The predicted swelling should occur only in a localised zone above the tunnel, and consolidation should occur at the sides of the tunnel at the tunnel axis level. (JT – 08)

【T1T2】

P: Both studies has shown that ANNs are capable of mapping complex relationships, such as those studied in complex finite element analyses, between the input parameters and the output variables for nonlinear, stress-dependent systems. (JT – 03)

C: The simplification introduced by equation (7) has been made considering the lack of data on turbulent viscosities of suspensions, and can be removed by conducting specific experimental investigations. (JT – 05)

CP: In Example 9 we have seen that theoretically there may be solutions which are locally optimal w. r. t. the smaller neighborhoods $N_{relocate}$ and N_{swap}, but that are not locally optimal w. r. t. the larger neighborhood MIN_+^2. (JT – 14)

【T1T3】

P: Both methods are found in [15, 21 – 26], which were not described here. (JT – 02)

C: A total of three ANN models for three CTEs of base layers were developed, and an example of prediction accuracy of the ANN models is shown in Fig 7. (JT – 02)

CP: The back-propagation technique was adopted in the ANN models; it is a supervised learning method, in which the difference between the calculated output and target output were reduced in each backward iteration until the required performance was satisfied. (JT – 02)

【T1T4】

P: The left contact point (red point in the figure) will gradually go down as the wheelset moves forward and the left wheel edge contacts the wing rail. (JT – 35)

C: A predetermination of the amount and distribution of α is impossible, but again it will be possible to choose appropriate values of it by back-analyzing the displacement field. (JT – 04)

CP: When the left wheel touches the crossing nose surface and separates with the wing rail, it will go up as the left wheel runs up on the slope of nose and finally becomes the contact point again. (JT – 35)

【T1T7】

P：Although the mechanisms of compaction grouting are not well understood, a basic understanding of the injection effect is developing. (JT – 07)

C：Grinding processes have many variables, including the depth of material removed, the frequency of grinding, the number of grinding stone passes in a single operation, and the rail profile the grinding is aiming to achieve. (JT – 34)

CP：The soil behaviour is elastic if the subloading surface is contracting (i. e. R is reducing), and is elastoplastic if the subloading surface is expanding (i. e. R is increasing). (JT – 08)

【T1T8】

P：Non-zero pore pressures computed at the tunnel crown extrados presented in Fig17 (c) suggest that the tunnel lining was acting as a partially permeable boundary. (JT – 08)

【T1T10】

P：The findings from the results of different permeability models emphasise that appropriate tunnel drainage conditions should be assigned for a long-term analysis. (JT – 08)

C：This deflection ratio depends on the position of the Observation Points and might not necessarily coincide with the definition used by Burland and Wroth [29] and Mair et al. [28]. (JT-06)

CP：Furthermore, because of the cement hydration, a variation of the apparent viscosity should be expected with time, but this can be neglected if the period between the preparation and the injection of the grout is relatively short. (JT – 05)

【T2T3】

P：In the present study the coefficient Λ has been evaluated by comparing equation (1) with the experimental data published by de Vleeshauwer & Maertens (2000), who measured the velocity decay along the axis of several submerged water jets expelled from a nozzle of 2.2 mm diameter. (JT – 05)

CP：To validate the BFA, energy and journey times were extracted for specific values of the variable parameters and compared to the results obtained by the STS, which have been independently validated using the analytical method described by Douglas et al. (2015). (JT – 24)

【T2T4】

P：It has been theorized by Graf (1969) that the effective radius of an individual grout point will be much larger at depth than near the surface due to the greater possible pressure. (JT – 07)

【T2T7】

P：Since the current version of the only software for analyzing rigid airfield pavements of the FAA (FEAFAA) is using isotropic linear elastic assumption of the pavement layers, the ANN models in the current study have been developed based on this assumption. (JT – 03)

【T3T4】

P：After we examined its behavior on R1 and C1, preliminary computational experiments on the rest of the problem sets indicated that this heuristic will, in general, require more vehicles than the number utilized by the other heuristics. (JT – 18)

【T3T7】

P: When the tunnel lining is acting as a partially permeable boundary, the pattern of excess pore pressures generated around the tunnel with the anisotropic model led to larger consolidation settlement above the tunnel centreline, causing the tunnel lining to squat in the long term. (JT – 08)

【T3T8】

P: Above these zones, the soil was settling as a rigid body, which resulted in continued settlement at the ground surface. (JT – 08)

C: The rail type in this curve was UIC54 (54.77 kgml), and both passenger and freight trains were running through this curve during this period. (JT – 36)

【T3T10】

P: Further investigation showed that the agreement between predictions and measurements could be further improved by reducing the value of K0 to 1.2 (Wongsaroj, 2005). (JT – 08)

C: This could then be viewed as the 'optimum' grinding frequency for that traffic type, and these individually determined grinding strategies were then applied to the mixed traffic case, and in addition, the 'optimum' for the mixed traffic case was determined. (JT – 34)

【T4T10】

P: It should be noticed that train A's driver will accelerate in order to meet its scheduled arrival time at station s1, as illustrated in Fig. 1. (JT – 28)

【T1T2T3】

P: Concerning the third hypothesis, it is recalled that the validity of Darcy's law for coarse-grained soils has been investigated by several authors (e. g. Rose, 1945, as reported by Bear, 1972; Muskat, 1946; Taylor, 1948; Scheidegger, 1957), who tried to find an upper limiting value of Reynolds number. (JT – 05)

【T1T3T4】

P: Graf (1969, 1992) indicated that, the grout material is forced into the holes under continuous pressure, and when the maximum compaction of the soil surrounding the grout bulb is achieved, the pressure available will normally cause a conical shearing of the soil above the grout bulb. (JT – 07)

【T1T3T10】

P: Since priority can only be provided once per cycle, K_i should exclude any cycle where a priority strategy was previously implemented. (JT – 31)

B. 时态与语步

图5.3.9是该学科文章中三种时态组合与语步的关系。如图所示，三种占比较高的时态组合中占比最高的前三个步骤中没有这三种类型时态组合共有的。M2.2b、M2.5a和M4.3a分别为两种类型时态组合共有，但是排序完全不同，数量和占比也不一样。此外，这三种时态组合形式中均包含了四个语步，就它们包含的步骤种类而言，T1、T3和T1T3中包含的步骤种类分别占四个语步中所有步骤种类的95%、86%和79%。

总体来说，不同时态形式的句子与语步的联系存在一定的差异，时态与步骤关系紧密度与该时态在所有句子中的占比有关，同时也与该步骤在所有步骤中的占比有关，但并不是决定性的。

以下是按照四种类型句子给出的三种时态组合中占比最高的前三个步骤的例句，但是有些步骤中不包含所有类型的句子。

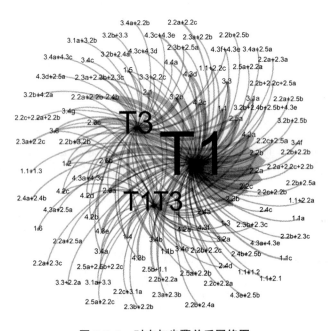

图5.3.9　时态与步骤关系网络图

【T1】

M 2.2b

S： A traction-slip relationship has thus to be used for the calculation of the torsional moment M.

（JT - 33）

P：A point mass is attached to the centre of the wheel so that the wheel has a total mass of 1025 kg. （JT - 33）

C：The second and fourth terms are primarily affected by bearing resistance and aerodynamics respectively and are predominantly not influenced by the application of a TOR friction modifier. （JT - 26）

CP：An initial damping coefficient kp of 4^*106 Ns/m is used and then reduced to a value of 53, 000 Ns/m, which is a realistic value for the primary suspension of the bogie. （JT - 33）

M 2. 2a

S：The crossing model uses the geometry of a manganese cast crossing of the standard design 760 - 1：15 for a UIC60 rail. （JT - 33）

P：This element possesses an angular frictional behavior, which is described in the following paragraphs. （JT - 33）

C：The x-axis denotes the lateral direction, y is the vertical direction and z is the longitudinal. （JT - 33）

CP：The parts of the model which are represented by explicit finite elements are dark grey and denoted by （Ia） and （Ib）. （JT - 33）

M 2. 3b

S：Tunnel installation is modelled in incremental lengths. （JT - 06）

P：To model this behaviour, grout elements are generated in the finite element mesh in horizontal planes in the locations where grout is assumed to flow. （JT - 06）

C：An increment of grout pressure $\triangle p$ is then applied; the applied grout pressure, pg1; at the end of this first increment is therefore pg1 = pg0 + $\triangle p$ [see Figure 5 （b）]. （JT - 06）

CP：If the Target Level is overshot, this analysis step is automatically discarded, and a smaller grout pressure increment is applied. （JT - 06）

【T3】

M 3. 2b

S：The cracks in the curve were measured visually （surface length）, with eddy current （depth） for small cracks （depth ＜ 2 mm） or with standard ultrasonic for larger cracks. （JT - 36）

P：It was unfortunately unknown what the exact contact environment was during the monitoring period. （JT - 36）

C：Several cracks were measured, with a real depth between 1. 5 and 7. 5 mm, but the standard ultrasonic measurements showed an average error of 5. 9 mm. （JT - 36）

M 2. 5a

S：The researchers reported a statistically significant association between the two-fluid model parameters and the two types of crash rate （rear-end and angle）. （JT - 29）

P：Cobb (1978, 1981) and Cobb and Zacks (1985) made a major step forward in resolving the problem by introducing a stochastic catastrophe model which included a stochastic noise term in the deterministic form of the catastrophe model. (JT – 29)

C：Gopalakrishnan et al. [3] mapped the solutions of nonlinear, stress-dependent finite element runs using ANNs and compared the ANN-based predictions of the flexible pavement layer moduli with the results obtained from the backcalculation programs using linear elastic assumption of the flexible pavement layers. (JT – 03)

M 4. 3a

S：The initial void ratio was kept constant. (JT – 20)

P：Above the tunnel crown the soil swelled, whereas at the sides and below the tunnel the soil consolidated. (JT – 08)

C：Soil elements adjacent to the tunnel springline extrados experienced more shearing and greater negative excess pore pressure than soil elements adjacent to the tunnel crown extrados; this was due to the initial K_0 (> 1) condition. (JT – 08)

CP：The soil porosity n was estimated to be equal to 0. 30, and the permeability coefficient k was evaluated as being variable in the range between 0. 5 and 4 cm/s by adopting the relation suggested by Hazen (1911), because direct permeability measurements were not performed. (JT – 05)

【T1T3】

M 2. 5a

P：The train resistance FX was used as an indicator of wheel-rail wear, which takes into account only the rolling resistance [13]. (JT – 35)

CP：The value for ktr was chosen according to [23] and for ctr the smallest possible value was chosen at which the vertical movement of the crossing stays in an acceptable range. (JT – 33)

M 4. 3a

P：Although, in this modelling exercise the grouting operations were able to reduce the values of deflection ratio, the control of deformations in a building was found to be a substantially more difficult task than that of controlling deformations at the ground surface when a building is absent. (JT – 06)

C：In particular the large amount of heave created and the small zone of influence of the grout injections are visible. (JT – 06)

M 2. 2b

S：The unit for the stress amplitudes was chosen to be MN m2, which influences the value of α'. (JT – 36)

P：As new capacity C'：$[n/K]$ was set, which implies that the resulting number of tours in a VR-PU solution is similar to the number of tours in a corresponding solution to the original VRP instance. (JT – 14)

（三）语态特征

A. 语态种类及组合

表 5.3.13 是该学科文章中使用的语态种类及不同语态组合及占比。如表所示，该学科文章中两种语态均有出现，同时还包含了这两种语态的组合形式。只包含 V1 的句子数量和占比最高，其次是只包含 V2 的句子，包含两种不同语态的句子数量和占比最低。所有文章中均有这三种形式的语态组合。同一种语态构成的句子中均包括了简单句、复杂句、复合句和复合复杂句这四种类型的句子。两种不同语态构成的句子中包括了除简单句以外的三种类型的句子。

以下是按照四种类型句子给出的三种语态组合中的例句，但是有些语态组合中不包含所有类型的句子。

表 5.3.13　　　　　　　　　　　语态种类及组合

语态	V1	V1V2	V2
句数	1569	724	1116
占比	46.03%	21.24%	32.74%

【V1】

S: Fig. 3 presents the flowchart of the load-related top-down cracking initiation model. (JT – 01)

P: A Grouting Strategy is a set of rules that compares the parameters derived from movements of the Observation Points [referred to as 'Settlement Control Parameters (SCPs)'] with predefined limits known as Trigger Levels and Target Levels. (JT – 06)

C: As mentioned before, these pavement responses yield different damage to pavement, and thereby need to compare against the limited strain energy of asphalt material in different modes of fracture (i. e. , Mode I and Mode II). (JT – 01)

CP: This prepares the ground for the second stage of grouting and ensures that any subsequent injections are immediately effective. (JT – 06)

【V2】

S: The description of the applied load pattern are found in Ling et al. . (JT – 02)

P: Further analyses in which buildings are included, are presented by Wisser [11]. (JT – 06)

C: Thermal cracking of asphalt pavements can be simulated in some widely-used commercial FEM programs (e. g ABAQUS), and the thermally induced J-integral can also be calculated. (JT – 02)

CP：The soil porosity n was estimated to be equal to 0. 30, and the permeability coefficient k was evaluated as being variable in the range between 0. 5 and 4 cm/s by adopting the relation suggested by Hazen (1911), because direct permeability measurements were not performed. (JT – 05)

【V1V2】

P：This is a consequence of the pressure-controlled approach that is adopted. (JT – 06)

C：ANN model predictions for critical pavement responses in each pavement foundation sublayer for both the B777 – 300ER and A380 – 800 cases were produced and compared with the FEM solutions. (JT – 03)

CP：When a stress point reaches a yield surface the stiffness is reduced (Figure 1) and those yield surfaces in contact with it follow its stress path (Figure 2). (JT – 06)

B. 语态与语步

图 5.3.10 是该学科文章中语态组合与语步的关系。如图所示，三种语态组合形式中语步占比最高的前三个步骤中均包含 M2.2a 和 M2.2b，它们在 V2 和 V1V2 中分别排在第一和第二，但是在 V1 中正好相反。虽然这两种步骤在 V2 和 V1V2 中排名一致，但由于这两种语态组合在文章中占比不同，这两个步骤的数量和占比也不同。各语态组合中占比排在第三的步骤均不相同。此外，这三种语态组合形式中均包含了四个语步。就它们包含的步骤种类数量而言，V1、V2 和 V1V2 中包含的步骤种类分别占四个语步中所有步骤种类的 98%、93% 和 81%。总体来说，语态与步骤关系紧密度与该语态在所有句子中的占比有关，同时也与该步骤在所有步骤中的占比有关。

以下是按照四种类型句子给出的三种语态组合中占比最高的前三个步骤的例句，但是有些步骤中不包含所有类型的句子。

【V1】

M 2.2b

S：The computation of maxExpr proceeds as follows. (JT – 09)

P：This latter quantity also equals the number of local trains that each express train passes during its journey. (JT – 09)

C：The binary variables Yst indicate the sequence of trains on the main line; they help to enforce the headway restrictions on the main line. (JT – 09)

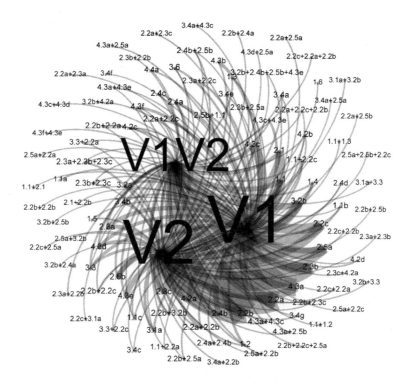

图 5.3.10 语态与步骤关系网络图

CP：Ds is the stopping（delay，dwell）time of each local train in station s，and Δ is the time when the first express train departs the origin.（JT – 09）

M 2. 2a

S：These approaches offer two fundamentally different means of modelling grout injection processes.（JT – 06）

P：In both cases，it is necessary to specify，at the start of the analysis，certain details relating to the way in which grout flows into the ground.（JT – 06）

C：This provides a specified reduction in cross-sectional area of the tunnel and is the means adopted in the analysis to prescribe the ground loss.（JT – 06）

CP：In the prescribed pressure approach，however，it may be possible to devise more detailed models to represent the way in which the grout actually flows in the ground；in this case fewer assumptions need to be made in advance by the analyst.（JT – 06）

M 4. 3a

S：The vertical displacement practically vanishes at about 2 diameters from the bulb center

(Fig. 6E). (JT – 04)

P： While the surface deformations agree very well between the three analyses outside the grouting zones, differences are noticeable above the activated grouting panels. (JT – 06)

C： With increasing distance, the effect of a grout injection on an Observation Point decreases and hence more injection steps are necessary for point 3 to meet the specified target. (JT –06)

【V2】

M 2. 2a

S： The radius of the cone rEq. at each distance x from the nozzle can be obtained by fixing vx/vx-max = ξ in equation (2). (JT – 05)

P： Once an arbitrary value of ξ is chosen, the evolution of the geometrical and mechanical characteristics of the equivalent submerged jet can be simulated by equations (3), (4) and (5) as functions of the relative kinematic viscosity N and of the injection parameters (d_0, v_0). (JT – 05)

C： Immediately out of the nozzle all the jet threads can be approximately assumed as having constant speed (v_0) and oriented along the x-direction. (JT – 05)

CP： Due to an interval ordering condition no sub interval can be inserted before position k – 1 and hence the k – 1st MOR is never removed, although it may be modified. (JT – 11)

M 2. 2b

S： According to equation (2) the velocity pattern in each cross-section is characterised by a bell-shaped surface, providing positive values of the mean velocity vx even for infinite distances r from the jet axis. (JT – 05)

P： For this purpose it is first recalled that the kinematic viscosity of a fluid is defined as the ratio between viscosity and density. (JT – 05)

C： Headways are viewed as sequence dependent setup times and are incorporated in the graph representation as additional disjunctive arc weightings. (JT – 11)

M 2. 3b

S： In such cases, the practical validity of this equation can be limited to > 30 Sror 40%. (JT – 22)

P： For the wet side of the ATL, i. e., $S_r \leqslant S_r^L$, the compression index K (S_r) for the constant degree of saturation is assumed to be a constant ksat, since Bishop's effective stress is considered to be valid. (JT – 22)

C： In the current model, the LC yield curve is defined for a certain plastic volumetric plastic strain v p and is derived from the volumetric yield surface developed through constant moisture content testing. (JT – 22)

【V1V2】

M 2.2a

P: As a consequence, part of the surrounding fluid mass is mobilised in the x-direction, while the speed of the threads located near the jet contour decreases. (JT－05)

C: Hence, the condition of spherical symmetry holds for the expansion process and the behavior could be described in terms of the spherical polar coordinates (r, θ, ω). (JT－07)

CP: When the injected fluid impacts on soils with permeability lower than gravel, grout seepage is largely inhibited and the jet threads turn back, dragging the soil aside from its initial position. (JT－05)

M 2.2b

P: It follows that the coefficient should be determined by performing specific experiments adopting various nozzle shapes. (JT－05)

C: Under such a hypothesis the resistance per unit area provided by the soil is dependent on its undrained cohesion cu, and can thus be expressed by the following relation. (JT－05)

CP: In Eqs. (9) and (10), vw L is the specific moisture volume at the nominal stress on ATL and C1, k1, C2 and k2 are assumed to be constants for a particular soil, which can be found by fitting experimental data. (JT－22)

M 2.2c

P: Punctuality at intermediate stations is not taken into account, since many railway networks penalise only delays at the terminus, as already mentioned above. (JT－28)

C: An optimisation problem is formulated and is to be solved subject to the satisfaction of the four constraints. (JT－28)

CP: Furthermore, because of the cement hydration, a variation of the apparent viscosity should be expected with time, but this can be neglected if the period between the preparation and the injection of the grout is relatively short. (JT－05)

第四节　车辆工程

车辆工程是机械工程学科一级学科下属的二级学科。该学科的实验方法主要分为建模仿真实验、台架实验以及实车实验等。其中建模仿真实验方法主要用于初步验证算法与模型，是车辆工程研究中必不可少的一环。

本研究共从该领域的 11 种国际知名期刊上选取了 20 篇建模实验类

专业学术论文，共 1539 句，33676 个单词。85% 的文章均为 2015 年后发表的，有 80% 文章的第一作者通信地址为英语国家或以英语为官方语言的国家。建模实验写作部分在文章中的占比最大值为 79%，最小值为 9%，平均值为 37%，标准差为 0.16。

一 标题特征分析

车辆工程与科学论文建模实验方法的写作一般会分成若干个平行部分，有些部分还会进一步细分，因此通常会包含不止一个一级大标题。所选的该学科文章中有四篇使用了 2 个大标题，占所选文章的 20%，其他各篇文章中均只有 1 个一级大标题。图 5.4.1 是所分析文章大标题词汇云图。如图所示，大标题中使用频率最高的是 model 这个单词，共出现了 5 次，其次是 algorithm 和 methodology，分别出现了 4 次。所选文章中有 90% 的文章使用了二级小标题，包含小标题数量最多的文章中有 11 个，最少的有 2 个。图 5.4.2 是小标题词汇云图。小标题中出现频率最高的单词也是 model，共出现了 12 次，其次是 fusion 和 data，这两个词分别出现了 7 次和 6 次。进一步分析还发现，architecture 和 development 这两个单词同时出现在了大小标题中，但是它们在大小标题中出现的频次不一样。

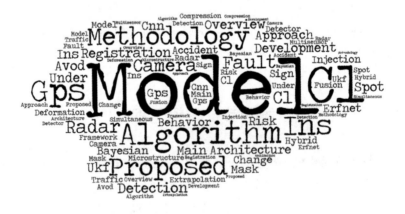

图 5.4.1　一级大标题词汇云图

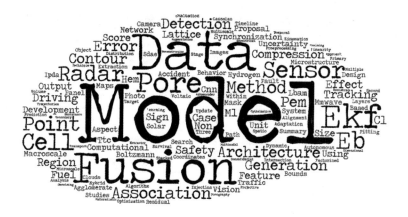

图5.4.2　二级小标题词汇云图

综上所述，该学科建模实验方法的写作均包含一级大标题，少部分文章中会有多个一级大标题。大部分文章中还包含二级小标题，不同文章中小标题数量存在差异。大小标题中会出现一些相同的单词，但是它们在大小标题中使用的频次和排名存在差异。总体来说，大标题中有些词汇与学科和实验手段关系不紧密，而小标题中词汇与建模实验所涉及的问题关系更紧密。

二　语步特征分析

本节主要分析该学科论文建模实验方法写作的语步特征。分析发现该学科建模实验内容写作的总体语步框架与本研究分析的其他四个学科一致，均可分成四个大的语步，但是该学科四个语步包含的步骤类型与其他学科存在一定的差异，本节各语步列表中只列出所分析的该学科论文中出现的步骤。

（一）语步一特征

表5.4.1是语步一中所包含的步骤种类。如表所示，该语步中共包括了5个步骤。表5.4.2是各篇文章语步一中各步骤在该语步中的占比情况。如表所示，有一篇文章中不包括语步一，其他各篇中均包含了该语步。在包含该步骤的文章中，该语步中各步骤占比情况不一。此外，

同一个步骤在不同文章中占比情况也存在差异。以下是针对每个步骤占比情况的具体分析及实例。

表 5.4.1　　　　　　　　　　语步一各步骤列表

M	语步一、问题陈述		
1.1	描述问题	1.3	问题解决难点
1.1a	章节介绍	1.4	创建新模型目的及必要性
1.2	前人研究的不足		

表 5.4.2　　　　　　　　　　语步一各步骤占比

M	1.1	1.1a	1.2	1.3	1.4
CZ－01	36%	—	—	36%	27%
CZ－02	50%	—	19%	25%	6%
CZ－03	100%	—	—	—	—
CZ－04	100%	—	—	—	—
CZ－05	80%	—	—	—	20%
CZ－06	59%	—	12%	9%	21%
CZ－07	50%	—	—	25%	25%
CZ－08	17%	—	—	17%	67%
CZ－09	—	14%	57%	—	29%
CZ－10	—	—	67%	—	33%
CZ－11	14%	—	43%	—	43%
CZ－12	67%	—	33%	—	—
CZ－13	67%	—	—	—	33%
CZ－14					
CZ－15	—	—	100%	—	—
CZ－16	—	—	100%	—	—
CZ－17	67%	—	—	25%	8%
CZ－18	—	100%	—	—	—
CZ－19	67%	—	—	33%	—
CZ－20	89%	—	11%	—	—

M 1.1 描述问题：所选文章中有 70% 的文章包含该步骤。在包含该步骤的文章中，该步骤在语步一中的占比最大值为 100%，最小值为 14%，平均值为 62%，标准差为 0.26。实例如下：

The goal of a targeted fault injector is to find situations in which $\delta > 0$, but under the injection of a fault f (which manifests as changes in the kinematic state of the EV) into the ADS stack, δdo $(f) \leqslant 0$. A solution to that problem involves speculating forward in time to after the fault has been injected, recomputing d stop under the fault, and then reevaluating the safety criteria for the EV. (CZ – 17)

Error bounds of heterogeneous sensors have different coordinate systems as stated above. Here we need to define how the fused system will behave compared to before and after the sensor fusion. (CZ – 01)

M 1.1a 章节介绍：所选文章中只有两篇包含该步骤。在这两篇文章中，该步骤在语步一中的占比分别为 100% 和 14%。实例如下：

In this Section, we describe their underlying formulas and describe how the properties of RSD can be used to cover risks in more general terms and in particular to integrate the prediction assumptions from both TH and TTC. (CZ – 18)

In this section, we introduce our efficient architecture for real-time semantic segmentation. (CZ – 09)

M 1.2 前人研究的不足：所选文章中有 45% 的文章包含该步骤。在包含该步骤的文章中，该步骤在语步一中的占比最大值为 100%，最小值为 11%，平均值为 49%，标准差为 0.33。实例如下：

3D Bounding Box Encoding：In [4], Chen et al. claim that 8 corner box encoding provides better results than the traditional axis aligned encoding previously proposed in [15]. However, an 8 corner encoding does not take into account the physical constraints of a 3D bounding box, as the top corners of the bounding box are forced to align with those at the bottom. (CZ – 16)

Originally, the Mask R-CNN selects ROIs randomly. This is done separately for foreground and background. However, when many small and large objects are present in the image at the same time the random selection introduces imbalance into the learning process. (CZ – 10)

M 1.3 问题解决难点：所选文章中有 35% 的文章包含该步骤。在包含该步骤的文章中，该步骤在语步一中的占比最大值为 36%，最小值为 9%，平均值为 24%，标准差为 0.09。实例如下：

As we argue in later sections, it is impractical (or highly difficult) to achieve the same objective using random FI. (CZ – 17)

Ideally we would like to predict the single most likely outcome, leading to a regression based approach. This does not work well as there are several distinct solutions, all of which may have some level of probability, but the average of these solutions is not another solution. (CZ – 07)

M 1.4 创建新模型目的及必要性：所选文章中有 55% 的文章包含该步骤。在包含该步骤的文章中，该步骤在语步一中的占比最大值为 67%，最小值为 6%，平均值为 28%，标准差为 0.16。实例如下：

Fusion takes advantages from both the sensors, which results in better range and angle resolutions. However, in this application, we do not solve for the elevation (height) due to the constraint of having a 1D antenna array from the mmWave radar sensor. (CZ – 01)

In this study, we characterize the three-dimensional microstructures of agglomerates of different sizes and compositions by extending this approach to incorporate the additional absorption contrast data for the local ionomer volume fraction. (CZ – 11)

综上所述，除一篇文章外，所有文章中均出现了语步一。在包含该步骤的文章中，M1.1 涉及的篇章数最高，共 14 篇，占所有文章的 70%，最低的是 M1.1a，共 2 篇，占比为 10%。各步骤涉及文章数平均值为 8.6 篇，占所有文章的 43%，标准差为 4.51。各篇文章中包含的步骤种类最多的有 4 种，占该语步中所有步骤的 80%，最低的只有 1 种，占比为 20%。各篇文章中涉及步骤种类平均值是 2.3 种，占所有步骤的 45%，标准差为 0.99。不同文章中该语步包含的步骤种类不一，同一个步骤在不同文章中的占比也有差异。各步骤平均值最高的是 M1.1，为 62%，最低的是 M1.3，为 24%，各步骤占比平均值为 44%，标准差为 17。

（二）语步二特征

表 5.4.3 是语步二中包含的步骤种类。如表所示，语步二共包括 5 个大的步骤，其中 M2.2 和 M2.3 分别包含 3 个和 4 个小的步骤，M2.4 和 M2.5 分别包含 3 个和 2 个小的步骤。该语步中共包含 13 种不同步骤。表 5.4.4 是各篇文章语步二中各步骤在该语步中占比情况。如表所示，所有文章中均包括了该语步，但是该语步中不同步骤占比情况不一，同一个步骤在不同文章中的占比情况也有所差异。以下是针对每个步骤占比情况的具体分析及实例。

表5.4.3　　　　　　　　　　　　**语步二各步骤列表**

M		语步二、模型研发	
2.1	介绍模型	2.3d	强调模型的科学性
2.2	模型及相关元素	2.4	模型预期结果
2.2a	描述公式/理论/方程/模块	2.4a	输出格式描述
2.2b	参数/变量/指标特点及关系	2.4b	运行结果
2.2c	模型假设/限制条件	2.4c	结果分析
2.3	构建模型	2.5	与前人研究的关系
2.3a	模型结构	2.5a	模型理论基础及原理
2.3b	实施步骤及最终结构	2.5b	相似之处及改进方面
2.3c	模型算法/优化		

表5.4.4　　　　　　　　　　　　**语步二各步骤占比**

M	2.1	2.2a	2.2b	2.2c	2.3a	2.3b	2.3c	2.3d	2.4a	2.4b	2.4c	2.5a	2.5b
CZ-01	5%	20%	15%	3%	1%	16%	22%	—	1%	7%	—	7%	3%
CZ-02	2%	27%	4%	3%	2%	37%	14%	—	—	—	—	3%	7%
CZ-03	5%	19%	6%	5%	1%	31%	30%	—	—	2%	—	2%	—
CZ-04	4%	22%	19%	4%	—	29%	19%	—	—	—	—	2%	—
CZ-05	—	43%	8%	21%	3%	10%	11%	—	—	—	—	2%	—
CZ-06	—	31%	25%	2%	3%	25%	—	—	3%	7%	—	2%	2%
CZ-07	3%	17%	16%	1%	20%	20%	9%	—	3%	4%	—	—	7%
CZ-08	3%	31%	11%	2%	19%	2%	7%	—	7%	—	—	7%	11%
CZ-09	—	13%	5%	—	45%	—	—	—	2%	—	—	20%	15%
CZ-10	8%	10%	3%	—	10%	31%	10%	—	4%	—	—	2%	20%
CZ-11	28%	28%	14%	17%	14%	—	—	—	—	—	—	—	—
CZ-12	19%	56%	22%	—	—	—	—	—	—	—	—	3%	—
CZ-13	—	—	44%	—	—	—	—	—	—	—	—	56%	—
CZ-14	27%	10%	47%	—	—	—	—	—	—	—	—	14%	3%
CZ-15	24%	22%	32%	—	—	—	—	—	—	—	—	12%	10%
CZ-16	3%	46%	28%	—	18%	3%	2%	—	—	—	—	—	—
CZ-17	1%	66%	12%	11%	—	—	—	—	1%	—	—	7%	2%

续表

M	2.1	2.2a	2.2b	2.2c	2.3a	2.3b	2.3c	2.3d	2.4a	2.4b	2.4c	2.5a	2.5b
CZ-18	—	71%	16%	2%	2%	5%	—	—	—	—	—	4%	—
CZ-19	3%	17%	14%	—	12%	6%	—	—	9%	23%	12%	—	3%
CZ-20	1%	10%	10%	18%	7%	8%	1%	1%	8%	19%	3%	6%	8%

M 2.1 介绍模型：所选文章中有75%的文章包含该步骤。在包含该步骤的文章中，该步骤在语步二中的占比最大值为28%，最小值为1%，平均值为10%，标准差为0.1。实例如下：

Below is the detail explanation of specific model applied in this work. (CZ-15)

Faster and Mask R-CNN are trained for the region proposal task as well as for the classification task. (CZ-10)

M 2.2a 描述公式/理论/方程/模块：所选文章中除一篇外，其他文章中均包含该步骤。在包含该步骤的文章中，该步骤在语步二中的占比最大值为71%，最小值为10%，平均值为30%，标准差为0.18。实例如下：

Typically, corrupted inputs are obtained by drawing samples from a conditional distribution p (x | ~x), for example the Gaussian white noise or salt-pepper noise. (CZ-06)

The adjacency matrix is expanded by adding an extra row and column to represent a target node in the two-dimensional tree structure. (CZ-12)

M 2.2b 参数/变量/指标特点及关系：所选文章均包含该步骤。该步骤在语步二中的占比最大值为47%，最小值为3%，平均值为18%，标准差为0.12。实例如下：

According to the microscale geometry of GDL, the time step was set to be as small as 0.001 to 1.0 microsecond per time step. (CZ-14)

Pt surfaces (subscript s) are considered active if they are in contact with ionomer. The oxygen reduction reaction (ORR) occurs at the active catalyst surfaces at a rate given by the following equation. (CZ-12)

M 2.2c 模型假设/限制条件：所选文章中有60%的文章包含该步骤。在包含该步骤的文章中，该步骤在语步二中的占比最大值为21%，最小值为1%，平均值为7%，标准差为0.07。实例如下：

Without loss of generality, we assume that there are only two vehicles in a platoon to simplify our notation. The two vehicles can have different combinations of sensors. (CZ-05)

If both sensors are presented, with a slight vertical difference in the positions of the camera and radar, shown in Fig. 1d, a fused system reconstructs the coordinate system with planes of vision and mmWave radar detections perpendicular to each other. (CZ – 01)

M 2.3a 模型结构：所选文章中有 70% 的文章包含该步骤。在包含该步骤的文章中，该步骤在语步二中的占比最大值为 45%，最小值为 1%，平均值为 11%，标准差为 0. 12。实例如下：

Loss：The loss for the MDN reconstruction is then the probability that the ground truth could be sampled from the output MDN distribution. A cross entropy loss is used for the padding output p, against the ground truth padding g. (CZ – 07)

As illustrated in Fig. 3a, the body of the agglomerate is filled by clustering the primary spherical C particles using sizes determined from the TEM data. (CZ – 11)

M 2.3b 实施步骤及最终结构：所选文章中有 65% 的文章包含该步骤。在包含该步骤的文章中，该步骤在语步二中的占比最大值为 37%，最小值为 2%，平均值为 18%，标准差为 0. 12。实例如下：

After building the geometry of the proposed simplified unit cell, three deformation modes were considered. (CZ – 20)

We partially address this issue with a pre-trained model, one learned on 1. 2 million images of ImageNet, but we also propose an additional data augmentation. (CZ – 10)

M 2.3c 模型算法/优化：所选文章中有 50% 的文章包含该步骤。在包含该步骤的文章中，该步骤在语步二中的占比最大值为 30%，最小值为 1%，平均值为 13%，标准差为 0. 08。实例如下：

Having established the association that relates a state vector to predicted observations, a key issue will be addressed in this subsection：how to determine a value of a state vector x (t) that best fits the observed data. (CZ – 04)

As there is random sampling during training, the gradients do not propagate through the sampler, but they do propagate through the recurrent layers of the RNN. (CZ – 07)

M 2.3d 强调模型的科学性：所选文章中只有一篇包含该步骤。在该篇文章中，该步骤在语步二中的占比仅为 1%。实例如下：

The number of steps used in this study is 500, which is large enough for our analytical model. (CZ – 20)

M 2.4a 输出格式描述：所选文章中有 40% 的文章包含该步骤。在包含该步骤的文章中，该步骤在语步二中的占比最大值为 9%，最小值为 1%，平均值为 5%，标准差为 0. 03。实例如下：

All these individual scores (a. k. a. local score) are then fused to compute the final decision to declare an incident as an accident. (CZ – 06)

H-net is fed with two subsequent frames stacked on the channel dimension and outputs the 9 parameters of the transformation, which are input to the spatial transformer layer ST LH, that warps Xt into X ~ tH + 1. (CZ - 08)

M 2.4b 运行结果：所选文章中有35%的文章包含该步骤。在包含该步骤的文章中，该步骤在语步二中的占比最大值为23%，最小值为1%，平均值为9%，标准差为0.08。实例如下：

The final output of this algorithm is the path from each leaf to the root, which correlates to each mode of the multimodal output. (CZ - 07)

As pressure is applied on CL, secondary pores become smaller so their contribution in total void vol- ume changes as well. (CZ - 20)

M 2.4c 结果分析：所选文章中只有两篇包含该步骤。在这两篇文章中，该步骤在语步二中的占比分别为12%和3%。实例如下：

The reason is that the deformation in larger pores are more and hence their volume reduction is more notable than that of smaller pores. If diameter of both large and small pores decreased by a same percentage, the volume of large pores would decrease more than the volume of small pores because volume is related to the third power of diameter. (CZ - 20)

The first section denotes the voltage drop caused by the sluggishness of the chemical reactions occurring at electrodes. Rely up on the operating pressure and temperature, electrode type and catalyst used, this section is relatively wide. (CZ - 19)

M 2.5a 模型理论基础及原理：所选文章中有80%的文章包含该步骤。在包含该步骤的文章中，该步骤在语步二中的占比最大值为56%，最小值为2%，平均值为9%，标准差为0.13。实例如下：

As demonstrated in [22], any 2D filter can be represented by a combination of 1D filters in the following way. (CZ - 09)

In previous work, the homogeneous CL was used to simulate the electrochemical kinetics by utilizing the macro-kinetics model. In this work, the detailed structure of the CL is introduced into this simulation, which is able to predict the local electrochemical kinetics by using the LBAM. (CZ - 15)

M 2.5b 相似之处及改进方面：所选文章中有60%的文章包含该步骤。在包含该步骤的文章中，该步骤在语步二中的占比最大值为20%，最小值为2%，平均值为7%，标准差为0.05。实例如下：

For this we use the trajectories over space-time interest points [39] and improved dense trajectories [40], [41]. (CZ - 06)

The key difference in our setup compared to other relevant work in this area is that (i) EBs are update by both sensors, and (ii) radar-camera fusion-EKF updates both vision BBox plane and radar localization BEV continuously. (CZ - 01)

综上所述，所有文章均包含 M2.2b。除一篇文章外，其他文章均包含 M2.2a。涉及文章篇数最少的为 M2.3d，只有一篇文章中包含了该步骤。各步骤涉及的篇章数平均值为 11.4 篇，占所有文章的 57%，标准差为 0.57。就各篇文章中包含的步骤种类而言，有一篇文章中包含了语步二中的所有步骤，共 13 种；最少的只包含 2 种，占所有步骤的 15%。各篇文章中包含的步骤种类平均值为 7.45 种，占所有步骤的 57%，标准差为 2.67。不同文章中该语步包含的步骤种类不一，同一个步骤在不同文章中的占比也有差异。各步骤平均值最高的是 M2.2a，为 30%，最低的是 M2.3d，仅有 1%，各步骤占比平均值为 11%，标准差为 7.37。

（三）语步三特征

表 5.4.5 是语步三中所包含的步骤种类。如表所示，语步三中共包括 4 个大的步骤，其中 M3.2 和 M3.4 分别又包含 2 个和 3 个小的步骤。该语步中共有 7 个不同步骤。表 5.4.6 是不同文章语步三中各步骤在该语步中的占比情况。如表所示，有部分文章不包括该语步。在包含该步骤的文章中，该语步中各步骤占比情况不一。此外，同一个步骤在不同文章中的占比情况也有所差异。以下是针对每个步骤占比情况的具体分析及实例。

表 5.4.5　　　　　　　　　　　语步三各步骤列表

M		语步三、模型验证或应用	
3.1a	实验所需设备/软件	3.4	数据收集及取样技术
3.2	模型运行时设置	3.4a	来源
3.2a	模型组件	3.4b	特征
3.2b	工作特征/参数	3.4c	取样技术
3.3	用于测试/评价的指标		

表 5.4.6   语步三各步骤占比

M	3.1a	3.2a	3.2b	3.3	3.4a	3.4b	3.4c
CZ – 01	100%	—	—	—	—	—	—
CZ – 02	—	—	—	100%	—	—	—
CZ – 03	100%	—	—	—	—	—	—
CZ – 04	67%	—	17%	17%	—	—	—
CZ – 05	—	—	—	—	—	—	—
CZ – 06	—	—	—	—	—	—	—
CZ – 07	—	—	—	—	—	—	—
CZ – 08	—	—	—	—	—	—	—
CZ – 09	—	—	—	—	—	—	—
CZ – 10	—	—	8%	—	81%	10%	—
CZ – 11	71%	—	—	—	—	14%	14%
CZ – 12	75%	—	—	25%	—	—	—
CZ – 13	67%	—	33%	—	—	—	—
CZ – 14	80%	—	20%	—	—	—	—
CZ – 15	100%	—	—	—	—	—	—
CZ – 16	—	—	—	—	—	—	—
CZ – 17	—	—	—	—	—	—	—
CZ – 18	—	—	—	—	—	—	—
CZ – 19	24%	6%	71%	—	—	—	—
CZ – 20	—	—	—	—	—	—	—

M 3.1a 实验所需设备/软件：所选文章中有 45% 的文章包含该步骤。在包含该步骤的文章中，该步骤在语步三中的占比最大值为 100%，最小值为 24%，平均值为 76%，标准差为 0.23。实例如下：

The radar used in our experiment can report as many as 15 pairs of range-azimuth observations with ID information at each scan. Each range-azimuth pair represents the location of a scattering center (SC). (CZ – 03)

In order to perform the calculations, STAR-HPC, a parallel solver, is used. STAR-HPC uses a domain decomposition approach to divide the computational geometry among the computational nodes. (CZ – 14)

M 3.2a 模型组件：所选文章中只有一篇包含该步骤。在该篇文章中，该步骤在语步三中的占比为6%。实例如下：

The fuel consumption is of 99. 56% and current turns to increase up to 133 Amps. (CZ – 19)

M 3.2b 工作特征/参数：所选文章中有25%的文章包含该步骤。在包含该步骤的文章中，该步骤在语步三中的占比最大值为71%，最小为8%，平均值为30%，标准差为0. 22。实例如下：

The surface tension of liquid-water was set to 0. 072 N/m, which corresponds to the surface tension of water in contact with air at 25℃. (CZ – 13)

We take 2000 regions and perform a non-maxima suppression (NMS) to eliminate duplicated ROIs. (CZ – 10)

M 3.3 用于测试/评价的指标：所选文章中有三篇包含该步骤。在这三篇文章中，该步骤在语步三中的占比分别为100%、25%和17%。实例如下：

The ellipses denote the uncertain measure of the observations. (CZ – 04)

Using the input parameters in Table I, iterations were repeated until residual (L2 norm of numerical solution) drops below 10 – 12. (CZ – 12)

M 3.4a 来源：所选文章中只有一篇包含该步骤。在该篇文章中，该步骤在语步三中的占比为81%。实例如下：

Additional synthetic traffic-sign instances are created by modifying segmented, real-world training samples. The traffic signs in the proposed dataset are annotated with tight polygons (see Figure 7), and can therefore be segmented from the training images. Two types of distortions were performed：(i) geometric/shape distortions (perspective change, changes in scale), and (ii) appearance distortions (variations in brightness and contrast). (CZ – 10)

M 3.4b 特征：所选文章中只有两篇包含该步骤。在这两篇文章中，该步骤在语步三中的占比分别为14%和10%。实例如下：

For the purpose of nano-CT imaging, the electrode sample was prepared by spraying the catalyst-ionomer ink electrode on a polytetrafluoroethylene (PTFE) sheet to achieve a loading of 0. 092 mg-Pt. cm-2. (CZ – 11)

At least two, and at most five, traffic signs were placed in a non-overlapping manner in random locations of each background image, avoiding the bottom central part where only the road is usually seen. (CZ – 10)

M 3.4c 取样技术：所选文章中只有一篇包含该步骤。在该篇文章中，该步骤在语步三中的占比为14%。实例如下：

As discussed previously, 9 the electrode sample was ion exchanged with Cs + to visualize ionomer prior to mounting on a tomography needle for nano-CT imaging. (CZ – 11)

综上所述，所分析的文章中有55%的文章包含语步三。在包含该步骤的文章中，各步骤涉及的文章数最多的是M3.1a，为9篇，占所有文章的45%，有三个步骤只涉及一篇文章，分别为M3.2a、M3.4a和M3.4c，分别占所有文章的5%。各步骤涉及篇章数平均值为3.14篇，占所有文章的16%，标准差为2.97。各篇文章中包含的步骤种类最多的文章中共有3种，占该语步中所有步骤的43%，最少的只有1种。各篇文章中涉及的步骤种类平均值为2种，占所有步骤的29%，标准差为0.89。不同文章中该语步包含的步骤种类不一，同一个步骤在不同文章中的占比也有差异。各步骤占比平均值最高的是M3.1a，为76%，最低的是M3.2a，为6%，各步骤占比平均值为38%，标准差为30.86。

（四）语步四特征

表5.4.7是语步四中所包含的步骤种类。如表所示，语步四中共包括同一个大步骤下的6个小步骤。表5.4.8是不同文章语步四中各步骤在该语步中的占比情况。如表所示，有一部分文章中不包含该语步。在包含该步骤的文章中，该语步中各步骤占比情况不一。此外，同一个步骤在不同文章中的占比情况也有所差异。以下是针对每个步骤占比情况的具体分析及实例。

表5.4.7 语步四各步骤列表

M	语步四、模型有效性验证		
4.3	有效性验证分析	4.3d	强调有效性查验的合理性
4.3a	对比实验与建模结果	4.3e	该模型的优点
4.3b	评价模型使用的评价指标	4.3f	该模型的局限性
4.3c	评价有效性检验结果		

表 5. 4. 8 　　　　　　　　　语步四各步骤占比

M	4. 3a	4. 3b	4. 3c	4. 3d	4. 3e	4. 3f
CZ – 01	—	25%	—	—	75%	—
CZ – 02	—	—	—	—	—	100%
CZ – 03	—	—	—	—	—	100%
CZ – 04	—	—	—	—	—	—
CZ – 05	—	—	—	—	—	—
CZ – 06	—	—	—	—	—	—
CZ – 07	—	—	—	—	—	—
CZ – 08	—	—	—	—	100%	—
CZ – 09	—	—	—	—	100%	—
CZ – 10	—	—	—	—	100%	—
CZ – 11	100%	—	—	—	—	—
CZ – 12	—	—	—	—	—	—
CZ – 13	—	—	—	—	—	—
CZ – 14	—	—	100%	—	—	—
CZ – 15	—	—	—	—	—	—
CZ – 16	—	—	—	—	100%	—
CZ – 17	—	—	—	—	—	—
CZ – 18	—	—	—	—	—	—
CZ – 19	—	—	—	—	—	—
CZ – 20	—	—	—	100%	—	—

M 4.3a 对比实验与建模结果：所选文章中只有一篇包含该步骤。在该篇文章中，该步骤也是该篇文章语步四中唯一一种步骤。实例如下：

The projection images were reconstructed into three-dimensional images with 12. 5-nm voxel size using TXM-Wizard. 21. Following the procedure in Ref. 22 images were acquired in both absorption and Zernike phase contrast modes without removing the sample from the tomography stage. The phase contrast mode facilitates imaging low electron density materials and resolves the secondary pore morphology and the structure of the solid electrode (C, Pt, ionomer, and primary pores), as shown in Fig. 1a. The absorption contrast relies on differences in the materials' electron density to show the high density Cs (which indicates the location of ionomer) in the electrode, as illustrated in Fig1 b. The absorption contrast image also includes contribution from the catalyst particles, but the volume of the catalyst particles is small compared to the volume of the ionomer. （CZ − 11）

M 4.3b 评价模型使用的评价指标：所选文章中只有一篇包含该步骤。在该篇文章中，该步骤在语步四中的占比为 25%。实例如下：

In the experiment, the EB of radar is measured and evaluated with RMSEs in range, Doppler and angle domains, respectively. (CZ − 01)

M 4.3c 评价有效性检验结果：所选文章中只有一篇包含该步骤。在该篇文章中，该步骤也是该篇文章语步四中唯一一种步骤。实例如下：

Therefore, the density and viscosity of the gas mixtures in the two flow channels are different and vary with location but the newly calculated values of the variables prevail throughout the time step. (CZ − 14)

M 4.3d 强调有效性查验的合理性：所选文章中只有一篇包含该步骤。在该篇文章中，该步骤也是该篇文章语步四中唯一一种步骤。实例如下：

The agglomerate size distribution obtained from this model is validated with experimental results, see the supplementary data of ref [4]. (CZ − 20)

M 4.3e 该模型的优点：所选文章中有 25% 的文章包含该步骤。在包含该步骤的文章中，该步骤在语步四中的占比最大值为 100%，最小值为 75%，平均值为 95%，标准差为 0.1。实例如下：

This module is faster (as in computation time) and has less parameters than the bottleneck design, while keeping a learning capacity and accuracy equivalent to the non-bottleneck one. (CZ − 09)

Notably, this framework requires no supervision other than the frame Xt + 1 itself, enabling the training of our model without ground-truth fields. (CZ − 08)

M 4.3f 该模型的局限性：所选文章中只有两篇包含该步骤。在该篇文章中，该步骤是这两篇文章中所包含的语步四中唯一一种步骤。实例如下：

In a particular case, when the parameter Rit is not consistent, one can use a self-tuning technique to tune the parameters online [31] which is not considered in this paper. (CZ − 02)

They are from radar and vision observations in which, although the radar range and angle could be independently distributed, the transformed x and y are not. The C point is derived from L and R points; its error could be correlated with them. (CZ − 03)

综上所述，所分析的文章中只有一半包含语步四。在包含该步骤的文章中，M4.3e 涉及的篇章数最高，有五篇，占所有文章的 25%，其次是 M4.3f，有两篇，其他几个步骤涉及文章数量均为 1

篇。各篇文章中包含的步骤种类最多为 2 种，占该语步中所有步骤的 33%，最低的仅有 1 种，占比为 17%。各篇文章中步骤种类平均值为 1.1 种，占所有步骤的 18%，标准差为 0.316。不同文章中包含的步骤存在一定的差异，同一步骤在不同文章中的占比也存在一定的差异。除 M4.3e 和 M4.3f 外，其他各步骤均涉及一篇文章，同时也是该篇文章语步四中包含的唯一一种步骤。M4.4e 在所出现的五篇文章中占比平均值为 95%，M4.3f 在所出现的两篇文章中占比均为 100%，即这两篇文章中只包含该步骤。总体来说，该学科包含语步四的文章中涉及的该语步中的步骤种类少，而且各篇文章中步骤种类差异较大。

（五）语步占比及轨迹

图 5.4.3 是所分析各篇文章中四个语步总体占比。如图所示，各篇文章中均包含了语步一和语步二，分别有 55% 和 50% 的文章包含了语步三和语步四。就各篇文章中四个语步占比而言，语步二在所有文章中的占比均远高于其他三个语步，其他三个语步在各篇文章中的总体占比均较低。

就各步骤在所有语步中占比平均值来看，占比最高的前三个步骤依次为 M2.2a、M2.2b 和 M2.3b，占比最低的分别为 M3.2a 和 M4.3e。占比最高的三个步骤涉及的篇章数也较高，占比较低的两个步骤分别只涉及一篇文章，但是占比和篇章数之间并不存在完全一一对应的关系。

就各篇文章中包含的步骤种类来看，在包含步骤种类最多的文章中有 18 种，最少的文章中有 6 种，各篇文章包含步骤种类的平均值为 11.8 种，标准差为 3.71。总体来说，各篇文章中包含的步骤种类存在一定的差异，包含的步骤种类均不高。

表 5.4.9 是所分析文章中语步组合情况。如表所示，所分析文章中共出现了 5 种语步组合。包含 3 个语步的文章占比最高，包含 2 个语步和 4 个语步的文章占比均较低。

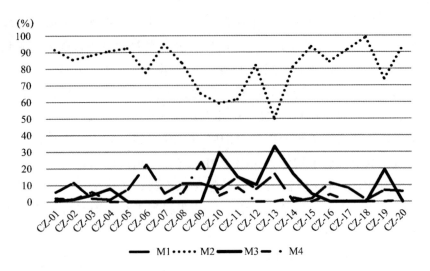

图 5.4.3　各篇文章中四个语步占比

表 5.4.9　　　　　　　　　　　　语步组合

学科	M1234	M123	M124	M234	M12
CZ – 01	√				
CZ – 02	√				
CZ – 03	√				
CZ – 04		√			
CZ – 05					√
CZ – 06					√
CZ – 07					√
CZ – 08			√		
CZ – 09			√		
CZ – 10	√				
CZ – 11	√				
CZ – 12		√			
CZ – 13		√			
CZ – 14				√	
CZ – 15		√			

续表

学科	M1234	M123	M124	M234	M12
CZ – 16			√		
CZ – 17					√
CZ – 18					√
CZ – 19		√			
CZ – 20			√		

图 5.4.4 至图 5.4.7 分别为四个语步在不同文章中的分布轨迹。如图所示，在包含四个语步的五篇文章中，语步二占比最高，分布也最广、最密集；其他三个语步中，除一篇文章中语步三占比略高，分布较集中外，其他文章中这三个语步占比均较低，分布也较分散。各篇文章中语步一分布差异较明显，以文章前部为主，但是也会分布在中间及后部。在三篇文章中语步二几乎覆盖了各部分，在另外两篇文章中分别覆盖了文章前四分之三和后四分之三的范围。语步三差异也较大，以文章前部为主，但是在一篇文章中同时分布在了文章中间及后部。语步四以前部和较后的位置为主。各篇文章中出现在最前的句子主要为语步二和语步三。各篇文章中语步二与三个语步均有交叉，其他三个语步之间也有一定交叉，特别是语步一和语步三之间。

该学科有五篇文章同时包含前三个语步，就语步占比及分布密集程度而言，语步二占比最高，分布也最广、最密集。其他两个语步占比均较低，语步一在其中两篇文章中分布较分散；除一篇文章外，语步三分布均较分散。就各语步分布轨迹而言，各篇文章中语步一分布差异较大，分别分布在文章的前部、中间及后部。在绝大部分文章中语步二从前到后几乎覆盖了文章的各部分。语步三分布主要以文章的中间及后部为主，但是也会出现在前部。在各篇文章中语步一和语步三均分布在语步二中，有两篇文章中三个语步均有交叉，在其他三篇文章中语步一和语步三没有交叉。

该学科中有四篇文章中同时包含语步一、语步二和语步四。语步二占比最高、分布最广也最密。语步一和语步四占比均较低，除一篇文章中只包含一句语步四外，其他文章中这两个语步分布均较分散。除一篇文章中最前位置为语步二，其他三篇文章中最前位置均以语步一为主。语步四分布位置以文章最后为主，语步二主要分布在语步一和语步四之间，但是在两篇文章中有一部分语步二分布在了文章的最后。三个语步均有交叉，特别是语步二与语步一和语步四之间，语步一和语步四之间交叉较少。

有一篇文章中同时包含语步二、语步三和语步四。在该篇文章中，语步二占比最高、分布最广最集中，其次是语步三，语步四占比最低，这两个语步分布相对较集中。语步三分布在文章的前部及中间位置，以前部为主。语步四也出现在了文章较前的位置，语步三和语步四均出现在了语步二中，三个语步均有交叉。

有五篇文章只包含语步一和语步二。各篇文章中语步二占比均高于语步一，分布也最广、最集中。有一篇文章中语步一只包含一个语句，该语句分布在文章中间偏后的位置。另外四篇文章中有两篇文章语步一分布较集中，主要分布在文章的最前及前部。还有两篇文章中语步一分散分布在文章的前部、中部和后部。所有文章中语步一和语步二均有交叉。

总体来说，同一学科不同文章中语步占比和分布轨迹既有相同之处，同时也存在一定的差异。该学科各篇文章中均包含了语步一和语步二，四个语步中语步二占比高于其他三个语步，该语步分布也最广，与其他三个语步均有交叉。其他三个语步分布均较分散，其中语步一以文章前部为主，也会出现在中间及偏后的位置。语步三和语步四分布位置也较灵活，以文章的前部及中间偏后的位置居多。语步四主要分布在语步三后，但是也会分布在语步三前，总体来说，这两个语步交叉的情况较少。有一半以上的文章中语步一和语步四之间有交叉，在一半的文章中语步四分布在语步一前。

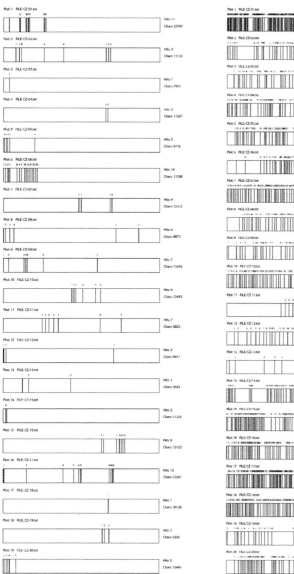

图 5.4.4 语步一分布轨迹

图 5.4.5 语步二分布轨迹

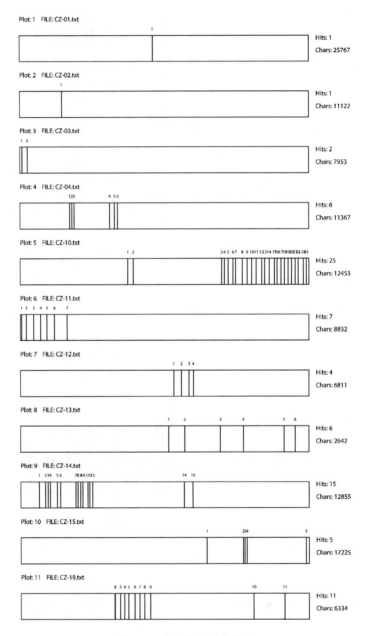

图 5.4.6　语步三分布轨迹

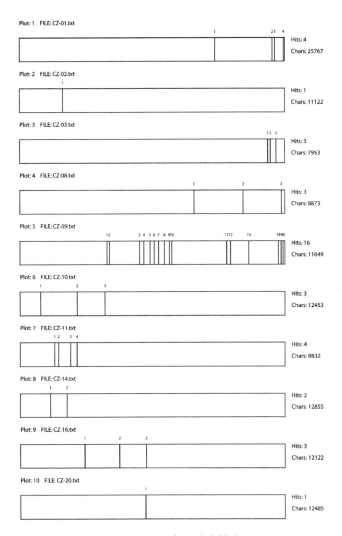

图 5.4.7　语步四分布轨迹

三　语言特征分析

（一）句子特征

表 5.4.10 是本学科文章中句子类型及占比。如表所示，简单句、复杂句、复合句及复合复杂句占所有句子的 91.24%。片段和有语法错误的句子，占所有句子的 1.04%。其他带有冒号、括号、破折号及 i.e. 的各类特殊句子占所有句子的 7.73%。

　　四类句子中简单句占比远高于其他三类句子，其次是复杂句，其他两类句子占比均较低，其中复合句占比略高于复合复杂句。特殊类型句子形式多样，有 21 种，其中占比较高的依次为 NWHS、NWS 及 NWP。以下例句为特殊类型的句子。

表 5.4.10　　　　　　　　　　　　句类及占比

句类	句数	占比	句类	句数	占比
S	851	55.30%	NSF	1	0.06%
P	391	25.41%	NSS	1	0.06%
C	118	7.67%	NWAS	7	0.45%
CP	44	2.86%	NWC	3	0.19%
BPF	3	0.19%	NWCP	2	0.13%
BSF	7	0.45%	NWHC	3	0.19%
BSS	2	0.13%	NWHP	6	0.39%
BWF	1	0.06%	NWHS	34	2.21%
IPF	1	0.06%	NWP	11	0.71%
IPS	1	0.06%	NWS	31	2.01%
ISCP	1	0.06%	PSC	1	0.06%
ISF	1	0.06%			
NCC	1	0.06%	F	4	0.26%
NSCP	1	0.06%	R	12	0.78%

BPF： In contrast to prior work [24], [30], which has reported significant SDC rates (as high as 20%) for the constituent deep-learning models (ConvNets that deal with perception: object recognition and tracking) of the ADS system, we observed that random injections rarely cause hazardous errors. (CZ – 17)

BSF： First, a shallow network provides a projective transformation embedding a motion field approximating the one of a static scene in presence of camera motion (that we refer to as homographic flow). (CZ – 08)

BSS： At t = 0 sec, RL load (opening current of the load is 0.1A) is applied by DC/DC converter with 100Vdc. (CZ – 19)

BWF： Indeed, for each pixel in X_t, two translation components u, v need to be estimated, resulting in a transformation with $2 \times h \times w$ parameters (where h , w represent the height and width of the two frames respectively) . (CZ – 08)

IPF：The equation describing proton transport can be derived with the electro-neutrality assumption, which is then reduced to Ohm's law, i. e. , divided from the 2, 000 × 2, 000 × 240 μm3 sample, which has a size of 470 × 800 × 240 μm3, as shown in Fig. 4. (CZ – 15)

IPS：The use of the 3-TBN-based-modeling formalism is based on the implicit assumptions that (a) the EV state can be completely determined by its previous state and the observed software variables, and (b) the transition parameters from one time step to another do not change with time, i. e. , the Markovian dynamic system is assumed to be homogeneous. (CZ – 17)

ISCP：These faults are masked because of the natural resilience of the ADS stack, i. e. , (a) for production ADS systems that make real-time inferences at 60 – 100 Hz, transient faults have little chance to propagate to actuators before a new system state is recalculated; (b) the ADS system architecture is inherently resilient, as it uses algorithms like extended Kalman filtering [37] (for sensor fusion) and PID control (for output smoothing) ; and (c) not all driving scenes/frames are hazardous even under faults. (CZ – 17)

ISF：The liquid-water was injected under the sample at the same locations and pressures as in the experiments (i. e. beginning at 500 Pa and increasing by 500 Pa until breakthrough pressure is reached) . (CZ – 13)

NCC：Downsampling (reducing the spatial resolution) has the drawback of reducing the pixel precision (coarser outputs) , but it also has two benefits：it lets the deeper layers gather more context (to improve classification) and it helps to reduce computation. (CZ – 09)

NSCP：This procedure can be briefly described as the following：i) the compression is applied in infinite number of steps and after each step, deformation due to a small force increment is found；ii) after each step, a new porosity is calculated based on Eq. (19) , which has been widely used in the literature to model different properties of porous media [23 – 30] ；iii) using the new porosity, a new simplified geometry is built；and iv) another force increment is applied and procedure is repeated. (CZ – 20)

NSF：Having established the association that relates a state vector to predicted observations, a key issue will be addressed in this subsection：how to determine a value of a state vector $X(t)$ that best fits the observed data. (CZ – 04)

NSS：Data association answers the question：given N observations, y_i from one or more sensors, how do we determine which observations belong together, representing observations of the same entity? (CZ – 04)

NWAS：For clarity, we further subdivide the ADS into two components：(a) an ML module (responsible for perception and planning) that takes as inputs It and Mt and produces raw-actuation commands UA, t, and (b) a PID controller [33] that is responsible for smoothing the output UA, t to produce At. (CZ – 17)

NWC：The full resolution feature extractor is shown in Fig. 3 and is comprised of two segments: an encoder and a decoder. (CZ – 16)

NWCP：Assume that the road direction of the preceding vehicle at time t_k is $\overrightarrow{\varphi}^p$ (tk); the following state constraints can be derived [27]: (equation) . (CZ – 05)

NWHC：In this model, the ionomer was considered as a spherical shell around agglomerates and its average thickness was found based on the geometry of unit cell and CL ink properties: Eq. 13 – 16. where, $A_{agglomerate}$ is the total area covered by ionomer which is the area around the agglomerate, and $t_{ionomer}$ is the thickness of ionomer covering agglomerate. (CZ – 20)

NWHP：Therefore, the unit cell size (i. e. a) can be found using Eq. (12) for different pore sizes obtained from PSD, which means unit cells in the simplified geometry have different sizes which is dependent on the sizes and volume percentage of pores in CL: Eq. , where, ξ can be found from Eq. (8) and φ can be found using Eq. (2), r_{pore} is the radius of the pore, and A_{sp} is area of the secondary pore. (CZ – 20)

NWHS：By considering an FCC arrangement for carbon particles inside the agglomerates, the following equations for agglomerate porosity ($\varepsilon_{agglomerate}$), volume of agglomerates ($V_{agglomerate}$), porosity of catalyst layer (ε_{CL}) and overlapping parameter (ξ) can be written: Eq. 3 – 9 where, V_{C-Pt} is the total volume of carbon and Pt particles in the agglomerate including the pores inside carbon particle, ε_{C-Pt} is porosity of carbon and Pt particles combined, ρ_I, ρ_{pt}, and ρ_C are the densities of ionomer, Pt and carbon particles, respectively. (CZ – 20)

NWP：In this case, the w noise matrix, which is the motion EB for the tracked model, can be expressed as: Eq. . (CZ – 01)

NWS：With all the resolutions discussed in Section III-A, the relations are below: Eq. . (CZ – 01)

PSC：This allows the network to be dynamic-it can take input and produce output of arbitrary sequence lengths. (CZ – 07)

B. 句类与语步

图 5.4.8 是四类句子与语步的关系。如图所示，M2.2a 和 M2.2b 在四类句子中占比最高的前三个步骤中分别排在第一和第二。在复合句中排在第二和第三的两个步骤占比相同。复杂句中排在第三位的是 M2.2c，简单句和复合复杂句中排在第三位的是 M2.3b。由于四种句

子在文章中占比不同，即使相同步骤在这四种句子中排序一致，数量和占比也不相同。

四种类型句子中只有复合复杂句中不包含语步三，其他三种句子均包含四个语步。就各类句子中包含的步骤数量而言，简单句、复杂句、复合句和复合复杂句中包含的步骤种类分别占所有步骤种类的91%、81%、72%和47%。

总体来说，不同句子类型与步骤之间的关系存在异同，句子与步骤关系紧密度与该类句子在所有句子中的占比有关，同时也与该步骤在所有步骤中的占比有关，但是不完全成一一对应的关系，句类与步骤之间没有明显的相关性。

以下是四类句子中步骤占比最高的前三个步骤的例句。

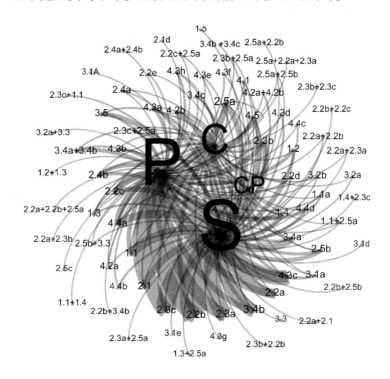

图 5.4.8　句类与步骤关系网络图

【S】

M 2. 2a: For the fused sensor system, we use a left-hand coordinate system, shown in Fig. 1a.

（CZ - 01）

M 2. 2b：z-axis is the elevation axis. （CZ - 01）

M 2. 3b：In this case, the fusion can be constructed with correlations of （u, v） and （ρ, θ, vd）. （CZ - 01）

【P】

M 2. 2a：With random error in measurement, the observation in the vehicle frame determined from o becomes a probability distribution whose extent can be characterised by the sensor's error variances. （CZ - 04）

M 2. 2b：The x-axis is the range axis which is radially away from the sensor center along the line of sight. （CZ - 01）

M 2. 2c：If both sensors are presented, with a slight vertical difference in the positions of the camera and radar, shown in Fig. 1d, a fused system reconstructs the coordinate system with planes of vision and mmWave radar detections perpendicular to each other. （CZ - 01）

【C】

M 2. 2a：In the proposed algorithm, the information fusion filter （16） - （19） is used as a basic framework and the decentralized datafusion form （20） has been applied. （CZ - 02）

M 2. 2b：The intrinsic parameters can be calibrated in the laboratory, but others have to be determined on the road. （CZ - 05）

M 2. 3b：Each patch is labeled as predefined types according to its position and normal vector; then, a grouping algorithm is used to group the small patches together to form the representation for the foreground object. （CZ - 03）

【CP】

M 2. 2a：Because the time tags for the GPS receivers on both vehicles are accurate, intervehicle communication latency has a negligible effect on the estimation accuracy, but the computing time might cause some small delay. （CZ - 05）

M 2. 2b：Measurements in the anechoicchamber are conducted and the antenna gain at 0 degrees isl0 dB compared to 0 dB at ±60 degrees for the TI mmWaveradar that we used in this study. （CZ - 01）

M 2. 3b：In what follows, we first explain the centralized information fusion and then, the decentralized information fusion is subsequently provided. （CZ - 02）

C. 句类与句长

表 5. 4. 11 是四类句子中句长占比情况。如表所示，简单句中句子长度占比最高的是单词数介于 11—20 的句子，其次是介于 21—30

的句子。复杂句和复合句占比最高的均为介于 21—30 的句子，其次均为介于 11—20 的句子，单词数介于 30—40 的句子占比略低于介于 11—20 的句子。复合复杂句中介于 21—30 和 31—40 的句子占比相同，均高于其他长度的句子，其次是介于 11—20 的句子。就四类句子覆盖范围而言，复杂句和复合复杂句略宽于其他两类句子，复合句覆盖范围最小，但是复杂句中短句占比高于复合复杂句。四类句子长度最大值简单句和复合句较接近，其中复合句略低于简单句，其次是复杂句，最长的是复合复杂句。最小值简单句最低，其次是复杂句，其他两类句子相同，均高于简单句和复杂句。

如果不排除特殊句子类型，将公式算为一个单词的话，所有句子中最长的句子为 NWHS，共有 140 个单词，最短的句子为简单句，共有 3 个单词。

综上所述，四种类型句子中，复杂句和复合句长度具有较大的相似性，简单句中短句较其他三类句子占比高，复合复杂句中长句较其他三类占比略高，四类句子中简单句和复合复杂句差异最大。

以下是所有句子中最长的 NWHS 例句及四类句子中最长和最短句子的例句。

表 5.4.11　　　　　　　　　　　句长分布

句长范围		1—10	11—20	21—30	31—40	41—50	51—60	61—70	MAX	MIN
S	句数	113	482	203	48	5	*	*	45	3
	占比	13.28%	56.64%	23.85%	5.64%	0.59%	*	*		
P	句数	4	118	162	89	16	3	*	53	9
	占比	1.02%	30.10%	41.33%	22.70%	4.08%	0.77%	*		
C	句数	*	28	66	21	3	*	*	43	14
	占比	*	23.73%	55.93%	17.80%	2.54%	*	*		
CP	句数	*	7	16	16	1	1	3	62	14
	占比	*	15.91%	36.36%	36.36%	2.27%	2.27%	6.82%		

NWHS/ [**Max：140**]：The expression for the agglomerate current is obtained as the following equations：Eq. ，where i_{agg} is the agglomerate volumetric current density，i is the current per unit volume in the CL，n is the number of electrons involved in the reaction per mole of reactant，F is the Faraday's constant，P_{O_2} is the oxygen pressure，P_{H_2} is the hydrogen pressure，H is the Henry's constant，E_r is an effectiveness factor of the spherical agglomerate，$^{\varepsilon}CL$ is the CL porosity，a_{agg} is the effective agglomerate surface area，r_{agg} or rr is the agglomerate radius，V_{agg} is the agglomerate volume，V is the total volume that agglomerate and thin-film occupy，δ is the thickness of the Nafion film，D_{O_2} is the diffusivity of the dissolved oxygen in Nafion，and D_{H_2} is the diffusivity of the dissolved hydrogen in Nafion. (CZ – 15)

S/［**Max：45**］In order to localize the accident incident, we divided the entire video into several smaller size volumes called spatiotemporal video volumes (STVVs) similar to［26］, with different scales in both space and time as well as across the modalities such as appearance, motion, and joint representations. (CZ – 06)

S/［**Min：3**］Fuse the Contour. (CZ – 03)

P/［**Max：53**］Here the mean μ_t and standard deviation σ_t are two dimensional vectors that exist over the parameters in $y_t = [x_t y_t]$ while the others are scalar, with p being the probability of this timestep being padding, π being the weight of each density in the mixture and ρ being the correlation coefficient. (CZ – 07)

P/［**Min：9**］Measure the time for which the object remains static. (CZ – 06)

C/［**Max：43**］Additionally, by giving an observation of distance (d_0) and azimuth (α_0) at frame zero, the initial EKF state vector can be set as Eq. , and its covariance is set as a diagonal matrix with relatively large variances to compensate the zero-velocity initial values. (CZ – 03)

C/［**Min：14**］The value of $\sigma_{0,i}^2$ quantifies measurement uncertainty and can be different for each TP. (CZ – 18)

CP/［**Max：62**］To accomplish that goal, DriveFI includes (a) an FI engine that can modify the software and hardware states of the ADS to simulate the occurrence of faults, and (b) an ML-based fault selection engine that can find the faults and scenes that are most likely to lead to violations of safety conditions and, hence, can be used to guide the fault injection. (CZ – 17)

CP/［**Min：14**］Therefore, as the porous CL is compressed, porosity decreases, and the material becomes stiffer. (CZ – 20)

（二）时态特征

A. 时态种类及组合

表5.4.12是该学科论文中使用的时态类型及组合形式。如表所示，除去片段和有语法错误的句子，该学科文章中共出现了7种不同时态，

其中 T8 没有单独使用，而是与其他时态共同出现在一个句子中。由不同时态构成的组合共有 11 种。不同时态组合中包含 T1 的最多，其次为 T3，分别占所有组合的 73% 和 36%，其他时态在组合中占比均较低。

只包含 T1 一种时态的句子占比最高，其次为由 T3 一种时态构成的句子，占比第三的为 T1 和 T3 两种不同时态构成的句子，其他相同或不同时态组合占比均较低。

以下是按照四种类型句子给出的三种时态组合中占比最高的前三个步骤的例句，但是有些时态组合中不包含所有类型的句子。此外，由于 T1T7T10 组合中不包含四类句子，因此只给出其所在的特殊句子。

表 5.4.12   时态类型及组合

时态	T1	T2	T3	T4	T7	T10	T1T2	T1T2T7	T1T3
句数	1271	13	117	14	5	6	10	1	38
占比	83.24%	0.85%	7.66%	0.92%	0.33%	0.39%	0.65%	0.07%	2.49%
时态	T1T3T10	T1T4	T1T7	T1T7T10	T1T10	T2T3	T3T8	T7T10	
句数	2	17	11	1	15	4	1	1	
占比	0.13%	1.11%	0.72%	0.07%	0.98%	0.26%	0.07%	0.07%	

【T1】

S： In this paper, a new fusion system for mmWave radar and camera is proposed. (CZ - 01)

P： It is a fundamental concept that is utilized in the fusion-EKF system for data association. (CZ - 01)

C： The approximation is estimated by two or more sensors' system, and the region takes advantages from the sensors' error bounds. (CZ - 01)

CP： On the other hand, when $H_k P_k H_K^T$ is much smaller than the R_k term, G is larger, and the fusion-EKF puts more weights on the current measurement. (CZ - 01)

【T2】

S： So far we have discussed the data fusion and multiple-object tracking framework for the proposed algorithm. (CZ - 02)

【T3】

S： In order to adapt it to the particular domain of TSD, we developed and implemented several domain specific improvements. (CZ - 10)

P: The original Faster R-CNN implementation performed this with a 4-step optimization process that alternated between the two tasks. (CZ – 10)

C: We modeled all changes with a Gaussian mixture model, but used a single mixture component, K = 1, for the geometry and appearance, and two mixture components, K = 2, for the scale. (CZ – 10)

【T4】

S: This will be discussed in Section Ⅲ – E. (CZ – 01)

C: Without any weighting the learning process will observe background objects more often and will focus on learning the background instead of the foreground. (CZ – 10)

【T7】

S: This process is overlying on the radar-camerafusion-EKF in Fig. 4. (CZ – 01)

【T10】

S: Additionally, from Equation (18) the H matrix should have a convertible formation to map radar detections from the state vector x to analyze y. (CZ – 01)

【T1 T2 T7】

CP: To alleviate this problem, we introduce a padding logit, to allow the network to nominate whether the vehicle has left the intersection, and the rest is padding data. (CZ – 07)

【T1 T7 T10】

ICPW: However, if the developed sensor system (i. e. , radar + CCD camera) is moving in a y-coordinate direction there must be an additional block to estimate the attitude of the sensor system and this effect should be taken into account to calculate the homography. (CZ – 02)

【T1 T3 T10】

P: This improvement is particularly important for the RPN, since regions missed at this point in the pipeline cannot be recovered later by the classification module and would lead to poor overall recall if not addressed. (CZ – 10)

【T1 T2】

P: However, if some abrupt motion or discontinued trajectories have occurred, then the possibility of a collision is high. (CZ – 06)

C: In the proposed algorithm, the information fusion filter (16) – (19) is used as a basic framework and the decentralized datafusion form (20) has been applied. (CZ – 02)

【T1 T3】

P: The reason we chose information fusion method is that it is simple in use and the optimality [26]. (CZ – 02)

C: This problem is well discussed in the previous research [32, 33] and thus, remained as a straightforward extension. (CZ – 02)

CP：Measurements in the anechoicchamber are conducted and the antenna gain at 0 degrees is 10 dB compared to 0 dB at ±60 degrees for the TI mmWaveradar that we used in this study. (CZ –01)

【T1T7】

P：The noise is typically dense when multiple targets are being detected. (CZ – 01)

C：Hence, faults are being injected into these memory units, but the variables are corrupted to emulate the faults. (CZ – 17)

CP：It represents the relative weight of the measurements compared to the current stateestimate, and is typically changing over time as the noise keeps changing throughout time. (CZ – 01)

【T1T4】

P：Here we need to define how the fused system will behave compared to before and after the sensor fusion. (CZ – 01)

C：Figure 1 outlines the block flow of the proposed system; the details of those blocks will be presented later. (CZ – 04)

CP：Beyond the work [30] that only learns homography, the novelty of the proposed algorithm is to consider a mathematical model of the uncertainty (e. g. , sensor noises) as given in (13) and reduce them by using Kalman filtering and two sources of measurements will be fused using the data fusion technique that will be explained in Section 3. 2. (CZ – 02)

【T1T10】

P：As vision data is not totally limited to one plane, blockage of some targets could exist on different range and azimuth locations. (CZ – 01)

C：The C point is derived from L and R points; its error could be correlated with them. (CZ – 03)

CP：When it comes to sensorfusion, the radial detections around corners are noisy and could lead to missed detections. (CZ – 01)

【T2T3】

C：This macroscale model has been validated with experimental data and the results were satisfactory of polarization data, water balance data, and local current mapping data. (CZ – 14)

【T3T8】

CP：In Scene 1A, the Ego vehicle (EV) was accelerating; however, target vehicle TV#1, operated by a human, initiated a lane change procedure, which decreased the safety potential delta from 20 m to 2 m as shown in "Scene 1B. " (CZ – 17)

【T7T10】

P：Large σ_i (t + s) at prediction times s $\gg$ 0 might unintentionally cover opposite lanes when a TP is turning. (CZ – 18)

B. 时态与语步

图5.4.9是该学科文章中各种时态及组合与语步的关系。如图所示，三种占比较高的时态组合中占比最高的前三个步骤均包含M2.2b，但是该步骤在这三种时态组合中排序不完全一致。T1和T1T3中均包含M2.2a，均排在第一位。其他排在前三的步骤在三种时态组合中各不相同。虽然M2.2a在T1和T1T3中均排在第一位，但由于这两种时态组合在文章中占比不同，该步骤在这两种时态组合中的数量和占比也不相同。此外，这三种时态组合形式中均包含了四个语步，就它们包含的步骤种类而言，T1、T3和T1T3中包含的步骤种类分别占四个语步中所有步骤种类的94%、56%和47%。

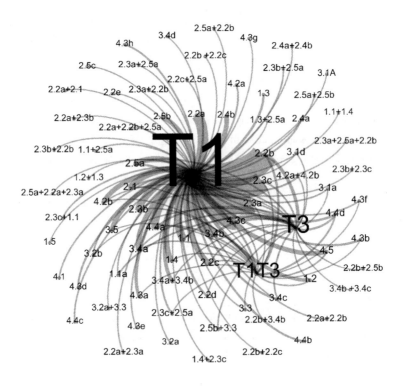

图5.4.9 时态与步骤关系网络图

总体来说，不同时态形式的句子与语步的关系存在一定的差异，时态与步骤关系紧密度与该时态在所有句子中的占比有关，同时也与该步骤在所有步骤中的占比有关，但并不是决定性的。

以下是按照四种类型句子给出的三种时态组合中占比最高的前三个步骤的例句，但是有些步骤中不包含所有类型的句子。

【T1】

M 2. 2a

S: To solve the multi-modal nature of the data, a Mixture Density Network (MDN) is used, allowing for a probabilistic output. (CZ - 07)

P: This makes this type of network ideal for time-series data, as the sequential nature of the network matches that of the sequential nature of the input data. (CZ - 07)

C: This is also true of most statistical techniques, and is usually done once during the data preprocessing step. (CZ - 07)

CP: This is a style of neural network that has a copy of the network for each time-step of the input data, and these networks are chained together to form a sequence. (CZ - 07)

M 2. 2b

S: During feedforward sampling, the final two parameters in x: v and θ can be determined via computing the magnitude and orientation of the vector between xt and xt - 1. (CZ - 07)

P: Here the mean μ_t and standard deviation σ_t are two dimensional vectors that exist over the parameters in $y_t = [x_t, y_t]$ while the others are scalar, with p being the probability of this timestep being padding, π being the weight of each density in the mixture and ρ being the correlation coefficient. (CZ - 07)

C: The values for μx and σx are determined for each element in x in the training set, and then are fixed as the first layer of the network. (CZ - 07)

CP: Thus, the input of the network is Xt, which is a track recording sample of length h, and at each time-step of the RNN the network is input with xt. (CZ - 07)

M 2. 3b

S: Then, DBSCAN [30] is run to group mixes together into several larger clusters. (CZ - 07)

P: To do this, less meaningful mixes are first ignored, where their assigned weight is less than a threshold t. (CZ - 07)

C: It groups all the possible outputs into paths, and ranks them according to their assigned probability. (CZ - 07)

CP: Afterwards, a tree can be constructed where the depth of each node is fixed to the timestep of that node, and children are assigned to the closest parent. (CZ – 07)

【T3】

M 2. 2b

S: For the operating condition, the average current density of 1. 0 A/cm^2 was applied to the re-action interface boundary. (CZ – 15)

C: In addition, we looked at typical accelerations at s = 0 plus velocity changes after s = 3 Sec. in NGSIM and fitted their standard deviations to ci. (CZ – 18)

M 2. 1

S: In this work, 3D time-dependent simulations of electrochemical kinetics and multi-physics/species transport inside porous layers for PEMFCs with the LBAM multiphase flow model were run for these GDL, MPL, and CL. (CZ – 15)

C: The MPL was assumed to be a porous region and the Darcy-Ergun equation was applied to calculate pressure drop across the medium and solve the mass transport inside the MPL. (CZ – 15)

M 3. 4a

S: Before applying geometric and appearance distortions we first normalized each traffic-sign instance. (CZ – 10)

P: For the appearance normalization, we normalized the contrast of the intensity channel in the L * a * b domain, while for the geometric normalization, we calculated the homography between the instance annotation points and a geometric template for a specific traffic-sign class. (CZ – 10)

C: We modeled all changes with a Gaussian mixture model, but used a single mixture component, K = 1, for the geometry and appearance, and two mixture components, K = 2, for the scale. (CZ – 10)

【T1T3】

M 2. 2a

P: The computational domain examined was divided from the 2, 000 × 2, 000 × 240 μm^3 sample, which has a size of 470 × 800 × 240 μm3, as shown in Fig. 4. (CZ – 15)

M 2. 2b

P: The parameter β is non-zero to promote the network to nominate the last known predicted position of a vehicle before the vehicle exited the scene. (CZ – 07)

CP: Measurements in the anechoicchamber are conducted and the antenna gain at 0 degrees is 10 dB compared to 0 dB at ± 60 degrees for the TI mmWaveradar that we used in this study. (CZ – 01)

M 2. 5b

P: Following the work of Shrivastava et al. [43], that introduced OHEM for Faster R-CNN, we replace the method for selecting regions of interest (ROIs) that are passed to the classification learning module. (CZ – 10)

C: This problem is well discussed in the previous research [32, 33] and thus, remained as a straightforward extension. (CZ – 02)

（三）语态特征

A. 语态种类及组合

表5.4.13是该学科文章中使用的语态种类及不同语态组合类型。如表所示，该学科文章中两种语态均有出现，同时还包含了这两种语态的组合形式。只包含 V1 的句子数量和占比远高于其他两种类型的句子，只包含 V2 的句子数量和占比略高于包含两种不同语态的句子数量和占比。所有文章中均包含这三种形式语态组合。同一种语态构成的句子中均包括了简单句、复杂句、复合句和复合复杂句这四种类型的句子。

以下是按照四种类型句子给出的三种语态组合中的例句，但是有些语态组合中不包含所有类型的句子。

表5.4.13　　　　　　　　　　　**语态类型及组合**

语态	V1	V1V2	V2
句数	771	251	505
占比	50.49%	16.44%	33.07%

【V1】

S: The radar used in our experiment can report as many as 15 pairs of range-azimuth observations with ID information at each scan. (CZ – 03)

P: Measure the time for which the object remains static. (CZ – 06)

C: The anomaly detection works in two steps, the first step is the automatic training of the deep features and the second step is to determine the outlier score for unknown incidents. (CZ – 06)

CP: Because the time tags for the GPS receivers on both vehicles are accurate, intervehicle communication latency has a negligible effect on the estimation accuracy, but the computing time might cause some small delay. (CZ – 05)

【V2】

S: It is composed of the blocks of initialization, prediction, data association, track update, track health monitoring, and track management. (CZ – 03)

P：Finally, the x and z values of the contour points are calculated from the centers of the patches that are located on the boundary of the group. (CZ – 03)

C：The C point is derived from L and R points; its error could be correlated with them. (CZ – 03)

CP：Many of these models are trained using a history of past movement, and then used to predict only one time-step in advance, which is then compared to ground truth to generate a loss for training. (CZ – 07)

【V1V2】

P：The contour fitting algorithm fits the line segments from a set of vision contour points such that the sum of perpendicular distances to the line (s) is minimized. (CZ – 03)

C：An MTT algorithm has been developed to estimate the locations and the velocities of the SCs, and the algorithm has the ability to dynamically maintain (create/delete) the tracked SCs by evaluating their track scores. (CZ – 03)

CP：As shown in Fig. 3 (b), we model both the host and threat vehicles as 2 – D rectangular boxes in the bird's-eye-viewing plane, and by considering the fact that only one or two sides of the threat vehicle can be seen by the cameras on the host one, we can use either one line segment or two perpendicular line segments to represent the contour. (CZ – 03)

B. 语态与语步

图 5.4.10 是该学科文章中语态组合与语步的关系。如图所示，三种语态组合形式中语步占比最高的前两个步骤完全一致，分别为 M2.2a 和 M2.2b。V1 和 V2 中排在第三的均为 M2.3b，V1V2 中还有一个步骤为 M2.2c，与该语态组合中的 M2.2b 占比相同。虽然三种语态组合中占比最高的前两个步骤相同，但由于 V1 占比远高于 V2 和 V1V2，这两个步骤在这三种语态组合中的数量和占比均不相同。此外，这三种语态组合形式中均包含了四个语步。就它们包含的步骤种类而言，V1、V2 和 V1V2 中包含的步骤种类分别占四个语步中所有步骤种类的 91%、75% 和 81%。总体来说，语态与步骤关系紧密度与该语态在所有句子中的占比有关，同时也与该步骤在所有步骤中的占比有关。

以下是按照四种类型句子给出的三种语态组合中占比最高的前三个步骤的例句，但是有些步骤中不包含所有类型的句子。

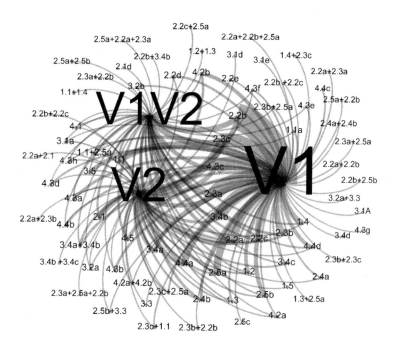

图 5.4.10 语态与步骤关系网络图

【V1】

M 2.2a

S： The faults injected into the architectural states of these processors can manifest as errors in the inputs, outputs, and internal state of the ADS modules described above (i.e., It, Mt, St, UA, t and At). (CZ – 17)

P： DriveFI can directly inject errors into ADS outputs by corrupting the variables that store ADS outputs. (CZ – 17)

C： However, TV#1 was behind another vehicle (TV#2), and the EV had no knowledge of TV#2; it was too late for the EV to recognize TV#2 and slow down in time to avoid an accident. (CZ – 17)

CP： In Scene 1A, the Ego vehicle (EV) was accelerating; however, target vehicle TV#1, operated by a human, initiated a lane change procedure, which decreased the safety potential delta from 20 m to 2 m as shown in "Scene 1B". (CZ – 17)

M 2.2b

S： The BN describes statistical relationships shown by black arrows between the variables Wt,

Mt, UA, t, and At at a time t, as well as relationships shown by red arrows between the variables over time. (CZ – 17)

P： Hence we convert time t to a discrete number k ∈ N such that t = kΔt, where Δt is the period of the sensor with the smallest sampling frequency. (CZ – 17)

C： DriveFI uses the BN to calculate the maximum likelihood estimate (MLE) 3 of the value M ^t + 1 and then uses the MLE value to calculate δ^do(f) based on the kinematic model of the AV described later in §III. (CZ – 17)

CP： It represents the relative weight of the measurements compared to the current stateestimate, and is typically changing over time as the noise keeps changing throughout time. (CZ – 01)

M 2. 3b

S： In other words, the gating performs a screen to eliminate the unlikely pairs, via heuristic knowledge or statistical hypothesis testing. (CZ – 04)

P： Given an observation oi, the first step involves querying candidate entities from the track database containing previously determined state vector (xj) of the tracks, which denote the current estimate of the entities' position, velocity and classification. (CZ – 04)

C： The anomaly detection works in two steps, the first step is the automatic training of the deep features and the second step is to determine the outlier score for unknown incidents. (CZ – 06)

CP： To alleviate this problem, we introduce a padding logit, to allow the network to nominate whether the vehicle has left the intersection, and the rest is padding data. (CZ – 07)

【V2】

M 2. 2a

S： ADS software input/output variables are ultimately stored in different levels of storage hierarchies, e. g. , registers or caches. (CZ – 17)

P： The extended notions of safety are not considered in this paper, as they can be nuanced based on the laws of the geographic regions in which they are applied. (CZ – 17)

C： Hence, faults are being injected into these memory units, but the variables are corrupted to emulate the faults. (CZ – 17)

M 2. 2b

S： The (unknown) fused observation in the vehicle frame is represented by a vector y, determined by a time invariant observation equation g (o, y) = 0. (CZ – 04)

P： At inference time, 300 proposals are used for the car class, whereas 1024 proposals are kept for pedestrians and cyclists. (CZ – 16)

C： Additionally, by giving an observation of distance (d_0) and azimuth (α_0) at frame zero, the initial EKF state vector can be set as 公式, and its covariance is set as a diagonal matrix with relatively large variances to compensate the zero-velocity initial values. (CZ – 03)

M 2.3b

S：These groups can then be assigned as nodes. （CZ – 07）

P：Finally, the x and z values of the contour points are calculated from the centers of the patches that are located on the boundary of the group. （CZ – 03）

C：Each patch is labeled as predefined types according to its position and normal vector; then, a grouping algorithm is used to group the small patches together to form the representation for the foreground object. （CZ – 03）

CP：Afterwards, a tree can be constructed where the depth of each node is fixed to the timestep of that node, and children are assigned to the closest parent. （CZ – 07）

【V1 V2】

M 2.2a

P：Those criteria form a "primal" definition of safety based on collision avoidance, which can be extended with other notions of safety, e. g., using traffic rules. （CZ – 17）

C：This is also true of most statistical techniques, and is usually done once during the data preprocessing step. （CZ – 07）

CP：This is a style of neural network that has a copy of the network for each time-step of the input data, and these networks are chained together to form a sequence. （CZ – 07）

M 2.2b

P：For easier integration into real-world data, we have chosen to implement this as the very first network layer, with weights and biases that are fixed in the model as the normalization parameters. （CZ – 07）

C：Hence, the spatial transformer layer ST LF warps Xt into $^{\sim \text{XFt}+1}$ and the reconstruction error with respect to the frame Xt +1 is minimized by means of the Charbonnier loss ［Eq. （5）］. （CZ – 08）

CP：The term $\gamma \frac{\text{tz}}{\text{d}\pi} (pw - e)$ instead, accounts for the parallax effect that is not negligible for points that do not lie on and it is directly modulated by L and suppressed by Z distances. （CZ – 08）

M 2.2c

P：Production ADSs use techniques such as those in ［34］, ［35］ to estimate vehicle and object trajectories, thereby computing dsafe whenever an actuation command is sent to the mechanical components of the vehicle. （CZ – 17）

C：As in Ref. 23, the agglomerates are identified by inscribing the largest possible spheres within the segmented phase contrast volume shown in Fig. 2b; Fig. 2c shows the size distribution of the extracted agglomerates. （CZ – 11）

CP：In our system, y-coordinate representing the vertical sensor position is fixed, and measurement noises are considered as additive terms which represent aforementioned measurement uncertainties that contains (1) signal noise and (2) measurement conversion error. (CZ – 02)

第五节　软件工程

软件工程是工科门类下属的一级学科，是一门研究用工程化方法构建和维护有效、实用和高质量的软件的学科。建模仿真是该领域主要使用的实验方法。

本研究共从 12 种软件工程与科学领域国际期刊上选取 16 篇建模实验类学术文章，用于分析的句子共 1324 句，单词数约 29606 个。所选文章中有 70% 的文章为 2010 年后发表的。除一篇文章以外，其他文章第一作者的通信地址均为英语国家或以英语为官方语言的国家。建模实验写作在论文中的篇幅总体占比最大值为 75%，最小值为 13%，平均值为 42%，标准差为 0.18。

一　标题特征分析

软件工程与科学论文中建模实验内容的写作一般会分成若干个平行部分，各部分还会进一步细分，因此通常会包含不止一个一级大标题。所分析的文章中有 30% 的文章该部分包含一个以上一级大标题，最多的有 4 个，最少的有 2 个。其他各篇文章中均只包含 1 个。图 5.5.1 为所分析文章建模实验部分大标题词汇云图。如图所示，大标题中 model 出现的频次最高，共出现过 5 次，其次是 data 和 network，均出现过 4 次。在所分析的文章中只有一篇文章中不包含二级小标题，其他文章中最多的有 12 个，最少的有 2 个。图 5.5.2 是小标题词汇云图。如图所示，在小标题中出现频率最高的词汇是 definition，共出现过 12 次，其次是 model，出现过 10 次，排在第三位的是 lemma 和 stage，它们分别均出现了 6 次。此外，对比以上两个词汇云图还可以发现，在大小标题中会出现一些相同的单词，如 learning、system、data、network。

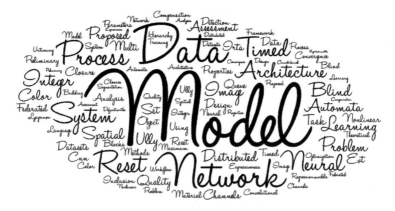

图 5.5.1　一级大标题词汇云图

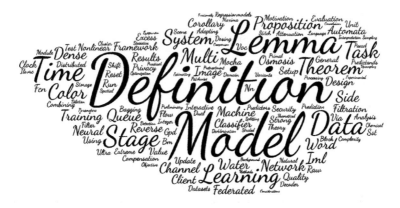

图 5.5.2　二级小标题词汇云图

　　综上所述，该学科建模实验方法的写作均包含一级大标题，部分文章中会有多个一级大标题。大部分文章中还包含二级小标题，不同文章中二级小标题数量存在差异。大小标题中会出现一些相同的单词，但是它们在大小标题中使用的频次和排名存在差异。大标题中有些词汇与学科和实验手段关系不紧密，小标题中词汇与建模实验所涉及的问题关系更紧密。

二　语步特征分析

分析发现该学科建模实验部分写作的总体语步框架与本研究分析

的其他四个学科一致，即均可分成四个大的语步，但是该学科四个语步包含的步骤类型与其他学科存在一定的差异，本节各语步列表中只列出该学科论文中出现的步骤。

（一）语步一特征

表5.5.1是语步一中所包含的步骤种类。如表所示，该语步中共包含5个步骤。表5.5.2是各篇文章语步一中各步骤在该语步中的占比情况。如表所示，有一部分文章中不包含该语步。在包含该步骤的文章中，该语步中各步骤占比情况不一。此外，同一个步骤在不同文章中的占比情况也存在差异。以下是针对每个步骤使用情况的具体分析及实例。

表5.5.1 　　　　　　　　　　　语步一各步骤列表

M	语步一、问题陈述		
1.1	描述问题	1.3	问题解决难点
1.1a	章节介绍	1.4	创建新模型目的及必要性
1.2	前人研究的不足		

表5.5.2 　　　　　　　　　　　语步一各步骤占比

M	1.1	1.1a	1.2	1.3	1.4
RJ – 01	—	—	—	—	—
RJ – 02	—	—	—	—	—
RJ – 03	—	—	—	—	—
RJ – 04	—	—	—	—	—
RJ – 05	—	—	—	—	—
RJ – 06	—	—	—	—	—
RJ – 07			100%		
RJ – 08	—	—	—	—	—
RJ – 09	—	—	—	—	100%

续表

M	1.1	1.1a	1.2	1.3	1.4
RJ－10	8%	—	—	69%	23%
RJ－11	33%	—	—	33%	33%
RJ－12	38%	—	19%	38%	6%
RJ－13	43%	29%	14%	—	14%
RJ－14	20%	—	10%	30%	40%
RJ－15	—	—	—	—	—
RJ－16	—	—	—	—	100%

M 1.1 描述问题：所选文章中有31%的文章包含该步骤。在包含该步骤的文章中，该步骤在语步一中的占比最大值为43%，最小值为8%，平均值为28%，标准差为0.13。实例如下：

After careful analysis of these images and their color channels statistics, we observed that all of them had a common characteristic: one color channel was made of large areas of zero values (see the peak in the origin in Fig. 4, where 60% of the pixels have 0 intensity, 90% of the pixels have lower than 25 intensity, and 98% of the pixels exhibit intensities below 40) or lacked scene-relevant spatial distribution of intensity. (RJ－10)

Since most vehicular applications rely on exchanging information with guaranteed low end-to-end latency (mission critical), such networks demand higher network resources. As such, our objective is to minimize the network-wide power consumption while ensuring URLLC. (RJ－12)

M 1.1a 章节介绍：所选文章中只有一篇包含该步骤。在该篇文章中，该步骤在语步一中的占比为29%。实例如下：

In this section, we suggest a general MTL framework for the federated setting, and propose a novel method, MOCHA, to handle the systems challenges of federated MTL. (RJ－13)

M 1.2 前人研究的不足：所选文章中有25%的文章包含该步骤。在包含该步骤的文章中，该步骤在语步一中的占比最大值为100%，最小值为10%，平均值为36%，标准差为0.37。实例如下：

Although COCOA can be extended directly to update W in a distributed fashion across the nodes, it cannot handle the unique systems challenges of the federated environment, such as stragglers and fault tolerance, as discussed in Section 3.4. (RJ－13)

Many segmentation architectures [2], [3], [4] share the same encoder network and they only vary in the form of their decoder network. (RJ－07)

M 1.3 问题解决难点：所选文章中有 25% 的文章包含该步骤。在包含该步骤的文章中，该步骤在语步一中的占比最大值为 69%，最小值为 30%，平均值为 43%，标准差为 0.16。实例如下：

Solving (7) which implies finding the optimal transmission control policy over time, is challenging due to two reasons. (RJ – 12)

While there are still many challenges to overcome until client-side ML becomes ubiquitous, progress is already under way: Two teams [6, 7] report on a new distributed NN model that needs much less communication than synchronized SGD. (RJ – 14)

M 1.4 创建新模型目的及必要性：所选文章中有 44% 的文章包含该步骤。在包含该步骤的文章中，该步骤在语步一中的占比最大值为 100%，最小值为 6%，平均值为 45%，标准差为 0.36。实例如下：

Our aim is to symbolically represent timed word where the time stamps of events which occur in any open interval $(i, i + 1)$ need not be distinguished. With this aim we can represent the timed word ρ over Σ by an untimed word $f(\rho)$ over $\Sigma \cup \{\delta, \sqrt{}\}$. (RJ – 16)

Therefore, new analytical tools are required to build a tractable model and to provide a distributed solution. (RJ – 12)

综上所述，只有一半的文章包含语步一。在包含该步骤的文章中，M1.4 涉及的篇章数最高，为七篇，占所有文章的 44%。M1.1a 涉及篇章数最低，只有一篇，占所有文章的 6%。各步骤涉及篇章数平均值为 4.2 篇，占所有文章的 26%，标准差为 2.17。各篇文章中包含的步骤种类最多的有 4 种，最低的只有 1 种，分别占所有步骤的 80% 和 20%。各篇文章中包含步骤种类的平均值为 2.63 种，占所有步骤的 52%，标准差为 1.41。不同文章中包含的步骤种类存在一定的差异，同一个步骤在不同文章中的占比存在一定的差异。各步骤在不同文章中占比平均值最高的是 M1.4，为 45%，最低的是 M1.1，为 28%，平均值为 36%，标准差为 7.79。

（二）语步二特征

表 5.5.3 是语步二中所包含的步骤种类。如表所示，在所分析的该学科论文中语步二共包括 5 个大的步骤，其中 M2.2 和 M2.3 分别包含 3 个小的步骤，M2.5 包含 2 个小的步骤。语步二中共有 10 种不同步骤。表 5.5.4 是各篇文章语步二中各步骤在该语步中的占比情

况。如表所示，所有文章中均包括了该语步，但是该语步中不同步骤占比情况不一，同一个步骤在不同文章中的占比情况也有所差异。以下是针对每个步骤占比情况的具体分析及实例。

表5.5.3 语步二各步骤列表

M	语步二、模型研发		
2.1	介绍模型	2.3b	实施步骤及最终结构
2.2	模型及相关元素	2.3c	模型算法/优化
2.2a	描述公式/理论/方程/模块	2.4	模型预期结果
2.2b	参数/变量/指标特点及关系	2.4b	运行结果
2.2c	模型假设/限制条件	2.5	与前人研究的关系
2.3	构建模型	2.5a	模型理论基础及原理
2.3a	模型结构	2.5b	相似之处及改进方面

表5.5.4 语步二各步骤占比

M	2.1	2.2a	2.2b	2.2c	2.3a	2.3b	2.3c	2.4b	2.5a	2.5b
RJ－01	—	—	7%	—	7%	—	85%	—	—	—
RJ－02	—	—	—	—	—	—	100%	—	—	—
RJ－03	—	—	4%	—	—	—	96%	—	—	—
RJ－04	—	—	—	—	38%	9%	53%	—	—	—
RJ－05	—	12%	—	4%	—	8%	77%	—	—	—
RJ－06	10%	10%	30%	—	—	7%	16%	13%	—	15%
RJ－07	3%	39%	19%	—	—	—	13%	—	15%	11%
RJ－08	2%	29%	5%	2%	—	16%	18%	—	17%	11%
RJ－09	4%	40%	14%	5%	—	—	5%	9%	23%	—
RJ－10	—	38%	41%	6%	—	—	—	9%	6%	—
RJ－11	9%	14%	9%	9%	18%	27%	5%	—	—	9%
RJ－12	4%	8%	13%	14%	4%	10%	31%	3%	8%	6%
RJ－13	7%	20%	14%	11%	3%	28%	6%	—	3%	8%
RJ－14	9%	—	—	4%	9%	43%	—	—	22%	13%
RJ－15	—	—	—	—	100%	—	—	—	—	—
RJ－16	—	77%	3%	—	6%	—	—	—	—	14%

M 2.1 介绍模型：所选文章中有 50% 的文章包含该步骤。在包含该步骤的文章中，该步骤在语步二中的占比最大值为 10%，最小值为 2%，平均值为 6%，标准差为 0.03。实例如下：

Our object detection system consists of three modules. The first generates category-independent region proposals. These proposals define the set of candidate detections available to our detector. The second module is a convolutional network that extracts a fixed-length feature vector from each region. The third module is a set of class-specific linear SVMs. (RJ – 06)

The spatial approach to NR IQA that we have developed can be summarized as follows. (RJ – 09)

M 2.2a 描述公式/理论/方程/模块：所选文章中有 63% 的文章包含该步骤。在包含该步骤的文章中，该步骤在语步二中的占比最大值为 77%，最小值为 8%，平均值为 29%，标准差为 0.2。实例如下：

Of the many possible transformations of our arbitrary-shaped regions, we opt for the simplest. Regardless of the size or aspect ratio of the candidate region, we warp all pixels in a tight bounding box around it to the required size. (RJ – 06)

A neural network in general consists of interconnected neurons, each acting as an independent computational element. The most common network is in the form of a multilayered perceptron with ability to approximate any continuous function (see Figure 2). (RJ – 05)

M 2.2b 参数/变量/指标特点及关系：所选文章中有 69% 的文章包含该步骤。在包含该步骤的文章中，该步骤在语步二中的占比最大值为 41%，最小值为 3%，平均值为 14%，标准差为 0.11。实例如下：

Let w be the block length (or time window) during which each VUE draws a maximum queue length sample. (RJ – 12)

With FCN-16s validation score improves to 65. 0 mean IU, and FCN-8s brings a minor improvement to 65. 5. At this point our fusion improvements have met diminishing returns, so we do not continue fusing even shallower layers. (RJ – 08)

M 2.2c 模型假设/限制条件：所选文章中有 50% 的文章包含该步骤。在包含该步骤的文章中，该步骤在语步二中的占比最大值为 14%，最小值为 2%，平均值为 7%，标准差为 0.04。实例如下：

Let formula be the dual vector history until the beginning of iteration h, and define formula. For all tasks t and all iterations h, we assume formula and formula. (RJ – 13)

Our hypothesis is that the MSCN coefficients have characteristic statistical properties that are changed by the presence of distortion, and that quantifying these changes will make it possible to predict the type of distortion affecting an image as well as its perceptual quality. (RJ – 09)

M 2.3a 模型结构：所选文章中有 50% 的文章包含该步骤。在包含该步骤的文章中，该步骤在语步二中的占比最大值为100%，最小值为3%，平均值为23%，标准差为0.31。实例如下：

> We adopted the architecture of a three-layered feedforward network with one input layer, one hidden layer, and one output layer (see Tangang et al., 1997, 1998 for details). (RJ - 01)

> This network has one receiving input layer, one broadcasting output layer, and one or more hidden (intermediate) layers in between. (RJ - 04)

M 2.3b 实施步骤及最终结构：所选文章中有50%的文章包含该步骤。在包含该步骤的文章中，该步骤在语步二中的占比最大值为43%，最小值为7%，平均值为18%，标准差为0.12。实例如下：

> We consider two regimes for batch size. In the first, gradients are accumulated over 20 images. (RJ - 08)

> In order to organize a perfect interplay of the components described above, we suggest the following sequence of interactions between the server (global sphere), client (local sphere), user (actually relevant data plus secure personal information) as well as the 'world' (all the information available on the Web or specialized online services. (RJ - 14))

M 2.3c 模型算法/优化：所选文章中有75%的文章包含该步骤。在包含该步骤的文章中，该步骤在语步二中的占比最大值为100%，最小值为5%，平均值为42%，标准差为0.36。实例如下：

> Finally, the following procedure was used to optimally select the number of hidden neurons (n_h). (RJ - 03)

> To adapt the CNN to the new task (detection) and the new domain (warped proposal windows), we continue stochastic gradient descent training of the CNN parameters using only warped region proposals. (RJ - 06)

M 2.4b 运行结果：所选文章中有25%的文章包含该步骤。在包含该步骤的文章中，该步骤在语步二中的占比最大值为13%，最小值为3%，平均值为9%，标准差为0.04。实例如下：

> The result of such sharing is that the time spent computing region proposals and features (10s/image on an NVIDIA Titan Black GPU or 53 s/image on a CPU, using TorontoNet) is amortized over all classes. (RJ - 06)

> We observed that increasing the number of scales beyond 2 did not contribute to performance much. (RJ - 09)

M 2.5a 模型理论基础及原理：所选文章中有44%的文章包含该步骤。在包含该步骤的文章中，该步骤在语步二中的占比最大值为23%，最小值为3%，平均值为13%，标准差为0.07。实例如下：

On the right in Fig. 3 is the FCN (also FCN-Basic) decoding technique. The important design element of the FCN model is dimensionality reduction step of the encoder feature maps. (RJ – 07)

Another intriguing aspect to our proposal comes from the field of ensemble learning, where Leo Breiman conceived the technique of Bagging [15] in 1994. (RJ – 14)

M 2.5b 相似之处及改进方面：所选文章中有 50% 的文章包含该步骤。在包含该步骤的文章中，该步骤在语步二中的占比最大值为 15%，最小值为 6%，平均值为 11%，标准差为 0.03。实例如下：

In our experiments, we find that in-network upsampling is fast and effective for learning dense prediction. (RJ – 08)

Most of our experiments use the Caffe [55] implementation of the CNN described by Krizhevsky et al. [8] (TorontoNet), however we have also experimented with the 16-layer deep network from Simonyan and Zisserman [24] (OxfordNet). (RJ – 06)

综上所述，所有文章均包含语步二。在该语步中 M2.3c 涉及的文章数最高，为 12 篇，占所有文章的 75%，最低的是 M2.4b，为 4 篇，占所有文章的 25%。各步骤涉及的文章数平均值为 8.4 篇，占所有文章的 53%，标准差为 2.22。各篇文章中包含的步骤种类最多的包含了该语步中所有步骤，最少的只包含 1 种步骤，占所有步骤种类的 10%。各篇文章中包含步骤种类平均值为 5.25 种，占所有步骤的 53%，标准差为 2.82。不同文章中包含的步骤种类存在一定的差异，同一个步骤在不同文章中的占比也存在一定的差异。各步骤在不同文章中的占比平均值最高的是 M2.3c，为 42%，最低的是 M2.1，为 6%，平均值为 17%，标准差为 11.31。

（三）语步三特征

表 5.5.5 是语步三中所包含的步骤种类。如表所示，语步三中共包括 7 个大的步骤，其中步骤 3.4 又包括 3 个小的步骤。语步三中共有 9 种不同步骤。表 5.5.6 是不同文章中语步三各步骤在该语步中的占比情况。如表所示，有一部分文章不包括该语步。在包含该步骤的文章中，该语步中各步骤占比情况不一。此外，同一个步骤在不同文章中的占比情况也有所差异。以下是针对每个步骤占比情况的具体分析及实例。

表 5.5.5   **语步三各步骤列表**

M	语步三、模型验证或应用		
3.1a	实验所需设备/软件	3.4	数据收集及取样技术
3.1b	介绍数据源	3.4a	来源
3.1c	模型应用流程概括	3.4b	特征
3.2	模型运行时设置	3.4c	取样技术
3.2a	模型组件	3.5	概述研究结果
3.3	用于测试/评价的指标		

表 5.5.6   **语步三各步骤占比**

M	3.1a	3.1b	3.1c	3.2a	3.3	3.4a	3.4b	3.4c	3.5
RJ－01	—	—	—	—	—	9%	35%	56%	—
RJ－02	—	—	—	—	—	20%	—	80%	—
RJ－03	—	—	—	—	—	17%	11%	72%	—
RJ－04	—	—	—	—	—	19%	48%	33%	—
RJ－05	—	—	—	—	—	13%	73%	13%	—
RJ－06	—	—	—	—	—	—	—	—	—
RJ－07	—	—	—	—	—	—	—	—	—
RJ－08	—	—	—	—	—	—	—	—	—
RJ－09	—	—	—	—	—	—	—	—	—
RJ－10	—	—	—	—	—	—	—	—	—
RJ－11	60%	—	—	—	—	—	40%	—	—
RJ－12	—	—	—	—	—	—	—	—	—
RJ－13	—	—	—	29%	71%	—	—	—	—
RJ－14	—	—	—	—	—	—	—	—	—
RJ－15	—	34%	28%	38%	—	—	—	—	—
RJ－16	79%	—	—	5%	12%	—	—	—	4%

M 3.1a 实验所需设备/软件： 所选文章中只有两篇包含该步骤。在这两篇文章中，该步骤在语步三中的占比分别为79%和60%。实例如下：

"Per iteration complexity" measures how many scalar multiplications are needed per iteration. "ε-accuracy iterations" measures how many iterations are needed to reach ε-accuracy. (RJ – 11)

Figure 2 shows timed automata based model (taken from [MRD + 08]) of a system which is a chain of n tasks working under the time triggered architecture. (RJ – 16)

M 3.1b 介绍数据源：所选文章中只有一篇包含该步骤。在该篇文章中，该步骤在语步三中的占比为 34%。实例如下：

Secured water treatment (SWaT) is a distributed control system for Reverse Osmosis (RO) water purification system comprises six stages or process connected using wired or wireless network (Fig. 1). Thus SWaT is considered as the most modern cyber physical test bed for research in the design of secure cyber physical system. (RJ – 15)

The Level 1 network comprises SCADA, Historian, HMI and an SDN controller operates periodically to query and apply policies in the PLCs to control the action of sensors if required. (RJ – 15)

M 3.1c 模型应用流程概括：所选文章中只有一篇包含该步骤。在该篇文章中，该步骤在语步三中的占比为 28%。实例如下：

Raw water processing contains dual control stations for managing sensors, actuators and their communication with I/O interfaces. Each of the six control stations were configured with six dual Programmable Logic Controllers (PLC). But each stage contains two PLCs where the primary PLC is used to monitor and secondary PLCs serves the same purpose when primary fails. The purpose of the controller at stage 1 is to manage the flow of raw water from the tank to the stage 2. The flow monitor (FIT101) checks the flow of water into the tank which is controlled by motorized valve (MV101) provided the measured value is less than 2.8. Then water is stored in the tank at stage 1, whose level is measured by the level indicator (LIT101) alerts at four levels. (RJ – 15)

M 3.2a 模型组件：所选文章中有三篇包含该步骤。在这三篇文章中，该步骤在语步三中的占比分别为 29%、38% 和 5%。实例如下：

MOCHA mitigates stragglers by enabling the t-th node to define its own θ_t^h. On every iteration h, the local updates that a node performs and sends in a clock cycle will yield a specific value for θ_t^h. (RJ – 13)

Consider the initial state of the system to be with all the analyzer indicator transmitter, pump, flow indicators, pressure indicators to be set to OFF (0) values. This module comprises various process includes pH analyzer, ORP analyzer, RO feed conductivity analyzer, RO feed pressure, RO permeate pressure, RO permeate conductivity analyzer and RO reject pressure. (RJ – 15)

M 3.3 用于测试/评价的指标：所选文章中只有两篇包含该步骤。在这两篇文章中，该步骤在语步三中的占比分别为 71% 和 12%。实例如下：

Let $A = (L1, L10, \Sigma1, C1, E1, F1)$ be a timed automaton and let $B = (L2, L20, \Sigma2, C2, E2, F2)$ be an IRTA or $\in$ -IRTA. (RJ - 16)

We define θ_t^h as a function of these factors, and assume that each node has a controller that may derive θ_t^h from the current clock cycle and statistical/systems setting. (RJ - 13)

M 3.4a 来源：所选文章中有31%的文章包含该步骤。在包含该步骤的文章中，该步骤在语步三中的占比最大值为20%，最小值为9%，平均值为16%，标准差为0.04。实例如下：

The data used in this study, covering the period from 1952 to 1992, came from the Comprehensive Ocean-Atmosphere Data Set (COADS) (Woodruff et al., 1987; 1993). The COADS monthly data were available in 2°latitude by 2°longitude grids. (RJ - 04)

The data used in this study came from two datasets: (a) the monthly SLP on 2.5° × 2.5° grids from the NCEP/National Center for Atmospheric Research (NCAR) reanalysis, (Kalnay et al., 1996; downloadable from ftp. cdc. noaa. gov/Datasets/ncep. reanalysis. derived/surface); and (b) the monthly extended reconstructed SST on 2° × 2° grids (ERSST version 2; Smith & Reynolds, 2004; downloadable from ftp. ncdc. noaa. gov/pub/data/ersst-v2). (RJ - 02)

M 3.4b 特征：所选文章中有31%的文章包含该步骤。在包含该步骤的文章中，该步骤在语步三中的占比最大值为73%，最小值为11%，平均值为41%，标准差为0.2。实例如下：

The data involves NCEP/NCAR global reanalysis products generated through assimilation and model and uses all ship and buoy SSTs and satellite derived SSTs from the NOAA Advanced Very High Resolution Radiometer (AVHRR). (RJ - 05)

The data used here extend from January 1948 to December 2005 (first set) and from January 1980, to December 2005 (second set) over the tropical Pacific Ocean (120°E - 70°W, 20°S - 20°N). (RJ - 03)

M 3.4c 取样技术：所选文章中有31%的文章包含该步骤。在包含该步骤的文章中，该步骤在语步三中的占比最大值为80%，最小值为13%，平均值为51%，标准差为0.25。实例如下：

Prior to the EEOF analysis, the SLP fields were averaged to coarser grids of 48 by 108 from the 28 3 28 COADS grids. (RJ - 01)

The data record (January 1948 - 2005) was divided into 10 equal segments. Data from one segment were withheld as validation data, while data from the other nine segments were used to train the models. (RJ - 02)

M 3.5 概述研究结果：所选文章中只有一篇包含该步骤。在该篇文章中，该步骤在语步三中的占比为4%。实例如下：

L (RMA) = $untime(L(MA))$ = $f(L(A))$. Proof. Follows from Theorems 1 and 5.

(RJ – 16)

    IRTA are closed under complementation. (RJ – 16)

    综上所述，在所分析的文章中约有56%的文章包含该语步。在包含该步骤的文章中，各步骤中涉及文章数最高的有五篇，占所有文章的31%。有三个步骤只涉及一篇文章，分别占所有文章的6%。各篇文章中包含的步骤种类最多的有4种，约占所有步骤的44%；最低的只包含2种，约占22%，平均值为2.78种，占所有步骤的31%，标准差为0.67。不同文章中包含的步骤种类存在一定的差异，同一个步骤在不同文章中的占比也存在一定的差异。各步骤在不同文章中的占比平均值最高的是 M3.1a，为70%，最低的是 M3.5，为4%，平均值为34%，标准差为19.55。

    （四）语步四特征

    表5.5.7和表5.5.8分别是语步四中各步骤列表和各步骤在不同文章中的占比情况。如表所示，语步四共涉及2个大的步骤，分为共4个不同步骤。

表5.5.7   **语步四各步骤列表**

M	语步四、模型有效性验证		
4.2	验证实验	4.3a	对比实验与建模结果
4.2a	实验条件和程序	4.3b	评价模型使用的评价指标
4.3	有效性验证分析	4.3c	评价有效性检验结果

表5.5.8   **语步四各步骤占比**

M	4.2a	4.3a	4.3b	4.3c
RJ – 01	——	——	——	——
RJ – 02	——	——	——	——
RJ – 03	——	——	——	——
RJ – 04	——	——	——	——
RJ – 05	——	——	——	——

续表

M	4.2a	4.3a	4.3b	4.3c
RJ - 06	28%	—	—	72%
RJ - 07	15%	39%	25%	21%
RJ - 08	—	—	—	—
RJ - 09	—	—	—	—
RJ - 10	—	—	—	—
RJ - 11	—	—	—	—
RJ - 12	—	—	—	—
RJ - 13	—	—	—	—
RJ - 14	—	—	—	—
RJ - 15	—	—	—	—
RJ - 16	—	—	—	—

M 4.2a 实验条件和程序：所选文章只有两篇包含该步骤。在这两篇文章中，该步骤在语步四中的占比分别为28%和15%。实例如下：

We test each architectural variant after each 1,000 iterations of optimization on the CamVid validation set until the training loss converges. (RJ - 07)

Following the PASCAL VOC best practices [3], we validated all design decisions and hyperparameters on the VOC 2007 dataset (Section 4.2). (RJ - 06)

M 4.3a 对比实验与建模结果：所选文章中只有一篇包含该步骤。在该篇文章中，该步骤在语步四中的占比为39%。实例如下：

When we compare SegNet-Basic and FCN-Basic we see that both perform equally well on this test over all the measures of accuracy. The difference is that SegNet uses less memory during inference since it only stores max-pooling indices. On the other hand FCN-Basic stores encoder feature maps in full which consumes much more memory (11 times more). SegNet-Basic has a decoder with 64 feature maps in each decoder layer. (RJ - 07)

M 4.3b 评价模型使用的评价指标：所选文章中只有一篇包含该步骤。在该篇文章中，该步骤在语步四中的占比为25%。实例如下：

We use the CamVid road scenes dataset to benchmark the performance of the decoder variants. This dataset is small, consisting of 367 training and 233 testing RGB images (day and dusk scenes) at 360 × 480 resolution. The challenge is to segment 11 classes such as road, building, cars, pedestrians, signs, poles, side-walk etc. We perform local contrast normalization [53] to the RGB input. (RJ - 07)

M 4.3c 评价有效性检验结果：所选文章只有两篇包含该步骤。在这两篇文章中，该步骤在语步四中的占比分别为72%和21%。实例如下：

Compared to their multi-feature, non-linear kernel SVM approach, we achieve a large improvement in mAP, from 35.1 percent to 53.7 percent mAP with TorontoNet and 62.9 percent with OxfordNet, while also being much faster. (RJ – 06)

In Table 1 we report the numerical results of our analysis. We also show the size of the trainable parameters and the highest resolution feature map or pooling indices storage memory, i. e., of the first layer feature maps after max-pooling and sub-sampling. We show the average time for one forward pass with our Caffe implementation, averaged over 50 measurements using a 360 × 480 input on an NVIDIA Titan GPU with cuDNN v3 acceleration. ⋯ From the Table 1, we see that bilinear interpolation based upsampling without any learning performs the worst based on all the measures of accuracy. All the other methods which either use learning for upsampling (FCN-Basic and variants) or learning decoder filters after upsampling (SegNet-Basic and its variants) perform significantly better. This emphasizes the need to learn decoders for segmentation. This is also supported by experimental evidence gathered by other authors when comparing FCN with SegNet-type decoding techniques [4]. (RJ – 07)

综上所述，在所分析的文章中只有两篇文章包含了该语步，约占所分析文章的13%。在该语步中 M4.2a 和 M4.3c 涉及两篇文章，M4.3a 和 M4.3b 分别只涉及一篇文章。就这两篇文章中包含的语步四步骤种类而言，有一篇中包含了该语步中所有步骤，另一篇中只包含2种，占所有步骤的50%。不同文章中包含的步骤种类存在一定的差异，同一步骤在不同文章中的占比也存在一定的差异。

（五）语步占比及轨迹

图5.5.3是所分析各篇文章中四个语步总体占比。如图所示，各篇文章中均包含了语步二，分别有50%、56%和13%的文章包含语步一、语步三和语步四。就各篇文章中四个语步占比而言，约有88%的文章语步二占比最高，12%的文章语步三占比最高。

就各步骤在所有语步中占比平均值来看，占比最高的前三个步骤依次为 M2.2a、M2.3c 和 M2.2b。占比最低的三个步骤依次为 M1.1a、M3.5 和 M1.2。占比最高的三个步骤涉及的篇章数也较高，占比较低的三个步骤涉及的篇章数也较少，但是步骤占比和篇章数之间并不存在完全一一对应的关系。

就各篇文章中包含的步骤种类来看，在包含步骤种类最多的文章中有 15 种不同步骤，在包含步骤最少的文章中有 3 种，各篇文章包含步骤种类的平均值为 8.5 种，标准差为 3.46。总体来说，各篇文章中包含的步骤种类存在一定的差异，包含的步骤种类均不高。

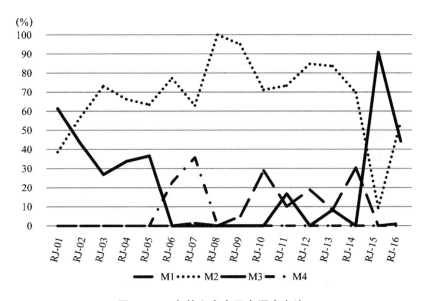

图 5.5.3　各篇文章中四个语步占比

表 5.5.9 是所分析文章中语步组合情况。如表所示，所分析的文章中共出现了六种语步组合，包含语步种类最多的文章中共有三种，占所分析文章的 25%。包含两种语步的文章占比最高，约为 69%，有一篇文章中只包含语步二一个语步。

表 5.5.9　　　　　　　　　　　　　　**语步组合**

学科	M123	M124	M23	M12	M24	M2
RJ - 01			√			
RJ - 02			√			

续表

学科	M123	M124	M23	M12	M24	M2
RJ – 03			√			
RJ – 04			√			
RJ – 05			√			
RJ – 06					√	
RJ – 07		√				
RJ – 08						√
RJ – 09				√		
RJ – 10				√		
RJ – 11	√					
RJ – 12				√		
RJ – 13	√					
RJ – 14				√		
RJ – 15			√			
RJ – 16	√					

　　图5.5.4至图5.5.7分别为四个语步在不同文章中的分布轨迹。如图所示，该学科有三篇文章只包含前三个语步，不同文章中三个语步占比及分布存在较大差异。在前两篇文章中语步二占比最高，分布也最广，语步一和语步三占比低，分布较集中。语步一主要分布在文章的前部及中间靠前的位置，语步二主要分布在文章前十分之一到文章最后，语步三主要集中在中间，文章最前偶尔也会出现语步三。其中一篇文章中三个语步均有交叉，另一篇文章中语步二分别与语步一和语步三交叉，语步一和语步三之间没有交叉。在第三篇文章中语步二和语步三占比相近，这两个语步分布也广，语步一占比低，集中分布在文章中间偏前的位置，语步一和语步三均分布在语步二中，三个语步均有交叉。

　　该学科中有一篇文章只包含语步一、语步二和语步四。语步二占比最高，语步四占比略低于语步二，语步一占比较低，三个语步分布均较集中。语步二主要集中在文章的前部，语步四主要分布在语步二后的位置，但是有少部分句子中同时包含了这两个语步，这两个语步分布存在一些交叉，语步一主要集中在前部、语步二中。

有四篇文章只包含语步一和语步二。各篇文章中语步二占比远高于语步一，分布也远比语步一广。在三篇文章中，语步一均集中分布在语步二前，两个语步之间没有交叉。在另一篇文章中，语步一从最前往后分散分布在四处，有三次分布在语步二中。

有六篇文章只包含语步二和语步三。其中四篇文章中语步二占比和分布均高于语步三，另外两篇文章中情况相反。所有文章中两个语步分布均较集中。除一篇文章外，其他五篇文章中语步二大部分语句均集中分布在语步三后，但是其中有一篇文章中有少量语步二分布在文章较前的位置、语步三中。还有一篇文章第一和第二句均为语步

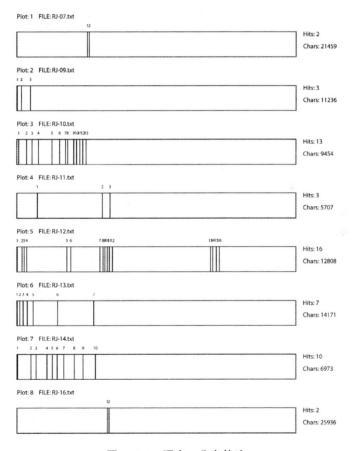

图 5.5.4　语步一分布轨迹

二。在其他三篇文章中两个语步之间没有交叉。除去这五篇，另一篇文章中语步二集中分布在语步三中、文章中间偏后的位置。

有一篇文章中只包含语步二和语步四。该篇文章中语步二占比较语步四高，分布也较语步四广。两个语步分布均较集中，语步二全部分布在语步四前，两个语步没有交叉。

图 5.5.5　语步二分布轨迹

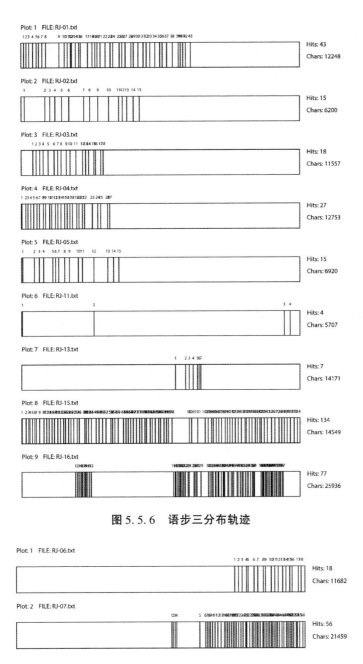

图5.5.6 语步三分布轨迹

图5.5.7 语步四分布轨迹

总体来说，同一学科不同文章中语步占比和分布轨迹既有相同之处，同时也存在一定的差异。该学科四个语步中，除一篇文章外，语步二占比均高于其他三个语步，该语步分布也最广。大部分文章中语步一分布以文章的前部、语步二之前为主，同时，语步一中少部分语句也会出现在语步二中。语步三占比总体上略高于语步一，分布也较语步一广且较集中，分布主要以文章前部为主，语步二之前，在个别文章中语步三也会分布在中间偏后或较后的位置。语步四分布均较集中，主要分布在文章最后的位置。语步二与其他三个语步在一定程度上均有交叉，特别是与语步一。

三　语言特征分析

本小节主要分析所选学科论文建模实验写作中使用到的语言特征。主要从句子结构、时态和语态三个大的方面进行分析。针对句子结构的分析主要包含句子类型、四类主要句子长度分布及句子类型与语步之间的关系。针对时态的分析主要包含时态种类、不同时态组合及时态与语步的关系。针对语态的分析主要包含语态种类、不同语态组合及语态与语步的关系。

（一）句子特征

表5.5.10是选取的本学科文章中所包含的句子类型及各类句子占比。如表所示，简单句、复杂句、复合句及复合复杂句占所有句子的89.57%。片段和有语法错误的句子占所有句子的2.26%。其他带有冒号、括号及i.e.的各类特殊句子占所有句子的8.16%。四类句子中简单句占比远高于其他三类句子，其次是复杂句，其他两类句子占比均较低，其中复合句占比略高于复合复杂句。特殊类型句子形式多样，共23种，其中占比较高的依次为NWHS、NWS、NWHP和NWP。以下例句为特殊类型的句子。

表5.5.10　　　　　　　　　　句类及占比

句类	句数	占比	句类	句数	占比
S	649	49.02%	NWP	8	0.60%
P	393	29.68%	NSS	1	0.08%
C	100	7.55%	NWS	21	1.59%
CP	44	3.32%	BCPS	1	0.08%
NPCP	1	0.08%	BCS	2	0.15%
NPCBP	1	0.08%	BPF	3	0.23%
NSC	3	0.23%	BPS	3	0.23%
NSCP	1	0.08%	BSISW	1	0.08%
NSIWS	1	0.08%	BSS	3	0.23%
NWAS	3	0.23%	IPS	1	0.08%
NWBSS	1	0.08%	ISC	1	0.08%
NWC	1	0.08%	ISP	1	0.08%
NWHP	9	0.68%	ISS	5	0.38%
NWHS	36	2.72%			
F	24	1.81%	R	6	0.45%

NPCP: Now that we have observed that the most challenging cases are characterized by the extinction of one color, due to attenuation or selective lighting spectrum, we better understand why conventional dehazing methods generally fail in those cases: the unbalanced attenuation induces color shifting; the dark channel prior, which associates a small minimal color value to a good transmission, systematically fails in estimating the transmission; and conventional enhancement methods, which attempt to reconstruct a pleasant image by resorting to some kind of histogram stretching (often guided by the inversion of an approximated light transmission model) for each channel, tend to amplify noise when the information is missing in one channel. (RJ－10)

NPCBP: After careful analysis of these images and their color channels statistics, we observed that all of them had a common characteristic: one color channel was made of large areas of zero values (see the peak in the origin in Fig. 4, where 60% of the pixels have 0 intensity, 90% of the pixels have lower than 25 intensity, and 98% of the pixels exhibit intensities below 40) or lacked scene-relevant spatial distribution of intensity. (RJ－10)

NSC: Simply decreasing subsampling within a net is a tradeoff: the filters see finer information, but have smaller receptive fields and take longer to compute. (RJ－08)

NSCP: Despite its effectiveness for underwater scenes, Equation 3 has two main limitations: first, if the red channel is entirely attenuated, then, based on Equation 3, the green channel values are transferred entirely to the red channel and will give the restored scene unwanted yellowish appearance. (RJ - 10)

NSIWS: There are two potential problems in nonlinear optimization: (a) local minima, i. e the optimization often terminates at a local (nonglobal) minimum of the cost function; (b) overfitting, i. e. the trained model fits to the noise in the training data. (RJ - 02)

NWAS: Examples include: objectness [51], selective search [21], category-independent object proposals [52], constrained parametric min-cuts (CPMC) [22], multi-scale combinatorial grouping [35], and Cire, san et al. [53], who detect mitotic cells by applying a CNN to regularly-spaced square crops, which are a special case of region proposals. (RJ - 06)

NWBSS: This loss of information is either the consequence of the illumination characteristics (some range of wavelengths is missing from the light spectrum) or due to the characteristics of the medium: selective attenuation, scattering phenomena (Rayleigh).

NWC: In the NN approach to nonlinear regression, nonlinear *adaptive* basis functions h_j (also called hidden neurons) ($j = 1, \cdots, n_h$) are introduced, so the linear regression is between y and h_j: Eq. (2) with typically Eq. (3). (RJ - 03)

NWHP: In either scenario, the m agents are connected through a communication network, which is modeled by an undirected graph: Eq. , where Eq. is the vertex set and Eq. is the edge set. (RJ - 11)

NWHS: The EOFs were calculated from the covariance matrix: Eq. (1) where su and sl are the zonal and meridional components of the wind stress anomaly respectively. (RJ - 04)

NWP: Interestingly, Equation 2 appears to be an extension, but also an elegant formulation, of the red channel compensation introduced by Ancuti et al. in [12], where the compensated red channel Ic r at every pixel location (x) has been defined as: Eq. , with Ir, Ig being the red and green color channels of the initial image I, each channel being in the range [0, 1], after normalization by the upper limits of their dynamic ranges; and Ir and Ig denoting the average of those channels over the whole image. (RJ - 10)

NSS: This turns a line topology into a DAG: edges skip ahead from shallower to deeper layers. (RJ - 08)

NWS: This functional form is maintained under composition, with kernel size and stride obeying the transformation rule: Eq. . (RJ - 08)

BCPS: Determining the crop that results in exact correspondence can be intricate, but it follows automatically from the network definition (and we include code for it in Caffe). (RJ - 08)

BCS: However, structure between models frequently exists (e. g. , people may behave similarly when using their phones), and modeling these relationships via multi-task learning is a natural strategy to improve performance and boost the effective sample size for each node [10, 2, 5]. (RJ – 13)

BPF: However, in underwater, since the attenuation is much higher and selective (in terms of wavelength), it becomes relevant to increase the correction for the red-green channel (because red is subject to higher attenuation in underwater medium), while keeping the generally recommended level of compensation for the yellowblue channel. (RJ – 10)

BPS: Our choice on the number of PCs to use for predictors and for predictands was based on Wu et al. [8], where A. Wu (pers. comm.) tested for the optimal number of PCs to use for the LR model (corresponding tests with NN models would be prohibitively expensive). (RJ – 03)

BSISW: We varied the lead time from 0 to 15 months [our definition of lead time follows that of Barnston and Ropelewski (1992) and Barnston et al. (1994), i. e. , the time between the end of the latest observed period and beginning of the predictand period]. (RJ – 04)

BSS: Dropout is included where used in the original classifier nets (however, training without it made little to no difference). (RJ – 08)

IPS: A smaller variant is one where the decoder filters are single channel, i. e. they only convolve their corresponding upsampled feature map. (RJ – 07)

ISC: The search for the hyperparameters was exhaustive; that is, a coarse grid search was first used to identify the region of minimum validated MSE, and then a finer grid search was used to pinpoint the optimal C, c, and σ values. (RJ – 03)

ISP: The high-dimensionality problem has finally been solved with the kernel trick, that is, although φ is a very high (or even infinite) dimensional vector function, as long as the solution of the problem can be formulated to involve only inner products like Eq. (with superscript T denoting the transpose), then a kernel function K can be introduced Eq. (6). (RJ – 03)

ISS: The temporal coefficient also clearly indicated ENSO connection, i. e. , it was high during E1 Niño and low during La Niña. (RJ – 04)

B. 句类与语步

图 5.5.8 是四种类型句子与语步的关系。如图所示，四类句子中占比最高的前三个步骤中均包含 M2.3c 和 M2.2a，但是这两个步骤在这四类句子中占比排序不完全一致。另外，在简单句和复合复杂句中排在第三的均为 M2.3b，在其他两类句子中均为 M2.2b。由于四种句子在文章中占比不同，即使相同步骤在这四种句子中排序一致，它们的数量和占比也不相同。

这四类句子中均包含了四个语步，就各类句子中包含的四个语步步骤种类而言，简单句中包含了四个语步中所有步骤，复杂句、复合句、复合复杂句中包含的步骤种类分别占四个语步中所有步骤种类的93%、86%和64%。

总体来说，不同句子类型与步骤之间关系存在异同，句子与步骤关系紧密度与该类句子在所有句子中占比有关，同时也与该步骤在所有步骤中占比有关，但是不完全成一一对应的关系，句类与步骤之间没有明显的相关性。

以下是四类句子中步骤占比最高的前三个步骤例句。

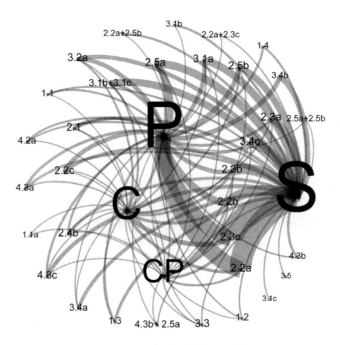

图 5.5.8　句类与步骤关系网络图

【S】

M 2.3c：The optimization, often referred to as network training, is an iterative procedure called the back-propagation method (Rumelhart et al., 1995; Smith 1993). (RJ – 01)

M 2.2a：Regardless of the size or aspect ratio of the candidate region, we warp all pixels in a tight bounding box around it to the required size. (RJ – 06)

M 2.3b：The GPD parameter estimation procedure using FL-based MLE is presented in Algorithm 1. （RJ－12）

【P】

M 2. 2a：Prior to warping, we dilate the tight bounding box so that at the warped size there are exactly p pixels of warped image context around the original box （we use p ¼ 16）. （RJ－06）

M 2. 3c：This form of a cost function represents a trade-off between residual error and model complexity, which have been shown to produce robust networks （Hanson and Part 1989; Ji and Psaltis 1990; Weigend et al. , 1990, 1991）. （RJ－01）

M 2. 2b：Less clear is how to label a region that partially overlaps a car. （RJ－06）

【C】

M 2. 3c：For the case of $a_3 \gg a_2$, more weight restriction is imposed on the output layer and hence the resulting net tends to be more nonlinear. （RJ－01）

M 2. 2a：Secondly, this solution has been tailored for underwater scenes and is not applicable to any color attenuation than the red. （RJ－10）

M 2. 2b：Hard negative mining converges quickly and in practice mAP stops increasing after only a single pass over all images. （RJ－06）

M 2. 3b：It can be easily selected based on M for many applications of interest; we provide details in Lemma 9 of the Appendix. （RJ－13）

【CP】

M 2. 3c：If the correlation skill of the NN model was higher than that of the LR model, and MSE of the NN model less than that of the LR model, the NN model was accepted; if otherwise, it was rejected. （RJ－02）

M 2. 2a：As we show later in this work, this lower memory storage results in a slight loss of accuracy but is still suitable for practical applications. （RJ－07）

M 2. 3b：Once the local sphere is instantiated, the actually relevant user data are prepared & visualized; the whole local sphere is instantiated within a clientside graph library in the background. （RJ－14）

C. 句类与句长

表 5. 5. 11 是四类句子中句长占比情况。如表所示，简单句中句子长度占比最高的是单词数介于 11—20 的句子，其次是介于 21—30 的句子，介于 1—10 的句子占比略低于介于 21—30 的句子。其他三类句子占比最高的均为单词数介于 21—30 的句子。复杂句和复合句中占比排在第二的均为介于 11—20 的句子，但是复合句中单词数介

于 21—30 的句子和介于 11—20 的句子占比差异不明显，只相差一句。复合复杂句中排在第二的为单词数介于 31—40 的句子。四种类型句子长度最大值复合句最低，其次是简单句，其他两类句子相似，但是复合复杂句略高于复杂句。句长最小值简单句最小，其他三类句子较接近，其中复合复杂句最高。

如果不排除特殊句子类型，将每个公式算为一个单词的话，所有句子中最长的为 NPCPBW，共有 109 个单词，最短的句子为简单句，共有 3 个单词。

综上所述，四种类型句子中，复杂句和复合句长度具有较大的相似性，简单句中短句较其他三类句子占比高，复合复杂句中长句占比较其他三类句子略高。

以下是所有句子中最长的 NPCP 例句及四类句子中最长和最短句子的例句。

表 5.5.11　　　　　　　　　　句长分布

句长范围		1—10	11—20	21—30	31—40	41—50	51—60	61—70	MAX	MIN
S	句数	127	318	149	47	6	2	*	54	3
	占比	19.57%	49.00%	22.96%	7.24%	0.92%	0.31%	*		
P	句数	8	124	158	75	20	4	3	62	9
	占比	2.04%	31.63%	40.31%	19.13%	5.10%	1.02%	0.77%		
C	句数	1	41	42	14	2	*	*	48	10
	占比	1.00%	41.00%	42.00%	14.00%	2.00%	*	*		
CP	句数	*	3	21	17	3	*	1	65	12
	占比	*	6.67%	46.67%	37.78%	6.67%	*	2.22%		

NPCPBW/［**Max：109**］Now that we have observed that the most challenging cases are characterized by the extinction of one color, due to attenuation or selective lighting spectrum, we better understand why conventional dehazing methods generally fail in those cases: the unbalanced attenuation induces color shifting; the dark channel prior, which associates a small minimal color value to a good transmission, systematically fails in estimating the transmission; and conventional enhancement methods, which attempt to reconstruct a pleasant image by resorting to some kind of histogram stretching (often guided by the inversion of an approximated light transmission model) for each channel, tend to amplify noise when the information is missing in one channel. (RJ – 10)

S/ [**Max：54**] We consider a dataset extracted from an EHR system, containing patients' demographic data such as age, gender, and race, physical characteristics such as weight, height, Body Mass Index (BMI), medical history captured by diagnoses, procedures, office visits, and a history of drug prescriptions, all captured by a feature vector $\varphi_i \in \mathbb{R}^d$, for each patient $i = 1, \cdots, n$. (RJ – 11)

S/ [**Min：4**] Skip architectures for segmentation. (RJ – 08)

P/ [**Max：62**] Under this assumption, which sounds like a transposition of the Gray World [3] assumption to the opponent color space, a simple way to mitigate the color shifts induced by severe spectral power discrepancies induced by a biased illuminant or a severe attenuation consists in subtracting the mean of each opponent color channel, as averaged on the whole scene, from the channel itself. (RJ – 10)

P/ [**Min：9**] We train the variants until the training loss converges. (RJ – 07)

C/ [**Max：48**]：The data used in this study were made available by Indian National Centre for Ocean Information Services (INCOIS) and pertained to monthly mean SST at six different locations in the North Indian Ocean, code named as AS, BOB, EEIO, SOUTHIO, THERMO, and WEIO as shown in Figure 1 (RJ – 05)

C/ [**Min：10**] The detailed construction is involved and is given in [SPKM07]. (RJ – 16)

CP/ [**Max：65**] White noise is very clearly separated from the pristine image set making it one of the easiest to gauge the quality of JPEG2000 and fast fading have (应为 has) a high degree of overlap as fast fading images in LIVE database are actually multi distorted, first compressed into a bitstream using a JPEG2000 codec, then passed through a Rayleigh fast fading channel to simulate packet loss [27]. (RJ – 09)

CP/ [**Max：12**] Let *Eq.* be a superstep that occurs in *MA*, and let *Eq.*. (RJ – 16)

（二） 时态特征

A. 时态种类及组合

表 5.5.12 是所研究文章中出现的各种时态及组合形式。如表所示，除去片段和有语法错误的句子，在所分析的文章中共出现了 7 种不同时态，其中 T5 没有单独使用，与其他时态共同出现在一个句子中。由不同时态构成的组合共有 12 种。在不同时态构成的组合中包含 T1 的组合最多，其次是 T3，分别占所有组合的 58% 和 42%，其他时态在组合中占比均较低。各种时态组合中，全部由 T1 构成的句子

占比最高，其次为全部由 T3 构成的句子，占比第三的是由 T1 和 T3 两种不同时态构成的句子，其他相同或不同时态组合占比均较低。

以下是按照四种类型句子给出的三种时态组合的例句，但是有些时态组合中不包含所有类型的句子。

表 5.5.12 时态类型及组合

时态	T1	T2	T3	T4	T7	T10	T1T2	T1T3	T1T4
句数	1007	6	163	7	1	13	20	40	11
占比	77.76%	0.46%	12.59%	0.54%	0.08%	1.00%	1.54%	3.09%	0.85%
时态	T1T4T7	T1T7	T1T7T10	T1T10	T3T4	T3T5	T2T3	T3T10	T4T10
句数	1	1	1	12	3	2	1	5	1
占比	0.08%	0.08%	0.08%	0.93%	0.23%	0.15%	0.08%	0.39%	0.08%

【T1】

S： The use of the EEOF technique in the preprocessing of the SLP field allows lag as well as spatial compressions of the data field into several dominant modes (Weare and Nasstrom 1982; Graham et al., 1987a). (RJ-01)

P： This is particularly advantageous in relation to neural network modeling since fewer inputs are required. (RJ-01)

C： No calculation is performed in this layer but each neuron distributes a copy of its input to all neurons in the hidden layer. (RJ-04)

CP： The advantage of using nonadaptive basis functions is that y does not depend on any parameter nonlinearly, and so only linear optimization is involved without the multiple minima problem. (RJ-03)

【T10】

S： The SSE could serve as the cost function to be minimized. (RJ-04)

C： Users' private data might even act as personalized ontologies and be combined with well-known knowledge extraction methods [17]. (RJ-14)

【T1T10】

P： It's clear that an image region tightly enclosing a car should be a positive example. (RJ-06)

CP： With our approach, 10 k detectors can run in about a minute on a CPU, and because no approximations are made mAP would remain at 59 percent with TorontoNet and 66 percent with OxfordNet (Section 4.2). (RJ-06)

【T1T2】

P: This form of a cost function represents a trade-off between residual error and model complexi-ty, which have been shown to produce robust networks (Hanson and Part 1989; Ji and Psaltis 1990; Weigend et al. , 1990, 1991). (RJ – 01)

C: We have tested other color-opponent spaces and the results are quite similar (see Fig. 5). (RJ – 10)

CP: Note that R^* depends on Ω , but for the sake of simplicity, we have removed this in our notation. (RJ – 13)

【T1T3】

P: Figure 2a shows the spatial patterns (at lag 9 months) of the first mode, which accounted for 26. 5% of the total variance. (RJ – 01)

C: Neural networks do not require data preprocessing as a precondition for training and hence the same was not performed. (RJ – 05)

CP: In Section 5, we give an overview of the ILSVRC2013 detection dataset and provide details about choices that we made when training R – CNNs on it. (RJ – 06)

【T1T4】

P: These form the first set of features that will be used to capture image distortion. (RJ – 09)

【T1T4T7】

P: We are interested in predicting whether or not a patient will be hospitalized in a given year, for instance in the next calendar year from the time the record is being examined. (RJ – 11)

【T1T7】

P: As nodes in such a federated approach have but a tiny sub-sample of a traditional, global da-tabase, new algorithms are being devised for this setting [8] . (RJ – 14)

【T1T7T10】

P: Let us assume there is a network of agents, each of which is holding part of the data and they all collectively would like to solve (1) utilizing all data. (RJ – 11)

【T2】

S: In an attempt to estimate the best timing, we have experimented with several different dura-tions of the wind stress in the predictor, to be discussed later in Sect. (RJ – 04)

【T3】

S: The same sea surface temperature (SST) data used in Tangang et al. (1997b) were em-ployed here. (RJ – 01)

P: The results confirmed that the climatologies (not shown) were almost identical and the indi-ces were highly correlated (0. 98 – 0. 99). (RJ – 01)

C: The Smith SSTs were reconstructed using the EOF method (Smith et al. , 1996) and were available in 28 latitude 3 28 longitude grids over the period 1950 – 92. (RJ – 01)

CP：Our results in Tangang et al. (1997b) showed that the SLP data were less noisy than the wind stress and, hence, became the better predictor at long lead times. (RJ – 01)

【T3T10】

P：However, since the EOF analysis could not capture propagating features by a single mode, the SLP EOF mode 2 in Tangang et al. (1998) had different spatial and temporal patterns than the SLP EEOF mode 2. (RJ – 01)

CP：This procedure was repeated until all 10 segments were predicted, and the correlation and root mean square error (RMSE) between the predicted SST anomalies and the corresponding observations could be calculated over the whole record. (RJ – 02)

【T3T4】

P：As will be discussed in section 6, we interpreted the SLP EEOF mode 1 as the low-frequency oscillation (LFO) mode and mode 2 as the LFO plus the tropospheric quasibiennial oscillation (QBO) mode, in relation to the LFO and QBO described in Barnett (1991), Ropelewski et al. (1992), and Goswami (1995). (RJ – 01)

【T3T5】

P：This entire procedure was repeated until 30 NN models had been accepted. (RJ – 02)

【T2T3】

P：While there have been conflicting arguments in recent years on whether the increasing trend in the trade winds or the SST in the Pacific ocean was real (Posmentier et al. , 1989; Cardone et al. , 1990), recent results of Wang (1995) seemed to indicate that this trend was real and important in characterizing the pre- and post-1977 ENSO events. (RJ – 04)

【T4】

S：In this study, the wind stress will be nonlinearly related to the SST by the neural network model. (RJ – 04)

【T4T10】

C：On the other hand, learning on very small, subjective subsets of 'reality' could be seen as a profound distortion of data, and algorithms will have to be tested for suitability as well as stability in such scenarios [11]. (RJ – 14)

【T7】

S：The run r is accepting *iff* $l_n \in F$. (RJ – 16)

B. 时态与语步

图 5. 5. 9 是该学科文章中三种时态组合与语步的关系。如图所

示，三种占比较高的时态组合中占比最高的前三个步骤中均包含了M2.3c，但是该步骤在三种时态组合中排序不完全一致。其他几个步骤在三种时态组合中均不相同。虽然三种时态组合中占比最高的前三个步骤中均包含了 M2.3c，但由于三种时态组合在文章中占比具有明显差异，该步骤在这三种时态组合中数量及占比也存在较大差异。此外，这三种时态组合中均包含了四个语步，就它们包含的步骤种类数量而言，T1 中包含了所有步骤，T3 和 T1T3 中包含的步骤种类分别占四个语步中所有步骤种类的61%和50%。

总体来说，不同时态形式的句子与语步的联系存在一定的差异，时态与步骤关系紧密度与该时态在所有句子中的占比有关，同时也与该步骤在所有步骤中的占比有关，但并不是决定性的。

以下是按照四种类型句子给出的三种时态组合中占比最高的前三个步骤的例句，但是有些步骤中不包含所有类型的句子。

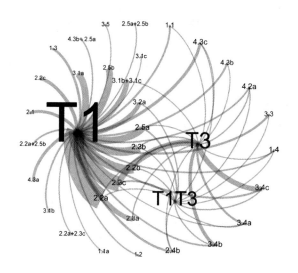

图 5.5.9　时态与步骤关系网络图

【T1】

M 2.2a

S: These are then batch normalized [50], [51]. (RJ-07)

P: The increasingly lossy (boundary detail) image representation is not beneficial for segmentation where boundary delineation is vital. (RJ-07)

C：Following that, max-pooling with a 22 window and stride 2 (non-overlapping window) is performed and the resulting output is sub-sampled by a factor of 2. (RJ – 07)

CP：As we show later in this work, this lower memory storage results in a slight loss of accuracy but is still suitable for practical applications. (RJ – 07)

M 2. 3c

S：The goal is to introduce a virtual queue for the aforementioned constraint instead of (4) and (5). (RJ – 12)

P：Let Eq. be a parameter which controls the tradeoff between queue length and the accuracy of the optimal solution of (10). (RJ – 12)

C：In order to scale this virtual queue with the actual queue size, both sides of the aforementioned constraint are scaled by the queues, and thus, it becomes Eq. . (RJ – 12)

CP：Note that the likelihood function is a smooth function of d and a summation over all the samples in Q, and thus, its gradient over a sample Q is given as follows. (RJ – 12)

M 2. 2b

S：Before proposing our federated method for solving (1), we make the following observations. (RJ – 13)

P：When fixing Ω, updating W depends on both the data X, which is distributed across the nodes, and the structure Ω, which is known centrally. (RJ – 13)

C：The matrix Eq. models relationships amongst tasks, and is either known a priori or estimated while simultaneously learning task models. (RJ – 13)

CP：In general, (1) is not jointly convex in W and Ω, and even in the cases where (1) is convex, solving for W and Ω simultaneously can be difficult [5]. (RJ – 13)

M 2. 3b

S：During MOCHA's federated update of W, the central node requires a response from all workers before performing a synchronous update. (RJ – 13)

P：To avoid stragglers, MOCHA provides the t-th node with the flexibility to approximately solve its subproblem $G_t^{\sigma'}(\cdot)$, where the quality of the approximation is controlled by a per-node parameter θ_t^h. (RJ – 13)

C：It can be easily selected based on M for many applications of interest; we provide details in Lemma 9 of the Appendix. (RJ – 13)

CP：Note that solving for Ω is not dependent on the data and therefore can be computed centrally; as such, we defer to prior work for this step [58, 21, 57, 16]. (RJ – 13)

【T3】

M 2. 3c

S：To avoid these problems, we adopted the following two strategies. (RJ – 02)

P：Bayesian regularization was used in the NN training, where the optimal weight penalty parameter was estimated by a Bayesian approach (MacKay, 1992), as coded by the program 'trainbr' in
the MATLAB Neural Network toolbox. (RJ – 02)

C：As in Tangang et al. (1997, 1998), we implemented the retroactive method by training the
networks over the period of 1952 – 81 and used the subsequent period from 1982 to 1993 as forecast
validation. (RJ – 01)

CP：If the correlation skill of the NN model was higher than that of the LR model, and MSE of
the NN model less than that of the LR model, the NN model was accepted; if otherwise, it was rejected.
(RJ – 02)

M 3. 4c

S：However, COADS had too many missing values in the 408 – 308S band, particularly in the
southeastern Pacific Ocean. (RJ – 01)

P：Several studies indicated that the surface wind and SLP anomalies, which eventually caused
most of the changes in the SST associated with ENSO, originated from the equatorial Indian Ocean and
propagated slowly eastward into the Pacific (Barnett, 1985; Yasunari, 1990; Gutzler and Harrison,
1987). (RJ – 01)

C：The climatological means were then removed and the anomalies were smoothed with a three-
point running average in time. (RJ – 01)

CP：Our results in Tangang et al. (1997b) showed that the SLP data were less noisy than the
wind stress and, hence, became the better predictor at long lead times. (RJ – 01)

M 3. 4b

S：Figures 1 and 2 showed the spatial pattern and the temporal coefficients of our first and second
modes. (RJ – 04)

P：This mode accounted for 4. 1% of the total variance as compared to 6. 8% in the Legler
analysis, where the seasonal cycle was not removed. (RJ – 04)

【T1 T3】

M 2. 3c

P：Since the error function contains many local minimum, there were potentially 50 different
models. (RJ – 03)

M 2. 5a

P：We consider the AlexNet2 architecture [1] that won ILSVRC12, as well as the VGG nets
[2] and the GoogLeNet3 [3] which did exceptionally well in ILSVRC14. (RJ – 08)

M 3. 4c

C：Neural networks do not require data preprocessing as a precondition for training and hence
the same was not performed. (RJ – 05)

（三）语态特征

A. 语态种类及组合

表 5.5.13 是该学科文章中使用的语态种类及不同语态组合类型。如表所示，该学科文章中两种语态均有出现，同时还包含了这两种语态的组合形式。只包含 V1 的句子数量和占比远高于其他两种类型的句子，只包含 V2 的句子数量和占比略高于包含两种不同语态的句子数量。所有文章中均有这三种形式语态组合。同一种语态构成的句子中均包括了简单句、复杂句、复合句和复合复杂句这四种类型的句子。两种不同语态构成的句子中包括了除简单句以外的三种类型的句子。

以下是按照四种类型句子给出的三种语态组合中的例句，但是有些语态组合中不包含所有类型的句子。

表 5.5.13 语态类型及组合

语态	V1	V1 V2	V2
句数	842	198	255
占比	65.02%	15.29%	19.69%

【V1】

S：For a given month, we stacked the SLP PCs of 3, 6 and 9 months before this month together with the SLP and SST PCs of this month, altogether yielding 37 time series. (RJ-02)

P：Table 1 shows the number of hidden neurons used in the NN, which gives the best correlation skill among the 8 NN models. (RJ-02)

C：Each neuron of the hidden and output layer sums up the weighted input, adds a bias term to it, passes on the result through a transfer function, and produces the output. (RJ-05)

CP：Our results in Tangang et al. (1997b) showed that the SLP data were less noisy than the wind stress and, hence, became the better predictor at long lead times. (RJ-01)

【V2】

S：These retained SLP and SST PCs were then separately normalized by dividing the standard deviation of their first PC. (RJ-02)

P: Data from one segment were withheld as validation data, while data from the other nine segments were used to train the models. (RJ – 02)

C: Only 85% of the training data (denoted by D85, randomly chosen from the nine segments of training data) were used to train the NN model and the remaining 15% (D15) were reserved for an overfitting test. (RJ – 02)

CP: A different pair of DT and DV was randomly chosen from the same D9 and the process was repeated until n_{h2} was determined. (RJ – 03)

【V1V2】

P: Although the ERSST data were available back to 1854, only data after January 1948 were used here. (RJ – 02)

C: By rotating the training and validation data, the MSE was computed over validation data for all of D9, for each set of C, ϵ, and σ values, and the lowest validated MSE gave the optimal values for the three hyperparameters. (RJ – 03)

CP: In this section, we present our design decisions for each module, describe their test-time usage, detail how their parameters are learned, and show detection results on PASCAL VOC 2010 – 12 and ILSVRC2013. (RJ – 06)

B. 语态与语步

图 5.5.10 是该学科文章中语态组合与语步的关系。如图所示，三种语态组合形式中语步占比最高的前三个步骤中均包含 M2.2a 和 M2.3c，但是这两个步骤在 V1 中排名与 V2 和 V1V2 不同。这三种语态组合中占比排在第三的步骤均不相同。虽然三种语态组合中占比最高的前三个步骤中均包含了 M2.2a 和 M2.3c，但由于这三种语态组合在文章中占比不同，这两个步骤在这三种语态组合中的数量和占比也不相同。此外，这三种语态组合形式中均包含了四个语步，就其包含的步骤种类数量而言，V1 中包含了四个语步中的所有步骤，V2 和 V1V2 中包含的步骤种类分别占四个语步中所有步骤种类的 82% 和 89%。

总体来说，语态与步骤关系紧密度与该语态在所有句子中的占比有关，同时也与该步骤在所有步骤中的占比有关。

以下是按照四种类型句子给出的三种语态组合中占比最高的前三个步骤的例句，但是有些步骤中不包含所有类型的句子。

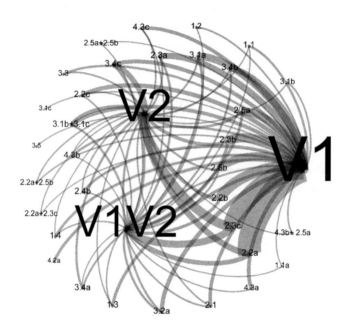

图 5.5.10　语态与步骤关系网络图

【V1】

M 2. 2a

S： Sub-sampling results in a large input image context (spatial window) for each pixel in the feature map. (RJ - 07)

P： While several layers of max-pooling and sub-sampling can achieve more translation invariance for robust classification correspondingly there is a loss of spatial resolution of the feature maps. (RJ - 07)

C： We fuse features by concatenation, and immediately follow with classification by a " score layer" consisting of a 1 × 1 convolution. (RJ - 08)

CP： As we show later in this work, this lower memory storage results in a slight loss of accuracy but is still suitable for practical applications. (RJ - 07)

M 2. 3c

S： The optimization, often referred to as network training, is an iterative procedure called the back-propagation method (Rumelhart et al. , 1995 ; Smith, 1993) . (RJ - 01)

P： However, our previous work, Tang (1995) , showed that this approach did not significantly inflate the forecasting skills. (RJ - 01)

C：As in Tangang et al. (1997, 1998), we implemented the retroactive method by training the networks over the period of 1952 – 81 and used the subsequent period from 1982 to 1993 as forecast validation. (RJ – 01)

CP：The softmax operation induces competition between classes and promotes the most confident prediction, but it is not clear that this is necessary or helpful. (RJ – 08)

M 2. 2b

S：The parameters κ and λ adjust the level of correction for the two opponent channels. (RJ – 10)

P：Therefore, we observe from our dataset that the severe color attenuation affects primarily one of the opposite colors in opponent color space. (RJ – 10)

C：Hard negative mining converges quickly and in practice mAP stops increasing after only a single pass over all images. (RJ – 06)

CP：In general, (1) is not jointly convex in W and even in the cases where (1) is convex, solving for W simultaneously can be difficult [5]. (RJ – 13)

【V2】

M 2. 3c

S：This is done by projecting from the present to the desired point h steps in the future, without any intermediate feedback. (RJ – 01)

P：This entire process was repeated until all 10 segments had been tested. (RJ – 03)

C：With this choice of n_h , a total of 50 models were trained using the entire D9 set and tested on D1. (RJ – 03)

CP：A different pair of DT and DV was randomly chosen from the same D9 and the process was repeated until n_{h2} was determined. (RJ – 03)

M 2. 2a

S：Max pooling is used to achieve translation invariance over small spatial shifts in the input image. (RJ – 07)

P：Once all layers have been fused, the final prediction is then upsampled back to image resolution. (RJ – 08)

C：Following that, max-pooling with a 22 window and stride 2 (non-overlapping window) is performed and the resulting output is sub-sampled by a factor of 2. (RJ – 07)

M 3. 4c

S：Based on the EOF and EEOF analyses of the near-global SLP of Graham et al. (1987a), most of the variability due to ENSO was contained in the 408S – 208N, 508E – 908W region. (RJ – 01)

P：Data from one segment were withheld as validation data, while data from the other nine segments were used to train the models. (RJ – 02)

C: The climatological means were then removed and the anomalies were smoothed with a three-point running average in time. (RJ – 01)

CP: This procedure was repeated until all 10 segments were predicted, and the correlation and root mean square error (RMSE) between the predicted SST anomalies and the corresponding observations could be calculated over the whole record. (RJ – 02)

【V1V2】

M 2. 3c

P: The values of a_2 and a_3 can be interpreted as " adjustment " toward linear or nonlinear net, as the hidden neurons have nonlinear transfer functions while the output neuron has a linear transfer function. (RJ – 01)

C: For the case of $a_3 \gg a_2$, more weight restriction is imposed on the output layer and hence the resulting net tends to be more nonlinear. (RJ – 01)

CP: If the correlation skill of the NN model was higher than that of the LR model, and MSE of the NN model less than that of the LR model, the NN model was accepted; if otherwise, it was rejected. (RJ – 02)

M 2. 2a

P: The score layer parameters are zero-initialized when a skip is added, so that they do not interfere with existing predictions of other streams. (RJ – 08)

C: In principle, this can be done using 2 bits for each 2×2 pooling window and is thus much more efficient to store as compared to memorizing feature map (s) in float precision. (RJ – 07)

CP: In contrast, our solution is general and can be used to solve severe attenuation conditions for turbid water or night-time scenes, where the blue channel may be significantly attenuated due to absorption by organic matter or the spectral power distribution of the artificial light spectrum. (RJ – 10)

M 2. 3b

P: To solve (1) across distributed nodes, we define the following data-local subproblems, which are formed via a careful quadratic approximation of the dual problem (3) to separate computation across the nodes. (RJ – 13)

C: It can be easily selected based on M for many applications of interest; we provide details in Lemma 9 of the Appendix. (RJ – 13)

CP: Note that solving for Ω is not dependent on the data and therefore can be computed centrally; as such, we defer to prior work for this step [58, 21, 57, 16]. (RJ – 13)

第六节 学科间对比

本节主要对比分析本章前五个小节所涉及的各学科论文中建模实

验方法写作的体裁特征。对比分析所涉及内容与第三章第三小节一致。

一　篇幅占比

各学科论文建模实验方法部分在全文中篇幅占比均存在学科内差异，差异最大的为管理和交通两个学科。不同学科中篇幅占比最大值较为接近，最高的为交通，最低的为软件。篇幅占比最小值也较为接近，最低的为电信，最高的为交通。篇幅占比平均值最高的为交通，最低的为电信，总体差异较小。

二　标题特征

各学科论文中建模实验内容通常包括两个或以上平行部分。因此绝大部分文章中会包含不止一个一级大标题。对比五个学科中大标题词汇云图发现，除电信工程与科学外，其他四个学科中出现频次最高的词汇均为 Model，电信中出现频次最高的为 method，共出现过 6 次，在该学科中 model 共出现过 2 次。

所有文章中均包含了二级小标题。在管理、交通和车辆这三个学科中小标题出现频次最高的词汇均为 model。在电信和软件中出现频次最高的分别为 learning 和 definition，但是在这两个学科中均出现了 model，占比分别为 20% 和 40%。各篇文章中小标题数量明显高于大标题数量，其中大小标题数量比最高的文章中小标题数量是大标题的 4 倍，为电信，最低的为 1.58 倍，为管理，各篇文章中平均值为 2.88，标准差为 0.99。

综上所述，model 是不同学科建模实验写作部分大标题和小标题中的常用词，但是不同学科也存在一定的差异，该单词在所研究的大部分学科标题中使用频率均较高。此外，建模实验部分的写作通常包括多个部分，各部分均有小标题，但不同学科在大小标题数量比上存在一定的差异。

三 语步特征

本小节主要讨论各学科论文中四个语步在以下三个方面的异同。1. 不同语步中包含的步骤种类；2. 各步骤涉及的篇章数；3. 各语步中不同步骤占比及分布轨迹。步骤占比中，平均值和标准差只涉及包含该步骤的文章。"＊"表示该步骤只涉及一篇文章，"—"表示文章中不涉及该步骤。

A 语步一

表 5.6.1 是语步一中各步骤在各学科中涉及篇章数及在所分析文章中的占比。如表所示，各学科共有的步骤共有 5 种，占所有步骤的63％。就各学科中不同步骤涉及的篇章数而言，管理学科中 M1.1 和 M1.4 最高，M1.5 最低；电信和软件中最高的均为 M1.4，其次是 M1.1，最低的均为 M1.1a；交通和车辆中最高的均为 M1.1，其次是 M1.4，最低的分别为 M1.1b 和 M1.1a。

就同一步骤在不同学科中涉及篇章数来看，M1.1 在车辆工程中最高，在软件中最低。M1.1a 在电信工程中最高，在交通和软件中最低。M1.2 在车辆中最高，在交通中最低。M1.3 在管理中最高，在交通中最低。M1.4 在电信中最高，在交通中最低。

各步骤在不同学科中涉及篇章数占比平均值最高的是 M1.1，其次是 M1.4，M1.1 与 M1.4 非常接近，最低的是 M1.1a，就各学科在这方面的差异来看，最大的是 M1.1，其次是 M1.4，最小的是 M1.1a。

表 5.6.1　　　各学科语步一中各步骤涉及篇章数及占比

M	GL	DX	JT	CL	RJ
	篇数—占比	篇数—占比	篇数—占比	篇数—占比	篇数—占比
1.1	15%—63%	10%—50%	19%—53%	14%—70%	5%—31%
1.1a	3%—13%	3%—15%	2%—6%	2%—10%	1%—6%
1.1b	—	—	1%—3%	—	—

续表

M	GL	DX	JT	CL	RJ
	篇数—占比	篇数—占比	篇数—占比	篇数—占比	篇数—占比
1.1c	—	—	3%—8%	—	—
1.2	9%—38%	8%—40%	8%—22%	9%—45%	4%—25%
1.3	9%—38%	4%—20%	6%—17%	7%—35%	4%—25%
1.4	15%—63%	16%—80%	12%—33%	11%—55%	7%—44%
1.5	2%—8%	8%—40%	4%—11%	—	—

表 5.6.2 和表 5.6.3 分别为不同学科语步一中各步骤在该语步中占比的最大值、最小值、平均值及标准差。其中平均值和标准差为包含该步骤的文章，不包含该步骤的文章不计入其中。最大值一栏显示，在五个学科中有四个学科 M1.1 和 M1.4 最大值为 100%，即有些文章中这两个步骤为语步一中唯一一步骤，有三个学科中 M1.2 和 M1.5 最大值为 100%，不同学科之间 M1.1a 和 M1.3 最大值差异较大。最小值一栏显示，不同学科在 M1.2 和 M1.4 中差异较小，在 M1.1a 和 M1.3 中较大，其次是 M1.1。此外，软件中 M1.1a 最大值和最小值相同，从表 5.6.2 中可以发现该学科中只有一篇文章包含了该步骤。

各步骤在语步一中占比平均值一栏显示，各学科之间存在一定的差异，但是总体来说除了软件学科，M1.1 在其他四个学科中占比均较高。电信中 M1.1a 和 M1.3 占比均较低，与其他几个学科差异较大。M1.3 中电信和交通占比最低，其次是管理和车辆，软件最高。M1.4 中电信、交通和软件相似，均明显高于管理和车辆两个学科，最低的是车辆。

标准差一栏显示，M1.1 中软件最低，其他四个学科相似，均高于软件。M1.1a 中管理和车辆相近，高于其他两个学科，而其他两个学科也较为相近。M1.2 中交通、车辆和软件相近，高于其他两个学科，这两个学科中管理高于电信。M1.3 中总体均较低，其中电信最低，管理最高。M1.4 中车辆最低，其他四个学科较为接近。

表 5.6.2　　　　各学科语步一中各步骤占比最大值和最小值

M	MAX（%）					MIN（%）				
	GL	DX	JT	CZ	RJ	GL	DX	JT	CZ	RJ
1.1	100	100	100	100	43	4	24	14	14	8
1.1a	88	25	60	100	29	15	7	33	14	29
1.1b	—	—	50	—	—	—	—	50	—	—
1.1c	—	—	22	—	—	—	—	3	—	—
1.2	74	43	100	100	100	7	7	3	11	10
1.3	60	11	22	36	69	4	6	5	9	30
1.4	100	100	100	67	100	4	2	10	6	6
1.5	100	100	100	—	—	15	6	8		

表 5.6.3　　　　各学科语步一中各步骤占比平均值和标准差

M	Mean（%）					SD				
	GL	DX	JT	CZ	RJ	GL	DX	JT	CZ	RJ
1.1	45	57	68	62	28	0.28	0.24	0.31	0.26	0.13
1.1a	41	13	47	57	29	0.33	0.09	0.13	0.43	*
1.1b	—	—	50	—	—	—	—	*	—	—
1.1c	—	—	14	—	—	—	—	0.08	—	—
1.2	37	23	43	49	36	0.23	0.12	0.36	0.33	0.37
1.3	22	8	11	24	43	0.19	0.02	0.07	0.09	0.16
1.4	37	41	46	28	45	0.3	0.33	0.32	0.16	0.36
1.5	58	40	41	—	—	0.42	0.28	0.35	—	—

综上所述，语步一中不同步骤涉及篇章数占比在各学科之间具有较大的共性，M1.1 和 M1.4 在各学科中涉及篇章数均较高，除去 M1.1b 和 M1.1c 外，M1.1a 在四个学科中均最低。在管理学科中最低的为 M1.5，M1.1a 也很低，仅比 M1.5 多一篇，高出 5%。同一步骤在不同学科中涉及篇章数占比平均值 M1.1 和 M1.4 也最高，学科间差异也最大。此外，电信中有三个步骤涉及篇章数占比高于其他学科，而交通学科中有四个步骤占比低于其他学科。各步骤涉及篇章数

与该学科语步中包含的步骤种类多少有一定的关系，种类多的占比低，但是它们之间不完全成正比的关系。

B. 语步二

表5.6.4是语步二中各步骤在各学科中涉及篇章数情况。如表所示，各学科论文语步二中共包含17种不同步骤，包含步骤种类最多的是管理学科，最低的是软件，有11种步骤为所有学科共有，约占所有步骤种类的65%。就各学科中不同步骤涉及的篇章数而言，除软件外，在其他四个学科中M2.2b涉及篇章数占比最高，其中在电信中M2.3c与M2.2b占比相同，在软件中M2.3c占比最高，其次是M2.2b，仅比M2.3c少一篇，约低6%。

就同一步骤在不同学科中篇章数占比来看，在涉及所有五个学科的10个步骤中，有5个步骤篇章数占比最高的均为车辆学科。篇章数占比最低的4个步骤均为软件学科，管理学科中有3个步骤篇章数占比低于其他学科，车辆学科中有1个步骤，电信学科中有2个步骤，M2.4b在电信和软件这两个学科中占比相同，均低于其他三个学科。篇章数占比最低的步骤均不涉及交通学科。各步骤在不同学科中涉及篇章数占比平均值最高的是M2.2b，最低的是M2.4b。就各学科在这方面的差异来看，最大的是M2.2c，最小的是M2.4b。

表5.6.4　　　　各学科语步二中各步骤涉及篇章数及占比

M	GL	DX	JT	CZ	RJ
	篇数—占比	篇数—占比	篇数—占比	篇数—占比	篇数—占比
2.1	14%—58%	13%—65%	20%—56%	15%—75%	8%—50%
2.2a	15%—63%	11%—55%	30%—83%	19%—95%	10%—63%
2.2b	22%—92%	17%—85%	34%—94%	20%—100%	11%—69%
2.2c	15%—63%	8%—40%	31%—86%	12%—60%	8%—50%
2.2d	4%—17%	—	—	—	—
2.2e	2%—8%	—	—	—	—

续表

M	GL	DX	JT	CZ	RJ
	篇数—占比	篇数—占比	篇数—占比	篇数—占比	篇数—占比
2.3a	18%—75%	16%—80%	20%—56%	14%—70%	8%—50%
2.3b	10%—42%	14%—70%	25%—69%	13%—65%	8%—50%
2.3c	13%—54%	17%—85%	23%—64%	10%—50%	12%—75%
2.3d	—	—	—	1%—5%	—
2.4a	3%—13%	5%—25%	12%—33%	8%—40%	—
2.4b	9%—38%	5%—25%	12%—33%	7%—35%	4%—25%
2.4c	—	—	1%—3%	2%—10%	—
2.4d	—	—	2%—6%	—	—
2.5a	14%—58%	10%—50%	26%—72%	16%—80%	7%—44%
2.5b	9%—38%	12%—60%	20%—56%	12%—60%	8%—50%
2.5c	1%—4%	—	—	—	—

表 5.6.5 和表 5.6.6 分别为各学科语步二中各步骤在该语步中的最大值、最小值、平均值及标准差。其中平均值和标准差为包含该步骤的文章，不包含该步骤的文章不计入其中。最大值一栏显示，在 M2.1、M2.2c、M2.3a、M2.3c 中，软件学科与其他学科差异较大。在 M2.2a 中，管理、车辆和软件这三个学科较接近，其他两个学科较接近，明显低于前三个学科。在 M2.2b 中管理学科明显高于其他各学科，其他四个学科较接近。在 M2.3b 中，电信和交通两个学科有差异，同时它们与其他三个学科也有显著差异。在 M2.3c 中，各学科之间均有明显的差异。在 M2.4b、M2.5a 和 M2.5b 中，与其他学科差异较大的分别为交通、车辆和电信。总体来说，交通和电信与其他学科差异较大。

最小值一栏显示，各学科间差异明显小于它们在最大值方面的差异。在多数步骤中软件最小值明显高于其他学科。各学科相似度最大的为 M2.1，其次为 M2.2c、M2.3a、M2.4b 和 M2.5a。在 M2.3b、M2.3c 和 M2.5b 中，除去软件，其他四个学科较为接近。在 M2.2a

中，材料和软件较为接近，其他三个学科较为接近。在 M2.2b 中，除电信外，其他四个学科均较为接近。

平均值一栏显示，各学科在 M2.1、M2.2c、M2.3b、M2.4b、M2.5a 和 M2.5b 中差异均较小。在 M2.2a 和 M2.2b 中，除管理学科外，其他各学科差异不大。在 M2.3a 中，交通最低，软件最高，其他三个学科差异较小。在 M2.3c 中，软件最高，管理和电信几乎没有差异，交通和车辆之间差异较小，平均值最低。

标准差一栏显示，在 M2.1、M2.2a、M2.2c、M2.3b、M2.4b、M2.5a 和 M2.5b 中，各学科差异较小，差异最大的是 M2.3c，其次是 M2.3a 和 M2.2b。在 M2.3c 和 M2.3a 中，软件学科标准差均高于其他各学科。在 M2.2b 中，管理学科远高于其他四个学科，其他四个学科之间没有明显差异。

综上所述，语步二中不同步骤涉及篇章数占比各学科之间具有较大的共性，M2.2b 在各学科中涉及篇章数均较高。

表5.6.5　　　　各学科语步二中各步骤占比最大值和最小值

M	MAX（%）					MIN（%）				
	GL	DX	JT	CZ	RJ	GL	DX	JT	CZ	RJ
2.1	24	25	35	28	10	1	1	1	1	2
2.2a	61	47	49	71	77	1	4	3	9	8
2.2b	92	46	56	47	41	1	7	3	3	3
2.2c	29	21	36	21	14	1	3	2	1	2
2.2d	18	—	—	—	—	3	—	—	—	—
2.2e	5	—	—	—	—	2	—	—	—	—
2.3a	51	42	20	45	100	1	2	1	1	3
2.3b	39	51	79	37	43	3	3	1	2	7
2.3c	69	87	18	30	100	2	2	1	1	5
2.3d	—	—	—	1	—	—	—	—	—	—
2.4a	28	5	35	9	—	1	1	1	1	—
2.4b	28	15	36	23	13	1	3	2	1	3
2.4c	—	—	7	12	—	—	—	7	3	—

续表

M	MAX（%）					MIN（%）				
	GL	DX	JT	CZ	RJ	GL	DX	JT	CZ	RJ
2.4d	—	—	4	—	—	—	—	2	—	—
2.5a	40	25	41	56	23	0.4	1	1	2	3
2.5b	30	42	21	20	15	1	1	0.3	2	6
2.5c	2	—	—	—	—	2	—	—	—	—

表5.6.6　　　　各学科语步二中各步骤占比平均值和标准差

M	Mean（%）					SD				
	GL	DX	JT	CZ	RJ	GL	DX	JT	CZ	RJ
2.1	7	8	11	9	6	0.08	0.07	0.09	0.1	0.03
2.2a	14	23	23	30	29	0.15	0.15	0.11	0.18	0.2
2.2b	36	20	24	18	14	0.28	0.1	0.13	0.12	0.11
2.2c	9	10	14	7	7	0.09	0.08	0.09	0.07	0.04
2.2d	8	—	—	—	—	0.06	—	—	—	—
2.2e	4	—	—	—	—	0.02	—	—	—	—
2.3a	16	13	7	11	23	0.15	0.13	0.06	0.12	0.31
2.3b	15	22	20	17	18	0.13	0.13	0.2	0.12	0.12
2.3c	26	25	6	13	42	0.22	0.23	0.04	0.08	0.36
2.3d	—	—	—	1	—	—	—	—	*	—
2.4a	10	3	7	5	—	0.12	0.01	0.09	0.03	—
2.4b	9	8	9	9	9	0.08	0.04	0.09	0.08	0.04
2.4c	—	—	7	8	—	—	—	*	0.05	—
2.4d	—	—	3	—	—	—	—	0.01	—	—
2.5a	11	9	13	9	13	0.1	0.06	0.09	0.13	0.07
2.5b	10	13	7	7	11	0.09	0.1	0.05	0.05	0.03
2.5c	2	—	—	—	—	*	—	—	—	—

C. 语步三

表5.6.7是语步三中各步骤在各学科中涉及篇章数情况。如表所

示，各学科均包含的步骤较少。包含步骤种类最多的是管理学科，共有 12 种，最少的是车辆，共有 7 种，分别占所有步骤的 60% 和 35%。就各步骤涉及的学科种类而言，有 11 种步骤只涉及一种学科，只有 5 种步骤为各学科共有，约占所有步骤种类的 24%。

就各学科中不同步骤涉及的篇章数而言，管理和交通这两个学科中最高的分别为 M3.4b 和 M3.2b，在电信和车辆中均为 M3.1a，而在软件学科中，M3.4a、M3.4b 和 M3.4c 这三个步骤占比相同，均高于其他各步骤。各学科中最低的均只涉及一篇。其中交通学科中有 4 个步骤只涉及一篇文章，其他四个学科均有 3 个步骤，各学科涉及篇章数最低的步骤之间重叠的较少，只有 M3.1c 同时涉及电信和软件两个学科。

在包含各学科的 5 个步骤中，对比同一步骤在不同学科中篇章数占比发现，管理中有 2 个步骤，交通、车辆和软件学科中分别有一个步骤高于其他四个学科。这五个步骤在各学科中的占比平均值最高的是 M3.1a，最低的是 M3.2a 和 M3.4c，总体来说，占比均较接近。标准差最高的是 M3.4b，最低的是 M3.4c。

表 5.6.7 　　　　　各学科语步三中各步骤涉及篇章数及占比

M	GL		DX		JT		CZ		RJ	
	篇数—占比		篇数—占比		篇数—占比		篇数—占比		篇数—占比	
3.1A	1%—4%		—		—		—		—	
3.1a	6%—25%		4%—20%		12%—33%		9%—45%		2%—13%	
3.1b	—		—		—		—		1%—6%	
3.1c	—		1%—5%		—		—		1%—6%	
3.1d	2%—8%		—		—		—		—	
3.1e	1%—4%		—		—		—		—	
3.2a	3%—13%		3%—15%		9%—25%		1%—5%		3%—19%	
3.2b	4%—17%		5%—25%		19%—53%		5%—25%		—	
3.2c	—		1%—5%		—		—		—	
3.2d	—		1%—5%		—		—		—	

M	GL	DX	JT	CZ	RJ
	篇数—占比	篇数—占比	篇数—占比	篇数—占比	篇数—占比
3.3	6%—25%	—	12%—33%	3%—15%	2%—13%
3.4a	13%—54%	2%—10%	6%—17%	1%—5%	5%—31%
3.4b	16%—67%	2%—10%	2%—6%	2%—10%	5%—31%
3.4c	7%—29%	3%—15%	2%—6%	1%—5%	5%—31%
3.4d	1%—4%	—	—	—	—
3.4e	—		1%—3%	—	—
3.4f	—		1%—3%		
3.4g	—		1%—3%		
3.5	8%—33%	—	—		1%—6%
3.6			1%—3%		

　　表5.6.8和表5.6.9为不同学科语步三中各步骤在该语步中的最大值、最小值、平均值及标准差。其中平均值和标准差为包含该步骤的文章，不包含该步骤的文章不计入其中。最大值一栏显示，各学科总体差异较大。最小值一栏显示，各学科间的差异明显小于最大值中的差异，其中在M3.2a、M3.4b和M3.4c中各学科间差异较小。在M3.4a中差异最大，主要原因是车辆学科中该步骤只涉及一篇文章。M3.1a在管理、电信和交通这三个学科差异较小，明显低于其他两个学科，软件中最高，其次是车辆。该步骤在软件学科中只涉及两篇文章。就各学科平均值而言，学科间差异较显著。各学科标准差差异不大，其中M3.2a最小。

　　综上所述，各学科中不同步骤涉及的篇章数存在一定的差异，各步骤在不同学科中分布比较分散。

表5.6.8　　　　各学科语步三中各步骤占比最大值和最小值

M	MAX（%）					MIN（%）				
	GL	DX	JT	CZ	RJ	GL	DX	JT	CZ	RJ
3.1A	7	—	—	—	—	7	—	—	—	—
3.1a	33	83	100	100	79	4	4	1	24	60

M	MAX（%）					MIN（%）				
	GL	DX	JT	CZ	RJ	GL	DX	JT	CZ	RJ
3.1b	—	—	—	—	34	—	—	—	—	34
3.1c	—	100	—	—	28	—	100	—	—	28
3.1d	33	—	—	—	—	2	—	—	—	—
3.1e	2	—	—	—	—	2	—	—	—	—
3.2a	15	14	33	6	38	1	8	6	6	5
3.2b	33	71	100	71	—	2	8	25	8	—
3.2c	—	15	—	—	—	—	15	—	—	—
3.2d	—	4	—	—	—	—	4	—	—	—
3.3	26	—	100	100	71	1	—	3	17	12
3.4a	100	100	50	81	20	3	26	2	81	9
3.4b	97	80	29	14	73	25	4	16	10	11
3.4c	50	33	11	14	80	5	13	1	14	13
3.4d	14	—	—	—	—	14	—	—	—	—
3.4e	—	—	7	—	—	—	—	7	—	—
3.4f	—	—	5	—	—	—	—	5	—	—
3.4g	—	—	10	—	—	—	—	10	—	—
3.5	100	—	—	—	4	5	—	—	—	4
3.6	—	—	—	—	—	—	—	—	—	—

表 5.6.9　　各学科语步三中各步骤占比平均值和标准差

M	Mean（%）					SD				
	GL	DX	JT	CZ	RJ	GL	DX	JT	CZ	RJ
3.1A	7	—	—	—		*	—	—	—	
3.1a	15	35	25	76	70	0.11	0.3	0.26	0.23	0.1
3.1b	—	—	—	—	34	—	—	—	—	*
3.1c	—	100	—	—	28	—	—	*	—	*
3.1d	18	—	—	—	—	0.16	—	—	—	—
3.1e	2	—	—	—	—	*	—	—	—	—

续表

M	Mean（%）					SD				
	GL	DX	JT	CZ	RJ	GL	DX	JT	CZ	RJ
3.2a	8	10	18	6	24	0.06	0.03	0.09	*	0.14
3.2b	14	47	63	30	—	0.12	0.25	0.23	0.22	—
3.2c	—	15	—	—	—	—	*	—	—	—
3.2d	—	4	—	—	—	—	*	—	—	—
3.3	11	—	33	47	42	0.11	—	0.32	0.37	0.3
3.4a	23	63	15	81	16	0.26	0.37	0.16	*	0.04
3.4b	60	42	22	12	41	0.21	0.38	0.06	0.02	0.2
3.4c	19	22	6	14	51	0.15	0.08	0.05	*	0.25
3.4d	14	—	—	—	—	*	—	—	—	—
3.4e	—	—	7	—	—	—	—	—	*	—
3.4f	—	—	5	—	—	—	—	—	*	—
3.4g	—	—	10	—	—	—	—	—	*	—
3.5	38	—	—	—	4	0.29	—	—	—	*
3.6						—	—	—	—	—

D. 语步四

表 5.6.10 是语步四中各步骤在各学科中涉及篇章数情况。如表所示，包含步骤种类最高的是管理学科，共有 16 种，最低的是软件，只有 4 种。只有 2 种步骤为各学科共有，占所有步骤的 11%。就各学科中不同步骤涉及的篇章数而言，管理学科中最高为 M4.4a，最低的有 5 个，只涉及一篇文章。电信和车辆中最高的是 M4.3e，最低的均只有一篇文章。语步四中只有 M4.3b 和 M4.3c 这两个步骤涉及了所有学科，占所有步骤的 11%。交通学科中这两个步骤篇章数占比均高于其他四个学科，而它们在车辆学科中均最低。

表 5.6.10　　　　各学科语步四中各步骤涉及篇章数及占比

M	GL		DX		JT		CZ		RJ	
	篇数—占比		篇数—占比		篇数—占比		篇数—占比		篇数—占比	
4.1	3%—13%		1%—5%		—		—		—	
4.2a	5%—21%		2%—10%		8%—22%		—		2%—13%	
4.2b	4%—17%		1%—5%		5%—14%		—		—	
4.2c	—		—		1%—3%		—		—	
4.2d	—		—		1%—3%		—		—	
4.3a	7%—29%		—		13%—36%		1%—5%		1%—6%	
4.3b	4%—17%		2%—10%		9%—25%		1%—5%		1%—6%	
4.3c	7%—29%		6%—30%		13%—36%		1%—5%		2%—13%	
4.3d	3%—13%		1%—5%		6%—17%		1%—5%		—	
4.3e	2%—8%		7%—35%		11%—31%		5%—25%		—	
4.3f	4%—17%		—		7%—19%		2%—10%		—	
4.3g	1%—4%		—		—		—		—	
4.3h	1%—4%		—		—		—		—	
4.4a	11%—46%		2%—10%		1%—3%		—		—	
4.4b	1%—4%		—		—		—		—	
4.4c	1%—4%		—		—		—		—	
4.4d	1%—4%		—		—		—		—	
4.5	3%—13%		—		—		—		—	

表 5.6.11 和表 5.6.12 为不同学科语步四中各步骤在该语步中的最大值、最小值、平均值及标准差情况。其中平均值和标准差为包含该步骤的文章，不包含该步骤的文章不计入其中。如表所示，各学科中 M4.3c 最大值较接近也较高，M4.3b 中电信较高，其他各学科均较低，没有显著差异。这两个步骤最小值各学科差异较大，车辆中这两个步骤分别只涉及一篇文章。软件中 M4.3b 也只涉及一篇文章。平均值一栏显示，与 M4.3b 相比，M4.3c 总体差异小，平均值也高。

M4.3b 中电信平均值最高，管理和交通差异不明显，均较低。两个步骤标准差没有明显学科差异。标准差 M4.3b 各学科差异均小于 M4.3c。

总体来说，各学科在最大值方面差异不明显，在最小值方面差异显著。标准差学科间差异小于不同步骤之间的差异。

表 5.6.11　　各学科语步四中各步骤占比最大值和最小值

M	MAX（%）					MIN（%）				
	GL	DX	JT	CZ	RJ	GL	DX	JT	CZ	RJ
4.1	13	9	—	—	—	3	9	—	—	—
4.2a	50	57	100	—	28	1	49	9	—	15
4.2b	62	33	100	—		7	33	1	—	
4.2c	—	—	7	—	—	—	—	7	—	—
4.2d	—	—	6	—	—	—	—	6	—	—
4.3a	50	—	100	100	39	8	—	3	100	39
4.3b	23	50	30	25	25	1	27	2	25	25
4.3c	97	100	65	100	72	10	11	2	100	21
4.3d	19	16	52	100	—	7	16	2	100	—
4.3e	18	100	100	100		4	17	3	75	
4.3f	38	—	14	100		2	—	1	100	
4.3g	2	—	—	—	—	2	—	—	—	—
4.3h	19					19				
4.4a	100	18	14			4	16	14	—	
4.4b	100	—	—	—	—	100	—	—	—	—
4.4c	11					11				
4.4d	100					100				
4.5	45	—	—	—	—	8	—	—	—	—

表 5.6.12　　　各学科语步四中各步骤占比平均值和标准差

M	Mean（%）					SD				
	GL	DX	JT	CZ	RJ	GL	DX	JT	CZ	RJ
4.1	7	9	—	—	—	0.05	*	—	—	—
4.2a	21	53	34	—	21	0.17	0.04	0.29	—	0.06
4.2b	36	33	38	—	—	0.25	*	0.35	—	—
4.2c	—	—	7	—	—	—	—	*	—	—
4.2d	—	—	6	—	—	—	—	*	—	—
4.3a	21	—	45	100	39	0.13	—	0.32	*	*
4.3b	12	38	10	25	25	0.08	0.12	0.09	*	*
4.3c	49	42	30	100	46	0.31	0.28	0.22	*	0.26
4.3d	13	16	17	100	—	0.05	—	0.17	*	—
4.3e	11	68	34	95	—	0.07	0.36	0.34	0.1	—
4.3f	17	—	9	100	—	0.13	—	0.05	*	—
4.3g	2	—	—	—	—	*	—	—	—	—
4.3h	19	—	—	—	—	*	—	—	—	—
4.4a	42	17	14	—	—	0.37	0.01	*	—	—
4.4b	100	—	—	—	—	*	—	—	—	—
4.4c	11	—	—	—	—	*	—	—	—	—
4.4d	100	—	—	—	—	*	—	—	—	—
4.5	28	—	—	—	—	0.15	—	—	—	—

　　表 5.6.13 为各学科中语步占比最高的文章占所有文章的百分比及各学科中各步骤在所有步骤中占比最高的前三个步骤。如表所示，各个学科中占比最高的均为语步二，其中电信和车辆两个学科中所有文章语步二占比均高于其他三个语步。管理学科中有一篇文章语步一占比最高，其他四个学科中均没有文章语步一占比高于其他语步。有三个学科中有少数文章语步三占比最高，有两个学科中有少数文章语步四占比最高。

　　就各学科四个语步中占比平均值最高的前三个步骤而言，各学科均包含 M2.2b，有四个学科包含 M2.2a，但是该步骤在各学科中排序不完全一致。有三个学科包含 M2.3c，有两个学科包含 M2.3b，只有一个学科包含 M2.2c。即使同一步骤在不同学科中排序一致，该步骤在不同学科中的占比也不相同。各个学科中占比最低的步骤均不相同。

表 5.6.13　　　　　　　　各学科语步占比分布及高占比步骤

学科	占比最高语步				占比最高前三个步骤		
	M1	M2	M3	M4	第一	第二	第三
GL	4%	88%	0.04	8%	2.2b	2.3c	2.2a
DX	—	100%	—	—	2.3c	2.2b	2.3b
JT	—	83%	0.03	14%	2.2b	2.2a	2.2c
CZ	—	100%	—	—	2.2a	2.2b	2.3b
RJ	—	88%	13%		2.2a	2.3c	2.2b

E. 语步组合及分布轨迹

表 5.6.14 是各学科出现的四个语步组合形式及占比。如表所示，共有八种形式，其中管理和车辆两个学科包含了 5 种组合形式，其他三个学科包含了 6 种组合形式。所有学科均包含了 M124，分别有四个学科包含了 M1234、M123 和 M12，这些组合中均包含了语步一和语步二。有四种组合中均不包含语步一，这类组合涉及的学科数为 2—3 种；此外，所有组合均包含语步二。

就同一学科不同组合涉及的篇章数占比而言，不同学科存在一定的差异。管理和交通两个学科中包含四个语步的文章占比明显高于其他组合，电信学科中只包含语步一和语步二的文章占比最高，车辆学科中有三种形式组合的文章占比相同。总体来说，除软件学科不包含四个语步的组合外，其他各学科中包含四个语步组合的文章占比均较高。软件学科中只包含语步二和语步三的文章占比最高，其次是包含语步一和语步二的组合。

表 5.6.14　　　　　　　各学科语步组合形式及占比

学科	M1234	M123	M124	M234	M12	M23	M24	M2
GL	46%	21%	17%	8%	—	8%	—	—
DX	30%	10%	15%	—	35%	—	5%	5%
JT	44%	—	3%	11%	25%	8%	—	8%
CZ	25%	25%	20%	5%	25%	—	—	—
RJ	—	19%	6%	—	25%	38%	6%	6%

综上所述，各学科中语步二在多数文章中占比均高于其他三个语步。不同语步组合形式数量各学科差异不大，同时包含语步一和语步二的组合涉及的学科种类均高于不包括语步一的组合。同一学科不同组合涉及的篇章数占比不同，存在一定的学科差异，但是除软件学科外，其他四个学科在 M1234 组合中相似度较大，而电信、交通、车辆和软件四个学科在 M12 组合中相似度极高。

M1234 组合分布轨迹：

有四个学科不同数量文章中同时包含了四个语步。就语步占比及分布密集程度而言，各学科中分布最广也最密集的总体来说均为语步二。除管理学科大部分文章中语步四分布也较广外，其他三个学科中除语步二以外的三个语步占比总体均较低，也较分散。但是各学科中这三个语步在这方面也存在细微的差异，电信一篇文章中语步一分布较广较分散；交通一篇文章中语步三占比最大，分布最广最密；车辆一篇文章中语步三占比略高，分布较集中。

就各语步分布轨迹而言，除车辆学科外，其他学科中语步一在大部分文章中主要集中分布在文章的最前及中间偏前的位置，个别文章中语步一会分布在文章的后部。车辆学科文章的最前没有出现语步一，该语步主要出现在文章前部，也有部分语句分布在了中间及后部。各学科语步二之间的差异不大于同一学科中不同文章之间的差异，主要分布在语步一后、语步三前，但是也有些文章中部分语步二会出现在文章的最前，有极少数文章中语步二会出现在最后。就语步三分布而言，车辆学科中语步三分布以文章前部为主，其他三个学科中该语步分布以文章中间偏后的位置为主，但是各学科中均有一部分文章语步三分别或同时出现在文章的最前、中间偏前及后部。就语步四分布而言，在车辆学科中主要以前部和较后的位置为主，在其他三个学科中语步四主要分布在文章的最后，但是在极少数文章中该语步也会出现在语步三前、语步二中或文章的中间。

就各语步之间交叉情况而言，各学科中均有较多文章中不同语步之间存在一定的交叉。在管理、电信和交通三个学科中，主要是语步一和语步二之间有交叉，其次是语步二与语步三之间，语步四与其他语步交叉的现象较少，但是在极少数文章中四个语步都有交叉。在车辆学科中，语步二与三个语步都有交叉，其次是语步一和语步三之间。

总体来说，各学科包含四个语步的文章在语步分布上存在较大的共性，同时也存在一定的差异，其中车辆与其他三个学科在语步一和语步三中存在的差异大于其他三个学科之间的差异。

M123 组合分布轨迹：

四个学科不同数量文章中同时包含了语步一、语步二和语步三。就语步占比及分布密集程度而言，各学科中语步二占比最高，分布也最广、最密集，但是在软件学科中有一篇文章语步三接近语步二。各学科中语步一占比均较低，但是分布密度存在一定的差异。总体来说，在车辆学科中分布较分散，而在其他三个学科中分布较集中。各学科中语步三的占比及分布密度不同文章中均存在差异。就各语步分布轨迹而言，各学科中语步一分布以文章前部为主，但是同一学科不同文章中也存在差异，在极少数文章中该语步也分布在文章的中间及最后。各学科语步二分布轨迹差异不大于学科内差异，各学科大部分文章中该语步几乎覆盖了文章各部位，也有少部分文章中该语步未出现在文章最前，主要分布在文章前部到最后，中间分别包含部分语步一和语步三。各学科中语步三分布较分散，在不同学科及同一学科不同文章中均存在一定的差异。在管理学科中，语步三分布以文章的前部和中间为主，在车辆学科中主要以文章的中间及后部为主，在软件学科中主要集中在文章的中部。但是在电信学科两篇文章中差异较大，在其中一篇文章中分布在文章较后的位置，在另一篇文章中分布在文章较前和最后两处。就各语步之间交叉情况而言，各学科少部分文章中存在三个语步均有交叉的情况，还有部分文章中语步二和语步三均有交叉。各学科部分文章中语步一与语步三没有交叉。

M234 组合分布轨迹：

有三个学科不同数量文章中同时包含了语步二、语步三和语步四。同一学科不同文章中在三个语步占比、分布广度和集中程度上存在一定差异。就语步占比及分布密集程度而言，管理和交通两个学科中均有部分文章语步二占比总体最高，分布最广也最集中。车辆学科只包含一篇文章，在该篇文章中，语步二占比最高，分布最广、最集中，其次是语步三，语步四占比最低，这两个语步分布相对较集中。在其他两个学科中语步三和语步四占比和分布密度在不同文章中存在一定的差异。就各语步分布轨迹而言，管理学科两篇文章中呈现两种不同情况，一篇文章中按照语步二、语步四、语步三顺序分布，各语步之间没有交叉；另一篇文章最前部是语步三，文章后部以语步四为主，中间以语步二为主，三个语步均有交叉。在交通学科中，各篇文章前部主要以语步二为主，最后都主要以语步四为主，语步三主要分布在中间偏后的位置，三个语步均有交叉。在车辆学科中，语步三分布在文章的前部及中间位置，以前部为主；语步四也出现在了文章较前的位置，语步三和语步四均分布在语步二中，三个语步均有交叉。

M12 组合分布轨迹：

除了管理学科外，四个学科分别有不同数量的文章中只包含语步一和语步二。各学科中语步二占比均高于语步一，分布也比语步一广。除软件学科外，其他三个学科中语步二分布均比语步一密集；软件学科中除一篇文章外语步一分布也较集中。不同学科中语步一分布轨迹存在一定的差异，在电信和软件两个学科中语步一主要分布在文章的前部；在交通和车辆两个学科中大部分文章的前部、中间及后部均有语步一分布，但是在车辆学科中大部分文章最前部也会出现语步一。就语步分布交叉情况而言，除软件学科中部分文章外，其他文章中语步一和语步二均有交叉，其中交通学科中语步一均分散分布在语步二中。软件学科有部分文章中这两个语步之间没有交叉。

M23 组合分布轨迹：

有三个学科不同数量文章中只包含语步二和语步四。就语步占比而言，管理和交通两个学科中语步二占比均高于语步三，但软件学科不同文章中存在一定的差异，大部分文章中语步二占比高于语步三，但也有少部分文章中情况相反。就这两个语步分布而言，同一学科不同文章之间存在一定的差异，但是学科间的差异大于学科内的差异。

M24 组合分布轨迹：

电信和软件两个学科中分别有一篇文章只包含语步二和语步四。这两个语步在这两个学科中的占比和分布具有高度相似性。在这两篇文章中语步二分布均较语步四广，均分布在语步四前，两个语步之间没有交叉。

四　语言特征

本小节主要对比分析各学科论文在句子结构、时态和语态三个方面的语言特征。具体内容与第三章第三节相同。

（一）句子特征

A. 句类及占比

表 5.6.15 是各学科中四类句子在所有句子中占比、特殊句子种类及特殊句类中占比最高的三类句子。如表所示，各学科论文中简单句、复杂句、复合句和复合复杂句这四种类型的句子占比总和均较高，均达到了 90%。四种类型句子中简单句占比均远高于其他三类句子，其次是复杂句，其他两类句子占比均较低，其中复合句占比略高于复合复杂句。电信学科论文中简单句占比高于其他四个学科，最低的是软件。复杂句占比最高的是管理，复合句车辆占比略高于其他学科。软件中复合复杂句占比略高于其他学科。总体来说，各学科四类句子占比分布差异不大。

就特殊类型句子而言，交通学科包含的类型最多，其次是管理学科，其他三个学科差异不大。所有学科中均包含了带有冒号、括号和 i.e. 的这三大类特殊句子，但是管理、交通和车辆三个学科中还包含带有破折号的句子。此外，除管理学科外，其他四个学科中占比排名最高的前两个特殊句类完全一致，管理学科中正好相反，占比排在第三位的交通和软件一致，其他三个学科均不相同。

表 5.6.15　　　　　　　　各学科句类及占比

学科	S	P	C	CP	特殊句类			
					种类	第一	第二	第三
GL	50.86%	34.14%	7.14%	2.05%	32	NWS	NWHS	BSS
DX	57.75%	26.95%	6.36%	2.32%	23	NWHS	NWS	NWAS
JT	52.34%	32.03%	6.44%	2.72%	38	NWHS	NWS	NWHP
CZ	55.30%	25.41%	7.67%	2.86%	21	NWHS	NWS	NWP
RJ	49.02%	29.68%	7.55%	3.32%	23	NWHS	NWS	NWHP

B. 句类与语步

表 5.6.16 是各学科中四种类型句子与步骤之间的关系。"种类比"一栏表示各类句子中出现的步骤种类在该学科所有步骤种类中的占比。右边三栏为各类句子中占比最高的前三个步骤。单元格中用斜线隔开的两个步骤占比相等，单元格中用 * 表示有多个步骤占比相同，但均较低。

如表所示，总体来说各学科四类句子中包含步骤种类占比最高的均为简单句，其次为复杂句，复合句次之，复合复杂句最低。简单句中学科性差异最小，复杂句中电信和车辆较低，其他三个学科均较高。复合句中电信也较低，软件最高，其他三个学科差别不明显，复合复杂句中软件最高，管理最低，其他三个学科较接近。

就四类句子中出现的占比最高的前三个步骤而言，有四个学科简单句中包含了 M2.2b 和 2.3b，分别有三个学科中包含了 M2.2a 和 M2.3c，只有一个学科中包含了 M2.3a。在复杂句和复合句中所有学科均包含了 M2.2b，有三个学科中均包含了 M2.3c，还有两个学科包含了 M2.2a，复合句中分别有三个学科包含了 M2.3b，两个学科包含了 M2.2a，有三个步骤只涉及一个学科。其他各步骤均只涉及一个学科。在复合复杂句中有四个学科包含了 M2.2b，三个学科包含了

M2.2a，两个学科中分别包含了 M2.3c 和 M2.3b，其他各步骤只出现在一个学科中。在各类句子中相同步骤在不同学科中排序不完全相同，即使在有些学科中排序相同，但是相同步骤数量和占比在不同学科中也有差异。

表 5.6.16　　　　　　各学科四类句子与高占比步骤

句类	学科	种类比	第一	第二	第三
S	GL	94%	2.2b	2.3c	2.3a
	DX	100%	2.3b	2.2b	2.3c
	JT	100%	2.2b	2.2a	2.3b
	CZ	91%	2.2a	2.2b	2.3b
	RJ	100%	2.3c	2.2a	2.3b
P	GL	92%	2.2b	2.3c	2.3a
	DX	72%	2.3c	2.2b	2.3b
	JT	91%	2.2b	2.2a	4.3a
	CZ	81%	2.2a	2.2b	2.2c
	RJ	93%	2.2a	2.3c	2.2b
C	GL	73%	2.2b	3.4b	2.3c
	DX	59%	2.3c	2.3b	2.2b
	JT	74%	2.2b	2.2c	1.1
	CZ	72%	2.2a	2.2b	2.3b
	RJ	86%	2.3c	2.2a/2.2b	2.3b
CP	GL	38%	2.2b	4.3c	2.4b
	DX	44%	2.3c	2.2b	*
	JT	53%	2.2a	2.2c	2.2b
	CZ	47%	2.2a	2.2b	2.3b
	RJ	64%	2.3c	2.2a	2.3b

C. 句类与句长

表 5.6.17 是五个学科中四类句子长度分布占比及句长最大值和最小值。如表所示，就简单句而言，各学科中句长占比从高到低排序

具有较高的一致性，占比最高的均为长度介于 11—20 个单词的句子，软件学科中该长度范围的句子占比较其他四个学科低，但是软件学科中句长介于 1—10 个单词数的句子占比略高于其他四个学科，管理和电信中长句及句子最大值均略高于其他三个学科，车辆学科中句子长度介于 11—20 个单词的占比高于其他四个学科，句子长度最大值最低。

就复杂句而言，各学科中占比最高的均为句长介于 21—30 单词数的句子，除电信外，占比排在第二的均为单词数介于 11—20 的句子，其次为介于 31—40 的句子，电信刚好相反。此外，电信中所有句子长度均大于 10，句子长度最小值高于其他四个学科。交通学科句子长度分布范围最广，即最大值最高，最小值最低。

就复合句而言，各学科中句长介于 21—30 单词数的句子占比最高，但是各学科句子单词数介于 11—20 和 31—40 的句子占比不完全一致；除电信外，其他四个学科中单词数介于 11—20 的句子占比均高于介于 31—40 的句子，其中软件中介于 11—20 的句子占比几乎等同于介于 21—30 的句子。各学科句子长度最小值较为接近，最大值管理最高，车辆最低，软件也较低，略高于车辆。

就复合复杂句而言，句子长度主要集中在单词数介于 21—30 和 31—40 这两个长度范围，其中车辆中这两个范围的句子占比相同，软件中范围在 21—30 个单词的句子占比高于范围在 31—40 个单词的句子，而在其他三个学科中情况正好相反。各学科句子长度最大值和最小值也存在一定的差异。最小值最高的是电信，其次是管理，其他三个学科较为接近。交通长度范围最广，即最小值最低，最大值最高。管理最大值低于交通，但是高于其他三个学科，其他三个学科较为接近。

总体来说，简单句、复杂句和复合句中句子长度分布没有明显的学科差异，但是复合复杂句中存在一定的学科差异。

表 5.6.17　　　　　　　　各学科四类句子长度分布

句类	学科	句长范围								MAX	MIX
		1—10	11—20	21—30	31—40	41—50	51—60	61—70	71—80		
S	GL	13.21%	54.29%	23.08%	7.12%	1.54%	0.45%	0.32%		69	5
	DX	14.68%	50.92%	24.77%	8.14%	1.26%	0.11%	0.11%		67	5
	JT	13.42%	50.06%	28.24%	6.60%	1.40%	0.28%	*	*	59	4
	CZ	13.28%	56.64%	23.85%	5.64%	0.59%	*	*		45	3
	RJ	19.57%	49.00%	22.96%	7.24%	0.92%	0.31%	*		54	3
P	GL	1.34%	27.79%	42.50%	21.20%	5.16%	1.81%	0.19%		63	8
	DX	*	19.90%	47.17%	24.82%	6.63%	1.47%	*		60	11
	JT	1.10%	24.89%	42.27%	21.41%	7.50%	1.74%	0.91%	0.18%	77	6
	CZ	1.02%	30.10%	41.33%	22.70%	4.08%	0.77%	*		53	9
	RJ	2.04%	31.63%	40.31%	19.13%	5.10%	1.02%	0.77%		62	9
C	GL	0.46%	26.03%	44.29%	19.18%	7.76%	1.37%	0.91%		62	10
	DX	*	21.88%	45.83%	26.04%	2.08%	4.17%	*		60	13
	JT	*	27.60%	44.80%	21.72%	5.43%	0.45%	*	*	53	11
	CZ	*	23.73%	55.93%	17.80%	2.54%	*	*		43	14
	RJ	1.00%	41.00%	42.00%	14.00%	2.00%	*	*		48	10
CP	GL	*	6.35%	33.33%	42.86%	11.11%	3.17%	3.17%		70	16
	DX	*	*	31.43%	34.29%	20.00%	8.57%	5.71%		61	23
	JT	1.08%	3.23%	34.41%	35.48%	17.20%	7.53%	*	1.08%	75	10
	CZ	*	15.91%	36.36%	36.36%	2.27%	2.27%	6.82%		62	14
	RJ	*	6.67%	46.67%	37.78%	6.67%	*	2.22%		65	12

（二）时态特征

A. 时态及组合

　　表 5.6.18 至表 5.6.20 为各学科中不同时态组合类型及占比。如表所示，不同学科中，管理学科中包含的时态种类最多，共 11 种，电信最少，有 6 种，其他三个学科均有 7 种。各学科共有的时态共有 6 种，分别为 T1、T2、T3、T4、T7 和 T10。T7 在电信中没有单独出现，而是与其他时态共在同一个句子中。T5 在交通和软件两个学科

中与其他时态共同出现在一个句子中，T8 在管理和车辆两个学科中与其他时态共同出现在同一个句子中。只有软件中包含了 T9，该时态没有单独使用，而是与 T3 共同出现在同一个句子中。T6 和 T11 只出现在管理中，这两个时态也没有单独使用，而是与其他时态共同出现在一个句子中。各学科相同时态组合中 T1 占比远高于其他时态，其次是 T3。T2 与 T4 占比较为接近，在管理、电信和交通中 T2 略高于 T4，而在其他两个学科中则相反。

就两种不同时态组合而言，所有学科中共出现了 21 种时态组合，有 6 种为各学科共有，其中 T1T3 在各学科中占比均最高，其他四种组合较接近，但在各学科占比排序存在差异。各组合中 T1 和 T3 出现次数均高于其他时态，但是 T1 略高于 T3。

就三种不同时态组合而言，所有学科中共出现 12 种，各学科差异较大，没有学科共有的，涉及学科最多的是 T1T3T10，共涉及四个学科。各组合中 T1 出现次数最高，其次是 T3。

表 5.6.18　　　　　　　　各学科相同时态组合及占比

学科	时态组合							
	T1	T2	T3	T4	T5	T7	T8	T10
GL	82.26%	1.24%	4.86%	1.21%	0.03%	0.10%	*	1.17%
DX	83.54%	1.00%	8.19%	0.67%	*	*	*	0.53%
JT	72.02%	1.70%	12.17%	0.88%	*	0.21%	0.03%	0.97%
CZ	83.24%	0.85%	7.66%	0.92%	*	0.33%	*	0.39%
RJ	77.76%	0.46%	12.59%	0.54%	*	0.08%	*	1.00%

表 5.6.19　　　　　　　　各学科两种时态组合及占比

学科	时态组合										
	T1T2	T1T3	T1T4	T1T6	T1T7	T1T8	T1T10	T1T11	T2T3	T2T4	T5T14
GL	1.34%	2.80%	1.66%	0.03%	0.65%	0.07%	1.76%	0.03%	0.10%	*	0.03%
DX	0.87%	2.33%	1.27%	*	0.60%	*	0.67%	*	0.07%	*	*
JT	1.58%	4.81%	1.91%	*	0.62%	0.03%	2.05%	*	0.15%	0.03%	*
CZ	0.65%	2.49%	1.11%	*	0.72%	*	0.98%	*	0.26%	*	*

学科	时态组合										
	T1T2	T1T3	T1T4	T1T6	T1T7	T1T8	T1T10	T1T11	T2T3	T2T4	T5T14
RJ	1.54%	3.09%	0.85%	*	0.08%	*	0.93%	*	0.08%	*	*
学科	T2T7	T3T4	T3T5	T3T7	T3T8	T3T10	T4T7	T4T10	T5T6	T7T10	
GL	*	*	*	*	0.07%	0.20%	0.03%	0.03%	0.03%	*	
DX	*	*	*	*	*	0.07%	*	*	*	*	
JT	0.03%	0.03%	*	0.06%	0.06%	0.32%	*	0.03%	*	*	
CZ	*	*	*	*	0.07%	*	*		*	0.07%	
RJ	*	0.23%	0.15%	*	*	0.39%	*	0.08%	*	*	

表 5.6.20 **各学科三种时态组合及占比**

学科	时态组合										
	T1T2T3	T1T2T4	T1T2T7	T1T3T4	T1T3T7	T1T3T10	T1T3T14	T1T4T11	T1T4T7	T3T5T6	T1T7T10
GL	0.03%	0.03%	*	0.03%	*	0.10%	0.03%	0.03%	*	0.03%	*
DX	0.07%	*	*	*	0.07%	*	*	*	0.07%	*	*
JT	0.06%	*	*	0.09%	*	0.12%	*	*	*	*	*
CZ	*	*	0.07%	*	*	0.13%	*	*	*	*	0.07%
RJ	*	*	*	*	*	*	*	*	0.08%	*	0.08%

B. 时态与语步

表 5.6.21 是各学科中三种主要时态组合与步骤之间的关系。"时态"一栏表示同一个句子中出现的时态组合形式。"种类比"一栏表示该时态组合形式中出现的步骤种类在该学科所有步骤种类中的占比。右边三栏为各学科时态组合中占比最高的前三个步骤。

如表所示，除电信外，其他各学科中步骤占比最高的均为 T1 组合，其次是 T3 组合，最低的是 T1T3 组合。在电信中，T1 组合中步骤占比低于 T3 组合，与 T1T3 组合相同。除电信外，T1 组合中各学科步骤占比较为接近，其中软件最高，车辆最低。T3 组合中交通占比明显高于其他四个学科，管理最低，其他三个较接近。在 T1T3 组合中，交通占比远高于其他四个学科，其他四个学科差异不明显。

就各学科时态组合中占比最高的前三个步骤而言，在 T1 组合中，各学科占比前三的步骤中均包含了 M2.2b，分别有四个和三个学科中包含了 M2.2a 和 M2.3c，但是各学科在步骤排序上均不相同。在 T3 组合中，学科性差异较大，只有三个学科包含了 M2.2b，只有两个学科包含 M2.2c 和 M3.4b，其他步骤各学科均不相同。在 T1T3 组合中，只有两个学科中包含了 M2.2a，分别有三个学科中包含了 M2.2b 和 M2.5a，其他步骤各学科均不相同。总体来说，这三种时态组合形式中均存在学科差异，但是程度不一，其中 T1 中差异较小，另外两种较明显。

表 5.6.21　　　各学科三种类型时态组合与高占比步骤

时态	学科	语步			
		种类比	第一	第二	第三
T1	GL	96%	2.2b	2.3c	2.3a
	DX	41%	2.2b	2.3c	2.2a
	JT	95%	2.2b	2.2a	2.3b
	CZ	94%	2.2a	2.2b	2.3b
	RJ	100%	2.2a	2.3c	2.2b
T3	GL	50%	2.2b	3.4b	4.4d
	DX	65%	2.3b	2.2b	2.3c
	JT	86%	3.2b	2.5a	4.3a
	CZ	56%	2.2b	2.1	3.4a
	RJ	61%	2.3c	3.4c	3.4b
T1T3	GL	42%	2.2b	2.5a	4.4d
	DX	41%	2.2a	2.3c	4.3e
	JT	79%	2.5a	4.3a	2.2b
	CZ	47%	2.2a	2.2b ＝ 2.5b	
	RJ	50%	2.3c	2.5a	3.4c

（三）语态特征

表 5.6.22 是各学科中不同语态组合及占比。"语态"一栏表示同一个句子中出现的语态组合形式。"种类比"表示该语态组合形式中出现的步骤种类在该学科所有步骤种类中的占比。最右边三栏分别是该语态组合中占比最高的前三个步骤。如表所示，不同学科中均包含三种类型语态组合。其中全部为 V1 主动语态构成的句子占比远高于全部由 V2 被动语态构成的句子及由 V1V2 两种不同语态构成的句子。在交通学科中使用两种语态的句子占比和使用被动语态的句子基本相同。在管理和软件学科中完全使用被动的句子占比略高于使用两种时态的句子。在其他两个学科中完全使用被动的句子占比均明显高出使用两种语态的句子。

表 5.6.22　　　　　　　　　**各学科语态组合及占比**

语态	学科	组合占比	语步			
			种类比	第一	第二	第三
V1	GL	63.60%	96%	2.2b	2.3a	2.3c
	DX	64.96%	97%	2.2b	2.3c	2.3b
	JT	46.03%	98%	2.2b	2.2a	4.3a
	CZ	50.49%	91%	2.2a	2.2b	2.3b
	RJ	65.02%	100%	2.2a	2.3c	2.2b
V2	GL	20.19%	83%	2.3c	2.2b	2.2a
	DX	22.19%	91%	2.3c	2.3b	2.2b
	JT	32.74%	93%	2.2a	2.2b	2.3b
	CZ	33.07%	75%	2.2a	2.2b	2.3b
	RJ	19.69%	82%	2.3c	2.2a	3.4c
V1V2	GL	16.21%	79%	2.3c	2.2b	2.3a
	DX	12.86%	71%	2.3c	2.2b	2.3b
	JT	21.24%	81%	2.2a	2.2b	2.2c
	CZ	16.44%	81%	2.2a	2.2b	2.2c
	RJ	15.29%	89%	2.3c	2.2a	2.3b

就三种语态组合涉及步骤种类而言，各学科中 V1 组合形式中步骤种类占比均最高，其次是 V2 组合，两种不同语态组合中步骤占比略低于 V2 组合。同一种组合形式中步骤种类占比学科间差异不大。但是软件学科中三种组合占比均略高于其他四个学科，在 V1 和 V2 组合中占比最低的均为车辆，V1V2 组合中占比最低的为电信。

就三种组合中占比最高的前三个步骤而言，各个学科有共性也有差异。在 V1 组合中，各学科均包含了 M2.2b，但是排名顺序不完全一致，在 V2 组合中交通和车辆完全一致，与其他学科有差异，分别有四个学科中包含了 M2.2a 和 M2.2b。在 V1V2 组合中，有四个学科包含了 M2.2b，且排序一致，其中车辆中该步骤与 M2.2c 占比相同，分别有三个学科中均包含了 M2.a 和 M2.3c。三种语态组合形式中 M2.2a、M2.2b 和 M2.3c 占比均较高。

附录 论文信息汇总

代码	期刊	卷期页	时间	论文题目	第一作者
GW – 01	*Supply Chain Management*	24(4)：524 – 539	2019	Trust, power and supply chain integration in Web-enabled supply chains	Carlo Mora-Monge
GW – 02	*International Journal of Project Management*	27(6)：638 – 348	2009	Trust in projects：An empirical assessment of owner/contractor relationships	Jeffrey K. Pinto
GW – 03	*Organization Science*	22(4)：1087 = 1104	2011	Foundations of Organizational Trust：What Matters to Different Stakeholders?	Michael Pirson
GW – 04	*Organization Science*	28(1)：74 – 92	2017	Mutual and Exclusive：Dyadic Sources of Trust in Interorganizational Exchange	Bill McEvily
GW – 05	*Strategic Management Journal*	37(4)：724 – 741	2016	When can you trust "trust"? Calculative trust, relational trust, and supplier performance	Laura Poppo
GW – 06	*Journal of Construction Engineering and Management*	146(4)：04020025	2020	Key Attitudes：Unlocking the Relationships between Emotional Intelligence and Performance in Construction Projects	Azadeh Rezvani
GW – 07	*International Journal of Project Management*	36(7)：954 – 967	2018	Why cultural intelligence matters on global project teams	Linda S. Henderson
GW – 08	*International Journal of Project Management*	38(1)：36 – 46	2020	Emotional intelligence：A preventive strategy to manage destructive influence of conflict in large scale projects	Pouria Khosravi

续表

代码	期刊	卷期页	时间	论文题目	第一作者
GW - 09	*Industrial Marketing Management*	34(3): 249 - 261	2005	Top management team diversity and innovativeness: The moderating role of interfunctional coordination	Seigyoung Auh
GW - 10	*Academy of Management Journal*	47(2): 175 - 192	2004	The Impact of Team Empowerment on Virtual Team Performance: The Moderating Role of Face-to-face Interaction	Bradley L. Kirkman
GW - 11	*Journal of Vocational Behavior*	114: 112 - 125	2019	Does holding a second job viewed as a calling impact one's work at the primary job	Brian D. Webster
GW - 12	*Human Performance*	32(2): 92 - 106	2019	Organizational Politics and Deviance: Exploring the Role of Political Skill	Wayne S. Crawford
GW - 13	*Personnel Review*	49(2): 597 - 619	2019	HRM reforms and job-related well-being of academics	Jie Xia
GW - 14	*Public Opinion Quarterly*	52(1): 100 - 124	1988	Underreporting of Substance Use In A National Longitudinal Youth Cohort: Individual and interviewer effects	Barbara S. Mensch
GW - 15	*Journal of Applied Social Psychology*	44(3): 175 - 189	2014	Generational differences in workplace behavior	John Bret Becton
GW - 16	*International Journal of Project Management*	27(1): 59 - 71	2009	Key project management practices affecting Singaporean firms' project performance in China	Florence Yean Yng Ling
GW-17	*International Journal of Project Management*	35(6): 1103 - 1119	2017	Critical success factors (CSFs) for integration of sustainability into construction project management practices in developing countries	Saeed Banihashemi
GW - 18	*Journal of Construction Engineering and Management*	140(7): 04014026	2014	Rationalizing the Implementation of Web-Based Project Management Systems in Construction Projects Using PLS-SEM	Hemanta Doloi
GW - 19	*Resources, Conservation and Recycling*	101: 73 - 83	2015	Improving waste management in construction projects: An Australian study	Nilupa Udawatta

代码	期刊	卷期页	时间	论文题目	第一作者
GW－20	*Journal of Construction Engineering and Management*	144(5)：04018025	2018	Preventive Mitigation of Overruns with Project Communication Management and Continuous Learning：PLS-SEM Approach	Jeffrey Boon Hui Yap
YW－01	Journal of Second Language Writing	23：17－30	2014	How do Planning Time and Task Conditions Affect Metacognitive Processes of L2 Writers?	Justina Ong
YW－02	Language Teaching Research	00(0)：1－29	2020	Target Language Use of Dutch EFL Student Teachers：Three Longitudinal Case Studies	Marjon Tammenga-Helmantel
YW－03	*Journal of Second Language Writing*	22(3)：307－329	2013	Written corrective feedback for individual L2 writers	Dana R. Ferris
YW－04	*Journal of Second Language Writing*	22(4)：406－424	2013	How do students of German perceive feedback practices at university? A motivational exploration	Vera Busse
YW－05	*Journal of Second Language Writing*	16(2)：82－99	2007	Teacher-written feedback：Student perceptions, teacher self-assessment, and actual teacher performance	Julie L. Montgomery
YW－06	*Journal of Computer Assisted Learning*	27(6)：557－574	2011	Effects of electronic outlining on students' argumentative writing performance	M. J. R. de Smet
YW－07	*The Modern Language Journal*	80(3)：287	1996	Some Input on Input：Two Analyses of Student Response to Expert Feedback in L2 Writing	John Hedgcock
YW－08	*Assessing Writing*	38：1－9	2018	Contract grading in the technical writing classroom：Blending community-based assessment and self-assessment	Lisa M. Litterio
YW－09	*International Journal of English Linguistics*	6(6)：8－18	2016	A Process Genre Approach to Teaching Report Writing to Arab EFL Computer Science Students	Hussein Taha Assaggaf
YW－10	*Assessing Writing*	36：3－18	2018	Going online：The effect of mode of delivery on performances and perceptions on an English L2 writing test suite	Tineke Brunfaut
YW－11	*Eurasian Journal of Applied Linguistics*	5(1)：131－151	2019	One Hand Washes the Other and Both Wash the Face：Individuality versus Collaboration in L2 Writing	Merve Savasci

代码	期刊	卷期页	时间	论文题目	第一作者
YW－12	*Written Communication*	35(1): 32－57	2018	The Role of Cognitive and Affective Factors in Measures of L2 Writing	Reza Zabihi
YW－13	*Language Teaching Research*	26(5): 1010－1033	2022	Motivation, self-regulation, and writing achievement on a university foundation programme: A programme evaluation study	James Wilby
YW－14	*Language Assessment Quarterly*	17(1): 43－59	2020	Motivational Factors in Computer-administered Integrated Skills Tasks: A Study of Young Learners	Judit Kormos
YW－15	*Journal of Second Language Writing*	20(2): 111－133	2011	Genre-based tasks in foreign language writing: Developing writers' genre awareness, linguistic knowledge, and writing competence	Sachiko Yasuda
YW－16	*Journal of Second Language Writing*	48	2020	English writing skills of students in upper secondary education: Results from an empirical study in Switzerland and Germany	Stefan D. Keller
YW－17	*The Journal of Asia TEFL*	16(1): 135－148	2019	Conceptualization of Second Language Writing Strategies and their Relation to Student Characteristics	Daniel R. Bailey
YW－18	*Journal of Language and Cultural Education*	4(3): 3－31	2016	Mexican university teacher-researchers' biliteracy beliefs and practices	Jitka Crhová
YW－19	*The Journal of Asia TEFL*	14(3): 464－481	2017	The Effects of University English Writing Classes Focusing on Self and Peer Review on Learner Autonomy	Hyoshin Lee
YW－20	*Journal of Second Language Writing*	24(1): 83－107	2014	Teacher assessment of grammatical ability in second language academic writing: A case study	Heike Neumann
SW－01	*ACS Chemical Biology*	13(2): 467－474	2017	CRISPR-Mediated Tagging of Endogenous Proteins with a Luminescent Peptide	Marie K. Schwinn

代码	期刊	卷期页	时间	论文题目	第一作者
SW－02	*Oncology Reports*	29(1)：149－154	2013	INSL5 is a novel marker for human enteroendocrine cells of the large intestine and neuroendocrine tumours	Thatchawan Thanasupawat
SW－03	*eLife*	6：1－20	2017	Tumor-promoting function of apoptotic caspases by an amplification loop involving ROS, macrophages and JNK in Drosophila	Ernesto Pérez
SW－04	*Cell Death and Differentiation*	23：1555－1564	2016	The initiator caspase Dronc is subject of enhanced autophagy upon proteasome impairment in Drosophila	TV Lee
SW－05	*Cell Reports*	1(6)：599－607	2012	The Drosophila Female Aphrodisiac Pheromone Activates ppk23 + Sensory Neurons to Elicit Male Courtship Behavior	Hirofumi Toda
SW－06	*eLife*	2013(2)：2013	2013	Apoptotic cells can induce non-autonomous apoptosis through the TNF	Ainhoa Pérez-Garijo
SW－07	*Genetics*	204(3)：1057－1064	2016	Discovering Single Nucleotide Polymorphisms Regulating Human Gene Expression Using Allele Specific Expression from RNA-seq Data	Eun Yong Kang
SW－08	*Genome Research*	27(11)：1950－1960	2017	A genome-wide interactome of DNA-associated proteins in the human liver	Ryne C. Ramaker
SW－09	*Genome Research*	22(5)：860－869	2012	Effects of sequence variation on differential allelic transcription factor occupancy and gene expression	Timothy E. Reddy
SW－10	*PloS one*	13(5)：e0196954	2018	Monoamines differentially modulate neuropeptide release from distinct sites within a single neuron pair	Tobias Clark
SW－11	*Nature*	529(7584)：92－96	2016	The C. elegans adult neuronal IIS/FOXO transcriptome reveals adult phenotype regulators	Rachel Kaletsky

代码	期刊	卷期页	时间	论文题目	第一作者
SW－12	*Cell*	172(5): 1022－1037	2018	NK Cells Stimulate Recruitment of cDC1 into the Tumor Microenvironment Promoting Cancer Immune Control	Jan P. Böttcher
SW－13	*Cell*	170: 1109－1119	2017	Oncolytic Virotherapy Promotes Intratumoral T Cell Infiltration and Improves Anti-PD-1 Immunotherapy	Antoni Ribas
SW－14	*Nature*	553 (7689): 496－500	2018	Monitoring T cell-dendritic cell interactions in vivo by intercellular enzymatic labelling	Giulia Pasqual
SW－15	*Nature*	553 (7686): 91－95	2018	Cyclin D-CDK4 kinase destabilizes PD-L1 via cullin 3-SPOP to control cancer immune surveillance	Jinfang Zhang
SW－16	*Cell Stem Cell*	10(1): 96－103	2012	Rejuvenation of Regeneration in the Aging Central Nervous System	Julia M. Ruckh
SW－17	*Biomedicine & Pharmacotherapy*	105 (2018): 753－757	2018	FAK and BMP-9 synergistically trigger osteogenic differentiation and bone formation of adipose derived stem cells through enhancing Wnt-β-catenin signaling	Cheng Yuan
SW－18	*International Journal of Obesity*	41(2): 299－308	2017	The role and possible mechanism of lncRNA U90926 in modulating 3T3－L1 preadipocyte differentiation	J Chen
SW－19	*Biomaterials*	35(10): 3172－3179	2014	BMP-9 as a potent brown adipogenic inducer with anti-obesity capacity	Mario Meng-Chiang Kuo
SW－20	*Journal of Molecular and Cellular Cardiology*	53(6): 790－800	2012	Endothelial differentiation in multipotent cells derived from mouse and human white mature adipocytes	Medet Jumabay
YXL－01	*Lupus*	27(9): 1437－1445	2018	Preconception antiphospholipid antibodies and risk of subsequent early pregnancy loss	K. J. Gibbins

代码	期刊	卷期页	时间	论文题目	第一作者
YXL－02	*Anesthesiology*	128(6)：1187－1192	2018	Effects of Prone Positioning on Transpulmonary Pressures and End-Expiratory Volumes in Patients without Lung Disease	Abirami Kumaresan
YXL－03	*Anesthesia and analgesia*	127(4)：920－927	2018	Resuscitation of Endotheliopathy and Bleeding in Thoracic Aortic Dissections：the VIPER-OCTA Randomized Clinical Pilot Trial	Jakob Stensballe
YXL－04	*Anesthesiology*	128(6)：1117－1124	2018	Positive End-Expiratory Pressure Alone Minimizes Atelectasis Formation in Nonabdominal Surgery	Erland Östberg
YXL－05	*Anesthesia and analgesia*	127(3)：759－766	2018	Readiness for Discharge After Foot and Ankle Surgery Using Peripheral Nerve Blocks: A Randomized Controlled Trial Comparing Spinal and General Anesthesia As Supplements to Nerve Blocks	Jacques YaDeau
YXL－06	*Journal of Dental Research*	97(11)：1207－1213	2018	Self-Limiting versus Conventional Caries Removal：A Randomized Clinical Trial	A. H. Ali
YXL－07	*Journal of Dental Research*	225(5)：406	2018	Five-Year Survival of Short Single-Tooth Implants (6 mm)：A Randomized Controlled Clinical Trial	N. Naenni
YXL－08	*Journal of Dental Research*	96(8)：875－880	2017	Cost-Effectiveness of Caries Prevention in Practice：A Randomized Controlled Trial	C. O'Neill
YXL－09	*Journal of Dental Research*	96(2)：163－170	2017	Esthetic and Clinical Performance of Implant-Supported All-Ceramic Crowns Made with Prefabricated or CAD/CAM Zirconia Abutments：A Randomized, Multicenter Clinical Trial	J. G. Wittneben
YXL－10	*Experimental Eye Research*	171：183－191	2018	Successful single treatment with ziv-aflibercept for existing corneal neovascularization following ocular chemical insult in the rabbit model	Ariel Gore

代码	期刊	卷期页	时间	论文题目	第一作者
YXL－11	*Biomaterials*	28(26)：3807－3814	2007	Immunological responses in mice to full-thickness corneal grafts engineered from porcine collagen	Lei Liu
YXL－12	*Peptides*	99：20－26	2018	Trophic effect of PACAP on human corneal endothelium	Grazia Maugeria
YXL－13	*Acta Biomaterialia*	64：346－356	2017	Mesenchymal stem cell therapy for retro-corneal membrane—A clinical challenge in full-thickness transplantation of biosynthetic corneal equivalents	Vijayalakshmi Rajendran
YXL－14	*BMC Infectious Disease*	15(1)：325	2015	Separation of Mycobacterium abscessus into subspecies or genotype level by direct application of peptide nucleic acid multi-probe-real-time PCR method into sputa samples	Kijeong Kim
YXL－15	*Journal of Clinical Microbiology*	52(1)：251－259	2014	Discrimination of Mycobacterium abscessus subsp. massiliense from Mycobacterium abscessus subsp. abscessus in Clinical Isolates by Multiplex PCR	Kazue Nakanaga
YXL－16	*Journal of Antimicrobial Chemotherapy*	67(11)：2606－2611	2012	Acquisition of clarithromycin resistance mutations in the 23S rRNA gene of Mycocaterium abscessus in the presence of inducible erm(41)	Florian P. Maurer
YXL－17	*Toxins*	4(12)：1427－1439	2012	Interleukin-l7 (IL－17) Expression is Reduced during Acute Myocardial Infarction：Role on Chemokine Receptor Expression in Monocytes and Their in Vitro Chemotaxis towards Chemokines	Maria Troitskaya
YXL－18	*Circulation Research*	96(8)：881－889	2005	CCL2/monocyte Chemoattractant Protein-1 Regulates Inflammatory Responses Critical to Healing Myocardial Infarcts	Oliver Dewald
YXL－19	*American Journal of Pathology*	164(2)：665－677	2004	Of Mice and Dogs：Species-Specific Differences in the Inflammatory Response Following Myocardial Infarction	Oliver Dewald

代码	期刊	卷期页	时间	论文题目	第一作者
YXL－20	*The Journal of Thoracic and Cardiovascular Surgery*	154(6)：2092－2099(e2)	2017	Survival and risk factors for progression after resection of the dominant tumor in multifocal, lepidic-type pulmonary adenocarcinoma	Rebecca W. Gao
YXJ－01	*Osteo Arthritis and Cartilage*	15(9)：1061－1069	2007	The surgical destabilization of the medial meniscus (DMM) model of osteoarthritis in the 129/SvEv mouse	S. S. Glasson
YXJ－02	*Osteo Arthritis and Cartilage*	25(8)：1335－1344	2017	Acute mobilization and migration of bone marrow-derived stem cells following anterior cruciate ligament rupture	T. Maerz
YXJ－03	*Osteo Arthritis and Cartilage*	22(8)：1158－1166	2014	Treatment efficacy of adipose-derived stem cells in experimental osteoarthritis is driven by high synovial activation and reflected by S100A8/A9 serum levels	R. F. Schelbergen
YXJ－04	*Osteo Arthritis and Cartilage*	25(9)：1541－1550	2017	Stepwise preconditioning enhances mesenchymal stem cell-based cartilage regeneration through epigenetic modification	S. Lin
YXJ－05	*Osteo Arthritis and Cartilage*	25(4)：554－560	2016	Intra-articular therapy with recombinant human GDF5 arrests disease progression and stimulates cartilage repair in the rat medial meniscus transection (MMT) model of osteoarthritis	W. R. Parrish
YXJ－06	*Osteo Arthritis and Cartilage*	23(3)：454－461	2015	The chemokine receptor CCR5 plays a role in post-traumatic cartilage loss in mice, but does not affect synovium and bone	K. Takebe
YXJ－07	*Cancer Research*	76(8)：2465－2477	2016	A three-dimensional organoid culture system derived from human glioblastomas recapitulates the hypoxic gradients and cancer stem cell heterogeneity of tumors found in vivo	Christopher G. Hubert
YXJ－08	*Cell Reports*	23(4)：1220－1229	2018	Glioblastoma Model Using Human Cerebral Organoids	Junko Ogawa

代码	期刊	卷期页	时间	论文题目	第一作者
YXJ－09	*Molecular Metabolism*	3(5)：544－553	2014	ER calcium release promotes mitochondrial dysfunction and hepatic cell lipotoxicity in response to palmitate overload	Robert A. Egnatchik
YXJ－10	*Hepatology*	63(1)：95－106	2016	Liver Receptor Homolog-1 Is a Critical Determinant of Methyl-Pool Metabolism	Martin Wagner
YXJ－11	*Clinical Cancer Research*	23(3)：707－716	2017	CD137 stimulation enhances cetuximab induced natural killer (NK)：dendritic cell (DC) priming of anti-tumor T cell immunity in head and neck cancer patients	Raghvendra M.
YXJ－12	*Clinical Cancer Research*	23(14)：3585－3591	2017	Agreement between Programmed Cell Death Ligand-1 Diagnostic Assays across Multiple Protein Expression Cutoffs in Non-Small Cell Lung Cancer	Marianne J. Ratcliffe
YXJ－13	*Clinical Cancer Research*	23(2)：454－465	2017	PD-1/PD-L1 Blockade Enhances T-cell Activity and Antitumor Efficacy of Imatinib in Gastrointestinal Stromal Tumors	Adrian M. Seifert
YXJ－14	*Clinical Cancer Research*	22(12)：2848－2854	2016	Phase Ib Study of PEGylated Recombinant Human Hyaluronidase and Gemcitabine in Patients with Advanced Pancreatic Cancer	Sunil R. Hingorani
YXJ－15	*Translational Oncol*	7(6)：694－701	2014	New Approach for Interpreting Changes in Circulating Tumour Cells (CTC) for Evaluation of Treatment Effect in Metastatic Breast Cancer	Peer Horn
YXJ－16	*BMC Cancer*	16：168	2016	Vimentin and Ki67 expression in circulating tumour cells derived from castrate-resistant prostate cancer	C. R. Lindsay
YXJ－17	*Journal of Circulating Biomarkers*	4：3	2015	Analytical Validation and Capabilities of the Epic CTC Platform：Enrichment-Free Circulating Tumour Cell Detection and Characterization	Shannon L. Werner

续表

代码	期刊	卷期页	时间	论文题目	第一作者
YXJ-18	*BMC Cancer*	15：458	2015	Categorical versus continuous circulating tumor cell enumeration as early surrogate marker for therapy response and prognosis during docetaxel therapy in metastatic prostate cancer patients	Mark Thalgott
YXJ-19	*Neuropsychopharmacology*	41：2893－2902	2016	The α7 Nicotinic Agonist ABT-126 in the Treatment of Cognitive Impairment Associated with Schizophrenia in Nonsmokers：Results from a Randomized Controlled Phase 2b Study	George Haig
YXJ-20	*Alzheimer's Research & Therapy*	8(1)：44	2016	ABT－126 monotherapy in mild-to-moderate Alzheimer's dementia：randomized double-blind, placebo and active controlled adaptive trial and open-label extension	Laura M. Gault
HX-01	*Nano Letter*	16(7)：4047－4053	2016	Supporting Information of General Thermal Texturization Process of MoS_2 for Efficient Electrocatalytic Hydrogen Evolution Reaction	Daisuke Kiriya
HX-02	*Journal of the American Chemical Society*	135(25)：9267－9270	2013	Nanostructured Ni_2P phosphide as an Electrocatalyst for the Hydrogen Evolution Reaction	Eric J. Popczun
HX-03	*Nano Letter*	13(12)：6222－6227	2013	Conducting MoS_2 nanosheets as catalysts for hydrogen evolution reaction	Damien Voiry
HX-04	*ACS Applied Materials & Interfaces*	9(44)：38959－38966	2017	Nonpolar Resistive Switching in Ag@ TiO_2 Core. Shell Nanowires	Hugh G. Manning
HX-05	*The Journal of Physical Chemistry C*	121(37)：20413－20418	2017	Formation of Metastable Water Chains on Anatase TiO_2(101)	Arjun Dahal
HX-06	*The Journal of Physical Chemistry C*	121(44)：24721－24725	2017	Direct Visualization of Au Atoms Bound to TiO_2(110) O. Vacancies	Andrew Mellor

代码	期刊	卷期页	时间	论文题目	第一作者
HX-07	*Dalton Transactions*	46(16): 5320 – 5325	2017	Anion exchange dynamics in the capture of perchlorate by a cationic Ag-based MOF	Ian R. Colinas
HX-08	*Advanced Materials*	23(37): 4248 – 4253	2011	Two-Dimensional Nanocrystals Produced by Exfoliation of Ti_3AlC_2	Michael Naguib
HX-09	*Advanced Energy Materials*	5(15): 1 – 4	2015	Probing the Mechanism of High Capacitance in 2d Titanium Carbide Using In Situ X-ray Absorption Spectroscopy	Maria R. Lukatskaya
HX-10	*Journal of Physical Chemistry Letters*	6(12): 2305 – 2309	2015	Two-Dimensional Vanadium Carbide (MXene) as Positive Electrode for Sodium-Ion Capacitors	Yohan Dall' Agnese
HX-11	*Advanced Energy Materials*	6(24): 1601372	2016	MXene-on-Paper Coplanar Microsupercapacitors	Narendra Kurra
HX-12	*Langmuir*	33(25): 6314 – 6321	2017	Controlling Photocatalytic Activity and Size Selectivity of TiO_2 Encapsulated in Hollow Silica Spheres by Tuning Silica Shell Structures Using Sacrificial Biomolecules	Kensei Fujiwara
HX-13	*Ceramics International*	44(5): 4577 – 4585	2018	Electrospinning amorphous $SiO_2 – TiO_2$ and TiO_2 nanofibers using sol-gel chemistry and its thermal conversion into anatase and rutile	Fei Huang
HX-14	*Catalysis Today*	302: 277 – 285	2018	Infrared analysis of methanol adsorption on mixed oxides derived from Mg/Al hydrotalcite catalysts for transesterification reactions	Gina Hincapié
HX-15	*ACS Applied Materials & Interfaces*	9(37): 31393 – 31400	2017	Selective Inactivation of Bacteriophage in the Presence of Bacteria by Use of Ground Rh-Doped $SrTiO_3$ Photocatalyst and Visible Light	Yuichi Yamaguchi

代码	期刊	卷期页	时间	论文题目	第一作者
HX – 16	*Nature Communications*	3	2012	A seamless three-dimensional carbon nanotube graphene hybrid material	Yu Zhu
HX – 17	*ACS NANO*	7(1)：58 – 64	2013	Three-Dimensional Metal-Graphene-Nanotube Multifunctional Hybrid Materials	Zheng Yan
HX – 18	*Nanotechnology*	18(18)：185605(1 – 5)	2007	A generic process of growing aligned carbon nanotube arrays on metals and metal alloys	Prahalad M. Parthangal
HX – 19	*ACS NANO*	11(3)：2724 – 2733	2017	Graphene Carbon Nanotube Carpets Grown Using Binary Catalysts for High-Performance Lithium-Ion Capacitors	Rodrigo Villegas Salvatierra
HX – 20	*Applied Catalysis B：Environmental*	228：130 – 141	2018	Sn modification of TiO_2 anatase and rutile type phases：2 – Propanol photo-oxidation under UV and visible light	María Fernanda Gálvez-López
SZ – 01	*Bioelectrochemistry*	118：123 – 130	2017	AQDS immobilized solid-phase redox mediators and their role during bioelectricity generation and RR2 decolorization in air-cathode single-chamber microbial fuel cells	Claudia M. Martinez
SZ – 02	*Water Science and Technology*	55(8 – 9)：43 – 49	2007	Evaluation of hybrid processes for nitrification by comparing MBBR/AS and WAS configurations	E. Germain
SZ – 03	*Biotechnol Lett*	36(10)：1981 – 1986	2014	High pH（and not free ammonia）is responsible for Anammox inhibition in mildly alkaline solutions with excess of ammonium	D. Puyol
SZ – 04	*Journal of environmental management*	142：53 – 59	2014	Laboratory study of nitrification, denitrification and anammox processes in membrane bioreactors considering periodic aeration	Rouzbeh Abbassi
SZ – 05	*Water Research*	131：110 – 121	2018	Relationships between DBP concentrations and differential UV absorbance in full-scale conditions	Nicolas Beauchamp

续表

代码	期刊	卷期页	时间	论文题目	第一作者
SZ-06	*Water Research*	133: 247-254	2018	Persulfate activation by glucose for in situ chemical oxidation	Richard J. Watts
SZ-07	*Chemosphere*	175: 170-177	2017	Remediating 1, 4-dioxane-contaminated water with slow-releasepersulfate and zerovalent iron	AnnKambhu
SZ-08	*Ultrasonics Sonochemistry*	38(1): 652-663	2017	Mechanistic investigations in sono-hybrid (ultrasound/Fe^{2+}/UVC) techniques of persulfate activation for degradation of Azorubine	Sankar Chakma
SZ-09	*Environmental Science & Technology*	45(20): 8683-8690	2011	Assessing the severity of rainfall-derived infiltration and inflow and sewer deterioration based on the flux stability of sewage markers	Jessica M. Shelton
SZ-10	*Water Science and Technology*	66(4): 704-711	2012	Integrated solutions for urban runoff pollution control in Brazilian metropolitan regions	A. C. D. Morihama
SZ-11	*Water Science and Technology*	40(3): 357-364	1999	Treatment of combined sewer overflows at small wastewater treatment works by constructed reed beds	M. B. Green
SZ-12	*Water Science and Technology*	56(12): 63-67	2007	Biocides used in building materials and their leaching behavior to sewer systems	M. Burkhardt
SZ-13	*Journal of Hydraulic Engineering*	144(6): 04018018	2018	Flow Structures in Evolving Scour Holes Caused by a Plunging Jet Downstream of a Weir	Jin-Hua Si
SZ-14	*Journal of Hydraulic Engineering*	129(9): 680-687	2003	Calibration of Submerged Radial Gates	A. J. Clemmens
SZ-15	*Journal of Hydraulic Engineering*	144(6): 04018019	2018	Clear-water Local Scour at Skewed Complex Bridge Piers	Yifan Yang
SZ-16	*Journal of Membrane Science*	603: 118047	2020	A novel stimuli-responsive and fouling resistant PVDF ultrafiltration membrane prepared by using amphiphilic copolymer of poly (vinylidene fluoride) and Poly (2-N-morpholino) ethyl methacrylate	Bharti Saini

代码	期刊	卷期页	时间	论文题目	第一作者
SZ – 17	*Water Research*	136: 84 – 94	2018	Neural networks for dimensionality reduction of fluorescence spectra and prediction of drinking water disinfection by-products	Nicolas M. Peleato
SZ – 18	*Desalination*	469: 114093	2019	Field validation of self-regenerating reversible ion exchange-membrane (RIX-M) process to prevent sulfate and silica fouling	Michael S. German
SZ – 19	*Journal of Nanoparticle Research*	22(5): 1 – 11	2020	Aerosol impaction-driven assembly produces evenly dispersed nanoparticle coating on polymeric water treatment membranes	Ariel J. Atkinson
SZ – 20	*ACS Applied Materials & Interfaces*	12(17): 19944 – 19954	2020	Dual-functional Nanofiltration Membranes Exhibit Multifaceted Ion Rejection and Antifouling Performance	John R. Hoffman
HY – 01	*Palaeogeography, Palaeoclimatology, Palaeoecology*	440: 22 – 32	2015	Carbon isotopic ratios of modern C3-C4 plants from the Gangetic Plain, India and its implications to paleo vegetational reconstruction	Sayak Basu
HY – 02	*Organic Geochemistry*	37(11): 1505 – 1513	2006	Paleohydrologic reconstruction based on n-alkane distributions in ombrotrophic peat	Jonathan E. Nichols
HY – 03	*Quaternary Science Reviews*	26(7 – 8): 1004 – 1015	2007	Paleohydrological changes during the last deglaciation in Northern Brazil	Jérémy Jacob
HY – 04	*Chemical Geology*	488: 44 – 55	2018	Estimating silicate weathering timescales from geochemical modeling and spring water residence time in the Kirishima volcanic area, southern Japan	Kiyoshi Ide
HY – 05	*Letters*	261: 476 – 490	2007	Iceland	R. B. Georg
HY – 06	*Litho*	274 – 275: 291 – 303	2017	Oceanic mafic magmatism in the Siletz terrane, NW North America: fragments of an Eocene oceanic plateau?	Bethan A. Phillips

代码	期刊	卷期页	时间	论文题目	第一作者
HY-07	*Lithos*	272-273: 69-83	2017	The pre-Atlantic Hf isotope evolution of the east Laurentian continental margin: Insights from zircon in basement rocks and glacial tillites from northern New Jersey and southeastern New York	N. Alex Zirakparvar
HY-08	*Lithos*	272-273: 128-146	2017	Zr-in-rutile resetting in aluminosilicate bearing ultra-high temperature granulites: Refining the record of cooling and hydration in the Napier Complex, Antarctica	Ruairidh J. Mitchell
HY-09	*Lithos*	276: 90-102	2017	Textures in spinel peridotite mantle xenoliths using micro-CT scanning: Examples from Canary Islands and France	K. K. Bhanot
HY-10	*Earth and Planetary Science Letters*	298 (1-2): 244-254	2010	The release of ^{14}C-depleted carbon from the deep ocean during the last deglaciation: Evidence from the Arabian Sea	Sean P. Bryan
HY-11	*Paleoceanography*	18(4): 10 (1-8)	2003	Atlantic Ocean circulation during the Younger Dryas: Insights from a new Cd/Ca record from the western subtropical South Atlantic	Rosemarie E. Came
HY-12	*Earth and Planetary Science Letters*	258 (1-2): 73-86	2007	Benthic foraminiferal B/Ca ratios reflect deep water carbonate saturation state	Jimin Yu
HY-13	*European Journal of Mineralogy*	18(4): 441-447	2006	OH in naturally occurring corundum	Anton Beran
HY-14	*Contributions to Mineralogy and Petrology*	133(4): 356-372	1998	Models of corundum origin from alkali basaltic terrains: A reappraisal	F. Lin Sutherland
HY-15	*Lithos*	260: 339-344	2016	Origin of sapphires from a lamprophyre dike at Yogo Gulch, Montana, USA: Clues from their melt inclusions	Aaron C. Palke

续表

代码	期刊	卷期页	时间	论文题目	第一作者
HY-16	*Palaeogeography, Palaeoclimatology, Palaeoecology*	203 (1-2): 73-93	2004	Contrasting glacial/interglacial regimes in the western Arctic Ocean as exemplified by a sedimentary record from the Mendeleev Ridge	Leonid Polyak
HY-17	*Quaternary Science Reviews*	79: 145-156	2013	Quaternary history of sea ice in the western Arctic Ocean based on foraminifera	Leonid Polyak
HY-18	*Geochimica Et Cosmochimica Acta*	73(2): 388-403	2009	Biogenic iron oxyhydroxide formation at mid-ocean ridge hydrothermal vents: Juan de Fuca Ridge	Brandy M. Toner
HY-19	*Applied & Environmental Microbiology*	81(23): 8066-8075	2015	Microbial Iron Oxidation in the Arctic Tundra and Its Implications for Biogeochemical Cycling	David Emerson
HY-20	*Marine Chemistry*	180: 42-50	2016	Suspended particle-associated PAHs in the open eastern Mediterranean Sea: Occurrence, sources and processes affecting their distribution patterns	Constantine Parinos
YY-01	*The Journal of the Acoustical Society of America*	125(6): 3962-3973	2009	Acoustic characteristics of clearly spoken English fricatives	Kazumi Maniwa
YY-02	*The Journal of the Acoustical Society of America*	108(3): 559-580	2000	Acoustic characteristics of English fricatives	Allard Jongman
YY-03	*Journal of Phonetics*	16(3): 295-298	1988	Acoustic characteristics of English voiceless fricatives: a descriptive analysis	Susan J. Behrens
YY-04	*Journal of Chinese Linguistics*	42(1): 150-171	2014	Acoustic characteristics of voiceless fricatives in Mandarin Chinese	Chaoyang Lee
YY-05	*Journal of Phonetics*	74: 18-41	2019	Acoustic correlates of anticipatory and progressive [ATR] harmony processes in Ethiopian Komo	Paul Olejarczuk
YY-06	*Journal of the Acoustical Society of America*	146(3): 1568	2019	Acoustic voice variation within and between speakers	Yoonjeong Lee

代码	期刊	卷期页	时间	论文题目	第一作者
YY－07	*Language and Speech*	1－21	2019	Sibilant Fricative Merging in Taiwan Mandarin: An Investigation of Tongue Postures using Ultrasound Imaging	Chenhao Chiu
YY－08	*Journal of Phonetics*	34: 202－240	2006	The acoustic and perceptual bases of judgments of women and men's sexual orientation from read speech	Benjamin Munson
YY－09	*Linguistics*	55(5): 1021－1044	2017	The development of gender-specific patterns in the production of voiceless sibilant fricatives in Mandarin Chinese	Fangfang Li
YY－10	*Phonetica*	77(2): 107－130	2020	Evidence for Incomplete Neutralization in Chilean Spanish	Mariška A. Bolyanatz
YY－11	*Journal of Phonetics*	10(3): 231－244	1982	Continuous and categorical perception of a fricative-affricate continuum	F. E. Ferrero
YY－12	*Journal of Phonetics*	39(3): 388－402	2011	Effects of the distribution of acoustic cues on infants' perception of sibilants	Alejandrina Cristià
YY－13	*Cognition*	98(2): B35－B44	2005	Categorical perception of speech sounds in illiterate adults	Willy Serniclaes
YY－14	*Journal of Phonetics*	38(1): 127－136	2010	On the perceptual basis of distinctive features: Evidence from the perception of fricatives by Dutch and English speakers	Keith Johnson
YY－15	*Brain and Language*	143: 52－58	2015	Categorical effects in fricative perception are reflected in cortical source information	Sol Lago
YY－16	*Clinical Linguistics & Phonetics*	31(1): 56－79	2017	Bias in the Perception of Phonetic Detail in Children's Speech: A Comparison of Categorical and Continuous Rating Scales	Benjamin Munson
YY－17	*Journal of Phonetics*	67: 49－64	2018	An order effect in English infants' discrimination of an Urdu affricate contrast	Mariam Dar

代码	期刊	卷期页	时间	论文题目	第一作者
YY-18	*International Journal of Pediatric Otorhinolaryngology*	79(2)：179-185	2015	Spectral features and perceptual judgment of place of affricate in Putonghua-speaking pre-adolescents with normal and cleft palate	Chenghui Jiang
YY-19	*Journal of Memory and Language*	112：104108	2020	Language-specific prosodic acquisition：A comparison of phrase boundary perception by French- and German-learning infants	Sanderien van Ommen
YY-20	*Journal of Phonetics*	40(1)：109-128	2012	Native-language phonetic and phonological influences on perception of American English approximants by Danish and German listeners	Ocke-Schwen Bohn
TM-01	*Journal of Structural Engineering（United States）*	138(1)：81-89	2012	Experimental Performance of Concrete Columns with Composite Jackets under Blast Loading	Tonatiuh Rodriguez-Nikl
TM-02	*Journal of Structural Engineering（United States）*	139(1)：98-107	2013	Performance of Steel Moment Connections under a Column Removal Scenario. I：Experiments	H. S. Lew
TM-03	*Physical review. E*	96(3)：032913	2017	Granular temperature measured experimentally in a shear flow by acoustic energy	Stephanie Taylor
TM-04	*Landslides*	6(3)：181-190	2009	Relations between hydrology and velocityof a continuously moving landslide—evidenceof pore-pressure feedback regulating landslide motion?	William H. Schulz
TM-05	*Nature Geoscience*	8：484-489	2015	Phase transformation and nanometric flow causeextreme weakening during fault slip	H. W. Green II
TM-06	*Journal of Geophysical Research：Solid Earth*	124(7)：6397-6408	2019	Energy Partitioning in Granular Flow Dependson Mineralogy via Nanoscale Plastic Work	S. E. Taylor
TM-07	*Geomorphology*	345：106835	2019	Causes and triggers of deep-seated hillslope instability in the tropics -Insights from a 60-year record of Ikoma landslide（DR Congo）	Antoine Dille

代码	期刊	卷期页	时间	论文题目	第一作者
TM - 08	*ACI Materials Journal*	111(5): 501 - 510	2014	Mechanical Performance of Reinforced Concrete and Steel Fiber-Reinforced Concrete Precast Tunnel Lining Segments: A Case Study	Safeer Abbas
TM-09	*Journal of Materials in Civil Engineering*	22(12): 1304 - 1314	2010	Effect of Wrinkles on the Circumferential Strength of a Cast-in-Place Composite Polymer Liner Used in Retrofitting Pressure Pipes	Nancy Ampiah
TM - 10	*Polymer Engineering and Science*	48(7): 1231 - 1239	2020	Material Characterization of Components and Assembled Behavior of a Composite Liner for Rehabilitation of Cast Iron Pressure Pipes	Michael Brown
TM - 11	*Rock Mechanics and Rock Engineering*	49(11): 4257 - 4272	2016	Analysis of the Behavior of Sedimentary Rocks Under Impact Loading	Oliver Millon
TM - 12	*Building & Environment*	73(1): 138 - 150	2014	Thermal assessment of heat mitigation strategies: The case of Portland State University, Oregon, USA	Mohammad Taleghani
TM - 13	*Structural Concrete*	15(3): 331 - 339	2014	Experimental investigations on the punchingbehaviour of reinforced concrete footingswith structural dimensions	Carsten Siburg
TM - 14	*Geotextiles and Geomembranes*	43(3): 240 - 249	2015	An evaluation of the interface behaviour of rail subballast stabilizedwith geogrids and geomembranes	M. Mahdi Biabani
TM - 15	*Engineering Structures*	216: 110790	2020	Effect of concrete cover on the pure torsional behavior of reinforcedconcrete beams	Mohammed Sirage Ibrahim
TM - 16	*Geotextiles and Geomembranes*	42(5): 494 - 504	2014	Experimental and numerical analysis of large scale pull out testsconducted on clays reinforced with geogrids encapsulated withcoarse material	M. R. Abdi

续表

代码	期刊	卷期页	时间	论文题目	第一作者
TM-17	*Engineering Structures*	101: 246-263	2015	Experimental evaluation of the seismic performance of reinforcedconcrete structural walls with different end configurations	Omar A. El-Azizy
TM-18	*Journal of Constructional Steel Research*	154: 149-160	2019	Experimental study of beams with stiffened large web openings	T. Al-Dafafea
TM-19	*Geotextiles and Geomembranes*	28(6): 570-578	2010	Investigation of factors influencing behavior of single geocell-reinforcedbases under static loading	Sanat K. Pokharel
TM-20	*Soil Dynamics and Earthquake Engineering*	27(4): 324-332	2007	Shaking table testing of geofoam seismic buffers	Richard J. Bathurst
TM-21	*Engineering Structures*	151: 633-647	2017	Shake table tests of a full-scale two-story sheathing-braced cold-formedsteel building	Luigi Fiorino
TM-22	*Engineering Structures*	125: 455-470	2016	Out-of-plane shaking table tests on URM single leaf and cavity walls	Francesco Graziotti
TM-23	*Composite Structures*	94(5): 1564-1574	2012	Shake table response and analysis of a concrete-filled FRP tube bridge column	Arash E. Zaghi
TM-24	*Engineering Failure Analysis*	18(8): 2305-2315	2011	Experiments into impact behaviour of railway prestressedconcrete sleepers	Sakdirat Kaewunruen
TM-25	*Engineering Structures*	29(7): 1343-1353	2007	FRP-confined concrete members: Axial compression experiments andplasticity modelling	Theodoros C. Rousakis
TM-26	*Cement and Concrete Composites*	77: 1-13	2017	Response of steel fiber reinforced high strength concrete beams: Experiments and code predictions	Luigi Biolzi

代码	期刊	卷期页	时间	论文题目	第一作者
CL－01	*ACS Nano*	13(9): 9927 － 9935	2019	Peptide Assembly Directed and Quantified Using Megadalton DNA Nanostructures	Juan Jin
CL－02	*ACS Nano*	6(7): 6122 － 6132	2012	Autonomous Motion of Metallic-Microrods Propelled by Ultrasound	Wei Wang
CL－03	*Advanced Materials Technologies*	2(12): 1700210	2017	Epidermal Tattoo Patch for Ultrasound-Based Transdermal Microballistic Delivery	Fernando Soto
CL－04	*Journal of the American Chemical Society*	136 (24): 8552 － 8555	2014	Ultrasound-Modulated Bubble Propulsion of Chemically-Powered Microengines	Tailin Xu
CL－05	*Nature Communications*	3: 710	2012	Precise hierarchical self-assemblyof multicompartment micelles	André H. Gröschel
CL－06	*Angewandte Chemie (International Edition)*	59(4)	2020	Unconventional Route to Oxygen-Vacancy-Enabled Highly Efficient Electron Extraction and Transport in Perovskite Solar Cells	Bing Wang
CL－07	*Angewandte Chemie International Edition*	55(30): 8599 － 8604	2016	Enhanced Intrinsic Catalytic Activity of λ-MnO_2 by Electrochemical Tuning and Oxygen Vacancy Generation	Sanghan Lee
CL－08	*Small (Weinheim an der Bergstrasse, Germany)*	15(29): e1804524	2019	N, P co-coordinated manganese atoms in mesoporous carbon for electrochemical oxygenreduction	Xiaofeng Zhu
CL－09	*Journal of the American Chemical Society*	141(16): 6680 － 6689	2019	Lithium-Doping Stabilized High-Performance P2 － $Na_{0.66}Li_{0.18}Fe_{0.12}Mn_{0.7}O_2$ Cathode for Sodium Ion Batteries	Lufeng Yang
CL－10	*Advanced Energy Materials*	7(17): 1700098	2017	K-Ion Batteries Based on a P2-Type $K_{0.6}CoO_2$ Cathode	Haegyeom Kim

续表

代码	期刊	卷期页	时间	论文题目	第一作者
CL-11	*Surface & Coatings Technology*	202(8)：1462－1469	2008	Influence of microarc oxidation and hard anodizing on plain fatigue andfretting fatigue behaviour of Al-Mg-Si alloy	B. Rajasekaran
CL-12	*Wear*	259(1－6)：271－276	2005	Quantitative analysis of fretting wear crack nucleation in 7075-T6aluminum alloy using fretting maps	Sachin Shinde
CL-13	*Materials*	9(3)：141	2016	Surface Characterizations of Fretting Fatigue Damagein Aluminum Alloy 7075－T6 Clamped Joints：The Beneficial Role of Ni-P Coatings	Reza H. Oskouei
CL-14	*Applied Physics Letters*	106(20)：202904	2015	Large magnetoelectric response inmodified BNT based ternarypiezoelectric $\{72.5(Bi_{1/2}Na_{1/2}TiO_3)-22.5(Bi_{1/2}K_{1/2}TiO_3)-5[BiMgmagnetostrictive(NiFe_2O_4)]$ particulate $(0-3)$ composites$\}$	Mintu Tyagi
CL-15	*ACS Nano*	13(8)：88760－88765	2019	Room-Temperature Electrocaloric Effect in Layered Ferroelectric $CuIn P_2 S_6$ for Solid-State Refrigeration	Mengwei Si
CL-16	*Science*	311(5765)：1270－1271	2006	Supporting Online Material for Giant Electrocaloric Effectin Thin-Film $PbZr_{0.95}Ti_{0.05}O_3$	A. S. Mischenko
CL-17	*Journal of Materials Chemistry C*	101：246－4(21)：4763－4769	2016	Perovskite ferroelectrics and relaxor-ferroelectricsolid solutions with large intrinsic electrocaloricresponse over broad temperature ranges	H. Khassaf
CL-18	*Science*	321(5890)：821－823	2008	Supporting Online Material forLarge Electrocaloric Effect in Ferroelectric Polymers Near RoomTemperature	Bret Neese
CL-19	*International Journal of Fatigue*	30(7)：1259－1266	2008	Effect of microarc oxidised layer thickness on plain fatigueand fretting fatigue behaviour of Al-Mg-Si alloy	B. Rajasekaran

续表

代码	期刊	卷期页	时间	论文题目	第一作者
CL-20	*Wear*	261 (3-4): 426-434	2007	Fretting fatigue behavior in 7075-T6 aluminum alloy	Sachin R. Shinde
GL-01	*Journal of the European Economic Association*	17(6): 1753-1796	2019	Banking and Industrialization	Stephan Heblich
GL-02	*The Journal of Finance*	65(5): 1637-1667	2010	Big Bad Banks? The Winners and Losers from Bank Deregulation in the United States	Thorsten Beck
GL-03	*The Review of Economics and Statistics*	99(3): 417-434	2017	Roads and Innovation	Ajay Agrawal
GL-04	*Journal of Financial Economics*	79(3): 469-506	2006	Partial adjustment toward target capital structures	Mark J. Flannery
GL-05	*Journal of Financial Economics*	84(1): 187-228	2007	Banking crises, financial dependence, and growth	Randall S. Kroszner
GL-06	*Transportation Research Part E*	46(3): 414-425	2010	Operational workforce planning for check-in counters at airports	Raik Stolletz
GL-07	*Transportation Research Part A*	35a(4): 289-308	2001	Multiple fleet aircraft schedule recovery following hub closures selection and tour-schedule construction	Benjamin G. Thengvall
GL-08	*Transportation Science*	34(3): 337-348	2000	Airline Crew Recovery	Ladislav Lettovsky
GL-09	*Annals of Operations Research*	127: 359-372	2004	Multi-Skilled Workforce Optimisation	Guy Eitzen
GL-10	*Computers & Industrial Engineering*	122(C): 1-14	2018	A multi-stage stochastic programming approach for blood supply chain planning	B. Zahiri
GL-11	*Transportation Research Part E: Logistics and Transportation Review*	48(1): 150-164	2012	Bioethanol supply chain system planning under supply and demand uncertainties	Chien-Wei Chen
GL-12	*International Journal of Production Economics*	195:27-44	2018	a bio-fuel supply chain network	Md Abdul Quddus

代码	期刊	卷期页	时间	论文题目	第一作者
GL - 13	*European Journal of Operational Research*	249(1)：76 - 92	2016	Hybrid robust and stochastic optimization for closed-loop supply chain network design using accelerated Benders decomposition	Esmaeil Keyvanshokooh
GL - 14	*Transportation Research Part E*	134：1366 - 5545	2020	Robust design of blood supply chains under risk of disruptions using Lagrangian relaxation	Bayan Hamdan
GL - 15	*Journal of Development Economics*	137(C)：36 - 65	2019	The surprising instability of export specializations	Diego Daruich
GL - 16	*The American Economist*	34(2)：55 - 59	1990	Commodity Concentration and Export Earnings Instability：The Evidence from African Countries	Abebayehu Tegene
GL - 17	*The Journal of International Trade & Economic Development*	8(2)：209	1999	Export instability, income terms of trade instability and growth：causal analyses	Teame Ghirmay
GL - 18	*Energy Policy*	88(4)：573 - 583	2016	Measuring the efficiency of energy-intensive industries across European countries	Georgia Makridou
GL - 19	*European Journal of Operational Research*	285(3)：1011 - 1024	2020	A data envelopment analysis and local partial least squares approach for identifying the optimal innovation policy direction	Panagiotis Tziogkidis
GL - 20	*Regional Science and Urban Economics*	54：99 - 115	2015	Neighborhood renewal：The decision to renovate or tear down	Henry J. Munneke
GL - 21	*Regional Studies*	54(6)：789 - 801	2019	Post-conflict area-based regeneration policy in deprived urban neighbourhoods	Gretta Mohan
GL - 22	*Journal of Urban Economics*	72 (2 - 3)：252 - 266	2012	Relaxing Hukou：Increased labor mobility and China's economic geography	Maarten Bosker，
GL - 23	*Journal of Urban Economics*	54(3)：474 - 498	2003	Understanding gentrification：an empirical analysis of the determinants of urban housing renovation deprived urban neighbourhoods	Andrew C. Helms

代码	期刊	卷期页	时间	论文题目	第一作者
GL−24	*Regional Studies*	54(3)：340−351	2020	The urban-rural gap in healthcare infrastructure：does government ideology matter?	Niklas Potrafke & Felix Roesel
DX−01	*Proceedings-IEEE International Conference on Robotics and Automation*	7276−7282	2019	MVX-Net：Multimodal Voxel Net for 3D Object Detection	Vishwanath A. Sindagi
DX−02	*Proceedings of the IEEE Computer Society Conference on Computer Vision and Pattern Recognition*	244−253	2018	Point Fusion：Deep Sensor Fusion for 3D Bounding Box Estimation	Danfei Xu
DX−03	*Proceedings of the IEEE Computer Society Conference on Computer Vision and Pattern Recognition*	4490−4499	2018	Voxel Net：End-to-End Learning for Point Cloud Based 3D Object Detection	Yin Zhou
DX−04	*IEEE Conference on Computer Vision and Pattern Recognition*	1−14	2017	Point Net++：Deep Hierarchical Feature Learning on Point Sets in a Metric Space	Charles R. Qi
DX−05	*IEEE Conference on ComputerVision and Pattern Recognition*	7337−7345	2019	Multi-Task Multi-Sensor Fusion for 3D Object Detection	Ming Liang
DX−06	*IJCAI*	1−8	2018	Behavioral Cloning from Observation	Faraz Torabi
DX−07	*ICML*	1−10	2019	Generative Adversarial Imitation from Observation	Faraz Torabi
DX−08	*CoRL*	1−13	2018	Task-Embedded Control Networks for Few-Shot Imitation Learning	Stephen James
DX−09	*ICLR*	1−16	2017	Third-Person Imitation Learning	Bradly C. Stadie
DX−10	*ICRA*	1−15	2017	Time-Contrastive Networks：Self-Supervised Learning from Video	Pierre Sermanet

续表

代码	期刊	卷期页	时间	论文题目	第一作者
DX – 11	*The International Journal of Medical Robotics and Computer Assisted Surgery*	16(2)：e2062	2020	Three-dimensional posture estimation of robot forceps using endoscope with convolutional neural network	Takuto Mikada
DX – 12	*IEEE Access*	7：99152 – 99160	2019	A Hybrid Deep Learning Model for Human Activity Recognition Using Multimodal Body Sensing Data	Abdu Gumaei
DX – 13	*IFAC Proceedings Volumes*	45(31)：115 – 120	2012	A Dynamic Prognostic Maintenance Policy for Multi-Component Systems	Adriaan Van Horenbeek
DX – 14	*Nucleic Acids Research*	45(9)：e69	2017	Computational approach for deriving cancer progression roadmaps from static sample data	Yijun Sun
DX – 15	*Nature Methods*	14(10)：979 – 982	2017	Reversed graph embedding resolves complex single-cell trajectories	Xiaojie Qiu
DX – 16	*Nature Communications*	11：1537	2020	Dimensionality reduction by UMAP to visualize physical and genetic interactions	Michael W. Dorrity
DX – 17	*Knowledge Discovery and Data Mining (Conference)*	765 – 774	2015	Dimensionality Reduction via Graph Structure Learning	Qi Mao
DX – 18	*bioRxiv*	1 – 76	2018	Visualizing Structure and Transitions for Biological Data Exploration	Kevin R. Moon
DX – 19	*Journal of Cleaner Production*	67：197 – 207	2014	Optimizing the production scheduling of a single machine to minimizetotal energy consumption costs	Fadi Shrouf
DX – 20	*Int. J. Production Economics*	146(1)：178 – 184	2013	"Just-for-Peak" buffer inventory for peak electricity demand reduction of manufacturing systems	Fernandez, Mayela

代码	期刊	卷期页	时间	论文题目	第一作者
JT-01	*Construction and Building Materials*	159：587-597	2018	Energy-based crack initiation model for load-related top-down cracking in asphalt pavement	Fan Gu
JT-02	*Construction and Building Materials*	206：130-139	2019	Enhanced model for thermally induced transverse cracking of asphalt pavements	Meng Ling
JT-03	*Transportation Geotechnics*	13：81-91	2017	Development of rapid three-dimensional finite-element based rigid airfield pavement foundation response and moduli prediction models	Adel Rezaei-Tarahomi
JT-04	*Computers and Geotechnics*	27(4)：249-272	2000	Modelling of a tunnel excavation in a non-cohesive soilimproved with cement mix injections	E. Nicolini
JT-05	*Géotechnique*	56(5)：335-347	2006	Theoretical modelling of jet grouting	Modoni, G.
JT-06	*International Journal for Numerical and Analytical Methods in Geomechanics*	29(5)：443-471	2005	Numerical modelling of compensation grouting above shallow tunnels	C. Wisser
JT-07	*Journal of Geotechnical and Geoenvironmental Engineering*	127(11)：955-964	2001	Model of compaction grouting	Adel M. El-Kelesh
JT-08	*Géotechnique: International Journal of Soil Mechanics*	57(1)：75-90	2007	Modelling of long-term ground response to tunnelling under St James's Park, London	J. Wongsaroj
JT-09	*Computer & Industrial Engineering*	66(1)：171-185	2013	Mixed integer programming for minimizing the period of a cyclic railway timetable for a single track with two train types	Mojtaba Heydar
JT-10	*Transportation Research Part B*	43(8-9)：821-836	2009	Techniques for inserting additional trains into existing timetables	R. L. Burdett

代码	期刊	卷期页	时间	论文题目	第一作者
JT – 11	*OR Spectrum*	32(1)：163 – 193	2010	A sequencing approach for creating new train timetables	R. L. Burdett
JT – 12	*Transportation Research Part C*	79：73 – 84	2017	Rescheduling through stop-skipping in dense railway systems	Estelle Altazin
JT – 13	*Transportation Research Part B*	135：143 – 155	2020	Optimal investment and management of shared bikes in acompetitive market	Zhoutong Jiang
JT – 14	*Computer & Operations Research*	120：104949	2020	The exponential multi-insertion neighborhood for the vehicle routing problem with unit demands	Jan-Niklas Buckow
JT – 15	*Computer & Operations Research*	112：104761	2019	Adaptive large neighborhood search for the commodity constrained split delivery VRP	Wenjuan Gu
JT – 16	*Transportation Research Procedia*	46：29 – 36	2020	A vehicle routing problem with movement synchronization of drones, sidewalk robots, or footwalkers	Glareh Amirjamshidi
JT – 17	*Lecture Notes in Computer Science*	10751：352 – 361	2018	Algorithms for Solving the Vehicle Routing Problem with Drones	Daniel Schermer
JT – 18	*Operations Research*	35(2)：254 – 265	1987	Algorithms for the vehicle routing and scheduling problems with time window constraints	Marius M. Solomon
JT – 19	*Géotechnique*	40(3)：405 – 430	1990	A constitutive model for partially saturated soils	E. E. Alonso
JT – 20	*Computers and Geotechnics*	32(7)：483 – 490	2005	On the undrained shear strength of gassy clays	J. L. H. Grozic
JT – 21	*Soils and Foundations*	58(3)：534 – 546	2018	Unsaturated elasto-plastic constitutive equations for compacted kaolin under consolidated drained and shearing-infiltration conditions	Harianto Rahardjo
JT – 22	*Computers and Geotechnics*	118：103332	2020	A generalised constitutive model for unsaturated compacted soils considering wetting/drying cycles and environmentally-stabilised line	J. Kodikara

代码	期刊	卷期页	时间	论文题目	第一作者
JT – 23	*Computers and Geotechnics*	98: 69 – 81	2018	A coupled hydro-mechanical constitutive model for unsaturated frictional and cohesive soil energy saving	Esmaeel Gholizadeh
JT – 24	*Journal of Rail Transport Planning & Management*	7:224 – 244	2017	A tool for the rapid selection of a railway signalling strategy to implement train control optimisation for energy saving	Robert Dunbar
JT – 25	*Journal of Rail Transport Planning & Management*	4(1 – 2): 14 – 27	2014	Comparative analysis of algorithms and models for train running simulation	Birgit Jaekel
JT – 26	*Wear*	314 (1 – 2): 155 – 161	2014	A predictive model of energy savings from top of rail friction control	Joel Vandermarel
JT – 27	*IEEE Conference on Control Technology and Applications*	270 – 277	2019	Non-linear Model Predictive Control of Wave Energy Converters with Realistic Power Take-off Configurations and Loss Model	A. Karthikeyan
JT – 28	*IET Intelligent Transport System*	10(1): 50 – 57	2016	Delay management and energy consumption minimisation on a single-track railway	Silvia Umiliacchi
JT – 29	*Accident Analysis and Prevention*	43(3): 1267 – 1278	2011	A stochastic catastrophe model using two-fluid model parameters to investigate traffic safety on urban arterials	Peter Y. Park
JT – 30	*2016 IEEE 19th International Conference on Intelligent Transportation Systems*	790 – 794	2016	Convex Signal Control Model in a Single-Destination Dynamic Traffic Assignment	Nam H. Hoang
JT – 31	*IEEE Transactions on Intelligent Transportation Systems*	20(4): 1269 – 1277	2019	Coordinated Transit Signal Priority Model Considering Stochastic Bus Arrival Time	Long Tien Truong
JT – 32	*Proceedings-1st International Conference on Intelligent Systems and Information Management, ICISIM* 2017	325 – 331	2017	Cooperative Multi-agent Reinforcement Learning Models (CM-RLM) for Intelligent Traffic Control	Deepak A. Vidhate

代码	期刊	卷期页	时间	论文题目	第一作者
JT-33	*Wear*	294-295：446-456	2012	A wheel set/crossing model regarding impact, sliding and deformation-Explicit finite element approach	M. Pletz
JT-34	*Journal of Mechanical Systems for Transportation and Logistics*	3(1)：216-225	2010	Planning Rail Grinding Using Crack Growth Predictions	Paul Hyde
JT-35	*Wear*	271 (1-2)：482-491	2011	A numerical method using VAMPIRE modelling for prediction of turnout curve wheel-rail wear	Y. Q. Sun
JT-36	*Fatigue & Fracture of Engineering Materials & Structures*	38(12)：1478-1491	2015	The development of a crack propagation model for railway wheels and rails	B. Dirks
CZ-01	*IEEE Access*	7：137065-137079	2019	Extending Reliability of mm Wave Radar Tracking and Detection via Fusion With Camera	Renyuan Zhang
CZ-02	*Information Sciences*	278：641-652	2014	Data fusion of radar and image measurements for multi-object tracking via Kalman filtering	Du Yong Kim
CZ-03	*IEEE Transactions on Intelligent Transportation Systems*	10(4)：606-614	2009	Collision Sensing by Stereo Visionand Radar Sensor Fusion	Shunguang Wu
CZ-04	*International Journal of Vehicle Autonomous Systems*	11(4)：384-404	2013	A target tracking system using sensors of multiple modalities	Shuqing Zeng
CZ-05	*IEEE Transactions on Intelligent Transportation Systems*	5(2)：84-98	2004	Simultaneous Registration and Fusion of Multiple Dissimilar Sensors for Cooperative Driving	Winston Li
CZ-06	*IEEE Transactions on Intelligent Transportation Systems*	20(3)：879-887	2019	Deep Spatio-Temporal Representation for Detectionof Road Accidents Using Stacked Autoencoder	Dinesh Singh
CZ-07	*IEEE Transactions on Intelligent Transportation Systems*	21(4)：1584-1594	2020	Naturalistic Driver Intention and Path Prediction Using Recurrent Neural Networks	Alex Zyner

代码	期刊	卷期页	时间	论文题目	第一作者
CZ - 08	*IEEE Transactions on Intelligent Transportation Systems*	20(9): 3294 - 3302	2019	Self-Supervised Optical Flow Estimationby Projective Bootstrap	Stefano Alletto
CZ - 09	*IEEE Transactions on Intelligent Transportation Systems*	19(1): 263 - 272	2018	ERFNet: Efficient Residual Factorized Conv Net for Real-Time Semantic Segmentation	Eduardo Romera
CZ - 10	*IEEE Transactions on Intelligent Transportation Systems*	21(4): 1427 - 1440	2020	Deep Learning for Large-Scale Traffic-Sign Detection and Recognition	Domen Tabernik
CZ - 11	*Journal of The Electrochemical Society*	165(13): F1051 - F1058	2018	Agglomerates in Polymer Electrolyte Fuel Cell Electrodes: Part I. Structural Characterization	Firat C. Cetinbas
CZ - 12	*Journal of The Electrochemical Society*	165(13): F1059 - F1066	2018	Agglomerates in Polymer Electrolyte Fuel Cell Electrodes: Part II. Transport Characterization	Firat C. Cetinbas
CZ - 13	*Journal of The Electrochemical Society*	165(13): F1115 - F1126	2018	Fundamental Understanding of Water Movement in Gas DiffusionLayer under Different Arrangements Using Combination of Direct Modeling and Experimental Visualization	P. Satjaritanun
CZ - 14	*Journal of The Electrochemical Society*	166(8): F534 - F543	2019	Multiscale Modeling of PEMFC Using Co-Simulation Approach	P. Satjaritanun
CZ - 15	*Journal of The Electrochemical Society*	167: 013516	2020	Numerical Study of Electrochemical Kinetics and Mass Transport inside Nano-Structural Catalyst Layer of PEMFC Using Lattice Boltzmann Agglomeration Method	P. Satjaritanun
CZ - 16	*2018 IEEE/RSJ International Conference on Intelligent Robots and Systems (IROS)*	5750 - 5757	2018	Joint 3D Proposal Generation and Object Detection from View Aggregation	Jason Ku
CZ - 17	*2019 49th Annual IEEE/IFIP International Conference on Dependable Systems and Networks (DSN)*	112 - 124	2019	ML-based Fault Injection for Autonomous Vehicles: A Case for Bayesian Fault Injection	Saurabh Jha

代码	期刊	卷期页	时间	论文题目	第一作者
CZ－18	*IEEE Transactions on Intelligent Vehicles*	4(3)：406－415	2019	Probabilistic Uncertainty-Aware Risk Spot Detector for Naturalistic Driving	Tim Puphal
CZ－19	*Materials Today：Proceedings*	17：246－253	2019	Analysis of PEM hydrogen fuel cell and solar PV cell hybrid model	Sendhil Kumar Natarajan
CZ－20	*International Journal of Hydrogen Energy*	44(41)：23396－23405	2019	Effect of compression on pore size distribution and porosity of PEM fuel cell catalyst layers	Ali Malekian
RJ－01	*Journal of Climate*	11(1)：3＝29－41	1998	Forecasting ENSO Events：A Neural Network-Extended EOF Approach	Fredolin T. Tangang
RJ－02	*Neural Networks*	19(2)：145－154	2006	Neural network forecasts of the tropical Pacific sea surface temperatures	Aiming Wu
RJ－03	*International Journal of Oceanography*	1－13	2009	Forecasts of Tropical Pacific Sea Surface Temperatures by Neural Networks and Support Vector Regression	Silvestre Aguilar-Martinez 1
RJ－04	*Climate Dynamics*	13：135－147	1997	Forecasting the equatorial Pacific sea surface temperatures by neural network models	F. T. Tangang
RJ－05	*Journal of Oceanography*	1－11	2013	Predicting Sea Surface Temperatures in the North Indian Oceanwith Nonlinear Autoregressive Neural Networks	Kalpesh Patil
RJ－06	*IEEE Transactions on Pattern Analysis & Machine Intelligence*	38(1)：142－158	2016	Region-Based Convolutional Networks forAccurate Object Detection and Segmentation	Ross Girshick
RJ－07	*IEEE Transactions On Pattern Analysis And Machine Intelligence*	39(12)：2481－2495	2017	SegNet：A Deep Convolutional Encoder-Decoder Architecture for Image Segmentation	Vijay Badrinarayanan

续表

代码	期刊	卷期页	时间	论文题目	第一作者
RJ－08	*IEEE Transactions on Pattern Analysis and Machine Intelligence*	39(4)：640－651	2017	Fully Convolutional Networksfor Semantic Segmentation	Evan Shelhamer
RJ－09	*IEEE Transactions On Image Processing*	21(12)：4695－4708	2012	No-Reference Image Quality Assessmentin the Spatial Domain	Anish Mittal
RJ－10	*IEEE transactions on image processing*	29：2653－2665	2019	Color Channel Compensation（3C）：A fundamentalpre-processing step for image enhancement	Codruta O. Ancuti
RJ－11	*International Journal of Medical Informatics*	112：59－67	2018	Federated learning of predictive models from federated Electronic Health Records	Theodora S. Brisimi
RJ－12	*IEEE Global Communications Conference*	1－7	2018	Federated Learning for Ultra-Reliable Low-Latency V2V Communications	Samarakoon，Sumudu
RJ－13	*Annual Conference on Neural Information Processing Systems*	1－11	2017	Federated Multi-Task Learning	Smith，Virginia
RJ－14	*Lecture Notes in Computer Science*	10410：367－373	2017	The More the Merrier-Federated Learning from Local Sphere Recommendations	Malle，Bernd
RJ－15	*Journal of Intelligent & Fuzzy Systems*	36(5)：4005－4015	2019	Intrusion detection system using timed automata for cyber physical systems	K. S. Umadevi
RJ－16	*Lecture Notes in Computer Science*	5215：78－92	2008	Timed Automata with Integer Resets：Language Inclusion and Expressiveness	P. Vijay Suman

参考文献

陈浩、文秋芳：《基于"产出导向法"的学术英语写作名词化教学研究——以促成教学环节为例》，《外语教育研究前沿》2020年第1期。

管李鑫、胡志清：《英语学术论文引言部分语步中词块的跨学科研究》，《外语教育》，2019年。

姜峰：《元话语名词：学术语篇人际互动研究的新视角》，《解放军外国语学院学报》2019年第2期。

姜峰：《基于多维分析的学术语篇语体特征的历时考察》，《外语教学与研究》2020年第5期。

姜亚军、赵刚：《学术语篇的语言学研究：流派分野和方法整合》，《外语研究》2006年第6卷。

李梦骁、刘永兵：《评价理论视域下中外学者期刊论文评论结果语步词块比较研究》，《外语与外语教学》2017年第5期。

梁文花、康淑敏：《"体裁理论"三个主要学派的比较研究》，《外语研究》2012年第1期。

刘国兵、张孝莲：《语料库驱动视角下学术英语动词搭配配价研究》，《外语电化教学》2021年第1期。

刘永厚、张颖：《中外学者国际期刊英语学术论文摘要写作的对比研究》，《外语界》2016年第5期。

秦秀白：《"体裁分析"概说》，《外国语》1997年第6期。

秦秀白：《体裁教学法述评》，《外语教学与研究：外国语文双月刊》2000年第1期。

王华、胡志清:《英语学术论文结论部分语步中词块的跨学科研究》,《外语教育》2020 年第 20 期。

王丽萍、吴红云、张军:《国际学术英语写作研究(1990—2015):基于 CiteSpace 的可视化分析》,《外语教学理论与实践》2017 年第4 期。

温植胜:《新修辞学派体裁研究的社会认知视角》,《天津外国语学院学报》2005 年第 6 期。

徐昉:《中国学习者英语学术词块的使用及发展特征研究》,《中国外语》2012 年第 4 期。

杨瑞英:《英语学术论文的体裁分析——理论与应用》,科学出版社2014 年版。

Aslam, Insaf, Dr. Asim Mehmood, "Genre Analysis of Conclusion Sections of Pakistani Research Articles in Natural and Social Sciences," *Journal of Natural Sciences Research*, Vol. 4, No. 22, 2014, pp. 106 – 112.

Azevedo, Luís. et al., "How to Write a Scientific Paper-Writing the Methods Section," *Revista Portuguesa de Pneumologia*, Vol. 17, No. 5, 2011, pp. 232 – 238.

Bahadoran, Zahra, et al., "The Principles of Biomedical Scientific Writing: Introduction," *Int J Endocrinol Metab*, Vol. 16, No. 4, 2018, p. e84795.

Baker, Paul, Jesse Egbert, *Triangulating Methodological Approaches in Corpus Linguistic Research*, New York: Routledge, 2016.

Basturkmen, Helen, "A genre-based Investigation of Discussion Sections of Research Articles in Dentistry and Disciplinary Variation," *Journal of English for Academic Purposes*, Vol. 11, 2012, pp. 134 – 144.

Basturkmen, Helen, "Commenting on Results in Published Research Articles and Masters Dissertations in Language Teaching," *Journal of English for Academic Purposes*, Vol. 8, 2009, pp. 241 – 251.

Bazerman, Charles, *Shaping Written Knowledge: The Genre and Activity of* the *Experimental Article in Science*, Madison: University of Wisconsin Press, 1988.

Bazerman, Charles, "Genre and Cognitive Development: Beyond Writing to Learn," in Bazerman, A. Bonini & D. Figueiredo (eds.), *Genre in a Changing World*, Fort Collins, CO: The WAC Clearinghouse and Parlor Press, 2009, pp. 283 – 298.

Berkenkotter, Carol A., Thomas N. Huckin, *Genre Knowledge in Disciplinary Communication: Cognition/Culture/Power*, Hillsdale, New Jersey: Lawrence Erlbaum Associates, Inc, 1995.

Bhatia, Vijay Kumar, *Analysing Genre: Language Use in Professional Settings*, London: Longman, 1993.

Biber, Douglas, et al., *Longman Grammar of Spoken and Written English*, Harlow: Pearson, 1999.

Bloor, Meriel, "Variations in the Methods Sections of Research Articles across Disciplines: The Case of Fast and Slow Text," *Issues in EAP Writing, Research and Instruction*, 1998, pp. 84 – 106.

Brett, Paul, "A Genre Analysis of the Result Sections of Sociology Articles," *English for Specific Purposes*, Vol. 13, 1994, pp. 47 – 59.

Bruce, Ian, "Cognitive Genre Structures in Methods Sections of Research Articles: A Corpus Study," *Journal of English for Academic Purposes*, Vol. 7, 2008, pp. 38 – 54.

Bruce, Ian, "Results Sections in Sociology and Organic Chemistry Articles: A Genre Analysis," *English for Specific Purposes*, Vol. 28, 2009, pp. 105 – 124.

Bruce, Nigel J., "Rhetorical Constraints on Information Structure in Medical Research Report Writing," in *ESP in the Arab World Conference, University of Aston, UK*, 1983.

Bunton, David, "The Structure of PhD Conclusion Chapters," *English for Academic Purposes*, Vol. 4, 2005, pp. 207 – 224.

Cortes, Viviana, "The Purpose of This Study is to: Connecting Lexical

Bundles and Moves in Research Article Introductions," *Journal of English for Academic Purposes*, Vol. 12, 2013, pp. 33 – 43.

Cotos, Elena, Sarah Huffman, Stephanie Link, "A Move/Step Model for Methods Sections Demonstrating Rigour and Credibility," *English for Specific Purposes*, Vol. 46, 2017, pp. 90 – 106.

Coxhead, Averil, "A New Academic Word Lit," *TESOL Quarterly*, Vol. 34, No. 2, 2000, pp. 213 – 238.

Dubois, Betty. L. , *The Biomedical Discussion Section in Context*, Greenwich, Connecticut: Ablex Publishing, 1997.

Durrant, Philip, "To What Extent is the Academic Vocabulary List Relevant to University Student Writing?" *Journal of English for Academic Purposes*, No. 43, 2016, pp. 49 – 61.

Evans, Stephen, Christopher Green, "Why EAP is Necessary: A Survey of Hong Kong Tertiary Students," *Journal of English for Academic Purposes*, No. 6, 2007, pp. 3 – 17.

Flowerdew, John, "Writing for Scholarly Publication in English: The Case of Hong Kong," *Journal of Second Language Writing*, Vol. 8, No. 2, 1999, pp. 123 – 145.

Freedman, Aviva, Peter Medway, *Genre and the New Rhetoric*, London: Talor & Francis, 1994.

Gardner, Dee, Mark Davies, "A New Academic Vocabulary List," *Applied Linguistics*, No. 35, 2014, pp. 305 – 327.

Gilbert, Nigel, Michael J. Mulkay, *Opening Pandora's Box: A Sociological Analysis of Scientists' Discourse*, Cambridge: Cambridge University Press, 1984.

Halliday, Michael Alexander Kirkwood, Rugaiya Hasan, *Language, Context, and Text: Aspects of Language in a Social-Semiotic Perspective* 2nd ed. , Oxford: Oxford University Press, 1989.

Hirano, Eliana, "Research Article Introductions in English for Specific Purposes: A Comparison between Brazilian Portuguese and English,"

English for Specific Purposes, Vol. 28, 2009, pp. 240 – 250.

Holmes, Richard, "Genre Analysis, and the Social Sciences: An Investigation of the Structure of Research Article Discussion Sections in Three Disciplines," *English for Specific Purposes*, Vol. 16, No. 4, 1997, pp. 321 – 337.

Hopkins, Andy, Tony Dudley-Evans, "A Genre-Based Investigation of the Discussion Sections in Articles and Dissertations," *English for Specific Purposes*, Vol. 7, 1988, pp. 113 – 122.

Hutchins, John, "On the Structure of Scientific Texts," in *University of East Anglia*, Vol. 5, No. 3, 1977, pp. 18 – 39.

Hyland, Ken, *Disciplinary Discourses: Social Interactions in Academic Writing*, London: Longman, 2000.

Hyland, Ken, Polly Tse, "Is There An Academic Vocabulary?" *TESOL Quarterly*, Vol. 41, No. 20, 2007, pp. 235 – 253.

Kanoksilapatham, Budsaba, *A Corpus-Based Investigation of Scientific Research Articles: Linking Move Analysis with Multidimensional Analysis*, Unpublished Doctoral Dissertation, Georgetown University, Washington, DC, 2003.

Kanoksilapatham, Budsaba, "Structure of Research Article Introductions in Three Engineering Subdisciplines," *IEEE Transactions on Professional Communication*, Vol. 55, No. 4, 2012, pp. 294 – 309.

Kanoksilapatham, Budsaba, "Distinguishing Textual Features Characterizing Structural Variation in Research Articles Across Three Engineering Sub-Discipline Corpora," *English for Specific Purposes*, Vol. 37, 2015, pp. 74 – 86.

Kaplan, Robert, et al., "On Abstract Writing," *Text*, Vol. 14, No. 3, 1994, pp. 401 – 426.

Lewin, Beverly A., Jonathan Fine, Lynne Young, *Expository Discourse: A Genre-Based Approach to Social Science Research Texts*, London: Continuum, 2001.

Lim, Jason Miin Hwa, "Method Sections of Management Research Articles: A Pedagogically Motivated Qualitative Study," *English for Specific Purposes*, Vol. 25, No. 3, 2006, pp. 282 – 309.

Lim, Jason Miin Hwa, "Commenting on Research Results in Applied Linguistics and Education: A Comparative Genre-Based Investigation," *Journal of English for Academic Purposes*, Vol. 9, 2010, pp. 280 – 294.

Lin, Ling, "Variability in the Rhetorical Structure of Research Article Introductions: The Case of Civil Engineering," *Revista Española de Lingüística Aplicada*, Vol. 27, No. 2, 2014, pp. 405 – 432.

Loi, Chek Kim, "Research Article Introductions in Chinese and English: A Comparative Genre-Based Study," *Journal of English for Academic Purposes*, Vol. 9, 2010, pp. 267 – 279.

Martin, James Robert, *A Contextual Theory of Language* [C] // B. Cope & M. Kalantzis, 1993, pp. 116 – 136.

Martínez, Iliana A., Silvia C. Beck, Carolina B. Panza, "Academic Vocabulary in Agriculture Research Articles: A Corpus-Based Study," *English for Specific Purposes*, Vol. 28, No. 3, 2009, pp. 183 – 198.

Miller, Carolyn R., "Genre as Social Action," *Quarterly Journal of Speech*, Vol. 70, No. 2, 1984, pp. 151 – 167.

Myers, Greg, "Texts as Knowledge Claims: The Social Construction of Two Biology Articles," *Social Studies of Science*, Vol. 15, 1985, pp. 593 – 630.

Nwogu, Kevin N., "The Medical Research Paper: Structure and Functions," *English for Specific Purposes*, Vol. 16, No. 2, 1997, pp. 119 – 138.

Omidian, Taha, Anna Siyanova-Chanturia, "Parameters of Variation in the Use of Words in Empirical Research Writing," *English for Specific Purposes*, No. 62, 2021, pp. 15 – 29.

Omidian, Taha, Hesamoddin Shahriari, Anna Siyanova-Chanturia, "A

Cross-Disciplinary Investigation of Multi-Word Expressions in the Moves of Research Article Abstracts," *Journal of English for Academic Purposes*, Vol. 36, 2018, pp. 1 – 14.

Otto, Philippa, "Choosing Specialized Vocabulary to Teach with Data-Driven Learning: An Example from Civil Engineering," *English for Specific Purposes*, Vol. 61, 2021, pp. 32 – 46.

Parkinson, Jean, Jill Musgrave, "Development of Noun Phrase Complexity in the Writing of English for Academic Purposes Students," *Journal of English for Academic Purposes*, Vol. 14, 2014, pp. 48 – 59.

Peacock, Matthew, "Communicative Moves in the Discussion Section of Research Articles," *System*, Vol. 30, 2002, pp. 479 – 497.

Pèrez-Llantada, Carmen, "An Interview with John Swales," *IBÉRICA*, Vol. 8, 2004, pp. 139 – 148.

Posteguillo, Santiago, "The Schematic Structure of Computer Science Research Articles," *English for Specific Purposes*, Vol. 18, No. 2, 1999, pp. 139 – 160.

Saeeaw Supachai, Supong Tangkiengsirisin, "Rhetorical Variation Across Research Article Abstracts in Environmental Science and Applied Linguistics," *English Language Teaching*, Vol. 7, No. 8, 2014, pp. 81 – 93.

Salager-Meyer, Françoise, "Discoursal Flaws in Medical English Abstracts: A Genre Analysis per Research and Text Type," *Text and talk*, Vol. 10, No. 4, 1990, pp. 365 – 384.

Samraj, Betty, "Introductions in Research Articles: Variations Across Disciplines," *English for Specific Purposes*, Vol. 21, No. 1, 2002, pp. 1 – 17.

Séror, Jérémie, Sandra Zappa-Hollman, "Research Genres: Explorations and Applications (Review)," *The Canadian Modern Language Review / La Revue Canadienne Des Langues Vivantes*, Vol. 62, No. 2, 2005, pp. 349 – 351.

Skoufaki, Sophia, Bojana Petrić, "Academic Vocabulary in An EAP

Course： Opportunities for Incidental Learning from Printed Teaching Materials Developed in-House," *English for Specific Purposes*, Vol. 63, 2021, pp. 71 – 85.

Soyer, Philippe, "Misuse of Semantics and Basic Statistical Terms in Original Articles," *Diagn Interv Imaging*, Vol. 98, 2017, pp. 825 – 826.

Soyer, Philippe, Michael Patlas, David Bluemke, "Writing A Successful Original Research Paper for a Radiology Journal," *Diagnostic and Interventional Imaging*, Vol. 103, 2022, pp. 285 – 287.

Spencer, Sarah, et al. , "Increasing Ddolescents' Depth of Understanding of Cross-Curriculum Words： An Intervention Study," *International Journal of Language & Communication Disorders*, No. 52, 2017, pp. 652 – 668.

Stanley, Rose M. , "The Recognition of Macrostructure： A Pilot Study," *Reading in a Foreign Language*, No. 2, 1984, pp. 156 – 168.

Swales, John, *Aspects of Article Introductions*, Birmingham, UK： The University of Aston, Language Studies Unit, 1981.

Swales, John, *Genre Analysis： English in Academic and Research Settings*, Cambridge： Cambridge University Press, 1990.

Swales, John, *Research genres： Exploration and Applications*, Cambridge： Cambridge University Press, 2004.

Tarone, Elaine, et al. , "On the Use of the Passive in Two Astrophysics Journal Papers," *The ESP Journal*, Vol. 1, No. 2, 1981, pp. 123 – 140.

Ventola, Eija M. , "Generic and Register Qualities of Texts and Their Realization," in Peter H. Fries and Michael Gregory (eds.), *Discourse in Society： Systemic Functional Perspectives*, Ablex Publishing Corporation, 1995.

Weissberg, Robert C. , "Given and New： Paragraph Development Models from Scientific English," *TESOL Quarterly*, Vol. 18, No. 3, 1984, pp. 485 – 500.

Weissberg, Robert C. , Suzanne Buker, *Writing Up Research*: *Experimental Research Report Writing for Students of English*, Prentice Hall Regents, 1990.

Williams, Ian. A. , "Results Sections of Medical Research Articles: Analysis of Rhetorical Categories for Pedagogical Purposes," *English for Specific Purposes*, Vol. 18, 1999, pp. 347 – 366.

Wright, Heidi R. , "Lexical Bundles in Stand-Alone Literature Reviews: Sections, Frequencies and Functions," *English for Specific Purposes*, Vol. 54, 2019, pp. 1 – 14.

Wu, Xue, Anna Mauranen, Lei Lei, "Syntactic Complexity in English as a Lingua Franca Academic Writing," *Journal of English for Academic Purposes*, Vol. 43, 2020, pp. 1 – 13.

Yang, Ruiying, Desmond Allison, "Research Articles in Applied Linguistics: Moving from Results to Conclusions," *English for Specific Purposes*, Vol. 22, 2003, pp. 365 – 385.

Yang, Ruiying, Christoper Edwards, "Problems and Solutions for Trainee Teachers Reading Academic Articles in English," in M. L. Tickoo (Ed.), *Reading and Writing*: *Theory into Practice* (Anthology Series 35) (pp. 366 – 382), Singapore: Regional Language Centre, 1995.